OLD FRIENDS, NEW ENEMIES

Admiral of the Fleet Sir Dudley Pound, First Sea Lord, June 1939–October 1943
c. 1944, probably from a photograph

OLD FRIENDS, NEW ENEMIES:
THE ROYAL NAVY AND THE IMPERIAL JAPANESE NAVY

STRATEGIC ILLUSIONS, 1936–1941

BY

ARTHUR J. MARDER

CLARENDON PRESS · OXFORD

1981

Oxford University Press, Walton Street, Oxford OX2 6DP
London Glasgow New York Toronto
Delhi Bombay Calcutta Madras Karachi
Kuala Lumpur Singapore Hong Kong Tokyo
Nairobi Dar es Salaam Cape Town
Melbourne Auckland
and associate companies in
Beirut Berlin Ibadan Mexico City

© Oxford University Press 1981

Published in the United States by
Oxford University Press, New York

All rights reserved. No part of this publication may be reproduced,
stored in a retrieval system, or transmitted, in any form or by any means,
electronic, mechanical, photocopying, recording, or otherwise, without
the prior permission of Oxford University Press

British Library Cataloguing in Publication Data
Marder, Arthur
    Old friends, new enemies.
    Strategic illusions, 1936–1941
    1. Great Britain. Royal Navy—History
    2. Japan. Navy—History
    I. Title
    359'00941   VA454

ISBN 0-19-822604-7

Typeset by CCC, printed and bound in Great Britain
by William Clowes (Beccles) Limited, Beccles and London

Arthur Jacob Marder—a personal memoir

'To look at yesterday with the eyes of yesterday, that is the historian's real task.' I cannot remember how many times Arthur said this to me but it was frequent enough to have made a deep impression. And it is, I think, the reason why he made himself the supreme historian, for he made it a rigid rule in all the history he wrote and taught. 'It's unfair to criticize a man because you know something he didn't know' was another of his rules, and this comes out vividly in the case of Tom Phillips in this, his last book, as indeed it does in the other works of history he has written.

But there is more to the writing of history than that. The basis of all good historical work is knowledge, and in this Arthur towered above so many of his contemporaries. His appetite for research was prodigious by any standards, and it was matched both by his own energy and by his powers of meticulous organization of the material he collected. The volume of his correspondence was immense—two or three letters a week from him was not uncommon while he was working—and if all this letter-writing produced one small nugget of relevant information, he counted it all worth while. His industry, his dedication, his knowledge, his judgement, his integrity, his happy facility with words, made him one of the giants of his profession.

Looking back over the thirty years I have known him, my lasting impression is one of great happiness and great courage. After the first volume of *From the Dreadnought to Scapa Flow* was published I was devastated to receive a letter from him to say that all the research he had done for the rest of the work had been accidentally destroyed. Knowing the volume of that research, the weeks spent in the Public Records Office and in museums, the immense personal correspondence, it appeared a blow from which he could hardly recover. Yet within a month I had a letter to say that he was on his way to England to start the research all over again. That was his courage, indomitable, undismayed. His love of life, of his children, of his friends, above all, his constant devotion to Jan, his wife, was his happiness, which is reflected in his work.

At the memorial service held in his University in California after his death the establishment of an Arthur Jacob Marder Prize was announced, to be awarded annually for the best historical essay by a student. Of all the honours he received in his life, this one, awarded in death, would I am sure have given him the greatest pleasure of all. With all his great qualifications, with all his personal distinctions, he was that sort of a man.

Peter Kemp

To
ALVIN COOX
With profound gratitude for his encouragement and help *ab ovo*

Preface

This volume is the first of two on the Royal Navy and the Imperial Japanese Navy in the crucial 1936–1945 decade, with, I trust, the woods standing out as clearly as the trees, and the impedimenta of scholarship kept to a minimum. I have found that, however regrettable the imbalance, I must give the prime position in my story to the Royal Navy. This is largely because of the vast discrepancy as regards sources. Take the British records. There is a plethora of Cabinet Office records (minutes and papers of the Cabinet and War Cabinet, the Committee of Imperial Defence, the Chiefs of Staff Committee, and so forth) and Foreign Office and Admiralty records, all at the Public Record Office. The Admiralty records are very full indeed (if miserably organized—the fault of the Admiralty, not of the Public Record Office). There is, besides, a wealth of source material in private collections, most of it now in the British Library, Churchill College, Cambridge, the Imperial War Museum, and the National Maritime Museum. By comparison the records of the Imperial Navy are pathetically meagre. The reasons are clear enough: the fire bombings of Tokyo in the last stages of the war (that of 25 May 1945, in particular, which half destroyed the Navy Ministry building) and the wilful destruction of the naval records at Yokohama, where many had been removed before the 25 May bombing, directly after the war had ended. (We cannot be certain who gave the directive, but it might have been the Navy Minister, Admiral Yonai.) Why this destruction? To cover up the tracks of the higher-ups, who were mindful of the Potsdam Declaration's directive that 'stern justice shall be meted out to all war criminals'? The result of the twin holocausts is indeed sad. And so, for example, there are no Naval Attaché reports from London and few records of the Naval General Staff. The naval records in the archives of the Military History Department of the National Defence College, National Defence Agency (Bōeichō Bōei Kenshūjo Senshibu Shiryōko) for the *whole* of 1868–1945 consist of twenty rows of documents, each some eight feet high and twenty-five feet long (very thin for 1936–45), and three rows of documents received since the war from individual officers or their families—mostly pretty low-level material. The holdings of the Bōeichō

Senshibu include the repatriated (1958) files of the operational and Navy Ministry records that were seized by the United States Occupation authorities.* The minutes of Cabinet meetings in my period do not exist, but we have those of the Liaison Conferences of 1941. The Official War History, *Senshi sōsho* (War History Series: 102 volumes on the war and its background, by a team of IJN and IJA officers), which includes some fourteen or fifteen volumes that I have found useful, have exploited the extant naval archival records as well as post-war interviews with and unpublished diaries and reminiscences of many responsible IJN officers. (These materials are at the Bōeichō Senshibu.) The consequence of the tremendous disparity in source material between the two sides is that I can usually determine the why and wherefores of British naval strategy and attitudes *vis-à-vis* the IJN at any given time, and in detail; it is not always possible to do the same for the IJN *vis-à-vis* the RN.

There is another reason why I pay more attention to the Royal Navy. Whereas the Imperial Navy was from 1935–6 an important, and from the summer of 1940 a critical, factor in the strategic calculations of the Royal Navy and the British Government, the Royal Navy never held quite the same position in the strategical thought and operational planning of the Imperial Navy. That Navy was so wrapped up in the problems of how to fight a war with the United States Navy—*the* enemy, potential, then actual, of Japan—that it had little time for, and even less interest in, thinking through the problems of a war with Britain. There seems also to have been a psychological block: the old Alliance, the traditional friendship of the two navies, memories of the Royal Navy as the teacher of the Imperial Navy, and a profound respect for Nelson and his heirs, all made for a deep-seated tendency in the Imperial Navy not to want to think seriously about a war with Britain. Indeed, the Imperial Navy went to war with Britain reluctantly. The greater danger to Japanese interests and security posed by the American Navy made the latter the principal enemy once hostilities commenced, and never after the first six months of hostilities was the Imperial Navy able to concentrate powerful forces against the Royal Navy in Eastern waters. British policy was to avoid a war

* Copies remain in Washington. Speaking generally, the operational records, portions of it in translation, are at the Operational Archives Branch of the Naval Historical Center, and the Navy Ministry records, untranslated, at the National Archives.

with Japan as long as possible—perils and commitments nearer home made this essential—and when war did come, the Royal Navy was unable to concentrate the force required to do the job in the East until the last year of the war, by which time the Pacific War was as good as won.

I would at this point comment on several problems that arose in the course of the research and writing. There was, first of all, the matter of informants. They were extraordinarily helpful on the RN side, but as a rule their information *supplemented* the records and provided a good deal of spice: amusing or revealing anecdotes and sidelights, and the kind of detail that one cannot as a rule find in the official records. In the case of the Imperial Navy, given the paucity of documentary material, the role of the informant is of greater importance. Yet the IJN officers I interviewed were *as a group* (there were a few notable exceptions) somewhat reluctant to speak frankly, whether about specific events or policies, or about brother officers, or their own roles when they held responsible positions. Word portraits tended to be one-dimensional: Admiral X was 'clever' or 'not clever', or Admiral Y was or was not a good Navy Minister, with reasons for judgements not given or only hinted at. I am certain that this generally bland, uncritical outlook goes beyond the natural reluctance to be critical of officers of the old Navy, who, as one Admiral said, 'have served the nation well and are now dead'. A factor may be that ancient Chinese saying which is well known in Japanese Service circles: 'Defeated generals should not talk of battles' (*Haigun no shō hei o Katarazu*). The force of this axiom is doubtless strengthened by the feeling of responsibility by Imperial naval officers to the nation as well as to the war dead. Japanese scholars have called my attention to other considerations as helping to explain the blandness and superficiality of statements from many of my informants: that history is traditionally written that way in Japan, and that this is due to 'groupism'. If you evaluate a person or a group with frankness, it necessarily involves pulling down another individual or group, which will not do. Add the fact that consensus-building is very important in the Japanese decision-making process, and that the Japanese people are collective-responsibility-minded: collective, not individual, responsibility is what matters. I am also advised by Japanese academics that 'what is left out [in an interview] can be judged by what is said. One must pay attention to what is omitted.' Having said all this, I must point out that my IJN informants did provide information of interest and value.

Not helpful to the Westerner is the indirectness and imprecision in speech, which is an outstanding trait of the Japanese national mores. One sees it in maddening form in the horrendous imprecision, confusion, and vagueness in the written language, which make for frequent semantic messes. Japanese, says Fosco Maraini, is 'incapable of constructing sentences of unequivocal meaning'. One of the problems lies in the *kanji*—the ideograms, which lend themselves to many alternative translations. The grammar is often no help, and so, for instance, the plural distinction is generally not made for nouns but is left to be understood from the context. This does not always work. The language is not the only culprit. Equally pertinent, and much more important in the view of many Western scholars, is the fact that the Japanese are given to expressing themselves indirectly; their speech and their writing are full of nuances. Professor Edwin O. Reischauer sums it all up this way—that 'it is easier to be ambiguous and vague in Japanese than in most Indo–European tongues', adding that there is nothing about the language 'which prevents concise, clear, and logical presentation, if that is what one wishes to make'.

It was a further handicap that IJN officers have not written much. In comparison with their Royal Navy counterparts, they have been remarkably reticent. The emphasis is on performance. As one flag officer put it, 'The men of the Imperial Navy pride themselves on not writing books.' When they did write, criticism was rare; objective writing on naval matters, even those of the past, was virtually impossible for IJN officers.

I encountered still another problem. I *know* what the British Government, the Chiefs of Staff, the Admiralty, or particular decision-makers are thinking and why they are thinking that way. The papers and minutes are plentiful, and the opinions expressed in them, especially in the minutes, are often quite frank. But even when I had a fair amount of source material on the Japanese side, whether from documents, autobiographies, interviews, etc., on a particular issue or policy or event, I was much less sure that I was getting the whole truth. It is the peculiarly Japanese problem of *tatemae* versus *honne*: *tatemae*, what is said or written *for the record* and which is not necessarily the truth or the whole truth, versus *honne*, the actual truth—what one intends or really means—which one expresses if one is courageous, though, normally, only to confidants or when one is in one's cups. *Honne,* I have reason to believe, does not always appear in the records or in autobiographies—or in interviews with historians. Of course, there have been courageous Navy Ministers—Admirals Inoue Shigeyoshi, Yonai Mitsumasa, and Yoshida Zengo are good examples—and there were other courageous senior officers who spoke their minds fearlessly (and let the Devil take the hindmost); but they were in a minority it would seem. So the historian, or the Western historian at any rate, has a problem in evaluating Japanese materials that he does not have in working with British materials.

Finally, there is the problem of what to include and what to exclude. Selectivity is always a problem for the historian; it has been an especially acute one in the case of this study. What does one do with such topics as the Imperial Navy in relation to the United States Navy, the German Navy, the political situation at home, Japanese foreign policy, and the movement for peace in the last months of the war; or the Royal Navy in relation to the American Navy, the problems of Australian–New Zealand defence, and problems of grand strategy? Books have been (or could be) written on any one of them. Some aspects of each of these topics have an integral connection with my principal theme, the Royal Navy *vis-à-vis* the Imperial Navy and vice versa, hence must be treated. But it would have been all too easy to get *too* involved in any of them. I have found myself constantly walking a tightrope and can only hope that I have not fallen flat on my face in executing this difficult balancing act!

I make no pretence to having examined all pertinent materials in Japanese. Rather have I made what I hope has been a broad and intelligent selection from the unpublished, untranslated records in Tokyo, as well as from the printed materials in Japanese (reminiscences, biographies, monographs, and, above all, the Official War History). Additionally, I have researched the American and German naval records on particular facets of my story.

I bring no theories of history to my research and writing, nor do I arrive at any startling conclusions. I am essentially a narrative historian. I want to tell a story and to tell it well, and with a liberal infusion of the personal, the human, component, for at bottom, to quote Sir Lewis Namier, 'The subject matter of history is human affairs, men in action, things which have happened and how they happened.' The world is indeed more a stage than a laboratory. One aspect of this outlook is my conviction that the writing of history must include a sense of how events appeared to the participants, bereft of the knowledge possessed by historians and others writing long afterwards. The story that I shall tell is, basically, a tragic one, with man's limitations all too prominently displayed, such as his moral cowardice at times and his short-sighted thinking. Yet it will also show man at his sublime best, for there are many instances of courage, moral as well as physical, of far-sightedness, and of an extraordinary spirit of self-sacrifice.

The research and the writing were greatly facilitated by fellowships from the Japan Foundation and the National Endowment for the Humanities, and by grants from the University of California, Irvine. A period of residence at the Rockefeller Foundation's Study and Conference Center at Bellagio was a much needed stimulant. To my university and to these foundations my heartfelt thanks.

It gives me pleasure to express my deep gratitude to the many individuals who have assisted the project in one way or another, a number of whom, unhappily, have since gone aloft. I must begin with my old friends Captain J. S. Litchfield, Lieutenant-Commander P. K. Kemp, and Mr Richard Hough, who gave the manuscript of this volume a thorough and constructive reading, as well as (the first two) answering countless queries and providing much useful information. For valuable recollections and in some instances papers: Admirals of the Fleet Earl Mountbatten of Burma, Lord Fraser of North Cape, Sir Caspar John, and Sir Algernon Willis, Fleet Admiral Arleigh Burke, USN, Admirals Sir Charles Daniel, Sir William Davis, Sir Desmond Dreyer, Sir Robin Durnford-Slater, Sir Guy Grantham, Sir Deric Holland-Martin, Sir Henry Leach, Sir Charles Madden, Bt, Sir Henry McCall, Sir Henry Moore, Sir Richard Onslow, Sir Arthur Peters, Sir Manley Power, Sir Frank Twiss, and Sir David Williams, Vice-Admirals Sir Ronald Brockman, Sir Dick Caldwell, Sir John Collins, Sir Kaye Edden, Sir Peter Gretton, Sir Charles Hughes Hallett, Sir John Hayes, Sir Louis Le Bailly, E. W. L Longley-Cook, Sir Charles Norris, B. B. Schofield, R. M. Servaes, Sir Richard Smeeton, and Sir John Stevens, Rear-Admirals Benjamin Bryant, Sir Kenneth Buckley, G. K. Collett, R. M. Dick, V. D. A. Donaldson, K. H.

PREFACE

Farnhill, J. G. C. Given, J. K. Highton, C. D. Howard-Johnston, C. H. Hutchison, Sir Rowland Jerram, A. W. Laybourne, R. H. Leir, A. D. Nicholl, R. W. Parker, O. W. Phillips, and M. St. L. Searle, Commodore Sir John Clerk, Bt, Captains Stephen Barry, L. H. Bell, G. M. Bennett, H. N. S. Brown, A. W. Clarke, G. T. Cooper, R. J. R. Dendy, D. H. Doig, R. M. Ellis, L. G. Goudy, K. L. Harkness, E. J. Hogg, R. H. Johnson, H. F. Layman, J. W. McClelland, C. W. McMullen, V. C. Merry, J. S. Milner, Hilary Norman, Revd T. A. C. Pakenham, Sir Richard Pim, George Pound, D. G. Roome, Sir Robert Stirling-Hamilton, Bt, G. S. Tuck, P. N. Walter, and F. J. Wylie, Commanders A. P. Barrow-Green, Peter Bartlett, Denis Calnan, T. C. Crease, R. D. East, F. W. B. Edwards, R. F. Harland, Sir Alan Noble, Reay Parkinson, T. V. G. Phillips, R. A. W. Pool, A. C. Reynolds, A. G. Skipworth, A. S. Tyers, M. Craig Waller, D. G. V. Williams, and Rodney Wrightson, Lieutenant-Commanders J. P. Banbury, Vivian Cox, Richard Dyer, R. D. East, W. F. B. Faulkner, S. W. Francis, A. G. C. Franklin, R. K. Hudson, C. H. Knollys, O. M. B. de Las Casas, P. G. Newton, P. W Ratcliffe, W. E. Rolfe, and J. A. F. Somerville, Lieutenant N. H. Power, Marshals of the Royal Air Force Sir Arthur Harris, Bt, and Sir John Slessor, Air Commodore R. W. Chappell, Lieutenant-General Sir Ian Jacob, Brigadier A. T. Cornwall-Jones, Colonels Humphrey Quill and H. P. Williams, Rear-Admiral Paul Auphan, French Navy, Sir Clifford Jarrett, Sir Michael Palliser and the Dowager Lady Palliser, the Dowager Marchioness of Cholmondeley, Lady Allan of Kilmahew, Lady Beatrix Evison, Lady Rawlings, and the Mesdames J. H. Godfrey, Thomas C. Hart, and A. W. Laybourne.

I owe a special debt of gratitude to my beloved mentor, the late Professor William L. Langer, and to Professor Edwin O. Reischauer and Mr A. J. P. Taylor, for encouragement and support; to Admiral of the Fleet Sir Terence Lewin, Admiral Sir Gordon Tait, and Surgeon Vice-Admiral Sir John Rawlins, and their staffs, for powerful strategic assists in certain important matters; and, in Japan, to the Authorities at the Bōeichō Senshibu and the Shiryō Chosakai (Historical Research Institute) for their splendid co-operation, and for invaluable assistance in a myriad of ways, to Professors Tsunoda Jun* and Nomura Minoru (Lieutenant, IJN),

* Except for authors of Japanese works translated into English, Japanese personal names cited in the Preface and in the text are given in the Japanese fashion: family name first and with macrons to indicate long vowels. I have also included macrons in place names, except for well-known ones like Tokyo.

PREFACE

Dr Hata Ikuhiko, and Commander Seno Sadao, JMSDF. Also helpful were Major-General Kenmi Ryōyū, JGSDF, Vice-Admirals Ishiwata Hiroshi, JMSDF, Nakazawa Tasuku, IJN, and Terabe Kineo, JMSDF, Rear-Admirals Chūdō Kan'ei, Horiuchi Shigetada, and Yamamoto Toshio, IJN, Captains Fukuoka Takeshi, IJN, Itō Tatsuji, JMSDF, Matsunaga Keisuke, IJN, Shioyama Sakuichi, IJN, Toyoda Kumao, IJN, Uesaka Yasushi, JMSDF, and Yoshimatsu Masahiro, JMSDF, Commanders Mizumura Hiroshi, JMSDF, Nagato Shigeo, IJN, Sekino Hideo, IJN, Yatsuka Hidenori, JMSDF, and Yoshida Toshio, IJN, Lieutenant-Commanders Akatsuka Ken, JMSDF, Ōhira Yoshirō, IJN, and Takai Sadao, IJN, Lieutenant Matsunaga Ichirō, IJN, Sub-Lieutenant Iwata Tomoo, IJN, Flight Petty Officer Arai Kiyoshi, IJN, Professor Ogawa Kunihiko, and Messrs Hayashi Yochikatsu and Inoue Masaru.

In a category by themselves are those former officers of the Imperial Navy who graciously afforded me lengthy interviews, often at considerable personal inconvenience (the second rank where two are given represents the JMSDF or JGSDF rank attained): Agawa Hiroyuki (Lt.), Chihaya Masataka (Cdr.), Fukuchi Nobuo (Capt./V.-Adm.), Fukui Shizuo (Lt.-Cdr.), Fukushima Tsutomu (Cdr.), Hoshina Zenshirō (V.-Adm.), Ihara Mitsugu (Capt./Adm.), Iki Haruki (Lt.-Cdr.), Irie Kazunao (Capt.), Isobe Tarō (Capt.), Kojima Hideo (R.-Adm.), Mikami Sakuo (Cdr./V.-Adm.), Miyo Kazunari (Capt.), Motora Isamu (Lt.-Cdr.), Nakajima Chikataka (Cdr.), Nakano Chujirō (Capt.), Nakayama Sadayoshi (Cdr./Adm.), Niimi Masaichi (V.-Adm.), Ōi Atsushi (Capt.), Okumiya Masatake (Cdr./Lt.-Gen.), Onozaki Makoto (Cdr.), Saito Kunijirō (Lt./V.-Adm.), Sanagi Sadamu (Capt./Gen.), Sanematsu Yuzuru (Capt.), Suekuni Masao (Capt.), Takahashi Kassaku (Lt.-Cdr.), Terai Yoshimori (Cdr./V.-Adm.), Terazaki Takaji (Capt.), Uchida Kazutomi (Lt.-Cdr./Adm.), Yamamoto Masuhiko (Cdr./V.-Adm.), Yokoyama Ichirō (R.-Adm.), and Yoshii Michinori (Capt.). I also received a number of informative letters from several of these officers, particularly Admiral Yokoyama, Captain Ōi, and Lieutenant-Commander Iki. Admiral Uchida graciously helped me to solve scores of problems.

I received considerable assistance from Commander R. C. Burton and Mr David Brown, successively Heads of the Naval Historical Branch and the Naval Historical Library, Ministry of Defence, and

PREFACE

Mr R. M. Coppock and the Misses Veronica Riley and Lesley Westgate of their staff, and from Rear-Admiral John D. H. Kane, Jr., and Dr Dean C. Allard, respectively, the Director of Naval History and the Head of the Operational Archives Branch, Naval Historical Center, Washington, D.C., and their extraordinarily efficient staff.

I also wish to thank Vice-Admiral R. H. Hillenkoetter, USN, Captain Stephen Roskill, Mrs Patricia Bradford and Miss Marion Stewart, successive Heads of the Archives Centre of Churchill College, and Mrs Margaret Tong and Miss Clare Stephens, of their Staff, Mrs Mollie Travis, the Archivist at Broadlands, Miss Margaret Browne, of the Historical Section of the Australian Department of Foreign Affairs, Mrs A. A. Bailey, of the Ministry of Defence, Mr R. F. Barker, Keeper of Aviation Records, RAF Museum, Messrs Norman Evans, E. Odell, E. K. Timings, and J. L. Walford, of the Public Record Office, Mr Alan Pearsall, of the National Maritime Museum, Air Commodore H. A. Probert, Head of the Air Historical Branch (RAF), Ministry of Defence, Mr R. W. A. Suddaby, Keeper of the Department of Documents, and Mr M. J. Willis, of the Department of Photographs, of the Imperial War Museum, Mr. H. L. Theobald, Head of the Cabinet Office Historical Section, and Mr J. W. Cheatle, of his staff, and Messrs Roger Berry and Eric MacDonald, and Mrs Cathy Smith, all of the University of California, Irvine, Professor Henry Smith II, of the Santa Barbara campus, and his wife Kimie, the Interlibrary Loan staffs of both campuses, notably Mrs Kathryn Uthe at Santa Barbara, Dr Bengt Ljunggren, Professors Carl Boyd, Raymond A. Callahan, Frank Iklé, J. M. McCarthy, Bryan Ranft, and J. R. Robertson, Dr John Horsefield, Commander James Auer, and Lieutenants B. A. McMunn and Charles G. Cooper III, USN, Messrs Patrick Beesly, J. D. Lawson, Paul Longrigg, Colin H. Mackenzie, Martin Middlebrook, C. F. Shores, A. F. Thompson and John Winton, Captain Duval, Head of the Service historique de la marine of the French Navy, Commander F. C. van Oosten, Director of Naval History, Royal Netherlands Navy, and Professor James William Morley, of Columbia University, who permitted me to see and to use (in Chapter Six) pertinent translated material from volume vi of the classic *Taiheiyō sensō e no michi* (The Road to the Pacific War) in advance of publication.

My once respectable command of Japanese having atrophied

PREFACE

almost to vanishing point over the years, I have relied for translations upon Commanders Fukushima Tsutomu and Sekiguchi Kōzō, IJN, and, in the United States, upon Mesdames Hisako Coox and Masako Ohnuki, all of whom performed superbly. Commander Sekiguchi, whose assistance extended to checking innumerable points and to a reading of the IJN sections of this volume, was a particular tower of strength.

Miss Carol Pfeil provided first-class typing assistance, no mean feat, given my handwriting and propensity for mucking up a manuscript.

Dr Oliver Metcalf did a superb job in editing the manuscript for the Press. I must also thank Mr John Callow in preparing the maps.

Grateful acknowledgement is made for permission to quote from the copyright material indicated: Cambridge University Press, from Ann Trotter, *Britain and East Asia, 1933–1937*; Cassell Ltd. and Houghton Mifflin Company, from Winston S. Churchill, *The Second World War*, volume iii, *The Grand Alliance*; Thomas M. Coffey, from *Imperial Tragedy*; Columbia University Press, from William T. de Bary (ed.), *Sources of Japanese Tradition*, Dorothy Borg and Shumpei Okamoto (eds.), *Pearl Harbor as History: Japanese–American Relations, 1931–1941*, James William Morley (ed.), *Japan's Foreign Policy, 1868–1941: A Research Guide*, and Morley (ed.), *Japan's Road to the Pacific War. Deterrent Diplomacy: Japan, Germany, and the USSR, 1935–1940*; Faber and Faber Ltd., from Captain Russell Grenfell, *Main Fleet to Singapore*; Harvard University Press, from Stephen E. Pelz, *Race to Pearl Harbor: The Failure of the Second London Naval Conference and the Onset of World War II*; Holt, Renehart, and Winston, from Commander James E. Auer, *The Postwar Rearmament of Japanese Maritime Forces, 1945–1971*; International Creative Management, from Captain Tameichi Hara (with Fred Saito and Roger Pineau), *Japanese Destroyer Captain*; Macdonald & Jane's Publishers Ltd., from Cecil Bullock, *Etajima: The Japanese Dartmouth*; Oxford University Press, from Peter Lowe, *Great Britain and the Origins of the Pacific War: A Study of British Policy in East Asia, 1937–1941*; Penguin Books Ltd., from Martin Middlebrook and Patrick Mahoney, *Battleship: The Loss of the Prince of Wales and the Repulse*; Random House, Inc., from Cecil Brown, *Suez to Singapore*; Stanford University Press, from Robert J. C. Butow, *Tojo and the Coming of the War*, and Nobutaka Ike (ed.), *Japan's Decision for War: Records of the 1941 Policy Conferences*; University of North Carolina Press, from

PREFACE

James R. Leutze, *Bargaining for Supremacy: Anglo–American Naval Collaboration, 1937–1941*; and the United States Naval Institute, from Captain Atsushi Ōi, 'Why Japan's Anti-Submarine Warfare Failed,' in the *United States Naval Institute Proceedings*, Vol. lxxviii. Transcripts of Crown-copyright records in the Public Record Office appear by permission of the Controller of H.M. Stationery Office.

A few explanations may be helpful. ADM (Admiralty), AIR (Air Ministry), CAB (Cabinet), PREM (Prime Minister), and FO (Foreign Office) documents cited in footnotes are in the Public Record Office at Kew. What we in the West know as the Pacific War (which the Imperial Navy itself preferred) the Japanese also know as the 'Greater East Asia War' (the Army's preference). I shall use the former throughout. References to South-east Asia, South-west Pacific, and the Far East may cause confusion without an indication of what I mean by these vague geographical areas. By South-east Asia I mean the land and sea areas bounded (clockwise) by (to use the place names of 1941) Burma, Thailand, French Indo-China, British Borneo, the Philippines, the Netherlands East Indies, and Malaya. By South-west Pacific I mean South-east Asia plus Australia and New Zealand, and by the Far East, China, Korea, Japan (including Formosa), the Soviet Far East, and the Pacific Ocean extending to 159 degrees east longitude and as far south as 20 degrees latitude.

Sea distances are given in nautical miles: one nautical mile = one minute of latitude, 6,080 feet, 1·15 statute miles, or 1·852 kilometres. Warship tonnage is for standard displacement (fully equipped and ready for sea, but excluding all oil and reserve feed water), and is given in (long) tons. In general, linear measures and weights are British in the case of warship and aircraft specifications and performance, but metric in the case of the 10 December action. An uneasy compromise! For those who do not mind simple calculations, herewith the equivalents:

British (and American), with metric equivalents

1 pound	0·4536 kilogram
1 (long) ton	1·016 tonnes
1 inch	25·4 millimetres or 2·54 centimetres
1 foot	0·3048 metre

PREFACE

1 yard	0·9144 metre
1 (statute) mile	1·609 kilometres

Metric, with British equivalents

1 kilogram	2·205 pounds
1 tonne (metric ton)	0·984 (long) ton or 2,205 pounds
1 millimetre	0·039 inch
1 metre	3·281 feet or 1·094 yards
1 kilometre	0·6214 mile

Santa Barbara, California
January 1980

Arthur Marder

NOTE

This volume went to press just before Professor Marder's death. It was planned as the first of two volumes on the Royal Navy and the Imperial Japanese Navy from 1936 to the end of the Pacific War in 1945. There is no bibliography, as Professor Marder intended this to appear in the second volume. Lieutenant-Commander P. K. Kemp has kindly undertaken the proof reading and the compilation of the index.

Contents

	Page
PREFACE	vii
ABBREVIATIONS	xxviii
ILLUSTRATIONS	xxx
MAPS	xxxii

PART ONE. COLLISION COURSE

CHAPTER I. 'A POTENTIAL AND POWERFUL FOE'

1. **FRIENDS, ALLIES, AND QUONDAM ALLIES** — 3
   RN influence on the IJN—The Anglo-Japanese Alliance—Its annulment—The process of alienation—Amicable relations between the navies continue—Naval contretemps—The naval limitation treaties—The Japanese proposal at the Second London Naval Conference—The Second London Naval Treaty—Japan refuses to subscribe—Invocation of the Treaty's escape clause.

2. **JAPANESE NAVAL EXPANSION** — 15
   The Third Replenishment Plan—The Fourth Replenishment Plan—British concern—Capital ship comparisons—The effect of the RN modernization policy.

3. **FAR EASTERN STAKES** — 19
   Japan's aggressive ambitions in China—British and American alarm—Motives underlying Japanese imperialism—The British stake in China—Their view of the Japanese goals.

4. **ANTI-BRITISH FEELINGS IN THE IMPERIAL NAVY** — 22
   The change in the IJN attitude towards the RN—*Japan Must Fight Britain*—The visit of HMS *Medway* to Keelung, Formosa—Evidence of the IJN's aggressive outlook—The Far Eastern situation begins to influence British policy in an important way.

CHAPTER II. BRITISH STRATEGIC DILEMMAS (1936–1939)

1. **DEFENCE ORGANIZATION AND PERSONALITIES** — 28
   The War Cabinet, CID, COS Committee, Joint Planning Staff, Board of Admiralty, Naval Staff—Role of First Sea Lord and First Lord—The First Lords—A. V. Alexander—Chatfield—Backhouse—Pound—Why the Navy's views on strategic matters carried exceptional weight.

2. **MAIN FLEET TO SINGAPORE: CONUNDRUMS AND UNCERTAINTIES** — 36
   RN strength in the Far East—The 'period before relief'—Strength of the main Fleet—Pressure from Australia and New Zeland—Assurances from the COS and Admiralty—The 'bombshell' of 20 March 1939—The Admiralty and Foreign Office proposals for battleships at Singapore—Their views on a foreign policy of limited liability—The Admiralty vis-à-vis Foreign Office initiatives in 1938–9.

CONTENTS

       Page

3. THE FRENCH CONNECTION   46
The Anglo–French naval conversations of spring 1939—The French position has powerful backing in Whitehall—Backhouse's view on Far Eastern naval strategy—Churchill's views.

4. STRATEGIC IMPASSE   50
The international situation in spring 1939—Extension of the period before the relief of Singapore—The debate over Main Fleet strategy—A. B. Cunningham's appreciation of the naval situation—Confusion and uncertainty over Main Fleet strength in a triangular war—Fresh assurances to the Australians—The Tientsin crisis drives home unpalatable strategic truths—The mood of the Services on the eve of the European War—The Molotov–Ribbentrop Pact.

5. HOW TO FIGHT JAPAN?   62
Far Eastern naval war plans, 1937–9—The Navy opts for a defensive strategy—Economic pressure—The COS consider IJN options—A measure of realism is introduced in spring 1939—Importance and status of Singapore—The importance of Hong Kong—Discussion of its standard of defence—The COS and Churchill oppose the reinforcement of Hong Kong.

6. THE AMERICAN NAVAL CONNECTION   69
American naval co-operation is seen as the key to Britain's strategic dilemmas—The Ingersoll–Phillips conversations, January 1938—Subsequent modifications of the agreement—The RN–USN conversations in Washington, June 1939.

CHAPTER III. THE NEW REALITIES (SEPTEMBER 1939–SEPTEMBER 1940)

1. THE DARKENING SCENE   75
Churchill and the Navy—Reduction of naval strength in the Far East—Craigie appeals for capital ships at Singapore—Churchill attempts to quiet Australian–New Zealand fears—The new realities, spring 1940—The COS are unable to spare a fleet for the East—Churchill puts a good face on a bad situation—Appeasement of Japan—The Admiralty's four principles.

2. 'FOLLY TO INVITE JAPANESE HOSTILITY'   81
The problem of the Dutch East Indies—Should Britain fight if Japan attacked the Islands?—COS and War Cabinet divisions—The COS 7 August 1940 paper on the Dutch East Indies—The COS 15 August revised Far East Appreciation—Prospects for peace in the Far East, summer 1940.

CHAPTER IV. THE IMPERIAL NAVY AND THE SOUTHWARD DRIVE

1. THE NAVY HIGH COMMAND   89
The Emperor's prerogative of supreme command—IGHQ—The Liaison and Imperial Conferences—The Navy Minister's powers—The bureaux of the Ministry—The Chief of the Navy General Staff *vis-à-vis* the Navy Minister—The divisions of the General Staff—The independence of the Supreme Command.

CONTENTS

Page

2. THE DECISION-MAKERS — 94
The purge of 1933-4—The Yonai–Yamamoto–Inoue team: personalities, views on a Tripartite Pact—'Whitehall warriors' v. sea officers—Yamamoto, target of the extremists—Yoshida succeeds Yonai as Navy Minister—Sumiyama succeeds Yamamoto as Vice-Navy Minister—Abe follows Inoue at the Naval Affairs Bureau—Pro- and anti-Pact forces in the Naval General Staff: Prince Fushimi, Koga, Kondō, Ugaki.

3. 'WE MUSTN'T MISS THE BUS' — 105
Captain Takagi's paper on foreign policy alternatives—Events play into the hands of the extremists—The 'legend of the Imperial Navy's moderation'—The Navy presses for an advance into the 'Southern Area'—A programme of 'footsteps'—The fresh drive in the Navy for the Tripartite Pact—'Outline of the Main Principles for Coping with the Changing World Situation' (4 July 1940)—Yonai is toppled as Prime Minister—Prince Konoe succeeds him—Matsuoka, the new Foreign Minister—The Liaison Conference of 27 July approves the 'Main Principles'—Progress towards a Tripartite Pact—Yoshida fights the Pact—His isolation at the ministry—His resignation—Oikawa succeeds him—Toyoda Teijirō, the new Vice-Navy Minister—The Navy's major reservation to the Pact—Matsuoka's assurances—The Navy takes the plunge—Provisions of the Pact—One reason for the Navy's metamorphosis: the pressures from within—Other factors.

4. 'A FORCE LET LOOSE' — 127
Reactions to the Pact—How Japan's leaders viewed the Pact—The Pact a failure in its main aspects—How Britain viewed the Pact—The larger significance of the Pact—The Navy National Defence Policy Committee and its Chief, Oka—Its First Committee: Ishikawa, Tomioka—Functions and importance of the First Committee—Prince Fushimi on the Southward advance—The four cases that would provoke Japanese military action.

CHAPTER V. 'WE MUST TRY TO BEAR OUR EASTERN ANXIETIES PATIENTLY'

1. BRITAIN AND THE TRIPARTITE PACT — 136
Japan occupies northern French Indo-China—The US reaction—The British consider possible deterrents—The COS prefer an interchange of information with the Dutch Services.

2. AGAIN THE AMERICANS — 141
The Bailey Committee is formed—RN–USN co-operation—Churchill intimates the desirability of a US naval force at Singapore—Ghormley arrives in London—British proposals for a reinforcement of the USN in the East—The problem of staff talks—The Americans are not eager to tie their hands—The Admiralty restate their case—Stark rejects British strategical views—The US 'Plan Dog'—Agreement on Washington staff talks—Churchill's views on the talks and strategic objectives in the Pacific—The Admiralty discuss their position re US views on Pacific strategy—The picture at year's end.

CONTENTS

Page

CHAPTER VI. TOKYO: COLLISION COURSE (JANUARY 1941–OCTOBER 1941)

1. 'TIME IS NOT ON OUR SIDE'   153

The Navy's attitude towards the use of force in the South—The Navy's policy re Singapore—The Navy and the Dutch East Indies—The policy statement of 30 January—Indo-China policy—The neutrality pact with the Soviet Union—Negotiations are opened in Washington—The decision of the 17 April IGHQ conference—The changes in the Navy High Command: Nagano, Kondō, Fukudome, Sawamoto—The pro-war party in the Navy is heard from—Germany invades the Soviet Union: the Japanese quandary—The Imperial Conference of 2 July—Konoe forms a new Cabinet—The move into northern French Indo-China—The Western response—The question of oil—Nagano sounds the alarm bell—The talks in Washington are deadlocked—Military considerations are uppermost after July—The policy statement on 'Essentials'—The Imperial Conference of 6 September—The Supreme Command regards war as inevitable.

2. THE EQUIVOCATION OF THE NAVY   175

The decision to continue the diplomatic negotiations—Tōjō's position—The Ogikubo conference on 12 October—Explanation of Oikawa's equivocation—Konoe cannot budge Tōjō—Tōjō becomes Prime Minister—Toyoda is considered as Oikawa's successor—Shimada, the new Navy Minister—Itō replaces Kondō as Vice-Chief of Staff—Tōjō agrees to start from scratch.

CHAPTER VII. ANGLO-AMERICAN COLLABORATION (1941)

1. 'THE FIRST THING IS TO GET THE UNITED STATES INTO THE WAR'   185

Signs of an imminent Japanese southward move early in 1941—British strategists debate Japan's intentions and British action—Churchill confides his fears to Roosevelt—A relaxation in the tension—The American-British staff conferences open—The two delegations—Fundamental differences emerge—Singapore is the crux—Admiral Turner outlines the role of the USN—Bellairs's paper—The US reply—Churchill is furious with the British appreciation—The air is cleared—A basic strategy, ABC-1, is agreed upon—The British mission to Pearl Harbor—Reflections on American strategy.

2. THE DUTCH EMBARRASSMENT   202

The position of the COS toward the Dutch East Indies—The recommendation of the Far Eastern Committee of the War Cabinet—The Admiralty state their position—The question of assistance to the Dutch surfaces again—Eden's minute of 30 July—Churchill proposes a more definite assurance to the Dutch—Eden at last offers the Dutch an unconditional agreement—The Anglo-Dutch staff talks: ADA, ADB, BD—The COS accept the ADB Report—The American Service Chiefs reject it—The basic point at issue—The Americans reject ADB-2—Agreement for a Phillips-Hart conference in Manila—Significance of the failure to draw up a common strategy against Japanese expansion.

CONTENTS

CHAPTER VIII. 'STRATEGICAL CLOUD CUCKOO LAND'

1. **THE GENESIS OF FORCE Z** — 213
   The threat of further Japanese moves to the south—Should Britain fight if Japan advanced into Thailand?—Roosevelt and Churchill warn Japan (August)—Evidence that the Japanese are preparing for operations—Australian pressures—Menzies in London—The Pacific Dominions have further cause for concern—Admiralty debates on whether to strengthen Far Eastern naval strength at the expense of the Mediteranean—Churchill is convinced Japan will not go to war—Menzies telegraphs Churchill on 12 August—Admiralty plans for the Far East—Churchill's 'Action this day' minute of 25 August—Pound's reply, 28 August—Churchill finds serious fault with it—Eden and the Far East and China Cs-in-C strengthen Churchill in his resolve to dispatch a deterrent force—The fall of the Konoe Government is the catalytic agent—The Defence Committee meeting of 17 October—A compromise decision is reached on 20 October—The *Prince of Wales* is to proceed to Singapore—The grounding of the *Indomitable*—Would the presence of a carrier with Force Z have made a great difference?—Tovey and the Naval Staff protest the dispatch of the *Prince of Wales*.

2. **'THEY THAT STAND HIGH HAVE MANY BLASTS TO SHAKE THEM'** — 231
   Churchill is savaged for the decision to send out an unbalanced force—A critique of his views—The case for Churchill—Roskill's charge re Pound and Churchill—A critique of Roskill—The controversy over Pound's health—Pound and the Sea Lords express their reservations to the First Lord—The political facet of the issue—A last word on the genesis of Force Z.

CHAPTER IX. 'LET SLIP THE DOGS OF WAR'

1. **TOKYO: POINT OF NO RETURN** — 242
   The debate over alternatives, 23 October–1 November—The confused position of the Navy—The inflexibility of the system—The historic Liaison Conference of 1 November—The Supreme War Council meets—The Imperial Conference of 5 November—Japan's 'A' and 'B' proposals to the US—The Hull proposal is received with consternation—The Emperor consults the Senior Statesmen—And Nagano and Shimada—The Imperial Conference of 1 December decides on war.

2. **RESPONSIBILITIES AND EXPECTATIONS** — 251
   Why the Navy opted for war—The pro-peace flag officers—The lack of moral courage at the top—The aggressive middle-echelon officers—The position of the individual Navy leaders: Nagano, Itō, Fukudome, Tomioka, Shimada, Sawamoto, Oka, Hoshina—Expectations about the outcome of the war.

PART TWO. COMPARISONS AND IMAGES

CHAPTER X. THE IMPERIAL JAPANESE NAVY. I. THE MEN

1. **THE 'JAPANESE DARTMOUTH'** — 265
   The social status of IJN officers—The competition for Etajima—

CONTENTS

Page

The Etajima routine—Discipline—The Emperor Meiji's rescript—The Great Hall—The Naval Museum—The 'Five Points of Self-Discipline'—Officers should be gentlemen—*Kun'iku*—The end product—The Naval War College—Criteria for the more important appointments—Comparisons between Etajima and Dartmouth.

2. THE IMPERIAL NAVY OFFICERS: EVALUATION   285

Physical condition—Strong points—Weaknesses—Senior-junior officer relations—Status of the engineering officers—Senior-junior relations in the RN—Quality of IJN enlisted men—Relations between officers and men in the IJN and RN—The differences between IJN and IJA officers—Poor inter-Service co-operation.

3. 'WAR IS SO EASY COMPARED WITH PEACETIME EXERCISES!'   292

Intensive training for battle—Illustrations—Combined Fleet training under Yamamoto—The Navy makes good use of the China Incident—Overstress on fighting spirit.

CHAPTER XI. THE IMPERIAL JAPANESE NAVY: II. MATÉRIEL, TACTICS, AND STRATEGY

1. OF SHIPS AND PLANES   296

Excellence of *matériel*—The leading characteristics of warships—The Yamato-class battleships—IJN-RN battleship comparisons—Aircraft carriers—Cruisers—Destroyers—Submarines—Total warship strength—Superiority in other *matériel*—RN advantages—IJN air: quality of officers—Yamamoto's boost to naval aviation—Intensification of air training—The Zero fighter—The Kate, Nell, and Betty bombers—Development of the oxygen torpedo—Wartime performance of the oxygen torpedo—Aerial torpedoes—The battleship *v.* carrier controversy—Shortcomings of IJN air—RN air problems.

2. 'FIGHT THE ENEMY ON SIGHT'   318

The tactical tradition: *kenteki hissen*—The concept of the decisive battle—Attritional tactics—Night action—The tactics of outranging—Shipping protection is slighted—Reasons—Other by-products of the offensive fetish—The RN, too, emphasizes the battleship and the decisive action.

3. GRAND STRATEGY   324

Formulations of defence policy—The Navy's operational plans—The first war game with the RN as the enemy—Singapore and Malaya—The 1941 manœuvres—Recognition that the US and Britain are inseparable—The Services clash on the sequence of operations in the south—Agreement on operational plans—The table-top manœuvres of September 1941—The Pearl Harbor operation—IJN relations with Germany.

CHAPTER XII. IMAGES

1. THE IMPERIAL NAVY LOOKS AT THE ROYAL NAVY   334

The role of Intelligence—Intelligence on the RN—The *King George*

CONTENTS

Page

V and her AA guns and radar—RN asdic—IJN opinion of the RN's capabilities—Pro-RN feelings and influences.

2. THE ROYAL NAVY LOOKS AT THE IMPERIAL NAVY 341

RN assessments of the IJN—Estimates of IJN air—A few RN officers see things differently—Captain Vivian's evaluation: 'national characteristics', etc.—Reactions in the Navy—Reasons for underrating the IJN—Difficulties in procuring Intelligence—Achievements of NID—The FECB—The OIC and JIC—'Where British Intelligence slipped up'.

PART THREE. THE SAGA OF FORCE Z

CHAPTER XIII. ODYSSEY

1. OF MEN AND SHIPS 365

Phillips is appointed C-in-C-designate, Far East—The general feeling about him—Why the appointment was made—A pen portrait of Phillips—The Admiral's staff—Leach—Tennant—The *Prince of Wales*—The *Repulse*—The bomb *v.* battleship controversy—The evolution of Phillips's position on the air threat.

2. MAIN FLEET TO SINGAPORE 388

Phillips is not optimistic—Most officers are—Force Z at Cape Town—On to Ceylon—The *Repulse* in the Indian Ocean—The Force arrives at Singapore—Layton's disappointment.

3. FORCE Z AT SINGAPORE 394

The reception of the fleet—A peacetime atmosphere pervades Singapore—The *Repulse* sails for Port Darwin—Phillips and Hart confer in Manila—It is abruptly terminated—Hart's promise of destroyers—The bombing of Singapore—Developments during November–early December: What were Japan's intentions?—Operation 'Matador'—Whitehall's obsession with Singapore as a fixed base—Pound suggests that Force Z leave Singapore—The COS emergency meeting, 6 December—The Japanese land troops in Thailand and Malaya—The staff conference in London, 9 December—Phillips returns to Singapore—The conference at the Naval Base, early 8 December—The conference with Layton and Palliser—The council of war in the *Prince of Wales*—The Admiral's plan is adopted—Considerations in Phillips's mind—Surprise and air support are crucial to success—The latter is denied.

4. 'WE ARE OFF TO LOOK FOR TROUBLE' 420

The composition of the Force—Expectations of disaster—But the officers in the flagship are absolutely confident—Confirmation of the lack of fighter support—The reasons—Was the Governor to blame?—Phillips chooses to stand on—The weather favours the fleet—The C-in-C's message to the ships' companies—The fleet is spotted from the air—The operation is abandoned—The reaction from the officers—Phillips's mood—Palliser's report on a Kuantan landing—Course is altered to Kuantan—The failure to notify Singapore—The reasons—The *Tenedos* is detached to Singapore—Disappointment off Kuantan—Notice of the enemy's near proximity—But Singapore is not informed—Phillips manœuvres the Force.

CONTENTS

CHAPTER XIV. ILIAD

1. CONTACT — 441
Components and responsibilities of the Southern Force—The 1st Air Force—Kondō, Ozawa, Kurita, and Matsunaga—What the Japanese knew about Force Z—Movements of the Southern Force—The landing at Kota Bharu—Ozawa's thinking—*I-65* sights Force Z—The response of the 22nd Air Flotilla—Uncertainty over British intentions—The aircraft sortie—Ozawa's strategy—Kondō alters his strategy—Ozawa's movements—His near meeting with Force Z—'We are the *Chōkai*!'—Kondō, Ozawa, and Kurita join forces—Contact with the British is lost—*I-58* sights Force Z—Kondō reverses course—Matsunaga orders a fan-shaped search—The attacking force—Bombs and torpedoes—The search is on—The *Tenedos* is mistaken for an enemy battleship—Reserve Ensign Hoashi sights the enemy.

2. THE NAVAL BATTLE OFF MALAYA — 465
Air tactics—The 'brutal actions of the Japanese'—The first (Mihoro) attack—The second (Genzan) attack: the *Prince of Wales* suffers two serious hits—The third (Mihoro) attack—Tennant's skill in dodging torpedoes—The fourth (Kanoya) attack: the *Repulse* receives some knocks—She sinks—The fifth (Mihoro) attack—The sixth (Mihoro) attack: the *Prince of Wales* receives her *coup de grâce*—She sinks—Phillips and Leach go down with her—What was the C-in-C's duty?—The Japanese aircraft retire—British fighters appear: The circumstances—Would their timely arrival have made a difference?—The high spirit, discipline, bravery, and humour of the ships' companies—Why so many survived—Layton is appointed C-in-C—His contretemps with the ships' companies—A note on IJN high-level bombing and torpedo tactics.

3. '... OR SURVIVED WITH HONOUR' — 483
Discipline in RN ships—Examples of courage in adversity—Return of the destroyers to Singapore—Admiral Layton's reactions—Note on Japanese bombing techniques.

CHAPTER XV. POST-MORTEM

1. 'ATTACKS MAGNIFICENTLY CARRIED OUT — 491
Statistics of bomb and torpedo hits—Damage and losses to IJN aircraft—British admiration of the Japanese performance.

2. 'I HAVE BAD NEWS...' — 494
The loss of the two ships a shock to British morale and prestige—Press reactions—How Churchill received the news—His statements in the Commons—How Alexander and Pound took the news—Pound defends Phillips—The Admiralty inquiry—The debate in the Navy and among naval historians—An appraisal of Phillips's strategy—'Where the hell was the air support?'—The failure of the inter-Service command at the top—Brooke-Popham's deficiencies—The fundamental mistake.

3. 'THE BISMARCK IS AVENGED' — 506
The bravery and fanaticism of the IJN pilots—The famous wreath incident—The wreck of the *Repulse* is located—The wrecks today—Japanese reactions to the victory.

CONTENTS

Page

4. **LESSONS AND RESULTS** — 512
   What the Royal Navy learned from the action—A factor in the loss of the *Prince of Wales* known to few—The Bucknill Committee—The IJN investigates the lessons of the battle—But fails to absorb all the lessons—The battle and the aircraft *v.* battleships controversy in the IJN—The RN is wiser in this respect—The strategic consequences of the battle—The RN and the British people are demoralized—It is different in Japan—The RN determination to pay the Japanese back.

INDEX — 523

ABBREVIATIONS

AA	anti-aircraft
ABCD	American–British–Chinese–Dutch
ABD	American–British–Dutch
A/C	aircraft
ACNS	Assistant Chief of Naval Staff
ACNS (F)	Assistant Chief of Naval Staff (Foreign)
ACNS(H)	Assistant Chief of Naval Staff (Home)
ADA	Anglo–Dutch–Australian
ADB	American–Dutch–British
AD of P	Assistant Director of Plans
AHQ	Air Headquarters
AOC	Air Officer Commanding
A/S	anti-submarine
BD	British–Dutch
CAS	Chief of Air Staff
C-in-C	Commander-in-Chief
CID	Committee of Imperial Defence
CIGS	Chief of Imperial General Staff
CNO	Chief of Naval Operations, USN
CNS	Chief of Naval Staff (alternate title of First Sea Lord)
CO	Commanding Officer
COIS	Chief of Intelligence Staff, Far East
COS	Chiefs of Staff or Chief of Staff to a Flag Officer Commanding
DCNS	Deputy Chief of Naval Staff
DDNAD	Deputy Director, Naval Air Division
DDOD(F)	Deputy Director of Operations Division (Foreign)
DNI	Director of Naval Intelligence
DNO	Director of Naval Ordnance
DOD(H)	Director of Operations Division (Home)
D of P	Director of Plans
FAA	Fleet Air Arm
FECB	Far East Combined Bureau
IGHQ	Japanese Imperial General Headquarters
IJA	Imperial Japanese Army
IJN	Imperial Japanese Navy
JGSDF	Japan Ground Self-Defence Force

ABBREVIATIONS

JIC	Joint Intelligence Committee
JMSDF	Japan Maritime Self-Defence Force
NID	Naval Intelligence Division
NID4	Naval Intelligence Division, Far East Section
OIC	Operational Intelligence Centre
RAF	Royal Air Force
RAN	Royal Australian Navy
RN	Royal Navy
RNAS	Royal Naval Air Service (until 1918)
RNVR	Royal Naval Volunteer Reserve
R/T	radio telephony
S/M	submarine
SO	Senior Officer
SO(I)	Staff Officer, Intelligence
SO(O)	Staff Officer, Operations
SO(P)	Staff Officer, Plans
T/B	torpedo-bomber
USN	United States Navy
VCNS	Vice-Chief of Naval Staff
W/T	wireless telegraphy

List of Illustrations

Admiral of the Fleet Sir Dudley Pound, First Sea Lord, June 1939–October 1943
(c. 1944, probably from a photograph; Institute of Directors, Pall Mall)   Frontispiece

PLATES APPEAR BETWEEN PAGES 256 AND 257

Plate
- 1(a) HMS *Prince of Wales* arriving at Singapore on 2 December 1941
  (*Imperial War Museum*)
- (b) HMS *Repulse*, April 1939
  (*National Maritime Museum*)

- 2(a) *Yamato*
  (*Historical Research Institute, Tokyo*)
- (b) *Hiei* (Kongo class)
  (*A water-colour by Mr Kaga Seijirō; original in the Historical Research Institute, Tokyo*)

- 3(a) Nell: Mark 22, IJN's standard land-based medium bomber in 1941.
  (*Japanese Defence Agency, Military History Department*)
- (b) Betty: Mark II, land-based medium bomber that gradually replaced the Nell from 1941.
  (*Japanese Defence Agency, Military History Department*)

- 4(a) Vice-Admiral Ozawa Jisaburō, commanding the Malaya Force, Naval Battle off Malaya
  (*Japanese Defence Agency, Military History Department*)
- (b) Vice-Admiral Kondō Nobutake, Vice-Chief of the Naval General Staff, October 1939–August 1941, commanding the Southern Force, Naval Battle off Malaya
  (*Japanese Defence Agency, Military History Department*)

- 5(a) Admiral Yoshida Zengo, Navy Minister, August 1939–September 1940
  (*Lieutenant Yoshida Kioyoshi, IJN; reproduced by Suzuki Photo Studio, Tokyo*)
- (b) Admiral Shimada Shigetarō, Navy Minister, October 1941–July 1944
  (*Japanese Defence Agency, Military History Department*)

- 6(a) Admiral of the Fleet Yamamoto Isoroku, C-in-C, Combined Fleet, August 1939–April 1943, on about D-day, 8 December 1941
  (*Historical Research Institute, Tokyo; reproduced by Suzuki Photo Studio, Tokyo*)

ILLUSTRATIONS

Plate

- (b) Admiral Oikawa Koshirō, Navy Minister, September 1940–October 1941
  (*Japanese Defence Agency, Military History Department*)

7(a) Admiral of the Fleet Prince Fushimi Hiroyasu, Chief of the Naval General Staff, October 1933–April 1941
  (*Japanese Defence Agency, Military History Department*)
- (b) Admiral of the Fleet Nagano Osami, Chief of the Naval General Staff, April 1941–February 1944
  (*Japanese Defence Agency, Military History Department*)

8(a) Admiral Yonai Mitsumasa, Navy Minister, February 1937–August 1939
  (*Japanese Defence Agency, Military History Department*)
- (b) Rear-Admiral Inoue Shigeyoshi, Chief of the Bureau of Naval Affairs, October 1937–October 1939
  (*Commander Sekiguchi Kōzō, IJN*)

9(a) Churchill mixing with US sailors in HMS *Prince of Wales* at Atlantic Conference, 16 August 1941
  (*Imperial War Museum*)
- (b) A. V. Alexander, First Lord of the Admiralty, May 1940–May 1945, at the Admiralty
  (Radio Times *Hulton*)

10(a) Admiral of the Fleet Lord Chatfield, First Sea Lord, January 1933–August 1938, Minister for Co-ordination of Defence, January 1939–May 1940
  (*Portrait by R. G. Eves, HMS* Excellent, *Portsmouth*)
- (b) Admiral of the Fleet Sir Roger Backhouse, First Sea Lord, August 1938–June 1939
  (Radio Times *Hulton*)

11(a) Vice-Admiral Sir Tom Phillips, Vice-Chief of the Naval Staff, June 1939–October 1941, C-in-C, Eastern Fleet (as Acting Admiral), October–December 1941, at the Admiralty c. January 1941
  (Radio Times *Hulton*)
- (b) Captain J. C. Leach, Captain of HMS *Prince of Wales*, in the ship in 1941
  (*Imperial War Museum*)

12(a) Vice-Admiral W. G. Tennant, Captain of HMS *Repulse* in 1941, visiting a carrier in June 1945
  (*Imperial War Museum*)

ILLUSTRATIONS

Plate
(b) Admiral A. F. E. Palliser, Chief of Staff to the C-in-C, Eastern Fleet, October–December 1941, as Fourth Sea Lord in 1944
(*Imperial War Museum*)

Maps

BETWEEN PAGES 521–523

Map 1. South-East Asia, the Far East, and Western Pacific, 1941
Map 2. The naval battle off Malaya
Map 3. British and Japanese naval movements, 8–10 December 1941

PART I
Collision Course

I

'A Potential and Powerful Foe'

> ... master and pupils have just reason to be proud of each other.
> *The Times*, 24 September 1894 (after the Battle of the Yalu in the Sino-Japanese War).

> The Japs lull us to sleep—one day when the moment is propitious they will cut our throats—because their policy cannot tolerate one having the position in the Western Pacific which we require.
> ADMIRAL SIR FREDERIC DREYER (C-in-C, China) to Admiral of the Fleet Sir Ernle Chatfield (First Sea Lord), 19 August 1933.

> The Japanese hope to be able to fight England alone, and consider themselves quite ready to do so now.
> An Australian naval officer early in 1938, on a conversation with IJN officers.

1. FRIENDS, ALLIES, AND QUONDAM ALLIES

FOR over half a century there were close and on the whole amicable relations between the Royal Navy and the Imperial Japanese Navy. It was the former which laid the foundations of the latter in the first generation of the Meiji Era that began in 1868. The Japanese, aware of Britain's naval predominance, naturally turned to the Royal Navy for help in educating and training the officers and men of their new Navy. British naval instructors were active in Japan from 1870—from shortly after the establishment in November 1869 of a Naval Training College (renamed the Naval Academy in 1876) in the Tsukiji district of Tokyo, now the site of a famed fish market and seafood restaurants. In October 1870 the Government decided that the system of naval education should be English, and this was quickly reflected in the adoption (January 1871) of RN-style uniforms for the cadets. In July 1873 Lieutenant-Commander A. L. Douglas, R.N., and 33 other officers and men dispatched by the Admiralty arrived to teach the practical side of naval affairs at the Naval College. Their educational philosophy was that of the English public school, and the organization and spirit of the College were made similar to those in the Royal Navy. Other British naval officers taught in the new schools for naval surgeons, paymasters, and engineers. By 1882 the naval instructors were gone, the Japanese by then feeling confident that they could manage their Fleet. But the influence of the Royal Navy remained strong.

In August 1888 the Academy was moved from Tokyo to Etajima in the Inland Sea. Until the red-brick building, which was both classroom and residence hall, was constructed (1893), the instructors and cadets lived in a training ship, an idea derived from the educational system of the Royal Navy. The red bricks of the main building were imported from England, the idea coming from the red-brick structure which the British instructors had built as their living quarters in Etajima. The bricks were expensive, each one costing the equivalent of 5·4 litres of rice, which for those days was a high sum indeed. The Navy Ministry building (popularly called *Akarenga*, the 'red brick' building) was put up in the same year, also with brick imported from England. The impact of the Royal Navy was felt in other ways. In February 1871 twelve cadets, including the future Japanese Nelson, Tōgō Heihachirō, were sent to the United Kingdom for training, and several to the United States. Tōgō first stayed in Portsmouth, then was attached to the Marine Officers' training ship *Worcester*, moored in the Thames. Later he studied navigation and mathematics at Cambridge, returning to Japan in 1878. Down to the Russian War of 1904–5, the Government continued to send the most promising young naval officers abroad, mostly to England or to British warships.

Although the Royal Navy was a prime factor in the splendid professional training received by the officers and men of the Imperial Navy, 'the intellectual impact of British naval assistance to the Japanese was slight. Save in a very few cases, the influence of the British on the thinking of the men of the Japanese Navy was superficial. There is no evidence, for example, that British attitudes toward politics, toward civil-military relations, affected the Imperial Japanese Navy. But British material aid to the Japanese Navy was substantial and significant.'[1]

Britain was the major foreign supplier of warships for the

[1] John Curtis Perry, 'Great Britain and the Imperial Japanese Navy, 1858–1905' (unpublished doctoral dissertation, Harvard University, 1961), p. 4.

Imperial Navy. Thus, in 1882, of its 28 warships 19 had been built in Britain. In 1894, on the eve of the Sino–Japanese War, seven of the 11 Japanese battleships had been constructed in British yards, and in 1904, on the eve of the Russo–Japanese War, six of the seven battleships (including Tōgō's flagship at Tsushima, the *Mikasa*) and four of the eight armoured cruisers. The Sino–Japanese and Russian wars boosted the prestige of British shipbuilding and of the Royal Navy generally in Japanese naval circles. The beginning of the manufacture of armour plate in 1902, however, marked the start of a Japanese policy of building their own warships, large and small. The battle cruiser *Kongō*, ordered from Vickers in 1910, was the last important Japanese warship to be constructed abroad.

The Anglo–Japanese Alliance of 1902, which was renewed in 1905 and again in 1911, worked on the whole reasonably well on the naval side. The two navies co-operated closely during the Russo–Japanese War, with, for instance, the Royal Navy keeping the Japanese informed on the movements of the Russian Baltic Fleet in its voyage to the Far East. Japanese naval attachés were permitted to attend British naval manœuvres, and the British attachés in turn were accorded various privileges. The two navies discussed arrangements for co-operation in the event of war. Yet relations were never intimate and were not without friction. For example, the exchange of technical data called for by the Alliance did not always go smoothly. Japan having achieved Great Power status through her defeat of Russia, her Navy was less inclined to seek guidance from its one-time mentor, and the latter was not so willing to teach her former pupil. The Royal Navy had little reason to be grateful to the Japanese in the First War. Japan refused to send any ships to fight Germany until 1917, when a destroyer flotilla was sent to the Mediterranean, and made hay in the Far East while the British were committed in Europe, as through the seizure of German-occupied Tsingtao and German islands in the Pacific—the Marshalls, Marianas, Carolines, and Palau.

The British renunciation of the Alliance at the Washington Naval Conference of 1921–2—it was held to be a fatal obstacle to a permanent improvement in relations with the United States—is 'where it all began'. The terms of an inoccuous Four-Power Treaty, which called for consultation among Great Britain, the United States, France, and Japan, if the aggression of a Third Power threatened the interests of the signatory powers, were read at a plenary session on 10 December 1921. The concluding words had the 'kicker': 'This agreement shall be ratified as soon as possible ... and thereupon the agreement between Great Britain and Japan ... shall terminate.' Exchanging an ally in the Far East for a potential rival was not a good bargain from the British point of view. 'We had turned a proved friend in military, if not in political, matters into a potential and powerful foe ten thousand miles away from our main bases' was the later judgement of Admiral of the Fleet Lord Chatfield.[2] The annulment of the Alliance was accepted by the Japanese, as Professor Nish has suggested, 'with the stoicism of the samurai'; but this was for public consumption. In reality, neither the Government nor the Navy wanted termination, but eventually decided to go along with the Western proposal. (The Navy was genuinely submissive to the political leadership in those days). It was bitterly resented by the Japanese, who regarded the annulment as a national insult. Viscount Ishii, once Foreign Minister, afterwards alleged that Britain had cast the Alliance aside 'like an old pair of sandals'. Whether the treaty abrogation helped to drive Japan into a more aggressive policy is an interesting speculation. The Government did not allow the termination of the Alliance to mar relations with Britain—something of the old special relationship lingered for a decade—but the rupture undoubtedly weakened the position of the moderates in the Imperial Navy; that is, the pro-English and pro-American officers.

The process of alienation between the erstwhile Allies was a gradual one. At the Admiralty, where the naval hero of the First War, Lord Beatty, was First Sea Lord between 1919 and 1927, there was a deep suspicion of Japan's naval ambitions and intentions, and the fear that her Navy might at its selected moment launch a surprise attack on British territory in the Far East. The Royal Navy could not meet such an attack without a substantial

[2] *It Might Happen Again* (London, 1947), p. 88. Churchill shared this opinion. "Many links were sundered which might afterwards have proved of decisive value to peace.' Winston S. Churchill, *The Second World War* (6 vols., London, 1948–54), i, *The Gathering Storm*, p. 11. This was being wise after the event. As Colonial Secretary at the time he had opposed the renewal of the Alliance: Japan was the only real threat to British imperial interests in the Far East. Martin Gilbert, *Winston S. Churchill* (London, 1971–7, 5 vols. to date; i and ii by Randolph Churchill), iv. 607. The Admiralty, too, had opposed renewal. In reply to a Foreign Office request for their position on the termination of the Alliance, their Lordships stated (12 Feb. 1920): 'They consider a continuation of the Alliance in its present form neither necessary nor desirable.' E. L. Woodward and Rohan Butler (eds.), *Documents on British Foreign Policy, 1919–1939*, 1st ser., vi (London, 1956), 1054.

new construction programme, which the Admiralty revealed in December 1924. Churchill, determined as Chancellor of the Exchequer to find the resources for social reform and to cut income taxes, pooh-poohed the Japanese danger. A ding-dong battle raged in the Cabinet and the Committee of Imperial Defence in the first months of 1925. Churchill viewed the position this way: 'I do not believe Japan has any idea of attacking the British Empire, or that there is any danger of her doing so for at least a generation to come. If, however, I am wrong and she did attack us "out of the blue", I do not think there would be any difficulty in defeating her. . . . We should be put to great annoyance and expense, but in three or four years we could certainly sweep the Japanese from the seas and force them to make peace.'[3] On 9 February of the same year the Committee of Imperial Defence declared that 'in existing circumstances' Japanese aggression against the British Empire 'is not a contingency seriously to be apprehended' within the next ten years.[4] The Cabinet ratified this conclusion. None the less, for the Admiralty a war with Japan remained a realistic possibility.

Reasonably amicable relations between the Royal and Imperial navies continued—not that they were ever close in a personal human sense. 'You can admire and do business with a Jap,' as one British naval officer put it, 'but you can't LIKE him as a friend.' The friendliness and respect of the Japanese Navy until the later 1930s was reflected in a visit of 1928 to the Boys Training Establishment at Portsmouth by Commander Oku, once Tōgō's ADC. He arrived disconcertingly dressed in a morning coat and silk hat. 'Tōgō', he told the officer delegated to look after him, 'hates Americans. He would like to have another Tsushima against the Americans. He admires and likes the English. When you go to England (Tōgō had said) see the English Navy very well. Study it. See all you can. Learn all you can. The English Navy is very great. All other navies are negligible beside it.'[5] When the British China Squadron visited Japan in the autumn of 1933, the C-in-C, Admiral Sir Frederic Dreyer, and his staff were entertained royally by the Imperial Navy, received expressions of friendship, and were told that the two Powers must continue to work together in close friendship, even though the Alliance was no more. The feeling in

---

[3] Churchill to Keyes, Mar. 1925, Gilbert, *Churchill*, v. 105.
[4] CID 1055-B, 'The Basis of Service Estimates', 23 June 1931, CAB 4/21.
[5] 18 Sept. 1928, unpublished diaries of Captain J. S. Litchfield.

the Royal Navy, however, was that it was an organized friendship, less than genuine—'all hisses and bows'—which could be instantly reversed on orders. The China Squadron had regular and good relations with the American, French, and Italian gunboats that operated in the Yangtse at the time, but very little intercourse with the Japanese gunboats beyond the formal exchange of visits required by protocol. Generally, the Japanese kept to themselves and were viewed with some suspicion.

Such practices as the following scarcely contributed to a truly friendly relationship. In 1926, when the new British cruiser *Enterprise* was fitted with a prototype of the 6-inch secondary armament turret which it was proposed to put into the battleship *Nelson*, the Japanese sent a deputation to inspect it. When the party returned to the wardroom, one was missing. He was found on the bridge, scraping away the paint on the director tower to see what sort of steel it was made of![6]

There was another contretemps in the same year. During Chatfield's time as Controller (1925–8), the Japanese Navy showed a growing reluctance to share technical data with its late Ally. 'While our naval officers on the China Station and our attaché in Japan were kept at arm's length and permission to visit naval yards became more and more restricted, Great Britain was on the contrary flooded with Japanese naval officers, ever on the prowl and claiming admission to our ships, dockyards, armament factories and colleges. It was necessary to try and establish greater equality of treatment.'[7] Japanese naval constructors had for some time been allowed to attend the annual naval construction course at the Royal Naval College at Greenwich, and this had continued despite the termination of the Alliance. In 1926, when the Japanese Embassy made the usual application for the admission of a number of students to the course, Chatfield, with Board of Admiralty approval, asked for a certain technical drawing of the new cruiser *Furutaka* as a *quid pro quo* for admitting the Japanese students. When, a month later, the Japanese Navy ministry refused Chatfield's request, he told their Naval Attaché: 'No *Furutaka*, no courses'; the admission of Japanese students to the naval construction course was ended.

The critical year was 1936, when the Washington Naval

---

[6] Vice-Admiral B. B. Schofield's letter to the author, 7 Nov. 1975. He was then Navigation Officer of the *Enterprise*.
[7] Chatfield, *It Might Happen Again*, p. 32.

Limitation Treaty of 1922 was due to expire. Japanese naval opinion had always regarded the Treaty as a disaster for Japan. It allowed her to have 315,000 tons of battleships to 525,000 tons each for Britain and the United States, and 175,000 tons each for France and Italy: the famous, or infamous, 5:5:3:1.67:1.67 ratio. Total tonnage of aircraft carriers was limited to 135,000 each for Britain and the United States, 81,000 for Japan, and 60,000 each for France and Italy. According to Article 23, the Washington Treaty would automatically be renewed on 31 December 1936 unless one of the signatory Powers notified its denunciation by 31 December 1934. Also running until 31 December 1936 was the London Naval Treaty of 1930, under which Britain, the United States, and Japan had agreed on an 8-inch cruiser ratio of 10:10:6, respectively, and a 6-inch cruiser and destroyer ratio of 10:10:7, with parity in submarines for the three Powers. A meeting of the five Washington Powers was to be held in London in 1935 to replace the expiring agreements with a new one.

In London, as in Washington, Japan's insistence on a 10:7 ratio in capital ships was rejected. When the United States in March 1934 passed the Vinson Act, designed to build up American fleet strength to the actual limits permitted by the naval treaties, the Japanese naval authorities reacted sharply. They saw the projected American expansion as giving the United States an offensive capability in Far Eastern waters. Japan made her intentions evident when Rear-Admiral Yamamoto Isoroku, who was to represent Japan in the preliminary conversations in London prior to the 1935 Conference, informed a Reuter's correspondent on his arrival at Southampton on 16 October 1934 that 'Japan can no longer submit to the ratio system. There is no possibility of compromise by my Government on that point.' The preliminary discussions in London predictably ended in failure, and on 29 December 1934, after the Conference had recessed, the Japanese Government gave formal notice of its intention to terminate the Washington and London naval treaties, effective 31 December 1936, that is, after the due two years' warning.

At the Second London Naval Conference in the winter of 1935–6, where the Washington Treaty Powers attempted to reach a new agreement before the existing 1922 and 1930 treaties ran out, the Head of the Japanese delegation, Admiral Nagano Osami (better known as Nagano Shūshin), made a bold plea (15 January 1936).

His thesis was that, owing to the great mobility of naval forces, no nation could be secure which possessed a navy smaller than any other. Equality of security could be achieved only through equality of armaments for all Powers, and, 'in order to establish as complete a state of non-aggression and non-menace as possible,' there should be a drastic reduction in all offensive weapons. These he defined as battleships, aircraft carriers, and A-class cruisers (10,000 tons, 8-inch guns). Nagano proposed equality or a common upper limit of total naval tonnage, which in the interests of genuine disarmament should be placed at a lower figure than that possessed by Japan. That figure settled, they should lay down the number and tonnage of each category of 'offensive' ships which any Power could have, and, finally, a 'global' figure for all other craft. All these figures should be common to all Powers, though adjustments to meet different degrees of vulnerability at sea could be arranged on the last figure only. The higher relative vulnerability of the British Commonwealth was recognized by the Japanese delegation in private and secret conversations. But, as the British appreciated, this admission had little practical value, since Japan considered her vulnerability to be at least as high as that of the United States. It was 'essentially a proposition of peace', Nagano emphasized, and years later, at the post-war Tokyo War Crimes Trials, Admiral Kondō Nobutake, Chief of the 1st Division (Operations) of the Naval General Staff at the time of the Conference, maintained that the Imperial Navy regarded it as 'a very just and fair proposal and because of that the Japanese navy desired from its very heart that this proposal would be accepted.... We had expected from our hearts that it would be accepted.'[8] It emphatically was not.

The other delegations in turn expressed their inability to accept the Japanese proposal: it was utterly impracticable. The British position, as stated by Lord Monsell, the First Lord of the Admiralty, was that equal security among the principal naval Powers would not be ensured by equal armaments. A country defending herself near her own territory (read: Japan) had an inherent advantage over any attacking force and therefore could defend herself with a lesser force than that brought against her. 'If, therefore, the fleets in the area of contact are numerically equal, that fleet which is operating in its own home waters will, in effect, possess the

---

[8] International Military Tribunal for the Far East, 'Record of the Proceedings' (unpublished material, Tokyo, 1946–8, hereafter cited as IMTFE), pp. 26,686, 26,691.

advantage in spite of equality in numbers.' The introduction of aircraft, moreover, Monsell went on, greatly strenghtened the defensive power of a fleet in its own home waters. A Power with world-wide responsibilities needed adequate defence in every area. Its forces could not be concentrated in one part of the world, for that would mean denuding its home waters of naval defence. A common upper limit would encourage a country whose resources and responsibilities were small to build up its naval strength to equality with its neighbours.[9] Neither the British nor the Americans would accept that equality of security, the Japanese goal, was obtainable for them with a common upper limit, without which a discussion of qualitative limitation, which the British wanted, was futile. Chatfield had told the Japanese (13 December 1935) that a common upper limit would signify permanent inferiority for the British Empire in the Pacific. On 15 January Nagano informed Monsell 'that as it has become sufficiently clear at today's sessions of the First Committee [where the main work of the Conference was done] that the basic principles embodied in our proposal for a comprehensive limitation and reduction of naval armaments cannot secure general support', Japan was withdrawing from the Conference.

Did the Japanese know that the Western Powers would not accept their proposal? Was it only a cloak for the unwillingness of the Imperial Navy to continue the shipbuilding limitations of the treaties when it was obvious that parity in naval armaments could not be obtained from Britain and the United States? On 21 August 1935 the Vice-Foreign Minister, Shigemitsu Mamoru, told Baron Harada (the Secretary to the Elder Statesman Prince Saionji) that the Navy was opposed to Britain's proposal of qualitative limitation, if there was no quantitative limitation. They felt that it would be advantageous not to be bound by restrictions in future. 'The Navy seemed to be rather emotional' about it.[10] The Official War History maintains that the Japanese delegates were pretty sure that the Western Powers would not accept Nagano's proposal, but that it was not necessarily a cloak for the unwillingness of the Navy to

[9] The two speeches, Nagano's and Monsell's, were reported in *The Times*, 16 Jan. 1936. The basic differences between the two positions are detailed in W. N. Medlicott, Douglas Dakin, and M. E. Lambert (eds.), *Documents on British Foreign Policy, 1919–1939*, 2nd ser., xiii (London, 1973), 725–81.

[10] Harada Kumao, *Saionji kō to seikyoku* [Prince Saionji and the Political Situation] (8 vols. and supplement, Tokyo, 1950–6), iv. 312.

continue the shipbuilding limitations. The Naval General Staff, in offering the low level of equality, had truly wanted to limit naval shipbuilding and save expenditure.[11] In any case, the Japanese proposals destroyed the whole idea of big-Power naval limitation and, in the retrospective opinion of at least some IJN officers, was a direct cause of the Pacific War.

Notwithstanding Japan's withdrawal, followed by that of Italy, the Conference ended with the signature of a new Treaty for the Limitation of Naval Armaments (the Second London Naval Treaty) between Great Britain, the United States, and France on 25 March 1936, to become effective on 1 January 1937, or as soon afterwards as all the signatories had ratified it, and would remain in force until 31 December 1942. (It actually came into force on 29 July 1937.) The treaty fixed qualitative limits on capital ships: 35,000 tons and 14-inch guns—16-inch, if Japan or Italy did not agree to the 14-inch by the time the treaty came into force; carriers: 23,000 tons, 6·1-inch guns; cruisers: 8,000 tons, 6·1-inch guns; and submarines: 2,000 tons, 5·1-inch guns. Corresponding bilateral agreements were signed with Germany and the Soviet Union. Italy did not adhere to the treaty until December 1938. Japan was another matter.

Japan twice, in March and June 1937, declined the invitation to subscribe, although the treaty abandoned quantitative limitation, which had been a major grievance of hers. She preferred to be free of all restrictions or limitations on her action if agreement could not be reached on a common upper limit and linking quantitative with qualitative limitation. The signatory Powers nevertheless proceeded with the treaty, hoping that Japan would eventually adhere, or at least would not exceed the treaty limits in her new construction. But persistent (false) reports were received by the British and Americans in 1937 that Japan might be building cruisers of about 15,000 tons with 9·2-inch guns. More seriously, Admiralty intelligence was that Japan probably intended to go to 16-inch guns and 42,000 to 43,000 tons in her capital ships, which tonnage would give them added qualities of protection, speed, or gun-power. The Admiralty resolved at the beginning of 1938 that it was

[11] Bōeichō Bōei Kenshūjo Senshi Shitsu (Military History Office of the National Defence College, National Defence Agency) (ed.), *Senshi sōsho* [War History Series], xci, *Daihon'ei kaigunbu: Rengō kantai* (1): *Kaisen made* [IGHQ Navy Department: Combined Fleet (1): Until the Outbreak of War] (Tokyo, 1975), p. 284. In 1976 the Military History Office (Senshi Shitsu) became the Military History Department (Senshibu).

desirable to take steps at once to determine whether the new Japanese capital ships exceeded 35,000 tons, so as to safeguard against Britain's new capital ships being outclassed. They recommended that Japan be informed bluntly that if she did not accept treaty standards or inform them of her intentions, Britain would invoke her far greater building capacity and financial strength to surpass Japan in anything she did. 'Even the rigid military mind, which at present holds power in Japan, might see the advantage of coming to terms under the circumstances, if they really thought we meant what we said.' The Admiralty also proposed that the United States and France make strong representations in Tokyo along the same lines as the British.[12]

On 5 February 1938 Sir Robert Craigie, the British Ambassador in Tokyo, handed the Japanese Foreign Minister a peremptory note (the United States and France sent identical notes) that referred to the 'persistent and cumulative reports' that Japan was planning to construct capital ships and cruisers above the Second London Treaty limits. The British Government would invoke their right of escalation under the treaty unless the Japanese Government furnished assurances by 20 February that they would not, prior to 1943, build ships not in conformity with the treaty 'without previously informing His Majesty's Government of their intent to do so and of the tonnage and calibre of the largest gun of the vessel or vessels concerned'. If Japan were exceeding, or intending to exceed, treaty limits 'and were willing to indicate forthwith the tonnages and calibres of guns of the vessels which they were constructing, or were intending to construct, His Majesty's Government for their part would be ready to discuss with the Japanese Government the question of the tonnages and gun calibres to be adhered to in future if Japan were not prepared to agree to some limitation'. On 12 February the Japanese Government flatly rejected the alternatives offered by the British. The main argument was the 'firm conviction' that 'qualitative limitation, if not accompanied by quantitative limitation, would make no contribution to the attainment of equitable disarmament'. Amplifying the note the following day, a Foreign Office spokesman issued a statement that, as reported by Craigie: 'Great Britain had started [a] colossal armament programme, alarming to other countries,

[12] Admiralty memorandum for the CID, 6 Jan. 1938, ADM 116/3735. The account that follows is based on the same ADM file.

and United States was probably about to start. It was not fair of them to expect Japan to disclose hers or to conclude from her refusal to do so that she must be constructing vessels not in conformity with a treaty to which she is in any case not a party. Other Powers must take responsibility for future developments but Japan is always ready to discuss any plan for disarmament which attaches primary importance to quantitative limitation.' The Japanese press unanimously supported the Government's reply. It was irate over the three Powers' *démarche*, which was 'insulting and unfriendly' to Japan and was only an attempt to justify their building programmes by putting the onus for the naval arms race upon Japan. Britain, as the prime mover in the joint *démarche*, was regarded as the villain.

A Japanese Foreign Ministry spokesman told a foreign correspondent (7 February) that Japan had no plans for building battleships of 43,000 tons. He was correct: rough plans drawn up in the autumn of 1934 and for which materials had been stockpiled called for mastodons of 64,000 tons, or nearly 72,000 tons when fully laden. And whereas the Admiralty—and the foreign press—believed that the Japanese were building capital ships mounting guns of at least 16 inches—18·1 inches was the actual calibre—the Imperial Navy denied they were exceeding 16 inches. 'These press reports', declared the Navy Minister, 'are sheer speculation with no foundation whatever and the Japanese Navy is prepared to deny them.'[13]

By the end of March 1938 the three Treaty Powers had agreed to invoke the escape clause. In the spring they discussed a new upper limit of tonnage and gun calibre of capital ships, and in the end signed a Protocol to the March 1936 treaty (30 June 1938) that increased the tonnage limit for capital ships to 45,000 tons, while retaining the 16-inch-gun limit permitted under the escalator clause. Ultimately, the British went in for nine 16-inch guns on a displacement of 40,550 tons: the four battleships of the Lion class authorized in 1938 and 1939.

The consequences of Japan's unwillingness to subscribe to the Second London Treaty, and her secretiveness in construction policy, was heightened suspicion and distrust of Japan's naval plans in British naval circles. 'It is difficult to understand the Eastern

[13] Admiral Yonai Mitsumasa, as reported in the *New York Times*, 21 May 1937. The decision to proceed with the two Yamato-class battleships had been made in July 1936.

mentality,' Chatfield observed on 21 February 1938, after the Japanese rejection of the joint *démarche*. 'They have without reason or consideration taken up an impossible attitude for two years, which has caused intentional anxiety to all Maritime Powers'.

2. JAPANESE NAVAL EXPANSION

Japan's denunciation of the Washington and London naval treaties and decision not to sign the Second London Naval Treaty led to a reappraisal of defence policy in 1936 and the decision to modernize her capital ships and cruisers and increase the size of her Fleet. The expansion of the Imperial Navy since 1930 had been carried out by means of a series of 'Naval Replenishment Plans', whose specifics— numbers and types of ships, aircraft, etc.—were not made public. The first two had been intended to provide Japan with the maximum strength permitted under the Washington and first London treaties (they did not include any capital ships), and the Third and Fourth were intended generally to meet the situation created by the expiration of the treaties and also to counterbalance the British and especially American programmes (the First and Second Vinson Acts, 1934 and 1938) as far as possible. The Third Replenishment Plan, launched in March 1937 with the 1937–8 estimates, had a total cost of 1,166,709,171 yen, which would be spread over the five financial years 1937–8 to 1941–2. Of this figure, new construction would consume 837,000,000 yen for the construction of 36 warships (two battleships, two aircraft carriers, 18 destroyers, 14 submarines) and 34 auxiliary vessels. (Three destroyers and a submarine were later cancelled in order to divert the funds to accelerating the construction of the two battleships.) The British Naval Attaché in Tokyo, Captain H. B. Rawlings, thought it significant that the new construction figure was nearly as much as the total in the first two Replenishment Plans. He was certain that capital ships were included in the total, perhaps as many as four, or two and several aircraft carriers, and that they would be completed in 1940. These would join what was already virtually a new Fleet, since the nine existing capital ships had been modernized 'to an extent that makes them virtually new ships'. A tenth capital ship, the training ship *Hiei*, demilitarized under the Washington Treaty, was to be converted back to a battleship, rebuilt into a fast unit, and brought back into service. Rawlings also singled out the air expansion programme in the Plan. The 75,000,000 yen, which might seem modest, allowed for the creation of eleven new air groups, bringing the total air strength to 50 air groups.[14] Indeed, the Third Plan aimed to double naval air strength in five years, in spite of the fact that it had taken over twenty years to expand it to its present strength.

Although it was a response to American naval expansion (the large Second Vinson Act of May 1938), and with the Third Plan was intended to provide the ships to defend the western Pacific, the Fourth Naval Replenishment Plan, voted by the Diet on 6 March 1939, intensified British concern over Japanese naval expansion. It was to run concurrently with the Third Plan from 1939–40 and was to be completed in April 1945. Its cost was 1,694,142,000 yen (£99 million), of which 1,205,780,000 yen (£70 million) were for the construction of 59 warships (two battleships, one aircraft carrier, six cruisers, 24 destroyers, 26 submarines) and 24 auxiliary ships, and 300,041,000 yen (£17 million) were for the construction of aircraft: 75 air groups (34½ operational, 40½ training), which would give the Navy a total of 128 air groups (approximately 6,144 planes). The 300-million yen figure was a significant sum greatly in excess of the expenditure for naval air in the Third Plan.

Captain D. N. C. Tufnell, the new British Naval Attaché in Tokyo, surmised (8 March) that the new Plan was intended to produce four capital ships, several carriers, and cruisers and smaller craft in proportion, and that it might be Japan's object to make herself superior to any other Power in submarines and aircraft. The sum for new construction, he pointed out, was 'the largest amount ever appropriated for shipbuilding in a single programme since the "eight-eight" plan [eight battleships, eight battle cruisers] which was cancelled by the Washington Treaty'. He drew attention to the statement of the Navy Minister, Admiral Yonai, who, in announcing the Plan to the Budgetary Committee of the Diet, was reported to have said that the main object of the Third and Fourth Plans combined was to make Japan the greatest naval power.

This statement, which almost amounts to a falsehood, was no doubt

---

[14] Rawling's report of 10 Aug. 1937, FO 371/21044. There were about 48 aircraft in an air group. His figures were subsequently revised (March 1939): to a 1,321,042,000 yen total (£77 million at about 17 yen to the pound) for new construction and 79,000,000 yen (£4·5 million) for air expansion. FO 371/23563. The actual air expansion figure was approximately 140,000,000 yen—200,000,000 yen with the addition of various subsidiary expenditures.

intended to inspire the public which is quite ignorant of the comparative economic strengths of Great Britain, the U.S.A. and Japan and their respective building capacities and which believes that Japan, free of the limitation Treaties, is steadily overtaking Britain and America and approaching parity.

There may, nevertheless, be an element of truth in the remark if it was intended to apply to aircraft and submarines in particular. Japan attaches the greatest importance to these arms and if she succeeded in making herself paramount in them, even though her strength in other types was inferior, she might well delude herself that she was superior in total strength—or in the type of strength appropriate to operations in the South Pacific—and might act accordingly.

The Ambassador, Craigie, agreed (14 March) that the increase in submarine and aircraft strength 'may give her such a feeling of power that she might embark on adventures in the South Pacific'. For the Admiralty it was difficult to see how Japan could overtake the Royal Navy in capital ships, aircraft carriers, and naval aircraft, though submarines were another matter. Still it was an ambitious programme, and the First Sea Lord, Roger Backhouse, minuted (24 April): 'Let us hope economic difficulties supervene.'[15]

Tufnell in a later report drew attention to the great significance of the doubling of the entry at the Naval Academy since the years 1935–7, when it was constant: from 243 in each of these years to 365 in 1938 and 458 in 1939. 'This entry indicates an anticipated increased demand for officers in 1942 and after [the period of training was four years for the Etajima class of 1938], which, in turn, points to a sudden increase in the Fleet at that time.'[16]

The alarming British estimates of Japanese capital-ship construction and potential were wide of the mark, which was inevitable perhaps in view of Japanese secrecy. Tufnell calculated that Japan had the capacity to complete eight capital ships by 1945, and on the eve of the European War the Admiralty officially estimated Japan's capacity at one capital ship a year, though she was reported to be making efforts to increase it. In March 1940 the Naval Staff credited the Japanese with the capacity to complete *two* capital ships a year 'on occasion'. In 1940–1 the Japanese were thought to be building five capital ships. Actually, the Third and Fourth Replenishment Plans called for a total of four battleships in the

---

[15] FO 371/23563.
[16] 'Imperial Japanese Navy. Annual Report. 1938', 4 Apr. 1939, ADM 1/9588.

'A POTENTIAL AND POWERFUL FOE'

eight-year period, 1937–45—the first in fifteen years. By contrast, the Japanese knew through published data and Parliamentary debates what the British building programmes were. We shall have to return to this intriguing topic of what each Navy knew about what the other was up to.

Capital-ship comparisons in the last years before the Pacific War showed Britain with 15: the two Nelsons (*Nelson, Rodney*), five Royal Sovereigns or R class (*Royal Sovereign, Royal Oak, Revenge, Resolution, Ramillies*), five Queen Elizabeths (*Queen Elizabeth, Warspite, Barham, Valiant, Malaya*), and the three old battle cruisers *Hood, Renown,* and *Repulse*. Building were five battleships of the King George V class (two in the 1936–7 programme and three in the 1937–8 programme), which were due to come into service in 1940–1. (All five were laid down in 1937, launched in 1939–40, but not completed until December 1940–August 1942.) Of the four battleships of the Lion class authorized in 1938 and 1939, two were laid down in June and July 1939, and the other two ordered in August 1939. All four were abandoned in 1940, when it was thought they could not be completed in time to be of use in the European War. Fifteen capital ships in commission, with five building, to the Japanese ten, with at least four more known to be building, gave the Royal Navy, with its heavy world-wide responsibilities, no reason for comfort. This is not the place to go into the 'business as usual' mentality, which, with other factors, delayed the beginning of a serious rearmament programme for all the Services until the last pre-war years. It was then too late to build up to levels that took into account the real possibility of a war against the Axis and Japan simultaneously.

A serious complication was the Admiralty policy from 1934 of laying up six of the battleships in rotation for modernization. 'If war were to be declared to-day against Japan,' Chatfield stated on 13 May 1936, 'we should have only seven battleships available for operations in the Far East. This position was a dangerous one.'[17] As late as the spring of 1939 three capital ships were undergoing modernization, one of which, the *Queen Elizabeth*, was not ready until 1941, whereas nine of the ten Japanese capital ships had been modernized between 1933 and 1937, and the tenth, the *Hiei*, in 1937–9. At no time in these years were more than 10 to 13 of

[17] COS(36) 174th M., CAB 53/6.

Britain's 15 capital ships actually in service. 'In crisis after crisis,' Chatfield afterwards lamented, 'this hampered the Admiralty and, indeed, the Cabinet in their foreign policy, and the Dominions especially, felt the weakness of the Fleet.' The outbreak of the European War only worsened matters, with the loss of the *Royal Oak* and with several capital ships under refit or repair at any one time.

3. FAR EASTERN STAKES

The expansion of the Japanese Navy in the later 1930s would not have appeared so ominous to Britain's policy-makers and the Navy were it not coupled with ample evidence of Japan's aggressive ambitions in China. This had been demonstrated in September 1931 with the Mukden Incident and the overrunning of Manchuria by the Japanese Army and the establishment under its protection of the puppet state of 'Manchukuo' in February–March 1932. The Japanese Government recognized the new state in September. The Manchurian affair by itself did not affect British attitudes towards Japan decisively, since that region was peripheral to Britain's real concerns in China. The clash between Japanese and Chinese Nationalist armies at Shanghai (January–March 1932) was quite another matter. The fighting gradually spread throughout China, and between 1934 and 1937 Japan extended her political and military influence over north China.

The disturbances that broke out in Tokyo on 26 February 1936, when 1,500 troops, led by chauvinistic young officers, occupied government offices and murdered several prominent politicians noted for their opposition to the military, 'sealed the fate of liberal government in Japan. It completely stifled any effective opposition to the Army, for such opposition meant instantaneous death by a volley of machine-gun fire.... Organized violence now ruled supreme in a land dominated by the military.'[18] The Army expansionists were now riding high. At the same time, the rightists, who were steadily increasing their influence in Japanese politics, took heart with the rapid successes of Hitler in Europe. The general public, too, became spellbound by Hitler's triumphs from the mid-1930s.

[18] Toshikazu Kase, *Eclipse of the Rising Sun* (London, 1951), p. 34.

'A POTENTIAL AND POWERFUL FOE'

The Japanese Army continued to extend operations in China, particularly from July 1937, when, following the Marco Polo Bridge Incident near Peiping, China and Japan were in a state of undeclared war. By September 1937 the Imperial Navy had enforced a complete blockade of the entire China coast, although Hong Kong and certain coastal ports were exempted out of consideration for foreign Powers. On 12 December Japanese shore batteries fired on the British gunboats *Ladybird* and *Bee* on the Yangtze off Wuhu, scoring four hits on the *Ladybird* and killing a naval rating and seriously injuring another. Later that day Japanese aircraft dropped bombs on a concentration of British merchant ships in the Yangtze near Nanking, and on the British gunboats *Scarab* and *Cricket*, which were guarding them. No hits were registered. The same day a flight of naval aircraft bombed and sank the American gunboat, *Panay* and three Standard Oil tankers in the Yangtze, 25 miles upstream from Nanking. Despite apologies, these incidents produced acute tension between Japan and Britain and the United States. In the same month the horrible atrocities committed by Japanese troops after the fall of Nanking further inflamed anti-Japanese feelings in Britain and the United States. By the end of the year practically the whole of China was in turmoil, with five northern provinces overrun by the Japanese. In May 1938 Japan invaded south China, landing troops at Amoy, 300 miles north-east of Hong Kong, and in October seizing Canton on the south coast of China and Hankow on the Yangtze. Japan now had control of the Chinese coast, and Hong Kong was sealed off from the mainland.

Britain, as well as the United States, was furious over the high-handed policy of the Japanese towards her nationals, property, and rights in China, and with their evasion of official protests, and there was alarm over the mounting evidence in 1939 that Japan was trying to drive Britain out of the China trade and was indeed seeking nothing less than a political hegemony in East Asia. Incidents occurred on the Yangtze, where severe Japanese restrictions on trade and movement of foreign nationals on the plea of military necessity particularly exhausted British patience. The atrocity stories coming out of China, some of which were horrific—Chinese babies being tossed into the air and caught on the bayonets of Japanese soldiers—fed the growing contempt for the Japanese as a people. It was left for Japan's *drang nach Sud* policy in 1940–1 to act as the catalyst in speeding up the deteriorating relationship between the one-time Allies.

It is not my intention to discuss in detail the motives underlying Japanese imperialism of the 1930s, a subject on which scholars continue to disagree. At one extreme are the traditionalists, who argue that Japan's agggressive policy resulted from a military conspiracy to achieve Japanese hegemony in East Asia and was the work of a military clique that rose to power after 1931 through violent means. At the other end of the spectrum are the revisionists, who hold that Japanese policy was but the pursuit of legitimate national aims by their civilian as well as military leaders. These aims were the attainment of security—really, national survival—and economic self-sufficiency. The latter was a compound of various factors, such as Japan's poverty in natural resources, the Great Depression, and the imposition of restrictions on Japanese trade. The former, the security factor, had to do with control of strategic areas essential to defence of the homeland, and an assured supply of raw materials, especially oil, vital to the Army and Navy as well as to the civilian economy. It was these objectives—legitimate national aims, say the revisionists—which explain Japan's expansionist policy. My own view is that Japanese imperialism was the product of the strategic–economic factors stressed by the revisionists *and* a militant nationalism that involved both Services. The end product of both factors was a policy of national expansion in China and South-east Asia.

The British stake in the Far East was based on their investment and trade in China,[19] the protection of their sea routes and possessions in the Pacific and Indian Oceans, notably India and the Dominions of Australia and New Zealand—Japan was supposed to

---

[19] A great deal of British capital was invested in China, but the China trade represented only about 2 per cent of total British trade. 'The myth of the China market', however, exerted a powerful influence on British policy. 'Again and again,' observes a scholar, 'the China market was referred to as a place on which the future development of British trade and employment would depend. In this circumstance, the influence of British business and financial interests in the China trade became paramount. . . . Those who walked the corridors of power in Britain were haunted by the thought that, despite the solid success of Britain in the East during two centuries, if British companies were forced to pull out of China, as they threatened to do unless the British government backed them up, the carry-over effect on India and the rest of the Empire would be incalculable. Britain's prestige had to be maintained, for it was on this national asset that possibilities for profitable trade and financial gain depended.' Stephen Lyon Endicott, *Diplomacy and Enterprise: British China Policy, 1933–1937* (Manchester, 1975), p. 184.

have long-range designs on these areas—and the prestige factor. To give ground in the Far East would, it was widely believed, undermine the Empire everywhere. These interests were, in the British view, threatened by Japanese imperialism-cum-naval expansion. They were not taken in by Japan's talk about a 'New Order' in East Asia (the first such statement was issued on 3 November 1938[20]) or her insistence that her foreign policy was motivated by a quest for 'self-sufficiency'. These were only seen as blinds for a drive to achieve hegemony in East Asia and to eliminate all foreign influence in the region, and to take over all foreign interests there. The official British view is well summed up in a Foreign Office memorandum to the Admiralty of 13 February 1939:

What appears to be necessary is the consideration from the broadest aspect of vital imperial needs of what measures should, and could most effectively, be taken permanently to defend British interests in the Far East against the threat inherent in Japan's plans for the setting up of what she calls 'a new order in East Asia'. The problem would appear to be one of preventing Japan from creating a vast closed area from which she would be able to draw nearly all the raw materials which are essential to her and thereby attaining such strength as might enable her subsequently to absorb into that area other territories producing two at least of the other raw materials of really vital importance to her, oil in the Netherlands East Indies and high-grade iron ore in Malaya. The power thus acquired by Japan would enable her to present, either in combination with Germany and Italy or even alone, a permanent and formidable threat to British interests throughout the Eastern Hemisphere.[21]

4. ANTI-BRITISH FEELINGS IN THE IMPERIAL NAVY

It was only after 1936 that the traditional pro-British sentiment of the Japanese Navy began to assume an anti-British cast, although important pockets of pro-British feelings remained. The abrupt

---

[20] The key passage read: 'What Japan seeks is the establishment of a new order which will ensure permanent stability in East Asia. The new order has for its foundations a tripartite relationship of mutual aid and coordination between Japan, Manchukuo and China, in the political, economic, cultural and other fields. Its object is to secure international justice, to perfect joint defence against Communism, to create a new culture, and to realize close economic cohesion throughout East Asia. This, indeed, is the way to contribute towards the stabilisation of East Asia and the progress of the world.'

[21] ADM 1/9909.

change was the result of the spread of the Japanese invasion to the Yangtze River region and South China, where British interests were so important and where friction between the two Powers, as mentioned, became chronic. At the same time, from the beginning of 1938, many IJA and IJN officers (though more particularly the former) held Britain responsible for Japan's inability to conclude the China war by urging China to continue her resistance. As relations between the former Allies cooled, there were many indications, direct and indirect, of a change in attitude of the Imperial Navy towards the Royal Navy. Thus, the officer in command of the British 8th Destroyer Division (1936–8), which ranged up and down the China coast during the opening phases of the 'Japanese Incident', as the Chinese referred to it, recalls; 'We often used to find Japanese destroyers in places like Amoy, Swatow, and the like, but both US and British relations with them remained strictly formal. The usual exchange of calls and that was all. They were always polite and would make "bon voyage" signals and so forth, but had evident instructions not to fraternise.... In 1938 the situation had become much more taut with the Japanese bombing Shanghai while we US and British ships stood by ready to intervene to protect our nationals.'[22] Friction in and over China was also a factor in the emergence of distinctly anti-Japanese attitudes in the Royal Navy.

Another reflection of changing attitudes was the publication in England in the spring of 1936 of the translation of a shrill book, *Japan Must Fight Britain*, by a Japanese naval officer, Lieutenant-Commander Ishimaru Tōta. It spoke of 'serious and irreconcilable economic and political differences', dwelt on all the evidence of British hostility (e.g. Britain's leadership of the League of Nations in opposition to Japanese expansion in Manchuria, and the building of the Singapore base, which was directed against Japan), expressed confidence in the ability of the Imperial Navy to hold its own or to defeat the British Navy in a sea fight in the South China Sea, and warned that Britain could avoid war only by reigning supreme in her own domain, the southern Pacific, while leaving the western Pacific to Japan. Ishimaru had been long retired from the Navy by 1936. Captain Ōi Atsushi recalls that the Imperial Navy did not take his book seriously and regarded it as 'rather ridiculous'. (But

---

[22] Rear-Admiral R. M. Dick's letter to the author, 9 July 1976.

cf. below.) The book, however, made quite an impression in British naval circles. It was not so much the actual contents of the book that caused any concern (except perhaps some hilarity at the sheer cheek of the idea of the Japanese thinking they could fight Britain at sea) as the fact that the author was believed to have been a guest student at the Naval Staff College. This sort of thing was not done; it was rather like accepting an invitation for a weekend visit to a country house and sleeping with your host's daughter.

During a visit of the submarine depot and repair ship HMS *Medway* to Keelung, Formosa, in October 1936, three British sailors were beaten up by the Japanese police for alleged failure to pay a taxi fare, and the officer sent to gain their release was insulted. When satisfactory apologies were not forthcoming, the British suspended all courtesy naval visits to Japanese ports. The Japanese Fleet perforce followed suit, except for attendance at the Coronation Review in 1937. This unfortunate state of affairs removed an important means of improving understanding between the two navies.

There was no dearth of evidence that influential elements in the Japanese Navy shared the aggressive outlook of the Army and the hawk-like elements in the Government and that it intended to thrust south, to the Netherlands East Indies and Australia. Late in 1937 the Naval Attaché wrote of the existence of

a strong party in the Japanese Navy calling for more drastic steps to be taken. The extremists of this band would quite happily embark on war with Great Britain but there is no reason to suppose as yet that they will succeed in attaining their desire. The pressure of what one may term the 'forward movement' cannot, however, lightly be dismissed for, quite apart from the fact that it contains highly placed Flag officers, the 'young officers' party is able to impose its opinions on the more balanced seniors.[23]

Early in 1938 a retired Royal Australian Naval Reserve Commander, now the Managing Director of an Australian shipping company, reported on a conversation with IJN officers he had met in Japan and whom he had drawn out with the aid of alcohol. ('He found that they drank two or three times as much as the average Englishman. Though particularly reserved when sober, they became very garrulous after a few drinks.')

[23] Rawlings, 'Disposition of the Japanese Fleet, November 1937', 3 Nov. 1937, FO 371/21044.

ANTI-BRITISH FEELINGS IN THE IMPERIAL NAVY

The Japanese Officers all agreed with the book, 'Japan Must Fight England'. The Japanese hope to be able to fight England alone, and consider themselves quite ready to do so now. They are, however, afraid of France and U.S.A. joining England.

It is their intention to dominate the whole of the coast of Eastern Asia.

They agree that Singapore is a great base, but they consider that it is vulnerable from the north, by land, and also that it is useless without a fleet. If England were sending a fleet east, Japan would know at once, and in the ensuing four weeks submarines and aircraft, concentrated in various straits and other focal points, would sink half the ships before they reached Singapore. If the whole British Navy were sent, they consider that they could still deal with it.

The Netherlands East Indies would be occupied within a week. Singapore would then be invested and blockaded, the N.E.I. ports being used for submarines....

They would not tackle Australia until they had command of the sea. A fleet would probably not be sent to Australia: only a 'Note'....

In general, the Japanese are all convinced that they have a 'mission' to improve the world.[24]

The Ambassador found anti-British feelings 'still very strong in naval circles' in the spring of 1938, and at the end of the year he could report that 'the Japanese Navy—and particularly its younger officers—are manifesting such strong anti-British sentiments'.[25] Admiral Takahashi Sankchi, C-in-C, Combined Fleet, 1934-6, and former Vice-Chief of the Naval General Staff and President of the Naval War College, was reported to have asserted: 'The Japanese Navy must expand suddenly South as far as New Guinea, Celebes and Borneo.'[26]

The Japanese occupation of Hainan Island and annexation of the disputed Spratly Islands in 1939 confirmed British fears, but to this as well as to other aspects of Imperial Navy policy we shall have to return. Here it is enough to point out that the British were not imagining anything. The increasingly hostile attitude of the Japanese Navy is borne out by a Naval General Staff memorandum of 1 September 1938 entitled 'Why Have Our Anti-British Feelings

---

[24] Australian Station Intelligence to DNI, 1 Feb. 1938, FO 371/22192.
[25] Craigie to Foreign Office, 7 May 1938, to Halifax (Foreign Secretary), 14 Dec. 1938, FO 371/21521, ADM 1/9909, respectively.
[26] Admiral Sir Frederic Dreyer, 'Some Historical Notes—Western Pacific', a memorandum for the First Sea Lord, 10 Feb. 1939, ADM 1/11326.

Been Aggravated?'[27] The three 'indirect causes' included the certainty that 'British support or instigation lies behind the contemptuous and anti-Japanese tendencies now prevailing among the Chinese people and the unfriendly policies towards us adopted by the Dutch East Indies Government in recent years'. 'Direct causes' were divided into sixteen concrete instances of Britain's antagonistic attitude over the China Incident and eight instances of how Britain treated Japan as though she were a third-class nation. The former included such charges as British merchant ships supplying Chinese 'guerillas' in the lower Yangtze area with weapons and ammunition, Britain's attempt to aggravate American opinion over the *Panay* incident, and her false report of Japanese atrocities on Amoy Island. The latter category included this item: 'Britain ignored China's blockade of the Yangtze through the use of sunken ships, blocking materials, and mines; but when Japan reopened the river, with great military effort and at the sacrifice of many lives, she forcefully demanded that we open it to her. This was an especially high-handed [or haughty: *gōman-fuson*] attitude, since she knew that our Army was in the midst of carrying out an important operation in that area.'

As early as 1933, especially from 1935-6, the Far Eastern situation had begun to influence British foreign and strategic policy in an important way. A major reason for the somewhat pusillanimous attitude of the Government and the Navy towards serious sanctions (oil, etc.) against Italy in the Abyssinian Crisis was the fear that Japan would seize the opportunity to attack Britain, should she become involved in a naval war with Italy in the Mediterranean and probably also with Germany in the North Sea and Atlantic. The Naval Staff and the Chiefs of Staff Committee realized how impossible it would be to fight Japan successfully under such conditions, since there would be a need to retain part or all of the Fleet in European waters.

In October 1935 the Chiefs of Staff declared flatly: 'Our strategic plans in the Far East are based upon the possibilities of conflict with an increasingly powerful Japan.' How could they meet the threat posed by Japan and, in particular, by her Navy? There were, basically, four ways to achieve this: through dispatching a force of

[27] 'Taiei kanjōwa naniyueni akka shitaka?', Tsunoda Jun (ed.), *Gendai shi shiryō* [Source Materials on Contemporary History], x, *Nitchū sensō* (3) [The Sino-Japanese Conflict (3)] (Tokyo, 1964), pp. 339-42.

capital ships to the Far East; completing the defences of Singapore and ensuring that the base would be held in a war; some form of naval co-operation with the United States; and, finally, through a foreign policy of appeasement. The strategic planners regarded all four as essential. But all were plagued with apparently insoluble difficulties.

II

British Strategic Dilemmas (1936–1939)

> ... we cannot foresee the time when our defence forces will be strong enough to safeguard our territory, trade and vital interests against Germany, Italy and Japan simultaneously.
>
> The Chiefs of Staff, 12 November 1937.

> Imperially we are exceedingly weak. If at the present time, and for many years to come, we had to send a Fleet to the Far East, even in conjunction with the United States, we should be left so weak in Europe that we should be liable to blackmail or worse.
>
> ADMIRAL OF THE FLEET LORD CHATFIELD to Sir Thomas Inskip (Minister for Co-ordination of Defence), 28 January 1938.

> Surely the real deterrent to Japanese aggression in the Far East can only be found in the willingness and open co-operation of the United States?
>
> A. V. ALEXANDER (First Lord) to Lord Halifax (Foreign Secretary), 29 November 1940.

1. DEFENCE ORGANIZATION AND PERSONALITIES

THE supreme authority in British defence, as in other matters, was the Cabinet—the War Cabinet, once the European War broke out in September 1939. In pre-war days, advising the Cabinet in matters of grand strategy, including strategic war plans, was the Committee of Imperial Defence, whose Chairman was the Prime Minister or his deputy on the CID, the Minister for Co-ordination of Defence (1936–40), and whose other regular members were the Foreign Secretary, the Chancellor of the Exchequer, the Home Secretary, and the three Service Ministers. The CID was abolished with the creation of the War Cabinet. The Chiefs of Staff Committee of the Cabinet, technically a sub-committee of the CID, made strategic recommendations to the CID—to the War Cabinet, once the war was under way. In practice, their recommendations were generally accepted without cavil. 'Ministers, with very few exceptions, either accepted the views of their professional advisers or criticised them from a limited, often single Service, rather than from an overall strategic point of view.'[1] Under the Service Chiefs was the Joint Planning Sub-Committee (called the Joint Planning Staff from September 1940): the three Service Directors of Plans and a small staff of officers from all Services.

The members of the Board of Admiralty, professional and civilian, had collective responsibility for all matters concerning the Navy.[2] The Board met to discuss and perhaps approve major matters of policy, for example, the warship building programme and characteristics of new ships. Operational matters, however, and strategy generally, were not referred to the Board. They were the province of the Naval Staff, consisting of the First Sea Lord, who was also Chief of the Naval Staff, the DCNS (retitled VCNS in April 1940), and the various ACNS, aided by the Directors of Plans, Operations, Intelligence, Trade, and other divisions and their staffs. But the First Sea Lord was in effect the Commander-in-Chief of the Navy at home and abroad. In other words, he could issue orders and instructions to flag officers and other operational authorities. Customarily, however, First Sea Lords did not abuse this power, but saw that their orders were agreed to and checked by the DCNS/VCNS and/or the ACNS concerned. The First Sea Lord made most of the final decisions; in certain matters he made recommendations to the First Lord, a civilian, who sat in the Cabinet (and, in 1939–40, when Churchill was First Lord, in the War Cabinet) and bore the ultimate responsibility for the work and decisions of the Admiralty. In naval strategy and operations and the big technical matters the First Sea Lord expected to have the last word. This was especially true in the last pre-war years and during the war, when the First Lords (except to some extent for Churchill's tenure) seldom interfered with their First Sea Lord, certainly not in strategic and operational matters.

The First Lords in 1936–45 were the 1st Viscount Monsell, June

[1] N. H. Gibbs, *History of the Second World War. Grand Strategy*, i (London, 1976), p. 775.
[2] The members of the Board when the war broke out were the First Lord, a civilian, the five Sea Lords, the DCNS, the ACNS (Trade) (four ACNS were added during the war— Home, Foreign, Weapons, and Air, not all of whom were members of the Board), and the civilian Civil Lord, Parliamentary and Financial Secretary, and Permanent Secretary. The Second Sea Lord was responsible for personnel, the Third Sea Lord and Controller, for *matériel*, the Fourth Sea Lord, for supplies and transport, and the Fifth Sea Lord, for naval air. A Deputy First Sea Lord was added in July 1942.

1935–June 1936; Sir Samuel Hoare, June 1936–May 1937; Alfred Duff Cooper, May 1937–October 1938; the 7th Earl Stanhope, October 1938–September 1939; Winston Churchill, September 1939–May 1940; and A. V. Alexander, May 1940–May 1945. Alexander, who will figure more prominently in our story than the others, excepting Churchill, was a man of medium height and solid build who could appear gruff and even forbidding but was essentially a kindly person with a great gift for friendship. As wartime First Lord, he displayed an extraordinary physical and mental stamina. He had a good quick intelligence and a real grasp of naval matters, which went back to his time as First Lord in the Labour Government of 1929–31. His gift for getting on with people, understanding of naval affairs, affection for the Navy, and, not least, his recognition that the direction of naval affairs was not his responsibility, account for the excellent relations which he was able to maintain with Churchill and the wartime First Sea Lords, Pound and Cunningham. In the Navy, however, Alexander had the reputation of being a 'rubber stamp' and a 'cipher', who did what he was told to do by the Prime Minister or First Sea Lord.

The Navy was fortunate in having effective spokesmen to present its ideas to the politicians and to the Chiefs of Staff Committee. The dominant personality in the formulation of British strategic policy from 1933 until 1938, and to a lesser degree in 1939 to the outbreak of war, was Admiral of the Fleet Sir Ernle Chatfield (created Baron in June 1937), First Sea Lord and Chief of Naval Staff, 1933–8, and Minister for Co-ordination of Defence from February 1939 until April 1940, when he resigned and the office was abolished. In the latter post he succeeded the first holder, the uninspiring and unimaginative Sir Thomas Inskip (May 1936–January 1939), who was, in Neville Chamberlain's words, not one to make 'friction with either the Chiefs of Staff or the Service Ministers'. Chatfield was without question the finest officer the Royal Navy produced between the wars. Though he lacked some of the more charismatic qualities of leadership—stories are rife of his lack of the personal touch—he had an unrivalled authority and prestige in the Service. He inspired confidence rather than devotion. He had been Beatty's Flag-Captain in the First War, held key Admiralty posts after the war, and commanded in succession Britain's two major fleets, the Atlantic and the Mediterranean. Chatfield had almost everything: character, charm (though he always looked rather severe and was somewhat lacking in a sense of humour), brains, energy, administrative ability, and exceptional professional competence. He was, as Admiral Sir William James once called him, 'the best "all-rounder" of his day and age'. No mean knack was Chatfield's ability to state the Admiralty view in CID or COS meetings with maximum effectiveness. An Assistant Secretary of the CID noted: 'He is extremely good at putting the Naval point of view and has an excellent grasp of detail.' The same observer remarked on how he 'puts his points most agreeably'. On the other hand, he was 'Not so good as a Chairman [of a CID committee] when he is apt to let the conversation wander ...'[3] Chatfield completely dominated the Board of Admiralty and the Chiefs of Staff during his time as First Sea Lord, and his views on strategic matters always carried a good deal of weight with the CID and the Government. His influence with the COS as Minister was appreciably lessened.

Backhouse and Pound were equal starters to succeed Chatfield in August 1938; the mantle fell on Backhouse ('RB' to the Service), much to the delight of Pound, who preferred an extra (third) year as C-in-C, Mediterranean. Admiral of the Fleet Sir Roger Backhouse was, like Chatfield, a man of the highest personal quality and integrity, and much respected in the Service. This sallow-complexioned officer with a tall (6 ft. 4 in.) spare figure had been a successful Third Sea Lord and Controller for over three years (1928–32), Commander of the 1st Battle Squadron and Second-in-Command, Mediterranean Fleet (1932–4), and C-in-C, Home Fleet (1935–8). Always serious minded and a hard taskmaster—a 'dedicated slave driver', as one of his officers described him—he did not tolerate fools gladly, and his wrath when aroused was truly devastating. He was a man of steel, who did not bend easily. Yet he could be most kind and considerate—he talked much more freely to junior officers than did Chatfield—and was generally well liked. His brain was first class (he was a 'five-oner'—a first class in all five of the qualifying examinations for promotion to lieutenant), but he did not have Chatfield's world-wide strategic outlook. Backhouse was more of a technical expert—he was a crack gunnery man—than a strategist yet he had a solid grasp of the essentials of the Far Eastern situation, and his strategic ideas were in some respects more

[3] Diary, 30 Mar., 6 Apr. 1936, Brian Bond (ed.), *Chief of Staff: The Diaries of Lieutenant-General Sir Henry Pownall* (2 vols., London 1972–4), i. 107.

realistic than Chatfield's, even if he did not carry as much weight in the Cabinet, CID, or Chiefs of Staff Committee.

Backhouse was a one-man band. He carried centralization much too far as C-in-C, having a built-in resistance to delegation to his staff. This and his concomitant adoration of paper work were his consuming weaknesses. His Staff Officer Operations in the Home Fleet writes 'His cabin was always full of dockets, on the tables, under the settees and armchairs, everywhere, so that I often had to go down on my hands and knees to rescue some important paper. He was very quick to grasp essential details, but his trouble was that he busied himself with minor matters like who was to sit on a board of seamanship exams for Boatswain!'[4] He never spared himself. Except when the flagship was in Portsmouth during leave periods, he took but five days' leave to go shooting during his years with the Home Fleet. As First Sea Lord Backhouse attempted to run the whole Navy on the same lines. He tried to do everything himself ('the arch centraliser', Admiral Sir William James called him) and he never stopped working. He could never be persuaded to take a genuine rest or go on holiday. The strain was too great. He fell sick in the spring of 1939 and had to be relieved by Pound on 12 June (–August 1943). He died not long afterwards from a brain tumour though overwork was probably a contributory factor.

Admiral of the Fleet Sir Dudley Pound was of average height and build, and a good-looking man—not the matinee idol of good looks, but what might be thought of as 'typical navy'. He was on the reserved side, seldom showed any emotion, and was absorbed in shooting and fishing. These traits may help explain why he had few intimate friends. Yet he was liked and admired by those who worked under him, partly because of his thoughtfulness—he always took the time to inquire about their little doings and about their families—his immense professional knowledge, and the impression he gave that he was firmly in command of whatever situation had arisen. He was an unusually modest man, who never employed the flamboyant approach and was singularly without affectation. He had a quiet, 'twinkle-in-the-eye' sense of humour and a great sense of fun, though he was not one to initiate escapades or horse-play. His humour could be of the mordant sort. He always drove his car at breakneck speed, and as C-in-C, Mediterranean, one of his

---

[4] Admiral Schofield's letter to the author, 11 Dec. 1975.

favourite ploys was to take Italian Admirals for a run and scare them stiff! 'Just as well to take the measure of one's possible enemies', he used to say. He had a great devotion to the Service and always wanted to establish that 'there is nothing the Navy cannot do'. Absolutely tireless, he went full out all the time in devotion to duty and seldom took a day off. He turned in very late, 1.30 to 2 a.m., sometimes 3 a.m., but did not usually start work again until 9 a.m. An officer who was a close friend referred in an obituary notice to his 'wonderful' patience and to other facets of his personality: 'He was always patient in listening to other people stating their views, whether he agreed with them or not. He was patient in getting all the facts on which to base his opinion. He was patient in working out and deciding what line he should take for whatever he considered to be the right course.'[5] 'He was not, perhaps,' as A. B. Cunningham believed, 'a man of great imagination or insight,' and there were those who thought that he interfered too much with the conduct of operations at sea, to the point of frequently giving tactical orders. Some of this was probably unavoidable with the exigencies of wireless silence imposed on seagoing commanders. One must remember, too, that the First Sea Lord's warrant of appointment empowered him to control operations of the Fleet everywhere, and that when Special Intelligence ('Ultra') was available, Pound had far better information than Commanders-in-Chief afloat. Not every C-in-C was briefed on Ultra, only those with the need to know, and some of it could not be sent to them even in edited form. All the same, Pound's 'interference' was felt to be generally unsettling.

Pound was a highly effective spokesman for the Admiralty point of view, and by all accounts was greatly respected by nearly everyone. His impact on the politicians was strong. Although no match for them in argument or advocacy, and though he disliked and was out of his depth in wide-ranging discussion on general strategy, he never missed a point affecting the Navy, and his obvious integrity and complete absence of deviousness was impressive. His rather blunt manner and rugged sea-dog presence, as well as his keen intellect and analytical mind, commanded conviction. He was never heard to raise his voice or strike the table;

[5] Anon., 'Admiral of the Fleet Sir Dudley Pound, GCB, OM, GCVO', *The Naval Review*, xxxi, 4 (Nov. 1943), 284. The author was Vice-Admiral Sir Geoffrey Blake, who had the assistance of officers who had known Pound.

it was not Pound's way; his was to state his case to ministers or the other Chiefs of Staff in a dry and factual manner. He had an absolutely iron self-control. His grasp of every detail of the naval implications of a problem was very persuasive on a naval or primarily naval problem: he had all the answers.

Chatfield had a superior brain and a more wide-ranging mind, and was better than Pound on the more intangible problems of grand strategy, and was able to speak to politicians in their own language; but on purely naval problems of a practical kind he was not better than, and perhaps not quite up to, Pound. Backhouse was not in the same class as Pound, though very able and sound enough. (Cunningham as First Sea Lord will concern us in volume ii.)

The Navy's views on strategic matters carried exceptional weight with the politicians and in the COS Committee in large part because of the calibre, as men and professionals, of the First Sea Lords, but also because the Chiefs of the Air Staff and Chiefs of the Imperial General Staff, down to 1940, anyway, were their inferiors in every way. The CAS to 1940 were Marshal of the Royal Air Force Sir Edward Ellington (May 1933–August 1937) and Air Chief Marshal Sir Cyril Newall (September 1937–October 1940). Ellington's own subordinates 'have no confidence in their own man', Pownall confided to his diary, 'and think he gets done down by the other two. That is an exaggeration, but it is a fact that he is a poor representative of their own case.'[6] Newall, a much better CAS than he was commonly made out, carried weight in the CID and COS Committee, though not to the same degree as Portal, his successor. But he was a tired man by 1940.

The Chiefs of the Imperial General Staff in this earlier period, Field-Marshal Sir Archibald Montgomery-Massingberd (February 1933–April 1936), Field-Marshal Sir Cyril Deverell (April 1936–December 1937), Lieutenant-General Viscount Gort (December 1937–September 1939), and General Sir Edmund Ironside (September 1939–May 1940) were not up to the quality of the First Sea Lords. The handsome and charming Montgomery-Massingberd, Rawlinson's Chief of Staff in the 4th Army in the First War, was becoming an anachronism in the 1930s. Duff Cooper, the War Secretary, found him 'very inadequate and out of date' as CIGS.[7]

---

[6] 23 Jan. 1936, Bond, *Chief of Staff*, i. 98.
[7] *The Memoirs of Captain Liddell Hart* (2 vols., London, 1968), i. 300.

Deverell was a mediocrity—a sound, honest infantryman with little personality and imagination. Gort too, though a first-class regimental soldier and an admirable man, had little imagination and was out of his depth as CIGS. He could hold his own with Backhouse and Newall, but did not have much influence with ministers in the CID. Pownall considered Newall and Gort 'both stupid in their different ways'.[8] Ironside was a disaster. He was a big strong man with a varied experience in many parts of the world who could have been a great CIGS if he had had any idea of how to use his staff and to think and act methodically. As it was, he relied entirely on his own judgement, and kept making statements and answering ministers' questions off the cuff. He had never been in Whitehall before, and was a bull in a china shop.

The situation was reversed in 1940. The successive CIGS, Field-Marshals Sir John Dill (May 1940–December 1941) and Sir Alan Brooke (December 1941–June 1946), were strong men and full of energy, who could stand up to the First Sea Lord. Dill was the most highly educated of the officers at the top. However, he could not cope with Churchill at all, whereas Brooke and Pound could. The CAS, Air Chief Marshal Sir Charles Portal (December 1940–December 1945), for all his faults (he was too inhuman and detached), was very highly regarded in all circles. Portal, Brooke, and Pound differed, but without acrimony. Theirs was an exceptionally harmonious relationship, assisted by their common enthusiasm for fishing! They were a first-rate team, all of whom were listened to with respect, and all of whom could hold their own with each other, with ministers, and with anyone else. This Chiefs of Staff Committee represented, in the view of Lord Mountbatten, who as Chief of Combined Operations was a member in 1942–3, the finest higher direction of the armed forces in British history.

In Far Eastern strategic matters the Navy's voice was the most influential, particularly down to the outbreak of the Pacific War. There was a special reason for this ascendancy. As Chatfield declared in 1937, 'In a war with Japan the navy would constitute, as it were, the forward line and the other two Services would form the backs.' This was inherent in the geography of the situation: the main lines of communications for the British and the Japanese lay across thousands of miles of ocean.

---

[8] 10 Nov. 1939, Bond, *Chief of Staff*, i. 254.

BRITISH STRATEGIC DILEMMAS (1936–1939)

2. MAIN FLEET TO SINGAPORE: CONUNDRUMS AND UNCERTAINTIES

The Service Chiefs envisaged two alternative situations for a war with Japan: (1) when Britain was at peace in Europe, but had to retain in Home waters a fleet sufficient to neutralize the German Fleet; (2) Japanese aggression when Britain was already at war with Germany. The Chiefs of Staff considered the latter contingency the more likely one. Thus Backhouse judged there was not 'the least chance of our having a row with Japan unless we first got involved in Europe, when possibly the Japanese might think the opportunity was good'.[9] This remained the position of the Admiralty and was shared by the Chiefs of Staff.

The strategic planners had, in either case, to take into account the possibility of hostilities with Japan alone. Britain's naval forces in the East were extremely modest. The ships on the China Station were based at Hong Kong but alternated between Hong Kong, Wei-hai-wei, and Singapore. (Not until June 1940 did the C-in-C, China station, shift his shore headquarters from Hong Kong to Singapore, and Wei-hai-wei was used until 9 October 1940, when the Japanese occupied Liu-kun-tao, an island off Wei-hai-wei.) The strength of this squadron in June 1937 was 5 cruisers (3 heavy, 2 old), an aircraft carrier, 9 destroyers and 2 old ones, 15 submarines, 18 gunboats, etc. The situation in June 1939 was similar. The Royal Navy's regular 'presence' at Singapore was variable and seasonal up to the summer of 1939, when nine submarines were based there. Other warships east of Suez—in the Royal Indian Navy and on the African, East Indies, Australian, and New Zealand stations—added little strength apart from a few cruisers in Australian and New Zealand waters.

The basis of strategy in a Far Eastern war was, therefore, the establishment of an adequate fleet at Singapore at the earliest possible moment after the outbreak of hostilities with Japan. This fleet was supposed to prevent any major operation against Australia, New Zealand, or India, keep open British sea communications in the Indian Ocean, including those to Egypt and the Middle East, and prevent the fall of Singapore. The 'period before relief', defined as the time during which the Singapore garrison would have to

---

[9] Backhouse to Vice-Admiral Sir Ragnar Colvin (First Naval Member of the Australian Commonwealth Naval Board), 9 Jan. 1939, ADM 205/3.

hold out, beginning on the day it was first attacked and ending on the day the 'Main Fleet' arrived and either defeated the enemy or forced him to withdraw, was fixed by the Chiefs of Staff at 70 days in March 1937. It was the basis of the Malayan defence plan and determined the size and composition of the garrison and the stores kept in Malaya in peacetime The 70 days were calculated as follows. The fleet could reach Singapore in 28 days via the Suez Canal and Malacca Straits (30 days, if the Sunda Straits were used), or 45 days if, because the position in the Central Mediterranean was not yet under control, the Cape of Good Hope route had to be used. Add 10 days for preliminary preparations (fuelling, storing, etc.) and 15 days for fuelling delays and possible adverse weather conditions *en route*. The maximum time, therefore, that had to be allowed for the arrival of the fleet at Singapore after the order to sail was 70 days. This was predicated on the assumption that the orders for the fleet to sail were give concurrently with the first Japanese act of war; it made no allowance for circumstances which might delay the sailing of the fleet, such as that its capital ships might be engaged in chasing the Germans in the Atlantic or convoying merchant shipping. They would have to retain sufficient strength in Home waters to contain the German Fleet, and to depend on the French Fleet to restrict Italian naval action in the Mediterranean. On 4 March 1938 the Committee of Imperial Defence officially accepted the 70-day period before relief.

What of the strength of the Main Fleet that would be sent to the Far East? As viewed by the Chiefs of Staff in 1937, the maximum strength of the Main Fleet that was available for Far Eastern operations, assuming Britain was at peace with Germany, was calculated as all British heavy ships other than those undergoing modernization (*Valiant, Renown, Queen Elizabeth*). This left 12 capital ships (10 battleships, 2 battle cruisers) to oppose Japan's 9 (not counting the *Hiei*).The British ships, however, would be operating far from their main repair facilities and sources of supply, with only the facilities of Singapore on which to rely, whereas the Japanese Fleet had its resources available close by. 'These facts in themselves are equivalent to an advantage of two capital ships to Japan, since at any average moment we could not rely on less than 2 ships being absent. On this basis our superiority in heavy ships is only 10 to 9.' Yet, practically speaking, they would have to keep four capital ships in Home waters to act as a deterrent to Germany, leaving only eight capital ships for the Far East (See further, below, pp. 51–2.) In cruisers, destroyers, and seaborne aircraft, though not in submarines, there would be an approximate equality once the Main Fleet arrived, including in the calculation the ships of the China Station and of the East Indies, African, Australian, and New Zealand squadrons. Reinforcements from Europe would ensure a definite superiority in these craft in about the third to fourth month of the war.

One of the crosses the Chiefs of Staff and the Admiralty had to bear was the regular pressure from Australia and New Zealand to maintan a battle fleet at Singapore in peacetime sufficient to deter Japanese aggression against the British Empire. (After all, as the Australian Prime Minister had exclaimed in October 1919, 'it is a long way from Tokyo to Whitehall, but we are within a stone's throw.') This ran counter to the basis of British strategy, which was to keep the Main Fleet in European waters, but to establish a fleet at Singapore as quickly as possible after the outbreak of war with Japan. Repeated assurances were given to the Australian and New Zealand authorities that in the event of such a war they would send an adequate fleet to Eastern waters irrespective of the situation elsewhere. 'No anxieties or risks connected with our interests in the Mediterranean can be allowed to interfere with the despatch of a fleet to the Far East.'[10]

There was a full discussion at the Chiefs of Staff meeting on 1 June 1937, which was attended by Australian and New Zealand representatives. Chatfield explained the two difficulties, political/strategic and administrative, which made it impossible to keep a fleet at Singapore in time of peace. As regards the first: 'We should have to send a force equal in strength to the Japanese Fleet, since to divide our forces, which were limited particularly as regards heavy ship strength, and run the risk of their defeat in detail should war break out, would be most unwise. But to send a Fleet equal to the Japanese out to the Pacific at the present moment would be a most challenging act from the diplomatic point of view.' The administrative problem was just as sticky.

We should have to maintain two-thirds of our Battle Fleet in the Pacific,

---

[10] CID 1305-B, 'Review of Imperial Defence by the Chiefs of Staff Sub-Committee', 22 Feb. 1937, CAB 4/25. The First Lord, Sir Samuel Hoare, had repeated the assurance at the Imperial Conference of 1937 on 26 May. E(PD)(37) 7th Mtg., CAB 32/128.

and that would mean a very much greater proportion of the Navy being permanently on foreign service. Already personnel did two commissions out of three on foreign service, and, if so large a force was maintained in the Far East, the proportion of foreign service would rise probably to four commissions out of five. Moreover, Singapore would have to be greatly expanded and made equivalent to, say, Portsmouth and Devonport in combination. This would involve a huge expense and involve closing dockyards at home.

It was therefore considered better to keep the Battle Fleet in European Waters. We must have a fleet at home ready for a European war, which might break out more suddenly than any war in the Pacific ... from the strategical point of view it was advisable to retain the major portion of our Fleet in European waters in peace. If the Fleet were stationed in peace in the Far East and hostilities suddenly broke out in Europe, the situation might be far more serious than if we had retained the Fleet in Europe and war broke out first in the Far East.

Chatfield answered the Australian fears of invasion by asserting that its exteme difficulty made such an operation unlikely unless the British fleet had been defeated in the Pacific. Raids were nothing to worry about. 'A raid was essentially a cut-and-run affair, and local forces and fixed defences provide a very strong deterrent against such operations.'[11]

Under Chatfield and Backhouse the Admiralty did not swerve an inch from their conviction that it was highly improbable that Japan would ever attempt to invade Australia in force—her lines of communication would be extended and vulnerable—so long as there was an undefeated British battle fleet in the Far East or *en route* to the Far East. Raids on Australian shipping or important ports could not be prevented except by the continued presence of strong local forces in Australian waters, although they would be less likely if there were a strong fleet at Singapore. In any case, such operations would not endanger the territorial integrity of the Dominion, however much local damage they did. A proposal by the Chiefs of Staff in the spring of 1938, repeated at the end of the year by the Admiralty, was that Australia contribute a capital ship for use in

[11] COS 209th Mtg., 1 June 1937, CAB 53/7. Chatfield emphasized the strategic factor in response to the request of the Cabinet Sub-Committee on the Far Eastern Situation for the Naval Staff view on the dispatch of two capital ships to Singapore to serve as a deterrent. 'Memorandum by C.N.S. Reinforcement of British Naval Forces in the Far East', n.d. (Sept. 1937), ADM 1/9909.

Australian waters as a deterrent against raids in strength before the arrival of the Main Fleet in the Far East, and as a reinforcement for that fleet. These proposals elicited no interest in Canberra. Indeed, Australia, 'in a state of fuss about her defences since the [Munich] crisis' (Backhouse), urged the British (autumn 1938) to send a capital ship to the East. Backhouse refused to do this, as he had none to spare. Also, 'any considerable Japanese attempt on Australia will be quite impossible at the present time'. The Pacific Dominions reluctantly and without conviction accepted the repeated assurances of the Chiefs of Staff that invasion of their countries could be ruled out indefinitely. Let it be said here that the Service Chiefs and the Admiralty never pressed hard for the assumption by the Dominions of a greater degree of responsibility for their own naval defence. That would have been heretical; it was taken for granted in British ruling circles in those days that the naval obligations of Britain towards the Dominions were one-sided, more or less.

In November 1938 the Admiralty gave what the Australian High Commissioner in London, Stanley Bruce, termed an 'unqualified reassurance' that, were there trouble with Japan, seven capital ships would be dispatched to Singapore. On 1 February 1939 the Chiefs of Staff promised that, even in a war with Germany, Italy, and Japan, a British fleet would have to be sent to the Far East. But the Australians worried that there might be delay in view of the possibility of German 'pocket battleships' breaking out on to the Atlantic. When on 19 March the Australian Government again asked for an assurance that in the event of war with Japan a fleet would arrive in time to contain the Japanese Fleet and deter Japan from 'a major act of aggression against Australia', Neville Chamberlain, the Prime Minister, send a telegram (20 March) to the Australian Prime Minister, J. A. Lyons, that came as a 'bombshell' to his Government. It struck them as a retreat from previous assurances, referring as it did to 'a combination never envisaged in our earlier plans', namely, the possibility of Britain having to fight Germany, Italy, and Japan at the same time, and it made the size of the fleet to be sent to the Far East dependent on the moment Japan entered the war and on the losses sustained by Britain and her opponents up to that time. 'It would, however, be our intention to achieve three main objects: (i) The prevention of any major operation against Australia, New Zealand or India; (ii) To keep open our sea communications; (iii) To prevent the fall of

Singapore.'¹² It could be inferred from this communication, and was undoubtedly so inferred in the Pacific Dominions, that a fleet only strong enough to perform these functions was no longer the Main Fleet that had been promised so many times during the preceding year. An Admiralty memorandum of 4 April attempted to calm Australian fears. Its thrust was that if war broke out in Europe and Japan intervened, Australia need fear nothing more than cruiser raids, for which her local defences were adequate. If Japan contemplated a 'major expedition' against Australia, she would tip her hand by acquiring an intermediate base in the Southwest Pacific, whereupon a British fleet would be sent to the Pacific 'of sufficient strength to make the position of any Japanese major expedition precarious'.¹³

The Admiralty had an equally difficult time with their own Foreign Office from 1937 on the issue of keeping a battleship squadron at Singapore as a peacetime deterrent. When in September 1937 the Far Eastern Committee of the Cabinet asked the Admiralty for their views on the dispatch of two capital ships to the Far East, Chatfield saw no merit in it. The ships would not serve as a deterrent because the Japanese would decide whether to go to war 'on the basis of her anticipation of the final outcome of such a war and not on the initial naval situation in the Far East'. The Japanese would only be concerned about Britain's ability to dispatch to the Far East a fleet capable of meeting and defeating their Fleet in battle. Besides, the dispatch of the two ships would lead to a 'division of our limited force of capital ships between the Eastern and Western hemispheres' and, 'far from acting as a deterrent to the Japanese, might even present a temptation to Japan in offering them at least a possibility of defeating the divided British forces in detail'.¹⁴ Such

---

[12] CID 355th Mtg., 2 May 1939, Appendix, CAB 2/8. In essence Chamberlain was reporting what the Admiralty had informed the Australian Naval Board three days earlier—that 'there has never been doubt that a force of Capital Ships would have to be sent to East in event of war with Japan', but that they were unable to make a firm commitment on its composition, as it would depend on the situation in Europe. ADM 1/9831. At about this time New Zealand expressed similar anxieties and received similar assurances at a Pacific Conference in Wellington in April.

[13] Stanhope (First Lord) to A. T. Stirling (Australian External Affairs Officer in London), CAB 21/893.

[14] Chatfield's memorandum for the Committee, 22 Sept. 1937, ADM 1/9909. The case that follows is from the same ADM file, and, for all but the Admiralty minutes, is also in E. L. Woodward and Rohan Butler (eds.), *Documents on British Foreign Policy, 1919–1939*, 3rd ser., viii (London, 1955), 320–2, 542–50.

common sense was sadly absent in the autumn of 1941, when precisely such a force, two capital ships, was sent out, and with the result predicted by Chatfield four years earlier.

The idea of sending out capital ships in time of peace refused to die. Craigie, the Ambassador in Tokyo, who was the Foreign Office's naval expert, touched off a flap by suggesting to Lord Halifax, the Foreign Minister (14 December 1938), that a permanent squadron of three or four capital ships be established at Singapore. It would uphold British prestige and influence throughout the Far East, and would force the Japanese to think twice before launching an attack on Singapore. The proposal stemmed from his feeling that events might be moving swiftly towards a crisis in the Far East. The Ambassador in China, Sir Archibald Clark Kerr, 'fully endorsed' Craigie's recommendation, as did G. G. Fitzmaurice, the Third Legal Adviser in the Foreign Office.

The Foreign Office sent copies of Craigie's dispatch, Clark Kerr's telegram, and Fitzmaurice's memorandum to the Admiralty on 13 February 1939 with the intimation that they, too, favoured the stationing of a powerful fleet in the Far East in peacetime. The Admiralty reply, which finally went out on 29 March, rejected the Foreign Office suggestion. They appreciated the political arguments advanced for stationing capital ships in the Far East, but their restricted number and the heavy commitments in the Mediterranean ruled this out. They hoped, nevertheless, to be able to station a capital ship at Singapore by 1942, and had recently so informed the Australian High Commissioner. If the situation envisaged by the Foreign Office materialized and the Japanese began to encroach upon Malaya or the Dutch East Indies, they would have to send a fleet out. 'But until the position is far more serious than it is now the Admiralty would hesitate to recommend such a step, which would involve the withdrawal of the greater part of our Fleet from the Mediterranean.' The letter concluded with a mini-lecture on the moral to be drawn from the situation that was a direct reflection of Backhouse's views. British foreign policy should be largely governed by the strength of the Navy.

Unless the Navy is maintained at a strength sufficient to secure our position in those parts of the world which are vital to the existence of the Empire, it is impracticable to carry out our chosen policy as and when we wish. But while, in theory, naval strength must be based upon foreign policy, in practice, there is a limit, governed by money, men and material, and determined by the Government of the day, beyond which our armaments cannot be advanced; and when this is reached the tables are turned, and foreign policy must depend upon naval strength, unless risk of war, and even of unsuccessful war, is to be incurred. A reduction in the number of our potential enemies is as definite an accretion to our strength as is an increase in the number of our battleships.

The last sentence refers to the Admiralty policy, and that of the Chiefs of Staff, in the last pre-war years of urging on their political masters a foreign policy of limited liability. The Joint Planners stated this in a paper of 1936: 'In order that our liabilities may bear some reasonable relation to our military capacity, until the latter has been very materially increased, the danger of simultaneous tension between ourselves and Germany, Italy and Japan must be eliminated ... the present situation dictates a policy directed towards an understanding with Germany'.[15] Six months later, Chatfield reminded the Foreign Office that, as a simultaneous war in the east and west would be fatal, Britain must 'make an agreement in one area or another'. His recommendation was for an understanding with Japan; it was 'the first essential', difficult though it would be to achieve.[16] The Chiefs of Staff adopted this approach, seeing that an improvement in relations with Japan offered a way of lightening defence problems. 'Moreover, the difficulties and dangers of conducting a war against Japan in the Far East, particularly if we were simultaneously engaged in Europe, are so great that it is manifest that no effort must be spared to establish such good relations with our former allies, the Japanese, as will obviate, as far as possible, the chances of their being aligned against us.'[17]

The Foreign Office were only too ready to oblige the Services, but they could find no concrete way of improving relations with Japan short of giving up their support of the Chinese nationalist regime under Chiang Kai-shek and writing off the British economic stake in China. The former was a policy that the Services would not countenance: it would risk alienating the United States and thereby

---

[15] JP158, 'Strategical Review', 3 July 1936, CAB 55/8.
[16] Chatfield to Sir Robert Vansittart (Permanent Under-Secretary of State for Foreign Affairs), 5 Jan. 1937, Chatfield Papers, CHT 3/1 (National Maritime Museum).
[17] COS596, 'Appreciation of the Situation in the Far East, 1937', 14 June 1937, CAB 53/32.

weaken Anglo-American collaboration in the Far East.[18] The latter policy, too, was a non-starter.

The British feared [writes a scholar] that a wider political and economic agreement with concessions to Japan in China would amount to an agreement to permit Japan to swallow up British interests. The loss of these interests would not have been economically shattering to Britain but it would have broadcast British impotence to the world. Once Japan had made it clear that she would not be a party to any naval limitation agreement, there was no *quid pro quo* which could be obtained from her which could compensate for a revelation that Britain could not police her interests or carry out her imperial role in the far eastern and Pacific areas. The Foreign Office was not prepared, therefore, to recommend that a step involving such risks to Britain's image as an imperial power should be taken.[19]

There was, finally, the belief in the Foreign Office that concessions in China would do nothing to temper the expansionist ambitions of Tokyo. There were, however, as Peter Lowe has pointed out, 'three examples of individual acts of appeasement made under pressure', of which one, the temporary closure of the Burma Road in July 1940, will concern us in a later chapter. (The other two were the Customs Agreement of 1938 and acquiescence in Japanese control in Tientsin.)

Admiralty views on relations with Japan come out most clearly in their response to Foreign Office initiatives in the summer of 1938 and the spring of 1939. In the first case the Foreign Office and Craigie were considerably exercised over Japanese restrictions on trade in the Yangtze and elsewhere in China. To prevent Japanese destruction of British trade interests that had been built up over a hundred years in regions controlled by their armed forces, Craigie and the Foreign Office proposed to strengthen the China Station, to show the flag more often in waters where British trade was moving, and to institute economic reprisals. But for the Admiralty it was not an opportune time to commence a forward policy in the Far East. As Chatfield tersely declared (20 July 1938): 'We are now facing a possible war in Europe and we are not strong enough to be sure of

[18] Air Ministry, Admiralty, and War Office to Foreign Office, respectively, 17 Feb., 2 Mar., 15 Mar. 1939, FO 371/23555. The particular point at issue at this time was whether co-operation with Japan in China would deter Japan from contracting a formal alliance with the Axis Powers.
[19] Ann Trotter, *Britain and East Asia, 1933–1937* (Cambridge, 1975), pp. 213–14.

waging a successful war in both the East and in the West. It would not seem wise, therefore, to take a very forward policy in China unless the situation is more serious than it appears to be. I doubt the moment has arrived for extreme measures on our part.... Another factor is that to get embroiled with Japan *now* would be an encouragement to Germany.' All he would countenance were diplomatic discussions with the Americans and French to try to adopt a joint policy seeking to remove trade restrictions in China waters. The First Lord, Duff Cooper, was just as cautious (22 July): 'No step in the direction of a more forward policy in the Far East should be taken without express Cabinet approval which I do not think would be given at the present time.'[20]

On 10 February 1939 the Japanese occupied China's Hainan Island, 250 miles south of Hong Kong, off the northern coast of French Indo-China, and, on 30 March, the Spratlys, a group of islands in the South China Sea claimed by France and Japan since the 1920s: some 400 miles east of the southernmost point of French Indo-China *and but 650 miles from Singapore.* There was a deep concern in London, since these annexations obviously had nothing to do with the needs of the war in China. Hainan and the Spratly Islands were regarded as Japanese advanced posts on the way to their long-term objectives, the oil of the Dutch East Indies and the high-grade iron ore of Malaya. And the threat to Singapore, once remote, was becoming a real one. How to deflect Japan from her attempt to form a self-contained economic bloc in the Far East was the problem. Assuming that the dispatch of a fleet to the East would, politically, be very difficult unless there was a direct Japanese attack on British or French possessions, Halifax raised the possibility of applying economic pressure on Japan, including a threat to denounce the Anglo-Japanese Commercial Convention of 1931. It was, he said, not now a question of protecting local vested interests, but of safeguarding Britain's whole world position. Economic reprisals had been discarded when last considered out of fear that Japanese countermeasures might lead to war. There was now less chance of this happening, since Japan had her hands full in China, and, besides, the attitude of the United States and the Soviet Union would act as a deterrent to any further large-scale campaign.[21] What did the Admiralty think?

[20] ADM 116/4087.
[21] CP76(39), 'Situation in the Far East', 18 Mar. 1939, CAB 24/284.

BRITISH STRATEGIC DILEMMAS (1936–1939)

The Admiralty response (3 May) was unequivocal. It was a most inopportune time to adopt a forward policy in the Far East. Japan had the capacity to adopt strong retaliatory measures, including the abolition of the British Concessions in China. The China hostilities had not involved the Japanese Fleet except to provide it with some first-class training, and Japan had enough uncommitted first-line troops to launch an operation against Hong Kong or Singapore. The deterrent value of the American and Soviet attitudes was overrated. Given the danger of war in Europe in the event of a state of emergency in the Far East, before using economic pressure against Japan it would be essential to be certain of American support—that she 'would, if necessary, not only come to our aid if either we or Japan should feel bound to regard as a casus belli any particular step taken by the other party, but be prepared to accept a large measure of responsibility for the conduct of the war against Japan, if war in Europe followed'. The prospects of obtaining such assurances, however, were not very strong. 'Finally,' and this was the nub of the matter,

> the present critical state of affairs in Europe provides, in our view, special reasons for extreme caution in approaching the question of economic pressure on Japan. In the event of war in Europe much will depend on our ability to keep Japan quiet so that we can exert all possible pressure on our opponents before having to release ships for the East. We should regard with the gravest misgiving any action calculated to drive Japan further into the arms of the Axis Powers so long as the persistence of the said Axis maintains the present tension in Europe.[22]

The question of economic retaliatory measures was raised again in June, with the onset of the explosive Tientsin crisis.

A major restraining factor on the dispatch of a sizable fleet to the East, whether in time of peace or war, was the Mediterranean situation.

3. THE FRENCH CONNECTION

Chatfield had made the point in December 1937 that if they sent a fleet to the East, it would be necessary to hold staff discussions with the French in order to arrange for them to help protect British trade and communications in the Atlantic, if necessary. Previously

[22] ADM 116/4087.

the Service Chiefs had opposed staff conversations with the French, mainly because of the reaction they would have upon Germany. On 8 February 1939 the Cabinet approved of staff conversations. A wary Backhouse did not believe that their Allies 'would like to hear that we were thinking of taking our heavy ships out of the Mediterranean'. It was well known in London that in the eyes of the French the decisive theatre of operations would be Europe— that if the war were lost there, it would be lost everywhere.

The Anglo–French naval conversations were held in London, 29 March–4 April and 24 April–3 May. There was agreement on the basics of the situation in time of war. Given the Allied preoccupation in the West, Allied Far Eastern strategy must be defensive at first. Although they must be prepared at some time to send naval reinforcements, 'The many incalculable factors make it impossible to decide definitely how soon after Japan entered the war these reinforcements would be sent or in what strength.' Plans for Allied co-operation had to provide for the two extremes: the practical abandonment temporarily of naval control in the Eastern Mediterranean or the Far East. The issue could not be decided in advance. They had to bear in mind the guarantees to the Eastern Mediterranean countries, and to hope that Italy could be disposed of fairly quickly. Until this happened, the French wanted to stay on the defensive in the Far East, relying on the Russians and the Americans, particularly the latter. They deemed it dangerous for British naval forces to leave the Mediterranean before the defeat of Italy.[23]

In the course of the conversations the French made it clear that they would be unable to control the Eastern as well as the Western Mediterranean without British support. If the Far Eastern situation necessitated a withdrawal of the British fleet in the Eastern Mediterranean, they would have no choice but to withdraw their two modern battle cruisers (Dunkerques) from the Atlantic (Brest) and send them into the Mediterranean, because the two Italian battleships had been modernized and were faster than the three modernized French battleships of the Lorraine class in that sea.

The French position had powerful backing in Whitehall. V. F. W. Cavendish-Bentinck, a Middle East expert at the Foreign Office, maintained that it would be practically impossible to retain

[23] COS914, 'Anglo–French Staff Conversations, 1939. United Kingdom Delegation', 11 May 1939, CAB 53/49.

Egypt and Palestine, and any influence in Iraq and Arabia, if control of the Eastern Mediterranean were lost as the result of the dispatch of a capital-ship force to the East. 'The consequences outlined above on our strategical position might be more disastrous for the Empire as a whole than the temporary loss by Australia and New Zealand of their sea borne trade and the risk to those Dominions of attack by Japan.'[24] Bentinck's pessimistic appraisal reflected the cleavage of opinion within the Foreign Office as to the prior claims on the Fleet of the Eastern Mediterranean and the Far East. They were in opposition to those of the Chiefs of Staff, who had laid down six months earlier that, once Japan had joined the Axis in a war against Britain, 'it would be imperative for us to send to Singapore a fleet of sufficient strength to enable us to stand on the defensive in the Far East. This would probably involve denuding the Mediterranean to an extent which might leave Italy in control of the sea communications in the Central and Eastern area, but no anxieties or risks connected with our interests there can be allowed to interfere with the dispatch of a fleet to the Far East.'[25]

This was, however, no longer the position of the Admiralty under the new First Sea Lord, Backhouse, who would not shut his eyes to the grim consequences of the fact that they had started to rebuild their battle fleet late in the day. He was irate at Bentinck's memorandum, exploding in a minute of 24 March that did not address itself directly to the main point but does reveal the First Sea Lord's thoughts on Far Eastern naval strategy and his impatience with advice from the non-Service ministries.

This paper is yet one more on the subject of whether the Fleet should remain in the Mediterranean or go to the Far East. . . .

I do not think that the Admiralty can be expected to answer every stray letter that comes in from the Foreign Office, and possibly other Departments, on this subject or we should never have time to do anything else. . . .

The fact of the matter is that at the present time the British Empire is not strong enough to fight the Germans, the Italians and the Japanese all at the same time, but unfortunately some of the good people who write essays on the subject seem to think that the Navy can carry all these wars

---

[24] 'Probable Effect on British Position in Egypt if a Large Fleet Is Sent to the Far East in the Event of War with Japan', 18 Mar. 1939, ADM 1/9909.

[25] COS755, 'Appreciation of the Situation in the Event of War against Germany in April, 1939', 5 Aug. 1938, CAB 53/40.

on its back to make up for the weaknesses of the Army and Air Force. Unfortunately this is not the case as the Navy has got behind hand also, and will not recover in strength for another year or two.

I do not personally believe that Japan will attempt to attack Singapore as a major operation unless the war is going badly for us in Europe, although I quite believe that they would attack Hong Kong if we were well occupied in European theatres. I am also of opinion that a squadron of three or four fast Capital Ships, with a force of Cruisers, Destroyers and Submarines, stationed in the East, should be quite capable not only of looking after itself but also of safeguarding our trade and our communications, although not strong enough to give battle to the whole Japanese Fleet in Japanese waters.

We have also to consider the possible effect on U.S.A. of any Japanese warlike action against us or our possessions. If the U.S.A. showed any inclination to interfere, I doubt very much whether the Japanese would attempt to do anything more than very restricted operations.

I do not feel that the paper in this docket should be given an official answer on a high level, for the reasons I have given earlier in this minute.[26]

Bentinck's position had strong support elsewhere. Writing independently to Halifax on 27 March, Churchill, then out of power, forcibly argued that no threats in the Far East should divert them from retaining wartime domination of the Mediterranean. Control of the Mediterranean would inflict serious injury on Italy and perhaps knock her out of the war. Her troops in Libya and Abyssinia would be 'cut flowers in a vase'; Egypt could be reinforced. 'Not to hold the Mediterranean would be to expose Egypt and the Canal, as well as the French possessions, to invasion by Italian troops with German leadership. We cannot tolerate this on any account.' If Japan joined the Axis in war, which was by no means certain, since she had her hands full, British interests and possessions would be 'temporarily effaced. . . . [But] we must bear the losses and punishment, awaiting the final result of the struggle.'[27] Halifax was in nearly complete agreement with Churchill, whose 'views as to the strategic necessity of dealing with Italy before attempting to send any large force to the Far East accord very closely with our own'.[28]

All the threads in the complex naval strategic picture were

[26] ADM 1/9909.
[27] 'Memorandum on Sea-Power, 1939', FO 371/23982.
[28] Halifax to Sir Ronald Lindsay (British Ambassador in Washington), 17 Apr. 1939, FO 371/23982.

brought together with the deterioration of the naval situation in the Far East in the spring of 1939: the problems of the period before relief, the size of the fleet to be dispatched and when, the Mediterranean, pressures from the Pacific Dominions, and foreign policy.

4. STRATEGIC IMPASSE

The Main Fleet strategy for the defence of the Empire in the East was feasible only in the absence of any other external threat—that is, so long as Britain had to contemplate a war against Japan alone. This was a possibility as late as 1938. The Abyssinian Crisis had created the strategic problem of a hostile Italy which could disrupt British communications through the Mediterranean. 'It now appears', Chatfield had told the Defence Policy and Requirements Committee of the Cabinet, 'that if we were to send the Fleet to the Far East we should, in future, have to maintain another Fleet in the Mediterranean to guard its communications.'[29] The crisis was, however, resolved after a fashion in the spring of 1936, and in 1937-8 the Chamberlain Government embarked on a policy of appeasing both Germany and Italy that offered some hope for the preservation of peace in Europe. By 1939, with the failure of Chamberlain's Italian policy and the deterioration in Europe—the Munich Crisis (September 1938), the German seizure of Czechoslovakia (15 March 1939), the Italian grab of Albania (7 April 1939), and the conclusion of an Italo-German political and military alliance (22 May 1939)—it was almost a certainty that a war would start in the West and that Italy would in all circumstances fight beside Germany. In this situation the British expected that Japan would exploit their difficulties and go to war after Britain had become involved in hostilities with the Axis Powers. The position of the Admiralty in such a contingency was that it might be some time before a fleet could be sent to the East, as in the first stages of a European war the Navy might be dispersed, tracking and destroying enemy raiders which had escaped on to the trade routes, and engaged on other operations. British strategy also called for knocking Italy out before being free to send out a strong fleet should the Japanese intervene.

The new situation raised difficult questions. In the first place, was

[29] 3 Oct. 1935, DRC, 15th Mtg., CAB 16/112.

the 70-day period before the relief of Singapore still valid, since it was based on the assumption that they would be undertaking a single-handed war with Japan? The Admiralty thought not, and the Chiefs of Staff had serious doubts. The feeling of the latter by early May was that, if war with Japan broke out simultaneously with or after the outbreak of war with Germany and Italy, naval conditions in European waters might prevent a fleet from reaching Singapore in less than 90 days after the outbreak of war. That is, the automatic dispatch of the Main Fleet might not be possible. What made it trickier still was the British commitments to Near Eastern countries: the treaty of alliance with Egypt (26 August 1936), the guarantees to Greece and Romania (13 April 1939), and the mutual assistance pact with Turkey (12 May 1939). These rendered it questionable whether a large portion of the Mediterranean Fleet would be removed in the early stages of a war. The CID approved the 90-day period before relief on 6 July. Provision was made that all kinds of reserves held in Malaya be increased as quickly as possible to a figure sufficient for a 90-day period before relief. After war commenced in September, the period before relief was extended to six months.

When the Navy began to quibble over the size of the fleet to be sent to the Far East, as well as over the period before relief, Chatfield, who was now Minister for Co-ordination of Defence, spoke out. He had, as Pownall noted in his diary, 'always been very keen on the Far East. He may kick pretty heavily.' Chatfield would rather they suffered losses in the Mediterranean and Middle East than allow the Japanese to gain undisputed control of sea communications in the Indian Ocean and in the Pacific. And he felt strongly about weakening the assurances they had given to the Dominions in 1937. It would have a very bad effect on opinion there. He would have a fleet of nine capital ships sent to the Far East, leaving four in European waters and the comparatively modern five French capital ships to counter the six German and Italian ships. Even seven or eight capital ships would contain the Japanese Fleet, 'in the same way as a vastly inferior German fleet contained the Grand Fleet for four years. . . . we must not lose sight of the superiority which the greater efficiency of our fleet conferred upon us. After all, we should have lost the battle of Trafalgar on a Staff Appreciation since our fleet was inferior to the French.'[30]

[30] CID 348th Mtg., 24 Feb. 1939, CAB 2/8.

BRITISH STRATEGIC DILEMMAS (1936–1939)

Chatfield held his ground at the first meeting of the Strategical Appreciation Sub-Committee of the CID (SAC) on 1 March 1939. It was in his view essential to send a fleet of at least seven capital ships to the East even if they found themselves fighting Germany, Italy, and Japan. To do otherwise would be to risk the Empire. The only new factor that had emerged since the assurances given to the Dominions in 1937 was that Italian as well as German and Japanese hostility had to be contemplated. He stated his position in these stark terms at the second meeting of the Committee on 13 March. 'The Chiefs of Staff had always maintained that we could not undertake a war against Germany, Italy and Japan simultaneously, but at the same time if we are faced with such a war he felt it would be better to lose the Eastern Empire by fighting than by default. In the first case it would be an honourable defeat: in the second case it would be a disgrace.' He added that 'if they did not show willingness to look after our Dominions they might consider whether it would not be advantageous for them to look to America for assistance'.[31]

The Chiefs of Staff did not share these views. The First Sea Lord, in particular, was cautious, though 'realistic' may be a better word. Backhouse had his doubts about the possibility of implementing the Main Fleet strategy: the assurances given to the Dominions in 1937 were 'optimistic in the light of present day circumstances'. He saw substantive changes for the worse over the 1937 position, with the fleet of a potentially hostile Italy nearly equal in strength to that of the French Fleet, and with nine of Japan's ten capital ships having been modernized, and that fleet having the advantage of fighting in its own waters. At least six capital ships would have to remain in Home waters to deal with the five German capital ships (three Deutschland pocket battleships and two battle cruisers), since if one or two German ships operated as commerce raiders in the Atlantic, they might need three or four to find them quickly and bring them to action. Even if all the remaining capital ships were sent to the Far East—five at first and a sixth late in the summer—this was hardly the 'adequate fleet' that had been promised to the Dominions. It would not be capable of relieving Hong Kong or of engaging the whole Japanese Fleet, though this force, as Backhouse claimed,

[31] CAB 16/209. SAC consisted of Chatfield as Chairman, the Chiefs of Staff, the Service ministers, and two other ministers.

should be able to safeguard communications in the Indian Ocean and prevent a major expedition against Australia and New Zealand. He was never able to be specific regarding the size of the fleet that would be sent to the East if Japan appeared to be threatening there. This would depend on what was happening in both the European and Eastern theatres, and on the American attitude towards an Anglo–Japanese war. The most promising way to solve the strategic problem was: 'if we could give the Italians a few hard knocks in the early stages of the war we might have no more bother from them at sea'. But he could never whip up much enthusiasm for sending a fleet out that could not meet the Japanese Fleet. What orders should be given to the C-in-C of such a fleet? And, 'On the assumption that he would have at his disposal five or possibly 6 capital ships, what action would he be expected to take if the whole Japanese fleet moved south with the obvious intention of seeking action?'[32] There was a solution which was no solution in the spring.

Influential in the deliberations on Far Eastern strategy at this time was Vice-Admiral Sir Andrew Cunningham, whom Backhouse had brought in as his DCNS in October 1938. It was Cunningham's first staff appointment and, as he tells us in his autobiography, he 'felt rather horrified at the prospect', believing that lack of staff experience made him unsuited for the appointment. His distress increased when, as could have been expected, the First Sea Lord gave him little of importance to do. But Backhouse's serious illness in the spring of 1939 (he did less and less work from the latter part of March) elevated Cunningham for some two critical months (through May) to the position of *de facto* First Sea Lord. (He succeeded Pound in the Mediterranean, when the latter took over from Backhouse in June.)

Pursuant to a request from the Strategical Appreciation Sub-Committee to the First Sea Lord (13 March), Cunningham prepared an appreciation of the naval situation in the event of (i) war with the Axis Powers with the threat of a hostile Japan, and (ii) with the three Powers simultaneously. This was to enable the Committee to make a recommendation on the question of the dispatch of a fleet to the Far East. The DCNS emphasized, in the case of (ii), that there were 'so many variable factors which cannot

---

[32] SAC4, 'The Despatch of a Fleet to the Far East. Note by the First Sea Lord', 28 Feb. 1939, CAB 16/209, and his statements at the SAC meetings on 1 and 13 March, ibid.

at present be assessed, that it is not possible to state definitely how soon after Japanese intervention a Fleet could be despatched to the Far East. Neither is it possible to enumerate precisely the size of the Fleet that we could afford to send.' The 'variable factors' were the number of capital ships available at the time; the strategical situation in Home waters and in the Mediterranean; Japanese strategy; and the reactions of the United States and the Soviet Union to Japan's intervention. 'It is not open to question that a capital-ship force would have to be sent, but whether this could be done to the exclusion of our interests in the Mediterranean is a matter which would have to be decided at the time.'[33] In a variety of guises the thrust of this analysis was to be repeated *ad nauseam* in succeeding months. On 2 May the CID approved the major conclusion reached in Cunningham's paper, that concerning the 'variable factors', and noted that this would necessitate a reconsideration of the reserves and defences of Singapore.

The problem of the exact strength of the fleet destined for Singapore in the event of a triangular war continued to be enveloped in confusion and uncertainty, there being no way to resolve the 'variable factors' with any precision. The Director of Plans at the Admiralty stated that in such a war, and with the United States remaining neutral, it was intended to despatch four capital ships, but only two, if the US were an ally. If Italy were neutral or had been eliminated when Japan intervened, seven capital ships would be sent out.[34] It was put more generally in June, when a revised Section XVII ('Situation in the Far East If War with Japan Breaks out When We, Allied with France, Are Already at War with Germany and Italy') of the Naval War Memorandum (Eastern) was sent to all Cs-in-C: 'While it is not open to question that a capital ship force would have to be sent to the Far East, its composition cannot be forecast at present. In the most favourable situation at home and in the Mediterranean a battlefleet of 7 or 8 ships might possibly be sent. In other circumstances, it might only be possible to despatch a small force in the form of a 'flying squadron'. In the latter event, it would be most desirable that

---

[33] SAC16, Cunningham, 'Despatch of a Fleet to the Far East', 5 Apr. 1939, CAB 16/209. We can assume that the paper had the First Sea Lord's approval. In any case, it reflected Backhouse's view that, given the many variables, detailed planning had little value.

[34] Captain V. H. Danckwerts's minute, 5 May, which was approved by the DCNS on 16 May. ADM 116/3863.

capital ships with high speed and large endurance should be sent.'[35]

With the likelihood that the Main Fleet would be dispatched to Singapore as soon as Japan entered the war becoming ever more remote, the nagging doubts of the Australians about British intentions and capabilities surfaced again. At two high-level meetings held in London in the early summer of 1939[36] the Australians were 'keenly anxious' to know whether a fleet would be dispatched to Singapore, were there armed conflict with Japan, and if so, of what size. The British had no answer: 'the position was still indeterminate'. A minimum of six capital ships must be retained in Home waters, and their new Allies (Greece, Romania and Turkey) would be very upset at the withdrawal of all capital ships from the Eastern Mediterranean. Chatfield, nevertheless, assured the Australians that 'although the plan was indeterminate, there was no question that in the event of war with Japan, we would abdicate our position in the Far East without fighting'. These assurances were not entirely satisfactory to the Australians, who were 'in the dark as to what would happen if trouble were to start in the East in the first place'. But no more so than were the Admiralty and the Service Chiefs.

The Tientsin crisis in the summer of 1939 drove home some unpalatable strategic truths to both the Government and the strategists. On 14 June 1939 the Japanese established a rigorous blockade of the British concession at Tientsin after the British authorities had refused to surrender to them four Chinese accused of terrorism. Japan publicly demanded (19 June) that Britain give up support of the Chinese Nationalist regime. Her tone throughout the crisis was harsh and bellicose. Japan, Chatfield later wrote, 'trading on our relatively weak naval position, was insulting British nationals in Tientsin, in a manner that would have made a Georgian or Victorian statesman issue violent ultimatums'. It was at this time, too, in June and July, that Japan bombed open, non-military cities and towns in China. These terror bombings horrified British and world public opinion.

The larger meaning of the crisis for the decision-makers in London was that, instead of the probability that Japan would join

[35] ADM 116/3863. This passage had been communicated in advance, on 16 May, to the C-in-C, China.
[36] The records of these meetings, on 28 June and 11 July, under the title 'The Situation in the Far East', are in ADM 205/1.

the Axis Powers after Britain had become involved in a war with them, it was now the other way round—that it was more likely that a war might start with Japan and then spread to Europe. If a fleet were dispatched to Singapore to deal with Japan, the Axis might find the temptation to take advantage of the situation irresistible. The new situation seemed to place in jeopardy the strategy of sending a fleet out in the event of trouble with Japan.

Halifax on 16 June advocated economic retaliatory measures against Japan as a counter to her action in Tientsin. It was, he asserted, the only way to turn the Japanese from their ambitions to dominate East Asia and advance southward against the British Empire. Chatfield at once asked the Chiefs of Staff as a matter of urgency to advise on the military implications. To deal adequately with Japan, they reported, would require at least eight capital ships; yet, to dispatch them would jeopardize the position in Home waters, the decisive theatre, since the Axis Powers would probably intervene in an Anglo–Japanese war. No more than two capital ships could be sent without relinquishing control of the Eastern Mediterranean, the assumption being that France would control the Western Mediterranean. The two ships would reinforce the ships on the China Station, which would be based in Singapore. Such a force might at best secure Britain's sea communications in the Indian Ocean against raids and deter the Japanese Fleet from undertaking major operations in the South China Sea or Australian waters. At the worst, if the Japanese Fleet moved southward in force, British naval forces would have to retire westward, leaving Singapore open to investment. To relieve Singapore would mean sending out a force that included at least eight battleships. Considering the limited results that a force with only two capital ships could hope to achieve, the COS concluded that 'without the active co-operation of the United States of America, it would not be justifiable from the military point of view, having regard to the existing international situation, to take any unavoidable action which might lead to hostilities with Japan'.[37] The dominating consideration for the Chiefs of Staff was that it was most undesirable for Britain to become involved in the Far East.

The Foreign Policy Committee of the Cabinet discussed the report at what Cadogan described as a 'very glum and sticky

[37] COS928, 'The Situation in the Far East', 18 June 1939, CAB 53/50.

meeting' on 19 June, 'when it was decided to stage as graceful a climbdown as possible by means of Craigie and the Americans—if the latter will play'.[38] Chatfield, though in 'cordial agreement' with the view that involvement in the Far East was most undesirable, and that they should do nothing to endanger their position in the decisive theatre, at home, thought the COS report painted the picture 'unduly black'. He asked the Chiefs of Staff to give further consideration to the strength of the fleet that might be sent to the Far East, while offering them his own opinion that if they could not dispatch more than two capital ships, which might be regarded as a confession of weakness, it might be better to send none at all.

The outcome was a cogent COS paper on 24 June that stated the fundamentals of the strategic problems that faced Britain's planners. It represented a shift in their thinking. Influenced by Chatfield, they were now prepared to consider the possibility of withdrawing the fleet from the Eastern Mediterranean to send a larger fleet to the East. The minimum capital-ship strength in that fleet was determined by the minimum strategic objectives of this force, viz., to secure Singapore and thereby British communications in the Indian Ocean, to secure Australia and New Zealand from large-scale Japanese attack, and to support by force the economic measures which they hoped would ultimately bring about the defeat of Japan. To achieve these objects, the Eastern Fleet must be strong enough to accept action with the Japanese Fleet, if it came south in full force. The Service Chiefs allowed for the need of the fleet to carry out periodical docking and fitting after arrival at Singapore; that, at Japan's selected moment, it might have to face her full capital-ship strength with one British capital ship in dock or refitting; that, even if they allowed for the Russian fleet at Vladivostok containing a proportion of Japan's light forces, the Japanese could bring south with their main fleet a superiority in aircraft carriers, cruisers, and destroyers; that the fighting efficiency of the Imperial Navy was only 80 per cent of the Royal Navy's; and that, if the British fleet did not move far north of Singapore, the Japanese, to engage it, would have to fight a fleet action at a great distance from their nearest repair base, and if this took place within the 190-mile radius of the shore-based torpedo-bombers at

---

[38] Diary, 19 June 1939, John Harvey (ed.), *The Diplomatic Diaries of Oliver Harvey, 1937–1940* (London, 1970), p. 298. Harvey was Private Secretary to Halifax, and Sir Alexander Cadogan was the Permanent Under-Secretary of State for Foreign Affairs.

Singapore, they would be subjected to the attack of these aircraft. From these considerations, positive and negative, the Chiefs of Staff emerged somehow with the figure of seven capital ships, 'but no less', as the size of the required fleet. 'It may be that the despatch of this force would be sufficient to bring Japan to heel at once. If, however, this did not prove to be the case, and, assuming, for example, that the Japanese did not commence hostilities, but merely continued with intensity their methods of freezing our people and trade out of China, the Fleet could do nothing to stop this process.' If the Japanese attacked Hong Kong, the fleet could not attempt to relieve it, since it would be too risky to engage the whole Japanese Fleet so far north, although 'it might well be possible that, after testing the efficiency of the Japanese fleet, our fleet could adopt a more offensive policy further northwards'.

But where were the seven capital ships to come from? Six of the 11 capital ships immediately available were required for Home waters: to deal with the five German capital ships, should they break out on to the trade routes, especially since the Royal Navy could not depend on the co-operation in the Atlantic of the two French battle cruisers if Britain abandoned the Eastern Mediterranean. This left one ship available from the seven in Home waters. Even by completely denuding the Eastern Mediterranean of its four capital ships, the total for the Far East would be five. To these could be added the *Revenge* on 1 August and the *Renown* early in September. The serious consequences, however, of withdrawing all their capital ships from the Mediterrean were brought out. (1) The French would probably concentrate all their five capital ships in the Western Mediterranean, and, to judge from the recent Staff conversations, were unlikely to be either willing or able to dispute control of the Eastern Mediterranean. (2) Although they would retain submarines and light forces at Malta and in the Eastern Mediterranean, and continue to exercise control in the Canal area and the Red Sea, they could not interupt Italian communications with North Africa or undertake offensive naval action in that area. This would permit an increase in the scale of the Italian attack against Egypt, by land and air, and possibly by sea. (3) Britain could not secure her communications in the Mediterranean to Turkey, Greece, or the Black Sea. (4) The political effect would be considerable on Britain's Eastern Mediterranean and Middle East friends and allies, especially Egypt and Turkey, and it might encourage Franco's Spain to side definitely with Germany and Italy.[39]

Chatfield summed up the principal questions which required immediate consideration by the Committee of Imperial Defence, of which the more crucial were these: If war broke out with Japan, should they adhere to the long-accepted policy of sending a fleet to Singapore with the responsibility of assuming a defensive posture initially, but of sufficient strength to accept action with the whole Japanese Fleet under favourable conditions? And since dispatching such a fleet involved loss of naval control of the Eastern Mediterranean, could this be accepted, having regard to British commitments in Europe and the Middle East? And as a way out of this cruel dilemma: 'Would it be preferable and practicable to concentrate any fleet destined for the Far East initially in the Eastern Mediterranean, viz., to threaten to send it, but not to act until the last possible moment?'[40]

The Committee of Imperial Defence examined the COS and Chatfield papers on 26 June. They agreed that nothing should be done to endanger the success of the impending negotiations at Tokyo. But would it be practicable and advisable, they asked the Admiralty, if the negotiations failed and hostilities with Japan appeared likely, initially to concentrate in the Eastern Mediterranean whatever fleet was earmarked for dispatch to the Far East? The Service Chiefs, in reply, stated on the authority of the First Sea Lord (Pound):

(a) The disadvantages of concentrating a Fleet for the Far East in the Eastern Mediterranean can be accepted if—
(1) War in the Far East appeared to be more probable than war in Europe.
(2) His Majesty's Government had already taken the decision that the Fleet would be despatched to Singapore and the Eastern Mediterranean abandoned in the event of war with Japan.
(b) Under existing conditions it is undesirable to accept the disadvantages of concentrating a Fleet for the Far East in the Eastern Mediterranean solely as a threat to Japan.[41]

---

[39] DP(P)61, 'Situation in the Far East. Report by the Chiefs of Staff Sub-Committee', 24 June 1939, CAB 16/183A. DP(P) was the Defence Plans (Policy) Sub-Committee of the CID, instituted in February 1937.
[40] DP(P)62, 'The Situation in the Far East', 23 June 1939, CAB 16/183A.
[41] COS949, 'Situation in the Far East', 28 July 1939, CAB 53/52.

And so round and round the same course went the discussions of the strategic planners and the decision-makers. It had long been accepted that it was beyond the capacity of Britain and France alone to provide adequate forces to deal with Germany, Italy, and Japan simultaneously in a major war. Short of a possible reconciliation with Italy, or a commitment of support from the Soviet Union, or, more importantly, the United States, there was no solution to the strategic dilemmas posed by a triangular war. It was accepted that in such a war they must send a fleet to the East—unless they were prepared to leave Australia and New Zealand to their fate and to face the loss of Singapore, with all the consequences this would involve. At the same time the great risks in Home waters and the Mediterranean involved in such a strategy, to say nothing of the political effects the naval evacuation of the Eastern Mediterranean would have on Greece, Turkey, and the Arab and Moslem world, made it impracticable and dangerous. British naval programmes, the strategists often reminded the politicians, had never allowed for a war with three major Powers. This line solved nothing. Indeed, there was no satisfactory solution in the context of British naval strength, the obligations to the Pacific Dominions, and the world situation.

The Services, *au fond*, favoured a strategy that retained all but one or two capital ships in Home waters and the Mediterranean, and concentrated on knocking Italy out, before sending a large battle fleet to Singapore, in the meantime remaining on the defensive in the East and relying on Russia and America to serve as deterrents to a major Japanese operation southward. This policy could never be pushed hard in face of Cabinet sensitivity to the fears of the Australians and New Zealanders—a sensitivity occasioned to a degree by anxiety lest, feeling abandoned by London, they opted for a policy of neutrality or of a closer association with the United States.[42] Under the circumstances the strategists felt that the wise policy was for the Government to do everything possible to avoid a showdown with Japan.

It was plain to Chamberlain that they 'could only send an effective Fleet to the Far East at the cost of abandoning our naval position in the Mediterranean. This was conclusive in favour of making every endeavour to reach an early settlement of the dispute

---

[42] See Foreign Office minutes, 24 May 1939, FO 371/22975.

at Tientsin. It was clear that we should only be prepared to run the risks involved in sending a Fleet to the Far East if Japan made our position there quite intolerable.'[43] Although towards the end of July the two sides apparently found a formula for solving the Tientsin crisis, the negotiations were rocky.

The mood of the Services on the eve of the war in Europe is captured in this extract from General Pownall's diary of 7 August:

Meanwhile things are not going at all well in the Tokyo discussions on Tientsin. The Japs are being extremely intractable, no doubt with an eye to the main chance if there is a European war. They are raising issues much larger than the local ones at Tientsin, and we are in a proper fix over the whole thing. It's a terrible condemnation of the conduct of our foreign policy that we are close to the position which the Chiefs of Staff have consistently warned the Government we *must* avoid—viz. a war against three first class powers—Germany, Italy and Japan.[44]

The negotiations over Tientsin continued to be deadlocked (a settlement was not reached until 12 June 1940), but the pressure on Britain's strategic planners was eased by the signing of the Molotov–Ribbentrop Pact on 23 August. It shook Japan profoundly. The Pact was viewed by the Joint Planners as weakening the Anti-Comintern Pact of November 1936 between Germany and Japan (Italy had adhered to it in November 1937), since Japan might well consider that it allowed Russia to pay more attention to the Far East and possibly to encourage Chinese resistance to Japan. 'This should have a salutary effect on the Japanese and, although it is unlikely to bring about an immediate cessation of anti-British activities in China, will probably discourage the Japanese from embarking on any major anti-British adventure until the European situation has been further clarified.'[45] A week later Britain and France were at war with the Axis, and now everything depended on the attitude of Japan. Before resuming the narrative, however, we must pause to further consider the naval plans formulated for a war with Japan.

---

[43] FP(36), 53rd Mtg., 20 June 1939, CAB 27/625.
[44] Bond, *Chief of Staff*, i. 217. Pownall was then Director of Military Operations and Intelligence at the War Office.
[45] JP529 (Revise), 'Military Implications of the New Situation in Europe and the Far East', 27 Aug. 1939, CAB 55/19.

BRITISH STRATEGIC DILEMMAS (1936–1939)

5. HOW TO FIGHT JAPAN?[46]

Far Eastern war plans in the later 1930s were predicated on the assumptions of no effective action by the League of Nations, peace in Europe, though with the possibility of being involved in a war with Germany (in which event France would be allied with Britain), and the arrival of the Main Fleet at Singapore. It was considered that the minimum size of the Main Fleet should be two less than the total Japanese capital-ship strength, or seven capital ships (the *Hiei* was not included in this reckoning). Four would come from Home waters and three from the Mediterranean, and a carrier from the Mediterranean. It was hoped that eight would be available in 1938–9 and ten in 1939–40. By August 1939, with a European war imminent, the maximum strength for the Far East was reiterated as seven capital ships and one aircraft carrier.

The Admiralty naturally regarded the decisive defeat of the Japanese Fleet as the ideal situation. It would mean complete British control of sea communications, which would probably force the Japanese to sue for peace. The distances involved in Far Eastern waters and the endurance of ships presented a difficult problem, however, if the Navy had no base nearer Japanese Home waters than Singapore. Thus, it was approximately 3,000 miles from Singapore to the Japanese coast off Yokohama, and the fleet could not remain in the area more than a few days. Under optimum conditions the Main Fleet would use Hong Kong, abour 1,500 miles from Japanese waters, as an advanced base and attempt to bring about a fleet action. Realistically, it came down to this: the Navy must adopt a defensive policy and base its plans on the assumption that it would be unable to undertake operations forward of the Singapore area. 'The decision to seek or decline a fleet action must rest with Japan. Our policy, therefore, should be to seek a fleet action under adequately favourable conditions and, as a corollary, to avoid exposing the fleet to any serious risk of attrition.' To put the matter in different words, the Naval Staff and the Chiefs of Staff

---

[46] The narrative that follows deals with the naval strategic thought of the Admiralty and Chiefs of Staff in 1937–9, prior to the outbreak of the European War, with a war-time extension in the discussion of Hong Kong. The principal documents are COS596 (14 June 1937) and 'Naval War Memorandum (Eastern)' (drawn up in December 1937 to give effect to this Appreciation by the Chiefs of Staff, with amendments as late as June 1939), ADM 116/4393.

held the firm view that 'the rôle of the Fleet in the Far East was not designed to seize control of the Sea of Japan, but rather to provide a defensive "fleet-in-being", so that before Japan could attack our main Imperial interests she would have first to defeat our Fleet under disadvantageous conditions.'[47]

With a fleet action unlikely, and invasion and victory by military action on Japanese soil declared to be out of the question, the Service Chiefs and the Admiralty looked upon the much slower process of economic pressure as the one practicable way to defeat Japan. The economic strain from her military operations in China made it improbable that Japan could support a war against Britain as well for any length of time. Economic pressure would lead to early decisive results only if they could carry the war into the China and Japan seas. This would require establishing a base closer to Japan than Hong Kong, like the Japanese Ryukyu Islands, which was not regarded as at all feasible. With a fleet based on Singapore, however, but mainly through the employment of a host of armed merchant cruisers, with some assistance from cruisers (whose main job would be the protection of British trade), they could impose such restrictions on enemy trade as to offer a good prospect of knocking Japan out of the war within two years—provided they could stop her trans-Pacific trade in addition to her European and British Empire trade. To this end, besides naval operations, they ought to persuade the United States to impose an embargo on supplies of war materials to Japan. She might be forced to accept a fleet action as the sole alternative to strangulation through economic pressure. By June 1939 the prospect of a triangular war forced a reappraisal of this strategy. 'Initially it is probable that our forces would be fully occupied in the protection of our own trade and attack on enemy trade could only take the form of occasional raids against Japanese shipping.'[48]

The Chiefs of Staff gave careful consideration to Japan's options. It was regarded as improbable that her Fleet would risk an action with the Main Fleet; nor were the Japanese likely to attempt the capture of Singapore in the period before relief, whether through a major expedition or a *coup de main*. The former would be risky with the Main Fleet *en route* to Singapore, and the latter would

---

[47] DP(P)60, 'The Situation in the Far East', 23 June 1939, CAB 16/183A.
[48] Revised Section XVII of the Naval War Memorandum (Eastern).

involve serious risks to capital ships and aircraft carriers. Nevertheless, they could not rule out the possibility of an offensive Japanese strategy, including a major offensive against Singapore, in view of the decisive results to which such a strategy could lead. At the other extreme, Japan might remain on the defensive, strengthening her military position in the Yangtze Valley and her already formidable defensive line of Japan–Luchu Islands–Formosa–Pescadores. But such a strategy would probably result in a protracted war for which Japan was not well prepared, financially and economically.

The Chiefs of Staff concluded that the most likely Japanese strategy would be a compromise between these two possible courses of action. 'After providing all necessary security measures, she might aim at the capture or complete neutralisation of Hong Kong, and the occupation of potential bases on the coast of China north and east of that base, at operations designed to delay the arrival of the British fleet, and to reduce its superiority by a process of attrition, and then at bringing about a fleet action if she could produce conditions of strategical or tactical advantage to herself.'[49] Additionally, Japan might take advantage of her great superiority before the arrival of the Main Fleet to do any of these things: dispatch a cruiser or armed merchant cruiser to attack British oil reserves at Trincomalee and Rangoon, and to capture oilers awaiting the arrival of the fleet; submarine and minelaying operations against the fleet in the Malacca Straits, should it use that route in preference to the Sunda Straits, which were less suitable for such operations; action by submarines, minelayers, and shore-based and carrier aircraft, as well as a destroyer night attack, if the British fleet attempted to move from Singapore to Hong Kong; raids on Indian, Australian, or New Zealand ports in the hope of forcing the dispatch of British naval forces for their local protection.

It was anticipated that the Japanese Navy would attack British trade. 'Although Japan's strategic position and lack of bases will probably preclude the possibility of any major offensive operations [against trade], there is no doubt that with carefully planned supply arrangements, Japanese submarines, armed merchant cruisers and

---

[49] COS596. And see COS755, 'Appreciation of the Situation in the Event of War against Germany in April, 1939', 5 Aug. 1938, CAB 53/40. It was thought that, to delay the British fleet, Japan might synchronize an attempt to block the Suez Canal with her declaration of war.

HOW TO FIGHT JAPAN?

possibly one or two heavy ships could operate in the Indian Ocean and in Australian waters.'[50] There was, however, no major threat in a strategy of trade warfare. 'The distances of our main trade routes from Japan, the alternative routes to and from the Far East via the Suez Canal, Cape of Good Hope, Panama Canal, and Cape Horn, the vast areas of oceans concerned, with the consequent possibilities of evasive routing, all operate towards the security of our trade.'[51]

All the thinking about the IJN's strategy was a grand exercise in futility—and a waste of countless man-hours—since, as we shall see, IJN operational planning paid scant attention to Great Britain before 1940–1, and even then its plans bore little relation to the cogitations of Whitehall planners. Of course, this is in the very nature of contingency planning. A measure of realism was introduced into the picture in the spring of 1939, when the change in the strategic outlook, with a triangular war as the most likely contingency Britain had to face, prompted a review of Japan's options by the DCNS. 'Experience shows that she fully understands the importance of getting in an early blow, and her plans are likely to be carefully prepared and put into execution simultaneously with her decision to intervene.' The investment of Hong Kong was probable, also attacks on Singapore, from a full-scale deliberate combined operation to occasional raids to damage the base facilities and reserves. As an alternative to a major operation against Singapore, the Japanese might attempt large-scale operations against Australia or New Zealand, particularly if they were satisfied that a considerable time would elapse before a British fleet could arrive in the East. It was certain that Japan would seize territory in the South-west Pacific—in French Indo–China, Borneo, the Netherlands East Indies, and New Guinea—and establish bases there for attacks on British trade in the vicinity of Australia or New Zealand and to carry out raids in the Indian Ocean. 'Each Squadron might be accompanied by one or two heavy ships and aircraft carriers. In the face of such a scale of attack the forces available for the protection of our interests would be ineffectual, and our sea communications would be paralysed.'[52] This was a more realistic estimate of probabilities, but, apart from the revision in June

[50] 'Naval War Memorandum (Eastern)', Dec. 1937.
[51] COS621(JP), 'Protection of Sea-Borne Trade', 11 Oct. 1937, CAB 53/33.
[52] Cunningham, 'Despatch of a Fleet to the Far East', 4 Apr. 1939, ADM 1/9897.

(above, p. 62n), it led to no changes in the Naval War Memorandum (Eastern). With the cornerstone of British strategic policy the operation of the Main Fleet in Eastern waters, and the conviction of the strategic planners that Japan could not be sure of securing her aims unless she captured Singapore (it would be a potential threat to her southward expansion so long as a British fleet remained in being anywhere), the security of the base was vital. Singapore, the 'gateway to the Pacific', on the shortest route between the Indian and Pacific Oceans, was not only what Beatty described in 1924 as the finest strategical position in the world; it was the only British naval base in the Far East capable of accommodating a modern fleet and possessing the requisite docking and repair facilities to deal with capital ships. Although unfinished (it had been under construction since 1923), the naval base was formally opened in February 1938. It would, however, be late 1940 before it was on a full war-time basis, able to undertake large repairs. Unless the fleet could operate from Singapore in a war with Japan, the British would be powerless to protect their Far Eastern and Australian interests, and the loss of the base would leave the coasts of India, Australia, and New Zealand, and the sea routes to these dominions, open to Japanese attack. 'Whereas the loss of Hong-Kong would be serious, the loss of Singapore would be an almost vital blow,' Chatfield had declared in December 1937.

In practical terms, these considerations meant that the fixed defences of Singapore Island (five 15-inch, six 9·2-inch, and nine pairs of 6-inch, covering the approaches to the naval base in the Johore Strait to the north and Keppel Harbour, the commercial port of Singapore City, in the south) and the four airfields in the Island must be completed in the shortest possible time (they were by September 1939), and the garrison (nearly 20,000 when war came in 1939) must be able to hold out against attack pending the arrival of the Main Fleet. 'With the arrival of the British Fleet the Japanese will either have to abandon their expedition or fight a fleet action. Provided that the naval repair facilities at Singapore can still be used by our ships, our Fleet would be at a great advantage compared with that of Japan, which could have no repair facilities nearer than its home waters.'[53]

[53] COS596.

HOW TO FIGHT JAPAN?

Hong Kong posed a special problem. It was an important naval base and 'a focus of British interests', as well as a centre of trade and shipping. Its loss or abandonment, moreover, would be a blow to British prestige and have the most far-reaching effects on Britain's position throughout the world—not only in East Asia. This was a point on which the Foreign Office in particular had strong feelings. No important steps had been taken to improve the defences since the expiration of the Washington Naval Treaty (Article xix had maintained the status quo over Hong Kong's fortifications). More important, the island lay in a zone dominated by Japanese naval, air, and military forces, and the Pescadores and Formosa were only 800 miles away. By 1937 the Chiefs of Staff held out little hope for the island 'if subjected to well-planned and well-executed Japanese land and air attack', even if they would not go so far as to recommend cutting their losses by evacuation in the event of war. They saw an advantage in trying to hold on to this outpost as long as possible. It would cause a dissipation of Japanese effort and gain time to secure Singapore.

There was much discussion in 1938–40 of the standard of defence that should be required: whether Standard 'A'—that required to protect the harbour, with its facilities, so that it might be used by the Main Fleet as a base on its arrival; or Standard 'B'—that required to give sufficient protection to the harbour, with the necessary facilities, to enable it to be used as a base for submarines and small craft; or Standard 'C'—that required to retain no more than a foothold in the colony, while denying the use of the anchorage to the enemy. The Chiefs of Staff recommended the adoption of 'C' in July 1938, and the CID had approved. The principal arguments which carried the day against Standard 'A' included these considerations: the value of the base for the Navy would be doubtful owing to the difficulty of countering air attack (ground suitable for aerodromes was extremely limited); the anchorage itself would be liable to bombardment by land artillery at long ranges; Hong Kong, as a base, was not vital to British security in the Far East; and the expense: £23·5m spent on a base, 'the use of which by the Main Fleet must remain open to doubt'.

Until the outbreak of the European War it was the Admiralty intention to hold Hong Kong as long as possible, but, given the difficulty of relieving it, they did not expect to be able to base the fleet there. In fact, the Far Eastern War Memorandum did not envisage the use of Hong Kong as a main fleet base either before or after the relief of Singapore. The China fleet would be based on Singapore at the outbreak of war. The main importance attached to Hong Kong in the War Memorandum was as a submarine base. But when war came in 1939, it was the Admiralty view, shared by the new First Sea Lord and the new DCNS, Pound and Rear Admiral Sir Tom Phillips, that Standard 'A' should be aimed for— a vain ideal. 'Personally,' Phillips minuted, 'I have always felt that this decision to adopt Standard "C" was fundamentally wrong and not in accordance with our position as a great maritime Power. Hong Kong is our most exposed outpost and ought to be properly defended with 15-inch guns and everything else we can put there. No other country would leave an outpost of this nature in an improperly defended state.' He was scornful of the CID report, which took 'a thoroughly defeatist view of the possibility of holding Hong Kong against the Japanese—and I believe that an adequate British garrison and adequate defences should make that hidebound nation think very hard. And there will always be the fear of the British Fleet coming out to interrupt the seige—they must always depend on seaborne supplies for their forces.'[54]

The Chiefs of Staff had the last word. In their Far East Appreciation of 15 August 1940 they laid down that:

Hong Kong is not a vital interest and the garrison could not long withstand Japanese attack. Even if we had a strong fleet in the Far East, it is doubtful whether Hong Kong could be held now that the Japanese are firmly established on the mainland of China; and it could not be used as an advanced naval base.

In the event of war, Hong Kong must be regarded as an outpost and held as long as possible. We should resist the inevitably strong pressure to reinforce Hong Kong and should certainly be unable to relieve it.[55]

Churchill, now Prime Minister, supported this position, showing more strategic common sense than had the Admiralty or the C-in-C in the Far East, Air Chief Marshal Sir Robert Brooke-Popham.

[54] Minutes of 3, 8 Jan. 1940, ADM 116/4271. The CID report in question was 471–C, 'The Policy for the Defence of Hong Kong', 15 July 1938, CAB 5/9. Phillips supported the recommendation of the D of P, Danckwerts, that the defences of Hong Kong be of sufficient strength for the island to hold out for at least six months, and indefinitely if reinforcements, ammunition, and provisions could be provided at the end of this period.

[55] COS(40)592 (Revise), 'The Situation in the Far East in the Event of Japanese Intervention against Us', CAB 80/15.

When the latter pressed for the reinforcement of Hong Kong, Churchill expressed strong disagreement:

> This is all wrong. If Japan goes to war with us there is not the slightest chance of holding Hong Kong or relieving it. It is most unwise to increase the loss we shall suffer there. Instead of increasing the garrison it ought to be reduced to a symbolical scale. Any trouble arising there must be dealt with at the Peace Conference after the war. We must avoid frittering away our resources on untenable positions. Japan will think long before declaring war on the British Empire, and whether there are two or six battalions at Hong Kong will make no difference to her choice. I wish we had fewer troops there, but to move any would be noticeable and dangerous.[56]

6. THE AMERICAN NAVAL CONNECTION

The outbreak of the European War bankrupted Far Eastern naval plans. Naval strength in Eastern waters was pitifully inadequate. The China Station had 4 cruisers, 1 aircraft carrier, 10 destroyers, 5 escort ships, 15 submarines, and about thirty lesser craft. The East Indies station could boast of 3 cruisers, 7 escort ships, and the Australian and New Zealand navies between them had 5 cruisers, 3 destroyers, and 4 escort ships. The Admiralty were in no position to dispatch a powerful fleet, or, indeed, any fleet, to the Far East if Japan intervened in the war, which meant that in many respects the strategic calculations and plans of 1937–9 were no longer applicable. As Britain's strategists had been only too aware from the beginning, there was but one way to get around the obstacles to sending a large naval force to the East: by securing American naval collaboration. Particularly from 1939 were the Admiralty and Chiefs of Staff convinced that the key to their apparently insoluble problem lay in the assurance of the active co-operation of the United States in the Pacific. The VCNS, Tom Phillips, put the matter in a nutshell. 'Without U.S.A. co-operation with us the stark fact was that we had not got the ships to take on the German,

---

[56] Churchill's minute to Ismay, 7 Jan. 1941, Churchill, *The Second World War*, iii, *The Grand Alliance* (1948) p. 157. Shortly before the outbreak of hostilities he weakened and allowed two Canadian battalions to be sent as reinforcements. But an adequate garrison and defences were not forthcoming.

Italian and Japanese fleets at the same time. We should either have to let the Eastern Mediterranean or the Far East go.'[57]

There were two principal ways in which the Americans could be helpful in the Far East. One, in the opinion of the DCNS in 1939, was for a strong US fleet to move to Honolulu, where its presence would have a restrictive effect upon Japanese strategy, enabling the British to delay the dispatch of a fleet to the East. Admiral Dreyer, the former China C-in-C, had the same thought, emphasizing the vulnerability of Japanese cities to the large number of aircraft in the US Fleet. The Director of Plans at the Admiralty, Captain C. S. Daniel, agreed.[58] To the Chiefs of Staff this would not of itself provide the necessary deterrent to a Japanese movement to the southward. It was only the active support of the United States Fleet in Far Eastern waters that would completely alter the situation. Either way, would the United States play? When the Australian High Commissioner in London was in the United States in the spring of 1939, he had asked the President what he would do if the Japanese were to send naval forces south of the Equator. Roosevelt had replied: 'You need not worry.'[59] Alas, the British had considerable cause for worry.

As early as 1936 the American and British navies had begun to exchange intelligence on the Japanese Fleet, and the two Governments had been in regular touch since the beginning of the China Incident in July 1937 to ensure a common approach to Far Eastern questions. Following the *Panay* incident in December 1937 (above, p. 20), President Roosevelt and the US Chief of Naval Operations, Admiral William D. Leahy, felt that the time had come to reach agreement with the Royal Navy for joint action in the event of both Powers finding themselves at war with Japan. The Admiralty had just rebuffed a Foreign Office call for possible deterrent measures against Japan in response to new infringements on British rights in China, especially at Shanghai. Chatfield could see no way to force the Japanese to behave, short of sending most of the battle fleet to the East, and this was out of the question. There was, accordingly, quick acceptance from the British of Roosevelt's

---

[57] COS(41), 8th Mtg., 4 Jan. 1941, CAB 79/8.
[58] Cunningham, 'Despatch of a Fleet to the Far East', 5 Apr. 1939, Dreyer, 'Plans for War in the Pacific', 10 Apr. 1941, and Daniel's minute, ADM 1/11326.
[59] Bruce's statement at the meeting with the Prime Minister and others, 28 June 1939 (above, p. 55).

proposal (16 December) that Anglo–American naval conversations be held on similar lines to those of 1915–17, since it opened up the possibility of US naval support. On 31 December Captain Royal E. Ingersoll, the Director of the War Plans Division, arrived in London for talks. Fearing serious political repercussions if the conversations leaked out in the press, the United States required that extreme secrecy be maintained. As a consequence, on the British Government side only the Prime Minister, First Lord, and Foreign Secretary (Chamberlain, Duff Cooper, and Eden) were kept informed.

Ingersoll met with Eden and Cadogan on New Year's Day 1938, with the DCNS, Vice-Admiral Sir William James, the same day, and with Chatfield and James on the third. But the substantive talks were held on 3 and 5 January with the Director of Plans, Captain Tom Phillips, and other Naval Staff officers. The conversations were purely exploratory, in accordance with Ingersoll's instructions. The agreement reached on 13 January by Ingersoll and Phillips was not a commitment by either Government. It merely outlined the nature of Anglo–American naval co-operation in the Pacific, *should* the two Governments decide to implement the agreement. The plan contemplated the approximately simultaneous arrival of an American battle fleet (nine or ten capital ships) at Honolulu fifteen or twenty days after the President had issued a Declaration of National Emergency, and of a British force at Singapore sufficient to engage the Japanese Fleet 'under normal tactical and strategical conditions' (para. 11). This force would include 8 battleships, a battle cruiser, and 3 aircraft carriers. The agreement said nothing about subsequent strategy in the event of war with Japan, although Ingersoll had spoken of a gradual US move westward to Truk and, if possible, Guam. Should the two Governments agree to institute a distant economic blockade or 'quarantine' of Japan, British naval forces would be responsible for stopping Japanese trade on the line Singapore–Dutch East Indies–New Guinea–New Hebrides–eastward of Australia and New Zealand; the US Navy would cut off Japanese trade with the west coast of the Western Hemisphere, including the Panama Canal and the passage round Cape Horn. 'Unity of command in a tactical or strategic sense' was not envisaged, nor tactical co-operation between the two fleets, since they would at first be widely separated, and no detailed information on war plans was exchanged. Strategic co-operation, however, would be necessary, to which end there was a discussion of codes, ciphers, calls, and signal procedure necessary if joint operations were undertaken.[60]

There were several things wrong with these arrangements from the British point of view. They would have preferred that *both* fleets proceed to Singapore, and that they should operate together tactically, as the British and American Fleets had in the First War.[61] The first consideration was tied to the British awareness, as expressed in paragraph 12 of the 13 January agreement, that in the event of Britain going to war with the Axis, 'it would almost certainly be necessary to effect a considerable reduction of British strength in the Far East'. Indeed, exactly a year later, 'in view of developments in the European situation that have taken place in the past year', the Admiralty informed the US Naval Attaché of unilateral amendments to paragraphs 11 and 12 of the Ingersoll–Phillips agreement. Paragraph 11 now read: the British Far Eastern Fleet would 'probably be sufficient only to engage the Japanese Fleet under *favourable* tactical and strategical conditions'. Paragraph 12 stated that the capital-ship component of this fleet was unlikely to exceed seven or eight battleships and two aircraft carriers. Three months later the Director of Plans minuted that the fleet they proposed to send to the East would 'probably be much smaller' than that suggested to the Attaché in January.[62] With all its shortcomings from the British vantage point, the Ingersoll–Phillips agreement was significant in initiating ever broader discussions for a common naval strategy *vis-à-vis* Japan.

To the Admiralty the most serious shortcoming of the first discussions was that they left uncertain the firmness of the American commitment of naval support in a war with Japan. When again on American initiative discussions were opened in the spring of 1939 for a renewal of the naval conversations, Backhouse gave vent to this concern.

I wish also to stress the great importance it would be to us to be able to be certain of American naval intervention on our side. Apart from the

---

[60] 'Record of Conversations', 13 Jan. 1938. ADM 116/3922. This had been drawn up by Phillips and Ingersoll. The US version of the talks is in the Strategic Plans Division Records, Box 116, Operational Archives, Naval Historical Center, Washington (hereafter cited as US Operational Archives).
[61] Phillips, 'Possible Staff Conversations with U.S.A.', 17 Dec. 1937, ADM 116/3922.
[62] 'Note of Meeting with United States Naval Attaché on 13th January 1939', Danckwerts's minute, 26 Apr. 1939, ibid.

greatly increased security this would give to our general situation in the Far East, it would also ensure that neither Australia nor New Zealand would have anything to fear from possible Japanese aggression. In fact, in my view it would make the whole difference to our strategic position in the Far East and give us a much freer hand to deal with our problems in Home Waters and in the Mediterranean. It would be impossible to exaggerate what this would mean to us in the event of a world war in which we were engaged with Germany, Italy and Japan.[63]

Since the Admiralty appreciated that the American Naval Staff was in no position to promise any such commitment, or even that their fleet would move into the Pacific in case of trouble with the Japanese, there was no optimism over what renewed conversations might achieve.

In May the Admiralty sent Commander T. C. Hampton, of the Plans Division (he had participated in the Ingersoll conversations), to Washington. Since as with Ingersoll's visit to London, a leakage would have had serious political repercussions in the United States, where isolationist sentiment was strong, he travelled incognito, as 'Mr Hampton', ostensibly on business as a land agent. On arrival he joined the Naval Attaché, Captain L. C. A. Curzon-Howe, in highly secret negotiations on 12 and 14 June with Admiral Leahy, the American CNO, and the Director of the War Plans Division, Rear-Admiral Robert L. Ghormley, in Leahy's home. The discussions took place in 'an atmosphere of complete mutual confidence and friendliness' (Hampton). The results were something else. At the outset Hampton informed the American representatives that the strategic situation had changed greatly since the Ingersoll discussions: the Admiralty had now to give priority to the threat from the Axis. In the event of Japan intervening in a British war with Germany and Italy, it was not possible to say at what stage a fleet would be sent to the Far East, nor how many capital ships it would include. Leahy, Hampton reported, 'was evidently reluctant to commit himself to a statement of naval plans in the event of the U.S.A. becoming allied to us ...' He would only say that it was Roosevelt's intention to move the US Fleet (or 'the major part of it', in the US version) to Hawaii as a deterrent to Japan, but that it was his, Leahy's, 'purely personal' opinion that if the United States entered the war, her Fleet should 'move to Singapore in sufficient

[63] Backhouse's minute, 27 Mar. 1939, ibid.

force to be able to engage and defeat the Japanese Fleet if met with on passage'. But whether this force would be dispatched depended to some extent on the ability of the Royal Navy to send 'an adequate token force to co-operate', including capital ships. American public opinion would otherwise be adverse to dispatching the Fleet. At least ten capital ships would be needed in the Far East. However hypothetical, it was a gain for the British that Leahy was favourably disposed to sending a strong American force to Singapore. It was otherwise with his disinterest in discussing plans for co-operation in detail, as when he did not follow up Hampton's statement that the Naval Staff thought it desirable that Britain's Far Eastern naval forces should be under the strategical control of the American C-in-C. 'It is evident that the US Navy have no detailed plans at present for active co-operation with the British Fleet in war.'[64]

The Admiralty, nevertheless, did not view the results of Hampton's visit as entirely disappointing. Captain Phillips's analysis was: 'Though little positive result was achieved and nothing was committed to writing, it is considered that his visit had been of value in keeping before the United States highest naval authorities, and probably the President, the difficulties facing us at the present time, and in obtaining some information as to the state of thought of the United States naval authorities as to their own possible actions.' The main advance over the Ingersoll conversations was the American idea that their fleet might go to Singapore. 'It seems probable that a "token" fleet say 2 or 3 battleships from us would suffice to meet US public opinion.'[65] The American factor in British Far Eastern naval strategy calculations assumed still greater importance after the outbreak of war in Europe in September 1939.

[64] Hampton's reports of the two meetings, ibid. No joint record of the conversations was made. The American reports, by Ghormley, are in the Strategic Plans Division Records, Box 116, US Operational Archives. The main difference is that in Ghormley's version there is no mention of Leahy's 'personal opinion' about sending a strong US force to Singapore.

[65] Minutes of 28, 29 June 1939, ADM 116/3922.

III

The New Realities (September 1939–September 1940)

> ... it would be folly to invite Japanes hostility in circumstances in which there is a good chance of avoiding it.
> ADMIRAL OF THE FLEET SIR DUDLEY POUND, 23 July 1940.

> ... our general policy must be to play for time, cede nothing until we must, and build up our defences as soon as we can.
> Chiefs of Staff Far East Appreciation, 15 August 1940.

1. THE DARKENING SCENE

THE famous 'Winston is back' signal from the Board of Admiralty to the Fleet on 3 September, the day Britain entered the Second World War, heralded Churchill's return to the Admiralty as First Lord. I have stated elsewhere my firm belief that 'the Churchillian forays into the concerns of the sailors did not apply to naval strategy and operations *while he was First Lord*, except when political considerations were involved. ... Churchill interfered more often in the prosecution of the war at sea after he went to No. 10 ...' (10 May 1940).[1] I shall have occasion to spell out some of the details of the Churchillian impact on the war at sea against Japan when he was Prime Minister, including the controversial story of his relations with Sir Dudley Pound, the First Sea Lord until shortly before his death in October 1943. Here it is sufficient to note that unlike his immediate predecessors at the Admiralty and at Number 10, Churchill had a deep knowledge of the role of sea power and was full of ideas on grand strategy and how best to use the Royal Navy.

The outbreak of war created a new situation in the Far East. Since the danger of the Japanese seizing the opportunity of the

---

[1] *From the Dardanelles to Oran: Studies of the Royal Navy in War and Peace, 1915–1940* (London, 1974), pp. 173, 175.

hostilities in Europe to launch attacks on Singapore and Hong Kong could not be dismissed, the Chiefs of Staff were eager that the 'greatest care' be exercised not to provoke them. There was, however, an early indication that the Japanese intended no aggressive act in the near future. On 5 September Japan offered 'friendly advice' to Britain, the United States, and France—that they should pull out their garrisons and river gunboats from Japanese-occupied China to eliminate the possibility of incidents. The British gradually withdrew 13 of the 20 gunboats on the West River and the Japanese-controlled section of the Yangtze. Most of them went to Singapore, where they were later refitted as minesweepers or A/S vessels. The Government decided not to disturb the garrisons (Peiping, Tientsin, and the International Settlement of Shanghai) for the time being, apart from reducing the battalion in Tientsin to a company. The ships being needed in the war theatres, the China Station was appreciably reduced in the first months of the war. The one carrier left at once; the four modern cruisers (5th Cruiser Squadron) were gone by January 1940 and were replaced by three old 6-inch cruisers sent from the Reserve Fleet at home; the nine destroyers of the 21st Destroyer Flotilla were quickly withdrawn, leaving five destroyers for the local defence of Hong Kong and Singapore; four of the 17 submarines left in October, and the rest in the spring of 1940.

The Royal Navy had its hands full with the German Navy and watching an Italian Navy that might at any time join the conflict. Naval reinforcements for the Far East were obviously out of the question. The loss of the battleship *Royal Oak*, torpedoed in Scapa Flow by *U-47* on 14 October 1939, obviously did not help. It left Britain with 14 capital ships, exclusive of the five King George Vs under construction. This situation did not discourage Craigie from reiterating his appeal of December 1938 (above, p. 42) that a small capital-ship squadron be sent to Singapore at the earliest possible moment. He had a fresh argument in the report that Germany planned to win Japanese assistance in some form through the offer of the Netherlands East Indies. 'The presence of such a squadron in Far Eastern waters would make any German offer much less palatable and assist moderates here to hold their "wild men" in check.'[2] All that the Foreign Secretary felt able to do was to remind

---

[2] Craigie's dispatch, 25 Sept. 1939, ADM 1/9909.

the Admiralty of the desirability of reinforcing the fleet in the East, 'if and when this becomes practicable ... not only from the point of view of reassuring the Dominions of Australia and New Zealand but of convincing the Japanese that His Majesty's Government do not intend to relinquish their interests in the Far East'.[3]

In November 1939 that other *bête noire* of the Admiralty was heard from. Feeling uncomfortable about the contemplated dispatch of their troops to the Middle East, which might leave their countries exposed to Japanese aggression, Australia and New Zealand sought assurances from the British Government that capital ships would be sent to Singapore if the need arose. Churchill attempted to quiet their fears so that they would proceed to dispatch their armies to the 'decisive battlefields'. He did not think the Japanese, so fully occupied in China, 'would embark upon such a mad enterprise' as an attack on Singapore. His paper formed the basis of a naval appreciation approved by the War Cabinet for the Pacific Dominions. The Government, it stated, expected that Japan would remain quiet so long as Britain and France were not getting the worst of it in the European war. However, should Japan begin to encroach upon the Netherlands East Indies, or should Britain find herself at war with Japan, 'the Admiralty would make such dispositions as would enable them to offer timely assistance either to a serious attack upon Singapore or to the invasion of Australia and New Zealand.... With our present limited forces we cannot afford to have any important portion of His Majesty's Fleet idle. All ships must play their part from day to day, and there are always the hazards of war to be faced, but the Admiralty can be trusted to make appropriate dispositions to meet events as they emerge from imagination to reality.'[4] Australia and New Zealand were sufficiently satisfied to agree to send troops to the Middle East.

The fact is that, once the war in Europe began and until the late spring of 1940, the British Government and the Services gave only passing thought to the Far Eastern strategic problem. Hostilities against Germany took absolute precedence: No. 1 priority was

---

[3] Foreign Office to Admiralty, 4 Oct. 1939, ibid. The Admiralty did not reply; none was required, the Foreign Office intimated later.
[4] WP(39)135, Churchill's memorandum for the War Cabinet, 'Australian and New Zealand Naval Defence', 21 Nov. 1939, CAB 66/3, R. G. Casey (leader of the Australian delegation to the meeting of United Kingdom and Dominion ministers in London) to R. G. Menzies (Australian Prime Minister), 23 Nov. 1939, R. G. Neale, *et al.* (eds.), *Documents on Australian Foreign Policy, 1937–49* (4 vols. to date, Canberra, 1975–80), ii (1976), 429–30.

Home waters and the Atlantic, and No. 2, holding the Middle East. Also, there was the expectation that the Russo–German cooperation would act as a restraining influence on further Japanese adventures. Italy's declaration of war against Britain and France on 10 June 1940, followed by the French capitulation on 22 June, changed everything. Britain's discomfiture—she was alone but for her Empire and Commonwealth, and the relatively small Polish, Dutch, Belgian, and Free French forces, naval and military, fighting on her side—and the prostrate conditions of France as well as the Netherlands, which had been overrun by the Nazis, promised to whet the Japanese appetite for further moves into South-east Asia. It was known that Japan had for months been concentrating forces on Hainan Island and Formosa for training in combined operations and jungle fighting. And London viewed the Soviet–Japanese treaty of 10 June fixing the frontiers between Manchukuo and the Soviet satellite state of Outer Mongolia as a possible forerunner to a neutrality and non-aggression pact which, by removing the Soviet threat in the north, would leave Japan freer to press on in South-east Asia. The vacuum created by the defection of the French Navy made what was extremely difficult before a strategic impossibility now. If the British pulled the four capital ships out of the Eastern Mediterranean and sent a fleet to the East, there would be nothing to contain the Italian Fleet and its six capital ships. The Italians would be free to operate in the Atlantic or reinforce the German Fleet, using bases in north-western France.

The Chiefs of Staff quickly drew a lugubrious conclusion from the new situation. They had to retain in European waters sufficient naval forces to contain the German and Italian Fleets, and therefore, as the Pacific Dominions were informed on 13 June, 'adequate naval reinforcements' were unlikely to be sent to Singapore if Japan declared war. Colonel L. C. Hollis, of the War Cabinet secretariat, minuted: 'The cold hard fact remains that no British government in their sane senses could possibly contemplate the despatch of even an inadequate Fleet to the Far East at the present time.'[5] The position was summed up in a telegram to the Government of Australia (copy to New Zealand) drafted by the Service Chiefs and approved by the War Cabinet. 'In spite of the deterrent effects of

---

[5] Hollis to Ismay, 3 July 1940, CAB 21/893. Hollis was Senior Assistant Secretary (Military) of the War Cabinet.

THE DARKENING SCENE

Japan's military commitments in China, the possible hostility of the United States of America and Russia and our military and economic strength, there are indications that Japan may be contemplating moves to improve her strategic and economic position.' War with Japan was not necessarily imminent, but, since the British were unable to spare a fleet for the East, it was all the more important to strengthen Malayan land and air defences by moving one division and two air squadrons from Australia to Malaya as an immediate deterrent.[6] The Pacific Dominions were, naturally, upset. What had happened to the oft-repeated undertaking to dispatch an adequate fleet to Singapore? When Bruce, the Australian High Commissioner in London, expressed his unhappiness with the telegram—he might, he said, have to advise his Government not to send the division that had been asked for—the Chiefs of Staff spelled out the reasons why no fleet could presently be sent to the Far East, and assured him that Japan could not undertake a serious invasion of Australia so long as the British Fleet was in being and Singapore was secure.[7] Something more needed to be done quickly to reassure the embittered Dominion Governments, lest they slacken in their war effort. On 11 August Churchill sent a personal message to the two Prime Ministers that had been approved by the War Cabinet. The telegram was a classic example of how to put a good face on a bad situation. 'Once Japan sees that Germany has either failed [in an invasion attempt], or dares not try, I look for easier times in the Pacific. In adopting against the grain a yielding policy towards Japanese threats, we have always in mind your interests and safety.' Should Japan, contrary to expectation, imprudently attempt a large-scale invasion of either Dominion (it would leave the US fleet between a large Japanese fleet and home), Britain would cut her losses in the Mediterranean 'and proceed to your aid, sacrificing every interest except only the defence and feeding of this island on which all depends. We hope that events will take a different turn. By gaining time with Japan, the present dangerous situation may be got over.'[8] It was, no doubt, an easy pledge for Churchill to make, given his confidence that Japan would never attempt a large-scale invasion of the Dominions.

These were worn-out themes and assurances. They masked the

[6] COS(40)501, 'Immediate Measures in the Far East', 28 June 1940, Annex I, CAB 80/14.
[7] COS(40) 209th Mtg., 5 July 1940, Annex II, CAB 79/5.
[8] WM(40) 222nd Conclusions, Appendix, CAB 65/14.

profound concern of the Service Chiefs and the Joint Planners over the unpromising situation in the Far East for which there appeared, immediately, to be only one solution. On 1 July the Chiefs approved a recommendation from the Joint Planners that the Government adopt a conciliatory line towards Japan. 'The overriding consideration in our Far East policy at present', the Planners had emphasized, 'must be the avoidance of an open clash with Japan, particularly as it is now clear that we cannot rely on active American support.'[9] At their 1 July meeting the Chiefs of Staff endorsed the suggestion of the CIGS, Sir John Dill, that Britain should offer to discuss with Japan proposals for a general settlement in the Far East which might include the withdrawal of the British garrison from Shanghai and even the demilitarization of Hong Kong. The Burma Road question, on which the Japanese held strong views, ought to be dealt with, too, in such a settlement.[10] The War Cabinet generally agreed (5 July) that 'the military situation did not justify us in taking action which might involve us in a war with Japan',[11] and they porceeded to do something about that.

Japan had taken advantage of the plight of Britain and France to bring pressure to bear on them in June and July to prohibit the transport of essential supplies to the Chinese Nationalists, whether by rail from Hanoi to South-west China, or by the Burma Road. The latter was a precarious 712-mile track which linked Kunming, the capital of China's Yunnan province, with Lashio in northern Burma, the terminus of the railway from Rangoon. It was the main supply route for Nationalist China from friendly countries. Goods arrived by sea at Rangoon and were then moved to Lashio by rail. On 20 June the Vichy regime in France agreed to stop shipments of war materials through Indo-China. On 18 July the British Government agreed to close the Burma Road for three months to the shipment of war *matériel* and other essential supplies. With the 'Battle of Britain' imminent, they were in no position to thwart Japan and risk war over the Burma Road, particularly after the strong COS recommendation on 4 July that the Government accede to Japan's request to close the road rather than run a real risk of war with Japan. On 9 August, in response to further Japanese pressure,

---

[9] JP(40)298, 'Policy in the Far East', 29 June 1940, CAB 84/15.
[10] COS(40) 222nd Mtg., CAB 79/5.
[11] WM(40) 194th Conclusions, CAB 65/8.

Britain announced that she would pull her garrisons out of Shanghai, Tientsin, and Peiping.

The hopelessness of the strategic position in the Far East was stressed by the Admiralty at this time. Four principles of crucial importance were offered for the guidance of the politicians and Chiefs of Staff. (1) They would have to retain a fleet in the Eastern Mediterranean capable of fighting the Italians. (2) Security in Home waters was the first esssential. (3) As important as their trade was in the Indian Ocean, it was less important than the Atlantic trade. (4) Since the French no longer controlled the Western Mediterranean for Britain, it was essential to have a force at Gibraltar as a deterrent to enemy ships breaking out into the Atlantic. (Force H, which included two capital ships, had been constituted for that purpose at the end of June.) These four principles, the Admiralty explained, made it impossible to send a fleet to Singapore, and there was no object in sending a fleet to Singapore unless it was strong enough to fight the Japanese Fleet.[12] The question of the Netherlands East Indies, which came to the fore during the summer, underscored Britain's parlous position in the East.

2. 'FOLLY TO INVITE JAPANESE HOSTILITY'

The German conquest of the Netherlands in May 1940 had added one more complication to Britain's strategic problems in South-east Asia. The Chiefs of Staff had considered the question of Japanese aggression in the Dutch East Indies at various times in the pre-war years and had always taken the view that the integrity of the islands was a major British interest. The Committee of Imperial Defence had accepted this position on 15 July 1936. The argument of the Service Chiefs was that the establishment of potentially hostile naval and air bases in these islands facing Singapore would jeopardize the security of the key to the whole British position in the Far East. Almost as important was awareness that Japanese control of the colony's oil resources would provide one of their principal requirements to sustain their aggressive efforts. There was, finally, the consideration that, in possession of the Dutch East Indies, the

---

[12] Alexander's minute (an appreciation by the Naval Staff) for the Prime Minister, 2 Aug. 1940, ADM 205/6.

Japanese would be standing across the British route to Australia and New Zealand.

In reviewing the problem early in the war, Churchill had professed to see no danger. The Japanese would be very unlikely to move, knowing that the United States would not stand by impassively while the Japanese acquired naval bases west and south-west of the Philippines. The contingency was, therefore, 'highly improbable, unless, of course, Great Britain and France are getting the worst of it, when many evils will descend upon us all'.[13] In May and June 1940, with the Allies definitely getting the worst of it, the problem of the Netherlands East Indies came to the fore as a leitmotiv in Far Eastern strategic calculations over the next year and a half.

A sharp divergence of views was revealed at the COS meeting on 23 July. There was agreement that, if Japan attacked the Islands, they should fight, irrespective of the Dutch attitude, *provided they were certain of active American support*; if the US did not co-operate and the Dutch did not resist the Japanese, the British should not fight. The disagreement was over whether to fight if the Americans did not fight, but the Dutch did. It was a case of the First Sea Lord *contra mundum*. The CIGS, Dill, the CAS, Newall, and Major-General H. L. Ismay[14] maintained that the integrity of the Islands was a vital British interest, to preserve which they should fight in support of the Dutch, *if they resisted*. Alone, the British could not prevent a Japanese take-over. Pound appreciated the strategical disadvantages of a Japanese occupation; yet he felt strongly that Japanese aggression in that area should on no account provoke them to go to war with them. They could do nothing to prevent a Japanese occupation, they were in no position to offer military support to the Dutch, and war with Japan would gravely prejudice their main object, the defeat of Germany. 'War with Japan may, of course, be forced upon us . . . but it would be folly to invite Japanese hostility in circumstances in which there is a good chance of avoiding it.' Counter-arguments stressed the awful consequences of doing nothing if the Japanese made a move. The capture of the

[13] WP(39)135, 21 Nov. 1939.
[14] Ismay was an additional member of the COS Committee, appointed to this position as Chief Staff Officer to the Minister of Defence (Churchill). He would join in the discussions, but he never signed the COS reports, as he felt that such reports could only emanate from the professional heads of the Services. He was also Deputy Secretary (Military) of the War Cabinet.

Islands 'would only be a first step towards the capture of Malaya and the elimination of British interests in the Far East'. Their Navy would have free access to the Indian Ocean and be able to make a heavier scale of attack on Britain's vital trade routes, seriously weaken the security of Singapore by establishing air bases within close range of that base, and, in the event of war, cut Malaya off from Australia. If they failed to support the Dutch, they would probably forfeit any chance of obtaining US support there. Standing idly by, moreover, if Japan moved against the Islands, 'would have a deplorable effect upon the Dominions, who would almost certainly conclude that we were pursuing an insular policy of paying attention to the security of the United Kingdom at the expense of that of the Empire'. Then there was the moral argument that the Dutch were their Allies and their naval and air forces were helping to defend British interests in the Home theatre. 'In these circumstances it would be, to say the least of it, difficult to refuse to assist them in the defence of their possessions in the East Indies.'[15] The Chiefs of Staff Committee were unable to resolve their difference at a meeting on 27 July. Pound held to his position that 'it would be better to have a non-belligerent Japan in occupation of these islands rather than Japan actively hostile'.[16]

The Committee had no choice but to submit this fundamental difference of opinion, which had far-reaching political as well as military repercussions, to the War Cabinet for an early decision. This discussion took place on 29 July. The politicians were themselves divided on what should be done. Halifax did not expect the Japanese to move on the Dutch East Indies. 'In the present case, would they not be likely to decide that their interests would be better served by remaining at peace with ourselves and the Americans, and thus remaining free to obtain economic assistance from us?' This was begging the question. Churchill, too, felt that 'On balance, the economic arguments told in favour of Japan's abstaining from war with the British Empire. Japan could not afford to see her shipping paralysed.' The Lord Privy Seal, Attlee, claimed that British prestige 'would suffer a terrible blow if we let the Dutch East Indies go without raising a finger in their defence, on the grounds that they were not British territory'. The Colonial

---

[15] COS(40) 230th Metg., CAB 79/5, with the arguments restated in COS (40)568 (Revise), 'Far Eastern Policy', 27 July 1940, CAB 80/15.
[16] COS(40) 236th Mtg., CAB 79/5.

Secretary, Lord Lloyd, though it might be decisive if they persuaded the Dutch to say they would blow up their oilfields if Japan attacked, and the Air Secretary, Sir Archibald Sinclair, opined that a British statement that they would regard aggression against the colony as a *casus belli* might well keep the Japanese from going to war. The Lord President of the Council, Neville Chamberlain, absent because of illness, registered his opinion that if the Dutch resisted the Japanese, Britain 'ought to go in with them and try to shame the United States into joining in ...' The First Lord, Alexander, reminded his colleagues that it was only a week or two since they had made a large concession to the Japanese in closing the Burma Road, on the principle that the country could fight no more than one war at a time.

Given this confusion of voices and the skittishness of the politicians in facing up to the central question involved, it was inevitable that the War Cabinet would make no clear-cut decision. They asked the Chiefs of Staff to prepare appreciations of the Far Eastern situation, 'the general assumption being that Japan commits an act of aggression against the Netherlands East Indies, that the Dutch resist and that this country comes to their assistance. The appreciations should indicate our general plan of campaign (a) with, and (b) without, the support of the United States.' The War Cabinet would settle the question of policy—whether to go to war in case of Japanese aggression against the Dutch East Indies—in the light of these appreciations.[17]

On 7 August the Service Chiefs produced their paper on the Netherlands East Indies. If the United States provided financial and economic support only, the direct military support the British could provide the Dutch was small. Their naval forces in the Far East could give the Dutch little assistance, but they could offer facilities for their Navy at Singapore. No assistance on land was possible: they had three brigades of regular British and Indian troops, which was inadequate to defend the whole of Malaya as well as Singapore. The 88 first-line British and Australian aircraft in Malaya were not sufficient for the defence of Malaya alone. More promising was the economic pressure which the British Empire and the United States could exert: it might bring Japan to commercial ruin at the end of twelve months. Active American

[17] WM(40) 214th Conclusions, CAB 65/14.

'FOLLY TO INVITE JAPANESE HOSTILITY'

military co-operation 'would make no difference to the direct military support which we ourselves could provide to the Dutch. On the other hand, we could offer the Americans the uses of Singapore and the presence of their fleet in these waters would jeopardise any continuation of Japanese aggression in Southern waters.'[18] The War Cabinet had this gloomy report before them, as well as the draft of a new COS Far East Appreciation, when they met on 8 August. Churchill thought that a decision on the question of assistance to the Dutch in case of Japanese aggression would be premature. The War Cabinet deferred consideration of the strategic issues raised in the two COS reports.

The Chiefs of Staff painted a sober picture on 15 August, when they finally brought out their revised Far East Appreciation. It was the first time since the exhaustive review of June 1937 and the last time before the outbreak of war with Japan that they considered the Far East as a whole. They made five assumptions. (1) The military situation at home and in the Middle East would not markedly change in their favour in the immediate future, meaning that they must retain a fleet in the Eastern Mediterranean. (2) The US attitude would not change, i.e. they could anticipate only economic and material support. (3) If Japan attacked British territory, they would fight her. (4) The decision whether to go to war with Japan if she attacked the Dutch East Indies and the Dutch resisted was one for the Government to make in the light of circumstances at the time. (5) It was, however, assumed for purposes of the Appreciation that they would go to war in this contingency; this did not prejudice the decision of the War Cabinet.

The security of India, Malaya, and Australia depended, the report continued, on the ability to control the sea communications leading to them, which meant basing an adequate capital-ship fleet at Singapore. Since this was not possible until they had defeated the Axis Powers or drastically reduced their naval strength, their object must be to limit the extent of Japanese damage to their Far Eastern

---

[18] COS(40)605, 'Assistance to the Dutch in the Event of Japanese Aggression in Netherlands East Indies', CAB 80/16. The report also examined the possibility of concentrating further naval forces in the Far East and concluded that 'any attempt to produce an adequate naval concentration at Signapore [nine of their 13 capital ships would be necessary to face Japan's 10] in the present world situation would be unsound . . .' The most they could do would be to send the battle cruiser *Renown* and aircraft carrier *Ark Royal* to the Indian Ocean, to be based on Trincomalee, Ceylon, for the purpose of protecting their communications in the Indian Ocean and round the Cape to the Middle East.

interests, 'and in the last resort to retain a footing from which we could eventually retrieve the position when stronger forces become available'. Japan was unlikely to risk war with Britain until the situation in Europe was clearer. Should the Japanese, however, decide to resort to force to improve their position in the Far East, they might suddenly attack the Dutch East Indies or Singapore. But since they would try to avoid war with Britain and the United States, and achieve their goals by stages, their 'most probable first move would be into Indo-China or Thailand, possibly followed later by an attack on the Dutch East Indies, if conditions at the time are judged favourable for such a move, before tackling Singapore itself'. The Service Chiefs recommended against going to war in the Indo-China or Thailand contingencies: '*under present world conditions* the threat to British vital interests would not be sufficiently direct to justify war'. An attack on the East Indies and the establishment of naval and air bases there was another matter, and if the Dutch resisted, they 'should offer them full military and economic support'. (What had happened to Pound's opposition? We do not know, though it was to be resumed.) They should, accordingly, hold Staff conversations with the Dutch in the Far East, though not before they were able to provide them with effective military assistance. The thrust of the report was contained in this paragraph.

Committed as we are in Europe, and without the help of France, we must avoid an open clash with Japan. A general settlement, including economic concessions to Japan, is desirable. But the prospects are not at present favourable. Failing this settlement, our general policy must be to play for time, cede nothing until we must, and build up our defences as soon as we can. At the same time we should aim at securing the full military co-operation of the Dutch.

The report ended on a low note. Until a fleet was available, they must rely primarily on air power in conjunction with available naval forces. Presently, those in the Far East (China, Australia, and New Zealand stations) were 'entirely inadequate' for a war with Japan: 1 8-inch cruiser, 2 modern 6-inch cruisers, 4 old 6-inch cruisers, 6 armed merchant cruisers, 5 old destroyers, 3 A/S escorts, and 8 motor torpedo-boats, The Dutch had but 2 cruisers, 7 destroyers, and 16 submarines in the Far East.[19]

---

[19] COS(40)592 (Revise), 'The Situation in the Far East', CAB 80/15. There was no War Cabinet discussion of the paper.

'FOLLY TO INVITE JAPANESE HOSTILITY'

Events in the summer of 1940 were a mixed bag as regards the prospects for peace in the Far East. On the one hand, there was the encouraging news from Tokyo early in September that moderate forces were in the ascendant in the Imperial Navy. The Naval Attaché reported that the Navy Minister, Vice-Admiral Yoshida Zengo, a moderate, had been succeeded by another moderate, Admiral Oikawa Koshirō, whose Vice-Minister, Vice-Admiral Toyoda Teijirō, was 'one of the best friends of England among Japanese flag officers'. Captain Tufnell entered a note of caution. Although developments indicated 'an absence of intention of joining the German camp or indulging in adventures, the motive is practical rather than political. It is realised by officers who are no less "patriotic" than their extremist colleagues that comparative tranquillity is, for the time, essential if serious delay in the naval rearmament programme is to be avoided.' The Ambassador added his own cautionary note:

This moderation may at any moment turn to advocacy of a forward policy if and when the Navy should have the power and material to carry out this policy, because it is not to be supposed that the Navy should be essentially less anxious to acquire an overseas empire for their country than any other section of the population. At present the issue of a conflict between Japan and the colonial Powers may still, in the opinion of the Japanese Navy, be in doubt. But caution and precaution are two of the outstanding points in the Japanese character and if, as is freely said in Japan, the East Indies area forms part of that Great East Asia which Japan intends to control, it may safely be assumed that Japan will continue building up her forces until she is sure of victory in any such conflict.[20]

Ominous indeed were the developments as the summer wore on. There was an ever-increasing tension in Anglo–Japanese relations as incidents multiplied. When Japan declared a blockade of China's coastal waters on 15 July, the Royal Navy protested. At about this time a number of British subjects were arrested in Tokyo, one of whom died in custody. The Cabinet retaliated with arrests of Japanese citizens in Malaya, India, and Great Britain. The tenseness in relations had reached the point where on 16 July the staff officers of Japan's China Area Fleet exchanged opinions on the measures to

---

[20] Tufnell and Craigie dispatches, 7, 12 Sept. 1940, FO 371/24723. There was a delay in the execution of the Third Replenishment Plan (above, p. 15), due largely to the shortage of raw materials.

be taken, should war suddenly break out.[21] On 1 August the new Japanese Government headed by Prince Konoe issued a national policy statement which spoke ominously of the 'construction of a new order in greater East Asia'—not 'East Asia', as formerly. This was recognized in London as a euphemism for extending Japanese control over South-east Asia. The new departure was not long in coming. On 22 September, in response to a Japanese ultimatum, the Vichy Government agreed to permit Japanese troops to be stationed in Tongkin, the northern province of the French Indo-China colony. Japan was now excellently positioned to take over Thailand and southern Indo-China, and from bases there directly to threaten Malaya. Four days later came the announcement of the signing of the German–Italian–Japanese Tripartite Pact. It quickly dispelled such optimism as may still have existed in London about Japan's intentions.

The Tripartite Pact was a watershed, but before discussing it, we must examine the structure and workings of the Japanese Navy High Command, a knowledge of which is essential to the story of the pact and beyond.

[21] Diary, 16 July 1940, of Commander (later Rear-Admiral) Yamamoto Yoshio, who was on the staff of the fleet; extracts from 3 Mar.–18 Sept. 1940 diary in possession of the author.

IV

The Imperial Navy and the Southward Drive

Japan should never be so foolish as to make enemies of Great Britain and the United States.
Vice-Admiral Yamamoto Isoroku, in a public statement quoted in the press early in 1937.

In employing armed strength [against the Southern Area], efforts will be made to limit the war adversary to Great Britain in so far as possible.
Liaison Conference decision, 27 July 1940.

The Strike South will be attempted in so far as possible by peaceful means.
Admiral of the Fleet Prince Fushimi Hiroyasu, at the Imperial Conference of 19 September 1940.

1. THE NAVY HIGH COMMAND

THE Royal Navy and the Imperial Japanese Navy were totally unlike in organization. The supreme commander of the Japanese armed forces in peacetime administration and in wartime operations was the Emperor. Article xi of the Meiji Constitution of 1889 read: 'The Emperor exercises the supreme command [*tōsui-ken*] over the Army and Navy'; xii: 'The Emperor determines the organization and peacetime strength of the Army and Navy'; xiii: 'The Emperor declares war, makes peace, and concludes treaties.' The Emperor's prerogative included the appointment of all generals and admirals. Although all actions were taken in the Emperor's name, in practice the Army and Navy Chiefs of Staff wielded the Emperor's prerogative of supreme command, and the Army and Navy Ministers, his prerogative of military administration. Or, as the Emperor's Grand Chamberlain in 1936–44, Admiral Hyakutake, put it: it 'was customary on the basis of the Japanese Constitution for the Emperor to approve plans and policies submitted to him through the proper channels or by the Chiefs of Staff of the Army and Navy as the product of agreed opinion'. He might question or criticize the Chiefs of Staff and the Service Ministers, but he would never give them orders. The Emperor's liaison with the Supreme Command [*Tōsuibu*], the Army and Navy General Staffs, was his Chief Aide-de-Camp, a post held by three generals in succession from 1936 to 1945.

The highest organ of the Supreme Command was the Imperial General Headquarters (*Daihon'ei*). It was first established in 1894 to oversee the Sino-Japanese War, was re-established in 1904 for the Russo-Japanese War, and again in November 1937 for the China Incident. It was continued throughout the Pacific War. IGHQ was concerned with operational and strategic matters. It supplied information on these and the progress of the war to the Emperor, and advised him on operations. It was supposed to be responsible to him, but, again, this was a polite fiction. IGHQ was headed by the Army and Navy Chiefs of Staff and consisted mostly of officers from the two Staffs, who served in a dual capacity. More precisely, on the Navy side Naval General Staff officers constituted the main body of IGHQ 'members'; the Navy Ministry's members were the Minister, Vice-Minister, Chief of the Naval Aviation Department, chief of the Naval Technical Department, and the Chiefs of the bureaux.[1] IGHQ was divided into various sections—operations, intelligence, and so forth. The important thing to note is that IGHQ bore little resemblance to the British Chiefs of Staff organization. There was no true Chiefs of Staff Committee, but rather two components—a Navy Department (*Kaigunbu*) and an Army Department (*Rikugunbu*), each acting independently in strategic planning and operations. There were joint discussions and exchanges of information on important operational plans which concerned both Services. (Less important plans were discussed at lower level conferences between the Army and Navy.) If they failed to agree, there was a stalemate. When inter-Service agreements were reached, separate orders went out from each department. There was no central office or special building that housed the IGHQ. The Navy Department operated from the Navy Ministry building, and

[1] There were two semi-independent *honbu* (departments or headquarters) under the Navy Minister: the *Kaigun Kōkūhonbu*, or Naval Aviation Department, and the *Kaigun Kanseihonbu*, or Naval Technical Department.

the Army Department from the Army General Staff building. When it was necessary to meet in the presence of the Emperor, the IJN/IJA staff officers, now functioning as IGHQ officers, went to the Palace for the meeting. 'The system, it has been said, led to "duplication, oversights, and mutual recrimination", for the two Services were in effect going their own ways.'[2]

One of IGHQ's more important functions was participation in the Liaison Conference (*Daihon'ei Seifu Renraku Kaigi*), an extra-constitutional body that came into existence in November 1937 to provide a medium for co-ordination of policy between the Government aand the Supreme Command. The Prime Minister, War, Navy, and Foreign Ministers, and other ministers as deemed necessary by the Prime Minister, represented the Government, and the Army and Navy Chiefs of Staff, and as necessary the Vice-Chiefs, spoke for the Supreme Command. The decisions of the Liaison Conference were carried out by the appropriate organs of the Government or the Supreme Command. Liaison Conferences were held whenever the need arose, but were usually held on a weekly basis after November 1940. The meeting place was moved from the Prime Minister's official residence to the Imperial Palace in July 1941. An Imperial Conference (*Gozen Kaigi*) was essentially a meeting of the Liaison Conference—the President of the Privy Council attended—to ratify its more important decisions in the presence of the Emperor, which gave them an almost sacrosanct aura, even if the Emperor rarely said anything. This made for inflexibility, since even if a majority subsequently wished to alter or revoke a decision of an Imperial Conference, a minority could block this by claiming that it would go against the Emperor's wishes. We shall see good examples of the irrevocable nature of decisions reached at an Imperial Conference.

The central organs of the Navy were the Navy Ministry (*Kaigunshō*) and the Naval General Staff (*Gunreibu*), whose functions were entirely separated. The Navy Minister was a distinguished vice-admiral or, more commonly, admiral, on the active list. He was appointed by the Emperor—actually, by the Prime Minister, customarily on the recommendation of the outgoing Navy Minister. The Navy Minister was responsible for the administration of naval

---

[2] Alvin D. Coox, 'The Japanese Army Experience', in Russell F. Weigley (ed.), *New Dimensions in Military History: An Anthology* (San Rafael, California, 1975), p. 141.

affairs. More precisely, he was concerned with the budget, ship construction, weapons procurement, personnel (including training), grand strategy, the Diet, and politics. All matters requiring money were his concern and that of his ministry. He enjoyed the power of managing Navy personnel affairs as he chose. The Navy Minister had nothing whatsoever to do with the drafting of operational plans or the operational movements of the Navy, which were functions of the Naval General Staff. Thus, Admiral Shimada, the Navy Minister, was not informed of the plans for the Midway operation (1942) until after they were drafted. So far as operations went, the Navy Minister's function was to get the equipment and the personnel necessary. Like the War Minister, the Navy Minister had the 'right of direct access to the throne', that is, to report directly to the Emperor. Because of this privilege, the Service Ministers were virtually equal to the Prime Minister in prestige. Moreover, they dominated the Government, since the resignation of either would topple a Cabinet, and failure of either Service to nominate a minister prevented the formation of a new Cabinet. No Prime Minister could tell a Service minister what to do; he advised, suggested, supervised.

The most important of the eight bureaux (*kyoku*) in the Navy Ministry was the Bureau of Naval Affairs (*Gunmukyoku*), which was in charge, *inter alia*, of naval administration, naval armaments, national defence policy, and public relations. The Chief of the Bureau, a vice- or rear-admiral, was, with the Vice-Navy Minister, the closest and most trusted adviser of the Navy Minister. In most cases he was handpicked by the Minister.

The Chief of the Naval General Staff was appointed by the Emperor, but the selection was really made by the Navy Minister, after consulting with the outgoing Chief. The *Gunreibu* Chief had exclusive responsibility for operations and war plans, although he consulted the C-in-C of the Combined Fleet. (The Combined Fleet under the aggressive Yamamoto practically became an equal partner with the Naval General Staff in planning operations.) He kept the Navy Minister *informed* in these areas. The *Gunreibu* Chief was, nominally, directly responsible to the Emperor, not to the Navy Minister. In reality, he *reported* to the Emperor, no more. As in the case of the Navy Minister, the Emperor listened and gave his opinions; he made no decisions and gave no orders. The *Gunreibu's* virtual independence of the Navy Ministry was one of the major defects of the Japanese system before and during the war. In the British and American systems, the First Sea Lord and the Chief of Naval Operations were, at least nominally (so much depended on the personalities of the principals involved), subordinated to the First Lord and the Secretary of the Navy respectively, each a member of the Cabinet. The *Gunreibu* Chief was inclined to go his own way, though he had to consult the Navy Minister on anything involving money or a political element. For example, in planning naval strength (categories and tonnages) it was necessary for the Naval General Staff to consult the Navy Ministry (Bureau of Naval Affairs) in the first instance. Commanders-in-Chief of fleets, nominally under direct orders of the Emperor, received orders from the Navy Minister in matters of naval administration, and instructions from the Chief of the Naval General Staff in matters related to fleet movements or operational plans, whether in peacetime or wartime.

The *Gunreibu* had four divisions (*bu*): Operations (1st), Armament and Mobilization (2nd), Intelligence (3rd), and Communications (4th). Most important was the Operations Division (*Sakusenbu*—officially, *Daiichibu*), whose 1st Section (*Sakusenka, ka* being a section), commonly called the 'Operations Section', was largely concerned with war plans, and the 2nd Section, among other things, with the protection of sea communications. Although the 1st Section was obviously of the highest importance, in the last two pre-war years it consisted of only a Chief (a captain) and *six* officers (commanders); there were about five times as many in the corresponding section of the Army General Staff.

'The independence of the supreme command was', in Professor Butow's words, 'the all-encircling reef upon which the ship of state eventually foundered.' In Great Britain the Service Chiefs had fundamental disagreements with the political leadership over strategy, but there was a basic acceptance by the Services of civil supremacy as the ultimate authority. It was entirely different in Japan, where the Supreme Command rarely kept the Prime Minister or the Cabinet informed of important strategy decisions or of the progress or results of operations. The classic example was that the Prime Minister and War Minister, General Tōjō, only learned *after the war*, at the Tokyo War Crimes Trials, that the Pearl Harbor Striking Force had been ordered on 10 November 1941 to assemble at Hitokappu Bay and had weighed anchor on 26 November.

Professor Butow has summed up the 'fatal flaw' in Japan's 'war guidance structure':

> On one side of the throne stood the cabinet, responsible for state affairs exclusive of military operations; on the other side stood the supreme command, responsible for the national defense *and anything related thereto*. In practical terms, this meant a continuous invasion by the army and navy general staffs of what was nominally the cabinet's sphere of authority. The traditional position of the Emperor was such that he could not provide the unity and the coordination which were lacking. The liaison conference procedure ... inevitably failed to solve the problem, since it perpetuated the divisive aspects of the existing structure. Presumably nothing short of constitutional amendment could have produced the needed revisions and reforms.[3]

One could argue, as Tōjō did after the war, that there were 'some good points' about the independence of the Supreme Command, 'for example, being able to conduct operations without political interference'. In time of peace, anyway, the results were disastrous.

For our immediate purposes the important thing to note is that the decisions to sign the Tripartite Pact in September 1940 and to go to war in December 1941 were made, so far as the Navy was concerned, by a very small circle: the Navy Minister, Vice-Navy Minister, and Chief of the Naval Affairs Bureau, on the one hand, and the Chief and Vice-Chief of the Naval General Staff and the Chief of its 1st Division, on the other. The former group was the more important in the decision to sign the Pact, since it was essentially a political issue.

2. THE DECISION-MAKERS

The Imperial Navy, it must be emphasized, suffered in the crucial years preceding the decision to go to war from a paucity of first-class admirals, especially those who were committed to peace. The Navy lost many able admirals experienced in Navy Ministry affairs when in 1933–4 Ōsumi Mineo, the Navy Minister, strongly backed behind the scenes by the one-time Chief of Staff Admiral Katō Kanji and the Vice-Chief of Staff Admiral Suetsugu Nobumasa, forced through a notorious purge. The key officers among those who were now retired were Admiral Yamanashi Katsunoshin (then

---

[3] Robert J. C. Butow, *Tojo and the Coming of the War* (Princeton, 1961), p. 421.

a Military Councillor), Vice-Admiral Sakonji Seizō (the Commander of the Sasebo Naval District and a former Vice-Navy Minister and C-in-C, 3rd Fleet), and Vice-Admiral Hori Teikichi (a former Chief of the Bureau of Naval Affairs). They were guilty of having supported the naval limitation agreement reached at the London Conference of 1930. The significance of the purge is that the moderate, Western-oriented forces in the Navy were fatally weakened. Had these Admirals, who were among the ablest and most respected officers in the Navy, been on the active list in 1940–1, they might have succeeded in blocking the Tripartite Pact and the subsequent acceleration of the drift to war.[4] As retired afficers they were not eligible for the Navy Minister's post, and the best the Navy could do were Oikawa and Shimada, who, we shall see, were not strong characters, able to hold out against the Army and the extremist forces in the middle echelons of the Navy. Even when the Pacific War began, the purge victims were not called back.

Until at least the summer of 1939 the *Gunreibu* and the Navy Ministry were united in their opposition to a Tripartite Pact with the Axis Powers. The Navy Ministers were Admirals Yonai Mitsumasa (February 1937–August 1939) and Yoshida Zengo (August 1939–September 1940). In the opinion of many surviving officers of the Imperial Navy, Yonai was the No. 1 admiral of the period and one of the greatest admirals the Imperial Navy ever produced. Admiral Inoue Shigeyoshi after the war classified Japanese admirals as of Class A, B, or C quality. Class A admirals were those with great professional ability, strong beliefs, and independence of judgement (based on confidence in their own ideas and judgements). He detected only four Class A admirals in the history of the Imperial Navy: the elder Katō (Katō Tomosaburō), Yamamoto Gonbei, Yamamoto Isoroku, and Yonai. (He might have added himself.) At the same time Yonai was one of the most respected Japanese, internationally as well as nationally.

Yonai came of a samurai family. He was a tall man by Japanese standards, stout, erect, handsome, and somewhat Caucasian in appearance. He had had a broad experience of sea duty, including the Combined Fleet command in 1936–7. Officers had the highest respect and admiration for him, not because of an exceptional

---

[4] Yamanashi was 56 at the time of his retirement (March 1933), Sakonji, 55 (March 1934), and Hori, 51 (December 1934). Age limits for retirement were: admirals, 65; vice-admirals, 62; rear-admirals, 58.

intellect, which he did not possess (he was only 68/125 in the Etajima class of 1901), but because he was kind and gentle (if usually reserved), straightforward, morally courageous, and gave the same feeling of confidence that the great Tōgō had given. He read widely, in newspapers, periodicals, and books. Russian literature was his favourite reading—in the original. (He spoke and read Russian, having been a language officer in Russia in 1915–17. His English was not fluent.) Yonai's capacity for *sake* and whisky (Johnny Walker, Black Label) was proverbial. He could drink the whole night, yet without noticeable effect. (He had been drunk only three times in his life, he told one officer.) His outstanding traits were his selflessness, integrity, and sound judgement, the last a product of balance and common sense. He was entirely without personal ambition, being free from any desire for wealth (though he came of a poor family and had money problems all his life) and power; he never compromised his principles, and the only way to persuade him was to convince him that a particular course of action was good for the country; and he made his decisions with a broad eye, taking all factors into account. As a politician he had his weaknesses; he was laconic, and when he did open up, he was a poor speaker—because, says one of his biographers, 'he told the conclusion too readily to be a good speaker'. Broadly speaking, Yonai was always right on the larger matters of policy. Thus, when Navy Minister, he made clear his dislike for the China War and said it should be stopped. But he lacked the power to do so. He was only the Navy Minister, and the Navy did not have the muscle of the Army, which was doing most of the fighting.

On the issue of the drift towards war with the United States and Great Britain Yonai constituted the most formidable barrier the pro-war forces had to face until the summer of 1940. Not only was his influence on the Navy great, but he had good friends among politicians and in business and Palace circles. To conclude a treaty with Germany meant, in his opinion, that Japan would be pulling Germany's chestnuts out of the fire. Working with Yonai to stop the pact were Yamamoto, Inoue, and Koga.

The charismatic and dynamic Vice-Admiral Yamamoto Isoroku (Admiral, November 1940) was Yonai's Vice-Navy Minister (December 1936–August 1939) and trusted friend, since they had both taught at the Naval Gunnery School in 1911–12. Mentally, this small (5 foot 3) heavy-set, impeccably dressed officer was very sharp (11/191 in the 1904 class at Etajima). He had great leadership and administrative talents, and he understood politics. He made his own decisions, quickly and clearly. Consulting others was not his style. He inspired confidence among officers senior to him, and at the same time was looked up to by junior officers. Although outwardly taciturn, he had a warm personality, was unpretentious, took a paternal interest in his subordinates, was very considerate to young officers, and was eminently approachable and easy to work for. His acts of kindness and thoughtfulness are legion. Even during the war he would receive many letters from all kinds of people, and, busy as he was as C-in-C, Combined Fleet, he would answer them in his own hand. His fondness for and skill in gambling (poker, bridge, mah-jong, and, when in Monte Carlo in 1936, roulette) are well known. Poker especially was his passion. His gambling instinct, it is often said, was reflected in his Pearl Harbor strategy. Though often joining his officers at *sake* parties, he scarcely drank; but he would sing and dance with them without restraint. When C-in-C, Combined Fleet, he once remarked: 'I have done a shameful thing to my Emperor.' The reference was to his connection with a geisha, which was not generally known in the Fleet.[5] Yamamoto was deeply in love with Kawai Ohiyoko, an attractive and highly intelligent girl who became his mistress in 1934. We have Craigie's perceptive estimate of Yamamoto in 1938: 'Speaks English well. Most able, strong-minded and quick-witted. Pleasant manners, and has a sense of humour. Would be a difficult man to bluff. Is one of the best brains in the navy, has foresight and originality. Will probably go far. Is probably largely responsible for the naval policy of Japan, and his strength of mind will ensure that that policy is carried through.'[6] The Naval Attaché shared this high opinion of Yamamoto, observing how considerably Yamamoto's reputation had grown. 'Among all Japanese, official and non-official, he is regarded with great admiration chiefly on account of the dignity and propriety of his behaviour in the Diet where his occasional statements are always loudly applauded. His calmness of manner and patience are frequently contrasted with the less impressive

---

[5] Not until revealed in 1954 in the periodical *Shukan* (the weekly *Asahi*). In 1969 Agawa Hiroyuki's biography *Yamamoto Isoroku* (English edition, *The Reluctant Admiral*, New York, 1979) added detail.

[6] 'Records of Leading Personalities in Japan', enclosure in Craigie to Halifax, 2 Apr. 1938, FO 371/22192.

attitude of other Cabinet Ministers . . . This officer does not attract very much public attention but his influence is probably at least as strong as that of Admiral Yonai himself. . .'[7] Like Yonai, Yamamoto had no interest in power or material possessions.

Yamamoto knew the United States and Great Britain and their strengths, especially the former. He had been a language officer in the United States, 1919–21, Naval Attaché in Washington, 1925–8, had spent nine months in Europe and the United States with the Vice-Navy Minister in 1923–4, and had participated in the First London Naval Conference and the preparatory talks of 1934 for the second Conference. His often expressed view was that war with the Anglo–Saxon Powers could only result in disaster for Japan. The Germans regarded him as pro-British, and to a degree he was. As Vice-Minister he tried to be cordial to the British. And so, for example, he accepted Craigie's invitation to visit the embassy. Yonai's obstinate opposition to a Tripartite Pact owed much to Yamamoto's staunch support.

Rear-Admiral Inoue Shigeyoshi (better known as Inoue Seibi, Vice-Admiral, November 1939), Chief of the Bureau of Naval Affairs (October 1937–October 1939), was a tall and slender man who gave the impression of being cold. He *looked* cold—he rarely smiled—but closer contact revealed him to be warm-hearted. He was an excellent musician, playing the piano and the koto surprisingly well. He posseseed a razor-sharp analytical mind (he was 2/179 in the class of 1909) and, like Yonai, was without personal ambition, never compromised his principles, and was farsighted. As Chief of the Naval Aviation Department in 1940, he submitted a recommendation for the entire reorganization of the Fleet, and in the same report accurately predicted the island-to-island-hopping strategy of the American Navy in a war with Japan, and advocated building up naval air power rather than warships. Little attention was paid to the report. As a commander of fighting forces in the war, there is some doubt about his ability (e.g. in the Wake operation and the Coral Sea action). But as an administrator he performed brilliantly, as witness his time as Chief of the Bureau of Naval Affairs and, late in the war, as Vice-Navy Minister. Inoue, who had once served as Naval Attaché in Rome (1927–30), could speak with expertise on Italy and the Italians. He disliked both,

[7] Tufnell, 'Imperial Japanese Navy. Annual Report. 1938'.

considering the former weak and the latter untrustworthy. He would refer to them as '*Itakō*', that is, 'wops'. The Navy regarded Italy as none too powerful, but the Military and Naval Attachés in Rome reported that Italy had become strong since the First World War under Mussolini and could be trusted. Inoue's response to this line was that 'national characteristics do not change that easily. Such rotten characteristics as Italy's can't be changed in ten or twenty years.'[8] (Opinion in Japan considered Italy much tougher than she really was.) Inoue supported Yonai's position on the Tripartite Pact and was very much against any policy that might lead to war with the United States and Britain.

The Yonai–Yamamoto–Inoue team worked together very well, no more so than in their firm opposition to an alliance with the Axis. At the time of the conclusion of the anti-Comintern Pact of 1936, which the Navy had not received with much enthusiasm, the target nation was the Soviet Union for both Japan and Germany. The target nations for Germany and Italy had, however, clearly shifted to Britain and France in the negotiations that began, on Germany's initiative, in the summer of 1938 to strengthen the Pact by converting it into a military alliance. The Japanese Government was under pressure from the Army, which believed that the strengthening of ties with the Axis would contribute to the settlement of the China Incident; it had reached a stalemate in 1939. A Tripartite Pact would, the Army believed, serve as a form of pressure on Britain and the United States to give up their assistance to Chiang Kai-shek, and it would lead the Germans to do the same. The latter had been training and arming the Chinese Army as well as giving the Chinese economic assistance.

Yonai and his lieutenants, joined by the Vice-Chief of Staff, Koga, always feared that a Triple Pact could lead to war with the United States as well as Britain—a war that the Imperial Navy could not possibly win, given the resources of the two Powers and the strength of the combined fleets. When the Finance Minister Ishiwata asked Yonai at a tense Five Ministers' Conference on 8 August 1939 for his opinion of the Pact, specifically, whether the naval forces of Japan, Germany and Italy would have any chance of defeating those of Britain, France, and the US, Yonai replied without hesitation: 'We would have absolutely no chance of

---

[8] Ikeda Kiyoshi, *Nihon no kaigun* [The Japanese Navy] (2 vols., Tokyo, 1966–7), ii. 210.

winning. The Japanese Navy is not made to fight against the US and England, to begin with. As for the Italian and German navies, they would be no help at all.'[9] Yonai, moreover, had a temperamental aversion to the Germans, based on a 2½-year stay in Germany and a reading of Hitler's *Mein Kampf*. Yonai and his supporters had no greater relish for a war with the Soviets, which a Pact would encourage the Army to start. In the sense that they were pro-peace and against close ties with Germany, the Yonai team were pro-American and pro-British.

These officers, as well as the purged Yamanashi and Hori, were, we might say, disciples of the great Admiral Katō Tomosaburō, Navy Minister and leader of the Japanese delegation at the Washington Conference, and who as Prime Minister had faithfully abided by its terms. (He had died in 1923.) He believed strongly in the enhancement of Japan's power through peaceful means. Other influential admirals of the period, like Suetsugu Nobumasa, were spiritual followers of the impetuous, hawkish, anti-British and anti-American Admiral Katō Kanji, and felt no hesitation about going to war with the United States and Britain, if forced to do so to realize Japan's national aims. This split in the Navy stemmed in part from the antipathy between the Tokyo officers (the 'Whitehall warriors', to use the Royal Navy's expression) and the sea officers. Typical sea Admirals included Suetsugu and Takahashi Sankichi (successively, C-in-C, Combined Fleet, 1933–6), and Nagumo Chuichi (Commander of the Pearl Harbor Striking Force). Typical Whitehall warriors were Yonai, Yamamoto, and Inoue, and it was the tendencies they represented that remained in the ascendant at least until the summer of 1940. Kept under control were Navy authorities directly involved who found the alliance 'attractive' because it did include France and Britain as target nations: Commanders Kami Shigenori and Shiba Katsuo, of the 1st Section, Bureau of Naval Affairs, Captain Yokoi Tadao, of the Operations Division of the *Gunreibu*, and Captain Kojima Hideo, the Naval Attaché in Berlin (February 1936–March 1939). After a dinner party in April 1939 that Yonai gave at the Navy Club in Tokyo, he took aside the Counsellor at the American Embassy, Eugene Dooman, and asked him to inform Ambassador Grew that he need

---

[9] Ogata Taketora, *Ichi gunjin no shōgai: kaisō no Yonai Mitsumasa* [The Life of a Naval Man: Recollections of Admiral Yonai Mitsumasa] (Tokyo, 1955), p. 58.

have no anxiety about a Japanese involvement in Europe. The pro-Axis element which wanted an alliance had been 'suppressed'.[10]

In the spring of 1939, when the Army intensified its campaign for the conclusion of the Tripartite Pact, extremist opinion became so inflamed against Yonai, Yamamoto, Inoue, and Koga, the anti-Pact leaders in the Navy, that their lives were in some jeopardy. There were rumours of an Army attempt to seize the Navy Ministry building to compel the Navy to accept the Pact. The naval authorities took precautionary measures, including the installation of machine guns. The Army and right-wing extremist elements excuriated Yamamoto as the central figure in the anti-Pact movement, and spread such stories as that he had a close relationship with the United States and Britain, as proven by his attendance at dinner parties at their embassies. In August Yonai, who had assigned Yamamoto a police bodyguard over his objections, appointed him C-in-C, Combined Fleet (it encompassed the main force of the Navy), to get him off to sea, as the only way to save his life. Many former Imperial Navy officers in retrospect are critical of this move, feeling that Yamamoto would have been better positioned as Navy Minister (see below)—that there would have been no war, had he stayed in Tokyo.

Yonai himself was forced to resign at the end of August, when the pro-Army, extremist Baron Hiranuma Kiichirō, who had been Prime Minister since January 1939, resigned (30 August) in the wake of the Molotov–Ribbentrop non-aggression pact. This blatant violation of the spirit of the Anti-Comintern Pact so shocked the Japanese that talk of a Tripartite Pact died down. The Axis supporters were demoralized. A moderate, on the whole pro-Western and anti-German, Government under General Abe Nobuyuki succeeded. It gave way on 16 January 1940 to a Yonai Government, with Yonai going on the Navy's retired list, despite the urgings of Prince Fushimi and Admiral Yoshida that, contrary to precedent, he remain on the active list.

Yonai's successor as Navy Minister (August 1939–September 1940) continued his opposition to a Tripartite Pact. He was Vice-Admiral Yoshida Zengo, lately C-in-C, Combined Fleet.[11] He

---

[10] Diary, 19 Apr. 1939, Joseph C. Grew, *Ten Years in Japan* (London, 1944), pp. 245–6.
[11] When sometime afterwards Admiral Toyoda Soemu asked Yonai why he had not recommended Yamamoto for his position, Yonai replied that it had been suggested, but that

(*continued*)

projected a gentle image: he was most agreeable, was forever smiling, had a sense of humour, and enjoyed the hobbies of calligraphy and Chinese literature. But he was tough, as befitted a man from Saga Prefecture in north-west Kyushu. Saga men are notoriously stubborn and independent, with strong minds and strongly held opinions. Vice-Admiral Fukuchi Nobuo, his Secretary at the time, calls him 'a typical Saga type'. Yoshida had a good brain in his large head (he was 12th in his 1904 class of 191) and was a hard worker. Unlike Yonai, who was content to let subordinates handle the details, Yoshida directed, checked, and decided everything himself. That was, as in the case of Roger Backhouse, his besetting weakness. One often found him gripping a red pencil, making corrections in drafts prepared by his staff. Like Yonai, he remained completely aloof from politics and had no ambitions outside the Navy. He supported the policy of Yonai, in particular good relations with the United States and Britain. There is a difference of opinion on his abilities as a Navy Minister. Rear-Admiral Takagi Sōkichi has written him off as a 'business-type admiral, not a fighter like Yamamoto'.[12] To the disinterested student Yoshida appears to have been a man of good sense and what his biographer, Captain Sanematsu Yuzuru, calls him: 'The Last Fortress'.

Yamamoto was succeeded as Vice-Navy Minister by Vice-Admiral Sumiyama Tokutarō (August 1939–September 1940, 24/175 in the class of 1906), a rather short, fat, bald courtier-type admiral (he had spent five years as an aide-de-camp to the Emperor when he was a captain), suave and gentle, but weak. The British

---

Yamamoto had stepped aside because his classmate, Yoshida, held higher seniority. Unconvinced, Toyoda repeated the question at a later date. This time Yonai said that Yamamoto might have been a better choice, but that he would have been assassinated, had he become Navy Minister. Toyoda Soemu, *Saigo no teikoku kaigun* [The End of the Imperial Navy] (Tokyo, 1950), pp. 47–8. Another authority has it that Yamamoto told Yonai that he could remain as Vice-Minister with his classmate Yoshida as Minister, but that Yonai, fearing for Yamamoto's life, talked him into taking the position of C-in-C. Ogata, *Ichigunjin no shōgai*, p. 59. Yamamoto himself, when Vice-Minister, was nonchalant about the threat to his life, though he took the precaution of making out his will. He was a man of iron nerves. Reporters, who often visited him at 11 or 12 at night, would find him answering the door, since the maids were sent to bed at 10 o'clock at his residence. He remained perfectly relaxed, enjoying *shōgi* (Japanese checkers) on Saturday afternoons and playing with his children whenever he found a little time.

[12] Takagi, *Taiheiyō sensō kaisenshi* [A History of Naval battles in the Pacific War] (Tokyo, 1949), p. 202. But Yamamoto thought that everything would be all right, since Yoshida's viewpoint was similar to his own. Ibid.

Naval Attaché welcomed his appointment. He 'appears to be well connected as he was educated at the Peers' School [*Gakushūin*] and for several years between 1927 and 1932 he was ADC to the Emperor. It is safe to say, therefore, that his tendencies are conservative and that his appointment as Vice-Minister of Marine indicates the absence of any radical tendencies in the Navy at the present time.'[13] Sumiyama was, however, not suited to the position of Vice-Minister. For example, whereas Yamamoto was always ready to talk to the press, Sumiyama would never receive the press, although good public relations were important for the Navy. He was apparently afraid to answer questions. Moreover, 'he was not a good wife to the Navy Minister', as an officer who knew him well says. He failed to support Yoshida in the latter's fight against the Tripartite Pact. Captain Sanematsu, Yonai's Secretary at the time, appraises Sumiyama as 'indeed a noble man, who had been nicknamed "The Principal of the Gakushūin Girls' School". But he was by no means a fighter, fit for this turbulent period.'[14]

Inoue was followed at the Bureau of Naval Affairs in October 1939–October 1940) by Rear-Admiral Abe Katsuo, who was not adequate in this important post at such a critical time. The glum-looking Abe had a good brain (10/144; class of 1912) and was a capable administrator, but he was very cautious and lacked any political sense. He had visited Germany and returned pro-German—the one advocate of the Pact among the top policy-makers in the Navy Ministry. It was Yoshida who, as Navy Minister, was ultimately responsible for the Sumiyama and Abe appointments, two unhappy ones, as it turned out.[15]

Pro- and anti-Pact forces in the Naval General Staff were

---

[13] Tufnell's report, 1 Sept. 1939, FO 371/23563.

[14] Sanematsu Yuzuru, *Saigo no toride: Teitoku Yoshida Zengo no shōgai* [The Last Fortress: The Life of Admiral Yoshida Zengo] (Tokyo, 1974), p. 26.

[15] Apparently, Yamamoto had recommended Sumiyama as Vice-Minister, in the belief that this gentle and amicable officer might serve as an effective mediator between the Army and Navy. Admiral Inoue Shigeyoshi interview, 14 Mar. 1962, Bōeichō Senshibu Archives. Sumiyama himself had said pretty much the same thing in an interview of 19 Dec. 1961, ibid. There is another version. Asked by a close friend, who was uneasy about Sumiyama's appointment, whether he could manage in such a period of emergency, Yamamoto had replied that the appointment was intended to show the Army that the Navy's position would never change even after such a gentleman became its leader. Sanematsu, *Saigo no toride*, pp. 26–7. Admiral Takagi thought that Yamamoto's 'biggest error and failure was the recommendation of Admiral Sumiyama as Vice-Minister, because of his weak personality. As an administrator he was very capable, but not as a statesman.' Takagi Sōkichi interview, 7 Mar. 1962, Bōeichō Senshibu Archives.

balanced. The Chief of the Naval General Staff since 1932 (–April 1941) was Admiral of the Fleet Prince Fushimi Hiroyasu, the Emperor's cousin, a member of a colateral branch of the Imperial family. He was a quiet man, slim, slightly stooped and looking the aristocrat that he was. He had the nickname of the 'Long-faced Prince' (*Chōmemkun*). He became the *Gunreibu* Chief not because of exceptional ability, but in order to create a balance between the two Services, since the Army had a prince for Chief of the Army General Staff, Field-Marshal Prince Kan'in Kotohito. Fushimi had his favourites in the Navy, among them, Admiral Shimada Shigetarō, Navy Minister when the war began. Fushimi was considered a bit of a tyrant, and he relied on his subordinates. An Admiral of the old Navy dismisses him with the comment: 'Just a prince—useless. He functioned only with a capable assistant.' Admiral Toyoda Teijirō considered him a mere figurehead. However, in those days it was taboo to talk about him in the Service, still less to criticize him. As a young officer the Prince had studied in Germany and was fluent in German. This may have disposed him to favour the Axis cause, but any such leaning was offset, initially anyway, by the views of his Vice-Chief of Staff, the *Gunreibu Jichō*, Vice-Admiral Koga Mineichi (December 1937– October 1939).

The tall and stout Koga, an aristocratic officer with Imperial Household connections, had had more service in Europe than most Japanese officers. He was a most agreeable person, kind, easy to work with, always calm, always smiling, full of common sense, and possessed of a good mind (14/174 in the Etajima class of 1906). He had two failings. He was an old-fashioned officer, a battleship man not *au courant* with developments, especially in naval air, and he was excessively deliberate and cautious. This explains why he was slow in making decisions: too much went through his mind. These weaknesses were more damaging when he was C-in-C, Combined Fleet, late in the war. Koga belonged to the group that had approved the London Naval Treaty of 1930, and he was dead against waging a war with the United States and Britain. But he was succeeded in October 1939 (–October 1941) by Vice-Admiral Kondō Nobutake. The heavy-set, round-faced, well-groomed Kondō had a commanding presence that concealed a gentle, affable nature. He made no enemies and was liked by all officers—and geisha! He graduated from Etajima at the head of his class (1/171,

1907), and was considered a brilliant staff officer. His besetting weakness was a passive character. He was not one to take the initiative. As Vice-Chief of Staff he was methodical and punctual—a good bureaucrat who always listened to others before making a decision. He had been Naval Attaché in London, but he had studied in Germany earlier. He was pro-German by 1940, albeit wary about a Tripartite Pact.

The Chiefs of the 1st Division of the Naval General Staff were Kondō Nobutake (December 1935–December 1938) and Rear-Admiral Ugaki Matome (December 1938–April 1941). The latter is an officer about whom I shall have more to say in the next volume (he was intimately associated with the 'Special Attack' forces in 1945). It is enough here to note that the humourless and arrogant Ugaki was evidently against the Tripartite Pact, though in the end he gave way.

3. 'WE MUSTN'T MISS THE BUS'

After signing the non-aggression pact with the Soviets, Germany worked on Japan, the Army especially, to join a four-Power alliance—Germany, Italy, Japan, and the Soviet Union. The idea won some favour in Navy circles. Thus, the Research Section Chief at the Navy Ministry, Captain Takagi Sōkichi, prepared a paper on 24 August 1939 on the 'Advantages and Disadvantages of Various Foreign Policies', in which he examined the alternatives of a lone and independent policy, an alliance with 'Britain and France (United States) [sic]', or an alliance with Germany, Italy, and the Soviets. He concluded that the first was unsuitable and the second disadvantageous; the third was 'the most favourable policy to be taken by Japan immediately and in the near future'.[16] So long, however, as Yonai and Yoshida were in power, pro-Tripartite Pact forces in the Navy were kept in check.

Yonai's Cabinet was destroyed in July 1940 by the Army because he had not only kept up his opposition to the Tripartite Pact, but he was at the same time reluctant to sanction a thrust into South-east Asia. Yonai, with his Foreign Minister, Arita Hachirō, was as fearful of war with Britain and the United States if Japan moved into South-east Asia as he was if a military alliance were concluded with the Axis. But events played into the hands of the extremists.

[16] *Senshi sōsho*, xci. 453.

Anti-British sentiment mounted as, increasingly, Britain was held responsible for the Army's inability to conclude the China Incident. A new source of friction occurred on 21 January 1940, when the British cruiser *Liverpool* stopped the Japanese steamer *Asama Maru* 35 miles east of Cape Nijima, in the approaches to Tokyo Bay, and forcibly removed twenty-one German passengers, on their way to Germany via Vladivostok. They were survivors of the German SS *Columbus*, which had scuttled herself some weeks earlier in the north Atlantic. Japanese maritime pride was touched, particularly by the nearness of the incident to the capital. Public opinion in Japan was shocked—'Everybody felt as though a burglar had broken into the entrance hall of a private home'—and the Government shot off a strong protest to London over the alleged abuse of belligerent rights. It was 'a serious and unfriendly act'. Although a compromise settlement was reached in February, the incident fed anti-British sentiment in Japan. Then came the dramatic turn of events in Europe in the spring—the German *blitzkrieg*, Italy's entry into the war, and the French collapse—which fired up the pro-German elements, primarily in the Army but also in the Navy. Supported by public opinion generally, they were determined to join an obviously unstoppable team, and were not impressed with the arguments of the admirals that Hitler could not defeat the British at sea and that the war was far from over.

When Yonai continued to oppose a full military alliance with the Axis, he was toppled by the Army. The Chief of the Army General Staff, Prince Kan'in, merely asked the War Minister, General Hata Shunroku (who, incidentally, sided with Yonai on the Pact) to resign and then refused to nominate a replacement. Elements in the Navy shared responsibility for Yonai's overthrow, especially the younger officers who wanted some of the glory the Army was winning in China since 1931. The American scholar Stephen E. Pelz has corrected the established view that the Navy was less ambitious and aggressive that the Army.[17] In particular has he challenged the 'legend of the Imperial Navy's moderation' in the later thirties with special reference to Yonai's policies. He writes (pp. 214-15):

From 1938 on, the navy had been resisting the Axis pact, because Yonai

[17] *Race to Pearl Harbor: The Failure of the Second London Naval Conference and the Onset of World War II* (Cambridge, Mass., 1974).

feared that the Germans would involve Japan prematurely in a war with the United States and Britain. In 1939, Yonai did agree to the first cautious steps south, such as taking Hainan, but he continued to shun any great leap into the western colonies as long as Japan's building programs were incomplete. It is from this period of Yonai's resistance to the Axis pact that the legend of the Imperial Navy's moderation dates, yet Yonai was no moderate. Shortly after the China incident began in the fall of 1937, Yonai agreed to send marines to Shanghai, thereby decisively expanding the hostilities. [IJN marines had been in Shanghai since 1927 to protect Japanese citizens. The 2,500 marines there at the outbreak of the China Incident on 7 July 1937 were reinforced to 4,000 by 12 August. On the next day, following a clash in Shanghai between the marines and the Chinese, Yonai asked and received Cabinet approval to send two Army divisions.] Rejecting all appeals for further arms restrictions, he presided over the adoption of the navy's Fourth Replenishment Program. As Navy Minister, Yonai demanded that Japan take Hainan and the Spratlys, and as Prime Minister, he warned of Japan's interest in the Dutch East Indies, and established a puppet government for all of China. Perhaps Yonai was an unwilling medium for the militarists, but there is a point at which reluctance ends and responsiblity begins; and Yonai certainly crossed that line with the attack on Hainan. In fact, Yonai was even willing to enter the Axis pact, granted one condition: inasmuch as Japan's naval building program was not complete, Germany would let the Japanese pick their own time to enter a war with the West. Hitler rejected Yonai's proposal in 1939.

The argument is persuasive—to a point; but it does not alter the fact that Yonai and those who followed his lead were vehemently opposed to a war with the United States and Britain. There was an obvious contradiction between this policy and Yonai's support of the 'New Order' in East Asia, which implied a Japanese advance to the south. Yonai, however, envisaged a southward expansion that would be achieved peacefully. He eschewed armed force and relied on diplomacy to achieve the expansionist objectives. Closer cooperation with the Axis might facilitate this advance, so was desirable. A military alliance was something else again—sure way to a disastrous war against the United States and Britain.

There was, however, from 1936 little to choose between the two Services as driving forces behind Japan's policy of imperialistic expansion. There were only differences in priority of strategic objectives and in the manner of achieving them. The Army focused on the need to deal with the Soviet menace to the north, whereas the Navy, categorically rejecting war with the Soviet Union, looked to the natural resources of South-east Asia, especially its oil, to break Japan's economic dependence on the United States and the British Empire. They supplied Japan with over half of her raw materials. The Navy accordingly pressed for an advance into the 'Southern Area', a vast region that included Indo–China, Thailand, Malaya, and the Netherlands East Indies. The German Naval Attaché summed up the essence of the southward policy in 1935: 'The target which, according to all my observations, has always been dangling in front of the Navy's eyes, is the realization of an aim which has already been set for some time—the expansion in a southerly direction by means of power politics. This is the seizure of areas which are in a position to solve two of the most urgent of Japanese problems—raw material supply and over-population.'[18] Opposition from the Army, which opposed a southward advance while Japan was occupied in the north, and, still more important, the lack of ships necessary to fight the American and British fleets until the Third Replenishment Plan was completed in 1941–2, operated as brakes on the Navy's ambitions. The Navy's goal, however, was adopted by a Four-Ministers' Conference (the inner cabinet: Prime Minister, Service Ministers, and Foreign Minister) on 7 August 1936, and, officially, by the Hirota Cabinet in a policy statement four days later, though it was to be carried out 'by gradual and peaceful means'. In pursuance of this policy statement, the Navy proceeded, through a programme of 'footsteps', to set the stage for decisive moves into the Southern Area, in part by establishing private development or exploitation companies (*takushoku*) there to exploit the resources—oil, tin, rubber, etc.[19] The

[18] Captain Paul W. Wenneker, 4 Sept. 1935, quoted in John W. M. Chapman, 'The Origins and Development of German and Japanese Military Co-operation, 1936–1945' (unpublished doctoral thesis, Oxford, 1967), p. 100. Wenneker was the Naval Attaché in 1933–7, and again, now a rear-admiral, in 1940–5. Between these tours of duty he commanded the pocket battleship *Deutschland*. He is described as a typical German naval officer, blond and good-looking. He got on well with IJN officers.

[19] This Southern Area policy was the responsibility of the Ministry of Overseas Affairs (*Takumusho*), since the Navy did not wish openly to play as conspicuous a role as the Army did in Manchuria. At the Navy's suggestion two companies were set up in 1936: the *Taiwan Takushoku*, which operated in the western Dutch East Indies, Malaya, Singapore, Thailand, French Indo–China, and Hainan Island, and the *Nanyō* (South Seas) *Takushoku*, which operated in the eastern part of the Dutch East Indies. The Navy had no jurisdiction over the business side of the overseas development companies, although the 1st Section of the Naval Affairs Bureau had one member who, working with the Ministry of Overseas Affairs, was

(*continued*)

taking over by the Navy of the government of Formosa late in 1936 after 20 years of civilian administration, which made possible the construction of bases needed for the push to the south, followed by the occupation of Hainan Island and the Spratly Islands early in 1939, were the next stages in the Navy's southward advance.

The smashing German victories in the spring of 1940 greatly impressed Japanese military and naval officers and opened up magnificent vistas in South-east Asia, whose colonial masters were in such desperate straits. The situation sparked a fresh drive in the Navy for the Tripartite Pact. The main consideration at this time, as viewed by Commander Shiba Katsuo, attached to the 1st Section of the Naval Affairs Bureau, and Captain Ōno Takeji, of the Operations Division, *Gunreibu*, was 'apprehension that Germany's influence, as the result of her victories, might extend to the Dutch East Indies and French Indo-China; so the Japanese sphere of influence should be clarified'.[20] But the Navy had no immediate intention, as Kondō told the German Naval Attaché on 14 May, of 'using force in the direction of the East Indies... Such action would lead Japan to a state of war with America as well as England.'[21]

The same events in the spring brought the Army round to the Navy's strategic orientation to the south. On 4 July a document entitled 'Outline of the Main Principles for Coping with the Changing World Situation', which had been drafted the day before by key officers in the War Ministry and Army General Staff, was put before the Naval General Staff. The Army was prepared for an advance to the south and was ready to use armed force if necessary, 'restricting insofar as possible its operations to Britain alone'. Thorough preparations for a war with the United States would proceed, however, 'as it may prove impossible to avoid war

---

responsible for promoting this policy of economic exploitation, with further political implications originating in the policy statement of the Hirota Cabinet.

[20] Rear-Admiral Ōno and Captain Shiba interviews, 22 Nov. 1961, 16 May 1962, respectively, Bōeichō Senshibu Archives. Captain Ishikawa Shingo (see below) also made this point at the time—that Japan should hurry and stake out her claims in the Southern Area before Germany incorporated it in her sphere. Rear-Admiral Yamaki Akira interview 6 Dec. 1961, ibid. (He was a captain in the Bureau of Personnel, Navy Ministry, during 1940.)

[21] War Diary of the German Naval Attaché, Tokyo, PG 32149, Admiralty Project, Reel 481, Naval Historical Branch, Ministry of Defence. Admiral Wenneker 'got the impression that the Japanese Navy's striking power for a war with the two major Powers, even bearing in mind the extent to which they would be tied down in the European theatre, was much too weak'.

with that country'. The prerequisites to this policy called for security from a Soviet attack, the early settlement of the China Incident, and a political alliance with the Axis.[22] The Navy was pleasantly surprised by the Army's acceptance of the southward advance, but 'wished to strengthen political collaboration with Germany and Italy, without concluding a tripartite alliance', and 'emphasized that the goal [of the southward expansion policy] must be achieved by peaceful means, if at all possible, and the use of military force must be determined with great prudence'.[23] On 15 July an inter-Service conference reached agreement on the Army's draft of 'Main Principles' which incorporated the Navy's reservations.

It was at this point, on the 16th, that the Army, despairing of a quick conclusion of the Pact with Yonai as Prime Minister, and hell-bent on taking advantage of the world situation to pursue its expansionist ambitions, overthrew him. 'Unquestionably,' writes Professor Crowley, 'the driving force behind the intrigue to oust Yonai was the army and the major personalities in the new political movement [those who were to found the hawkish Imperial Rule Assistance Association, into which all political parties were merged in October 1940], but some share of the credit or blame should be traced to the outlook in naval circles which produced a passive reaction to Hata's resignation.'[24] There was not only opposition in the Navy to Yonai's reluctance to sanction a southern expansion by force, if necessary, but also a feeling, as Admiral Kondō pointed out in 1953, that 'the preparations for the defence of Japan might be seriously threatened if she maintained her attitude of opposition' to the Pact. That is, that deepening of the Army–Navy split would be

[22] The document is reproduced in James William Morley (ed.), *Japan's Road to the Pacific War. Deterrent Diplomacy: Japan, Germany, and the USSR, 1935–1940* (New York, 1976), pp. 208–9. (Hereafter cited as Morley, *Deterrent Diplomacy.*) This is volume iii of the projected five volumes of translations of selected portions of the classic *Taiheiyō sensō e no michi: kaisen gaikō shi* [The Road to the Pacific War: A Diplomatic History before the War] (7 vols. Tokyo, 1962–3), edited by the Nihon Kokusai Seiji Gakka Taiheiyō Sensō Gen' in Kenkyūbu [The Japan Association on International Relations. Study Group on the causes of the Pacific War]. *Deterrent Diplomacy* draws on volumes iv and v. Where I cite the original work volumes vi and vii), I use the abbreviation TSM.
[23] Japanese Monograph No. 146, *Political Strategy Prior to the Outbreak of War*, Pt. ii (1953), 14–20. The Japanese Monographs are a series of 182 operational monographs written by former IJN and IJA officers for the Japanese Research Division of the Military History Section, US Army Headquarters, Far East Command.
[24] James B. Crowley, 'Japan's Military Foreign Policies', in James William Morley (ed.), *Japan's Foreign Policy, 1868–1941: A Research Guide* (New York, 1974), p. 86.

'WE MUSTN'T MISS THE BUS'

a serious handicap to inter-Service collaboration 'in time of a national emergency'.[25] After the war, Yonai lamented to Ogata Taketora, Editor of the newspaper *Asahi*: 'Our opposition to the Pact was almost like trying to row a boat a few hundred metres upstream from Niagara Falls.' Asked by Ogata whether he and Yamamoto would have continued their opposition to the Pact to the very end, had they remained in office, Yonai had replied: 'Of course, we would have, but we probably would have been assassinated.'[26]

Prince Konoe Fumimaro, who had been Prime Minister between June 1937 and January 1939, formed his second Government on 22 July. Konoe was a cultivated Westernized gentleman of liberal outlook who read English poetry as a relaxation. A contemporary has described him as 'quick-witted and clear-minded; he was universally liked and a typical gentleman. He was by no means anxious to see government by the militarists, nor was he in sympathy with their aims. ... a member of the aristocratic circle most intimate with the Court ... Surely such a man was not cast to be the puppet of the militarists ... He did in fact become the puppet of the Army'.[27] Because he was weak and vacillating, although opposed to the attempts to strengthen Japan's ties with the Axis, in the end Konoe succumbed to pressure from the Army, exerted through the new War Minister, Lieutenant-General Tōjō Hideki, and from the new Foreign Minister, the ardent nationalist, Matsuoka Yōsuke. The latter, a brilliant and fiery University of Oregon Law School graduate who spoke English fluently, was an ambitious schemer with extraordinary self-confidence. 'Matsuoka was a genius, dynamic and erratic. His mind worked as swiftly as

---

[25] Japanese Monograph No. 146, p. 55. We have a further clue to Kondō's thinking in the early summer of 1940. Wenneker reported a meeting with him on 9 July. 'I took the opportunity, as on many previous occasions with this close friend and very influential officer, to impress upon him just how much the events in Europe could mean to Japan, especially in presenting the opportunity finally to drive England out of East Asia. Kondō readily agreed that it was almost criminal not to act now. He endeavoured to put my mind at rest by assuring me that the new Cabinet would probably effect a change. But the impression I got was that he himself did not really believe this. In any case, he returned to the subject of the slowness of the Japanese military and political leadership, which could not be changed overnight.' War Diary, German Naval Attaché, PG 32149, Admiralty Project, Reel 481.

[26] Ogata, *Ichigunjin no shōgai*, p. 61.

[27] Mamoru Shigemitsu (Foreign Minister, 1943–5, 1954–6), *Japan and Her Destiny: My Struggle for Peace* (London, 1958), p. 134. The American scholar Gordon Mark Berger has advanced the unconvincing thesis that Konoe was no 'robot' of the military. Berger, *Parties out of Power in Japan, 1931–1941* (Princeton, 1977), pp. 269–70.

lightning. People were dazzled by his brilliance. He was eloquent and could plead a cause with passion.... Matsuoka wanted to use the Axis alliance as an instrument for restraining the United States from intervening in the European war... an event which he feared might involve Japan in the struggle.'[28] Yoshida regarded him as a 'madman. It was a great error to appoint him Foreign Minister.'[29]

On 22 July, the day the new Government was formed, a conference of the top leaders of the armed forces met to confirm the agreement reached on the 15th. It soon became clear that the Army and Navy were still far apart on the nature of a pact with the Axis. The Army talked about a *military* alliance, whereas the Navy contemplated only the strengthening of ties *without* a military alliance. The differences were concealed with the vague conclusion that 'Japan will reconsider the possibility of a military alliance if it should be proposed by Germany and Italy'. For the time being, 'Japan will proceed to strengthen political ties', and this became the Government's policy on 27 July, when a Liaison Conference, the first in over two years, approved the principles of foreign policy agreed to by the Services in the 'Outline of the Main Principles for Coping with the Changing World Situation'. It was now official policy that the southern advance would proceed and that political ties with the Axis would be strengthened. The latter was seen as a crucial means of winning Japanese hegemony in South-east Asia. It would pre-empt the area before Germany claimed it for herself, and it would deter the Soviet Union from attacking in the north and the United States from interfering with Japan's expansion to the south. Without American support, the British could do little. In fact, both policies inevitably involved a clash with Britain and the United States.

The Army interpreted the vague language in the agreement with the Navy to mean the Government could go ahead and negotiate a military alliance with the Axis. Public opinion as well as the Foreign Office were on its side. On 1 August Matsuoka asked the German Ambassador, General Eugen Ott, to sound out his Government's intentions. This eventually led, on 23 August, to news from Berlin that Heinrich Stahmer would be sent to Tokyo as

[28] Kase, *The Eclipse of the Rising Sun*, pp. 43–4.
[29] At the round-table conference of Navy leaders, 17 Jan. 1946. Shinmyō Takeo (ed.), *Kaigun sensō kentō kaigi kiroku* [Recollections on the Circumstances of Japan's Going to War] (Tokyo, 1976), p. 76. On these conferences, see below, p. 120n.

a special envoy. With his arrival on 7 September, progress towards a Tripartite Pact moved swiftly. The turning point had come on 5 September, when Admiral Oikawa replaced Yoshida as Navy Minister. Yoshida had stayed on as Navy Minister in the new Konoe Government. He stubbornly and vigorously continued his resistance to the Pact, mainly because of his cautious attitude towards the United States, as well as his scepticism of a German victory. He was worried about American economic pressure, because of the dependence of the Japanese economy on the United States as well as on Britain. At a meeting of the Navy's leaders held at Yoshida's official residence on 2 August, a report was made that if imports from the United States and Britain ceased, Japan would have key war materials for only one year. At the close of the meeting, Yoshida, with a grave expression, made a plea for 'not being dragged into anything. . . . Only a fierce but reckless tiger will rush into hostilities with a war potential sufficient for but a year. . . . Germany's wishful thinking [about a victory over] Britain should not be trusted. The [Japanese] Empire may be heading for disaster.'[30] The Naval Attaché in Berlin, the Anglophile Rear-Admiral Endō Yoshikazu, kept getting instructions from the Navy Minister to be wary. The American–British destroyers–bases agreement announced on 2 September (50 US destroyers were transferred to Britain in exchange for a 99-year lease of naval and air bases in Newfoundland and the West Indies) indicated that the United States would eventually enter the war on Britain's side, hence that Japan had to be careful about allying herself with Germany.

Unhappily, with the fall of the Yonai Government in July 1940 and the precarious situation of Britain, the pro-German forces in the Navy began to assert themselves. The most authoritative Japanese study of the genesis of the Pact explains the situation:

What draws our attention here is the fact that not only the Foreign Ministry and the army but those within the navy concerned with this matter as well were already inclined to approve a triple military alliance against Britain. However, . . . Navy Minister Yoshida had consistently refused to support such an alliance . . . Clearly there existed a grave difference of opinion between top and middle-ranking officers in the navy. But by the middle of August the idea of a tripartite pact had gained

[30] Sanematsu, *Saigo no toride*, pp. 76–7.

support even among the navy's top leaders, such as Chief of the Naval Affairs Bureau Abe Katsuo, and it was increasingly apparent that Yoshida was becoming isolated. Nevertheless, Yoshida held steadfastly to the views he had expressed when the cabinet was formed. The August 12 entry in the Army General Staff's *Confidential War Diary* reads: 'Negotiations with Germany and Italy stalled. Still being studied by the navy minister. Ugh!'[31]

As late as 27 August the Navy Ministry and Naval General Staff were on record as being opposed to the Pact. But the situation was about to change.

Yoshida found himself more and more a lone figure at the ministry. The brilliant Commander Shiba Katsuo, of the Bureau of Naval Affairs, which was in charge of political matters, and his Chief, Abe Katsuo, favoured an alliance with the Axis, with the former believing that Japan should participate in the war, once the China Incident had been settled. Abe had been a close associate of Yoshida, but had gradually come under the influence of Shiba and the Army. By the summer of 1940 he was their captive. Nor did Yoshida receive much support from his Vice-Minister, Sumiyama, who was essentially weak and irresolute and anything but a fighter and now sat on the fence. Although, like Yoshida, Rear-Admiral Oka Takazumi, Chief of the *Gunreibu*'s Intelligence Division (October 1939–October 1940), 'positively and strongly' opposed the conclusion of the Tripartite Pact,[32] many of his associates were not in the same mind. At least two of the Naval General Staff's Big Three, however, Prince Fushimi and Kondō Nobutake, maintained a relatively neutral attitude. Captain Ōi remembers that when he visited Tokyo that summer, he was told by many of his naval friends that the Minister stood alone on the question of the Pact. Vice-Admiral Nakazawa Tasuku, who was then a captain and Chief of the 1st Section (war plans) of the *Gunreibu*'s Operations Division, stated in a lecture on 11 July 1977 that he was often called upon by Yoshida to give advice on the problems related to the Alliance, and that he, Nakazawa, who was strongly against it, might have been the only officer in whom Yoshida had real confidence. A slight exaggeration, perhaps; but Nakazawa unfor-

---

[31] Hosoya Chihiro, 'The Triple Pact, 1939–40', in Morley, *Deterrent Diplomacy*, pp. 228–9.
[32] Rear-Admiral Horiuchi Shigetada's letter to the author, 18 June 1970. The Admiral, then a Captain, was Chief of the 8th Section of the Intelligence Division, which included British Intelligence, November 1939–September 1941.

'WE MUSTN'T MISS THE BUS'

tunately lacked the ability to influence people. Yamamoto, Koga, Inoue, and the two former Prime Ministers, Admirals Yonai and Okada Keisuke, were not in a position to intervene, beyond providing moral support behind the scenes. In the Japanese naval tradition, it was deemed improper to interfere with another officer's responsibilities. Besides, they had confidence in Yoshida's ability to prevent the conclusion of the Alliance.

Matters came to a head on 3 September. On that day Captain Ishikawa Shingo (see below) called on Yoshida and told him about the attitudes and atmosphere prevailing in various circles regarding the Pact, and then advised him: 'If you, the Minister, are determined to oppose the Treaty, let us stage a gigantic quarrel with the Army.' Yoshida replied: 'It is not a good policy to get into a quarrel with the Army at this time.' Ishikawa asked: 'Then are you going to agree to the Tripartite Alliance?' Yoshida protested: 'But we are not prepared for war with the United States.' Ishikawa pressed the Minister. 'This is the time for the Navy Minister to decide one way or the other. This is a matter of your guts, not a problem of reasoning, I believe!' Yoshida complained, 'I am at a loss, indeed!' Admiral Oka, who was standing next to Ishikawa, signalled with his eye for him to finish the interview. Ishikawa left the Minister's room at once. That evening Yoshida suffered a severe nervous breakdown—probably, says Ishikawa, because of accumulated exhaustion from his continuous hard work since his service as C-in-C, Combined Fleet.[33] He was rushed to hospital, leaving all

---

[33] Ishikawa Shingo, *Shinjuwan made no keii* [The Road to Pearl Harbor] (Tokyo, 1960), pp. 229–30. Yoshida's collapse was surely due at least as much to the fact that the anxieties and pressures related to the Pact had finally got to him. In his last days in office Yoshida was visibly fatigued as well as under severe emotional stress. He was snowed under by work and overwhelmed by important problems needing decisive action, and distressed by the misconduct of his eldest son as well as by his inability to rally the Navy against the Pact. The Chief of the Navy's Medical Bureau, Vice-Admiral Nakano Tarō, who examined the Minister at Captain Nakazawa's request, advised him to retire from his post. He also advised the family not to leave any knives or swords around, lest Yoshida find the means to commit suicide. Vice-Admiral Sumiyama Tokutarō interview 19 December 1961, Bōeichō Senshibu Archives. (There is an unproven story, though it comes on respectable authority, that Yoshida tried to commit suicide while in hospital.) Normally, a man of cool judgement and firm will, he had by August begun to act unreasonably, as when he ordered his Secretary to go and tell a certain Bureau Chief in the Ministry that he was a big fool. (The childish order was disregarded.) Captain Kojima told Admiral Wenneker on 13 September that Yoshida's departure 'was only in part for health reasons. In fact his excessive respect for England and more especially for America had annoyed the younger, activist circles so much that he could not hold out any longer.' War Diary, German Naval Attaché, PG 32150, Admiralty Project, Reel 481.

the business of the ministry to Abe. The next day he resigned, and on the 5th a new minister was appointed. For all practical purposes the tug of war in the Navy had ended, even if important pockets of resistance and doubts remained.

Yoshida's successor, the Commander of the Yokosuka Naval District, was appointed largely on the recommendation of Prince Fushimi, though Yoshida, too, had recommended him. He was the tall, handsome, heavily built (he was said to eat for two!) Admiral Oikawa Koshirō. The gentle and refined Oikawa had been an excellent Superintendent of the Naval Academy (1933–5), although his addresses, of a philosophical nature, were over the heads of the cadets. He was a Chinese classical scholar. Indeed, he was more a scholar than a naval officer. (This was belied by his class standing: 76/187 in the class of 1903.) Even while the Pacific War was on, he was always reading books, usually Chinese books. When he spoke, he might introduce an historical allusion, for example: 'About 3,000 years ago in China . . .' He was easy to work for: he was pleasant, smiled easily, and had a sense of humour. But he was a disaster as Navy Minister. For one thing, he was not a politician and had never been in the Ministry before. Worse, he had a passive, weak character, and was notorious for his desire to please everybody at the same time. In Admiral Inoue's words, 'He was a great man but not a man of firm convictions'. Oikawa's Vice-Minister from April to October 1941, Vice-Admiral Sawamoto Yorio, described him as 'too mild and gentlemanly, and does not like a fight', and went so far as to call him a 'figurehead Minister'.[34] He had no ideas or opinions of his own; he followed the prevailing wind and was inclined to agree with whomever had his ear last.

Worst of all was Oikawa's attitude towards the Army. One can divide IJN officers of that generation into two groups as regards the Army. Some hated the Army for its interference in politics and swashbuckling ways, and could not get along with it. Yonai, Yamamoto, Inoue, and Toyoda Soemu (he was especially hated by the Army) are good examples. Others were willing to co-operate, which group included Oikawa and his successor, Shimada, and Prince Fushimi's successor, Nagano. It was the Army which in the end overrode the naval and political opposition to the Pact. The

---

[34] 'Kaigun taishō Sawamoto Yorio shi shuki' [Private Notes of Admiral Sawamoto Yorio] (1962), Bōeichō Senshibu Archives.

military and other extremists viewed the European situation, with France and the Netherlands conquered and occupied, and an isolated Britain facing the expected German onslaught, as an ideal occasion for realizing their expansionist ambitions. 'The victories of Germany have intoxicated them like strong wine,' Ambassador Grew recorded in his diary (1 October). But only if Germany won could Japan hope to inherit the estates of Britain, France, and the Netherlands in the Far East.

It is unfortunate that Oikawa's Vice-Minister (appointed on 6 September), who was, no doubt, requested by him, was the soft-spoken Vice-Admiral Toyoda Teijirō. He was a fairly tall, handsome man, blessed with a first-class mind (he was at the top of the class of 1905 at Etajima: 1/171), wealth (through marriage), an attractive personality, and a cosmopolitan outlook. He had spent many years in the 1920s as Naval Attaché in London, spoke English fluently, and looked and carried himself like an English gentleman. He became so identified with the Royal Navy that, soon after he returned to Japan, he gave a talk to naval officers in which he remarked, in a slip of the tongue, with reference to the Royal Navy: 'In our Navy . . .', for which he was much criticized. He never realized his ambition to become Navy Minister, but he did become Foreign Minister in 1941 and Minister of Munitions in the Suzuki Cabinet of 1945. Toyoda had excellent administrative ability and the reputation of being a slick operator. Although he had been one of the most pro-British naval officers, he knew which way the wind was blowing. He joined the pro-German forces, playing a major role in the conclusion of the Tripartite Pact. People spoke of 'Navy Minister Toyoda and Vice-Navy Minister Oikawa'. Matsuoka was at this time putting almost daily pressure on the Navy, using all manner of argument, for example, that if Japan refused to conclude the Pact, Hitler would agitate the 40 million Americans of German and Italian descent to pressure the Government to make war on Japan.[35]

There was apparently one formidable obstacle to the Navy's acceptance of the Pact. 'In particular,' as Oikawa testified at the Tokyo Trials, 'I remained absolutely opposed to accepting the obligation to go to war automatically.' He feared Japan's involvement in a war with the United States, if the Pact were

---

[35] Admiral Toyoda Teijirō, 17 Jan. 1946, Shinmyō, p. 78.

signed in the form to which Stahmer and Matsuoka had agreed on 11 September, with the crucial Article 3 reading: 'in case one of the three is attacked by a power not presently involved in the European war or the China Incident, the three countries shall aid one another by every means, political, economic, and military'. The Naval General Staff, too, had the same major reservation to the Pact. Once Matsuoka assured them on the 13th that Japan would not be obliged to go to war automatically, and would be free to make her own decision on the time and circumstances of her entry into the war, their main objection was immediately removed. In addition, Matsuoka had convinced Oikawa that 'Germany not only did not desire Japan to enter the European war at that time but was even more determined than we to keep the United States out of the war.' Oikawa concluded that 'the navy no longer had any grounds for opposing the proposal. Not only that, but it seemed to me that for the navy to insist stubbornly on its own views (regardless of public opinion...) would lead to a violent internal confrontation.'[36] The top officers in the Ministry and the Naval General Staff, though worried about the implications of the Pact, now regarded it as unavoidable and, with varying degrees of reluctance, accepted it. Actually, the Navy's opposition to the Pact was more fundamental than the mere objection to the automatic participation clause, but it had marshalled no back-up arguments in case. This is what I believe Kondō had in mind when he stated at the Navy leaders' conference on 17 January 1946 that 'as the Vice-Chief of the *Gunreibu*, I was distressed'. Distressed, because the Navy was still against the Pact but could say no more, its main argument taken away.[37]

The Navy took the plunge on 13 September at a meeting of the

[36] Oikawa's affidavit, IMTFE, Defence Document No. 1664. Elsewhere Oikawa used the arguments that Matsuoka had persuaded him that the pressure of the Triple Pact countries plus Russia would be powerful enough to keep the US out of war, and that signing the Pact would contribute to the early termination of the China war. Kudō Muchihiro, 'Nihon kaigun—Shinjuwan e no michinori' [The Japanese Navy and the Road to Pearl Harbor], *Gunji Shigaku* [Military History], xiii, 49 (June 1977), p. 48.

[37] Statements made by Kondō and Enomoto Shigeharu (who had been Legal Adviser to the Navy Ministry) at the Navy leaders' conference, 17 Jan. 1946, Shinmyō, pp. 78–9. Admiral Inoue made the point at the same conference that the *Gunreibu* should have been fully consulted, which it was not, and its full support obtained, since the matter of war was involved in the Treaty as well as foreign relations. He made the further point: 'If the whole Navy did not want the Pact, the Navy should have played its trump card,' i.e., withdrawn its minister from the Cabinet. Ibid. 82. He must have had in mind the Army's use of its trump card when it toppled the Yonai Government in July 1940.

'Five Leaders' at the Navy Minister's official residence. The three officers on the ministry side—Oikawa, Toyoda, and Naval Affairs Bureau Chief Abe—signified their agreement to the Pact. The Vice-Chief of Staff, Kondō, was silent, and only Ugaki, the Chief of Operations Division, was opposed.[38] On the following day, the 14th, a Liaison Conference met and approved the Pact. The next day a meeting of the Navy's top brass was held. Present were all five of the Navy's Military Councillors (Ōsumi Mineo, Nagano Osami, Hyakutake Gengo, Katō Takayoshi, and Hasegawa Kiyoshi), the fleet commanders (Combined Fleet and 1st Fleet, Yamamoto, and 2nd Fleet, Koga), and all Naval District commanders. (On the Military Councillors, see below, p. 245n.) Toyoda chaired the meeting, and Abe briefed it, after which Prince Fushimi stated that 'there is nothing we can do, as the matter has gone so far'. This set the tone for the meeting. Ōsumi, in the naval tradition that the purpose for such meetings was to receive briefings from the responsible authorities, not for consultation, responded that 'the Navy [the Navy's Military] Councillors agree'. But Yamamoto rose and said that if the Pact were concluded, it might cause a clash with the United States, for which the Navy was not ready. In particular, the air force was insufficient, and they would have to double the number of land-based attack-planes. It was not a forceful statement. He had arrived in Tokyo primed with comparison charts depicting the military strength of Japan and the United States. His intention was to restate his opposition to the treaty, which would cause a confrontation between the two Powers, since victory was not probable in view of Japan's insufficient military preparation. However, it appears that he confined himself to secondary matters due to the atmosphere of the meeting.[39]

An Imperial Conference on the 19th reached a final decision to conclude the Pact. It was signed in Berlin on 27 September. Japan

---

[38] *Senshi sōsho*, xci. 458.

[39] Ibid. 458–9. At the Navy leaders' conference on 17 January 1946 Oikawa stated that he had asked Yamamoto to come to Tokyo and had listened to his opinion on the Pact. The occasion appears to have been a different one than that mentioned above, though whether earlier or later we have no way of knowing. To judge from Yamamoto's reaction to the signing of the Pact (below, p. 127), it was earlier. Oikawa claimed that Yamamoto judged that the Navy had to give its approval—it could not be helped, as the situation had become so critical—but that he had asked for a night to think the matter through. Yamamoto returned the next morning. 'Admiral Oikawa,' he said, 'you should give your approval to the conclusion of the Pact; it can't be helped. There is no other means left—i.e. to prevent a great internal upheaval'. Shinmyō, p. 80.

recognized the establishment of a New Order in Europe under the leadership of the Axis Powers (Article 1). Germany and Italy, in turn, acknowledged the leadership of Japan in establishing a New Order in Greater East Asia (Article 2). Article 3 obligated the three Powers 'to assist one another with all political, economic, and military means when one of the three Contracting Powers is attacked by a power at present not involved in the European war or in the Sino-Japanese conflict'. This indirectly referred to the United States and the Soviet Union, but had the United States in mind. So far as Japan was concerned, this article was nullified by a secret note from Ambassador Ott to Matsuoka on 27 September which stated: 'Needless to say, the question, whether an attack within the meaning of article 3 of the Pact has taken place, must be determined through joint consultation of the three contracting parties.' In effect, this reserved to Japan the right to decide whether an 'attack' had taken place. In the next sentence Germany waived the right for herself: 'If Japan, contrary to the peaceful intent of the Pact, be attacked by a power so far not engaged in the European War or the China conflict, Germany will consider it a matter of course to give Japan full support and assist her with all military and economic means.'[40]

Hosoga writes that 'the change in the navy's attitude following Oikawa's appointment as navy minister had great consequences. The reasons for this change are still being debated.' This is because the documents that might show precisely why the Navy finally consented to the Pact, after fighting it for two years, are no longer extant. The main reasons for the Navy's metamorphosis are, however, fairly clear.[41]

[40] Ott had sent this note without authorization from his Government, which was not even aware of it for some time. There was, consequently, from the beginning a serious misunderstanding between the two Governments on the meaning of Article 3. Hosoya, 'The Tripartite Pact', p. 254. On the same day another secret note from Ott confirmed Japan's possession of the former German islands in the central Pacific (the Marianas, Caroline, and Marshall archipelagoes), Japanese League of Nations mandates since the First World War.
[41] To try to find out the motives for the dramatic reversal in the Navy's position the 2nd Demobilization Bureau of the Navy Ministry arranged round-table discussions of the problem on 22 December 1945 and 17 January 1946, which were attended by Yoshida, Toyoda Teijirō, Kondō, Sawamoto, and Inoue, among others who had served in the Navy Ministry or the Naval General Staff. The full proceedings are in Shinmyō. Some of the data obtained is in Japanese Monograph No. 146, pp. 32-5, supplemented by statements made in February 1953 by Captain Omae Toshikazu (1st Section, Naval Affairs Bureau, 1939–42), Admiral Takada Toshitane (former Chief of the 1st Section of the Naval Affairs Bureau), and Admiral Kondō, pp. 36, 53–6.

'WE MUSTN'T MISS THE BUS'

It is important to re-emphasize that the Pact had widespread support in 1940. Many of the flag officers and most of the middle-rank officers, captains and commanders, including section chiefs in the Navy Ministry and Naval General Staff, bent with the prevailing wind and supported the Pact. Many of these, the younger officers particularly, were pro-German in their sympathies, and the German Naval Attaché Admiral Wenneker made a practice of cultivating these officers. There is, for example, this diary entry of 12 July 1940: 'Reception for 140 Japanese officers. My speech was warmly received, and the Vice-Chief of the Naval Staff, Kondo, replied. A very interesting evening, as was evidenced by the large number of younger officers. Bearing in mind that in Japan much of the pressure comes from below, it is of the utmost importance to influence this circle.'[42] Captain Ichimiya Yoshiyuki, the First Adjutant to the Navy Minister, Yoshida, was always most co-operative towards the Germans. He was the leading figure in obtaining permission from the Japanese side regarding sailings, cargoes, etc., of German supply ships and blockade runners. Thus, on 9 January 1940, Ichimiya, apparently on his own initiative, discussed with the German Naval Attaché the suitability of islands near Japan where U-boats and pocket battleships could find anchorages: two in the Aleutians and three in the Marshalls and Carolines. Ichimiya demanded the strictest secrecy. In the event of a British or French protest, the Japanese would deny all knowledge. Unfortunately for the Germans, Ichimiya retired from his post in November 1940. Identified as very pro-German by the German Naval Attaché were Vice-Admiral Kondō, the Vice-Chief of Staff, and Rear-Admiral Abe, the Chief of the Bureau of Naval Affairs. The former told Wenneker on 3 April 1940 that the Imperial Navy would welcome the presence of German naval forces in East Asian waters, especially U-boats, which he believed would have great prospects of success. Vice-Admiral Yamagata Seigó, Chief of the Management Division of the Naval Aviation Department, informed the Attaché on 2 May 1940 that for some time feeling among naval officers up to the rank of captain had been almost 100 per cent pro-German, although a certain proportion of the flag officers still favoured England. 'This was not surprising,' Yamagata went on, 'considering that the Navy had been modelled on the British Navy.

[42] War Diary, German Naval Attaché, PG 32149, Admiralty Project, Reel 481.

But the spirit of the younger officers would carry the older ones along with them.'[43] Another of the senior officers identified as pro-German was retired Vice-Admiral Kobayashi Seizaburō, who was described on 26 February 1940 as a very strong nationalist and leader of the anti-British movement, and said to have great influence in like-minded naval circles. Admiral Ōsumi Mineo, the affable and opportunistic former Navy Minister, whom the Attaché originally regarded as pro-British, showed himself to be thoroughly pro-German in a conversation with the German Ambassador and the Naval Attaché on 25 July 1940. Other extremely pro-German naval officers identified by Wenneker in 1940 included the former Naval Attaché in Berlin, Captain Kojima Hideo, who was now (1939–41) Chief of the 7th Section of the Intelligence Division (Continental Europe, including the USSR). Wenneker described him on 19 September 1940 as 'quite openly pro-German'. Another was Commander Shiba Katsuo, of the Bureau of Naval Affairs. In 1939 he passed intelligence items on the Royal Navy to the Germans.

Shiba was only one of a number of middle-echelon officers in the Ministry and on the Naval General Staff who wanted the alliance. Another was Captain Ishikawa Shingo, section chief of the political division of the *Kōain*, the Asia Development Board (November 1939–November 1940), an agency attached directly to the Prime Minister that handled Chinese political matters. Ishikawa came from Yamaguchi Prefecture, the same one as the Foreign Minister, Matsuoka, and the two had been close friends at least since the early 1930s. He was well known in the Navy for his hard line on the United States and Britain and had long believed that Japan's China policy was destined to collide with that of the United States. From 1935–6 he perceived that Japan was encircled by the ABCD Powers and the Soviet Union, and was concerned with how Japan was to break through these encircling forces. He belonged to that stream of flag officers, represented by flag officers like Katō Kanji, Suetsugu Nobumasa, and Takahashi Sankichi, who held strong views against foreign countries. On a visit to Germany in 1936 he was strongly impressed by Hitler's success in the Rhineland Crisis. He shared the pro-German and anti-American and-British views of the Assistant Naval Attaché in Berlin, the brilliant Lieutenant-Commander

[43] Ibid

'WE MUSTN'T MISS THE BUS'

Kami Shigenori (the top graduate of the Naval War College in 1933), a great admirer of Hitler. Ishikawa and Kami were both very sharp and of the same temper—fire-eaters, extremists, activists, zealots, men given to reaching hasty conclusions. Kami's successor in Berlin was Lieutenant-Commander Shiba Katsuo. In May 1939, when Commander Kami was transferred from the 1st Section of the Bureau of Naval Affairs to 5th Fleet Headquarters (and in November of the same year to the 1st Division of the Naval General Staff)—the Bureau Chief, Rear-Admiral Inoue Shigeyoshi, deemed him altogether too pro-German—Shiba again succeeded him in the same post. Of the four officers who played prominent roles in the push for the Triple Alliance—Abe, Kami, Shiba, and Ishikawa—it was the last named, closely followed by Kami and Shiba, who acted as the driving force. Ishikawa, who had close personal relations with Oikawa, appears to have worked behind the scenes to get the new Navy Minister to conclude the Pact.[44] 'Ishikawa was unusually political among navy men, who were not supposed to get involved in politics.'[45]

Professor Asada has pointed out how in the course of the 1930s Germany replaced Britain as the preferred nation to which the Navy sent its most promising young officers; how upon their return to Japan, these officers 'formed the influential "nucleus group" of the pro-German and anti-American elements in the navy'; and how 'by 1940 the "German faction" had come to occupy some of the key middle-echelon posts that provided the driving force in the navy's policymaking.'[46] The more pro-German officers were generally former naval attachés, assistant naval attachés, and technical officers in Berlin, or officers sent there to study the language, naval architecture, etc. Shiba is a good example, and others are Kami, Kojima, Yokoi Tadao, and Takada Toshitane.[47] I would add that the three top *Gunreibu* officers at this time, Prince Fushimi, Kondō, and Ugaki, had spent some years of their early

---

[44] Ishikawa, *Shinjuwan made no keii*, p. 239.
[45] *Senshi sōsho*, xci. 499.
[46] Sadao Asada, 'The Japanese Navy and the United States', in Dorothy Borg and Shumpei Okamoto (eds.), *Pearl Harbor as History: Japanese–American Relations, 1931–1941* (New York, 1973), pp. 228–9.
[47] The rise in the total number of officers sent to Germany in whatever capacity increased significantly after the termination of the Anglo-Japanese Alliance in 1922 and the need to acquire technological know-how that was no longer available through the Royal Navy:

(*continued*)

123

naval careers in Germany, although this did not seem to have affected Ugaki. By the same token, those officers with experience in the United States or Britain were generally favourable to those Powers. Yamamoto, Toyoda Teijirō, and Toyoda Soemu are good examples. Exceptions included Nagano Osami, who served in the United States in 1913–14 and as Naval Attaché in 1920–3, and Admiral Suetsugu Nobumasa, who had studied English in London in 1914-15 and had then been attached to the battle cruiser *Queen Mary*. The pro-German pressures from within the Navy are an important explanation of the great reversal. There were other factors that finally persuaded the Navy's leaders to conclude the Pact. (1) Matsuoka's assurance that the Pact would permit Japan to decide for herself whether and when to go to war, even if the United States intervened in the European war. (2) His persuasive argument that an alliance would force the United States to act more prudently towards Japan. This would not only improve the prospects of concluding the China Incident (American and British assistance were held to be responsible for China's continuing resistance), but also enable Japan to expand southward without fear of American armed intervention or German claims to the region. There was fear in the Navy that the Germans might extend their influence to the Netherlands East Indies and French Indo-China. As Rear-Admiral Ōno Takeji put it after the war, 'The Navy wanted to demarcate the Japanese and German spheres of influence.' (3) The feeling that the Army, because of its larger role in China, would continue to enjoy priority over the Navy in budgetary allocations, unless the Navy 'adopted a broader view, including the possibility of involvement in war in the South under certain circumstances. The army was already saying that if the navy were so opposed to war with Britain and the United States, it would not need either money or matériel.'[48] A military alliance aimed at the two Powers might, then, reverse the priority enjoyed

---

1906–11: 16; 1912–15: 9; 1916–20: 3; 1921–5: 28; 1926–30: 34; 1931–5: 42. (There are no later figures.) Contrast this situation with the post-war decline in the British figures: 1906–11: 92; 1912–15: 76; 1916–20: 119; 1921–5: 71; 1926–30: 65; 1931–5: 42, the same number as were sent to Germany. The US figures were quite stable from 1916 to 1920: 46 then, and 54 for 1931–5. This material is with the interview records in the Bōeichō Senshibu Archives. We also have figures for 1940: Germany, 16; Britain, 10; US, 14. *Senshi sōsho*, xci. 333.

[48] Butow, *Tojo and the Coming of the War*, p. 167.

by the Army. (4) The pressure of public opinion, as reflected in the leading newspapers, which had become intensely pro-Axis. The catchword in Japan was: 'We mustn't miss the bus.' The Navy was far from immune to this feeling. (5) The fear that a confrontation between the Services might precipitate civil war. When, after the war, Admiral Inoue asked Oikawa why he had signed the Pact, the latter replied that if he had not, there would have been a *coup d'état* by the Army.[49] (6) The confidence of the pro-Germans that a German invasion of England would be successful, an attitude that persisted as late as the spring of 1941, despite the reports of the Naval Attaché in London and the frequently expressed views of the British (8th) Section of the Intelligence Division.[50]

Finally, although most of its leaders distrusted Germany, as

[49] Interview with Admiral Nakayama Sadayoshi, 15 July 1976. Vice-Admiral Fukuchi Nobuo, who was Oikawa's Secretary, confirms that Oikawa was strongly influenced by the strong pro-German feeling in the country and the fear that the Navy's continued refusal to conclude the Pact would lead to civil war. Interview, 15 June 1976. Vice-Admiral Toyoda Teijirō, the Vice-Minister, told Kone, when asked to explain the circumstances of the Navy's reversal: 'To speak the truth, the Navy at heart is opposed to the Tripartite Pact, but since the domestic political considerations no longer permit further opposition on the part of the Navy, the Navy unavoidably approves it.' *The Memoirs of Prince Fumimaro Konoye* (Tokyo, 1946), p. 2. The Prime Minister rebuked him: the Navy should examine the situation from the military standpoint only and should continue its opposition to the Treaty if it considered that it would worsen relations with the US and was not confident it could win a war against her. 'This is the only way the Navy can show its loyalty to the Emperor.' Toyoda replied: 'The situation being what it is, Mr. Prime Minister, please understand and give your sympathy to the Navy's viewpoint.' Kudō Muchihiro, 'Nihon kaigun—Shinjuwan e no michinori', p. 48. Toyoda said much the same thing at the Navy leaders' conference on 17 January 1946: 'The confrontation between the two Services was extreme, and I was under the impression there was a real possibility of an Army *coup d'état*, which would have created an upheaval in the country.... so I felt the Navy should make every effort to avoid such a situation.' Shinmyō, p. 79.

[50] The splendid Attaché in London (February 1939–November 1941) was the tallish, stout, round-faced Captain Kondō Taiichiro (Rear-Admiral, October 1941), who is described by all who knew him as 'a real gentleman' and 'a really nice person'. He had a happy disposition and he spoke English fluently. Although the Admiralty, hitherto friendly to Kondō, changed its attitude to one of suspicion when the Pact was announced, Kondō continued to send reports that Hitler could not possibly launch a successful invasion, because the English Channel was narrow and could be held by the Navy and the RAF, and German landing craft were inadequate. He also spoke of the high state of British morale even after the Dunkirk evacuation. In the case of Captain Horiuchi, the Chief of the 8th Section of the Intelligence Division, against the view of the 7th Section Chief, Kojima, who confidently predicted an early surrender by the British, he always insisted during the Battle of Britain that the British would not surrender, and that, despite the big fanfare, Hitler would not dare to attempt an invasion of England. His judgement was based on the Naval Attaché reports from London, his knowledge of British patience and resourcefulness in the anti-submarine

(*continued*)

reflected for example, in the coolness of the Navy towards the Anti-Comintern Pact, the Navy had by this date become accustomed to co-operation with the Germans. From the early 1920s the Imperial Navy had been receiving technical data about equipment being produced in Germany and had imported submarine engines, torpedoes, aero-engines, and other equipment from German arms manufacturers. Beginning in 1934 there was intimate collaboration until 1945 between the IJN and Hitler's Navy. In June 1936, after prolonged negotiations, the German Naval Attaché had received permission to inspect Japanese ships, shipyards, bases, and other installations. Exchange of naval intelligence about third Powers was initiated by an agreement in August 1937. Initially confined to the Soviet Union, it was extended in April 1939 to include Britain, France, and the United States. The two navies continued to exchange technical information. Thus, the Imperial Navy gave the Germans a blueprint of the aircraft carrier *Akagi* in 1935, following which the Germans sent a naval constructor, a pilot, and a naval officer to Japan. They came on board the *Akagi* and were shown how to fly off and on, and so forth. The German carrier *Graf Zeppelin* was designed on the basis of the data furnished by the Japanese. (Since Goering, the Air Minister, neglected to produce carrier aircraft, the *Graf Zeppelin* was never used effectively in the war.) It was, however, not a one-sided relationship. With the expansion of the Imperial Navy in the later 1930s, experts on marine engines, armour-plating, naval ordnance, range-finders, submarine construction, torpedo manufacture, explosives, and naval aircraft design were dispatched to Germany. The German Navy supplied the Japanese with motor torpedo-boats, Krupp armour plate, and smokeless powder. Fleet Admiral Raeder, the German C-in-C, went out of his way to be kind to the Japanese Naval Attaché, Kojima, often coming with his wife to the Kojima's for dinner. (General Ōshima Hiroshi, the Ambassador, was envious, having had no luck in getting the Army C-in-C to his home!) The Imperial Navy gave little help to German naval operations after

---

campaign of the First World War, and the feeling that the United States would eventually join Britain in the war. Horiuchi made his views known at the weekly meetings of Intelligence Division section chiefs, the Division Chief, and the Vice-Chief of the Naval General Staff, but partly because he was the youngest of the section chiefs, he made no impression. My remarks on Horiuchi's position are derived from Captain Ōi's interview with him on my behalf (Ōi's letter to the author, 24 Nov. 1977) and Admiral Horiuchi's memorandum for me, Nov. 1978.

war broke out in Europe until the overwhelming German successes in the West. German surface raiders in the Indian and Pacific Oceans were permitted the use of Japanese bases from July 1940 for refuelling, etc. (The Japanese were less co-operative in 1941, as will be noted.) The important thing is that the relations between the two navies were quite friendly and co-operative; an alliance, therefore, did not seem too far fetched to many Imperial Navy officers.

4. 'A FORCE LET LOOSE'

The enemies of the Pact in Japan were more farsighted than its supporters, always fearful of a collision with the United States as well as with Britain. Yamamoto was upset, calling the Pact 'impulsive' and 'irrational', and as sure to lead to a Pacific war with the United States. He regretted having taken on the appointment of C-in-C, Combined Fleet, which had kept him away from Tokyo. He even told friends that he was considering retiring to tend the chestnut trees in his garden. When he asked Oikawa for his opinion on the future, the latter replied optimistically: 'It's all right' (*daijōbu*).[51] Oikawa was, in truth, not elated over the Pact. Wenneker's War Diary on 28 September reads: 'German and Italian Naval Attachés called on the Navy Minister and the Chief of the Naval General Staff to express officially the good wishes of their navies as regards the Pact. The Minister extremely cool, but the reception from the Naval Staff was ever so warm.'[52] There was, in fact, considerable unhappiness over the Pact in the *Gunreibu*. The Chief of the 1st Section of the Operations Division, Captain Nakazawa Tasuku, resigned because of it, so certain was he that it would involve Japan in war with Great Britain and the United States. (He had, incidentally, served in the United States.)[53] There

---

[51] Yamamoto to Koga, 23 Jan. 1941, Koga, '*Gohō roku*' [Private Record of Gohō, which was Admiral Koga's pen name], Bōeichō Senshibu Archives. This is a collection of letters and memoranda written by Yamamoto Isoroku, Hori Teikichi, Koga Mineichi, 1940–4.

[52] PG 32150, Admiralty Project, Reel 481.

[53] 'Because I had been against the conclusion of the treaty, I told my senior officers [in the *Gunreibu*] that I could not be responsible for carrying out my duties as a section chief. I repeated this three times before my application for resignation was finally accepted and I was appointed to the command of the heavy cruiser *Ashigara* in October 1940.' Nakazawa claims that almost all the Navy's leaders were against the conclusion of the treaty, but that the Army had pushed it through. Lecture at the Maritime Staff College, 9 June 1971, 'Taiheiyō sensō kaiko to hansei' [Recollections and Reminiscences of the Pacific War], *Kaikankō Hyoron* [Staff College Review] x, 2 (Mar. 1972), 8–9.

was a general feeling in the *Gunreibu* that, contrary to the opinion of the Army General Staff, Britain and the United States could not be separated. This is why when the Navy spoke of war with the 'United States', we must always read 'United States and Britain' or the 'Allied Powers'. The 8th (British) Section of the Intelligence Division had harboured 'a feeling of hatred towards the Pact because its conclusion meant a definite separation from the United Kingdom and the US. It was now definitely clear that the final and unavoidable result would be war with the Allied Powers'.[54] The Ambassador in London, Shigemitsu, the Military Attaché, General Tatsumi, the Naval Attaché, Captain Kondō, and the Counsellor were all shocked when the news of the Pact was announced; the Assistant Naval Attaché, Commander Yoshii Michinori shed tears. The Ambassador in particular was angry at not having received any warning from Tokyo. The Embassy was unable to understand how the many sane elements in Japan had been pushed aside, in view of the Ambassador's reports about the stubbornness of British resistance and their prospects of final victory.[55]

From Japan's point of view, the main purpose of the Pact was to deter the United States from entering the European war and from interfering with Japan in China and her southward advance. The Pact was, secondarily, directed against Britain. American non-intervention in the European war would ensure Britain's defeat by the end of the year, thereby removing her military opposition to Japan's southward drive. A further advantage to Japan was that the Alliance was expected to keep the Soviet Union in check, Germany and the USSR being on friendly terms. The first secret note declared: 'With regard to the relations between Japan and Soviet Russia, Germany will do everything within her power to promote a friendly understanding and will at any time offer her good offices to this end.'

When at this time (September) Captain Yokoyama Ichirō visited Oikawa to say goodbye before leaving for Washington to assume the post of naval attaché, the Navy Minister told him: 'You are not the usual sort of naval attaché, so please don't work hard to collect military information. You should help Ambassador Nomura to

[54] Admiral Horiuchi's memorandum, Nov. 1978.
[55] Major-General F.S.G. Piggott (late Military Attaché in Tokyo), 'Note on Anglo-Japanese Relations with Special Reference to Proposed Mission to Tokyo as Affected by German–Italian–Japanese Pact', 30 Sept. 1940, CAB 63/127. This was inside information that Piggott had obtained from the Japanese Military Attaché.

prevent war with the United States; the Tripartite Pact is a defensive, not an offensive, alliance.'[56] That there was a danger of being sucked into war with both the United States and Britain through Japan's close Axis ties was a contingency not foreseen by Oikawa and the Navy when they finally gave up their opposition to the Alliance. For the pro-Pact forces in the Navy the Alliance was purely defensive. The mere existence of this formidable military combination was expected to keep the United States from resorting to armed force against Japan. In actuality, as Professor Morley brings out, the Pact, by strengthening the aggressive expansionist forces in Japan, was an important step on the road to the Pacific War. 'Deterrence may, of course, be utilized to protect an offensive or a defensive posture. Japan's posture was clearly offensive; but that is not to say that Japan had resolved to go to war with the United States and other western countries at this time. Rather, Japan sought to achieve its offensive or aggressive aims in Asia by deterring its opponents from military intervention, itself not reaching the decision for war with them until a year later when the Hull–Nomura talks had broken down.'[57]

The Pact was a failure in its main aspects. The China Incident was not settled—Germany's good offices were without result (though the German Army, on Hitler's direct order, brought home its military mission in China)—and the Pact brought the United States closer to war, for it spurred the Japanese armed forces, the Navy in the van, to step up the southward advance. This could only lead to war against Britain, with the highly likely support of the United States. Britain would not go to war over her stake in China; a direct threat to her possessions in South-east Asia, indirectly to Australia and New Zealand, was an entirely different matter. In London the Tripartite Pact was viewed as aimed principally at the United States, but as, nevertheless, posing grave dangers to Britain herself. It was Craigie's judgement that the Pact probably contained clauses 'giving Japan a reasonably free hand in Indo-China and Netherlands East Indies, while Germany may also have agreed to take certain definite steps to secure an improvement in Japanese–Soviet relations, leading each to conclude a non-aggression pact'.[58]

[56] Interview with Rear-Admiral Yokoyama, 4 June 1976.
[57] Morley's introduction to Hosoya, 'The Triple Pact, 1939–1940', *Deterrent Diplomacy*, p. 183.
[58] Craigie to Foreign Office, 28 Sept. 1940, COS(40)802, Annex I, CAB 80/20.

Article 1 of the Pact virtually gave Japan that 'reasonably free hand', and the first secret note took care of the Soviet facet.

As Admiral Nagano Osami, who became the *Gunreibu* Chief in 1941, remarked after the war, the Tripartite Pact was 'a force let loose, similar to the water in Lake Erie flowing into the upper rapids and in turn into Niagara; it could not be stopped'. Of those days after the signing of the Pact, Admiral Inoue later remarked, 'I observed that many officers, especially senior officers, were changing their minds and were now inclining towards Germany, together with the Army.'[59] Pro-Pact naval officers saw no big difference between the original Matsuoka–Stahmer automatic participation clause and the revised clause, believing that each country still had the obligation of automatic participation. Of the larger significance of the Pact, Admiral Ōno Takeji asserted: 'If there had been no Tripartite Treaty, there would have been no war between Japan and the United States. The existence of the Treaty was the most significant cause of the Pacific War. The conclusion of the Treaty showed clearly that Japan was against the Allied Powers.'[60]

From the Tripartite Pact until the outbreak of war the pro-war element had the upper hand in the Navy Ministry and the Naval General Staff. Anti-Pact officers were transferred to less important positions, and pro-Pact officers came into the more important positions. In Tokyo four of the leading middle-echelon pro-German naval officers, all with first-class minds, were loosely associated in the very influential 'First Committee' (*Dai Ichi Iinkai*).

The parent of this First Committee was the Navy National Defence Policy Committee (*Kaigun Kokubō Seisaku Iinkai*) established on 12 December 1940 and commonly called the 'Policy Committee' (*Seisaku Iinkai*). Its Chief was the Chief of the Naval Affairs Bureau, whom we have already met as Chief of the *Gunreibu*'s Intelligence Division: Rear-Admiral Oka Takazumi, who had succeeded Abe

---

[59] Inoue Shigeyoshi, *Omoide no ki* [Recollections of an Age] (2 parts, Tokyo, 1956–7), ii. 31–2. Inoue titled the section from which the quotation is taken 'The Navy Took the Wrong Bus.'

[60] Ōno interview, 22 Nov. 1961, Bōeichō Senshibu Archives. Ōno claimed that he had been against the Pact at the time it was concluded. Rear-Admiral Takagi Sōkichi was another who saw 'the close and deep relationship between the Tripartite Pact and the coming of the Pacific War. But nobody can tell whether the war would have broken out without the Pact.' Admiral Takagi interview, 7 Mar. 1962, ibid.

on 15 October 1940 (–July 1944). Oka was not particularly sharp or shrewd, and was cautious in making decisions. He never married; the Navy was his whole life. 'He practically became an Army officer,' a contemporary notes, 'so close was he to the Army and its pro-German views.' The Policy Committee's members came from other jobs in the Navy Ministry and Naval General Staff. Its function was to serve as 'the nerve-center of the Navy's activities, expediting the management of affairs by the regular organs, improving the liaison among departments concerning research projects, and ensuring co-operation among departments for the purpose of achieving prompt results'.[61] Oka said after the war that the Committee 'did not have great significance', but its First Committee (there were four committees) certainly did. Its members were all captains: Takada Toshitane (Chief of the 1st Section of the Bureau of Naval Affairs, November 1940–July 1942); Ishikawa Shingo (Chief of the Bureau's 2nd Section, November 1940–June 1942); Ōno Takeji (1st Division of the Naval General Staff, September 1939–November 1941); and Tomioka Sadatoshi (Chief of the 1st Section, 1st Division, Naval General Staff, October 1940–January 1943). Tomioka and Ishikawa merit special mention.

An important reorganization of the Naval Affairs Bureau had taken place soon after Oka became its Chief. The function of the 2nd Section, which had been naval mobilization, was changed; it now dealt with political and diplomatic affairs, (Naval mobilization was transferred to a newly created bureau, the *Heibikyoku*.) With this reorganization the 1st Section relinquished jurisdiction over political and diplomatic affairs. Captain Ishikawa was appointed the first Chief of the 'new' 2nd Section on Oka's strong recommendation. Oka and Ishikawa had been in a 'junior–senior relationship' ever since their middle-school days in Tokyo, when Oka was Ishikawa's senior by two years. It was Oka who had rescued Ishikawa when the latter was facing severe punishment in connection with the 26 February 1936 Incident (see above, p. 19). It is believed that Oka had selected Ishikawa because he could get 'information' from the Army, but, as the saying goes, he 'went for wool but came home shorn' in his negotiations with the Army authorities.[62] That is, he was dominated and influenced by the

---

[61] *Senshi sōsho*, xci. 494.
[62] Ibid. 524. Ishikawa's reputed ability to get along with the Army, his knowledge of
(*continued*)

Army. As 2nd Section Chief of the Naval Affairs Bureau, Ishikawa promoted his strong ideas whenever opportunity offered, and as the most senior, he took the lead in the Section Chiefs' Conferences. Ishikawa had especially close contact with politically active Army officers and extreme rightist politicians and organizations. The Personnel Bureau Chief, Rear-Admiral Itō Seiichi, had made the Ishikawa appointment reluctantly. His 1st Section Chief advised against it, feeling that it was dangerous to place Ishikawa in such an important position.

As for Tomioka, four generations of his family had served in the Navy, beginning with his paternal grandfather under the Tokugawa Shogunate. His father had been created a baron and promoted to vice-admiral for his services in the Russo–Japanese War. Sadatoshi's son represented the fourth generation in the Navy. Tomioka, the second Baron, was a nice-looking man, a little above medium height and a bit on the stout side, pleasant, rather gentle, courteous, and possessed of a good brain. (This was reflected in his Etajima class standing: 20/89, 1917.) He was widey respected and admired in the Service. Tomioka had spent most of his naval career as a staff officer since his promotion to commander. (He spent over half of the war in the *Gunreibu*. Such a long service there was rare.) His talents ran to operational matters. As a strategy instructor at the Naval War College, he had shown confidence in Japan's ability to fight the United States and Britain, and he carried this confidence with him to the War Plans Section of the Operations Division, when he succeeded the pro-American Nakazawa.

The First Committee existed until the end of the war, but fell into disuse after 1941. Its precise functions are not clear. According to *Senshi sōsho*, it was 'mainly to conduct the planning for concrete implementation measures for the development of national strength and national defence policies, and to conduct liaison with all departments in the Navy, and liaison and guidance with the Army and the *Kōain* [Asia Development Board]'.[63] Professor Asada is

---

Army types, and his presumed capability of eliciting information were qualifications for his posting to the job. The 'information' feature referred to Ishikawa's ability to communicate with the Army, which was quite a precious asset for a ranking IJN officer. Early in 1943 Yamamoto reminisced that 'the Navy had been too permissive towards Ishikawa'. Ibid. He was eventually, in June 1942, transferred to the Yokosuka Munitions Department as the General Affairs Section Chief. He considered it as exile, which it apparently was intended to be.
[63] Ibid. 494.

'A FORCE LET LOOSE'

more helpful: 'This machinery, designed to provide strong "collective leadership", was an outgrowth of the mounting impatience of energetic junior-grade officers with the "vacillation" and "inaction" of upper-echelon leaders. Their aims were to create a consensus of views among the key section chiefs in both the ministry and the General Staff, draft policy recommendations, and press them upon their superiors.... in the pervasive atmosphere of *gekokujō* (rule from below) their recommendations met with little resistance from their superiors, so that for all practical purposes the navy's policymaking came, in the words of one of its members, to "revolve about the First Committee".'[64]

Commander Shiba, who was transferred from the 1st Section of the Naval Affairs Bureau to the 2nd Section in November 1940, and Captain Kami, of the 1st Section of the Operations Division of the *Gunreibu*, were allied with these officers, who, in Asada's words, played a 'catalytic role ... in crystallizing the navy's "determination" to go to war with the United States'.[65] And war with the United States, it was recognized, meant war with Britain as well.

[64] 'The Japanese Navy and the United States', p. 233. The reference to 'rule from below' (or inferiors controlling superiors, or the tail wagging the dog) requires explanation. Two important characteristics of decision-making in Japanese public and private bureaucracies in the period 1868–1945 are the behaviour patterns known as *ringisei* and *nemawashi*. To simplify, under *ringisei* policy was drafted at lower levels and circulated for approval to successively higher levels of an administrative hierarchy. When, in the case of the Navy, the document reached the Minister or Chief of the Naval General Staff and he affixed his seal, it was official policy. This is not to say that the real power of decision rested at lower levels; initiatives might come from the top, and the leaders might closely supervise the preparation of documents. 'To be sure, leaders uncertain of their own authority are influenced by the convictions of people at lower levels in the organization, but more commonly, those at the lower levels of the organization are given leeway to draft documents only when they have the confidence of their superiors.' *Nemawashi* often had a more important role in the decision-making process. This refers to the practice of broad consultation and the achievement of a consensus before taking action. It is *nemawashi* that explains, for example, the *modus operandi* of Liaison and Imperial Conferences, whereas *ringisei* helps to explain the great influence exerted by middle-echelon officers in the Navy's bureaucracy. See Bernard S. Silberman, '*Ringisei*—Traditional Values or Organizational Imperatives in the Japanese Upper Civil Service: 1868–1945', *Journal of Asian Studies*, xxxii, 2 (Feb. 1973), 251–64, and especially Ezra F. Vogel (ed.), *Modern Japanese Organization and Decision-Making* (Berkeley and Los Angeles, 1975), from which (p. xvii) the above quotation is taken. *Ringisei* and *nemawashi* have parallels, of course, in the West (e.g. the clearance system and 'buttonholing' respectively in the United States), but there are differences in the application of the concepts.

[65] According to the post-war recollections of Captain Sanagi Sadamu, a commander in the 1st Section of the Operations Division, the officer who held the strongest opinions in the *Gunreibu* was its senior member, Kami, and that there was a tendency for Tomioka to be led by him. *Senshi sōsho*, xci. 525. Shiba was even-tempered as compared with the firebrands Ishikawa and Kami.

The First Committee officers also shared the view that if Britain were defeated in Europe—it was only a matter of time—Japan would without much difficulty be able to take over British possessions in South-east Asia. They were not averse to helping on the inevitable by entering the war on Germany's side if the United States joined the fray. Kami reflected the views of these and other staff officers in middle-echelon positions when, on 28 October 1940, he told the Army General Staff that Japan's policy vis-à-vis the Netherlands East Indies was bound to lead to war with Britain and the United States. The time to initiate a war would be in April or May 1941, when the Navy would be at 75 per cent of US fleet strength.[66]

At the Imperial Conference on 19 September, Prince Fushimi had restated the Navy's position on the southward advance: that it would be 'attempted as far as possible by peaceful means, and that useless friction with third parties will be avoided'.[67] This was not because of any pronounced pacifist sentiment, but, as his remarks make clear, because the Navy was simply not ready for a war with the United States, let alone the United States and Britain, that would in all likelihood follow the use of force in the south. The Navy's war preparations, especially as regards oil supplies, must be completed before a protracted war could be risked. There was also the consideration, though not mentioned at the Conference, that by early 1942 the Third Replenishment Plan would be completed (the two monster Yamato-class battleships and the two Shōkaku-class carriers were expected to be operational late in 1941), and the Fourth Plan, with its many destroyers and submarines, well on the way to completion.

There were, however, it was generally understood, four cases which would provoke military action because they would threaten Japan's 'very existence'. (1) An all-out American embargo on exports to Japan, in which other Powers joined, 'thus rendering it

[66] TSM, vii, *Nichi-Bei kaisen* [The Outbreak of War between Japan and the United States] (1963), p. 80.
[67] Nobutaka Ike, *Japan's Decision for War: Records of the 1941 Policy Conferences* (Stanford, California, 1967), p. 13. Fushimi on this occasion had offered two other desiderata in agreeing to the Tripartite Pact: that 'every conceivable measure will be taken to avoid war with the United States', and that 'unrestrained discussion of the conclusion of this Pact will not be permitted, and that harmful anti-British and anti-American statements and behavior will be restrained'.

impossible for Japan to acquire essential materials'. (2) American–British co-operation 'to exert pressure upon Japan', and American use of British strategic bases. (3) British or American measures that posed 'a direct threat to the existence of Japan', like a large reinforcement of military strength in East Asia, including the Philippines. (4) 'In case it could be estimated that Great Britain could be defeated, that America would not open hostilities against Japan and that Great Britain and America were completely separated.'[68] Realistically, though, the Navy's leaders did not think it would be possible to separate the two, and that war with one meant war with the other. 'The Navy was of the opinion that once war was declared against Great Britain, Japan would have to be prepared militarily and psychologically to fight also the United States.'[69]

There is no doubt [according to Butow] that the army shared these views. Matsuoka and other members of the diplomatic corps also appreciated the use to which force could be put in certain circumstances. What the members of the Japanese government did thereafter, perhaps more inadvertently than by design, was to create the very conditions in the Far East which the army and navy had already said would require Japan to go to war. And in so doing, the leaders in Tokyo endangered the security of American and British possessions in that area and thus unintentionally provided, *by virtue of their own reasoning*, a clear justification for hostile action against themselves.

The occupation of Hainan, the annexation of the Spratlys, the dispatch of troops to northern French Indo-China, the conclusion of the Tripartite Pact, the creation of a puppet government at Nanking [30 November 1940], the role played in the border dispute between Thailand and French Indo-China [see Chapter Six], and the continuing pressure for an ever-larger share in the economic opportunities of the Netherlands East Indies [Japanese–Netherlands East Indies negotiations re the procurement of oil had begun in September 1940]—separately and together—demanded an Anglo-American response of the type envisaged in the first three instances specified by the Japanese navy.[70]

A harbinger of the type of response envisaged in the first instance occurred in October 1940, and growing Anglo-American co-operation in 1940–1 presaged responses contemplated in the second and third instances.

[68] Japanese Monograph No. 146, pp. 18–19.
[69] Ibid. 19.
[70] *Tojo and the Coming of the War*, p. 203.

V

'We Must Try To Bear Our Eastern Anxieties Patiently'

> The Pact gives us greater reason for supposing that Japanese aggression against the Netherlands East Indies would ultimately be directed against ourselves.
>
> The Chiefs of Staff, 7 October 1940.

> It is only the U.S. Navy which can provide the reinforcement of the naval forces in the Far East necessary to contain the Japanese fleet and provide for the security of all Allied territories and communications.
>
> The Chiefs of Staff, 8 November 1940.

1. BRITAIN AND THE TRIPARTITE PACT

IN August 1940, in pursuance of the policy enshrined in the 'Outline of the Main Principles for Coping with the Changing World Situation' (above, p. 109), Japan presented the Governor-General of French Indo-China with the demand that their troops be allowed into the northern part of the colony (Tongkin), adjacent to the borders of China, for the purpose of blocking off the supply route to Chiang Kai-shek via French Indo-China. An understanding was reached with the Vichy Ambassador in Tokyo on 30 August, but it was not until 22 September, after a Japanese ultimatum on 19 September with a three-day time limit, that an agreement was reached with the Indo-China Government. It provided for the Japanese use of four air bases in Tongkin, the stationing of up to 6,000 Japanese troops to guard the air bases and supplies, and the passage of up to 25,000 Japanese troops through Tongkin north of the Red River. On 23 September troops began to occupy the area. It was the first major move in the southward advance, set the stage for the move into southern French Indo-China the following year. Hattori admits: 'Although the sending of troops into northern French Indochina was intended primarily for an early termination of the China Incident, it was an undeniable fact that some quarters in the Supreme Command desired to make it the initial step in the southward expansion, which was against the will of the Army authorities. However, the sending of troops into French Indochina actually meant that Japan had taken her first step in [the] southward movement.'[1] Middle-echelon naval officers, among them Kami Shigenori, Shiba Katsuo, and Ishikawa Shingo, had supported the aggressive aims of their Army counterparts, 'although their manœuvrings were less conspicuous'.[2]

Posing as it did a threat to Singapore, Malaya, the Philippines, the Netherlands East Indies, and indeed all of South-east Asia, the United States and Britain took a serious view of the occupation. On 26 July the United States had imposed licensing restrictions on aviation fuel and No. 1 heavy melting iron and steel scrap. Now, on 26 September, the United States announced an embargo (effective on 16 October) on the export of all iron and steel scrap, except to the Western Hemisphere and Great Britain. It was patently aimed at Japan, which obtained 91 per cent of these vital war necessities from the United States in 1939. This was extended to iron ore, pig iron, ferroalloy, and certain steel products on 10 December, to various metals on 10 January 1941, and well and refining machinery on 4 February. These sanctions had the effect of cutting Japan off by the winter of 1940–1 from a major source of many strategic commodities. The only item vital to her still being shipped by the United States was oil. On 8 October 1940 (effective on 18 October) the British reopened the Burma Road. (The agreement had been due to expire on the previous day.) What else could Britain do to deter the Japanese or to prepare for the worst?

Craigie suggested on 28 September that a countermove of an early visit of an American naval force to Singapore would have a favourable effect on the Japanese political situation by giving the extremists pause. The Chiefs of Staff had no objection, but when Churchill picked up the cue and suggested to Roosevelt on 4 October that, action speaking louder than words, an American

---

[1] Colonel Takushirō Hattori, *The Complete History of the Greater East Asia War* (4 vols., Center of Military History, Library of Congress, Washington, D.C.), i. 61. This is a direct translation of the Japanese text of Hattori's indispensable *Dai Tōa Sensō zenshi* [The Complete History of the Greater East Asia War] (4 vols., Tokyo, 1953) made by the Headquarters, 500th Military Service Group, in 1953. The pagination differs from the original. Hattori was Private Secretary to Tōjō, 1941–3, then Chief of the Operations Section, Operations Bureau, of the Army General Staff.

[2] TSM, vi, *Nampō Shinshutsu* [The Southward Advance] (1963), p. 243.

'WE MUST TRY TO BEAR OUR EASTERN ANXIETIES PATIENTLY'

squadron, 'the bigger the better', might visit Singapore, the President's advisers recommended against such a provocative step. In December, responding to an Admiralty request for their views, the Naval Attaché in Tokyo, Captain Tufnell, and the Ambassador recommended that the United States send a cruiser division to Manila as a deterrent to a Japanese advance south of Indo-China. Its units could visit British ports independently, 'thus', as the Attaché put it, 'foreshadowing solid British–American co-operation in the event of future dangers'. But the visit of more than a single ship to Singapore in present circumstances, they felt, would be a provocation to the Japanese Navy, as would the dispatch of a *moderately* strong force' to Manila.³

Another proposed form of deterrence emanated from the Foreign Office in November. R. A. Butler, Parliamentary Under-Secretary of State for Foreign Affairs and Chairman of the Far Eastern Committee of the War Cabinet, saw indications that Japan intended to seize control of the rest of French Indo-China (Annam, Laos, Cochin China, and Cambodia), and that she hoped to establish a naval base at Camranh Bay. 'This would facilitate pressure upon Thailand, and any further advance which Japan may contemplate towards Malaya and the Netherlands East Indies. In these circumstances there is an urgent need to strengthen our defences in the Far East, not only with the object of offering successful resistance to any attack which may be made, but even more for the purpose of showing Japan by our preparedness that she would be unwise to make the attempt, and also of strengthening the courage and stiffening the resistance of the territories which Japan seeks to penetrate.' Butler raised the question whether it might be possible to revert to the course that the Chiefs of Staff had reluctantly been prepared to consider in their appreciation of 7 August (above p. 85n), namely, that a battle cruiser and an aircraft carrier should be based on Ceylon. 'They would ostensibly be sent there as a

---

³ Craigie to Foreign Office, 13 Dec. 1940, ADM 116/4657. Matsuoka, in one of his typical long monologues, had explained to Craigie that there was no thought of attacking Malaya unless the Americans moved a powerful squadron to Singapore. 'Nothing would provoke this [war with either Britain or the United States] except American entry into the European war or some serious provocation such as the visit of a powerful American squadron to Singapore.' Matsuoka apparently had in mind the moving of a powerful squadron, not just a courtesy visit of individual American warships, to Singapore. Churchill marked the Malaya/Singapore reference: 'Foreign Secretary. A serious warning.' Craigie to Foreign Office, 9 Nov. 1940, PREM 3/156/6.

deterrent to commerce raiders in the Indian Ocean.... Meanwhile, they would have a stimulating effect upon the morale not only of countries such as Indo-China, Thailand and the Netherlands East Indies which are most susceptible to Japanese pressure, but also upon the people of China and upon our own peoples in Malaya and Burma. The dispatch of these ships would also hearten Australia and New Zealand and help to reassure them as to the safety of their lines of communication with Africa, the Middle East and Europe.'[4]

Halifax passed the memorandum to the First Lord with a mild endorsement. The Admiralty reply contained no surprises. Despite the success at Taranto on the night of 11 November (British torpedo aircraft had attacked the Italian warships in the harbour, sinking three battleships, half the Italian battle fleet), they were unable to send reinforcements to the East because at least five armed raiders were out on the Atlantic trade routes, and they had lost the battleship *Resolution* (heavily damaged in the Dakar operation, 25 September) for many months. The Admiralty 'must put first things first' and 'concentrate our forces on beating Italy and Germany. The Navy, despite Taranto, is still stretched to the utmost in coping with this task.'[5]

The Chiefs of Staff had quite different ideas than the Foreign Office on how to cope with the new situation. After examining the implications of the Tripartite Pact, they concluded that Japan had not gained any advantage commensurate with her obligations under the Pact, unless she had obtained some further *quid pro quo* not yet divulged, such as the acknowledgement of her right to annex Allied possessions in the Far East. Were that the case, Japan might be tempted to take advantage of the impending American

[4] FE 40(65), Butler's memorandum for the Foreign Secretary, 'Far Eastern Situation', 23 Nov. 1940, CAB 96/1. The Far Eastern Committee had been established in October 1940 to monitor British policy in the Far East.

[5] Alexander to Halifax, 29 Nov. 1940, ADM 1/10865. Butler was not impressed with this line of reasoning. As he informed the Far Eastern Committee: 'diplomatic persuasion and economic pressure depend for their ultimate effectiveness upon a backing of potential force. It is true that it is difficult to build up our defences in the Far East without imperilling our position elsewhere, but Japan will continue to be a real danger on our flank in the present war until, by increasing our own armed strength in the Far East and by creating a firm front with the United States we can convince her that it will not be worth her while to intervene.' WP(40)484, 'Report by the Far Eastern Committee. Memorandum by the Secretary of State for Foreign Affairs', 18 Dec. 1940, CAB 66/14. The Alexander and Butler communications point up so neatly the perennial conflict over priorities between the Admiralty and the Foreign Office. Which considerations came first, the naval/strategical or the political? Each side believed it had the right answer.

presidential election and Britain's 'embarrassment in Europe' to obtain control of the Netherlands East Indies and Indo-China in the near future.

(i) The Pact gives us greater reason for supposing that Japanese aggression against the Netherlands East Indies would ultimately be directed against ourselves. If we failed to support the Dutch there would be a grave risk to our whole position in the Far East.

(ii) We have now a better chance of obtaining American support and the danger of our having to fight Japan alone is correspondingly reduced. Failure to support the Dutch would, moreover, seriously alienate American opinion and this might indeed result in our having subsequently to fight the Japanese alone after they were established in the Netherlands East Indies and possibly in Indo-China as well.[6]

For the moment, at least, all the Service Chiefs were after was an interchange of military information with the Dutch Services similar to the interchange that was already in progress between representatives of the US and British navies. It was based on the hypothesis that war had broken out with Japan and the two countries were allied; no political commitment was implied, and the stage of considering joint plans had not been reached. As soon as the Government's approval was given, the Foreign Office approached the Netherlands Government-in-exile (London) with the suggestion of a British–Dutch exchange, which would facilitate full cooperation in war between their forces, if the time came for them to act together. The C-in-C of the Dutch Naval Forces, Vice-Admiral Furstner, at a meeting with Rear-Admiral Bellairs at the Admiralty, expressed the displeasure of his Government with the evasive replies his Government had received from the British and American Governments as to whether they would come to the assistance of the Netherlands East Indies in case of a Japanese attack. His Government was, nevertheless, willing to proceed with the exchange of information, and this took place. Thus, on 21 November the Admiralty received answers to the questions handed to Furstner on 31 October regarding naval bases in the Dutch East Indies, etc. At the end of November, when the Dutch Chief of the General Staff visited Singapore for discussions with the British Cs-in-C, Far East, agreement was reached on the broad lines of

[6] COS(40)808, 'The Far East: Implications of the German–Italian–Japanese Pact. Draft Report', 7 Oct. 1940, CAB 80/20. There was no final report.

wartime co-operation—for example, that the Dutch would be responsible for local naval defence up to certain geographical limits. It was understood by both sides that no political commitment was involved. The two Governments approved the agreement in principle and also adopted other forms of co-operation such as a common code, the interchange of liaison officers, and, when it became possible, British provision of armament and equipment for the Netherlands East Indies forces.

The Service Chiefs had their eyes on the Dutch East Indies for the rest of the year and beyond. There were reports at the end of October that the Japanese were growing increasingly dissatisfied with the progress of negotiations with the Dutch for an increase of oil shipments. Other reports had it that Japan might occupy the Islands if she thought the United States planned to sign an agreement with the Dutch for bases in the East Indies (similar to the bases/destroyers agreement with the British). Early in November the Admiralty received intelligence that the Japanese were withdrawing sizable military forces from China, possibly for 'the much heralded advance south'. It was more imperative than ever for the naval planners to enlist the support of the US Navy in the Far East and to co-ordinate strategy with it for such a contingency.

2. AGAIN THE AMERICANS

On 17 June 1940 the British Ambassador in Washington, the Marquess of Lothian, reported President Roosevelt as favouring Staff talks. The Chiefs of Staff were all for them, and the Admiralty at once began to make preparations. Already, on 15 June, at the suggestion of the new Director of Plans, Captain Charles Daniel, which was endorsed by Pound, and with the approval of Churchill (as Defence Minister) and the War Cabinet, a special Admiralty committee had been established under Admiral Sir Sidney Bailey, with officers representing divisions of the Naval Staff. The Committee was in regular touch with the First Sea Lord through his principal Naval Assistant, Rear-Admiral R. M. Bellairs. The directive to Bailey was 'to formulate proposals for co-operation with US Naval Forces in the event of the intervention of the U.S.A. on the side of the Allies'.

At the beginning of July, the Prime Minister authorized the exchange of information with the United States regarding secret equipment, provided that the specific secrets and items for exchange were reported to the Cabinet beforehand. On 24 September discussions were initiated between Admiral Ghormley and the US Naval Attaché in London, Captain Alan G. Kirk, and the Bailey Committee and NID representatives for co-operation between the two naval intelligence services in the Far East.

These were, however, marginal matters so far as the British authorities were concerned. All along they hoped for active American naval assistance in the event of a Japanese attack. Especially did they want the US Pacific Fleet, or a contingent of it, to join a British fleet at Singapore. The first suggestion that the major part of the US battle fleet be shifted to Singapore, as a peacetime deterrent or for wartime offensive operations in the South-west Pacific and South China Sea, had been made in Hampton's conversations with Leahy and Ghormley in May 1939. Early in 1940 Lothian had discussed such a possibility with Roosevelt. In a personal message of 15 May 1940 to Roosevelt, Churchill had intimated that the stationing of a US naval force at Singapore was one of the most helpful forms of assistance the US could render the British. 'I am looking to you to keep the Japanese dog quiet in the Pacific, using Singapore in any way convenient.'[7] The Admiralty communicated a similar proposal to the US Naval Attaché on 17 May. But Roosevelt and the State Department were not interested, nor was the Chief of Naval Operations. The Americans decided in July to keep their main naval force, the Pacific Fleet, at Pearl Harbor and not send a detachment to the Far East, whether to Manila or Singapore. (The Pacific Fleet, normally based on San Diego, had been concentrated at Hawaii since the completion of manœuvres in May 1940.)

Nor had anything come of the initial American interest in Staff conversations. This became all too clear when Rear-Admiral Ghormley, now Assistant CNO, arrived in London on 15 August to serve as 'Special Naval Observer'. With him were two Generals representing the Army. Their brief was to form an 'objective estimate of Great Britain's ability to resist invasion' and to gather information for future planning. Genuine Staff talks on strategy and co-operation in war, the British quickly learned to their dismay, were not within the scope of the mission's functions. This did not

[7] Churchill, *The Second World War*, ii, *Their Finest Hour* (1949), pp. 22–3.

discourage them from putting their strategic concerns before the Americans. On 31 August Pound stressed the immense importance of American co-operation in a war with Japan: the support of her battle fleet would transform the entire strategical situation in the Far East. Under existing conditions, he pointed out, no more than a battle cruiser and an aircraft carrier, to be based on Ceylon, could be sent out. The Royal Navy consequently would have to confine its activity in the Far East to an attempt to control the Indian Ocean. However, Pound did not believe the threat from the Japanese was imminent. They were 'a cautious people' and seemed 'anxious to avoid hostilities with us'. What he had in mind was that a strong detachment of the US Fleet, sent to reinforce the small US Asiatic Fleet and acting in concert with British and Allied naval and air forces in the South-west Pacific, might make Japan hesitant to advance southward. British policy 'must obviously be a temporizing one of playing for time by giving way on non-vital points, and by building up our resources as fast as we can. Our first object is the defeat of Germany and war with Japan would certainly jeopardize this.'[8] Ghormley explained why his Government could not consider the British proposal: the need to keep the US Fleet concentrated; the serious, perhaps insuperable, logistical difficulties if US forces operated 6,000 miles from American supply and repair bases; and the probability that US naval forces would be required in the Atlantic, if priority in a two-ocean war were given to the defeat of Germany and Italy.

The British recommendation was repeated in a different form at a series of meetings at the Admiralty between Ghormley and the Bailey Committee (17 September–16 October). On the assumption that the US Fleet would be concentrated in the Pacific, the Committee proposed that strong forces be moved into the South-west Pacific and South China Sea—specifically, to Singapore, Australia, or the Philippines—to deter Japan from any move to the south, particularly to the Netherlands East Indies. Ghormley was once more cool, while stating that his views were his own, not necessarily those of the Navy Department. Besides reiterating the

---

[8] Captain Tracy B. Kittredge (USN), 'United States–British Naval Co-operation, 1940–1945' (unpublished MS, 1946? US Operational Archives), Sec. iii, Pt. C, App. A, pp. 278–9. The US Pacific Fleet was composed of battleships, aircraft carriers, cruisers, and the necessary smaller forces. The US Asiatic Fleet, a much smaller force based on Manila, consisted of cruisers, destroyers, and submarines only.

logistical argument, he pointed out that the First Sea Lord and other Naval Staff officers had themselves suggested that the Royal Navy was not sufficiently strong in the Atlantic, and therefore US naval assistance would probably be required there, in addition to whatever action might be taken in the Pacific. American strategy, he went on, envisaged a naval offensive from Hawaii, where the Fleet was concentrated, into the Western Pacific as soon as possible *after* the beginning of a war with Japan.

And still there had been no formal Staff conversations. Ghormley had operated as little more than a 'a quasi-official fact-finder', and his conversations with the Bailey Committee and other Naval Staff officers in the autumn were limited to an exchange of technical information, disclosure by the British of their war experience, discussion of arrangements for closer co-operation between the two naval commands in Asiatic waters, including an exchange of visits between officers of the staffs of the C-in-C, Asiatic Fleet, and of the British Naval Commander at Singapore, and an agreement to work out combined communication methods, procedures, and systems for use in a war that found the two navies allied. All this, however, was a profound disappointment to the Admiralty, which had hoped that Ghormley's instructions included a discussion of the strategical and tactical employment of the combined fleets in the event of the US entering the war. But it was evident that the Americans were for domestic political considerations (the strength of the isolationist forces) still not eager to tie their hands. It would be 'political dynamite', in the words of the CNO, Admiral Harold Stark. 'Get in on any and all staff conversations you can,' he instructed Ghormley on 17 October. 'Go as far as you like in discussions—with the full understanding you are expressing only your own personal views as to what best to do—"if and when"—but such must not be understood to commit your government in any manner or to any degree whatever.'[9] In a personal letter to Ghormley on 16 November Stark went a step further: 'a theoretical plan, which can be a practical plan, can and should, in my opinion, be drawn up ... with the other fellow fully understanding *that it is on our own, without any backing from State Department or the White House or anyone else*'.[10]

[9] Ibid. 239.
[10] Ibid. 241. Samuel Eliot Morison gives us this pen portrait of the CNO. Stark, 'with his
(*continued*)

Roosevelt, while making it plain at the end of October that genuine Staff conversations could not be undertaken at that time, wanted to know what Britain would like from the US Navy. This gave the Admiralty a fresh opportunity to make their case for the concentration at Singapore—all along, their first preference—of the minimum force necessary to hold the Japanese while all other forces were concentrated on defeating the Axis Powers in the European and Atlantic theatres, which alone could bring about the termination of the war. The paper was not coy about pointing out that of the naval forces required at Singapore (at least eight capital ships, three carriers, and a number of cruisers, destroyers, and submarines), 'the greater part' would have to be provided by the United States.[11] The First Sea Lord elaborated the basic British strategical idea to the American Naval Attaché, Captain Kirk, on 19 November. The assumption was that the United States and Japan entered the war simultaneously. The Royal Navy could be counted on to safeguard Allied interests in the Atlantic, leaving the US Fleet free to operate against Japan. The vital theatres were in Europe and the Mediterranean, since the primary objective of the war was the defeat of Germany and Italy. Once that was accomplished, they would deal with Japan. In the meantime, Japan must be contained, and here the US Fleet had a key role to play:

if the Japanese could be prevented from extending their operations southward to the Dutch East Indies–Singapore area, the resulting economic pressure on the Japanese would be sufficient to curtail her effective participation on the side of the Axis powers, at least until such time as more aggressive measures could be taken. . . .

In explaining this basic strategical idea, it was pointed out that Singapore must be held at all costs. This, in their judgement, was the key position. It was an adequate fleet base from which allied forces could prevent the Japanese from extending the Asiatic theatre of the war into the Indian Ocean. . . .

With the U.S. Fleet, or a substantial portion of it, based upon Singapore,

---

pink complexion, benevolent countenance, rimless spectacles and thick shock of white hair, looked more like a bishop than a sailor. Gentle in manner and unobtrusive in personality, he had one of the best brains in the Navy . . .' *History of United States Naval Operations in World War II* (15 vols., Boston, 1947–62), i. 41. Stark was slow to make up his mind, but it had been made up as regards US priorities: if the US became involved in war, hemispheric defence would be the Number One objective, with a defensive strategy employed in the Pacific.

[11] 'Allied Naval Dispositions in the Event of Japan Joining the Axis and the United States Entering the War on Our Side', n.d. (late Oct.), ADM 205/6. Pound and Phillips had redrafted a Bellairs paper.

it was their considered opinion that the Japanese Fleet would be contained north of the whole chain of Islands comprising the Dutch East Indies. The balance of the U.S. Fleet could then assist the British Navy in operations against the Germans and Italians.[12]

At an important meeting held at the Admiralty on 22 November between Ghormley and Kirk and the Bailey Committee the British estimated the force the Americans should send to Singapore at nine capital ships to contain Japan's 10 battleships and, if necessary, operate against them. The US Navy Department, however, were apparently prepared to contemplate the loss of Singapore, as well as of the Dutch East Indies and the Philippines, since they proposed to keep only a few capital ships at Hawaii and to send the greater part of their forces into the Atlantic. It was Ghormley's personal view that 'it would be difficult to educate American public opinion to understand the necessity for denuding Hawaii' to the extent of dispatching nine of the 12 battleships there to the Far East. Besides, 'the presence of a striking force at Hawaii would almost certainly prevent the Japanese from moving the whole of their fleet south. In any case, he felt certain that if 8 or 9 capital ships were to go to the Far East, it would be impossible to withdraw any battleships from the Pacific to operate in the Atlantic.' These views were hardly consonant with the Admiralty's proposed distribution of US capital ships: nine at Singapore (plus the battleship in the Asiatic Fleet), none at Hawaii, and the remaining five in the Atlantic, where there were presently three.[13]

Admiral Stark bluntly rejected the strategical views expressed by Pound on 19 November and by the British representatives at the 22 November meeting. He instructed Ghormley (7 December) to inform the Admiralty that

> The disposition of U.S. naval forces proposed above does not provide sufficient support of U.S. interests and is therefore not acceptable. Please inform British Authorities that their representatives for Staff Conversations [see below] should have instructions to discuss concepts based on equality of considerations for both the United States and British Commonwealth and to explore realistically the various fields of war co-operation. The Chief of Staff of the U.S. Army and the Chief of Naval Operations are

---

[12] Kirk, 'Notes on Conversation with the First Sea Lord', 19 Nov. 1940, ADM 199/691.
[13] 'Record of a Meeting Held at the Admiralty on 22nd November, 1940', 25 Nov. 1940, ADM 199/1159.

agreed that no useful purpose would be served by Staff Conversations at this time if British conferees are restricted in their instructions as to the concept of co-operation, the only basis of discussions being that set forth above in the conversations with the First Sea Lord and with the Bailey Committee.[14]

Ghormley so informed Admiral Bailey on 9 December. Bailey's explanation of the tone of the Navy Department's message, derived from Ghormley, was that they (the Navy Department) had to consider three things: 'The press in formulating policy, and may therefore appear unduly cautious of United States interests in the Atlantic and Eastern Pacific'; the fact that 'a section of public opinion is not convinced that Britain can win even with full United States assistance at sea'; and that the presence of US forces at Singapore 'would be misinterpreted "as pulling British Chestnuts out of the fire"—a cry constantly raised by the Isolationists. Unfortunately the vital importance of Singapore to the British Empire, and therefore indirectly to the United States, is not grasped by public opinion and possibly not by the Navy Department.'[15]

In the meantime Stark had already stated on 12 November the basic American naval strategy (what came to be known as 'Plan Dog' or 'Plan D') in a memorandum to the Navy Secretary Frank Knox. If the US became a British ally in war against the Axis and Japan, the European theatre would be the decisive one, with a strictly defensive strategy adopted in the Pacific. One concept of this 'limited war' strategy was the reduction of Japan's offensive power through an economic blockade. This would involve among other things the British and Dutch 'holding the Malay Barrier [Singapore–Timor]', which would require help from the US Asiatic Fleet and ships and aircraft drawn from the fleet at Hawaii. An alternative form of limited war would call for the capture by the main fleet of the Marshalls or the Carolines (or both), 'for the purpose of diverting away from Malaysia important Japanese forces to oppose it, and thus reducing the strength of their assault against the Dutch and British'. 'It is out of the question to consider sending our entire Fleet at once to Singapore. Base facilities are far too limited, the supply problem would be very great, and Hawaii, Alaska, and our coasts would be greatly exposed to raids.' 'Admiral

[14] ADM 199/1232.
[15] Bailey, 'Disposition of US Naval Forces', 9 Dec. 1940, ibid.

'WE MUST TRY TO BEAR OUR EASTERN ANXIETIES PATIENTLY'

Stark's unwillingness to risk an unlimited war in the Pacific rested', two scholars claim, 'on his belief that the British were not strong enough by themselves to hold their empire together and perhaps not strong enough to hold even the British Isles.'[16] The CNO had concluded his Plan Dog memorandum by advising the immediate commencement of secret and formal Staff conversations with the British naval and military authorities to reach agreement on strategy, should the two Powers be allied in a war against Germany, Italy, and Japan.[17] On 29 November the President had agreed to such talks taking place in Washington, and the invitation went out to the British Chiefs of Staff on 2 December. Staff talks being precisely what they had been pressing for, the Chiefs of Staff wasted no time in expressing agreement (4 December). Pound tried to erase Stark's impression that the British representatives would take a cast-iron stand in the forthcoming talks. With the approval of the COS Committee he informed the CNO on 12 December that the British representatives would 'not be bound by any rigid instructions', and would 'take into full account all interests involved'. Churchill backed this diplomatic approach at a meeting of the Defence Committee (Operations) of the War Cabinet on 17 December.[18]

It would be most unwise to try and force our views on naval strategy in that [Pacific] theatre upon the United States Naval authorities. Our delegation should open the discussion by saying that they recognised that

---

[16] Maurice Matloff and Edwin M. Snell, *United States Army in World War II: Strategic Planning for Coalition Warfare, 1941–1942* (Washington, 1953), p. 26.

[17] The full text of Stark's memorandum is in James H. Herzog, *Closing the Open Door: American–Japanese Diplomatic Negotiations, 1936–1941* (Annapolis, 1973), pp. 241–55. Captain A. W. Clarke, who had since July been acting as a liaison between the Admiralty and the US naval authorities, was shown a copy on 20 November. Plan Dog was the dominant US naval strategy from then until the Pacific War broke out a year later. On US naval strategical thinking generally in the pre-war years, see Waldo H. Heinrichs, Jr., 'The Role of the United States Navy', in Borg and Okamoto, *Pearl Harbor as History*, pp. 641–9.

[18] The Ministerial Committee for Military Co-ordination (1937–40) (Minister for the Co-ordination of Defence, Chairman, the three Service Ministers, and the Minister of Supply, with the Service Chiefs in attendance) made recommendations to the War Cabinet or took decisions which were presented to the War Cabinet for confirmation. On becoming Prime Minister in May 1940, Churchill replaced it with the Defence Committee. The latter was chaired by the Prime Minister in his capacity as Defence Minister. This Committee worked in two panels, one for Operations and one for Supply, of which the former, the more important one, was at this time composed of the Prime Minister, Deputy Prime Minister (Attlee), the Service Ministers, the Foreign Secretary, the Minister of Supply, and the Chiefs of Staff. All references to the Defence Committee hereafter will be to the Operations panel.

the United States Navy would be in charge in the Pacific, and that the American views on strategy in that theatre must prevail. They would not be asking the Americans to come and protect Singapore, Australia, and India against the Japanese, but would offer the use of Singapore to the Americans if they required it. If the delegation adopted this attitude, it might well be that as the war proceeded the Americans might spontaneously wish to enter more fully into the conflict against Japan, and thus be led of their own volition to send more considerable forces to Singapore. Nothing should stand in the way of the main principle, which was that all efforts should be directed to the defeat of Germany—the minimum force being left to hold Japan in check.

The Chiefs of Staff, Pound declared, fully agreed with the view that the delegation should not try to exert pressure on the Americans to fall in with their views on Pacific strategy.[19]

The Admiralty and the Prime Minister were, however, in complete disagreement on strategic objectives in the Pacific. Churchill found Plan D

strategically sound and also most highly adapted to our interests. . . .

Should Japan enter the war on one side and the United States on ours, ample naval forces will be available to contain Japan by long-range controls in the Pacific. The Japanese Navy is not likely to venture far from its home bases so long as the superior battle-fleet is maintained at Singapore or at Honolulu. The Japanese would never attempt a siege of Singapore with a hostile, superior American Fleet in the Pacific. The balance of the American Fleet, after providing the necessary force for the Pacific, would be sufficient, with our Navy, to exercise in a very high degree the command of all the seas and oceans except those within the immediate Japanese regions. A strict defensive in the Far East and the acceptance of its consequences is also our policy. Once the Germans are beaten the Japanese would be at the mercy of the combined fleets.[20]

Professor Leutze has drawn attention to the weaknesses in Churchill's thinking. 'Did the prime minister see that if the U.S. Navy shifted major units to the Atlantic the United States would no longer have a "superior" fleet on Japan's flank protecting Singapore? And did he realize that Far Eastern requirements would

---

[19] DO(40) 51st Mtg., CAB 69/1. The Prime Minister gave particular directions to the British delegation that their attitude in the discussions on naval strategy 'should be one of deference to the views of the United States in all matters concerning the Pacific theatre of war'. COS(40) 1052, 'British–United States Technical Conversations', 19 Dec. 1940, CAB 80/24.
[20] Churchill's minute to Alexander and Pound, 22 Nov. 1940, CAB 84/24.

have to assume a higher priority for the British if they were to assume a lower one for the Americans? These details Churchill was willing to skim over; everything paled next to getting the United States committed to some forward policy.'[21] Plan Dog was anathema to the Admiralty, to say nothing of the Foreign Office. They had no use for a strategy that wrote off the Western Pacific, above all, Singapore, which must be held at all costs, and opposed basing the combined fleet at Singapore, the best place from which to contain the Japanese.

A meeting of the VCNS (Phillips), ACNS(F) (Rear-Admiral Sir Henry Harwood), D of P (Daniel), and Admirals Bailey, Bellairs, and Danckwerts on 10 December discussed the attitude to be adopted towards the American views on Allied strategy in the Pacific. Singapore, they agreed, was the 'proper place' for the combined fleets in a war with Japan, but there might be great difficulty in persuading the American naval, and even more the political, authorities to accept this view. It was also agreed that they 'might accept the presence of their main Pacific Fleet at Hawaii instead of Singapore', if that fleet were prepared to threaten Tokyo and other Japanese cities with carrier aircraft. The mere threat of such action would probably be enough to prevent the Japanese from sending their fleet to the south, or to withdraw it if already dispatched. 'If, on examination, however, they [the Americans] found such an offensive policy impracticable it seems quite possible that they themselves would suggest the necessity of basing their Fleet further to the westward, which means, of course, Singapore.' If the British accepted the US main fleet at Hawaii, they should ask the Americans to strengthen their Asiatic Fleet by two capital ships and base this force on Singapore. The Royal Navy would probably send the *Renown* and a carrier to the Indian Ocean to deal with Japanese raids in that area.[22] No such flexibility, however, was revealed in the First Sea Lord's position on 7 January 1941, on the eve of the departure of the British delegation for Washington. He advised Ghormley that 'Singapore is the only naval base in the Far East available' to Allied Forces; Singapore was 'most important' because of British interests in Persia, South-east Asia, and the Pacific Dominions; if Singapore were held, it would probably prevent the

[21] James R. Leutze, *Bargaining for Supremacy: Anglo-American Naval Collaboration, 1937-1941* (Chapel Hill, North Carolina, 1977), p. 200.
[22] 'Minutes of Meeting held in D. of P.'s room on 10th December, 1940', ADM 199/1232.

Japanese from taking the Philippines; nine US battleships and support craft would hold Singapore 'until such time as Germany and Italy are disposed of', at which time, if Japan were still fighting, a united effort would be made against her; three American battleships and support craft 'would prevent any raids against the American West Coast or North Pacific holdings'; and the present US force in the Atlantic was capable of assisting convoy work, dealing with German raiders, and preventing Axis aggression against the Western Hemisphere.[23]

The official US position on the eve of the Staff discussions closely followed Plan Dog. The United States would stand on the defensive in the Pacific; the principal military effort would be directed towards the crushing of the Axis Powers. Neither side had succeeded in convincing the other of the correctness of its strategic priorities regarding Pacific strategy. The Washington talks did not bode well.

The year ended pretty much as it had begun so far as the naval situation in the Far East was concerned. In a telegram of 8 December to the Australian Prime Minister, R. G. Menzies, thanking him for his promised help at Singapore, Churchill first gave the bright side of the picture. The danger of Japan going to war with the British Empire was 'definitely less' than in June, after the collapse of France, and the naval and military successes in the Mediterranean had weakened Italy and made the mobility of the Mediterranean Fleet 'potentially greater'. Until the Italian Fleet had been knocked out, however, and Italy herself 'broken as a combatant', they could not send a strong naval force to Singapore. 'We must try to bear our Eastern anxieties patiently and doggedly until this result is achieved, it always being understood that if Australia is seriously threatened by invasion we should not hesitate to compromise or sacrifice the Mediterranean position for the sake of our kith and kin.'[24] It was a tired refrain, reiterating once more that, failing a crushing blow to the Italians, and barring an emergency, a strong fleet could not be sent to the Far East. There was as always only one effective way out of the cruel dilemma: American naval assistance. The First Lord's letter to Halifax of 29

---

[23] Leutze, *Bargaining for Supremacy*, pp. 212–13.
[24] PREM 3/156/6.

'WE MUST TRY TO BEAR OUR EASTERN ANXIETIES PATIENTLY'

November had concluded: 'Surely the real deterrent to Japanese aggression in the Far East can only be found in the willing and open co-operation of the United States?' The Staff conversations in Washington were about to determine how far the Americans were prepared to go. But first we must examine the backdrop in Japan against which this and other developments in 1941 occurred.

VI

Tokyo: Collision Course
(January 1941–October 1941)

[To achieve her objectives in the South] Japan will not refuse war with Great Britain and the United States.

Imperial Conference, 2 July 1941.

In the event that there is no prospect of our demands being met by the first ten days of October through the diplomatic negotiations mentioned above, we will immediately decide to commence hostilities against the United States, Britain, and the Netherlands.

Imperial Conference, 6 September 1941.

The 2 July Imperial Conference decision had made a Pacific war inescapable; that of 6 September made it definite.

SHIGENORI TŌGŌ, The Cause of Japan (1956).

1. 'TIME IS NOT ON OUR SIDE'

THE Tripartite Pact was for the Japanese armed forces only the first step: the means to an end. Caution, nevertheless, continued to prevail until the spring of 1941. The Navy was still for an advance that proceeded in easy stages and would not provoke hostilities with the Western Powers, at least not before war preparations were completed and the China Incident settled. When on 10 February 1941 the competent authorities of the Army Department of IGHQ presented a draft statement to their opposite numbers in the Navy Department that called for seizing a favourable opportunity to employ force against Malaya and the Dutch East Indies in order to solve the Southern Area problem once and for all, the Navy officers would not play. This policy, they pointed out, would provoke war with the United States as well as Britain, the two being inseparable. As spelled out towards the end of March in a series of conferences between the two High Commands, the Navy was for the use of force in the Southern Area only if the United States increased her military pressure upon Japan or imposed an all-out embargo against her. Let us see how the Navy's circumspect policy applied in particular situations.

After Britain's Dunkirk evacuation in June 1940, the Army General Staff had proposed to the Naval General Staff an operation to capture Singapore. The Operations Division would not agree, since it would mean instant war with the United States as well as Great Britain.[1] The same argument was made by the Navy when, early in 1941, the Germans proposed on several occasions that Japan attack Singapore as soon as possible. Thus, on 4 March the German Ambassador, General Ott, informed Kondō that all preparations had been completed for the invasion of Britain; the time of execution only awaited Hitler's decision. In concert with the invasion, Japan should not miss the golden opportunity of attacking Singapore without delay. Kondō's response made clear that Japan had no intention of employing force against Singapore (or the Dutch East Indies). There was a 'great possibility' that the United States would go to war if Japan used force, and the Dutch East Indies would immediately suspend the shipment of raw materials to Japan of which she had dire need for the survival of the nation and the acceleration of the buildup of her war potential.[2] When Matsuoka visited Berlin late in March, Hitler and Ribbentrop

[1] Interview with Captain Miyo Kazunari, 17 May 1976. Miyo was then a commander in the 1st Section of the Operations Division, the war plans section. It was Miyo who had rejected the proposal. His Section Chief, Captain Nakazawa Tasuku, agreed with his estimate.

[2] *Senshi sōsho*, ci, *Daihon'ei kaigunbu: Dai Tōa Sensō kaisen keii* (2) [IGHQ Navy Department: The State of Affairs until the Outbreak of the Greater East Asia War (2)] (1979), pp. 214–16. From a conversation with Kondō on 8 March, during which the Vice-Chief of Staff stressed the possibility of American entry into the war if Japan attacked Singapore, and the danger in that eventuality of vigorous cruiser warfare by the US Navy on Japanese supply lines to the Southern Area, Admiral Wenneker got 'the impression that Japan's will to attack had weakened somewhat as compared to six months ago. The reason probably lies in the Italian setbacks as well as in the present lull.' PG 32220, Kriegstagebuch 1. Sk1. Teil C Heft xv, 'Zusammenarbeit mit Japan', Admiralty Project, Reel 54. The causes went far beyond these. Ambassador Ott reported on 25 March that, according to inquiries put to Kondō, the Navy was 'vigorously preparing for an attack on Singapore. Preparations were expected to be concluded by the end of May'. *Documents on German Foreign Policy, 1918–1945*, Ser.D, xii (Washington, 1962), 361–2. This was, however, no more than contingency planning. No decision to attack Singapore had been made. On 10 June, after conversations with 'influential officers', Wenneker telegraphed Berlin that the attack on Singapore had been abandoned. 'All authorities agreed that such action would make American entry into war unavoidable. At best the action will be undertaken if it should become essential in order to forestall America gaining a footing in the South China Sea. Against action: (a) Navy, although fully

(*continued*)

worked hard to persuade him that an attack on Singapore would be 'a very decisive factor in the speedy overthrow of England', which would solve the Southern Area problem for Japan. Matsuoka was careful not to commit his Government, although personally sympathetic to the proposal.

There was moderation, too, as regards the Netherlands East Indies. At the conclusion of a war game late in November 1940 whose subject was operations against the Netherlands and China, Yamamoto had written to Prince Fushimi, at the latter's request, that war with the United States was inevitable if they started the Dutch East Indies operation, unless American war preparations were much delayed or Britain's war against Germany went very badly, and that this would very probably develop into a war against the ABD Powers. 'Therefore, we should not start the southern operation unless we are ready for it and we have made sufficient war preparations.'[3]

In the latter part of 1940 the Navy realized that, with the possibility of a cessation of American oil supplies, they must reduce their dependence on the United States and obtain oil elsewhere. Their idea was to procure it from the Dutch East Indies. The Islands had an annual petroleum output of 8,000,000 tons, or nearly twenty times as much as Japan's. Japan's requirements at the time were over 5,000,000 tons a year; domestic production satisfied less than 10 per cent of those requirements. Negotiations had been proceeding in Batavia since mid-September 1940 to achieve closer economic relations with the Dutch East Indies. The Navy, eschewing a military policy toward the East Indies, saw to it that the negotiations were confined to economic issues, meaning, above all, the question of oil. The Indonesian authorities were pressed for a five-year guarantee of 3·75 million tons of oil a year in lieu of the 600,000 tons annually imported. The best the Japanese could get was agreement on 2,000,000 tons for the six months beginning 1 November, or less than half of Japan's annual needs (5,370,000 tons

prepared, because it fears a long war, which the country is not equal to. (b) Army, because preparations are incomplete and the study plan showed that complete success of attack over land was very doubtful.' War Diary, German Naval Attaché, PG 32144, Admiralty Project, Reel 481.

[3] *Senshi sōsho*, xxiv, *Kaigun shinkō sakusen: Hitō Marē hōmen* [Naval Attack Operations: Philippines and Malaya] (1969), p. 25. He wrote along similar lines to the China Area Fleet Commander, Admiral Shimada Shigetarō, in December 1940. Shimada and Fushimi agreed completely with Yamamoto. Ibid., xci. 508–9.

annually, 1937–40). The rest would have to come from the US, and this was uncertain if relations with the US did not improve. After a hiatus, the negotiations were resumed on 2 January 1941, with the Japanese delegation presenting a list of proposals designed to obtain control of Indonesian natural resources: the Japanese sought the right to prospect for oil and minerals and to send more Japanese to the Islands, freedom of access of Japanese ships to unopened ports for the purpose of transporting raw materials, and a Dutch promise to furnish large set quantities of oil, tin, and other essential materials. The negotiations dragged on.

A Liaison Conference on 30 January 1941 considered a policy statement, the 'Outline of Policy towards French Indo-China and Thailand', that reveals the outlook of the Supreme Command and the Government on the southward expansion programme at this time. 'The objective of the measures toward French Indochina and Thailand, who confront Japan on the road to the creation of the Greater East Asia Co-prosperity Sphere, lies in the establishment of a close military, political, and economic union with French Indochina and Thailand, for Japan's self-preservation and self-defence.' To attain this objective, Japan 'should apply the necessary pressure, and if unavoidable, employ military force against French Indochina. Regardless of the manœuvres by Britain and the United States, this group of measures should be enforced immediately, in order to attain the objectives as soon as possible.' The 'procedure' called for (1) Japanese mediation in the localized war between French Indo-China and Thailand, which had broken out on 16 January over a boundary dispute, with the purpose of gaining 'a dominant influence' in both territories, and (2) a pact with Thailand, and one with French Indo-China that would permit the establishment or utilization of air bases and port facilities, and the acquisition of facilities for the billeting and movement of Japanese troops. And the French were to agree not to co-operate in any manner with a third Power on Indo-China matters. 'Efforts shall be made to attain the objective by increasing pressure at the proper time. ... In the event that French Indochina resists such acts of pressure with force, Japan shall forcibly carry out the plan of action even by resorting to the use of arms.'[4] Before the Conference approved this policy statement, at Matsuoka's insistence this passage

[4] Hattori, *The Complete History of the Greater East Asia War*, i. 82–3.

was deleted. A supplementary decision merely stated that the objectives of the policy should be achieved by the beginning of April through diplomacy. If French Indo-China refused to conclude a military pact, a decision would then be made as regards military operations against her. The statement received the Imperial sanction on 1 February.

Her offer to mediate having been accepted by Thailand and French Indo-China, on 7 February Japan began negotiations in Tokyo that resulted in a settlement on 11 March. Included with it was an agreement between Japan and the two that neither French Indo-China nor Thailand would co-operate with a third Power, in any manner, for political or military purposes. There was, however, no progress towards the achievement of what for the Services, the Navy in particular, was the important thing: the use of air and naval bases in southern Indo-China as a springboard for the occupation of Thailand, from whose territory they could mount an attack on Malaya. But the Navy was not keen on risking a confrontation with Britain and the US for this goal by taking military action. Yamamoto warned Oikawa in a letter of 25 February 1941 of a strong American and British reaction to the use of force in French Indo-China. Admiral Shimada was remonstrating with Tokyo at this time along similar lines. Oikawa and Prince Fushimi were themselves unenthusiastic about the use of force towards Indo-China.

There was one absolute prerequisite to a southward advance: an agreement with the Soviet Union, which by securing the Manchurian frontier would enable Japan to run the risk of war with Britain, and the United States if need be, in the drive to the south. It was primarily this objective that concerned Japan's policy-makers from November 1940 until April 1941, after German good offices had proved of no avail. Matsuoka proceeded to negotiate with the Soviets directly. On 13 April 1941 a neutrality pact was signed between the two Powers: they agreed to respect each other's territorial integrity and to observe neutrality if either was attacked by one or more Powers. The Japanese were now free to continue the southward advance, encouraged, moreover, by the British reverses in Greece and North Africa.

In the meantime, the Government had decided to open discussions in Washington to find a peaceful solution to the inherent conflict between the policy of the southward advance and the American hostility towards it. The negotiations began on 14 April, after the arrival of the new Japanese Ambassador, the moderate Admiral Nomura Kichisaburō. On 11 May he presented a scheme for a settlement of outstanding issues. It included such proposals as a US hands-off policy as regards China if China refused an American request to conclude peace with Japan, and in general showed scant regard for the four principles of a settlement that Secretary of State Hull had proposed to Nomura on 16 April: respect for the territorial integrity and sovereignty of all nations; non-intervention in the domestic affairs of other countries; the principle of equality, including equality of commercial opportunity; and non-disturbance of the status quo in the Pacific, except by peaceful means. All the same, negotiations for an agreement continued in Washington. The British were not involved, and not till later in the year were they much consulted by the United States. They were content to allow the United States to carry the ball. By June the negotiations were at a standstill.

On 17 April an IGHQ conference decided to proceed with the plan to gain control of the Southern Area 'for the purpose of self-preservation and self-defence'. But since the Navy was in no position to endure a long war and therefore remained sceptical about the prospects of success in a war with the United States and Britain, it insisted that there should be no recourse to force unless the ABD Powers imposed a trade embargo on Japan, or the United States, alone or in alliance with Britain, the Netherlands, and China, threatened her existence by encirclement and there was no way to break through it.

Professor Crowley has made the significant point that the decision

marks a subtle but crucial change in attitude among many of the most influential officers of the army and navy. What was desired in 1940 as part of a future new order had, by April 1941, become essential to the security of the empire. ... Since the anticipated results of the Axis pact had not materialized, the national objectives of July 1940 were clearly being stymied by the policies of the United States. Faced with this situation, the initial motive of extending the principles of the 'national polity' throughout Asia by means of a New Order was transformed into a matter of the 'existence and defence' of the nation. Thus, the policies of the colonial powers and of the United States became identified as an 'encirclement' of imperial Japan. At the moment it is not possible to pinpoint precisely when this change in vocabulary and thought-pattern occurred. Nevertheless, it was basic to the policies adopted by the Imperial Headquarters, the Liaison Conference, and the cabinet throughout 1941, and judging by the available documents, it emerged sometime between January and mid-April [above, p. 156]. Moreover, it also marked a growing consensus between the Army Ministry and the Navy General Staff that the 'southern advance' was the key to the nation's defence.[5]

The other important development in April was the changes in the Navy High Command. Although the influence of the extremist junior officers in the Navy was not as great as that of the 'Young Turks' in the Army, the difference was only a matter of degree. The Navy's Young Turks wanted to have at the top officers who would be amenable to their advice and recommendations. As a consequence, the Navy Minister and the Chief of the Naval General Staff were sometimes appointed from among those admirals who lacked the ability to form their own opinions and therefore had to rely upon the advice and recommendations of subordinates. In Admiral Nagano Osami, who succeeded the ailing Prince Fushimi as Chief of the *Gunreibu* on 9 April 1941 (–February 1944), chiefly on the Prince's recommendation (Yamamoto had hoped it would be Yonai), they had such a man. He was reported to have said on one occasion, when *Gunreibu* Chief, that he was ready to follow 100 per cent the recommendations presented by his subordinates of captain's rank, because he believed that they had studied and discussed the particular issue.[6]

We have met the stately Nagano before, as the plenipotentiary to the London Naval Conference of 1935–6 who had led the Japanese delegation out of the Conference. Subsequently, he was Navy Minister in 1936–7 (Yonai's immediate predecessor), when he had been, Professor Pelz states, 'the prime mover behind the adoption of the southern advance by the Hirota cabinet'. (See above, p. 105.) In 1937 he became C-in-C, Combined Fleet. His earlier career, until he reached flag rank, was more successful than the later. He was a clever and brilliant young officer (2/104 in the class of 1900), who gave the impression of being a 'superman' to the cadets when he was the Superintendent of the Naval Academy

---

[5] 'Japan's Military Foreign Policies', pp. 91–2.
[6] Captain Ōi Atsushi, who served under Nagano in 1943, has 'some reason to believe that this story is not so wide of the mark'. Ōi interview, 24 May 1976. On the other hand, Commander Sekiguchi Kōzō, who was Nagano's ADC in 1944–5, describes him as a strong-willed man who knew his mind.

(1928–9). Especially after promotion to full admiral in 1934, his considerable natural ability was somehow atrophied. By 1941 he was past his prime. He became lazy and let others do the work. He married three times, all to young wives (No. 3 was very beautiful—and very young), which, Navy gossip had it, explained why he was always tired. He slept at meetings and in conferences. His vanity worsened with age. When, in 1944, he realized his ambition to become an admiral of the fleet, he went to his native prefecture to show off, and that at a most critical time for the Navy. As Chief of the *Gunreibu* he was anything but outstanding; he did not enjoy the confidence of the Naval Staff or the Emperor, nor was moral courage his strong point. He was also criticized for being prone to impulsive action. Nagano knew the United States and had a healthy respect for its power. He had served in Washington as Naval Attaché when a captain, and as a rear-admiral he had commanded the training squadron that had visited the United States. By the middle of 1941, nevertheless, he had become strongly influenced by the First Committee and its view that war with the United States was inevitable.

The pliant Kondō Nobutake remained as Vice-Chief of Staff. Nagano's Chief of the 1st Division, also appointed in April in succession to Ugaki, was Rear-Admiral Fukudome Shigeru (–June 1943), whose previous appointment was as Chief of Staff, Combined Fleet, under Yamamoto. (He returned to that post under Koga in 1943–4.) Fukudome was a stocky man, reserved, unexcitable, and of a warm, attractive personality. There was no question about the quality of his mind: it was sharp and clear. (He had been 8/144 in the class of 1912 at Etajima and at the top of his Naval War College class.) He impressed the Americans after the war as being 'a markedly superior Japanese Officer'. And so he was, at least so far as his forte, operational planning, was concerned. His weaknesses were, however, not negligible. He could not satisfy himself—he had doubts about his ability—and he obeyed orders from superiors without questioning them. Nagano was in general inclined towards war. Kondō and Fukudome, being dovish, tended to counterbalance Nagano's hawkishness, but neither was a forceful enough character to put the brakes on their Chief.

On the ministry side, Oikawa stayed on until October, but his Vice-Minister, Toyoda Teijirō, was followed by the moderate Vice-Admiral Sawamoto Yorio on 22 April (–July 1944). He was of average height, fat, slightly bald—'like a village schoolmaster in appearance'. He had been an excellent navigation officer and was a clever man and a hard worker, and had an exceptional memory: he never forgot anything. 'An excellent bureaucrat' might sum him up. Oka Takazumi was still Chief of the Bureau of Naval Affairs. Sawamoto and Oka were not keen on war, but neither was a strong character, able to exercise an effective control over hawkish subordinates.

The important consideration is that the Oikawa–Nagano combination was an excellent one—for the Army and Navy extremists. They were infinitely manipulable.

It was hardly surprising, therefore [as Professor Asada brings out], that the middle-echelon 'nucleus group'—now asserting a sort of 'collective leadership' through the First Committee—became the virtual locus of the navy's policymaking. As part of their assigned duties, these officers formulated naval policy from a strategic standpoint—that of war planning. There was nothing irregular about this, but as their recommendations were almost automatically approved by their superiors, strategic requirements came to have excessive influence in the making of national policy. Their demands for 'war preparations' were to drive the ranking naval leaders into an impasse that finally forced their 'determination' for war. The decision to march into southern Indochina was a case in point.[7]

By the summer the Section Chiefs Conference[8] was openly favouring war with the United States. Tomioka and Ishikawa were overheard saying: 'Now is the time to strike; we won't be defeated.' It was against this background that a policy statement emerged in the First Committee on 5 June, on Captain Ishikawa Shingo's initiative. It called for 'the military advance into French Indo-China and Thailand to be carried out as soon as possible'. The moves to the south were put forward under the guise of pre-emptive measures against encirclement by the ABD Powers. Japan must be ready to resort to military action against them in any of these eventualities: an oil embargo on Japan; a rice embargo by the Netherlands East Indies, Thailand, and French Indo-China; the latter two refusing to agree to military co-operation that Japan regarded as indispensable to her self-defence; the strengthening of ABD armed forces in

---

[7] 'The Japanese Navy and the United States', p. 252.
[8] A section chiefs conference could be within the Navy Ministry, the Naval General Staff, or both. I am here referring to the last-named, the *Shōbu Kachō Kaigi*. The chief of a section (*kachō*) was usually a captain.

South-east Asia to a point that was strategically unacceptable to Japan; the United States and Britain interfering militarily with Japanese operations in China; these two Powers initiating military action against Thailand.[9] The document was submitted to Oikawa. Although it was not formally approved by the Navy's leaders, Nagano endorsed the outlook of the hawks in the Navy Ministry and Naval General Staff. At Liaison Conferences on 11 and 12 June he bluntly asserted that if the ABD Powers interfered with the establishment of bases in French Indo-China, they must fight them. 'We must resolutely attack anyone who tries to stop us' (11 June).[10] Oikawa, if only through his silence, accepted the policy advocated by the fire-eaters.

The pro-war group received an important reinforcement at this time with the conversion of the 5th Section Chief of the Intelligence Division in charge of North and South America, Captain Yamaguchi Bunjirō (May 1940–May 1942). It seems that his change from his moderate stance happened after a visit to the US in March 1941 when he was badly treated by (?Customs) authorities on his departure in June. Thereafter he became unfriendly and even hostile towards the United States, and ready to join the extremists.[11]

Events in June suddenly altered the entire situation and played into the hands of the pro-war party. On 17 June the Japanese–Netherlands East Indies talks, which had been utterly deadlocked by the end of May over rubber and tin exports, broke down completely. The policy of gaining peaceful access to the wealth of the Netherlands East Indies had proven a chimera. The apprehension of the Services about their oil supplies was intensified when, on 20 June, the US Government, because of domestic scarcity, banned oil exports from the Eastern seaboard, except to Britain and certain other Western countries. On the 22nd Germany invaded the Soviet Union, which took the Japanese completely by surprise. They were in a quandary. Should they abandon the Co-Prosperity sphere and the drive to the south for war with the Russians? Or ought they to take advantage of the neutrality pact with the Soviets and the German invasion to move into South-east Asia, even at the risk of war with Britain and the United States? At almost daily Liaison

[9] *Senshi sōsho*, ci. 322–5.
[10] Ike, pp. 50–1.
[11] Private source.

'TIME IS NOT ON OUR SIDE'

Conferences between 25 June and 1 July,[12] Matsuoka, though incensed when he got the news of the invasion (the Government had received no advance official notification from Germany), heatedly argued that Japan was honour-bound under the Tripartite Pact to attack the Soviets, and that, as he had been arguing all month, the southern advance would probably lead to war with Britain and the United States. Now was the time to rid themselves of the Soviet menace; they should strike north, not 'start a fire in the South'. The Services felt differently. The Army could not fight the Soviet Union so long as most of its troops were tied down in China. The Navy knew that such a war would not solve Japan's oil and raw materials problems. Moreover, as Oikawa declared (25 June), 'The Navy is confident about a war against the United States and Britain, but not confident about a war against the United States, Britain, and the Soviet Union'. The Services decided that Japan would maintain her neutrality, and they reconfirmed their support for the priority of the southward advance. The IGHQ draft outlining this policy, the 'Outline of National Policies in View of the Changing Situation', was sanctioned by a Liaison Conference on 28 June, approved by the Cabinet on 1 July, and confirmed at an Imperial Conference on 2 July.

The 'Outline' declared for a policy of non-intervention in the German–Soviet war 'for the time being'. Japan would endeavour to settle the China Incident, using increasing 'pressure applied from the southern regions' to force China's capitulation. Japan would advance south in order to establish for herself 'a solid basis for the security and preservation of the nation'.[13] The northern problem would be dealt with in accordance with developments there—a sop to the supporters of the Northern orientation. Measures would be taken against French Indo-China and Thailand 'with the purpose of strengthening our advance into the southern regions'. To achieve her objectives in the South, Japan 'will not refuse [or not hesitate to engage in or refrain from: *jisezu*] war with Great Britain and the United states'. 'We will immediately turn our attention to putting the nation on a war footing.'

The decisions of 2 July differed significantly from those of a year

---

[12] See Ike, pp. 56–90, for the proceedings, including the crucial Imperial Conference on 2 July.

[13] 'Security and preservation of the nation', *ji-son ji-ei*, is, literally, 'self-existence and self-defence'.

earlier through (1) the introduction of the 'security and preservation' reference, and (2) the fact that Japan was now prepared to use force to achieve her objectives in the Southern Area. These would begin with the occupation of southern Indo-China. Thailand would await her turn. A move in that direction, as General Sugiyama, the Chief of the Army General Staff, said, 'might have serious consequences, since Thailand is near Malaya. This time we will go only as far as Indo-China'. Nagano's statement at the Imperial Conference makes clear that these crucial decisions had the full backing of the Navy.

Britain, the United States, and the Netherlands are currently stepping up their pressure against Japan. If they obstinately continue to obstruct us, and if our Empire finds itself unable to cope with this, we may, it must be anticipated, finally have to go to war with Great Britain and the United States. So we must get ready, resolved that we will not be deterred by that possibility. As the first step, it will be necessary for us to carry out our policy with respect to French Indo-China and Thailand... and thereby increase our ability to move southward.

The decision of the 2 July Imperial Conference set in motion the events that led to the Pacific War five months later.

The Imperial Conference had also decided that Japan would continue diplomatic negotiations with the United States to solve the Far Eastern problem, though, of course, in accordance with Japan's ideas. The Services meanwhile were to prepare for a war with the United States and Britain in the event of a breakdown of the negotiations. The gist of the decisions taken at the 2 July Conference were known to these Powers through the Americans having cracked the Japanese diplomatic cipher system ('Purple'). Konoe had some hopes for success in Washington. The Services, too, wanted the conversations to continue, at least until the occupation of southern French Indo-China was complete and the outcome of the Russo–German war was clearer. Because of Matsuoka's opposition to the conversations, which jeopardized their success, Konoe asked for the resignation of his Cabinet on 16 July. (Under the Japanese system the Prime Minister could not force a minister to resign; a dissolution of the Cabinet was the only way to effect a change.) It was re-formed without Matsuoka on the 18th—Konoe's third Cabinet. The new Foreign Minister was Admiral Toyoda Teijiro, Commerce Minister in the previous Cabinet, who was believed to be *persona grata* to the United States. Ambassador Grew found him 'cheery and very friendly', and 'sound and sensible'.

Meanwhile, the Japanese were preparing to take over southern French Indo-China. This would strengthen their strategical position in a variety of ways: the acquisition of the resources of that area (rice and raw rubber, in particular), as well as bases; the prevention of an expected American and British pre-emptive move into French Indo-China (with the collusion of Gaullist and other anti-Japanese forces in the colony), which would complete the ABCD encirclement of Japan; the containment of Thailand; the completion of the blockade of China; and, not least, the ability of Japan to threaten the use of force against the Netherlands East Indies to compel the Dutch to come to terms as regards oil. The last-named was *the* reason, Admiral Tomioka later recalled.[14] No foreign complications were expected by the Service staffs or by most ministers, and certainly nothing so drastic as an ABD freezing of assets and a total embargo against Japan. 'When seen from subsequent developments', remarks Hattori, 'this was a grave misjudgment, and the fateful die was cast here!' Oikawa had made up his mind after two reports, one from Admiral Maeda, who had returned from an inspection trip to Thailand and French Indo-China in April, and the other, in June, from Captain Chūdō Kan'ei, the chief of the IGHQ Navy Department's French Indo-China Expeditionary Committee.[15] Both assured the Navy Minister that the advance could be executed peacefully without war with Britain and the United States. Nagano had wavered till the last, apprehensive that an advance would lead to war.

An ultimatum to the Vichy Government on 14 July—the Japanese asked for approval to move their armed forces into southern Indo-China and for the use of eight air bases there, including Saigon, and the naval bases at Camranh Bay and

[14] Interview, 13 Feb. 1962, Bōeichō Senshibu Archives. Admiral Sawamoto singled out the China blockade factor as the primary objective. At the same time the invasion of southern Indo-China would furnish bases en route to the oil of the Dutch East Indies. Sawamoto, 'Shi shuki'. Captain Miyo Kazunari, whose Chief then was Tomioka, also testifies that the China factor was pre-eminent. IMTFE, Defence Document No. 2097. On the other hand, the Chief of the Intelligence Division (October 1940–June 1942), Rear-Admiral Maeda Minoru, declared after the war that the primary objective was to take a 'preliminary step for preparing for war with the United States and Great Britain, by carrying out the pre-emptive occupation of this strategically important area in the Southern Area before our two opponents could seize it for the same purpose as our own'. *Senshi sōsho*, ci. 331.
[15] *Senshi sōsho*, xci. 528, ci. 331.

Saigon—gave the French until 19 July to cave in peacefully. The French yielded on 21 July, and an agreement, in the guise of a defensive alliance, was concluded at Vichy on 22 July and was formally signed on 29 July. Washington knew what was in the offing. On the 24th Japanese warships were reported off Camranh Bay, and troop transports headed south from Hainan. On the 25th Matsuoka informed the American Ambassador that Vichy had agreed to admit Japan to a joint protectorate of Indo-China. The reaction in Washington and London was swift. The occupation of southern Indo-China would all but complete the encirclement of the Philippines and bring nearer the threat of attack on British and Dutch possessions in South-east Asia. From Camranh Bay the Japanese Navy could develop a serious threat to British sea routes in the Indian Ocean, even while Singapore remained in British hands. As a warning to Japan, as well as a measure of self-defence, on 26 July President Roosevelt issued an executive order freezing Japan's assets in the United States and halting all trade with Japan, including the highly important oil exports. Although the British Service chiefs had consistently advised against involvement in a war over French Indo-China or provoking Japan in any way without the firm promise of American support, the Government believed, with the Foreign Secretary, that it was essential to act alongside the United States. The British Government, therefore, at once denounced the Anglo-Japanese Commercial Treaty of 1911 and the Supplementary Convention of 1925 and imposed their own freezing order, and the Netherlands followed suit on the 28th. In effect, the three Western Powers had severed their trade relations with Japan. This strong reaction, though coming as a complete surprise to the Supreme Command, was too late to serve as a deterrent. On 28 July Japanese troops began to occupy southern Indo-China; by the end of the month 40,000 were there. Hull suspended the talks with Nomura.

The imposition of the earlier embargoes was a grave matter for the Services, but it was the embargo on oil exports that hit them at their most vital spot. In 1940 Japan produced less than 10 per cent of her civilian and military needs, with the United States alone providing 80 per cent and the Netherlands East Indies 10 per cent of her oil imports. Admiral Shimada, who was to succeed Oikawa in October, stated the matter tersely after the war: 'if there were no supply of oil, battleships and any other warships would be nothing more than scarecrows', and this went for the tanks and planes of the Army, too. Heavy industry also depended to a great extent on oil. It became clear that even if Japan increased the production of synthetic petroleum to record levels, and took into account the exploitation of oil in northern Sakhalin and the purchase of oil from Iran or Peru, there was no way she could meet her civilian and military needs. The Bureau of Naval Affairs immediately conducted studies of oil supply and demand after the American and Dutch total oil embargo and came up with these figures. Expected demand, first to third years, 5,400,000 kilolitres per year, or a total of 16,200,000kl, to which they added 500,000kl for the decisive battle between the main forces. Expected supply was: in stock, 9,400,000kl, to which they added: from domestic sources, synthetic production, and the oil from the Southern Area they would secure 800,000kl in the first year of war, 3,340,000 in the second, and 6,670,000 in the third, for a grand total of 20,210,000kl available in the three years. Stock at year-end (in parentheses this figure less 500,000kl reserve for the decisive battle, 1,000,000 reserve for civilian use, and 800,000 for scorching at the bottom of oil tanks) would be:

1st year	4,800,000	(2,500,000)
2nd year	2,740,000	(440,000)
3rd year	4,010,000	(1,710,000)

The most important conclusion from these figures was that, 'considering the fact that approximately 400,000kl of oil would be reduced monthly from the amount of oil stocks after August due to the actual oil embargo against Japan imposed by the United States and the Netherlands, if we did not start operations in October there would be the danger of concern over the fuel situation by the end of the second year of the war'.[16] These calculations became the rationale behind the Navy's attitude towards the policy statement, 'The Essentials for Carrying out the Empire's Policies', adopted by the Imperial Conference on 6 September (below).

The various oil estimates in 1941 had one feature in common: they overlooked (among other things) the elementary fact that the rate of consumption in war is much higher than in peacetime. Thus, cruising distances and fuel consumption in pre-war exercises

[16] The entire paragraph is based on *Senshi sōsho*, xci. 537–8. Cf. the figures produced on 5 November, below, p. 246n. A kilolitre was equal to 1,000 litres or 220 imperial gallons.

and training were nothing like what they were in war, when ships cruised longer distances and at high speed. Also, everything in wartime would depend on the exploitation of the rich Indonesian oil fields and the ability to ship the oil back to Japan. Yet no serious attention was paid to the question of tankers to ship the oil—that is, scant allowance was made for the attrition of the tanker force by submarines and aircraft, and the need to replenish that force by continual production in Japan.[17]

It was only with the total stoppage of trade that war suddenly became a reality in Navy circles, especially in the Naval General Staff. The German Naval Attaché recalled how 'the number of those who considered the supply of vital raw materials from the East and South the only means of keeping the nation alive increased steadily after the blockade came into effect'.[18] There was a widespread feeling that 'if there is going to be a war, the sooner, the better'. Peace at the price of the Navy being deprived of its oil supply, its life-blood, was intolerable. In the judgement of the Official History, 'The hopeless prospects for oil supply was one of the main motives which forced Japan to resolve on the Greater East Asia War.'[19] In retrospect, too, Nagano and Oikawa thought that the question of oil was one of the important reasons why Japan went to war. Admiral Shimada called it 'one of the factors but it was not the fundamental factor'.

Nagano sounded the alarm bell at the first Liaison Conference of the new Government on 21 July. There was, he said, a chance of defeating the United States now, but the odds would diminish with time. 'If we could settle things without war, there would be nothing better. But if we conclude that conflict cannot ultimately be avoided, then ... as time goes by we will be in a disadvantageous position.'[20] This was the position that the *Gunreibu* Chief took on 30 July, when the Emperor, who was distressed by the 'inevitability of war' talk in the Services, gave him a long, 55-minute audience. Nagano reported that he and his predecessor, Prince Fushimi,

---

[17] See e.g., Captain Ōi Atsushi, *Kaijō goei sanbō no kaisō: Taiheiyō sensō no senryaku hihan* [Recollections of a Convoy Escort Staff Officer: Criticism of the Strategy of the Pacific War] (Tokyo, 1975), pp. 3-4.

[18] Wenneker, 'My Stay in Japan', 20 Mar. 1946, p. 5, German Naval Records, US Operational Archives.

[19] *Senshi sōsho*, xxxi, *Kaigun gunsenbi* (1): *Shōwa jūrokunen jūichigatsu made* [Naval Armaments and Preparations for War (1): Until November 1941] (1969), p. 730.

[20] Ike, p. 106.

whom the Emperor had asked him to consult, were agreed that war must be avoided, if at all possible. If, however, no settlement were reached with the United States, and the oil embargo continued, Japan would be left with two years of oil stocks in peacetime, or a year and a half in case of war. Were this the prospect, Japan would have no alternative to war, even though the prospects of victory were not satisfactory (*jūbun de nai*). By contrast, the Army's position after the American freezing order was that further negotiation was a waste of time.

Events seemed to bear out the Army. The talks in Washington, though resumed, were deadlocked by the end of August. The United States would not rescind her restrictions on trade with Japan, discontinue aid to the Chinese Nationalists, or recognize Japan's special position in French Indo-China. Konoe fired the one shot left in his locker. After preliminary soundings earlier in the month, on 26 August he sent a personal message to President Roosevelt, suggesting a meeting between them 'to explore the possibility of saving the situation'. The Japanese mission was scheduled to include, in addition to the Prime Minister and Foreign Minister, key Army, Navy, and Foreign Ministry personnel. The *Nitta Maru*, escorted by four cruisers, would transport this imposing party to Hawaii, which the Japanese preferred, or to Juneau, Alaska, which was the American preference. The Americans proposed (3 September) a deferment until an agreement could be reached on the fundamental points at issue between the two countries, such as the Japanese military occupation of China. A 'patch-work' solution would not do. For the next month the Japanese continued without success to press for a leaders' conference as soon as possible.

Military considerations were uppermost after July, as Admiral Hoshina has brought out:

Until the invasion of southern French Indo-China of 28 July 1941, Japanese national policy was directed from the political standpoint only, without any definite plans of military strategy. Originally, the Navy had opposed any policy that would pit Japan against the United States and Britain as adversaries. Those who were enchanted with the glorious victories of Germany in the European war, together with the Army, strongly supported the Triple Alliance against the belief of the mainstream in the Navy. . . . Despite the impatience of the Supreme Command, Japanese national policy was still controlled by political strategy.

There was now, from the end of July 1941, a definite shift from an emphasis on political strategy to an emphasis on military strategy in the formulation of national policy.[21] The Supreme Command—the two Chiefs of Staff—was in the driver's seat, and the Navy Ministry and the politicians, including the Prime Minister and the Foreign Minister, with their more moderate approach on major policy questions, became increasingly powerless. Nagano now spoke for the Navy; Oikawa had a back seat.

Reports of a rapid buildup of American and British air, naval, and land forces in Malaya and the Philippines, as well as of the strengthening of joint defence arrangements among the ABCD Powers, provoked an even greater sense of urgency in the Services than the continued threat to Japan's oil reserves. A Supreme Command paper of 1 October estimated that military co-operation among these Powers had reached 'almost total understanding'. (How far off the mark this was we shall see in the following chapter.) The Services knew that weather and sea conditions made early November, or December at the latest, the most favourable time for landing operations in the south and a naval strike against Pearl Harbor. Otherwise, there would have to be a postponement until the spring, which, because of the steadily decreasing oil supply, could only work to Japan's disadvantage. It was also necessary to move swiftly, if they were going to move, so that, if the Soviet Union attacked, operations in the south could be completed during the winter, when climatic conditions in the north were unsuitable for military operations.

The tempo of naval war preparations was stepped up in August and September. They included the requisitioning of an additional 265 ships, totalling 490,000 tons, and increasing air strength. To counter the huge Third Vinson Act in the United States (June 1940), which had been followed a month later by the 'Stark Plan' for a 'two-ocean Navy', a Fifth Replenishment Plan (1942–50) had been informally adopted by the Navy Minister and the Naval General Staff in May 1941. At a cost of nearly 4½ billion yen, it provided for the construction of 159 vessels, of 650,000 tons,

---

[21] Vice-Admiral Hoshina Zenshirō, *Dai Tōa Sensō hishi* [The Secret History of the Greater East Asia War] (Tokyo, 1975), p. 27. Japanese Monograph No. 150, *Political Strategy Prior to the Outbreak of War*, Pt. vi (1952), 17, prefers a later date—that it was in September that 'military strategy became the underlying factor of national policy and political strategy assumed a subordinate role'.

including 3 super-battleships mounting six *20-inch* (50·8 cm) guns, 2 super-cruisers (17,000 tons, six 12-inch main batteries), 3 carriers, 9 cruisers, 32 destroyers, and 45 submarines, with an additional two billion yen for 1,320 combat aircraft and 2,138 training aircraft. The Japanese battleship ratio of 70 per cent of US battle-fleet strength in 1941 would decline rapidly thereafter and drop to approximately 40 per cent by 1945, if the building plans did not go beyond the Fourth Plan. 'This fact,' as the Official History points out, 'together with the fuel problem, contributed to the view that if war was unavoidable, the sooner the better; and it was also connected with the fear of a long drawn-out war. At that time, when the concept of the supremacy of the air was still weak, in order for the Japanese Navy to endure a long drawn-out war against the United States, Japan would have to maintain an appropriate ratio of battleships vis-à-vis the United States...' There was talk in November 1941 of a Sixth as well as of a Fifth Replenishment Plan, calling for 197 warships of about 800,000 tons, including four battleships and 88 operational air groups. But it was recognized that matching the American rearmament was beyond Japan's resources, especially as regards steel. Little that was definite had been decided about new Replenishment Plans when war broke out beyond the execution of the modest Emergency Armament Plan of August 1941. This involved the construction of 63 vessels, including a carrier, 2 cruisers, 26 destroyers, and 33 submarines.

At a Liaison Conference on 3 September, Nagano demanded that, failing a peaceful settlement, they must resort to war. 'We are', he asserted, 'getting weaker. By contrast, the enemy is getting stronger. With the passage of time, we will get increasingly weaker, and we won't be able to survive.... Although I am confident that at the present time we have a chance to win a war, I fear that this opportunity will disappear with the passage of time.' They had to prepare for a long war 'by getting essential resources and by making the best of our strategy' (of seeking a decisive battle). The Conference adopted with minor changes a fateful policy statement, 'The Essentials for Carrying out the Empire's Policies', that had been drawn up by the Army and Navy Departments of IGHQ.

The Cabinet accepted it on 5 September, and the historic Imperial Conference of 6 September ratified it. The statement read: In view of the current critical situation, in particular, the offensive attitudes that such countries as the United States, Great Britain, and the Netherlands are taking towards Japan, and in view of the situation in the Soviet Union and the condition [limits] of our Empire's national power, we will carry out our policy toward the South, which is contained in the 'Outline of National Policies in View of the Changing Situation' [of 2 July, above], as follows:

I. Our Empire, for the purposes of self-defense and self-preservation, will complete preparations for war, with the last ten days of October as a tentative deadline, resolved to go to war[22] with the United States, Great Britain, and the Netherlands if necessary.

II. Our Empire will concurrently take all possible diplomatic measures vis-à-vis the United States and Great Britain, and thereby endeavor to attain our objectives. The minimum objectives of our Empire to be attained through negotiations with the United States and Great Britain and the maximum concessions therein to be made by our Empire are noted in the attached documents.

III. In the event there is no prospect of our demands being met by the first ten days of October through the diplomatic negotiations mentioned above, we will immediately decide to commence hostilities against the United States, Britain, and the Netherlands.

An attached document listed the minimum demands to be achieved through negotiations with the United States (and Britain) and the maximum Japanese concessions. The former called for (1) American and British non-interference with Japan's disposition of the China Incident, the closing of the Burma Road, and the cessation of aid to Chiang Kai-shek. (2) The US and Britain should 'refrain from actions that may threaten the defense of our Empire in the Far East': they should not obtain military bases in Thailand, the Dutch East Indies, China, and the Soviet Far East, or strengthen further their armed forces in the Far East, nor should they demand any alteration in the Japanese–French agreement on Indo-China. (3) The US and Great Britain should assist Japan economically by restoring trade relations with her, supplying her with urgently needed materials from their South-West Pacific territories, and contributing to Japan's economic co-operation with Thailand and the Netherlands East Indies. If all these demands were met, Japan would agree not to advance militarily from French Indo-China except against China, would be prepared to evacuate her forces

---

[22] The Japanese words *sensō o jisezaru ketsui* may be translated as 'resolved not to refuse war', or 'would be prepared for war'.

from Indo-China after a just peace had been established in the Far East, and to guarantee the neutrality of the Philippines. If the US entered the European war, Japan would make an independent judgement as regards the interpretation of the Tripartite Pact.

Three things should be noted about the vital Clause III in the 'Essentials'. First, how the Government and the Services interpreted the word 'prospect' of successful negotiations in early October was to be a crucial point. Second, only the decision on *whether* to go to war would be made in early October. There was as yet no *resolve* to go to war. Third, should the decision be for war, there was no stipulation as to the date for its commencement, which would be determined by a fresh decision. Konoe, in a prepared statement at the Imperial Conference, put the emphasis on diplomacy. They must 'try to prevent the disaster of war by resorting to all possible diplomatic measures'. Nagano's statement, which followed, played down diplomacy and talked more about war preparations and, if need be, war itself:

in the event that a peaceful solution is not attainable, and we have no alternative but to resort to war, the Supreme Command believes, from the standpoint of operations, that we cannot avoid being finally reduced to a crippled condition [if we delay for too long]. A number of vital military supplies, including oil, are dwindling day by day. This will cause a gradual weakening of our national defense. ... Meanwhile, the defenses of American, British, and other foreign military facilities and vital points in the Far East ... are being strengthened with great speed. ...

Accordingly, if our minimum demands, which are necessary for the self-preservation and self-defense of our Empire, cannot be attained through diplomacy, and ultimately we cannot avoid war, we must first make all preparations, take advantage of our opportunities, undertake aggressive military operations with determination and a dauntless attitude, and find a way out of our difficulties.

Nagano then spoke about the naval strategy and the prospects of a war against the United and Britain, if war became inevitable. They must, he concluded, spare no efforts to settle the present crisis peacefully. 'We must never fight a war that can be avoided.' At the same time they must not be forced into a position in which they would have to fight under extremely disadvantageous conditions. The Army, stated its Chief of Staff, Sugiyama, was 'in complete agreement' with Nagano's statement. Oikawa had little to say. He was prepared for war if diplomacy did not secure Japan's demands.

Indeed, no dissenting voices were raised at this conference to the momentous decisions on policy.

The custom at the conclusion of an Imperial Conference was for the Emperor to indicate his acceptance of the decisions reached by nodding and leaving the room without uttering a single word. On this occasion, however, Hirohito amazed those present by clearing his throat and proceeding to read from a piece of paper he had taken from his pocket. It was a poem that his grandfather, the Emperor Meiji, had composed:

> All the seas in every quarter are
> as brothers to one another.
> Why, then, do the winds and waves of strife rage
> so turbulently throughout the world?

He counselled the assembly to ponder the meaning and take appropriate action.[23] Amid the solemn silence that ensued—the participants were deeply moved by this break with precedent—Nagano and Sugiyama stated that the Supreme Command was in accord with the Government in awarding diplomacy priority over war preparations. The difference was that Konoe was still hopeful of a peaceful settlement; the Supreme Command was pessimistic. And well might they be, as the history of the negotiations showed there was virtually no prospect of American acceptance of Japan's minimum demands.

The Services accelerated their war preparations, while Konoe went about the thankless task of pulling off a miracle in Washington. The two Chiefs of Staff, impatient with 'the unexpectedly slow progress of the diplomatic negotiations, the shortage of time and the increasing urgency of operational demands', demanded in a memorandum of 25 September that the Government set a 15 October deadline for the negotiations and decide on war or peace by that date. To complete war preparations by the end of October, it was necessary to make the decision for war at least two weeks in advance. 'Each day's delay increases Japan's operational disadvantages.' The two Chiefs argued their case at the Liaison Conference on 25 September. Konoe was shocked by the deadline; but the hard-line American reply on 2 October to the Japanese proposals

---

[23] Ike, pp. 133–63, has the proceedings and documents of the 6 September Imperial Conference, including this translation of the poem.

of 6 September practically snuffed out any hope of a diplomatic solution by confirming the four principles and demanding the withdrawal of Japanese troops from China and French Indo-China, respect for the principle of non-discrimination in China, and the abandonment of the Tripartite Pact. The negotiations were deadlocked. The Army judged there was no more room for negotiation and that war was inevitable. Nagano was of the same mind. At the Liaison Conference on 4 October he uttered that famous remark: 'There is no longer time for discussion. We want action.' Other Navy leaders, on the other hand, and especially Oikawa, were reluctant to see the talks ended, being pessimistic about the Navy's chances in a long war. A crisis was fast approaching.

2. THE EQUIVOCATION OF THE NAVY

Oikawa had called the Prime Minister's attention on 1 October to the critical oil situation. The Combined Fleet was consuming 10,000 tons a day, and if this situation continued, the day would come when the Fleet would have no oil. Only successful negotiations with the United States could prevent this. If absolutely necessary, they should be prepared to swallow all the American proposals. Konoe 'fully agreed' with Oikawa's opinion. At a meeting of Navy VIPs on 6 October in Oikawa's official residence (Navy Minister, Vice-Navy Minister, Chief and Vice-Chief of the *Gunreibu*, Chief of the Naval Affairs Bureau, and Chief of the Operations Division), the decision was reached that the diplomatic negotiations should be continued, and that it would be absurd to get involved in a war with the United States over the issue of maintaining troops in China. In principle, Japan should accept the US requirement of a gradual withdrawal of the troops from the continent. Oikawa promised to make every effort, for the sake of the country, to persuade the Army, while avoiding a direct confrontation between the two Services. Then, addressing himself to the *Gunreibu* Chief: 'Do you, Admiral Nagano, agree that I should proceed this way, with determination, and that if worst comes to worst, the Navy is prepared to come to blows with the Army?' Nagano's reply threw a chill over the gathering: 'I cannot definitely say yes.'[24] There was,

[24] Sawamoto, 'Shi shuki'.

nevertheless, hope that the Army would come round to the Navy's position. At the end of a conference between the two Service Ministers on the 7th, General Tōjō said, with a pathetic expression: 'Japan has lost over 200,000 officers and men in the China War. This should not have been in vain. If, however, Japan went to war with the United States, there would be many more casualties. Accordingly, we should consider carefully the American request that we withdraw our troops from China. I am at a crossroads as to which path to take. I have not yet decided which it is to be.'[25] By 12 October he had made up his mind: that to withdraw from China would have a devastating effect on the morale of the troops. Furthermore, meeting the American demand would only postpone the evil day; in two or three years there would be a more serious crisis—and war.

On 12 October a crucial Five Ministers' 'Ogikubo' conference (named after its setting, Konoe's villa in the Tokyo suburb of Ogikubo) was held between the Prime Minister, the Foreign Minister, the Service Ministers, and the Planning Board President, Lieutenant-General Suzuki Teiichi, to debate the question of war or peace, specifically whether there was a possibility of a successful conclusion of the negotiations in Washington, in view of the fact that it was already near the middle of the month, which was set as the deadline. The conference revealed a split between the Service Ministers on what should be done. Oikawa, speaking first, was equivocal. He was obviously worried about the outcome of a war, yet would not come right out and say so. 'We are at the crossroads,' he said. The time had arrived for the big decision; but the Navy was prepared 'to leave matters entirely to the Prime Minister',[26] that is, on whether to continue the negotiations. If Japan were to rely on diplomacy, she must stick to it and achieve success. If war were to be resorted to, that decision should be made at once, for, if the negotiations were to continue for two or three months, then given up, 'the Navy will be troubled', that is, it would be too late to fight. Konoe replied that he was determined to avoid war with the

[25] Ibid.
[26] Prior to the conference, Konoe received a message from Oka, the Chief of the Bureau of Naval Affairs, that stated: 'The Navy does not desire to have the American–Japanese negotiations disrupted. The Navy desires to avoid war as much as circumstances permit. But the Navy cannot say it openly. At today's conference the Navy Minister will propose "entrusting to the Prime Minister the matter of deciding either for peace or war." Please understand this point.' *The Memoirs of Prince Fumimaro Konoye*, p. 54.

United States and to settle all matters through diplomatic negotiations. He indicated that he was prepared to make concessions on the central issue of the troops in China. He had no confidence in case of a long drawn-out war, and if the choice had to be made then between diplomacy and war, he would choose diplomacy, because a war should be fought only by those who were confident of success. The Foreign Minister, Toyoda, supported the Prime Minister. The national policy decided on 6 September was, he said, 'a little hasty'. Tōjō was disgusted. 'It would be a serious matter if we continued the hopeless negotiations and thus miss the chance. Does the Foreign Minister have any confidence of success in the negotiations?' None at all, was Toyoda's answer, unless the Army was prepared to make a concession on the issue of troop withdrawal from China. To which Tōjō retorted that the Army could make no such concession; it would nullify the enormous sacrifices made by the Army during four years of fighting. No conclusion had been reached when, after four hours of heated discussion, the conference broke up. On returning to the Navy Ministry, Oikawa told Oka that the Prime Minister was 'too weak-kneed to control the Services, and the situation is approaching the crisis stage'.[27]

Oikawa's equivocation made him equally culpable. When the question was asked after the war, at the navy leaders' round-table conference on 22 January 1946, why he had not clearly articulated the Navy's 'no war' position and, in Admiral Inoue's words, 'continued to resist the Army courageously like a man', Oikawa's reply was twofold. 'My mind was dominated by the words which Admiral of the Fleet Tōgō had stated to *Gunreibu* Chief Taniguchi, who was opposed to the Manchurian Incident, that "the *Gunreibu* has been presenting operational plans every year to the Emperor; therefore, if we were to say that we were not able to carry out operations against the United States, it would have meant that we had been lying to the Emperor." I also have been reporting to the Emperor, agreeing with the plan every year; so that would have meant that I, too, had been lying to the Emperor. How could we tell the Emperor things like that now?' In second place, Oikawa continued, 'At that time there was a saying, "Don't let Konoe put *geta* [wooden clogs] on you" [i.e. don't let him hand over the full responsibility to the Navy]; and the Navy had been on its guard. I

---

[27] Vice-Admiral Oka Takazumi, 'Oboe' [Recollections], Bōeichō Senshibu Archives.

was warned about it also by the *Gunreibu* and the Navy Ministry Bureau of Naval Affairs. So far as the Navy was concerned, it was not a matter of "giving carte blanche to Kanoe", but was only meant to get him to take the lead' (i.e. encouraging him to exercise stronger leadership). To Admiral Inoue's query whether he believed that Konoe was competent to solve the problem, Oikawa replied: 'I believed that the Navy could not solve the problem that even the Prime Minister could not solve,' to which Inoue retorted: 'You should have resigned from the Cabinet. Why didn't you? That would have been to play the Navy's trump card.'[28] Another explanation of Oikawa's reluctance to speak clearly and frankly may have been his fear, and that of many senior naval officers, of an Army *coup d'état* if the Government gave in to the American demands.[29] Finally, there is the plausible explanation advanced by Admiral Toyoda Soemu in his memoirs, that Oikawa was being subjected to pressures from the hawks among upper- and middle-echelon naval officers, who were hand in glove with extremist Army officers.[30]

It has been said that 'Oikawa lost the last chance' (to prevent war).[31] This is going too far, since it must be emphasized that the Navy itself was split. Nagano was of the same mind as the Army that operational requirements dictated the end of the palaver in Washington and the resort to war by November. He summarized his position in these words: '1. Extension of the negotiations will handicap operations. 2. If the negotiations are to be continued, they must be conducted with the conviction of success. We cannot help you, should the negotiations be deadlocked. Now is not the time to be conducting test-firing without a conviction of hitting the target.'[32]

---

[28] *Senshi sōsho*, xci 559, Shinmyō, pp. 178–80. The *Senshi sōsho* comment is that the first point 'displayed a misunderstanding of the real substance of the annual operational plans, which must be implemented by an Imperial order under a war plan in case of an emergency'. The second point 'indicated that the Navy, following its tradition of [respecting] political supremacy, expected the Prime Minister to exercise the fullest leadership'.

[29] See, for example, Oikawa's affidavit at the Tokyo Trials, IMTFE, Defence Document No. 2761.

[30] *Saigo no teikoku kaigun*, p. 65. Professor Asada leans towards Toyoda's analysis as the best explanation of Oikawa's behaviour. 'The Japanese Navy and the United States', p. 255. It fits in with Oikawa's character.

[31] TSM, vii. 288.

[32] Hattori, *The Greater East Asia War*, i. 191. This is the note from which Nagano was going to speak at the Liaison Conference on 9 October when he was 'checked' by Oikawa.

THE EQUIVOCATION OF THE NAVY

Konoe saw Tōjō on the 14th, but had no luck in getting him to reconsider. 'If we yield to the United States at this time, the latter will become more arrogant and more overbearing.' At the Cabinet meeting that followed, Tōjō reiterated his position with some heat; the negotiations should not continue. There was no response, and the meeting went on to other business. The impasse was complete.

Tōjō saw no hope for the completion of the negotiations; it would be irresponsible to change the national policy adopted on 6 September, which had decided for war against the ABD Powers if there was no prospect for the acceptance of Japan's demands by early October, and here it was already 14 October. Besides, there was no room for compromise about the troops in China and French Indo-China, which was the key to a settlement. Whereas the Prime Minister and Foreign Minister wanted to continue the negotiations with the United States and were prepared to compromise on the troop withdrawal issue, the Army wished to break off the talks and plunge into war before Japan's military position worsened yet more relative to the United States. And the Navy once again at the Cabinet meeting on the 14th refused to commit itself, preferring to entrust the matter of peace or war to an exasperated Prime Minister. That evening Tōjō sent a message to Konoe advising that the Cabinet should resign. They must 'return to a clean slate position and new plans will have to be made all over again'.

Placed in a dilemma between the Services and not knowing how to solve it, and with the breach between him and the War Minister having reached the point where Tōjō would no longer speak to him, Konoe handed in the resignation of his Cabinet on 16 October. The Navy leaders shed no tears. They had felt that he should make way for a stronger man. Rumours flew around Tokyo that the next Prime Minister would be the hawkish Admiral Suetsugu, or the one time War Minister General Koiso Kuniaki, or Tōjō. On the 17th a conference of seven elder statesmen (the *Jūshin*)—former Prime Ministers, including Admirals Okada and Yonai—met and unanimously accepted Lord Keeper of the Privy Seal Kido's recommendation of Tōjō, *faute de mieux*, as they could not agree on anyone else. (The duties of Marquis Kido, the Emperor's chief political adviser, included the recommendation of a new prime minister whenever a new Cabinet was being formed.) The next day Tōjō received an Imperial mandate to form a new Cabinet and was at the same time promoted from lieutenant-general to full general.

His appointment as Prime Minister while retaining his active status in the Army was a departure from precedent. He retained the War Ministry in order to be able to exert influence on the Army. The solidly built Tōjō, with the small, egg-shaped, practically bald head and horn-rimmed spectacles, became the caricaturists delight in the west. Although hard-working, he was not up to the premiership, as events were to prove. He was irascible and lacked a broad vision.

Oikawa's shillyshallying had doomed him so far as the Army was concerned, although he testified at the Tokyo Trials that he had 'decided not to succeed himself as Navy Minister before I ever heard that Lt. General Tojo was to become the new premier. I had made up my mind that a new man might better function in that capacity than I had and that as a matter of political morality it was best that I not succeed myself.' By 'political morality' he meant that it would not have been proper for the old Cabinet ministers to have stayed on in the new Cabinet, whose duty was expected to be to 'wipe the slate clean and start afresh'.[33]

The outgoing Navy Minister was responsible for recommending his successor to the Prime Minister, after consultation with the Vice-Minister, the Chief of the Naval Affairs Bureau, and other officers. Prince Fushimi was always the strong man in such a case. On this occasion Oikawa consulted the Vice-Navy Minister, Sawamoto, the Vice-Chief of Staff, Itō Seiichi, the Chief of the Naval Affairs Bureau, Oka, the Chief of the Operations Division, Fukudome, and the Chief of the Personnel Bureau, Rear-Admiral Nakahara Yoshimasa. All five agreed to recommend the very able Admiral Toyoda Soemu, then C-in-C of the Kure Naval District. But when Oikawa reported this recommendation to Prince Fushimi on the 17th the latter objected that Toyoda was 'too talkative and has a strong tendency to be disruptive [*hakai-teki*]. You should stay.'

---

[33] Oikawa's affidavit, Defence Document No. 3559, and testimony, IMTFE, pp. 34,570–1, 34,590–1. The Emperor's distrust of Oikawa, of which the latter was presumably aware, must have been another reason for his resignation. When Admiral Shimada, his successor, visited the Palace on 20 October, he was told by the Emperor's ADC, General Hasunuma, that His Majesty had a deep anxiety over US-Japanese relations, and that he had not been satisfied with Oikawa because of his indecisive attitude, sometimes being in favour of war and sometimes against war; he would change his views overnight. 'Shimada Shigetarō taishō muhyōdai bibōroku (Taishō jidai kara shūsen go made)' [Admiral Shimada's Collection of Memoranda without Title (From the end of the Taishō Era to the End of the War)], Bōeichō Senshibu Archives, Shimada interview, 13 April. 1964, Bōeichō Senshibu Archives. What follows, on the appointment of Oikawa's successor, is based on the full account in Sawamoto, 'Shi shuki'.

But he was not entirely against the appointment. Whereupon Admiral Nakahara telephoned Toyoda at Kure and asked him to come to the Navy Ministry immediately, taking his decorations with him (for use, if appointed, in the appointment ceremony). A happy Toyoda reported to Oikawa late in the afternoon of the 17th. While they were talking, Oikawa was called to the Palace by telephone. He returned a half hour later to his official residence (next door to the Ministry) and told the assembled Navy VIPs (the above five) who had gathered there: 'General Tōjō [the newly appointed Prime Minister] told me: "I don't care for Toyoda as Navy Minister. He is quite unpopular with the Army leaders, and he lacks a co-operative attitude. Therefore, if you insist on recommending Toyoda as the next Navy Minister, I will resign."' Sawamoto, with support from Itō and Nakahara, strongly opposed yielding to the Army under those conditions; it would set a bad precedent. Oikawa pointed out that if he recommended Toyoda over the objections of the Army, the new Cabinet would be aborted. 'In the past there have been instances of naval appointments where we asked for the Army's opinion, and vice versa. Accordingly, if Tōjō ... insists on his objection to the Toyoda appointment, we shall have to accept it.' Sawamoto suggested that if they had to accept Tōjō's veto, it should be reported that Toyoda had refused of his own free will, not through Army pressure, to be Navy Minister, but that he, Sawamoto, preferred that Oikawa stay on. Itō and Nakahara supported him. Oikawa, refusing to consider this option, proposed Shimada as his successor, and the five Admirals agreed. In the meantime, poor Toyoda had been waiting for the happy tidings in Oikawa's office. Oikawa returned and broke the news. 'I am sorry, Admiral Toyoda, but various reasons have made it impossible for you to assume the post of Navy Minister.' Toyoda accepted the situation and, after dining with Oikawa, returned to Kure.[34] The larger significance of the episode is that, conceivably,

---

[34] Toyoda apparently fell in with the scheme that it should be got out that he had refused the appointment of his own free will. The story was that on arrival in Tokyo he had asked Oikawa who the new Prime Minister was going to be. Told it would to Tōjō, Toyoda is supposed to have blurted out: 'I don't want to be Navy Minister under General Tōjō. I don't like the Army!' And he had gone back to Kure. Toyoda was famous for his hatred of the Army. 'I don't like khaki,' he often said. He called the Army *maguso* (horse-shit), and spoke of 'those *rikusuke*' (landlubbers or countryfolk). Interviews with Commander Chihaya Masataka, 7 July 1976, and Lieutenant Agawa Hiroyuki, 19 July 1976. Toyoda's extreme dislike of the Army is said to have originated in a severe confrontation he had with it when he captured Tsingtao as 4th Fleet Commander during the China Incident.

Toyoda's appointment might have stemmed the steady drift towards war. He firmly believed that a war with the United States and Britain would be unrealistic.

Later in same evening of the 17th, Shimada was summoned to Tokyo from Yokosuka and was offered the post. He demurred, feeling that he had been out of touch with naval affairs, having been away from Tokyo since December 1937, had never served in the Navy Ministry, and had a distaste for politics. But he asked for time, until the next morning, to make a final decision. He returned to Tokyo in the morning, and in a half-hour talk with Nagano was persuaded to accept the post.

Admiral Shimada Shigetarō, the new Navy Minister (–July 1944), was a former Vice-Chief of the Naval General Staff (1935–7), when (1936) the *Gunreibu* had forced the Southern policy on the Cabinet of Hirota Kōki. He had just assumed the post of C-in-C of the Yokosuka Naval District, following his command of the China Area Fleet, in which post he had succeeded Oikawa in May 1940. He was, like Oikawa, tall for a Japanese, and was rather stout. He was agreeable, charming, jovial, very clever,[35] and very religious. He often worshipped at the Meiji shrine in Tokyo. Shimada was dedicated to peace, but was as poor a Navy Minister as Oikawa had been. Admirals Hori and Yamamoto, as close friends of Shimada, were well aware of his weaknesses. It was common knowledge, Hori once said, that Shimada was very much like Oikawa, and Yamamoto criticized him as a 'fool' or 'simpleton' (*medetai*).[36] He had no mind of his own—he was known in the Service as a 'yes man'—and co-operated with Tōjō to the point where one admiral (Takagi Takeo) called him a 'bedfellow' of Tōjō. Senior naval officers referred to him as Tōjō's 'lackey'. Shimada was convinced that the Army and Navy had to work together, and he had no taste for quarrelling with the senior Service. He was a protégé of Prince Fushimi, whose Vice-Chief of Staff he had been for a while. Captain Ōi Atsushi was once advised: 'If you want to get promoted, imitate Shimada: be very cautious towards and subservient to your superiors.' Shimada was never known to have opposed the Prince;

---

[35] Shimada was 27/191 in the Naval Academy class of 1904. Admiral Fukuchi, who was Secretary to three successive Navy Ministers, rates him as smarter than Yoshida or Oikawa. It was Craigie's estimate of Shimada in 1938 that 'Outwardly he does not give the impression of a clever man, but in reality he is shrewd, able and obstinate.' 'Records of Leading Personalities in Japan', in Craigie to Halifax, 2 Apr. 1938, PO 371/22192.
[36] TSM, vii. 311.

he had the reputation of putting forth opinions that would be acceptable to his Chief. As Navy Minister, Shimada did not make decisions by himself when important matters came up. He invariably went to the Prince, who was a supporter of the Army's vigorous line, and followed his advice.

Sawamoto and Oka remained as Vice-Navy Minister and Chief of the Bureau of Naval Affairs. On the *Gunreibu* side, Nagano continued as Chief of Staff, and Fukudome as Chief of the 1st Division. But Vice-Admiral Itō Seiichi had replaced Kondō as Vice-Chief of Staff on 1 September. The highly respected Itō, one of the best Japanese naval officers of his generation (15/148, class of 1911), was a vast improvement over Kondō. He was in respects ideal for the appointment. The tall, bulky square-faced Itō was pleasant and very approachable. He made good use of his subordinates, while giving much of himself. He looked after everything for his Chief, which permitted Nagano to sleep and rest whenever he liked. He had his own opinions, yet was eager to listen to anybody's views, and he was adept in naval politics. Itō, moreover, understood the United States. He had been there and had an appreciation of the country and its Navy. Could a moderate, however able, instill common sense into a naval leadership headed by the likes of Nagano and Shimada?

When the Emperor commanded Tōjō to form a government, he also instructed him to disregard the decision of the Imperial Conference of 6 September and to re-examine the situation freshly before determining the national policy. Tōjō accordingly instructed the new Cabinet to 'go back to a blank sheet of paper', and he announced that his Government was not bound by previous decisions on national policy and would continue the negotiations. Indeed, the new Foreign Minister, the 'grim, unsmiling, and ultrareserved' Tōgō Shigenori (a Foreign Office official who had been Ambassador in Moscow in 1938-40), like Shimada had agreed to serve only after Tōjō had assured them that his Government was sincerely committed to continuing the negotiations and exploring every possible avenue. In his interview with Shimada on the 18th, Tōjō had 'emphatically agreed that it would be the policy of the government to start from scratch in attempting to wholeheartedly and sincerely reach a diplomatic understanding to the end of preventing war in accordance with the Emperor's wish'. He also accepted Shimada's condition that the new Cabinet should make every effort to accelerate the Navy's war preparedness programme.[37] The dovish elements among the Navy's leaders feared the worst. Admiral Oka's reaction to Tōjō's appointment was: 'I felt that war between Japan and the United States was inevitable.'[38] Despite the new Government's proclamation of their good intentions, the distrust of Tōjō was such in the United States and Britain, where he was considered to be closely identified with the Army extremists, that the new Cabinet was regarded as a War Cabinet. This produced an immediate response in London that was to have the gravest consequences. At this point we must retrace our steps to the strategic scene as viewed from London at the beginning of the year.

[37] Shimada's testimony, IMTFE, p. 34,654, Shimada, 'Nikki' [Diary], 18 Oct. 1941, Bōeichō Senshibu Archives.
[38] Koyanagi, 'Kaigun chūjō Oka Takazumi danwa shūroku.'

VII

Anglo–American–Dutch Collaboration (1941)

> ... the issues at stake are so fundamental that the loss of Singapore would be a disaster of the first magnitude, second only to the loss of the British Isles.
>
> Appreciation by the United Kingdom Delegation at the US–UK Staff Conference in Washington, 11 February 1941.
>
> The eastern Dominions, the Netherlands East Indies and China look upon its [Singapore's] security as the guarantee of their safety. Its value as a symbol has become so great that its capture would be a serious blow. But many severe blows have been taken by these various nations, and other severe blows can be absorbed without leading to final disaster.
>
> Appreciation by the United States Delegation at same, 19 February 1941.

1. 'THE FIRST THING IS TO GET THE UNITED STATES INTO THE WAR'

THE coming of 1941 inaugurated a time of Far Eastern jitters in London. Signs of an imminent Japanese southward move multiplied in late January and early February—that they would attack Singapore (there was no knowledge of Ribbentrop's attempts to induce Japan to attack Singapore) and perhaps the Netherlands East Indies as well, and seize southern French Indo-China for good measure. Japanese warships were active off the southern coast of Indo-China. This was Japan's effective way of putting pressure on the French colony to agree to a cease-fire in the localized war with Thailand. It was signed in the *Natori*, anchored at Saigon, on 31 January. Japanese mediation suggested to the British the possibility that Japan might secure for her trouble a naval base at Camranh Bay and maybe even agreement with the Thais for an attack on British or Dutch possessions. Additionally, there was a report (false) of a landing force off Singora (Songkhla) on the Kra Isthmus of Thailand near Malaya, and reports of the cancellation of sailings of Japanese ships and of the Government commandeering them. Suspicions were further raised when the tapping of Japanese Embassy telephones in London revealed an excited state of affairs. Most important in stirring British apprehensions about the Far East was a report of 5 February from the Joint Intelligence Sub-Committee. It drew attention to the gravity of the situation in the Far East and reinforced this warning by a 'most secret intelligence report', from which it appeared that the Japanese had decided on a policy which they knew might in the near future lead to war with the British Empire.

Requested by the Chiefs of Staff to submit a short recommendation as to British action in this event, the Joint Planners stated that there was no military move they could make in the Far East in the near future apart from the reinforcement of Malaya by one or two Indian or Australian infantry brigades, but that this was unlikely to deter the Japanese. The solution of the problem lay with the United States. If they could persuade the Japanese that their action would bring the United States into the war as well as the British Empire, this would probably deter them. The time had come to take up this question with the US Administration at the highest level. 'Even if the United States is unwilling at this stage to make an open declaration of her policy, she might be persuaded to make a significant gesture in the Far East such as increasing her Naval forces at Manila and sending a detachment to Singapore.' Also, Britain should herself convey a strong warning to Japan that if she continued her policy of southward expansion, the British would be compelled to react in self-defence. 'We are of the opinion that the stronger the line we take the more likely are the Japanese to believe that the United States is behind us. In any case we would be instilling doubt and hesitation in their minds.'[1] The Service Chiefs approved the report (6 February) and discussed it that night with the Prime Minister.

They proceeded to consider the strategical implications of a Japanese thrust to the south in response to a War Cabinet directive of 5 February. Japan, they believed, would 'almost certainly not confine her activities to Indo-China alone but carry them into Thailand ... Japan will probably take advantage of her role as mediator between the Thais and the French to gain bases from which to threaten Malaya, the Netherlands East Indies, North

---

[1] JP(41)95, 'Measures to Avert War with Japan', 5 Feb. 1941, CAB 84/27.

'THE FIRST THING IS TO GET THE UNITED STATES INTO THE WAR'

Borneo and possibly Burma. With these bases in her hands we think that Japan will probably select the Netherlands East Indies as her first objective, and that any move she makes will be timed to fit in with a German major offensive.' The conclusions drawn were that Japanese control over Indo-China alone would bring the threat of attack on British possessions nearer but would not in itself directly affect our vital interests. It would increase the ability of the Japanese to control the South China Sea and threaten the line of communication between Singapore and Manila. This would be in accordance with Japan's traditional step-by-step policy, and would almost certainly lead to the acquisition of bases in Thailand.

A Japanese penetration of Thailand would threaten Singapore, and make the defence of Burma and Malaya far more difficult. It would be an added threat to our communications in the Indian Ocean.[2]

Churchill confided his fears to Roosevelt in a telegram of 15 February that stressed the serious consequences of Japanese naval attacks on British trade and communications in the Pacific and Indian Oceans, and tried to convince the President of the urgent need to take deterrent action against Japan.

Many drifting straws seem to indicate Japanese intentions to make war on us or do something that would force us to make war on them in the next few weeks or months. I am not myself convinced that this is not a war of nerves designed to cover Japanese encroachments in Siam and Indo-China. However, I think I ought to let you know that the weight of the Japanese Navy, if thrown against us, would confront us with situations beyond the scope of our naval resources....

Everything that you can do to inspire the Japanese with the fear of a double war may avert the danger. If however they come in against us and we are alone, the grave character of the consequences cannot easily be overstated.[3]

The President had already warned the Japanese Ambassador that another move might find Japan at war with the United States.

From this date, however, there was for some months a relaxation in tension. Matsuoka's assurances to Craigie in Tokyo, and Shigemitsu's in London, about Japan's peaceful intentions *vis-à-vis* the United States and Britain, and reports that Matsuoka was restraining the Army and Navy, and especially that he was going

---
[2] COS(41)104, 'Implications of the Japanese Southward Move', 15 Feb. 1941, CAB 80/26.
[3] Sir Llewellyn Woodward, *British Foreign Policy in the Second World War* (5 vols., London, 1970–6), ii. 124.

to visit Berlin, Rome, and Moscow in March, suggested that no bold move was imminent in the Far East. Not that London thought that Japan had given up her plans for a southward advance; she had only postponed them. Churchill, however, was almost alone among the decision-makers to view developments in the Far East hopefully. On 4 March, after a visit of the Japanese Ambassador, he minuted: 'I do not think Japan is likely to attack us unless she is sure we are going to be defeated', an opinion he reaffirmed late in April. And he comforted himself with the thought that if Japan attacked Great Britain, the United States would come in. But *would* they? And if they did, would there be a well co-ordinated Allied naval strategy to contain and then defeat her Navy? The Staff talks agreed to in December might provide the answers.

The American–British Staff Conference (ABC), began in Washington at the Old Navy Building on Constitution Avenue on 29 January 1941 and ended, after fourteen plenary sessions, on 29 March.[4] To maintain secrecy, the members of the British Mission were in plain clothes and were accredited as additional members of the British Purchasing Mission. The fact of the conversations as well as their substance were top secret, and the British Delegation was left in no doubt about the importance the President attached to this. Rear-Admiral Bellairs, who headed the British delegation, was very experienced in the RN planning world, but he lacked personality ('to look at him he was more like a bishop than an admiral', observes one member of his team) and was overshadowed by the other members, the former D of P, Rear-Admiral V. H. Danckwerts, Major-General E. L. Morris, Air Vice-Marshal J. C. Slessor, and Captain A. W. Clarke, RN. Although not in good health, Danckwert's 'first-class brain and wide experience made a great contribution to the success of the conversations', in Slessor's opinion. The delegation represented the Chiefs of Staff and was guided by their views. The American side was headed by an experienced planner, the colourless Major-General S. D. Embick, who acted as Chairman of the Conference, and included, on the naval side, Rear-Admirals Ghormley and R. K. Turner, Head of the Navy's War Plans Division. Kelly Turner, 'a very able and forcible officer whose influence in the Navy Department was

[4] The minutes and papers of the Washington Conference are in the BUS(41) and BUS(J)(41) series in CAB 99/5. The former contains the memoranda circulated to the UK Delegation, the latter, the minutes and papers of the joint meetings.

'THE FIRST THING IS TO GET THE UNITED STATES INTO THE WAR'

perhaps more powerful than his position warranted' (he was a prime mover in the formulation of Plan Dog, gave the British delegates an extremely difficult time. 'In 1940 he could be what one of his colleagues called "as ornery as hell," and . . . was rather liable to start from the assumption that he was right and everyone else either fools or knaves. . . . Nevertheless he was a splendid chap, a doughty champion of what he believed to be right, and he had an endearing trick, at the height of a terrific argument when he was being as difficult as he could be, of suddenly laughing at himself and coming to meet our point of view.'[5] 'Terrible Turner', as he was known, was to make his reputation as an amphibious commander in the Pacific War.

The main difference between the delegations was that the British were an inter-Service team, practised in thrashing out policy and plans, and meeting their opposite numbers with an agreed inter-Service view. The Americans, in contrast, were not a team in the British sense. They had not met each other to develop a single inter-Service view before the Conference. Moreover, the Army and Navy components, unlike the British, usually met separately before the plenary sessions. Lacking an agreed policy, the American delegates sometimes brought their differences to the table, and occasionally the British delegation found itself in the position of referee. Personal relations between the Americans and British were on the whole excellent. Differences of opinion there were, and the need for someone to pour oil on troubled waters was recognized in a cartoon the US delegation presented to Slessor which showed him doing just that from the bow of a very small boat in a very rough sea.

The basic purpose of the Staff Conference was 'to determine the best methods by which the Armed Forces of the United States and British Commonwealth, with its present Allies, could defeat Germany and the Powers allied with her, should the United States be compelled to resort to war'. The early meetings brought out a serious difference of views on Far Eastern strategy. The British strategy called for a concentration of almost the whole of the US Pacific Fleet at Singapore, instead of being locked up in Hawaiian waters nearly 6,000 miles to the east from where it could not serve as an effective deterrent to a Japanese southward advance. It was only through a strong Allied fleet based on Singapore, which was

[5] Marshal of the RAF Sir John Slessor, *The Central Blue: Recollections and Reflections* (London, 1956), pp. 355–6.

half the distance from Japanese home waters as Pearl Harbor, that the Malay Barrier (the great arc of islands from Sumatra to Timor) could be defended. Moreover, as the Japanese moved south, they would approach Singapore but get farther from Pearl Harbor. And a fleet so based would deter a Japanese move against Hawaii, to say nothing of California. We must appreciate that Singapore was a great deal more than a powerful base. It was a symbol of British might and prestige, and of Commonwealth unity and security in the Far East. As expressed in a British delegation paper on 11 February, the maintenance of a fleet base at Singapore was based, 'not only upon purely strategic foundations, but on political, economic and sentimental considerations which ... are of such vital importance to the British Commonwealth that they must always be taken into serious account'. The major British concern was the strategic one. As explained by Pound, the 'economical method' of controlling the Pacific was to have one battle fleet at Singapore strong enough to meet the whole Japanese Fleet. The Royal Navy was unable to provide such a fleet, and the Americans would not, although the 'economical and correct strategical disposition' of their Pacific Fleet was to base it on Singapore. 'If there is only one Fleet in the Pacific at Hawaii, it is doubtful whether the pressure on the Japanese will be sufficient to deter them from expanding their land operations to the southward.'[6] This strategy was in direct opposition to the American strategy of basing their Pacific Fleet on Honolulu, with a limited offensive role, and putting their main effort in the Atlantic.

There were no surprises in the positions put forward by the two sides; but they generated much heat and constituted a formidable obstacle to a successful conclusion of the meetings. The essential point was Singapore. Politically, it was unthinkable for the United States, if at war, to dispatch the bulk of her main fleet to a foreign base so distant from the Pacific Coast, thereby leaving the direct route to her own shores uncovered. Moreover, as the Americans declared at the second meeting (31 January), 'It was difficult to believe that the Japanese would actually penetrate the Indian Ocean, and seriously threaten British sea communications to the Middle East, even if Singapore had fallen. It was contrary to the traditional Japanese policy of caution.' The British riposte was:

[6] Pound's minute to Churchill, 13 Feb. 1941, ADM 205/10.

'THE FIRST THING IS TO GET THE UNITED STATES INTO THE WAR'

'Japanese penetration of the Indian Ocean would be greatly facilitated if the Japanese had the use of Malaya as a base.' Other considerations on the American side with which the British could not cope were the vast distance of the supply route, the unsatisfactory state of Singapore's defences—the base would be vulnerable to air attack as well as to attack from the land side—and the inadequacy of repair facilities for capital ships. Unspoken was the extreme American reluctance to do anything that might imply a commitment to defend the British Empire in the East. There was, as Slessor detected, 'even the light-hearted assumption that it didn't matter all that much if Singapore did fall, we could always get it back when we won the war—and I still find it very difficult to understand. I have sometimes wondered ... whether it was in any way connected with the traditional American dislike of "colonialism" and to a feeling that it was not up to them to protect British trading interests in Malaya with American arms.'[7]

Admiral Turner outlined the role of the US Navy in the Pacific and Far East at the third meeting (3 February). It was prepared to assume responsibility for American and British interests in the Pacific east of the 180th meridian, and, south of the equator, to support British naval operations as far west as 155° East. The objectives of the Pacific Fleet would be to sever Japanese sea communications east of the 180th meridian, deny Japan the Marshall Islands, and raid to the westward, to support 'associated [the US euphemism for 'Allied'] forces in holding the Malay Barrier. The objective of the supporting operations would be the diversion of Japanese forces toward Japan or into the Mandates and thus weakening their power against Malaysia.' The US Asiatic Fleet would defend the Philippines. If its position became untenable, it would continue operations from another base, 'probably either Singapore or Surabaya'. The Americans proposed that, since the British line of communications to the Far East was secure, whereas their own was 'extremely hazardous', they should augment British naval forces in the Atlantic and Mediterranean, which would permit the British to strengthen their naval forces in the Far East. Danckwerts brought out that

the crux of the matter was the extent to which the operations of the United States Pacific Fleet would in fact restrain Japan. If this fleet was to remain

---

[7] Slessor, *The Central Blue*, p. 347.

comparatively inactive, then the fear of the British Chiefs of Staff was that they might be forced to despatch forces to the Far East in fulfillment of their assurances to the Dominions and for the maintenance of the Eastern war effort of the British Commonwealth.

This would be a wasteful distribution of force in the Pacific at the expense of the more immediately important European theatre. If, on the other hand, the operations of the United States Pacific Fleet were to be such as to restrain Japan, then the joint object of restraining Japan while concentrating the maximum force in the principal theatres would have been achieved'. . . .

If the Pacific Fleet were to remain passive in Pearl Harbour, this would place no restraint at all on Japan, who would thus be free to operate to the southward. It would seem, therefore, that in these circumstances greater strength would be required in the Asiatic Fleet.

The American position was that the proposed strength of their Pacific Fleet (nine battleships) would be sufficient 'to prevent any Japanese major move to the southward. It was considered strategically unsound to reduce the strength of the Pacific Fleet in order to reinforce the Asiatic Fleet, since, if this were done, neither fleet would be strong enough to accomplish a decisive effort.' It was by now apparent to the British delegation that it was improbable that they would succeed in getting the Pacific Fleet moved to the westward to Singapore, and that the Pacific Fleet based on Hawaii would not pose a 'sufficient threat' to Japan.

The minutes of the sixth meeting (10 February) registered the impasse. 'It was generally agreed that Great Britain and the United States each had a fundamental policy with reference to the Far East. For Great Britain it was fundamental that Singapore be held. For the United States it was fundamental that the Pacific Fleet be held intact and not become firmly committed in the Far East, although detachments might be sent to the Atlantic.' The impasse was registered afresh the next day, when the British delegation submitted a massive paper which had been prepared by Bellairs and which again emphasized their concern over Singapore.

We still feel that the issues at stake are so fundamental that the loss of Singapore would be a disaster of the first magnitude, second only to the loss of the British Isles.

From the narrow military point of view, we feel it to be of the utmost importance to retain a card of re-entry, so that, in the event of Japanese naval operations against our shipping in the Indian Ocean and the Western Pacific from bases in the South China Seas or the Archipelagoes

'THE FIRST THING IS TO GET THE UNITED STATES INTO THE WAR'

becoming intolerable, we shall still be in a position to base a substantial fleet in that area, though, admittedly, we could only do so by accepting serious risks elsewhere. But it is necessary to take a broader view of the results, which can be summed up by saying that Japan would become the undisputed master of East Asia, of the East Indies and of the Western Pacific. The British Empire and the United States would lose the immensely important resources in food and vital war materials, such as rubber, tin and oil... The Japanese Empire would become self-supporting and... would be free from one of the gravest consequences of war with the United States—economic pressure. Our morale and prestige, especially among the peoples of the East, would suffer a resounding blow, and those of the Axis Powers and Japan would be correspondingly enhanced, with almost incalculable consequences, both during and after the war. All hope of Chinese resistance would be at an end, and Russia, faced with a Japan supreme in the Orient, might well throw in her lot definitely with the Axis....

This is a black picture; but we do not think it over-drawn. ... even if Germany as well as Italy were defeated, it is at least highly problematical whether we could ever restore the position in the East. To carry out a successful attack and gain a foothold against opposition in east Asia and the Indies, thousands of miles from our nearest base, would be a colossal undertaking. It is open to doubt whether it would be a practicable operation of war in any circumstances. In the conditions in which it would have to be faced, when we should be exhausted by the strain of a long and desperate struggle from which we had only just emerged, we are doubtful whether we should even be able to attempt it. ...

The only real solution of the problem is to base a naval force, including a cover of capital ships, at Singapore. ...

In the absence of a capital ship force [i.e. the dispatch of most of the US Pacific Fleet to Singapore] this can only be done if the United States or British Asiatic naval forces are reinforced to an extent which would constitute a real threat to Japanese advanced sea communications and enable us at least to interrupt them. In our view, reinforcements of the order of one carrier, a division of heavy cruisers, and the necessary auxiliary naval craft in proportion would be the minimum required to fulfil this rôle in the early stages.

In view of the fact that the main theatre of war will be in the Atlantic and Mediterranean, it is obviously desirable that any naval reinforcement of the Asiatic naval forces should not be at the expense of those areas, which means that it should be found from the United States Pacific Fleet.

As for the US Pacific Fleet, its role 'must include activity, not only in the Marshall–Caroline area, but against Japan itself by sweeps, carrier-borne air attack and raids on Japanese shipping in their home waters. In other words it must constitute a live and active threat.' In the light of this appreciation, the British delegation invited the United States Staff Committee to agree with the British Government's basic position that: 'The security of the Far Eastern position, including Australia and New Zealand, is essential to the maintenance of the war effort of the Associated Powers. Singapore is the key to the defence of these interests and its retention must be assured.'[8]

The persistence of the British in pushing for an American naval presence at Singapore is a puzzle. It may be that they were aware that Plan Dog had never been approved by the President or the State Department, hence was open to change. At any rate, the British paper upset the US delegation. Their sharp reply took the form of a paper on 19 February, mostly Kelly Turner's work, that incorporated the Plan Dog strategy and once and for all shut the door on any British hopes of US support for the retention of Singapore by putting their Pacific Fleet or any part of it there or, at the least, by strengthening the Asiatic Fleet.

The general moral effect of the loss of Singapore and the Philippines would be severe. Singapore has been built up in public opinion as a symbol of the power of the British Empire. The eastern Dominions, the Netherlands East Indies and China look upon its security as the guarantee of their safety. Its value as a symbol has become so great that its capture would be a serious blow. But many severe blows have been taken by these various nations, and other severe blows can be absorbed without leading to final disaster.

There is no question that the loss of Malaysia to Japan would be unfortunate from moral, economic and strategic viewpoints. Nevertheless, the United States Staff Committee holds the view that this loss need not have a decisive effect upon the issue of the war....

The United States Staff Committee agrees that the retention of Singapore is very desirable. But it also believes that the diversion to the Asiatic theatre of sufficient forces to assure the retention of Singapore might jeopardize the success of the main effort of the Associated Powers.[9]

[8] BUS(J)(41)13, 'The Far East. Appreciation by the United Kingdom Delegation'.
[9] Leutze makes this shrewd observation: 'it was logical to inquire why the United States could not at least put a battle fleet into Singapore to deter Japanese action. This matter, however, had to be approached delicately, and it was, even though it went to the very heart of American defense strategy and involved its oldest and darkest fears about Britain's chances. The way it was put was that since hemispheric defense took priority, American military power must be deployed so that forces from both the Atlantic and the Pacific could

(*continued*)

'THE FIRST THING IS TO GET THE UNITED STATES INTO THE WAR'

There would (to continue with the US appreciation) be no reinforcement of the US Asiatic Fleet, which, with the British and Dutch forces in the Far East, would defend the Malay Barrier through 'submarine, mine, and air offensives against exposed naval forces, naval communications, and embarked troops', 'cruiser offensives against raiders south of the Malay Barrier', and so forth. At the same time the US Pacific Fleet would adopt an offensive strategy—severing Japanese sea communications at the 180th meridian, capturing or blockading merchant shipping to the eastward, and supporting the defence of the Malay Barrier 'by diverting Japanese naval and air strength toward the Mandates and home waters through raids on exposed naval forces, sea communications and positions; and by the denial or capture of advanced positions in the Marshalls and possibly Carolines.' The US delegation, in rejecting the invitation to subscribe to the British position, advanced their own view that:

(a) The broad military objective of the United States operations will be the defeat of Germany and her allies, but the United States necessarily must also maintain dispositions which, under all eventualities, will prevent the extension in the Western hemisphere of European or Asiatic political and military power.

(b) The objective of the war will be most effectively attained by the United States exerting its principal military effort in the Atlantic or navally in the Mediterranean regions.[10]

The US side had an unknown ally on the most important of the strategic problems. Churchill was furious with the British appreciation of 11 February. It was 'far too long' and contained 'such extreme arguments' as that Singapore had priority in Empire considerations.

What has been the use of all this battling? Anyone could have seen that the United States would not base a battle-fleet on Singapore and divide their naval forces, enabling the Japanese to fight an action on even terms

be thrown into the defense of the hemisphere if the British were defeated. In other words, Britain's tenuous hold on life, which Churchill himself had spoken of so often and so dramatically, was the best argument against heavy American commitments far from the major theater of war.' *Bargaining for Supremacy*, p. 243. Of course there were all the other factors, noted above and which Leutze mentions, for the American aversion to stationing a battle fleet in Singapore.

[10] BUS(J)(41)16, 'Statement by the United States Staff Committee. The United States Military Position in the Far East'.

with either of them. They said so weeks ago, and I particularly deprecated the raising of this controversy....
  The first thing is to get the United States into the war. We can then settle how to fight it afterwards. Admiral Bellairs is making such heavy weather over all this that he may easily turn the United States Navy Board into a hindrance and not a help to the main object, namely the entry of the United States.
  I do not see why, even if Singapore were captured, we could not protect Australia by basing a fleet on Australian ports. This would effectively prevent invasion.[11]

It was really the strategic views of the Chiefs of Staff, the views essentially of Pound and the Naval Staff that Churchill was pilloring, yet the Chiefs had no choice but to 'cool it'. It was that or a confrontation whose consequences would be too terrible to contemplate. Besides, they were as aware as the Prime Minister that to push the Americans too hard might jeopardize the main prize—that of 'getting the Americans into the war'. Accordingly, on the 19th Bellairs was instructed not to 'press his views further'. Thereafter Singapore was no longer a stumbling block in the talks. Irreconcilable differences did, however, remain.

At the eleventh plenary meeting, on 26 February, the British delegation agreed with the propositions in the last paragraph of the US paper of 19 February—that the object must be the defeat of Germany, and the principal American effort should be made in the Atlantic and Mediterranean theatres; and they accepted the decision that the US Pacific Fleet would be based at Hawaii, and that the Asiatic Fleet would not be reinforced. But they 'found it impossible to agree with the contention of the United States Staff Committee that the security of the Far East was not essential to the associated war effort. In the opinion of the United Kingdom Delegation, the security of the Far East *was* essential.' The British then brought out that their Chiefs of Staff, if the situation demanded it, were prepared to send a fleet, including about six capital ships, to the Far East. This force would be drawn from the Atlantic and the Mediterranean, but, unless the Mediterranean were to be abandoned, could be sent only if there was 'a very generous and substantial United States reinforcement of the Atlantic'. It was obviously of the utmost importance that this reinforcement arrive as quickly as possible after the US entry into the war. Admiral

---

[11] Churchill's minute to the First Sea Lord and First Lord, 17 Feb. 1941, ADM 116/4877.

'THE FIRST THING IS TO GET THE UNITED STATES INTO THE WAR'

Turner, however, said it was impossible to be precise about either the forces that might be shifted from the Pacific to the Atlantic, or about the time of arrival of the reinforcement in the Atlantic; there were too many variable factors, among them the Japanese attitude. As regards operations of the US Pacific Fleet, Turner tried to reassure the British about the effectiveness of the proposed strategy of severing Japanese sea communications at the 180th meridian and supporting the defence of the Malay Barrier: 'the rôle of the Fleet would be one of continued activity aimed at achieving its primary objectives—that of containing the major part of the Japanese Fleet in or near its own home waters, and of reducing Japanese strength by economic starvation'. 'The ideal would be to bring the Japanese Fleet to action' by attacking a vital objective (such as the Marshall and Caroline Islands) that it would be forced to defend.

The Americans would not meet any of Britain's important strategic objectives in the Pacific and South-east Asia. They would not send any part of the Pacific Fleet to Singapore or, in lieu of that, strengthen the Asiatic Fleet, since this would create two under-strength fleets, at Manila and at Pearl Harbor. They would not accept the British definition of the role of the US Pacific Fleet; a defensive strategy of containment of the Japanese Fleet was all they would contemplate. Finally, and most crucially, there was, as the US paper of 19 February frankly stated,

serious doubt that the United States would immediately declare war against Japan were that nation to move against Malaya, British Borneo, or the Netherlands East Indies, unless the United States were previously also at war with Germany and Italy. The Congress, before deciding whether or not to declare war against Japan for attacking Malaysia, almost certainly would require a considerable period for debate. . . .

Therefore, the Staff Committee concludes that it would be a serious mistake for the United Kingdom, in making their strategical dispositions to withstand a Japanese attack against Singapore, to count upon prompt military support by the United States.

The air had, at least, been cleared; there was agreement on some of the fundamentals and on where the two sides disagreed. The thirteenth meeting, on 27 March, approved the Joint Report on the Staff conversations, which was formally approved at the fourteenth and last meeting on 29 March for submission to the CNO, the Chief of Staff of the US Army, the British COS Committee, and the two Governments. The joint basic war plan, later known as ABC–1,[12] was based on the premiss that the European theatre was the decisive one. 'The paramount territorial interests of the United States' being in the Western Hemisphere, the principal American effort would be in the Atlantic and European theatres. They would strengthen their naval forces there, which would permit Britain to dispatch 'the necessary forces' to the Far East. The US Asiatic Fleet would not be reinforced. The United States recognized ('somewhat unwillingly', Slessor observes, 'and probably because we made it quite clear that it was no good their doing anything else') that Britain's 'retention of a position in the Far East such as will ensure the cohesion and security of the British Commonwealth and the maintenance of its war effort' was a cardinal principle of her strategy, but would not accept any commitment in that theatre beyond support for the defence of the Malay Barrier 'by diverting Japanese strength away from Malaysia'. The precise tasks of the US Pacific Fleet were defined as:

(a) Support the forces of the Associated Powers in the Far East Area by diverting enemy strength away from the Malay Barrier through the denial and capture of positions in the Marshalls, and through raids on enemy communications and positions.
(b) Destroy Axis sea communications by capturing or destroying vessels trading directly or indirectly with the enemy.
(c) Protect the sea communications of the Associated Powers within the Pacific Area.
(d) Support British naval forces in the area south of the Equator, as far west as Longitude 155° East. [This included New Zealand but not Australia.] ...
(e) Protect the territory of the Associated Powers within the Pacific Area, and prevent the extension of enemy Military power into the Western Hemisphere, by destroying hostile expeditions and by supporting land and air forces in denying the enemy the use of land positions in that Hemisphere.
(f) Prepare to capture and establish control over the Caroline and Marshall Islands area.

Allied naval tasks in the Far East and the South-west Pacific were defined as:

(a) Raid Japanese sea communications and destroy Axis forces.

[12] 'United States–British Staff Conversations. Report', BUS(J)(41)30. The US Joint Army and Navy War Plan, Rainbow 5, which was officially adopted in May 1941, was based on it. My discussion of ABC–1 is confined to the naval aspects *vis-à-vis* Japan.

'THE FIRST THING IS TO GET THE UNITED STATES INTO THE WAR'

(b) Support the land and air forces in the defense of the territories of the Associated Powers....
(c) Destroy Axis sea communications by capturing or destroying vessels trading directly or indirectly with the enemy.
(d) Protect sea communications of the Associated Powers by escorting, covering, and patrolling, and by destroying enemy raiding forces.

In this theatre the British Naval C-in-C, China, would be responsible for the 'strategic direction' of the Allied naval forces, except that the C-in-C, US Asiatic Fleet, would be responsible for directing the naval forces engaged in the defence of the Philippines. After the transfer of three battleships and an aircraft carrier to the Atlantic (as provided in the agreement) in April and May, the US Fleet at Pearl Harbor included nine battleships and three aircraft carriers. The US Asiatic Fleet would consist of two cruisers, 13 destroyers, 17 submarines, and supporting vessels. The British forces available for the Far East were stated as:

		Immediate reinforcements	*Ultimate reinforcements*
Battleships	–	–	5
Battle cruisers	–	1	–
Aircraft carriers	–	1	–
8-inch cruisers	1	1	2
6-inch cruisers	3	3	5
6-inch cruisers (old)	4	–	4
Destroyers	–	5	27
Destroyers (old)	5	–	–

The projected buildup of the British Fleet in the East was a reflection of the British resolve to face reality. Pound had anticipated this: 'If we are prepared to burn our boats entirely as regards getting the American Fleet to Singapore, we should no doubt be in a better position to guard our interests in the Indian Ocean and in the Far East if we sent a capital ship force to the Far East ... to consist of *Nelson*, *Rodney*, *Renown* or *Repulse*, and three "R" class battleships.'[13] And this is what the British settled for at Washington, except that an aircraft carrier was added to the projected force.

It is important to note that, although a basic strategy was agreed upon for the two alternatives, the US supporting Britain, but not engaged in war, and the US at war with the Axis Powers and

---

[13] Pound's minute to Churchill, 13 Feb. 1941.

Japan, *the United States neither accepted an obligation to go to war, nor stated the circumstances in which she was prepared to do so.* There was only the 'assumption' that 'when the United States becomes involved in war with Germany, it will at the same time engage in war with Italy. In these circumstances, the possibility of a state of war arising between Japan and an Association of the United States, the British Commonwealth and its Allies, including the Netherlands East Indies, must be taken into account.' The uncertainty of the American posture if Japan entered the war—a definite US commitment was not forthcoming until forty-eight hours before the attack on Pearl Harbor—continued to have a serious cramping effect on British Far Eastern naval strategy.

As an important by-product of the Conference, which had recommended the immediate provision of a regular machinery for joint war planning, a British Joint Staff Mission was set up in Washington. Its members represented, as a corporate body, the Chiefs of Staff Committee, and, individually, the professional head of their own Service. It was the forerunner to the Combined Chiefs of Staff which became operational when the United States finally entered the war and 'by whom, under the Prime Minister and President, the higher direction of the combined war effort was conducted in an intimate and integrated manner without precedent in the history of alliances'.[14]

The British Chiefs of Staff recommended approval of ABC-1, as did the Defence Committee of the War Cabinet on 15 May. The CNO and Chief of Staff of the US Army recommended approval to the President, but he withheld formal approval, indicating, however, that he would do so in case of US entry into the war.

ABC-1 was for Britain's strategists a setback. They knew they were unable to protect an area they considered vital without American naval assistance of a far more substantive kind than ABC-1 had produced. Early post-Washington developments gave them no cause for jubilation over the results. During the Washington talks (5 February) the British were horrified to discover that it would be left to the 'discretion' of the C-in-C of the US Pacific Fleet to determine how to meet the US commitment to restrain the Imperial Navy. Days after ABC-1 was signed, Admiral Danckwerts, now Head of the Naval Staff Mission (the naval side of the Joint

---

[14] Slessor, *The Central Blue*, p. 352.

'THE FIRST THING IS TO GET THE UNITED STATES INTO THE WAR'

Staff Mission and which, after the Pacific War broke out, was renamed the British Admiralty Delegation), and his Chief of Staff, Captain A. W. Clarke, hustled out to Pearl Harbor (9–11 April) to learn for themselves how the C-in-C, Admiral Kimmel, and his staff interpreted the role assigned to their force. They did not like what they heard. The Americans gave the impression that the 'mere existence' of the Pacific Fleet would restrain the Japanese. They thought that direct operations against Japan would be too risky, and such operations useless unless repeated continually. They had no more use for operations in the Aleutions; here the bad weather was the obstacle. Bases in the Marshalls and the Carolines would be suitable targets, 'but they do not appear to have any definite plan for the purpose, nor detailed knowledge of Japanese defences and preparations there, nor necessary means of overcoming Japanese shore resistance'.[15]

The difference over Singapore continued to bother the Royal Navy. On 11 July the Admiralty reiterated their view to Admiral Ghormley that the dispatch of an American capital-ship force to Singapore might deter the Japanese from aggression, and, if it failed, would assure the defence of the base against Japanese attack. To the end the Americans adhered to the policy of keeping their main fleet at Hawaii. This may have been one of the biggest mistakes of the whole war. The division of naval forces and their subsequent annihilation as a consequence of this destroyed Allied Far Eastern naval strategy and left the whole field wide open. The US Navy had to fight an appallingly costly campaign to regain all that was lost then. Yet, politically, it was impossible for the American Government in 1940–1 to have sent the Pacific Fleet or a substantive contingent of it to Singapore.

[15] Danckwert's telegram to the Chiefs of Staff, 17 Apr. 1941, CAB 105/36. At this very time, Slessor, in his 'Secret and strictly Personal' impressions of the American defence system, after five months in that country, was making these disparaging remarks: 'Their naval policy strikes me as being distressingly defensive (though Turner was constantly cheering us on to be awfully offensive during the conversations). In the Pacific they have almost a Maginot complex in respect of Hawaii and the protection of the West coast of America— though what threat there can be to that coast we have never been able to elicit. They are set on getting a great Grand Fleet in being sitting at Hawaii ... and are full of staff college clichés about dividing their forces and laying themselves open to defeat in detail, not realising that the days of Grand Fleets are passed, particularly when the nearest enemy is several thousand miles away. They strike one also as having a tendency, not unknown in other navies in times of peace, to shrink at the possibility of loss of any important units of the fleet.' Slessor papers, AC 75/28/76 (RAF Museum, Department of Aviation Records). Except perhaps for the last sentence, the Naval Staff could have written this appreciation.

The ABC-1 Report recommended that the American and British Chiefs of Staff convene 'without delay' a conference of their military commanders in the Far East, with Dutch representatives invited to attend.

2. THE DUTCH EMBARRASSMENT

As the New Year began, the Dutch were still annoyed by their inability to get a categorical assurance of support from Britain or the United States if Japan attacked the Netherlands East Indies. On 18 December 1940 the Foreign Office had proposed that an informal and oral communication be made by the Foreign Secretary, Eden, to the Dutch Minister in London to the effect that if the Islands were attacked, 'we should do our best to help them'. The stumbling block was the persisting division of opinion in the Chiefs of Staff Committee, with the Admiralty holding that to give Japan an excuse for attacking the Dutch East Indies would be a most unwise move, and the CIGS and CAS, Dill and Portal, arguing that the failure of the Dutch East Indies to resist Japanese aggression for lack of British support would be 'disastrous'.

The Far Eastern Committee of the War Cabinet, after considering the views of the Chiefs of Staff and the Foreign Office on 16 January, recommended that the Foreign Secretary by permitted to exchange orally with the Netherlands Government reciprocal assurances of mutual help in the event of a Japanese attack upon British or Dutch territory in the Far East. 'The view was expressed that co-operation with the Dutch on economic matters would be greatly facilitated by some assurance of the nature proposed, and that the prevailing uncertainty of our relations hindered fruitful collaboration. There was little danger of their taking an unduly stiff attitude if, as was likely, they adhered to their long established practice of making concessions to the Japanese without yielding the whole demand.'[16] Eden accepted the recommendation and submitted it to the War Cabinet on 5 February. On the 7th, at Churchill's request, Eden discussed the proposal with the Chiefs of Staff, emphasizing the awkward political position in which the Government would be placed *vis-à-vis* the Dutch Government in London if Britain failed to go to the aid of the Dutch East Indies. The Chiefs, but particularly

---

[16] FE(41) 3rd Mtg., CAB 96/2.

THE DUTCH EMBARRASSMENT

the First Sea Lord, were reluctant to approve the exchange of assurances, which went beyond the original Foreign Office proposal of limited assurances. On purely military grounds it would be most unwise to get involved in war with Japan over an attack upon the Dutch East Indies unless they were certain of full American support. Simply put, they had not sufficient force to deal with the Japanese Fleet. Though impressed with these arguments, Eden recommended to Churchill that they proceed with the suggested exchange of oral assurances with the Dutch.

On 13 February Churchill told Cadogan he was going to dictate a minute giving his final conclusion upon this matter. But first he asked for a full statement of the Admiralty position, which was quickly forthcoming.

The implications of war with Japan, when we have not got American support, can be stated simply. It is not the threat to our Far Eastern possessions, although the loss of Singapore would obviously have most serious repercussions, that is of primary concern. The real threat lies in the vulnerability of our sea communications east of Aden to Japanese attack that at once arises when we go to war with Japan; for our naval forces are so occupied with Germany and Italy that we cannot simultaneously provide against the above Japanese attack.

But if the Japanese display resolution and enterprise, our supply of troops and material that we draw from India, Malaya, Australia and New Zealand, and our line of communication from the Cape to Aden wherewith we support our war effort in the Middle East, may be seriously endangered. In these circumstances we may be forced into sending important naval forces to the Indian Ocean. These can only come from the Mediterranean; and their withdrawal might jeopardize our whole position in that area, negativing the successes we had so far gained. Germany would obtain further oil and other supplies, and the effectiveness of our action against her would be correspondingly reduced. Thus, Japan would have weakened our whole effort against Germany and Italy, offsetting, perhaps completely, the material aid being given to us by America. . . .

To sum up, a guarantee to the Dutch regarding the Netherlands East Indies will avoid an awkward political situation, and may, to some extent, facilitate the co-ordination of our joint plans. As opposed to this we stand the risk of being involved in war with Japan, with all the incalculable consequences that would spring therefrom, in circumstances where this might have been avoided had freedom of action remained with us. In the Admiralty view, therefore, we should on no account give any assurance either formal or informal to the Dutch unless we have previously been assured of complete American co-operation.

But present indications were that such a US assurance could not be expected.[17] Soundings in Washington bore out the Admiralty, and on 20 February the War Cabinet decided to take no action. They adhered to this decision when Eden brought the matter up again on 27 March, after the Dutch had once more pressed for a British guarantee.

The question would not go away, since the Dutch authorities continued to be difficult. It surfaced again in May and in July. Eden, who was embarrassed by Dutch insistence on an unequivocal statement of British support, was not to be put off. 'The Netherlands Government lose no opportunity to comment on our hesitation to exchange some kind of assurances and the position with them is becoming rapidly more difficult.... All that is suggested is that we should let the Dutch know that we will help them, in the event of a Japanese attack, to the best of our ability. It is not suggested that we should be committed to any "chalk line" entailing automatic military action.'[18] Churchill reluctantly authorized Eden (1 August) to promise the Dutch Government the limited assistance proposed by him: 'an attack upon the Netherlands East Indies would lead us to do the utmost in our power. We must however remain the sole judge of what actions or military measures are practicable and likely to achieve our common purpose.'[19] On the same day Eden made an oral statement to the Dutch Minister that followed Churchill's minute practically verbatim; it was confirmed in writing on 5 September. It was somewhat indefinite and gave neither side assurance that it could count on the immediate support of the other if it became involved in a war with Japan.

The installation of the Tōjō Government in Japan on 18 October,

---

[17] Alexander to Churchill, 16 Feb. 1941, PREM 3/326. There was considerable feeling against the Admiralty, the chief prop of the COS position, in high governmental quarters. For example, L. S. Amery, the Secretary for India, who had a poor opinion of Pound and felt that the Admiralty was 'rotten at the top', was 'appalled by the pusillanimous and shortsighted attitude' of the Admiralty spokesmen at the War Cabinet of 6 February. 'However weak we are in the Far East we shall gain nothing by letting the Japanese first mop up such Dutch forces as there are out there as well as occupy every strategic position in the Dutch East Indies up to the doors of Singapore, and then cut our throats at leisure. ... That is the material side. But how can we morally take the line of not helping Allies who have sacrificed their own home country ... in order to stand with us? What of the Dutch sailors and airmen who are fighting with us if they hear that we propose to leave their comrades out East in the lurch? What of American opinion? ... what of our own opinion at home?' Amery's minute to Churchill, 6 Feb. 1941, PREM 3/326.
[18] Eden's minute to Churchill, 30 July 1941, ibid.
[19] Ibid.

which was read in London as to all intents and purposes putting the Government in the hands of the Army and signalling further military moves, caused Churchill to propose a more definite assurance be offered to the Dutch. On 31 October Eden proposed to the War Cabinet that they authorize him to seek 'a formal defensive agreement with the Netherlands Government whereby each party would undertake to co-operate immediately to the fullest extent of its available resources in the event of the other party being forced to take military action to counter an attack upon any of its territories in the Far East'. Such an agreement should be made public, unlike the secret assurances of 1 August and 5 September, if it was to have a deterrent effect on Japan.[20] When the War Cabinet discussed Eden's proposal on 3 November, they were unable to reach any conclusion because the Services, above all the Admiralty, still hesitated to endorse an agreement with the Dutch. As before, their position turned on the consideration that their own resources, especially naval, were not large, and on the absence of an assurance of American support. Also, Churchill preferred to wait until the fleet that had been dispatched to Singapore on 25 October (see below) had arrived in the Far East. A further reason for a go-slow attitude was the possible American resentment over a public declaration, which might be interpreted as an attempt to force their hand. When, however, Churchill reported Roosevelt's remark to the War Cabinet on 4 December, that 'we should obviously all be in it together' if the Japanese attacked British or Dutch possessions, Eden was at last able to offer the Dutch (5 December) an unconditional agreement for mutual assistance if Japan attacked either. Two days later (8 December, Far East time), before anything could be finalized, the Japanese began their invasion of Malaya and war was on in the Far East. Binding agreement or no binding agreement, it had been generally understood all along, even at the Admiralty, that in the crunch they would have to come to the aid of the Dutch if they resisted, since Japanese control of the Netherlands East Indies would put Singapore in jeopardy.[21]

All the political difficulties notwithstanding, there had been four

---

[20] WP(41)254, Eden, 'Defensive Co-operation in the Far East with the Netherlands East Indies and the United States', CAB 66/19.
[21] See, for example, the revealing Admiralty response to a paper prepared for the First Sea Lord by Admiral Dreyer: Dreyer, 'Plans for War in the Pacific', 10 Apr. 1941, and the D of P's (Captain Charles Daniel) minute, 25 Apr. 1941, ADM 1/11326.

sets of secret Anglo-Dutch staff talks, which had gone off quite well and promised that defence plans would be co-ordinated in the Far East. Yet it was clearly understood at these talks that no political obligations were involved. In other words, the absence of a guarantee had proved no obstacle to the holding of staff conversations. This was why the Admiralty could not accept the Foreign Office argument that without a guarantee joint plans could not be prepared. The first talks had taken place in Singapore at the end of November 1940 (above, p. 140). Then had come the Singapore Conference (ADA) between the British, Dutch and Australians (who also represented New Zealand), with an American observer present, on 22–5 February 1941. The conference had made three assumptions: active US intervention in the early stages of a war could not be counted upon; Japan would not attempt to invade Australia and New Zealand while Singapore remained available as a base for a fleet in being; and Japan would not attack Malaya and the Dutch East Indies simultaneously—initially, an attack on Malaya from Thai and Indo-China bases, with the object of capturing Singapore, was more probable. In that case the security of Singapore would be the most important Allied object. There was an understanding on what Japanese actions would constitute an act of war: a 'direct act of war' against the territory of any of the four Associated Powers; the movement of Japanese forces into any part of Thailand west of longitude 100° East or south of latitude 10° North; the movement of a large number of Japanese warships, or of a convoy of merchant ships escorted by Japanese warships, towards the east coast of the Kra Isthmus or the east coast of Malaya, or if such a force had crossed the parallel of latitude 6° North between Malaya and the Philippines; the movement of Japanese forces into Portuguese Timor or into New Caledonia or the Loyalty Islands off New Caledonia; an attack on the Philippines. Any of these actions 'would create a situation in which our failure to take active military counter-action would place us at such military disadvantage, should Japan subsequently attack, that we should advise our respective Governments to authorise such action'. Plans for mutual reinforcements were drawn up, as was a policy for meeting Japanese threats to Allied sea communications. Spheres of operational control of naval and air forces were laid down.[22]

[22] COS(41)406, 'Report of the Anglo-Dutch-Australian Conference, held at Singapore, February 22–25, 1941', CAB 80/29.

THE DUTCH EMBARRASSMENT

The Chiefs of Staff approved the military clauses of the ADA Report as a basis for planning, but not the prior definition of an act of war and automatic reaction without reference to London, because a decision to co-operate with the Dutch could only be taken by the British Government when Japanese aggression had taken place. 'This meant', as General Kirby has pointed out, 'that Japan would retain the initiative and be able to choose the moment of aggression.'

Two months later, the American–Dutch–British Conference (ADB), recommended at the Washington Staff conference, was held in Singapore (21–7 April), with Australian, New Zealand, and Indian representatives in attendance. The object was to prepare a plan on the basis of the ABC–1 agreement for combined action in the event of the three Powers finding themselves at war with Japan and the Axis. 'No political commitment is implied.' Although the agreement (ADB–1) was all about concerted action in war, its hoped-for deterrent effect was stated: 'If it is clear to Japan that the united forces of the British Empire, the United States and the Dutch would meet aggression on her part, her immediate intervention in the war is unlikely.' Still, 'such is the national psychology of the Japanese that acts of hysteria which might lead to the plunging of Japan into war must be faced'. The Japanese object was assumed to be complete political and economic domination of South-east Asia, to achieve which the Japanese must take the offensive. Reiterated were the Japanese moves specified in the ADA agreement of February as calling for concerted military action—except for the reference to an attack on the Philippines. It was replaced by this move: a Japanese convoy clearly destined for the Philippines.

In the first phase of naval operations in the Pacific and Indian Oceans, the basic principle stated was that the Atlantic and Europe were the decisive theatres, and, accordingly, the main strategy in the Far East must at first be defensive. The chief force would be the US Pacific Fleet. It must be maintained in strength at least equal to the Japanese Fleet, in order to act offensively against Japanese forces and bases, as provided in the report on the Washington conference, so as to counter the certain Japanese offensive against the ADB position in the Eastern theatre. The US Asiatic Fleet would be based on Manila initially. It would operate against the flank of any Japanese southward advance, using Hong Kong as an advanced base. It was, however, recognized that this fleet might have to withdraw to Singapore. The remaining naval forces would concentrate on local defence of bases and protection of vital sea communications, while attacking whenever they could.

As for British naval forces specifically, their functions were phrased in generalities. Apart from the local defence of bases, they would defend the vital sea communications and attack Japanese sea communications. Since the British forces available were inadequate for the introduction of a general convoy system, evasive routings or sailings under cover must be the main defence of trade. The Dutch naval forces would be employed mainly for the defence of the Netherlands East Indies and of the narrow passages between the Islands. But their naval and air force should reinforce the British as necessary. In phase two, the arrival of the British Far Eastern Fleet would alter the balance of strength considerably against Japan. The immediate object of this fleet would be to operate from Singapore. Although alone it would be inferior to the Japanese Fleet, it would be strong enough to seize the initiative, launch 'powerful counter-attacks' against any Japanese forces in their territories, and intensify the attack on Japanese forces, territories, and sea communications. If unable to operate from Singapore ('an unlikely event'), the British Fleet would operate from Indian Ocean bases to secure vital Allied sea communications, despite any further enemy advance to the southward or westward, and, if possible, relieve pressure on Malaya by operations in the Malacca Straits.[23]

Immediately after the ADB Conference, on 27 April conversations were held between the British and Dutch alone (the American participants in the ADB Conference attended as observers) to clear up outstanding points in the ADA Report of February. A definite plan emerged (BD agreement) for the disposition and employment of British and Dutch forces in the Far East, with the usual rider attached that no political commitment was implied.[24] The British formally approved the BD agreement, as well as the ADA agreement, in Eden's letter of 5 September.

The British Chiefs of Staff approved the ADB Report except for two points: Hong Kong, being more a liability than an asset, could

[23] COS(41)387, 'Report of the American–British Conversations Held at Singapore, April 1941', 21 June 1941, CAB 80/28. The Report included this prescient sentence: 'It is probable that her collapse will occur as a result of economic blackade, naval pressure and air bombardment.'
[24] COS(41)388, 'Report of the British–Dutch Conversations Held at Singapore, April 1941', CAB 80/28.

not be regarded as an advanced base for the US Asiatic Fleet, and, as in the case of the ADA Report, they could not agree that any specific Japanese move should be regarded as a *casus belli*—not until they could be sure what the American attitude would be at the outbreak of war in the Far East. The American Service Chiefs, on the other hand, rejected the ADB Report (3 July). It covered too large an area: from the East Indies Station to New Zealand; the Report should be limited to the Far Eastern Area (that in ABC–1). They were unhappy over the C-in-C, US Asiatic Fleet, being under the C-in-C, British Eastern Fleet, since this might lead to the deployment of the Asiatic Fleet in waters of no strategic significance to the United States. This related to the proposed dispositions of the British naval forces, which stuck in the American craw. Despite the importance of the Malay Barrier to the security of Singapore and the whole of their position in the Far East, so often emphasized by the British, only three of their 48 ships in the Far East were assigned to operate in its vicinity. No British ships were committed either to the defence of the Barrier against a Japanese naval move southward, or to offensive operations aimed at closing the Barrier to enemy raiders. British naval forces were instead allocated to escort and patrol work, the security of sea communications, as well as the security of Singapore, being defined as the most important Allied interests in the Far East. Until such time as a plan was drawn up that gave the Royal Navy a predominant role in the defence of the British position in the Far East, the United States was averse to her Asiatic Fleet operating under British strategic direction. As Professor Herzog has summed up the basic point at issue: 'The incongruity between the British position in Washington that Singapore was *sine qua non* to their Far Eastern security and the British position in Singapore of assigning none of their ships directly to support that theory was undoubtedly the major provocation for American rejection of the ADB Report.'[25] Admiral Hart, C-in-C of the US Asiatic Fleet, put the central issue in terms of 'a rather basic conflict between British and American views; the British navy seemed always to primarily feature the control of trade routes over broad areas (with particular regard to ocean escort of the Empire's troop and supply convoys), whereas we tended to minimize the requirements in that respect to the consequent availability of naval

[25] *Closing the Open Door*, p. 132.

concentrations prepared for direct combat'.[26] The ADB Conference did not, accordingly, result in a joint plan in the event of a Far Eastern war.

Churchill and Roosevelt met at sea, in Placentia Bay, off Argentia, Newfoundland, on 9–12 August 1941 (The 'Atlantic Conference') to talk over Far Eastern problems *inter alia*. The American and British Service Chiefs, meeting personally for the first time, discussed ADB Report problems. One troublesome point was disposed of. 'US naval forces, including naval aviation, would in all circumstances remain under the orders of C-in-C, Asiatic Fleet, who would, on bringing his force south, receive strategic direction from C-in-C, Eastern Fleet.' On the other hand, as Admiral Turner remarked, British naval dispositions remained 'unsound'. Their forces were to be 'employed on British trade routes instead of operating along the northern line of the Dutch East Indies'.[27] Afterwards, on 25 August, the British planners drew up a revised agreement (ADB–2). Although it met some of the American objections, it was rejected (3 October) on the ground that the fundamental defects remained, especially that the defence of the Malay Barrier was not recognized as primarily a British and Dutch concern. At this point the American naval authorities were prepared to forget about ABD–2. An effective combined plan of operations appeared impossible, and all they now envisaged was collaboration by mutual co-operation between local commanders.

With the advent of the Tōjō Cabinet Pound tried a new approach. On 5 November, two weeks after the decision to send two capital ships to Singapore under Admiral Phillips (see the following chapter), Pound admitted to Stark that ADB–1 and ADB–2 were dead, and he spoke of the urgent need for a fresh conference in the Far East, after Phillips's arrival in Singapore, to draw up an operational plan to implement the broad directives in ABC–1. There was a complete change in outlook on the sticking point. 'In the new conditions we are considering the possibility of disposing a capital ship force north of the Malay barrier, and it is, therefore, important that joint plans for its employment in the Far East Area

[26] Hart, 'Narrative of Events, Asiatic Fleet, Leading up to War and From 8 December 1941 to 15 February 1942' (June 1942), p. 2, US Operational Archives.
[27] COS record of the joint Staff discussions during the Atlantic Conference, 20 Aug. 1941, CAB 99/18.

THE DUTCH EMBARRASSMENT

should be drawn up as soon as possible.'[28] Stark promptly agreed, and by the end of November the US and British Chiefs of Staff had developed the procedure for coming up with a detailed joint plan in the Far East. There would, first, be a naval conference in Manila, to be attended by Phillips and Hart. They would use ADB–2 as a point of departure in drawing up a broad outline for joint naval operations, which could be developed later, in ADB conversations, into detailed joint operational plans. To the Manila conference, held on the eve of the outbreak of war, we shall return in connection with the Force Z story. It is enough here to say that no ADB naval operational plan was in effect when the Japanese struck. There was only a joint British–Dutch operational plan, PLENAPS (Plans for the employment of Naval and Air Forces of the Associated Powers), which Vice-Admiral Sir Geoffrey Layton, C-in-C, China Station, had prepared (12 November 1941) on the basis of the British–Dutch conversations of 27 April 1941 (the BD agreement). PLENAPS was concerned only with the opening phase of the war, until the arrival of naval and air reinforcements. It used the small forces in the theatre to the best advantage and ensured that action would be co-ordinated. And so, for example, two Dutch submarines were placed under the orders of the C-in-C, China, on 1 December. When hostilities began, they proceeded to their assigned war stations, although these were distant from Java, the heart of the Netherlands East Indies.

'The period of pre-war conferences was over,' Herzog comments. 'The attempts to derive a plan of action against the Japanese expansion had failed, one after the other. The reasons for the failure were many. From an American point of view, the countries involved were too concerned with their own interests, commerce, and position. National jealousies were very much in evidence.'[29] For the British the failure of the United States in any of the 'agreements' (ABC–1, ADB–1, ADB–2) to make a definite political or military commitment in case of a Japanese attack on the British or Dutch, to say nothing of harmonizing their strategic ideas with those of the British, was a severe trial. All they had was a general plan of action (ABC–1) that would be operative *if* the United States should enter the war, and *provided* it was approved by the proper authorities. The British recognized that constitutional difficulties

[28] ADM 116/4877.
[29] *Closing the Open Door*, pp. 135–6.

prevented a formal American commitment. They would have been content with an intimation from Roosevelt that, in the event of a war resulting from a Japanese attack on British or Dutch Far Eastern possessions, he would ask Congress for authority to fight at Britain's side. But when Churchill asked for such an assurance at the Atlantic Conference (10 August), the President would give none. How a definite American commitment would have affected developments is one of history's intangibles. Apart from boosting British morale immeasurably, it just might have led to the co-ordination of ADB naval operational plans that would have stood a better chance of withstanding or at least slowing down the Japanese juggernaut in the winter of 1941–2.

The advent of the Tōjō Cabinet, which had, albeit late in the day, spurred the British into making a firm commitment to the Dutch, and the Americans and British into agreement for an urgent conference at Manila to implement ABC–1, also precipitated the British decision to send a capital-ship force to Singapore immediately.

VIII

'Strategical Cloud Cuckoo Land'

I cannot feel that Japan will face the combination now forming against her of the United States, Great Britain and Russia, while already preoccupied in China.... Nothing would increase her hesitation more than the appearance of the force I mentioned [25 August] ... and above all of a *K.G.V.* This might indeed be a decisive deterrent.

Churchill's minute to Pound, 29 August 1941.

It would have been to Britain's advantage had he [Churchill] left the decisions on naval strategy in the hands of his professional advisers.

MAJOR-GENERAL S. WOODBURN KIRBY, *Singapore: The Chain of Disaster* (1971).

1. THE GENESIS OF FORCE Z[1]

A number of developments in the summer and early autumn of 1941 explain the decision to hustle out a capital-ship force to the East immediately. One was the threat of further Japanese moves to the south, now that the German invasion of the Soviet Union had decreased the threat to Japan's flank. The Naval Staff expected that the Japanese would do nothing to provoke war with the Western Powers until the outcome of the European war was clearer, but that they would probably move into southern French Indo-China and then use it as a base for a fresh advance in the south. The Chiefs of Staff were agreed (16 July) that military action to deter Japan from such a move was out of the question. We have seen (above, p. 166) that the Japanese marched into southern French Indo-China at the end of July, and how the British and Americans had reacted.

Evidence mounted from the latter part of July that the Japanese were about to make demands upon Thailand similar to those on Vichy with respect to Indo-China. In a speech in the Commons on

---

[1] 'Force G' until code-named 'Force Z' just prior to its sailing from Singapore on 8 December, though, for convenience sake, I shall refer to it throughout as Force Z.

6 August, Eden warned that 'any action which would threaten the independence and integrity of Thailand would be a matter of immediate concern to this country, more particularly as threatening the security of Singapore'. A Japanese move into northern or eastern Thailand was not regarded in London as constituting a direct threat, but the occupation of the Kra Isthmus, adjacent to Malaya, would be another matter. The Defence Committee on 8 August (Churchill was not present) discussed the question whether Britain should fight if Japan tried to occupy the Isthmus. The Chiefs of Staff advised that, lacking ships and men, they should avoid war as long as possible unless American support was certain. The contrary view was expressed at the meeting that, though strategically the Kra Isthmus might not be vitally important, from the political point of view Britain could not possibly remain inactive in face of a Japanese advance to the Malayan border. The Committee could only agree on this much: to recommend to the Prime Minister that an 'oblique' Anglo-American warning against any aggression in Thailand be issued to Japan.[2]

The danger of further Japanese moves was a main topic of conversation at the Atlantic Conference in August. The British were after parallel (US–British–Dutch) warnings to Japan that further Japanese aggression in South-east Asia would mean countermeasures, even if these resulted in war. Roosevelt was asked whether in such a case he would seek from Congress an undertaking to help any Power Japan attacked as a consequence of these warnings. The President would make no such commitment, nor were there the parallel warnings of the sort Churchill had in mind. Roosevelt did warn Japan, through Ambassador Nomura on 17 August, that further Japanese aggression would compel the United States 'to take immediately any and all steps which it may deem necessary toward safeguarding the legitimate rights and interests of the United States and American nationals, and toward insuring the safety and security of the United States'. The British naturally found unsatisfactory a warning with no reference to Great Britain or the use of the word 'war', and with the emphasis on American security. To stay in step with American policy, in a broadcast on 24 August Churchill warned Japan that Britain would 'range herself unhesitatingly at the side of the United States', if her efforts to stop Japanese aggression led to war between the US and Japan.

[2] DO(41) 56th Mtg., CAB 69/2.

THE GENESIS OF FORCE Z

Signs multiplied that the Japanese Combined Fleet was being readied for operations, possibly combined operations, in the near future. Early in September the Naval Attaché reported that the main units of the Combined Fleet and the China Area Fleet were at their principal home ports, and that large numbers of naval reservists had been secretly called up with instructions to report at their depots 'at earliest possible moment'. NID4—the Far Eastern Section—graded this intelligence as 'A.1' (a report from a completely reliable source confirmed by other reports) and commented: 'It is abnormal for ships to be at their home ports at this time of the year when the Fleet should be at the peak of the exercise programme.'[3]

Another important factor in the decision to send a capital-ship force to the East with a minimum of delay was a telegram from the Australian Prime Minister, Menzies, to Churchill on 11 August. This was the culmination of persistent Australian pressure in 1940–1 for the strengthening of defences in the East. In December 1940, when the Australian Government had asked if the improved situation in the Mediterranean (as a result of the Taranto strike) did not permit the basing of three or four battleships on Singapore, Churchill had offered no encouragement. Despite the improved situation in the Mediterranean, the imminent addition of the powerful battleships *Tirpitz* and *Bismarck* to the German Navy, the appearance of a German pocket battleship in the Atlantic, and the possibility of the French Fleet being turned over to the Germans meant 'we are at the fullest naval strain I have seen either in this or the former war. The only way in which a naval squadron could be found for Singapore would be by ruining the Mediterranean situation. This I am sure you would not wish us to do unless or until the Japanese danger becomes far more menacing than at present.'[4] Menzies, an exceptionally able man of forceful character, and a passionate Australian, was not one to be fobbed off easily. When he arrived in London in March 1941 for high-level discussions on his

---

[3] NID4/19, 'Situation Report. Mobilization of Japanese Fleet', 11 Sept. 1941, FO 371/27963. NID4 reported on 7 October that the main units of the Combined Fleet were still at their home ports. 'Grand manoeuvres have apparently been cancelled and the Fleet is undergoing the annual reorganization, two months ahead of the normal time.' 'Disposition of the Japanese Fleet', FO 371/27964. From the Naval Attaché came the intelligence on 17 October that the Japanese Fleet was now fully mobilized and on a complete war footing.

[4] Churchill to Menzies, 23 Dec. 1940, Churchill, *Their Finest Hour*, pp. 628–9.

country's strategic concerns, the British found him still obsessed with the idea that they should send three or four capital ships to Singapore. He expressed himself firmly to the First Lord and VCNS, Alexander and Phillips, on 8 March. Australia could, he said, no longer be satisfied with the British position that, if war broke out with Japan, they would, if necessary, abandon the Mediterranean and come to the assistance of the Pacific Dominions with capital ships. Their public opinion, he insisted, would not tolerate that the substantial Dominion land forces in the Middle East should be left improperly protected by a naval withdrawal from the Mediterranean. He did, however, 'strongly welcome' the news that the dispatch of a battle cruiser and an aircraft carrier into the Indian Ocean for the protection of trade routes was under discussion.[5] The Admiralty could not promise a larger reinforcement for the East in the near future because they needed to keep a battle fleet in Home waters sufficiently strong to contain the German Fleet; to provide strong escorts for troop convoys to the Middle East; to form hunting groups to cope with surface raiders; to maintain a fleet in the Eastern Mediterranean. To prevent the Italian Fleet from entering the Atlantic; to carry out offensive operations in the Western Mediterranean; and, to protect trade in the North Atlantic, a small capital ship and carrier force had to be maintained at Gibraltar (Force H). These requirements, in the words of the D of P, Daniel, were placing 'a greater strain on the Royal Navy than it has probably ever experienced before in its history'.

Scarcely put off, on 29 March Menzies shot off a memorandum to the British Government referring to the total inadequacy of Malaya's defences in the absence of a main fleet in the East to meet a major attack, and asking for a definite plan of naval reinforcement east of Suez on a progressive basis, according to events in the Mediterranean. It was their intention, the Chiefs of Staff responded, to send a battle cruiser and an aircraft carrier to the Indian Ocean

---

[5] Alexander's note on the conversation, A. V. Alexander Papers, Churchill College, Cambridge (AVAR) 5/5/13(a), which refers in slipshod fashion to battle cruisers and aircraft carriers. The Australian version of the 8 March discussions includes these points made by Phillips: the war plans had never contemplated that the Empire would be fighting Germany, Italy, and Japan together, since there were not sufficient capital ships for Home waters, the Mediterranean, and the Far East; the prospect in such a war depended primarily on the US coming in; left alone against the three Powers, it would would be necessary to withdraw from the Mediterranean. *Documents on Australian Foreign Policy, 1937–49*, iv. 482.

at the start of a war with Japan. The dispatch of further heavy ships would depend on the strength and disposition of the German Fleet, the course of the war in the Eastern Mediterranean, their own capital-ship strength, and the likelihood of an invasion of the United Kingdom, none of which factors could be accurately forecast. There was the ritual promise of cutting their losses in the Mediterranean in the event of Japanese naval action constituting a real threat to Australia, and, something new, the mention of how the changing attitude of the United States had lessened the threat to Australia. 'Though nominally neutral, they are now so closely identified with our cause that the potential threat of the United States Fleet at Hawaii must alone impose a most powerful restraining influence on Japanese freedom of action to move southwards. It would, we feel, certainly prevent the use of the whole Japanese fleet in support of an expedition to the South Seas.'[6] Menzies returned to Canberra with no firm commitments.

The Pacific Dominions had further cause for concern when the impending transfer of some of the battleships and carriers of the US Pacific Fleet to the Atlantic was announced. Afraid that this reduction of American naval strength in the Pacific might encourage Japanese aggression, the Dominions asked on 5–6 May for 'the release against the event of war with Japan of adequate British capital units to at once reinforce Singapore'.[7] The response in London was a *non possumus*. It was, as the First Lord stated to the Defence Committee, 'impossible to get away from the fact that until the United States came into the war, we could get no relief from capital ship escorts for convoys and we had to maintain Force H at Gibraltar. It was from these two sources that any Fleet destined for the Far East would have to come.'[8]

From the perspective of the Pacific Dominions the situation worsened after the German invasion of the Soviet Union in June. This greatly relieved the pressure on Britain, but it ran counter to the interests of Australia and New Zealand in two respects. The Russo-German War put a fresh burden on the hard-pressed Royal Navy, which had now to protect the supply route to Archangel,

---

[6] COS(41)230, 'Visit of the Australian Prime Minister', 11 April. 1941, CAB 80/27. This reply to Menzies closely followed the thinking of Churchill and Pound at a Defence Committee meeting on 9 April.
[7] COS(41)80(O), 'Despatch of a Fleet to the Far East', 18 May 1941, CAB 80/57.
[8] DO(41) 31st Mtg., 19 May 1941, CAB 69/2.

and it diverted British attention from the Far East. The defence of the United Kingdom, including the threat of invasion and the U-boat warfare in the Atlantic, was the No. 1 priority, followed by the operations in the Mediterranean and Middle East, and the dispatch of supplies to the Soviet Union. Resistance to a Japanese attack took fourth and last place in Churchill's list of priorities. 'It was however always understood that if Japan invaded Australia or New Zealand the Middle East should be sacrificed to the defence of our own kith and kin. This contingency we all regarded as remote and improbable because of the vast abundance of easier and more attractive conquests offered to Japan by Malaya, Siam, and above all the Dutch East Indies.'[9]

On his return from a visit to London in June, Menzies reported to his Government that Churchill tended to dismiss from his mind defence problems the farther they were from London. He had a point. At the Atlantic Conference Churchill pointed out that 'nothing that might happen in Malaya could amount to a fifth part of the loss of Egypt, the Suez Canal, and the Middle East'. The Chiefs of Staff, though more especially the CIGS, Dill, regarded the Far East rather than the Middle East as being second in importance only to home defence. Churchill was, however, not without support at the Admiralty, where there were some very active debates during 1941 on whether they should reduce their Mediterranean strength to back up their Far Eastern strength. Admiral Sir William Davis, then a Captain, who was DDOD(F), February–August 1941, then AD of P until September 1942, recalls: 'My own views—which were not wholly accepted—was to the effect that the Middle East must have priority over the Far East, as, to put it simply, if the Middle East falls, Japan is free to join forces with her main Axis European allies, whereas if the Far East falls, we still have a powerful barrier in our Middle East position which would prevent the junction of the Axis European allies with Japan. I think bye and large the majority of folk were to my way of thinking.'[10] Pound, who kept a pretty open mind on the question of priorities between the Mediterranean and the Far East, tended to favour the majority position. He knew they had nothing like sufficient forces to provide both theatres with adequate numbers of up-to-date ships and

---

[9] Churchill, *The Grand Alliance*, pp. 522–3.
[10] Memorandum for the author (from recollections written at various times after the war), 3 Apr. 1975.

aircraft, and therefore thought it was best in the circumstances to have enough in the Mediterranean and take a chance on the Far East. His thinking seems to have been that if they lost control of the Mediterranean, the Far East would go anyway, but if they kept the Mediterranean, they could at least come back to the Far East later in conjunction with the United States.

Among Churchill's reasons for putting the Far East at the bottom of his priorities was the conviction since 1939, expressed repeatedly during 1941, that Japan would not declare war on Britain or provoke her into hostilities. She was bogged down in an interminable war in China, and she feared that the United States would enter the war. He put special emphasis on the deterrent effect of the American battle fleet in Hawaii on the flank of a major Japanese thrust to the south. Earlier in the year he was saying that Japan would not go to war before she was sure that Britain was beaten. Later in the year the argument was that the Japanese would not risk war with the ABD Powers 'unless or until Russia is decisively broken'. As he declared at the Lord Mayor's banquet on 10 November, 'It would seem a very hazardous adventure for the Japanese people to plunge, quite needlessly, into a world struggle in which they may well find themselves opposed in the Pacific by States whose populations comprise nearly three-quarters of the human race.'

The Japanese advance into southern Indo-China and the threat to Thailand caused Menzies to telegraph to Churchill on 11 August: 'My colleagues and I have given anxious consideration to Far East position. We have, as you know, always regarded Singapore and Malaya as our vital outposts ... We have also assumed that in the event of war with Japan, naval reinforcements as discussed in London with a nucleus of five capital ships would be sent to the Far East. We now say and emphasize that an early despatch of capital ships east of Suez would itself be most powerful deterrent and first step.'[11]

On his return from the Atlantic Conference on 19 August, Churchill pondered the urgent Australian message against this background. ABC-1 included the principle that the United States would reinforce her Atlantic Fleet (which she had done in June), and that this would permit the Royal Navy to send out a battle cruiser and an aircraft carrier from Force H on the outbreak of

[11] PREM 3/156/1.

war, to be followed eventually by five battleships. In May the VCNS, Phillips, had received the dormant appointment of C-in-C of this projected 'Eastern Fleet'. On 10 June the Chiefs of Staff had declared: 'We constantly feel that at the present time the need for a deterrent against Japan is greater than it was...'[12] In August the Admiralty went a step further than they were prepared to go in the Washington talks, now proposing to form an Eastern Fleet consisting of 7 capital ships (the battleships *Nelson* and *Rodney*, the 4 R-class battleships *Revenge, Royal Sovereign, Ramillies,* and *Resolution,* and the battle cruiser *Repulse* or *Renown*), 1 aircraft carrier, 10 cruisers, 24 destroyers, and eventually submarines. Such a fleet would be powerful enough to remain at Singapore if war broke out and to sever Japanese communications in a southward advance. This strength, however, could not be reached before March 1942 on account of the necessity for refits, fitting modern radar, the repair of action damage to certain ships, and the unavailability of the cruisers and destroyers until then. In the meantime, there would be only a few old cruisers and destroyers at Singapore, and the small obsolete carrier *Hermes* at Ceylon, 1,500 miles to the west.

The Australian telegram of 11 August caused Churchill to consider what could be done *now* to impress on the Japanese the absolute determination of Britain to go to war with them if they persisted in their southward advance. His 'Action this day' minute of 25 August to Pound and Alexander began: 'It should become possible in the near future to place a deterrent Squadron in the Indian Ocean. Such a force should consist of the smallest number of the best ships. We have only to remember all the preoccupations which are caused us by the *Tirpitz*[13]—the only capital ship left to Germany... to see what an effect would be produced upon the Japanese Admiralty by the presence of a small but very powerful and fast force in Eastern waters.' He proposed the dispatch to the East by the end of October of a 'formidable, fast, high-class Squadron,' consisting of the new King George V-class battleship

[12] COS to Joint Staff Mission, COS(41)365, 'Dispositions of the United States Fleet', CAB 80/28.

[13] This new and powerful German battleship had been completed in February 1941, but did not become operational until 20 September 1941. She was working up during the summer, based mainly at Kiel but also operating from other Baltic ports. British intelligence sources kept sighting her in different places and hearing of her up to different activities, some of which led the powers-that-were to believe that she was more ready for operations than was the case.

Duke of York, the *Repulse* or *Renown,* and an aircraft carrier of high speed. 'This powerful force might show itself in the triangle Aden–Singapore–Simonstown [the Cape]. It would exert a paralyzing effect upon Japanese naval action.' The *Duke of York* could work up on her long voyage to the East.[14]

The idea of sending out a deterrent force struck a responsive chord at the Admiralty. The problem was the number and quality of the capital ships that could be dispatched in the very near future, and here there was a sharp disagreement with what the Prime Minister had in mind. Pound, in his reply of 28 August, did not feel that any of the latest battleships, the first three of the five King George V class,[15] should be sent out until fully worked up, and this could be done effectively only in proximity to a dockyard or contractor's yard. More important, the Atlantic being the vital area, it was essential to have two of the King George Vs there to guard against a breakout by the *Tirpitz,* with the third available in case one was damaged or was refitting. The capital-ship situation was tight. Of the 15 in commission, only eight were immediately operational; the other seven were working up, in dock for repairs or refitting, with two of these due to be operational in the first week of September. The strongest force that Pound could recommend to be sent to Singapore (it would have to withdraw to Trincomalee if war broke out) *by the beginning of 1942* were the *Nelson* and *Rodney,* the *Renown,* and the small carrier *Hermes,* with the carrier *Ark Royal* to follow in April 1942. In an emergency the carrier *Indomitable* would be added. This force would deter the Japanese from sending 8-inch cruisers to attack trade in the Indian Ocean. Another form of deterrence would be provided in the meanwhile by the four old unmodernized R-class battleships, which would go to the Indian Ocean for troop convoy escort. The hope was that, in conjunction with the US Pacific Fleet, they would deter the Japanese from sending any battleships to the area. It was further hoped that the presence of the two forces in the Indian Ocean that would eventually become part of the Eastern Fleet 'will go some way to

---

[14] This and the following minutes (Pound's of 28 August and Churchill's of 29 August) are in ADM 199/1934, ADM 205/10, and Churchill, *The Grand Alliance,* pp. 768–74. Churchill's versions have taken a number of minor editorial liberties.

[15] *Prince of Wales* (completed in March 1941), the *King George V* (December 1940), and the *Duke of York* (November 1941). The *Anson* and *Howe* were not completed until June and August 1942, respectively. The last wartime battleship, the *Vanguard,* laid down in October 1941, was not ready until after the war (August 1946).

meet the wishes of Australia and New Zealand for the Far East to be reinforced'. Until they could put together a fleet in the East 'capable of meeting a Japanese force of the strength they were likely to send south', they would rely on the two forces to deter Japanese action in the Indian Ocean.

Churchill found serious fault with the proposed dispositions (29 August). 'It is surely a faulty disposition to create in the Indian Ocean a fleet considerable in numbers, costly in maintenance and man-power, but consisting entirely of slow, obsolescent or unmodernized ships which can neither fight a fleet action with the main Japanese force nor act as a deterrent upon his modern fast heavy ships, if used singly or in pairs as raiders. Such dispositions might be forced upon us by circumstances: but they are inherently unsound in themselves.' Nor did he like the use of the four Rs, with their low speed and the short range of their guns, for convoy work. They would be good against 8-inch cruisers; but if the Japanese detached a fast modern battleship to raid convoys, the Rs and their convoys would be 'easy prey'. In their present state the Rs would be 'floating coffins'. To justify their use for convoy work, it would be necessary to have one or two fast capital ships to prevent the enemy from detaching a capital-ship raider without fear of punishment. 'The potency of the dispositions I ventured to suggest in my M.819–1 [25 August] is illustrated by the Admiralty's own extraordinary concern about the *Tirpitz*. *Tirpitz* is doing to us exactly what a *K.G.V* in the Indian Ocean would do to the Japanese Navy. It exercises a vague, general fear and menaces all points at once. It appears, and disappears, causing immediate reactions and perturbations on the other side.' He expressed dismay that the Admiralty considered that the King George Vs were 'evidently judged unfit to fight their opposite number in a single ship action'. An 'excessive provision' was being made in the Atlantic to contain the *Tirpitz*, having regard '(a) to the American dispositions which may now be counted upon and (b) to the proved power of Aircraft Carriers to slow down a ship like *Tirpitz* if she were loose'. 'Nothing', he concluded, 'would increase her hesitation more than the appearance of the force I mentioned ... and above all of a *K.G.V.* This might indeed be a decisive deterrent.'

There was patently a clash between the Prime Minister's conception of a small but 'high-class' squadron that would through a show of strength act as a deterrent to Japanese aggression, and the

Admiralty's, which envisaged two larger forces of older capital ships to deter the Japanese Navy. For the time being no decision was reached. That the Admiralty was operating in a different time frame than the Prime Minister was demonstrated by the approval in mid-September of Vice-Admiral Sir Henry Moore to relieve Phillips as VCNS, with the latter going out as C-in-C-designate, Eastern Fleet, in the *Nelson* or *Rodney* towards the end of the year.

Two developments at the end of September strengthened the Prime Minister in his resolve that a deterrent force, whatever its composition, must be dispatched to Singapore forthwith. On 30 September Eden submitted a memorandum to the War Cabinet that made these principal points: (1) a stronger reaction to Japanese moves had become possible with the buildup of the Malayan defences and the strengthening of co-operation with the Americans and the Dutch; (2) faced with the prospect of economic isolation unless she made a major policy change, Japan would be compelled to reach a decision as to her future course; (3) a 'display of firmness is more likely to deter Japan from war than to provoke her to it'.[16] A day later the Cs-in-C, Far East and China, Air Chief Marshal Sir Robert Brooke-Popham and Vice-Admiral Sir Geoffrey Layton, telegraphed the Chiefs of Staff in similar, but more specific, terms. They pointed out that, since Japan was concentrating her forces against Russia, and knew that war with one of the ABD Powers would probably mean war with all three and possibly with Russia as well, 'the last thing Japan wants at this juncture is a campaign in the south. Consequently she must now be susceptible to pressure'. The opportunity should not be lost to insist on a withdrawal of Japanese armed forces from Indo-China. The telegram referred to the recent conference they had attended at Singapore and the 'emphatic opinion' there expressed that 'the only real deterrent to further Japanese aggression would be a British fleet based on Singapore and in absence of this fleet there is little doubt Japan could strike at her selected moment.... we would stress propaganda value of even one or two battleships at Singapore'.[17] This was, of

---

[16] WP(41)230, 'Far Eastern Policy', CAB 66/19.
[17] JP(41)816, 'Japan—Our Future Policy', 7 Oct. 1941, Annex I, CAB 84/35. The Singapore Conference, held on 29 September, was chaired by Duff Cooper, Chancellor of the Duchy of Lancaster, and was attended by Sir Shenton Thomas, Governor of the Straits Settlement, Sir Archibald Clark Kerr, the Ambassador to China, Sir Josiah Crosby, the Minister to Thailand, and Sir Earl Page, special Australian envoy to the War Cabinet, as well as the Cs-in-C, Far East and China.

course, Churchill's view and must have strengthened his determination to have it accepted.

The catalytic agent in the formation of Force Z was the fall of the Konoe Government on 16 October. This was viewed by Eden as 'an ominous sign'. It presaged the formation of a Cabinet

> more under the influence of extreme elements. The Russian defeats must inevitably be having their effect upon the Japanese appetite. There is nothing yet to show in which direction Japan will move, if any. But it is no doubt true that the stronger the joint front that the A.B.C.D. Powers can show, the greater the deterrent to Japanese action.
>
> In this connexion you will recall that we discussed some little time ago the possibility of capital ship reinforcements to the Far East. The matter has now become more urgent, and I should be glad if it could be discussed at the Defence Committee to-morrow afternoon.[18]

The meeting on 17 October, which was of crucial importance, was attended by Churchill (in the chair), Attlee, Beaverbrook (Minister of Supply), Eden, Cadogan, Ismay, the Service Ministers, and the Chiefs of Staff—Dill, Portal, and Phillips, acting for Pound, who was in Scotland visiting the Home Fleet. The Prime Minister opened the discussion of Eden's minute by expressing his disagreement with the Admiralty's proposal. The gradual buildup of a fleet in the East comprising mostly obsolete ships would solve nothing. It 'seemed to him wrong to send a squadron of Capital Ships that were neither strong enough to engage the weight of the Japanese Navy, nor yet fast enough to avoid action except in circumstances of their own choosing'. Again using the analogy of the *Tirpitz*, which immobilized a force three times her weight, he argued that a single modern capital ship in Far Eastern waters would have a similar effect on the Japanese Navy, 'and thereby on Japanese foreign policy'. His specific proposal was that the *Repulse*, which was then in the Indian Ocean on convoy escort duty, should proceed to Singapore, and that the *Prince of Wales* be rushed out to join her there. (The *Duke of York* would not be ready until the end of the year.) 'We could afford to accept some risk of the *Tirpitz* breaking out into the Atlantic in the knowledge that we ought by air action from aircraft carriers to be able to slow her up to become a prey for the heavy metal of our Capital Ships.'

[18] Eden's minute to Churchill, 16 Oct., DO(41)21, 'Capital Ship Reinforcements to the Far East. Note by Major-General Sir Hastings L. Ismay', 17 Oct. 1941, CAB 69/3.

THE GENESIS OF FORCE Z

Alexander, using the arguments provided by Pound and Phillips, spoke against the proposal, noting that the analogy with the *Tirpitz* did not apply to the Far East, for 'whereas the *Tirpitz* was a threat to our trade convoys in the Atlantic, our dispositions in the Far East would be governed more by the need to protect our own trade routes than to raid Japanese shipping'. He added that a strong reason for retaining all three KGVs in Home waters was the need to have modern capital ships available for important operations in the Western Mediterranean. Phillips used the argument against Churchill's proposal that Japan's 'oldest battleships were inferior to the R Class ships which it was proposed to send out to the Far East. There four R Class ships together with the *Rodney*, *Renown* and *Nelson* (when repaired) should, in their own waters, and operating under cover of shore-based aircraft, be a match for any forces the Japanese were likely to bring against them.'

Eden and Attlee gave the Prime Minister strong support from different points of view. For Eden, a modern ship like the *Prince of Wales* 'would have a far greater effect politically than the presence in those waters of a number of the last war's battleships. If the *Prince of Wales* were to call at Cape Town on her way to the Far East, news of her movements would quickly reach Japan and the deterrent effect would begin from that date.' Attlee, on the other hand, stressed the potential offensive role of the force sent out. The VCNS's arguments 'assumed that we would be prepared to remain on the defensive in Malayan waters even if Japan attacked Russia. We should find such action hard to justify in the circumstances.'

Churchill wound up the proceedings by inviting the First Lord 'to consider the proposal to send as quickly as possible one modern Capital Ship, together with an aircraft carrier, to join up with *Repulse* at Singapore. He would not come to a decision on this point without consulting the First Sea Lord, but in view of the strong feeling of the Committee in favour of the proposal, he hoped that the Admiralty would not oppose this suggestion. The Committee would take its final decision on Monday, 20th October...'[19]

---

[19] DO(41) 65th Mtg., CAB 69/2. It is hard to detect in the minutes 'the strong feeling... in favour of the proposal': two speakers had been critical of it and three (including Churchill) had supported it. The others present, so far as the minutes show, had been silent. Lieutenant-General Sir Ian Jacob (then a Colonel), who wrote up the minutes, has the explanation. It 'lies in the usual method of writing minutes during the war. Provided the arguments on each side were adequately recorded, we used not to bother with individual statements. It is evident

(*continued*)

The period of agonizing debates ended on 20 October, when the Defence Committee met in what was essentially a duel between Churchill and Pound. The former alluded to the great deterrent effect the arrival of a fast modern ship in the Far East would have, and to the improvement on the naval position in Home waters since the sinking of the *Bismarck* in May and the more active role of the US Fleet in the Atlantic. The War Cabinet, he said, were quite prepared to face the shipping losses which might occur if the *Tirpitz* broke out into the Atlantic. Pound's forceful response was that if the *Tirpitz* came out, they would have to run her down. 'How long this would take it was not possible to say, but the chances would obviously be improved if we had three K.Gs. at our disposal. In such an event we should be able to feel that the losses of shipping which we might sustain were incurred in spite of the sound dispositions we had made. If we detached the *Prince of Wales* to the Far East, we should then lay ourselves open to incurring additional losses as a result of unsound dispositions.' As for the Pacific, the First Sea Lord did not believe that one fast battleship would deter the Japanese, who 'could easily afford to put four modern ships with any big convoy destined for an attack in Southern Waters'. What would deter them would be the presence of six battleships (the *Nelson, Rodney,* and the four Rs at Singapore (note that Pound had originally proposed basing the Rs in the Indian Ocean), even if the Rs were obsolescent, since this would force the Japanese to detach the greater part of their Fleet, and thus uncover Japan to the American Navy. This exchange followed:

The Prime Minister said that he understood that the R Class battleships would be used in the Indian Ocean for escort duties for convoys.

Sir Dudley Pound said that this would be so until it became necessary to concentrate in the Far East. The aim had always been to constitute a battle fleet with this as the nucleus.

---

that those present other than Alexander and Phillips must have indicated their support for the P.M. either by saying something or simply by nodding. If they had supported Phillips, they would have been recorded, but as they didn't, the P.M. was able to make his statement even though the argument for had only been stated by himself, Attlee and Eden.' Jacob's letter to the author, 23 Feb. 1976. Jacob, incidentally, kept the records he made at high-level wartime meetings (War Cabinet, COS, both Defence Committees, and others), which he used for the minutes afterwards. They were contained in foolscap hard-backed notebooks, of which as time went on he collected 'quite a shelf-full'. Unfortunately, he left these notebooks behind when he left office, and when a few years later he asked to see them, he was told they had been burnt. All part of the confidentiality of Cabinet discussions, he presumes, but what a loss to historians!

THE GENESIS OF FORCE Z

The Prime Minister said that he did not foresee an attack in force on Malaya. He thought the main danger would be to our trade from Japanese battle-cruisers. The former would be sufficiently powerful to sink an R Class battleship and the convoy it was protecting. The only thing which would induce caution in the Japanese would be the presence in Eastern Waters of a fast striking force. This would be still more true before war had actually begun.

Supported by Eden, the Prime Minister reiterated that he wished to see the *Prince of Wales* sent out and the situation reviewed when the *Nelson*, which had been torpedoed on 27 September, had been repaired (November, it was expected).

At this point, with the views of the First Sea Lord and the Prime Minister backed by the Foreign Office so divergent, Pound offered a compromise. Realizing the value of a report from Cape Town of the arrival there of the *Prince of Wales*, he proposed that 'she should be sailed forthwith for that destination, a decision as to her onward journey being taken in the light of the situation when she arrived at Cape Town'. The idea of reviewing the movements of the *Prince of Wales*, which would, if she preceeded, include her joining the *Repulse* in the Indian Ocean, stemmed in part, anyway, from the danger of the *Tirpitz* breaking out and other operational possibilities before the *Duke of York* was ready in December. The Committee approved the First Sea Lord's proposal.[20] Under an agreement reached by Churchill and Pound a few days later, in case of war the four R-class battleships would be moved as ready to Eastern waters for convoy duty, and it was hoped later on to relieve the *Repulse* with the *Renown*, which had a greater radius of action and was about a half knot faster.

It was a relief to ministers, as it always is, to feel that they could postpone a decision, hence their silence at these meetings. The ships were to go to the Cape, and the further destination could then be determined. The question was never brought up again, and was presumably settled between Churchill and Pound. And here I must stress that the Chiefs of Staff as such normally did not discuss or raise purely naval questions. It was left for the First Sea Lord to

[20] DO(41) 66th Mtg., Confidential Annex, CAB 69/8. In a letter to Churchill on 7 March 1942 (ROSK 5/124), Pound made the extraordinary statement that the *Prince of Wales* and *Repulse* had been sent to the Far East 'in accordance with my advice'. The only explanation of this *mea culpa* that occurs to me is that his compromise proposal had ultimately led to the dispatch of the two capital ships to Singapore—and disaster.

decide naval positions, getting such approval from the Prime Minister (the Minister of Defence) as might be needed.

The decision as to the subsequent movements of the *Prince of Wales* was made long before she reached Cape Town. An Admiralty signal on 21 October to all concerned mentioned that she would shortly leave for Singapore. This contravened the decision reached only the day before, yet was 'probably intended mainly to ensure that adequate administrative preparations were made for a not improbable movement'.[21] The Admiralty informed the American CNO, Stark, on 23 October that the *Prince of Wales*, wearing the flag of Admiral Phillips, 'will leave the United Kingdom this week for Singapore via the Cape'.[22] Phillips left the Clyde in the *Prince of Wales* on 25 October apparently in the knowledge that it was already virtually decided that he would go on to Singapore.[23] And yet, on 1 November Churchill minuted Pound: 'If it is decided that P. of W. should go on to Singapore ...', and the next day Pound minuted Churchill: 'It is my intention to review the situation generally just before P. of Wales reaches the Cape.' He would consult with the Prime Minister as regards that decision.[24] On 5 November Churchill informed the War Cabinet that the *Prince of Wales* was *en route* to Cape Town and was 'likely to proceed to Singapore'.[25] This had become a certainty by 7 November, on which day Pound, in reviewing the general situation with Allied admirals (Free French, Polish, Dutch, and Norwegian), stated that Phillips, in the *Prince of Wales*, 'was on his way to Singapore via Freetown ... and the Cape'.[26] On the 9th, a week before the *Prince of Wales* reached Cape Town, Phillips was ordered to Singapore after a short stay at Cape Town. On the 11th the Admiralty ordered him to rendezvous with the *Repulse* in Ceylon, and to proceed in company to Singapore. They were to be only the nucleus of the larger and more powerful Eastern Fleet they hoped to have out there early in 1942.

[21] Post-war official source, Naval Historical Branch records.

[22] Central Security-Classified Records, Secretary of the Navy/Chief of Naval Operations, Secret File, (SC) A–4–3EF13, US Operational Archives.

[23] Indeed, Admiral of the Fleet Lord Fraser of North Cape says: 'It was understood when *Prince of Wales* sailed from the Clyde that her destination would be Singapore.' Lord Fraser's replies (Aug. 1979) to a questionnaire submitted to him by the author. Other Fraser quotations below are from the same source. He was Third Sea Lord and Controller, March 1939–May 1942.

[24] ADM 205/10.   [25] WM(41) 109th Mtg., Conclusions, CAB 65/24.

[26] ADM 205/7.

I must at this point interject Lord Fraser's statement, for which I can find no direct corroboration, but which cannot be dismissed lightly: 'D.P. put up a very tough fight re the *Prince of Wales*. He refused to send out *Repulse* and *Prince of Wales* until Winston changed the destination to Australia, under the cover of the Australian Air Force.' The *Prince of Wales* would refit at Singapore, then proceed to Australia. If this is what happened, the probable date was between 5 and 7 November. This revelation must be borne in mind in the discussion of responsibilities in the following section. And cf. below, p. 398.

Nothing had been said on 20 October about the dispatch of an aircraft carrier with the *Prince of Wales*. The Admiralty had always emphasized that a carrier must accompany any capital ships sent to the East, and Churchill at the Defence Committee on 17 October had wanted one. Yet none was immediately available to accompany the *Prince of Wales*. Alexander and Pound dug in their toes and 'stood out against sending a battle squadron without a Carrier. On pressure we agreed to try and speed up the "working up" of a new Carrier just completed, and on the understanding that after working up in the West Indies she would rendezvous with Prince of Wales at Cape Town.'[27] She would help to form the core of a balanced fleet. Unfortunately, the Captain of the carrier in question, H. E. Morse, of the *Indomitable*, damaged her when he put her aground on a reef off Kingston Harbour, Jamaica, on 3 November during a fog.[28] As she had to be docked and repaired (the work was performed at the Norfolk (Virginia) Navy Yard between 11 and 19 November, the rapid turn-round being due entirely to the ingenuity of the Navy Yard), it was not possible for her to join the *Prince of Wales* before the latter's arrival at Singapore. No other suitable carrier was available. The *Ark Royal* was sunk on 13 November, the

[27] Alexander to Roskill, 14 Nov. 1952, ROSK 4/79.
[28] For this Morse lost his command. He was a six-oner and, it has been suggested, would have reached the top of the Service but for this mishap. Part of the problem on 3 November lay in Morse's refusal to take a pilot, and therein lies this precious yarn. 'That delightful Chaplain and Naval Instructor, the Reverend William Hall, was responsible for his decision. During one of his pleasant rambling dissertations during Navigation instruction at Dartmouth, he had said: "Don't forget that as a naval officer you must feel able to take your ship into any harbour without a pilot, except of course where pilotage is compulsory." A remark that Harold Morse never forgot.' Captain G. D. Owen, 'Unrecorded History', *Naval Review*, lxvi, 2 (Apr. 1978), 162. What astonishes me is that the Navigating Officer of the *Indomitable*, who was actually the one who put the ship on the reef, was subsequently promoted to commander (31 December 1943) and was awarded an OBE for War Services. He even returned to the *Indomitable*, as SO(Plans) to the C-in-C, Home Fleet, 1950–2.

Illustrious and *Formidable,* heavily damaged in the Mediterranean, were under repair in the United States, the *Furious* was undergoing a major refit, and the *Eagle,* besides being old and slow, was in dock. The *Hermes* was too old and too slow (26 knots), and carried too few aircraft (generally, 12) to qualify for a striking force. The ancient *Argus,* though reconstructed in 1937–8, was no improvement (18.75 knots, 12–18 aircraft). The small 15-knot auxiliary carrier *Audacity* (converted from the German merchant ship *Hannover* in July 1941) carried only six aircraft. Of the carriers that could have met the requirements of Force Z, only the recently commissioned *Victorious* (23,000 tons, 31 knots, 33 aircraft) remained in service, but she could not be spared from the Home Fleet because of the possible breakout of German capital ships. And so, in spite of the lessons of the war to date that in modern warfare it was not possible to operate capital ships safely without air cover, the *Prince of Wales* and *Repulse* arrived at Singapore without the protection of a carrier. It was hoped that shore-based air strength provided by the RAF in Malaysia would be sufficient.

It is fascinating to speculate whether the presence of a carrier would have made a great difference or whether the disaster would have been even worse. My view is the more or less orthodox one—that the presence of the fast *Indomitable* (23,000 tons, 30.5 knots) and her 45 aircraft (12 Fulmars, 24 Albacores, and 9 Sea Hurricanes) would not have made any decisive difference in the result on 10 December, and she might indeed have been lost as well, though the Japanese would have had to pay a much higher price for their success.[29]

The decision to dispatch the *Prince of Wales* to the East, albeit conditionally, was taken over the strong protest of the C-in-C, Home Fleet, Admiral Sir John Tovey, who was deeply concerned over the danger of a breakout of the *Tirpitz,* the battle cruisers *Scharnhorst* and *Gneisenau,* and the pocket battleship *Admiral Scheer,* on to the Atlantic trade routes. Without the *Prince of Wales,* he had only one capital ship immediately available, the *King George V.* (The

---

[29] The Fulmars were respectable low-level fighters and had an excellent endurance for long-range reconnaissance, but they were slow, in level speed and climb. The Hurricanes were faster but of low endurance (approximately two hours without drop tanks). The armament of both types, eight 0.303s, though superior to the Buffalo's, would have been outmatched by the armament of the IJN bombers, though perhaps not seriously, since the 20mm of the Nells and Bettys had indifferent arcs of fire and primitive mountings. On the Nells and Bettys, see further, below, p. 308. The Albacore was an ideal night-attack aircraft.

'THEY THAT STAND HIGH HAVE MANY BLASTS'

Duke of York was having a final pre-completion docking at Rosyth, and the *Malaya* left Scapa Flow for the Clyde and Gibraltar on 20 October.) The Naval Staff, too, particularly the officers in Plans and Operations (Foreign), were solidly against sending the *Prince of Wales* to the Far East, as it were almost by herself. They argued against the unwisdom of dispatching a wholly unbalanced force, lacking a carrier, cruisers, and an adequate destroyer screen (only two went out with the *Prince of Wales*, and were later joined by two more), into an area where they did not know the strengths or capacities of the potential enemy. They suggested that such action would make the *Prince of Wales* a hostage to fortune, and they considered the deterrence argument advanced by the Prime Minister and the Foreign Office as utterly unrealistic—that it would need a force far greater than they could possibly provide to 'deter' Japan from any course of action on which she decided.

2. 'THEY THAT STAND HIGH HAVE MANY BLASTS TO SHAKE THEM'

Churchill has been savaged by Captain Roskill, Vice-Admiral K. G. B. Dewar, Major-General S. Woodburn Kirby, and many others for the decision to send out a totally inadequate and seriously unbalanced force, lacking especially the air element of naval power, to an insecure base in a theatre where air cover would be scanty to say the least. As Dewar charged after the war, 'British naval policy in Far Eastern waters was based on unrealistic threats and imaginery deterrents, conceived in Mr Churchill's strategical cloud cuckoo land.' The critics are on solid ground.

Churchill's principal object was to deter Japan from entering the war by constituting what he described in his history of the war as 'that kind of vague menace which capital ships of the highest quality, whose whereabouts are unknown, can impose upon all hostile naval calculations'. This overlooked the differences between the Atlantic and the Pacific, and between the British problem in the former and the Japanese problem in the latter. It was sheer fantasy to believe that the presence of the two capital ships in the Aden–Singapore–Simonstown triangle 'would exert a paralyzing effect upon Japanese naval action'. Churchill thought that because the *Tirpitz* posed a serious threat to the vital convoy routes in the North Atlantic and pinned down strong naval forces at Scapa Flow, the *Prince of Wales* and *Repulse* would exert similar pressure on the

Imperial Navy. As he said of the *Prince of Wales*, 'There is nothing like having something that can catch and kill anything.'[30] The circumstances, however, were completely dissimilar. The 'triangle' would be devoid of Japanese shipping in time of war, and the distances were enormous: Singapore to Aden and to the Cape was 3,600 and 5,600 miles respectively. There was no earthly reason why British warships in that area should paralyze the Japanese Navy. The chances of the two big ships threatening Japan's vital communications to the northward of Singapore were equally negligible because of the great distances involved—Singapore to Japan was some 2,500 miles—and the powerful naval forces between them and this objective. Again it was unlikely that they could establish effective local control even in the Malaya–Singapore area, where greatly superior forces, based on Camranh Bay in French Indo-China, were almost certainly concentrated to support Japan's southward drive. Being on the offensive, the Imperial Navy would launch a major expedition in the Southern Area only if they could cover its voyage with sufficient strength. They could take account in their dispositions of the existence in the offing of one or two capital ships, no matter where they happened to be. The Admiralty plan of gradually building up a fleet in the Indian Ocean seems to be the best strategy that was possible, though it could have had no effect on an invasion of Malaya. Also, it would have been sensible to stop worrying about capital ships and to do everything they could during 1941 to build up a modern air force in Malaya.

In Churchill's defence, it could be said that this was one of the occasions when political requirements of a situation must override operational doubts. It was operational madness to send the *Prince of Wales* and the *Repulse* to Singapore without a carrier and a proper screening force, but it made *political sense* in the context of those critical days. A comparatively small reinforcement like the two capital ships *might* tip the scales in favour of caution on the part of Japan. And here we must remember that Churchill had been brought up in the day of the battleship, constantly thought in terms of fleet actions, and had had his ideas of the immense influence exercised by a powerful capital ship confirmed by the exploits of the *Scharnhorst, Gneisenau,* and *Bismarck.* He therefore felt that the

---

[30] Telegram to Roosevelt, 1 Nov. 1941, PREM 3/469.

presence of one or two capital ships in South-east Asia would exert the same kind of influence on the Japanese as these had done on the British. In exaggerating the value of capital ships he was only following majority opinion in the Navy. And nobody in the higher decision-making levels in Whitehall asked whether the arrival of two capital ships might not just as likely prove a provocation rather than a deterrence to the Japanese, who might regard it as final indication of ABCD encirclement and decide they had better strike without delay.

Sending a token force to a war area where the enemy is in far greater strength has always been an invitation to disaster. Yet, war had *not* broken out and the enemy was only a *potential* enemy. In the light of our knowledge of what happened seven weeks later, it is difficult to realize that the idea of the Japanese going bald-headed at the United States, Britain, and the Netherlands simultaneously and in such a complete and ruthless fashion came as a big surprise. It is fair to say that no one involved in the decision to send out Force Z, from the Prime Minister downwards, imagined that Japan would behave in so ultimately suicidal a fashion. Pound himself expected that Japan 'would attack northward', which presumably meant against the Soviet Union. They all thought that Japan would push things cautiously. Immediately after the Singapore Conference on 29 September, Lady Diana Duff Cooper told a number of Service wives that they could all relax, as the top brass had said that the Japanese would not attack for another six months, at least.[31] General Jacob heard Churchill 'more than once say to the COS that he would give them three months notice of Japan entering the War. This was when he was deprecating the tying up of more troops in Malaya. He also said that as a Japanese entry into the war would bring in the Americans, the temporary disasters that might occur would not matter because with America on our side victory was certain and all would be restored.'[32]

It has been charged that 'if the Admiralty had been more strongly represented at the top some of the worst naval disasters of the war (notably the dispatch of the *Prince of Wales* and *Repulse* to Singapore without air cover in the autumn of 1941 and the scattering of the

[31] Captain D. H. Doig, 'Misfortune off Malaya, 10th December 1941' (unpublished MS, revised, 1977), p. 2; copy in my possession. Doig was the quiet, unassuming, but very efficient Secretary to Admiral Layton.
[32] Letter to the author, 25 Feb. 1975.

Arctic convoy PQ 17 in July 1942) might well have been averted'.[33] This disparagement of Pound stems from the legend that he could not stand up to Churchill on critical issues, being intensely loyal to him and deprived by poor health (a long-standing osteoarthritis of the left hip, extreme fatigue, insomnia, and perhaps the onset of the brain tumour that finally killed him in 1943) of the stamina and the will to cope with his interventions in naval operations and strategy.[34] There is no denying that Churchill could be difficult. Edwin Montagu said of him in 1922: 'Nobody learns more readily from experience or yields with more difficulty to argument.' Yet Pound knew how to handle Churchill. Lord Fraser declares that 'D.P. was not Winston's "stooge". He would fight hard on strategical and operational policy.' Admiral Sir Henry Moore, who succeeded Phillips as VCNS, admitted that 'Pound was still a bit fixed in his ideas, but at least he could deal with Churchill!'[35] This from the No. 2 man on the Naval Staff, who obviously had an insider's view on the relationship between the two men. Rear-Admiral A. D. Nicholl was another who was in a good position to judge the Pound–Churchill relationship. 'He was completely loyal to Churchill ... At the same time, Pound would if necessary stand up to Churchill firmly and it was the First Sea Lord's toughness and loyalty that endeared him to Winston as time went on.'[36] Admiral of the Fleet Sir Arthur Power, ACNS (H) in 1940-2, thought 'the greatest service' that Pound did for the Navy was 'to stonewall the bowling of W. S. C.'.[37] Subjected to constant pressure from Churchill, on top of the heavy responsibility he held for the conduct of the war at sea, Pound decided early that he would fight him only on the really vital matters—the Churchill-sponsored Plan 'Catherine' early in the war, the passage of the R-class battleships into the Baltic, is an

---

[33] Captain Stephen Roskill, *Naval Policy between the Wars* (2 vols., London, 1968, 1976), ii. 467.

[34] In my *From the Dardanelles to Oran* (Chapter Four), I spelled out in detail my views on the Pound–Churchill relationship. What I say above is an addendum to that statement. I am not concerned here with how effective a First Sea Lord Pound was. This is an entirely different (and in respects equally controversial) matter.

[35] Letter to the author, 20 Apr. 1976.

[36] Nicholl's memorandum for Donald McLachlan, 6 Apr. 1968, Nicholl Papers, 77/122/1 (Imperial War Museum). He was Naval Assistant Secretary, War Cabinet, 1939-41, and DOD(F), 1942-4.

[37] As quoted by Rear-Admiral M. W. St. L. Searle, his COS in the East Indies Fleet (1943-5); Searle to Roskill, 18 July 1977, Roskill Papers, Churchill College, Cambridge (ROSK) 5/57.

example—but that the wise policy was not to oppose him directly. It was absolutely no good answering him with a blunt 'No'. The idea was to appear to agree, then wean him from his untenable projects by wearing him down with subtle opposition. When C-in-C, Mediterranean, he explained his method to an officer on his staff when he had to reply to a Foreign Office telegram on policy for the defence of Egypt with which he strongly disagreed: 'Never say No unless it's really impossible. Say Yes—and this is what it would mean in terms of resources and other commitments. Then they'll turn it down themselves.'[38] Pound did not always win out in his many rough and tumbles with Churchill—Force Z is a conspicuous instance where he did not—but he did, as General Jacob and so many other first-hand observers maintain, and as I maintain, hold his own very well.

Then there is the alleged health factor, which is supposed to have weakened Pound's resistance to Churchill's pressures. The charge of bad health does have support from contemporaries. One instance is the remark of the Mediterranean Fleet Medical Officer (Surgeon-Captain E. Moxon Browne) in the spring of 1939: 'If the war comes, I don't believe he is fit enough to command this fleet.' His evidence was Pound's arthritic left hip and the consequent sleeplessness, which caused him often to walk about the ship in the small hours of the morning.[39] Then there is the evidence in 1941-2 of Alanbrooke, a man of keen intelligence with sharp powers of observation, who pictures the First Sea Lord as a tired and worn-out old man.[40] It is on the basis of such evidence[41] that Roskill concludes that Pound 'was never really fit to carry the great responsibilities which fell on his shoulders; and that, but for

---

[38] Captain J. S. Litchfield's letter to the author, 18 Dec. 1979.
[39] Roskill's letter in the *Daily Telegraph*, 7 Mar. 1970. I like Nora Loft's mischievous letter in the *Daily Telegraph* of 11 Mar. 1970: 'So Captain S. W. Roskill seems to think that arthritis and insomnia make a man unfit to command. One wonders how he would have assessed an admiral with one arm, one eye and a background of considerable emotional stress. Unfit for Trafalgar?'
[40] e.g. in his diary on 17 Feb. 1942: 'Am getting more and more worried by old Dudley Pound as First Sea Lord. . . . He is asleep 75 per cent of the time he should be working.' Arthur Bryant, *The Turn of the Tide, 1939-1945* (London, 1957), p. 308. Rear-Admiral Godfrey, the DNI, was another who, by the end of 1941, was deeply concerned about the First Sea Lord's sleepiness. He tried unsuccessfully to get two retired Admirals, men nearer to Pound's age, to persuade him to consult a physician. Patrick Beesly, *Very Special Admiral: The Life of Admiral J. H. Godfrey, CB* (London, 1980), pp. 235-6.
[41] There is much more in a dossier in Roskill's papers (ROSK 5/125), some of which is cited in his *Churchill and the Admirals* (London, 1977), pp. 296-8.

Churchill's strong affection for him, he would and should have been relieved of his office much earlier than 1943'.[42]

Let us examine the charge. It is not suggested here that Pound was 100 per cent physically fit when he took over as First Sea Lord. He had had three and a half years hard 'crisis' work in the Mediterranean without any leave. But this is a far cry from the picture, given by Pound's detractors, of a physical wreck who had no business taking over the supreme command of the Navy on the eve of a world war. Vice-Admiral Sir Charles Norris, then a Captain, who left the Mediterranean at the end of April 1939, is positive that Pound was 'in top form then. I saw him again, *en famille*, on his recall to the UK, June/July. He was his usual self.' 'He was as strong, purposeful, and unflappable as ever.'[43] Certainly, the osteoarthritis of the left hip did not seem to worry Pound much; he would put in a whole day's walking after partridge or woodcock, without apparent fatigue. Nor had disability from his hip anything to do with his 'sleeplessness', which itself was no reflection of poor health. During the eighteen years that Admiral Norris knew him, Pound 'never slept like the majority of people. [He did not require more than a few hours sleep at night.] He was a master of "catnapping", and I should say was able to throw off his problems for a nap at any time it was possible.' This trait was well known in the family and in the Mediterranean Fleet. It may have all started when as a young man he often turned out at ungodly hours to get in an hour's shooting and be back onboard for early morning work. As for the 'dozing' at meetings of which so much has been made, it was not very profound: the moment anything to do with the Navy came up, he was, as Lord Mountbatten told me and as others have noted, instantly awake and alert. Vice-Admiral Brian Schofield was in frequent contact with Pound when Director of the Trade Division (March 1941–August 1943), not only at the Admiralty but on special occasions, as when he accompanied the First Sea Lord to the Atlantic Conference in August 1941, the Casablanca Conference in January 1943, and to Washington in May 1943. It was on this first occasion, in the numerous meetings in the *Prince of Wales* on the way over, that he

became familiar with Pound's habit of closing his eyes in order the better

---

[42] Letter in the *Daily Telegraph*; and see *Churchill and the Admirals*, pp. 165, 204, 210, 230.
[43] Letter to the author, 5 Nov. 1978, and tape of Jan. 1979.

to listen to what was being said. I remember the C-in-C Coastal Command [1937-41, Air Chief Marshal Sir Frederick], 'Ginger' Bowhill, remarking on it to me one day, and he added it only needed someone to mention the word 'destroyer' or 'cruiser' for Pound to instantly spring to life, and it was evident that he had heard every word that had been said. Never once, in the great many conferences I attended with him did he fail to show that despite outward appearances of slumber, he was fully aware of what had been said. I left the Admiralty in August 1943, and I can honestly say that up to that time I never once saw Pound unable to cope with what was going on.[44]

Sir Ian Jacob saw Pound at COS meetings and Churchill's staff conferences, and during the trips across the Atlantic, as in the *Prince of Wales* to the Atlantic Conference, in the *Duke of York* to Norfolk, Virginia (December 1941), and in the *Queen Mary* to the Quebec Conference (August 1943). He has this to say on the matter of Pound's health:

From the beginning of the war Pound gave the impression of being half asleep at meetings, and yet as Ismay says really very much alive if naval matters were mentioned. We knew he was a night bird, and had always worked late so as to be able to shoot and fish, so we weren't surprised to see him as he was. As time went on he seemed to get worse in this respect, but the war was having its effect on everyone. When did his deterioration in health begin to affect his work? I can't really say. Unless you know that a man is ill, you tend to put down a degree of slowness or lack of sharpness just to fatigue. I believe that in 1943 we thought that he was beginning to show his age. He never spoke much at COS meetings, and he still drove his fast Bentley [one foot hard on the accelerator], and he seemed full of keenness on the voyage to Halifax [Quebec Conference]. I had no idea he was ill, but thought he was wearing out. If I had to make a definite statement it would be that Pound's illness affected not more than the last year of his life, and was barely detectable even then.[45]

It is true that Pound was under tremendous strain in 1942-3 with the convoy losses in the Battle of the Atlantic, and that he tired more easily. But tiredness, a habit of closing one's eyes during meetings, and of catnapping when the occasion permitted, are *not*

---

[44] Letter to the author, 5 July 1979.
[45] Letter to the author, 22 Jan. 1979. Commander David Joel, who was Flag-Lieutenant in the *Colossus* in the First War when Pound was Flag-Captain, and served again with him in the Second War as Duty Signal Officer, is another first-hand witness: 'He seemed always alert and little changed.... His being asleep at meetings is a myth. After a certain age many peoples' eyes grow tired and though wide awake they close them to rest this tiredness and often to help them concentrate their thinking.' Letter in the *Daily Telegraph*, 13 Mar. 1970.

to be confused with poor health and declining mental power. Lord Fraser states categorically: 'There was nothing wrong with Dudley Pound's health when he was First Sea Lord. He was mentally alert.' There was no appreciable deterioration in Pound's health until shortly before the end. Admiral Norris, who saw Pound at various times in 1941–3, found him 'as imperturbable as ever—perhaps a little more weary. Who wouldn't be? But otherwise no obvious change, physically or mentally.' Vice-Admiral Sir Ronald Brockman, Pound's Secretary from January 1940, remembers the first time the Admiral made any complaint about his health. It was in July of 1943, when Pound told him he was having trouble with his right leg and was occasionally losing a sense of feeling in his foot.[46] Pound's records in the Medical Director-General's Department reveal no serious illness or ailment during all his time at the Admiralty—he had appeared to be in normal health—until 8 July 1943, when he complained of some dulling of sensation of the outer side of his right thigh and some stiffness of the neck. These were the first symptoms of the very malignant brain tumour that led to his resignation in September and death in October. From its rate of progress, it might be deduced (from modern medical records) that the tumour was very unlikely to have been present for much more than a month prior to the first symptoms. There is, however, room for caution, since in the absence of a post-mortem the final diagnosis can never be positively confirmed. The rate at which brain tumours grow varies enormously from case to case, and whether in this case there was a haemorrhage into an existing tumour or whether it was simply a very rapidly growing primary malignant glioma can never now be known. Opinions will differ as to whether Pound could have been adversely affected by the tumour during the last years of his life. Although it is true that a loss of vivacity and concentration, accompanied by mental drowsiness, are common features in the earlier stages of a brain tumour, there is nothing to suggest that such was the case here. This should cast serious doubts on the charges that have been made that Pound's earlier decisions were affected by the developing tumour. Indeed, Pound 'got through the Quebec Conference [19–24 August 1943] magnificently,' says Admiral Brockman, 'and I, who probably saw him more than anyone else, noticed no diminution in his powers.'

[46] Admiral Brockman's letter to Captain George Pound, 16 Feb. 1979 (copy in the author's possession), as slightly amended in a letter to the author, 15 Nov. 1979.

'THEY THAT STAND HIGH HAVE MANY BLASTS'

Pound's integrity and immense sense of duty would never have allowed him to assume the post of First Sea Lord in 1939 and to hold it, had he been physically unfit to carry out his duties. Had this been the case, Churchill, who admired Pound's naval knowledge and the 'intensity' of his thought in naval matters, surely would not have kept him on and have continued to rely on him. It represents, in any case, a quantum leap to argue that Pound's ill health disposed him to knuckle under to Churchill. I can only repeat what I have written elsewhere, that for anyone 'to impugn the character of the professional head of the Navy in the first four years of the War by accusing him of being too acquiescent, even servile, to Churchill is grossly unjust and, not to put too fine a point on it, is sheer nonsense as well'.

Pound it is alleged, said that on the matter of the dispatch of Force Z Churchill had 'worn him down', as he had worn down Fisher in 1915.[47] I am prepared to accept that Pound made some such statement. It tells a scant half of the story. There was a feeling in the Admiralty of grave doubt and disquiet about the dispatch of the *Prince of Wales* to the Far East. They would have much preferred waiting until early in 1942, when a balanced fleet could have been sent out. (As matters developed, the Admiralty's preference would not have been possible after the *Ark Royal, Barham,* and two cruisers had been sunk in the Mediterranean in November, and the *Queen Elizabeth* and *Valiant* had been seriously damaged at Alexandria in December.) But with Churchill pressing him to make this move, Pound had given up his strong objections and proposed a compromise at the meeting on 20 October as the best that was possible. This was not, however, before an unusual happening took place.[48]

Pound was dismayed at sending out such a completely unbalanced force that he felt it his duty to call a meeting of the Sea Lords and other professional members of the Board to discuss their position. As

---

[47] *Naval Memoirs of Admiral J. H. Godfrey* (8 vols. in 11, privately printed, 1964–6), viii. 66.

[48] For this incident I am indebted to a memorandum of 5 Mar. 1975 from Rear-Admiral Sir Rowland Jerram, who was then Secretary to the ACNS (Home), and to his letter to me of 5 Apr. 1978. It is not substantiated in the extant Admiralty records, and Lord Fraser has no recollection of it, which is no reason for not giving it credence. Jerram certainly was in a position to know what was going on at the highest levels, and his recollection is 'very clear' on this point. Admiral Brockman, moreover, in a letter of 15 November 1979 to me, confirms Admiral Jerram's statement. The date of this incident is not certain, but I would assume that it was sometime between the 17 and 20 October meetings of the Defence Committee.

a result, their unanimous opinion against the strategically unsound disposition was expressed in a memorandum to the First Lord.

It is not known [says Admiral Jerram] whether Alexander forwarded this representation to Churchill—probably not, for it was unconstitutional. What he did do, as I well remember, was to direct Markham (Sir Henry, Permanent Secretary) to draft a memorandum for him to address to the Sea Lords reminding them that it was the duty of the *First Sea Lord* to give his professional advice to the Government, that the decision on such advice would be entirely a political one, and that there was no provision in the Constitution for the collective opinion of the Sea Lords to be proferred to the Government. The first of these had been covered on this occasion by the advice already expressed by the First Sea Lord to the Prime Minister, and there the responsibility of the former ended.

This long established machinery was of course well known to and understood by the Sea Lords, who felt their unprecedented action was justified by the concern they felt at a decision which, in their view, could only lead to disaster.

My own Chief (Power, ACNS) and doubtless some other Sea Lords expected that Pound might feel bound to resign over this issue, which, as forecast, resulted in one of the worst disasters ever incurred by the British Navy. However, resignation of a First Sea Lord, particularly in war and at that critical stage, could well be regarded as a disservice to the country [as indeed it was in the case of Lord Fisher's resignation in May 1915], and he remained at his post. The sequel is well known.

Alexander shared the reservations of the Sea Lords and the Naval Staff, but he was finally persuaded that the situation in the Far East was so critical that the risks had to be taken.

It is true that, as General Kirby says, Churchill, 'despite opposition from the Admiralty based on naval and strategic factors, used political pressure to force the Admiralty to put his plan into action'. After the loss of the two big ships, Pound never ceased to regret that he had succumbed to Churchill's pressure, severe though it was, to dispatch the unbalanced force. It is difficult to see that he had much choice, since the issue was indeed as much a *political* as it was a strategic matter. There comes a time when political requirements must be balanced against strategic considerations. In the crunch they are paramount. There are other examples in the war, such as the movement to Wavell's Army to Greece after his successful campaign in Cyrenaica. As Pound's Secretary sums up the essential point: 'I think anyone who was in the Admiralty at the time will remember how hard Dudley Pound and the Naval Staff fought, but when a political decision is given, it has to be accepted.'[49] Something had to be done, and swiftly, to reduce the grave apprehensions of the Pacific Dominions, to say nothing of Britain's, by persuading Japan not to pursue her southward drive.

The story of the genesis of Force Z goes to show how a strongly rooted mode of thought persists regardless of developments. For years the British had promised the Australians and New Zealanders that if Japan went to war, they would send a fleet to Singapore, if necessary sacrificing the Mediterranean. This assurance had been reiterated *ad nauseam*. Yet, after France fell, they ought to have reviewed the policy fundamentally and withdrawn so obviously an unfulfillable promise and made a new plan based primarily on air and land reinforcements. Instead they persisted in the general idea, even if it meant sending only two big ships for the moment. In his speech at a secret session of the House of Commons on 19 December 1941, Alexander explained that the anxieties of the Dominions had been a major consideration in the decision to send Force Z and not wait for the larger force the Admiralty planned to dispatch early in the New Year.[50] 'It was too late to go back on the promise made to Australia and New Zealand,' as he later remarked.[51]

Churchill and, with less conviction, the Admiralty hoped that the Japanese would regard the *Prince of Wales* and *Repulse*, which were faster than any Japanese capital ship afloat (the *Yamato* was not completed until 16 December), as a powerful raiding force and would be deterred by it from entering the war; or, if they went to war anyway, that the presence of these ships, together with the containing power of the strong American fleet at Hawaii, would deter them from dispatching their expeditionary forces into the Gulf of Siam. Did Force Z have any of these effects on the Japanese? The answer obviously lay in Tokyo—to be precise, in the calculations of the Supreme Command in the crucial weeks following the advent of the Tōjō Cabinet.

[49] Admiral Brockman's letter to the author, 31 Dec. 1975. Or as a post-war Secretary of the Cabinet phrased it, 'It was evident that that decision was taken largely on the basis of the political considerations which it was no part of the responsibility of the Naval Staff to assess. ... [Pound] *accepted* the decision—in the sense that he accepted it as a decision of Ministers and was prepared loyally to carry it out.'
[50] ADM 1/11043.
[51] Alexander to Roskill, 14 Nov. 1952.

IX

'Let Slip the Dogs Of War'

The time for war will not come later!
ADMIRAL NAGANO OSUMI, at the Liaison Conference of
1 November 1941.

... in my opinion the gradual progress toward war followed by Japan was partly due to the impetus provided by the younger officers, and this tendency could be described as a disease which I believe spread from the younger officers in the Army to the younger officers in the Navy. The disease spread through both services...
ADMIRAL BARON SUZUKI KANTARŌ, interrogation, 26 December 1945.

1. TOKYO: POINT OF NO RETURN

DURING the ten days 23 October–1 November national policy was deliberated almost daily at a series of eight, often heated, Liaison Conferences.[1] The decision that had to be made was whether to accept the American demands—that is, a policy of peace at any price—or to break off the negotiations and start war immediately; or to be patient and continue the negotiations *pari passu* with war preparations and the intention to fight in the event of a rupture in the negotiations. The first alternative was a non-starter, being equated with national suicide: specifically, the loss of Japan's position in China and leadership in East Asia, reduction to a third-class nation, and economic stagnation and the concomitant of greater dependency on the Western Powers. The Army General Staff supported the second plan, but the Emperor was opposed. The third course was favoured by the Emperor, Tōjō, and Foreign Minister Tōgō. The argument of the Army was that the negotiations had demonstrated the bankruptcy of diplomacy and that, with the approach of the monsoon season, the rapid dwindling of oil reserves, and other factors, they should immediately resort to war, or 'self-

[1] See Ike, pp. 184–207, for the proceedings of these meetings.

defence' measures, as it was phrased. The Navy's position was a confused one.

In his first days of office, Shimada had often aired his view that war must be avoided, to which end the negotiations in Washington must continue. It had been a condition of his acceptance of the post. On 30 October, however, after his mentor, Prince Fushimi, had advised him on the 27th that 'If we do not open war soon, we will miss the opportunity' (to fight on favourable terms), Shimada expressed his 'resolve' (*ketsui*) to the Vice-Navy Minister, Sawamoto, and the Naval Affairs Bureau Chief, Oka, in favour of war for the very reason the Prince had given him. The Navy, moreover, 'could not buck the trend towards war. The final result will be war. The Navy should, therefore, be completely prepared for war. There is no alternative. We should proceed in full co-operation with the *Gunreibu*.'[2] Sawamoto and Oka were doves, but the authorities in the Ministry who were directly concerned, the 2nd Section of the Naval Affairs Bureau, whose Chief was the ultra-hawk Ishikawa, were very aggressive. The Naval Staff in general were of the opinion that the decision on war or peace must be made soon: Japan must quickly decide on the prospects of the talks in Washington, as she could not afford any loss of time. Here, too, however, there were differences of opinion. The directly concerned authorities, the 1st Section of the 1st Division, were aggressive, whereas Vice-Chief Itō and 1st Division Chief Fukudome were cautious. Nagano was with the first group. As he declared at the 23 October Laision Conference, 'The Navy is consuming 400 tons of oil an hour. The situation is urgent. We want it decided one way or the other quickly.'

Tōgō discovered at the Conference on 23 October 'that although the 6 September decision was to be re-examined, the war preparations which the high command had undertaken following the 2 July Imperial Conference remained, undisturbed, like a mine in the path of diplomatic activity, encouraging the military services

---

[2] Shimada interview, 13 Apr. 1964, Bōeichō Senshibu Archives, 'Shimada Shigetarō taishō muhyōdai bibōroku', Oka, 'Oboe', Sawamoto, 'Shi shuki'. Shimada had, nevertheless, not given up all hope for the negotiations. He had told Prince Fushimi on the 27th that, before deciding on war, they should exhaust every diplomatic means. It is clear from the sources, however, that his main purpose in wishing the continuation of the negotiations was to achieve complete national unity, which would be indispensable in war. The people should be able to understand that the Government had made every possible effort to avoid war. On Shimada's hot-and-cold attitude towards war and peace, see further, below, pp. 257–9.

to a bellicose attitude and constituting a formidable obstacle to any progress.... 'the "limits" set by the September decision tended to be taken as a point of departure for any renewed examination of the subject, and a resulting sort of psychological inertia made it very difficult to obtain relaxation of those limits.'[3] There was agreement that 'Because of the close relationship between the United States and Great Britain and their interest in the Netherlands, it would be impossible to limit the war to the Netherlands or to Great Britain and the Netherlands.... Undoubtedly, an understanding exists between Great Britain, the United States and the Netherlands, to stand united in the event of an armed invasion of the southern area by Japan.'[4]

The historic Liaison Conference of 1 November met in the palace grounds at 9 a.m. and did not adjourn until 1.30 the following morning. Nagano argued that the opportunity for a successful war would be lost if they waited. 'The future is uncertain; we can't take anything for granted. In three years enemy defences in the South will be strong, and the number of enemy warships will also increase.' Asked by the Finance Minister, Kaya Okinori, when they could go to war and win, Nagano responded with great emphasis: 'Now! The time for war will not come later!' The Finance Minister and the Foreign Minister held out against the precipitate start of war. They were not convinced the time had come for that. The minutes of the conference read:

Nagano, Navy Chief of Staff, is clearly determined that we must go to war now. Navy Minister Shimada, who has said that the future prospects of a war are not clear, appears to think, like Nagano, that there is no alternative but to go to war now. But he does not state this in a positive manner. Army Chief of Staff Sugiyama states strongly that now is the best time for war. He says he is confident that Army operations, given Navy protection of transportation on the high seas, would assure control of the occupied areas. Finance Minister Kaya and Foreign Minister Togo are completely unable to decide, on grounds that we don't know what would happen several years hence if we went to war.... Director of the Planning Board Suzuki ... argues that there is no alternative but to decide on war now, and that from the point of view of materials it would be better to go to war now.

[3] Tōgō, *The Cause of Japan*, p. 124.
[4] 'Conclusions Reached after Study of "The Outline for the Execution of the Empire's National Policy", at the Liaison Conference[s] from 23 to 30 October 1941', Japanese Monograph No. 150, p. 85.

The Services were not willing to let the negotiations drag on much longer. The Army General Staff held out for 13 November; the more pliant Naval General Staff would accept 20 November. What emerged after heated controversy (mainly between the Army General Staff on the one side and Tōjō and Tōgō on the other) was the decision to continue negotiations until midnight, 30 November/1 December. War would commence at the beginning of December if diplomacy were unsuccessful by the deadline, but war preparations would be cancelled at once, should the negotiations have proved successful. The negotiations would proceed on the basis of two sets of proposals, 'A' and 'B', presented by the Foreign Minister.

On the afternoon of 2 November, Tōjō, accompanied by the Chiefs of Staff, reported to the throne in a tearful voice the details of the debate and the decisions reached. 'The Emperor', according to Hattori, 'seems to have agreed.' On the 4th a meeting of the Supreme War Council was held in the Emperor's presence, ostensibly to give him their opinion on the advisability of the Services drawing up operational plans to meet the situation that would arise if the negotiations failed.[5] The Chiefs of Staff reiterated their views, which were endorsed by the Council. The following day, 5 November, IGHQ Navy Order No. 1 was sent to Yamamoto (as well as to the C-in-C, China Area Fleet): 'In view of the great possibility of being compelled to go to war against the United States, Great Britain and the Netherlands ... Japan has decided to complete various operational preparations within the first ten days of December.... The Commander-in-Chief of the Combined Fleet will make the necessary operational preparations.'[6] This included assembling the Pearl Harbor Task Force at Hitokappu Bay in the Kuriles.

---

[5] The Supreme War Council (*Gunji Sangikan Kaigi*) was composed of the 'military venerables'—the Military Councillors: the *Gensui* (Generals of the Army and Admirals of the Fleet), the Service Ministers and Chiefs of Staff, and other generals and admirals (including Oikawa and Yoshida) appointed from the active list by the Emperor without regular term. It was the chief advisory body on non-operational military policy. There were nineteen Military Councillors present on this occasion.

6 The IGHQ 'Orders' and 'Directives' to the Fleet, 5 Nov.–2 Dec. 1941, are in Japanese Monograph No. 97, *Pearl Harbor Operations: General Outline of Orders and Plans* (1953), and in No. 152, *Political Strategy Prior to the Outbreak of War*, pt. v. (1953). IGHQ Navy and Army operational 'Orders' carried the Imperial chop, in accordance with the constitutional principle that the prerogative of supreme command rested with the Emperor. 'Directives'

(*continued*)

On the same day an Imperial Conference confirmed the decisions of the 1 November Liaison Conference.[7] In his statement Nagano remarked that naval war preparations would be 'almost completed by the end of November. Hereafter we will go forward steadily with our war preparations, expecting the opening of hostilities in the early part of December. As soon as the time for commencing hostilities is decided, we are prepared for war.' All present agreed that war was inevitable if the United States rejected Japan's demands. These were contained in the 'A' and 'B' proposals that had been cabled to Nomura in Washington on 4 November. The 'B' proposals were a fall-back position if 'A' proved unsuccessful. Under 'A', Japan would pull her troops out of French Indo-China after the China Incident had been settled or an equitable peace established in East Asia; and for a 'necessary period of time' (twenty-five years) after a Sino–Japanese peace treaty, she would maintain troops in certain areas of North China and Inner Mongolia, and on Hainan Island, but would withdraw her troops elsewhere from China within two years of the establishment of peace. As regards the 'interpretation and execution of the Tripartite Pact', Japan would act 'independently'.

This proposal having been rejected by 15 November, Proposal 'B' was put forward on the 20th. Under it the two Governments would undertake no armed advance in South-east Asia and the South Pacific, except for French Indo-China, where Japanese troops already were in occupation; but with the conclusion of the

---

were Naval General Staff or Army General Staff explications without the chop. Both, in the case of the Navy, went out over Nagano's signature, prefixed in the case of an 'Order' with the words 'By Imperial Order.'

[7] The proceedings are in Ike, pp. 208–39. The President of the Planning Board, Lieutenant-General Suzuki Teiichi, produced the latest figures for the three-year outlook on oil in case of war that had been prepared by the Government and the Services. They gave 8,400,000kl as the domestic stockpile (Army, Navy, Civil combined) before the war. Prospective wartime production (homeland, synthetic, Netherlands East Indies), with prospective wartime consumption (Army, Navy, Civil) in the next column, and amount in stock at year end in the last column, were:

First year	850,000	5,200,000	4,050,000
Second year	2,600,000	5,000,000	1,650,000
Third year	5,300,000	4,750,000	2,220,000

When one subtracted 1,000,000kl as reserves for the homeland and 500,000 as reserves for decisive battle from the amount in stock at year end, it would leave 2,550,000 for the first year, 150,000 for the second, and 720,000 for the third. They would, said Suzuki, 'just be able to remain self-supporting'. *Sensho sōsho*, xxxi. 731–2, xci. 538–9.

agreement, Japan would move her troops from southern to northern Indo-China, and from the north as well upon the settlement of the China Incident or the establishment of a 'just peace' in the Pacific area. The United States would co-operate in securing the commodities Japan needed from the Netherlands East Indies, restore trade relations to those existing before the freezing of assets, and supply Japan with the oil that she needed. Finally, the United States was to take no actions 'as may hinder efforts for peace by both Japan and China'. There was no mention of the Tripartite Pact. In essence, Proposal 'B' was a *modus vivendi* based on a return to the position in June, before the Japanese occupation of southern Indo-China and the American freeze of Japanese assets in July.

Secretary of State Hull found these demands totally unacceptable, in which position he had firm British support. He countered on 26 November with a demand for the full and unconditional withdrawal of Japanese troops from China and French Indo-China, that Japan support no Chinese regime other than that of Chiang Kai-shek, and that she nullify the Tripartite Pact and conclude a non-aggression pact with the ABCD Powers, the Soviet Union, and Thailand. In return, the United States offered to lift the oil and steel embargo and the freeze on Japanese assets.

The Hull proposal was received with consternation in Tokyo on 27 November. Like the Japanese proposals, it involved a complete reversal of policy for the other side. To have agreed to it would have meant abandoning all Japan's hard-won gains since 1931. Her leaders were shocked and dumbfounded. Admiral Sawamoto recalled: 'The American reply was interpreted in naval circles as a virtual ultimatum, revealing an unbending and non-compromising attitude that promised no hope of negotiations succeeding. I believe this note destroyed all but a faint hope for peace in the minds of many naval men who had previously held out against war.' Shimada put it this way: 'Here was a harsh reply from the United States Government unyielding and unbending. It contained no recognition of the endeavours we had made toward concessions in the negotiations. There were no members of the Cabinet nor responsible officials of the General Staff who advocated acceptance of the Hull Note. The view taken was that this communication was an ultimatum threatening the existence of our country. The general opinion was that acceptance of the conditions of this note would be tantamount to the defeat of Japan. It seems clear that no nation willingly relegates itself to a secondary position as a world power if it can help it.'[8]

Given the seemingly unalterable goals of expansion, to which both Japanese society and the military were geared, it is difficult to see how *in the context of those times* war could have been avoided. Peter Lowe summarized the position cogently:

> The only way in which conflict could have been avoided was by British and American withdrawal from East Asia and the western Pacific. Such a withdrawal would have been easier for the United States than Britain, for American territorial interests were confined to the Philippines and the American economic stake in China was not large. For Britain, on the other hand, it would have connoted surrender of the portions of the British empire lying east of India, would have encouraged the collapse of British authority in the Indian sub-continent, and have had disastrous consequences on relations with Australia and New Zealand. Furthermore it would have included the liquidation of investments in China. Looked at from the vantage point of the 1970s, it might be argued that such a policy would have been sensible. The United States has learned painful lessons from overextending herself in East Asia and is intervening in the area less than at any time since 1941; the British empire has vanished into history and Britain sees her future as part of the European Community. Was it all worthwhile? Would Japanese hegemony perhaps have been preferable? These questions are unhistorical and in essence irrelevant. Politicians and diplomats have to resolve the problems of today and let tomorrow take care of itself.[9]

A gravely concerned Emperor arranged for an 'informal talk' with the Senior Statesmen or ex-prime ministers (*Jūshin*) to seek their advice before giving his sanction for war. Eight former Prime Ministers, including two Generals, Hayashi and Abe, and two Admirals, Yonai and Okada, as well as Hara Yoshimichi, president of the Privy Council (it advised the Emperor on constitutional issues), Tōjō, Shimada, Tōgō, and other ministers, gathered at the Palace on 29 November. During the morning the *Jūshin* received an analysis of the situation from Tōjō, who explained why the Government felt that war with the United States and Britain was inevitable, and asked questions of ministers about the negotiations in Washington and the country's war potential. Each was invited

[8] IMTFE, pp. 34,611, 34,665.
[9] *Great Britain and the Origins of the Pacific War: A Study of British Policy in East Asia, 1937–1941* (Oxford, 1977), pp. 286–7.

to give his views on a possible war against the United States and Britain, and this was continued in the afternoon after they had been given lunch by the Emperor. Most of the Senior Statesmen spoke out for moderation and peace, whether through a strong desire for peace for its own sake, doubts (in the case of Baron Wakatsuki Reijirō) about the self-defence rationale for war advanced by the war party (would it not rather be a war to promote the Greater East Asia Co-Prosperity Plan?), or fear of the outcome of a prolonged war, given the country's parlous raw materials situation, and of how the public would react to a protracted war. To Wakatsuki it was 'incredible that Japan has to open war without any hope of victory, thus risking the 2600 years of the Empire's undefeated history'. The suspension of negotiations, he pleaded, did not necessarily mean the start of war immediately; there should be a cooling-off period. Konoe also asked for a cooling-off period. Yonai and Okada pledged their support to the Government if it came to war, but hoped there would be none, and that even if these negotiations failed, they should plan for new ones, with Yonai arguing that they should not take the road to sudden decline, war, in an attempt to avoid a gradual decline. Okada gave eight reasons for it not being the time to begin war. Thus, he raised questions about the sufficiency of oil tankers and about Japan's ability to wage war in the South as well as in China, and to cope with a concentration of US–British power against Japan after the end of the war in Europe. He sharply attacked the national policy of the establishment and maintenance of the East Asia Co-Prosperity Sphere, equating it with the robbery of native peoples, whose hatred of Japan would jeopardize the supply of raw materials. Only three Senior Statesmen, Hirota, Abe, and Hayashi, spoke out for war as the only course left with the collapse of the negotiations. Tōjō 'argued against each opinion for the maintenance of the present conditions, and finally all the senior statesmen were obliged to acknowledge the determination of the government for commencing hostilities'.[10] The general atmosphere was one of helplessness. The Emperor merely listened throughout the discussion.

The *Jūshin* had no power, and their opinions carried no weight

[10] Hattori, *The Complete History of the Greater East Asia War*, i. 291. The principal sources for this meeting include Admiral Shimada, 'Bibōrku' [Memoranda], Bōeichō Senshibu Archives, *Okada Keisuke Kaikoroku* [The Memoirs of Okada Keisuke] (Tokyo, 1950), pp. 200–1, Kido's diary of 29 November (IMTFE, pp. 16,187–91), and Tōjō's testimony in Japanese Monograph No. 150, Appendix 4, especially p. 98.

with Tōjō, who proceeded to hold a Liaison Conference as soon as they had left the palace. It discussed the agenda for the Imperial Conference scheduled for 1 December that would formally sanction war in accordance with the decision made at the Imperial Conference of 5 November. To Tōgō's plea that he be told the zero hour, so that he could carry on diplomacy, Nagano replied *sotto voce* that it was 8 December. The date was not yet official.

On the morning of the 30th the Emperor was informed by his brother, Prince Takamatsu, a commander in the war plans section of the *Gunreibu*, that the Navy appeared to have misgivings about war, not being confident it could win. On the advice of Marquis Kido, Hirohito sent for Nagano and Shimada that afternoon to determine what the Navy's real thinking was. The three conferred for two hours. When the Admirals left, the Emperor summoned Kido and told him that they had answered his questions 'with considerable confidence'. He then instructed Tōjō to proceed with the Imperial Conference planned for the next day. Long afterwards, at the Tokyo Trials, Shimada explained that 'the question of confidence in the ultimate outcome of the war was not the theme of our conversation but only whether we were confident of the preparations which the Navy had made'. The inquiry from the Emperor to Nagano was 'What was the state of the operational plans?', and to Shimada, 'What was the state of preparations as far as the Navy Ministry was concerned?' Both had answered, Shimada claimed, that 'preparations were completed'. That is, that the Navy had made 'adequate preparations'. In essence, the Navy affirmed that it was better prepared to fight at that time than at a later date.[11]

The following afternoon, 1 December, an Imperial Conference unanimously accepted Tōjō's opinion that, a peaceful settlement having finally failed, Japan must go to war against the United States, Britain, and the Netherlands.[12] The American demands, said Tōjō,

---

[11] IMTFE, pp. 31,045–7 (Kido's testimony), 25,416–18, 34,667, 34,698–702 (Shimada's testimony). The Prosecution interpretation was that Shimada and Nagano had answered affirmatively as to the success of the war.

[12] The proceedings are in Ike, pp. 262–83. Present were the Prime Minister, the Chiefs and Vice-Chiefs of Staff, the Navy Minister, the Finance Minister, the Foreign Minister, seven other ministers, the President of the Privy Council, and three 'observers': the Chief Cabinet Secretary, the Chief of the Military Affairs Bureau of the War Ministry, and the Chief of the Naval Affairs Bureau of the Navy Ministry.

not only belittled the dignity of our Empire and made it impossible for us to harvest the fruits of the China Incident, but also threatened the very existence of our Empire. It became evident that we could not achieve our goals by means of diplomacy.

At the same time, the United States, Great Britain, the Netherlands, and China increased their economic and military pressure against us; and we have now reached the point where we can no longer allow the situation to continue, from the point of view of both our national power and our projected military operations. Moreover, the requirements with respect to military operations will not permit an extension of time. Under the circumstances, our Empire has no alternative but to begin war against the United States, Great Britain, and the Netherlands in order to resolve the present crisis and assure survival.

Speaking on behalf of General Sugiyama and himself, Nagano affirmed that preparations were completed and the Services were ready to commence operations. The Emperor uttered not a word during the whole meeting. He merely 'nodded in agreement with the statements being made', and afterwards formally sanctioned the decision reached.

IGHQ Orders went out immediately, informing commanders that hostilities would commence against the ABD Powers early in December. The date, 8 December, was set the next day, 2 December. That evening the historic radio message went out from Combined Fleet Headquarters: 'Niitaka Yama Nobore 1208,' or, literally: 'Climb Mt. Niitaka [the highest mountain in Formosa] 1208.' It meant: 'Start war against the Allies 8 December.' On that day, 2 December, the *Prince of Wales* and *Repulse* arrived at Singapore to prevent the unpreventable.

2. RESPONSIBILITIES AND EXPECTATIONS

The Imperial Navy went to war in the sincere belief that the continuation of existing conditions would force Japan to the wall: she would be destroyed sooner or later, if the situation continued. Viewed in this light, the resort to war was only a last-ditch attempt, in the interest of national self-defence, to break the 'economic encirclement' of Japan by the ABD Powers; Japan had no alternative but to fight for national preservation by capturing and exploiting the raw materials in the Southern Area essential for the maintenance of the Japanese economy both in peace and war. The

Army saw it the same way. This was the meaning of Japan's stated reason for going to war as expressed in the decision on national policy taken on 6 September, the IGHQ Navy Order No. 1 of 5 November to the C-in-C, Combined Fleet, the 'Draft Proposal for Hastening the End of the War Against the United States, Great Britain, the Netherlands, and Chiang', approved by the Liaison Conference on 15 November, and the Imperial Rescript on the declaration of war: Japan went to war exclusively for the purposes of 'self-defence and self-preservation'. That was not all, however. To this was added, in the policy decision on 5 November, the establishment of a 'New Order in Greater East Asia', which, despite idealistic slogans like 'universal harmony' (*hakkō ichiu*) and the 'Greater East Asia Co-Prosperity Sphere' (*Daitōa Kyōei Ken*), meant nothing more than Japan aiming to become the dominant Power in East Asia by taking over territories and emulating Western colonialism. This reason, Admiral Shimada claimed after the war, was far from the true intention of the Navy's central authorities, although such an opinion arose in Navy circles after the war started. That is, as Shimada and others said, the *main* intention of the Navy was Japanese 'self-defence and self-preservation'. True enough, yet there can be no denying that the Navy—and the country—had been driven into this desperate position by policies that it had supported. Yamamoto's Chief of Staff, Rear-Admiral Ugaki Matome, stated the case fairly in a diary entry the day before the Pearl Harbor strike: 'When we concluded the Tripartite Alliance and moved into Indo-China, we burned our boats in our march towards the anticipated war with the United States and Great Britain.'[13]

When it came down to the choice between war and peace, the majority of the Navy's elder statesmen wanted peace. Their position was that Japan was *not* invincible—that the war supply situation would be her Achilles heel. They had a keen appreciation of American industrial might. Admirals Yonai, Okada, Toyoda Soemu, and Suzuki Kantarō clearly felt that way. Suzuki, a former C-in-C, Combined Fleet, and Chief of the Naval General Staff, who was to become Japan's last wartime Prime Minister in 1945, thought that against the 'overwhelming odds' represented by American and British naval might and American resources 'Japan

---

[13] Diary, 7 Dec. 1941, Ugaki, *Sensō roku* [War Diary] (Tokyo, 1968), p. 31.

would probably lose, so that from the very beginning, although I thought things might go well for a while, I believed Japan would eventually lose the war'.[14] Yamamoto was in agreement with the Navy's elders that the Navy had no business fighting the American and British navies, since Japan's chances of winning were very slim in a prolonged war. When, in September 1940, Konoe asked Yamamoto about Japan's chances in a war against the United States and Britain, the Admiral had replied bluntly: 'If I am told to fight regardless of consequences, I shall run wild considerably [sic] for the first six months or a year but I have utterly no confidence for the second and third year.'[15] Sawamoto learned that Yamamoto had gone to Tokyo on 29 September 1941 and warned Nagano that in two years of war Japan would have consumed all her war *matériel*, and the majority of her fighting ships would have been destroyed or damaged, with their replacement a difficult task for a country as poor as Japan. Moreover, as the tide of war went against Japan, the people of Taiwan, Manchuria, and Korea would rise against Japan. All the Cs-in-C of the Combined Fleet shared his opinions, he said. 'Nagano was deeply shocked.' Sawamoto quotes Yamamoto as saying after the war had broken out: 'If I had been the Chief of the Naval General Staff or the Navy Minister, I would have clearly stated that the Navy had no prospect of defeating the United States.'[16] Toyoda Soemu, at the briefing in Tokyo of commanders of naval districts and key port commanders after the Imperial Conference on 5 November, had taken the attitude that war was unrealistic. 'Was the Navy serious about a war with the United States?' he had asked.[17]

These were, unfortunately, lone voices crying in the wilderness. There were few listeners in the Navy—or outside the Navy. 'It

[14] 26 Dec. 1945, United States Strategic Bombing Survey (Pacific), Naval Analysis Division, 'Interrogations' (unpublished material, National Archives, Washington), No. 531. Hereafter USSBS (Pacific), 'Interrogations'.
[15] *The Memoirs of Prince Fumimaro Konoye*, p. 2. Yamamoto repeated the 'six months or a year' prediction to Konoe in January 1941, but in the same month he told Fukudome that the Navy could fight successfully for a year and a half. Fukudome Shigeru, *Kaigun no hansei* [Reflections on the Navy] (Tokyo, 1951), p. 72.
[16] Sawamoto, 'Shi shuki'. Even after Pearl Harbor, Yamamoto judged that the Navy could fight only two or three years—after that, *trouble*. Yamamoto's predicament was an anguished one. To Hori Teikichi he had written on 11 October 1941: 'I find my present position extremely odd—obliged to make up my mind to pursue unswervingly a course that is precisely the opposite of my personal views'. Agawa, *The Reluctant Admiral*, p. 231.
[17] *Senshi sōsho*, xci. 560.

was', as the German Naval Attaché saw it, 'mainly the Company Grade Officers (Lt. Commanders to Captains) or the so-called *Gumbu* who demanded a war. Older officers, even from the Admiral Staff [*Genreibu*], indicated in their conversations that a war with America could not be brought to a successful conclusion because they could not visualize how Japan could possibly protect a line extending from Tokyo to New Guinea, corresponding to the distance between New York and London. They realized that it was impossible to maintain free traffic within that territory.'[18]

The Naval High Command was in a position, legally and strategically, to influence decisively the national policy in the autumn of 1941: legally, in the sense that the Tōjō Government, or *any* Government, could not function without the Navy's approval of the Navy Minister; and, strategically, because to an island nation the outcome of a war with the two leading naval Powers depended on mastery at sea, and the achievement of the 'Greater East Asia Co-Prosperity Sphere' demanded the same command of the sea. Being in the driver's seat, the Navy would have been able to prevent war by stubbornly refusing to go along with the Army; but the consequences of such a policy, an Army *coup d'état* or a direct clash between the Army and Navy, were regarded by Nagano and Shimada as too terrible to contemplate. Nagano told his wartime aide, Commander Yoshida Toshio, that the result of an inter-Service clash would have been more serious and prolonged than a war with foreign countries. 'We could not go through such a hell.'[19] Tomioka admitted after the war that if the Navy had strongly opposed the commencement of war in 1941, there would have been no war. However, he added, if the Navy had said No, there would have been a great possibility of a *coup*.[20] Moreover, the hard realities made a strong and independent Navy initiative for peace a practical impossibility. The origins of the war were cumulative and date back to the Manchurian and China Incidents. The Japanese commitment to expansion in China and in the Southern Area was too deep-rooted by 1941 to have been changed by people appointed for the most part only a few months before the outbreak of the war.

It is a thousand pities that the officers of the Naval High

---

[18] Wenneker, 'My Stay in Japan'.
[19] Mori Shirō, *Kaigun sentōkitai* [History of the Navy's Figher Force] (3 vols., Tokyo, 1973–7), iii. 77.
[20] Tomioka interview, 12 Dec. 1961, Bōeichō Senshibu Archives.

Command—particularly the two at the top, Nagano and Shimada—lacked the moral courage of a Yonai or a Yamamoto, though, of course, one cannot be at all sure that a Yonai or a Yamamoto (or both) would, in their places, have made any difference.[21] The Naval High Command vacillated and in the end capitulated to the Army and to the aggressive middle-echelon naval officers, who were to be found especially in the Bureau of Naval Affairs and the Operations and Intelligence Divisions. They were led by Captain Ishikawa, the 2nd Section Chief of the Naval Affairs Bureau, and Rear-Admiral Maeda Minoru, the 3rd Division (Intelligence) Chief of the Naval Staff. Konoe's Secretary, Hosokawa Morisada, on 4 August 1941 named Ishikawa and Maeda to the Research Section Chief of the Naval Affairs Bureau (Takagi Sōkichi) as 'the aggressors' in the Navy.[22] Ishikawa went so far as to tell a Section Chiefs Conference that those materials indicating that Japan was unable to fight the Allied Powers because of *matériel* and personnel shortages were not to be shown to the Navy Minister, Oikawa, but were to be kept at the section chiefs level.[23] The hard-liners in the middle echelons did not take the 1941 negotiations in Washington seriously. So far as they were concerned, the talks were only a front to conceal the Navy's real intentions and to convince Japanese public opinion that Japan had exhausted diplomacy before going to war.[24] After the war, Maeda frankly admitted that he belonged

---

[21] Admiral Inoue indicated as much, of Yonai at least, when he declared that he and Okada had not 'positively opposed' the start of hostilities, because they feared a *coup*. Interview, 29 Nov. 1961, ibid. Admiral Hoshina believes that the Navy could have stopped the war, had the top positions been filled with pro-peace officers: Yonai as Navy Minister, Inoue as Vice-Minister, Yamamoto as *Gunreibu* Chief, Itō as Vice Chief (which he was), Shimada as C-in-C, Combined Fleet, and Rear-Admiral Yamaguchi Tamon as COS of the Combined Fleet. Such a leadership would have arranged for a summit conference with the United States and been agreeable to troop withdrawal from China. *Dai Tōa sensō hishi*, pp. 197–8. When Vice-Admiral Ozawa Jisaburō, the newly appointed C-in-C, Southern Expeditionary Fleet, visited Yamamoto in his flagship in the latter part of October 1941, instead of talking strategy, as Ozawa had expected, Yamamoto asked him why they had not appointed Inoue Navy Minister. 'He would be the one who could cope with Prime Minister Tōjō.' Ozawa teitoku denki henshū iinakai [Committee for the Publication of Admiral Ozawa's Biography], *Teitoku Ozawa Jisaburō den* [Biography of Admiral Ozawa Jisaburō] (Tokyo, 1969), p. 46.

[22] *Senshi sōsho*, xci. 568.

[23] Rear-Admiral Shimamoto Kyūgorō interview, 23 Dec. 1962, Bōeichō Senshibu Archives. Shimamoto, then Chief of the 1st Section, Personnel Bureau, was present at this conference, but he gives no date for it.

[24] Chapman, 'German and Japanese Military Co-operation, 1936–1945', p. 481, quoting statements made by Captains Maeda and Shiba (26 Nov., 6 Dec. 1941, respectively) to this effect.

to the pro-war faction, as did many of his section chiefs. They believed there was no way to save Japan except by going to war, because, said Maeda, 'they did not expect successful negotiations with the United States, and because Japan lacked raw materials' (and needed to obtain them from the Southern Area).[25]

The pro-war officers had on their side what Admiral Hoshina refers to as 'the dominant atmosphere of the time, "to adapt to the trend of the time", among people who, tantalized by the steady progress of the German Army in Europe, had lost their perspective'. Another factor that played into the hands of the extremists was the Navy's fear of weakening its position. As Admiral Sawamoto recalled: 'the Navy was not in a position to say, "The Japanese Navy cannot wage war", because if the Navy had said this, it would have lost its *raison d'être* and the morale of the officers and men would have dropped'. Further, Japan was suffering an acute shortage of war materials, and the Army would get a larger share if it could argue that the Navy would not fight.[26]

What of the position of individual Navy leaders? Nagano's position had shifted during 1941 from the peaceful solution of Japan's problems, based on a lack of confidence in victory (*vide* what he told the Emperor in July, above, pp. 168–9), to a conviction by the late summer that national suicide was inevitable if they did nothing, and that the Navy stood a chance, especially in the initial operations.

As for the Vice-Chief of Staff, Itō, we must remember that he had been appointed on 1 September 1941, which was too late to stem the tide. There is little documentation on his attitudes. From what we know, he did not like the idea of war, but thought it could not be avoided.

Fukudome, the Chief of the Operations Division of the *Gunreibu*, frankly declared at an Army–Navy conference of chiefs of divisions and bureaux on 6 October 1941 that 'the Navy was not confident that it could carry out the Southern operations successfully because

[25] *Senshi sōsho*, ci. 331, Maeda interview, 19 June 1962, Bōeichō Senshibu Archives. Maeda has been described as a man of 'noble appearance and gentle character' who possessed no particular prejudice against the Anglo-Saxon countries. Rear-Admiral Chūdo Kan'ei's letter to the author, 13 July 1979. He was, as a Captain, Chief of the British Section of the Intelligence Division, September 1941–August 1943. The Admiral also mentions Captain Ogawa Kanji, Assistant Chief of the Intelligence Division (December 1940–May 1942), as a member of the war party.
[26] Sawamoto at the Navy leaders' Conference, 22 Jan. 1946, Shinmyō, pp. 177–8.

PLATE 1(a) HMS *Prince of Wales* arriving at Singapore on 2 December 1941

PLATE 1(b) HMS *Repulse*, April 1939

PLATE 2(a) *Yamato*

PLATE 2(b) *Hiei* (Kongo class)

PLATE 3(a) Nell: Mark 22, IJN's standard land-based medium bomber in 1941

PLATE 3(b) Betty: Mark II, land-based medium bomber that gradually replaced the Nell from 1941

PLATE 4(b) Vice-Admiral Kondō Nobutake, Vice-Chief of the Naval General Staff, October 1939–August 1941, commanding the Southern Force, Naval Battle off Malaya

PLATE 4(a) Vice-Admiral Ozawa Jisaburō, commanding the Malaya Force, Naval Battle off Malaya

PLATE 5(b) Admiral Shimada Shigetarō, Navy Minister, October 1941–July 1944

PLATE 5(a) Admiral Yoshida Zengo, Navy Minister, August 1939–September 1940

PLATE 6(a) Admiral of the Fleet Yamamoto Isoroku, C-in-C, Combined Fleet, August 1939–April 1943, on about

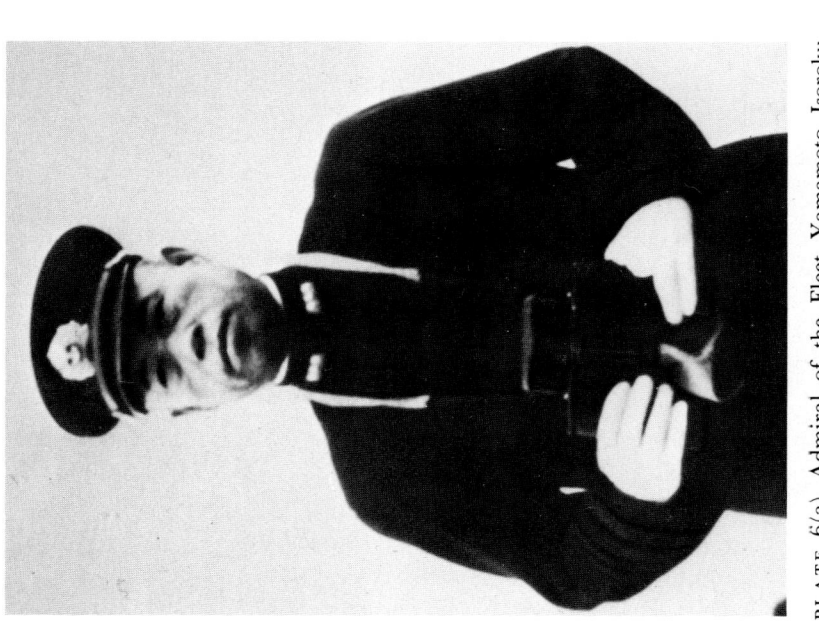

PLATE 6(b) Admiral Oikawa Koshirō, Navy Minister, September 1940–October 1941

PLATE 7(a) Admiral of the Fleet Prince Fushimi Hiroyasu, Chief of the Naval General Staff, October 1933–April 1941

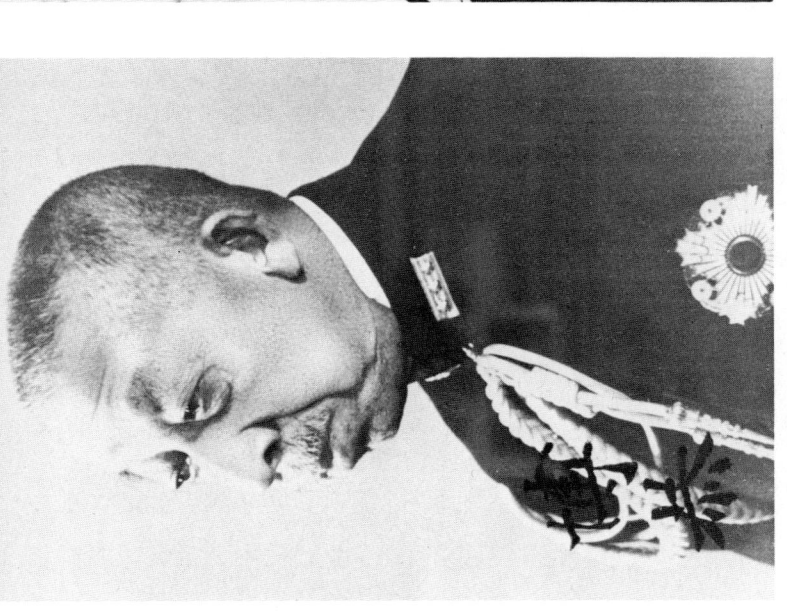

PLATE 7(b) Admiral of the Fleet Nagano Osami, Chief of the Naval General Staff, April 1941–February 1944

PLATE 8(a) Admiral Yonai Mitsumasa, Navy Minister, February 1937–August 1939

PLATE 8(b) Rear-Admiral Inoue Shigeyoshi, Chief of the Bureau of Naval Affairs, October 1937–October 1939

PLATE 9(a) Churchill mixing with US sailors on HMS *Prince of Wales* at Atlantic Conference, 16 August 1941

PLATE 9(b) A. V. Alexander, First Lord of the Admiralty, May 1940–May 1945, at the Admiralty

PLATE 10(b) Admiral of the Fleet Sir Roger Backhouse, First Sea Lord, August 1938–June 1939

PLATE 10(a) Admiral of the Fleet Lord Chatfield, First Sea Lord, January 1933–August 1938. Minister for Co-ordi-

PLATE 11(a) Vice-Admiral Sir Tom Phillips, Vice-Chief of the Naval Staff, June 1939–October 1941, C-in-C, Eastern Fleet (as Acting Admiral), October–December 1941, at the Admiralty
c. January 1941

PLATE 11(b) Captain J. C. Leach, Captain of HMS *Prince of Wales*, in the ship in 1941

PLATE 12(a) Vice-Admiral W. G. Tennant, Captain of HMS *Repulse* in 1941, visiting a carrier in June 1945

PLATE 12(b) Vice-Admiral A. F. E. Palliser, Chief of Staff to the C-in-C, Eastern Fleet, October–December 1941, as Fourth

the estimated loss of shipping during the first year would reach 1,400,000 tons'.[27] Yet he, too, eventually thought that the Navy had no choice but to fight and had voted for war.

There are differing opinions about Tomioka, the Chief of the 1st Section of the Operations Division. There are those who say he was for war and pushed to start it quickly; others say the opposite. Which interpretation is correct? The extant documents do not give us a clear answer.[28]

Shimada at heart was a man of peace. His letters to Yamamoto reveal that he had an earnest wish not to fight the United States and Britain. One of his conditions for accepting the navy portfolio was that the negotiations 'be pursued to the utmost with the firm determination to seek a peaceful solution ...'[29] On assuming his post, he was shocked when he realized how serious the situation was. He instructed the Vice-Minister and bureau chiefs to make the greatest of efforts to avoid war—that all difficulties must be overcome and a settlement reached. But the well-intentioned Shimada was swept along in the pro-war current. His first priority became one of not revealing any inter-Service split. Shimada's views come out most clearly in his *Dai Iōa sensō ni itaru kaiko* [Recollections on the Outbreak of the Greater East Asia War] (1946):

I had gained a great deal of confidence from the hard training of the Combined Fleet, which had been zealously conducted from the beginning of the year.... The atmosphere of the [Navy] circles also gradually became clear: if war was unavoidable, the sooner the better, considering that the [success of the] Pearl Harbor attack would become uncertain after early December as the last [opportunity].... I judged that even if I did resign, there was no hope for us to be able to avoid war, given the

---

[27] Daihon'ei rikugunbu [IGHQ Army Department], *Kimitsu sensō nisshi* [Confidential War Diary], iv, Bōeichō Senshibu Archives. In April 1941, soon after his appointment, Fukudome had proposed at an Army and Navy conference that the only path to peace was their withdrawal from the Tripartite Pact and from China. There was silence. After the meeting, Oka, the Chief of the Naval Affairs Bureau, told him: 'Don't ever mention the matter of withdrawal from the Tripartite Pact, because there is no way to do it.' Fukudome, *Kaigun no hansei*, p. 64.

[28] Admiral Chūdo places Tomioka with the war school. Chūdo's letter to the author, 13 July 1979. There is also this indication. Tomioka criticized the Chief of the Mobilization Section of the *Gunreibu* (4th Section, 2nd Division) for saying that the *matériel* shortage precluded a prolonged war with the United States. This, Tomioka asserted, was a 'counsel of defeatism', and his duty lay in carrying on the war with the resources at hand. Asada, 'The Japanese Navy and the United States', p. 287.

[29] Shimada's testimony. IMTFE, p. 34,654. And see Sawamoto, ibid., pp. 34,607–10.

internal and external situation of that time. After all, there was no way left under the circumstances of that time, no matter how hard we tried to avoid a war, and also it would add confusion at a very important time and would only result in losing the fighting opportunity. I therefore regretfully reached the decision that war was unavoidable.

He had, practically speaking, reached that conclusion by 30 October.[30]

As for the role of Sawamoto, the Vice-Navy Minister, it appears that he opposed the war, but was bypassed by Shimada and the younger officers. They simply went around him. He strikes a plaintive note in his reflections of 1962. 'I, from the beginning to the end, believed that Japan should not go to war with the United States. My opinion never changed before the war commenced. . . . I kept saying that Japan should not go to war.'[31]

Similar in important respects was the attitude of the Chief of the Naval Affairs Bureau. Oka's diary reveals that he was thoroughly cautious and not one to be driven into support of a conflict with the Western Powers. Indeed, he constantly advised his subordinates that war must be avoided by all means. At the Army–Navy conference on 6 October 1941 he insisted that withdrawal from the China mainland might effect a substantive improvement in relations with the United States. But he felt powerless to stem the tide. Sometime after Konoe's resignation, which Oka deeply regretted as it dimmed the prospects of the negotiations in Washington, he told Tomita Kenji, the Chief Secretary of the Cabinet in Konoe's Government, that 'he did not think Japan should under any circumstances engage in a full-scale conflict with a powerful country like the United States. However, he frequently expressed himself as being a subordinate who would be compelled

[30] *Senshi sōsho*, xci. 563. Cf. p. 243.
[31] Early in October Sawamoto visited retired Admirals Yonai and Okada and asked each his opinion on whether Japan should go to war. Both strongly insisted that Japan should stay at peace. 'In retrospect, I, with the support of those two Admirals, should have worked harder for peace. Because I did not, I am very ashamed.' Sawamoto, 'Shi shuki'. He claims to have offered his resignation after Shimada on 30 October had told him and Oka of his prowar stance. Sawamoto noted that Vice-Admirals Iwamura Seiichi, Chief of the Naval Technical Department, and Katagiri Eikichi, Chief of the Naval Aviation Department, felt as he did: they were absolutely against war. Had the three of them resigned, he said, it might have weakened the determination of the Navy Minister, and if, in addition, more admirals had offered to resign, it might have been powerful enough to have caused Shimada to change his mind. Sawamoto expressed shame for not having taken this additional step of getting other admirals to join him. Ibid.

to follow orders whether or not they were in accord with his own personal views. During the many times that I came in contact with Oka I observed that he was a man who worked under orders and did not disregard the wishes of his superiors.'[32] He wept when Hull's note of 26 November arrived, realizing at once that war was unavoidable.

The position of Rear-Admiral Hoshina Zenshirō, the very studious and exceptionally hard-working Chief of the Bureau of Mobilization and War Preparations in the Navy Ministry, is not clear. There are those in the old Navy who told me that Hoshina, who originally estimated that the Navy lacked the resources to fight a long war, changed his views at some point in the autumn of 1941. Professor Asada confirms this, citing evidence that, whereas on 31 October 1941 he had 'stated at a Bureau Chiefs Conference that it was impossible to prepare adequately for war with the United States, yet subsequently Captain Ishikawa was able to pressure him into reversing his conclusions'.[33] In my interview with the Admiral, however, he stressed that he was a man of peace in those days, that the Army and the mass media, aware of his attitude towards war, levelled accusations against him, and that he was often threatened, and received blackmailing letters for opposing war. There is evidence (Hoshina, *Dai Tōa sensō hishi*, pp. 58–9, the substance of which has been confirmed for me by Captain Ōi) that Hoshina worked for peace in the early autumn of 1941, in the sense that he opposed the prevailing opinion that Japan should stand firm in the face of American pressure even at the risk of war. It is, none the less, my judgement that he did alter his position. Through October he could have remained a man of peace, irrespective of the pressure of Ishikawa's group. But once his Navy Minister had determined firmly at the end of October that it was no longer possible to stop the war, Hoshina must have changed his position. He could not help but obey and comply with the Navy Minister's intentions. Besides, he was a man noted for loyalty to his superiors.

---

[32] IMTFE, p. 33,302. Admiral Hoshina, who, too, was closely associated with Oka, socially as well as officially, claimed that he 'worked hard to avoid war with the United States.... When the negotiations ended unsuccessfully, he was very much disappointed.' Ibid. 33,309–10. Captain Shiba Katsuo offered similar testimony (ibid. 33,320–1) about Oka's views and how he encouraged his subordinates not to be discouraged over peace prospects. Oikawa affirmed that Oka 'was not the type of person who acted in disregard of his superiors'. IMTFE, Defence Document No. 2761.

[33] 'The Japanese Navy and the United States', pp. 256–7.

'LET SLIP THE DOGS OF WAR'

The hawkish middle-echelon naval officers were sanguine about the outcome of the war. The Naval High Command and most naval officers were not so sure. They were confident of achieving victory in the initial operations. But this, they knew, would not end the war, which would continue long after the Southern Operations, because of the vastly superior resources of the United States especially, and because Japan could not possibly invade the United States and force peace on her. There was, however, the expectation that with the success of the initial operations, Japan would secure the sources of strategic raw materials in the 'Southern Resources Area'—the crude oil, rubber, tin, bauxite, nickel, and copper of Java, Sumatra, Borneo, Malaya, and the Celebes, while depriving the United States and Britain of these—as well as strategic positions like Singapore, Hong Kong, Manila, Guam, and Wake for the subsequent protracted fighting. What then? Admiral Fukudome, in post-war testimony, said 'there was general agreement in the upper levels of the Navy that this war could be continued only two or three years'. Three years was the upper limit because they 'would come to the end of the rope, especially in such matters as heavy oil, gasoline, lubrication oil, steel, special metals, ships, machine tools, etc.'. Exploitation of the raw materials in the Southern Area was no certain solution, since, even if the South was captured and controlled, the raw materials would have to be shipped to Japan under war conditions. Also, surface-ship losses in operations (predicted on three major fleet engagements a year and perhaps a few minor engagements) would begin to mount after the opening stage of the war and would reach an annual loss of 30 per cent. They would be able to replace only 10 per cent. Having lost over half the total strength of the surface fleet at the end of three years, 'continuation of the war would become impossible'.[34]

Sawamoto ('Shi shuki') spoke of 'at least two years', after which period they would be unable to go on fighting. Nagano thought that Japan could carry on the war successfully for about two years. He was foggy on what would transpire then. 'The outcome of a long war', he said at the Supreme War Council meeting on 4 November, 'depends on various physical and metaphysical factors, on our total war potential and on the development of the world situation. It is difficult, under these circumstances, to foretell now

[34] 12 Dec. 1945, USSBS (Pacific), 'Interrogations', No. 524.

whether we have a chance of winning the war several years hence.'³⁵ He was just as imprecise in retrospect. 'I do not believe that in the mind of even the most optimistic there was any idea that we could drive either America or Great Britain to their knees. The general idea must have been that this would be a very long, protracted war, that in time it would end somehow. That was the idea prior to the outbreak of the war.'³⁶ Tomioka was just as vague in his post-war statement: 'The Japanese planned at the outset of the war that they could carry on the war for fifteen months with the supplies (chiefly oil) they had at hand, but the flow of oil from the Dutch East Indies would, from the second year on, determine the situation.'³⁷ The Navy's leadership thought that if Japan held on long enough, her opponents would tire of the war or be pressured by public opinion to abandon the war. This would make possible a compromise peace that would enable Japan to retain a large part of her conquests. There was some hope that the Germans would successfully invade Britain and force her to surrender, which would demoralize the United States and hasten a compromise settlement.³⁸

---

³⁵ Japanese Monograph No. 152, p. 11.
³⁶ 30 Nov. 1945, USSBS (Pacific), 'Interrogations', No. 498.
³⁷ 25 Mar. 1947, United States Army, General Headquarters, Far East Command, Military History Section, 'Interrogations of Japanese Officials on World War II' (2 vols., unpublished materials, National Archives, Washington). A decade later he wrote: 'It is embarrassing, but we could not foresee the progress of the war after three years of conflict. In the game of "Go" we are supposed to be able to predict about fifty moves ahead. But in this war, as Yamamoto Isoroku said, the Navy's true feeling was that, although we would be able to fight for over two years holding our superior position, we did not have any idea what would happen after that.' Rear-Admiral Tomioka Sadatoshi, *Kaisen to shūshen: hito to kikō to keikaku* [The Making and the Losing of the War: Men, Organization, and Plans] (Tokyo, 1968), p. 64.
³⁸ This expectation, perhaps rooted in wishful thinking, flew against the judgement of Rear-Admiral Kondō, the last pre-war Naval Attaché in London. Just after his return to Japan in November 1941, he asserted in his oral report to the Navy Ministry's and *Gunreibu*'s top-ranking officers that it would be extremely difficult for Germany to subdue Britain by air bombings and cutting her lines of communication, that Hitler, it appeared, had given up the plans for an invasion, and that Britain would not accept a German proposal for a cease-fire and a peace treaty. 'The war in Europe will be a prolonged one.' 21 Nov. 1941, Shimada, 'Nikki'. Kondō was heard out in complete silence; there were no questions. His appraisal was probably a reason for the displeasure of his Chief, Admiral Maeda, who failed to invite him to a dinner party (on which occasion there would be acknowledgement of his services), as was customary after a naval attaché returned from overseas duty and made his formal report. Captain Chūdo was another who, at periodic senior staff officer conferences at the *Gunreibu* attended by Nagano and Maeda, often expressed his judgement that Great Britain would never be invaded by the German Army. The Naval Attaché in Berlin (September 1940–September 1943), Captain Yokoi Tadao, several times in the spring of 1941 advised

(*continued*)

'LET SLIP THE DOGS OF WAR'

Much of the Imperial Navy's confidence in its ability to put on a good show was rooted in an unquestioning belief in the qualitative superiority of their personnel and *matériel* and the soundness of the strategy and tactics they planned to adopt in war. How justified was this confidence?

---

the Navy Minister that the Germans could not successfully invade England. She lacked the resources in landing craft, and, besides, there were no large-scale preparations for an invasion, as he had observed in a tour of France. TSM, vii. 333, interview with Rear-Admiral Kojima Hideo, 15 June 1976.

PART TWO
Comparisons and Images

X

The Imperial Japanese Navy: I. The Men

> We lag behind in the material agencies of war; we therefore try and keep our personnel equal or superior to that of any other Navy.
> VICE-ADMIRAL TOYODA SOEMU (Chief of the Naval Affairs Bureau) to the British Naval Attaché, 29 June 1937.

> There stands the beautiful Mt. Fuji,
> High up on the Tokaido.
> Our hearts throb more and more with the hot blood
> Of the sons of the Sacred Land.
> We shall never stop sacrificing ourselves
> To defend the glorious foundations of our country.
> From the Etajima cadets' song, 'Etajima kenji no uta' ('The Song of the Etajima Strong Ones').[1]

1. THE 'JAPANESE DARTMOUTH'

It was a truism in the Imperial Navy that its quantitative inferiority in warships could be made up by superiority in the efficiency of the personnel. The development of a superior officer corps began at the Imperial Naval Academy at Etajima (*Kaigun Heigakkō*), which educated line officers. There was no shortage of candidates.

The social status of naval officers was very high—higher than that of Army officers. (The Army's military police in particular, were hated by the public, who also deplored the political assassinations of the 1930s in which the Army was deeply implicated). Even ordinary enlisted men had status; petty officers were considered good husband material. The high status of naval officers was due in part to the fact that they were, in the best

---

[1] Cecil Bullock, *Etajima: The Dartmouth of Japan* (London, 1942), p. 127. Bullock, whom I shall be quoting below, was an Englishman who taught English at the Naval Academy in 1932–5.

tradition of the Royal Navy, taught to regard themselves as gentlemen; the broadening expertise of the training cruise, something the Army never had, was another factor, as was the attractiveness of the pay scales—by Japanese standards, that is.

Although a midshipman graduating from the Naval Academy might have had an initial salary slightly below that of a university graduate, he soon caught up with his university contemporaries. All officers of flag rank had salaries at least equivalent to those of college professors, vice admirals and above exceeding the pay of a full professor of a national university. Enlisted men were also adequately compensated, chief petty officers drawing salaries generally comparable to those of university graduates. Senior officers had liberal expense accounts for entertainment, and retirements were made comfortable for all career men. A chief petty officer could retire in his fifties with enough money to buy a home and live comfortably as an honorable and respected member of his community.[2]

Such reasons as these explain the lure of Etajima, which, writes one of its graduates, was 'a shrine and a subject of dreams to millions of youngsters in pre-war Japan'. The cream of the young generation applied—many more than could be accepted. For example, in 1928 there were approximately 5,500 applicants for 130 vacancies, or about 42 candidates for each place; in 1934, over 7,100 for 240 places, about 30 for each one. (No comparison with Dartmouth is possible, the only figures available being those of the actual entries). They had to be between 16 and 19 (18 was the usual age) and in the great majority of cases a middle-school graduate (or student entering his final year).[3] An annual competition was held in the principal cities and towns. If a candidate passed the rigorous medical check by naval surgeons on the first day (approximately 50 per cent were eliminated: a minor flaw like a few missing teeth was enough to reject a candidate), he went on to three days of written examinations in English, mathematics (trigonometry and algebra), Japanese and Chinese Classics, geography, history (Japanese,

---

[2] James E. Auer, *The Postwar Rearmament of Japanese Maritime Forces, 1945–1971* (New York, 1973), p. 20. The pay scale in the 1930s ranged from £60 or £66 (1,020 yen or 1,130 yen) per annum for a sub-lieutenant (*chūi*) to the full admiral's (*taishō*) £388 (6,600 yen). The comparable figures for the Royal Navy in 1939 were £164 and £2,311, which, making allowance for comparable living costs, were not appreciably higher that the IJN scale.

[3] Elementary school (six years: ages 7–13) was obligatory in Japan; the middle school (five years: 13–18) was not. One had to pass an examination to get in and to pay fees. There were no public, i.e. private, schools in the British sense, except perhaps the Peers School in Tokyo.

Chinese, European, and American), physics, chemistry, and essay writing. Candidates who failed to get passing scores in that day's subjects (results were posted the following morning) were not permitted to take further exams. Those who survived underwent an oral interview by a naval officer, who tested the applicant's personality, attitudes, and so forth. He would be asked such questions as 'Why do you want to enter Etajima?' 'If you are rejected, what will you do?' One of the things the interviewer looked for was whether the candidate spoke standard Japanese, not a dialect, and whether he stammered. The final stage in the selection process was a check by the local police with the candidate's middle school, his neighbours, and the family itself to determine how reputable the candidate and his family were—whether, for example, there was any criminal record or whether the father was addicted to gambling. The successful candidate faced one last hurdle: a final medical check upon arrival at Etajima that might eliminate a few.

The cadets came from every social class—from the sons of humble farmers to the sons of the nobility and of Imperial princes (at least nineteen of whom attended the Academy); but they were mostly from lower middle-class families: farmers, small businessmen, shopkeepers, artisans, many of whom had made sacrifices to see their sons through middle school.

The Naval Academy was located on the small island of Etajima (6 square miles), which lies in the western part of the beautiful Inland Sea, opposite the naval base of Kure, near Hiroshima. The buildings, placed round two sides of a large parade and playing field facing the bay, are not especially impressive, but the wooded setting of the campus (pine trees on the far side of the playing field) and the well-maintained grounds, with the sacred Mount Furutaka in the background and the beautiful Etauchi Bay on the northern side, were—and are.

The young cadets enrolled in August, proudly wearing for the first time the white uniform, with seven shining brass buttons and with the short ornamental dagger slung on his waist belt.[4] It was a very demanding regimen. The cadets were awakened by bugles at

---

[4] Beginning with the class of 1923, the cadets were enrolled in April and wore winter (navy blue) uniforms. For the cadets who graduated in the 1920s the course varied between 2 years 11 months, and 3 years 8 months; in the 1930s, between 3 years 4 months, and 4 years; for the class of 1940 it was 3 years; and it was then shortened to 2 years 11 months, for the classes of 1941–3, and to 2 years 4 months, for the last graduates in 1944 and 1945.

05.30 (06.00 in winter), and were hard at it, with classes, practical training, athletics, and study until lights out at 21.30 (22.00 in winter). Except for Sunday, which was a rest period most of the day, they had only one free period: a 'special period' at 14.10–15.20 to pursue individual interests. 'Except for summer vacations [four weeks] and a few short days of home leave' [mainly three weeks at Christmas], writes an officer of the old Navy, 'we lived on this island in complete isolation from the outer world. . . . On days off, no students were allowed to leave the immediate vicinity of the town. Sunday routine was to climb hills, hike around the island, or sprawl in the club.'[5] A favourite Sunday activity was to climb Mount Furutaka ('Old Hawk Mountain', 1,279 ft.), which dominated the island.

As for the course of study, in addition to the technical naval subjects, seamanship, navigation, gunnery, and the rest, there were general education subjects like mathematics, physics, foreign languages, and history—Japanese history and world history. There was no naval history as such. Engineering was not an important subject, engineers being separately educated at the Naval Engineering Academy (*Kaigun Kikangakkō*) at Maizuru, north of Osaka, whither it had been moved after the destruction of the naval engineering school at Yokosuka in 1923. There was military as well as naval training at Etajima, because there was no separate marine corps as in the Royal Navy: rifle and revolver practice, bayonet drill, and one week each year was devoted to training in assault landings. English was an important aspect of the academic programme, being studied in every year (on top of five years of English in middle school).[6] Learning at Etajima was by rote, and there was no place for originality.

Physical fitness, endurance, and toughness were stressed, the cadets spending $2\frac{1}{4}$ hours daily at hard exercise, whether at judo, kendo (a modern form of the old samurai swordplay, using bamboo sticks about four feet long), sumo wrestling, tennis, soccer, rugger,

---

[5] Captain Tameichi Hara, with Fred Saito and Roger Pineau, *Japanese Destroyer Captain* (New York, 1961), pp. 15–16. Hara was in the class of 1921.

[6] Before the war, all the cadets studied English and either French or German. During the war, all first-year cadets studied English (the Naval Academy was the one Japanese university to continue teaching English during the war), and in the following years 60 per cent of the class studied English only, with the rest in equal numbers doing French, German, Russian, or Chinese. The cadets emerged with a greater proficiency in reading than in speaking English.

baseball, sailing, swimming, or rowing. There were gymnastic exercises before breakfast daily. Rowing and swimming were regarded as especially important. The most strenuous part of the athletic programme was the 10-mile summer swim from the *torii* (gateway) of the Shinto shrine at the sacred island of Miyajima to Etajima: some 12 or 13 hours in the water. This gruelling experience, which often led to pleurisy developing into tuberculosis, was responsible for most of the 10 per cent of each class that had to withdraw from the Academy for health reasons. Nearly as strenuous as the summer swim was the running race on an autumn day to the summit of Mount Misen (1,700 ft.), the highest point on Miyajima. A game peculiar to Etajima called *Botaoshi* (pole-fighting), played several Saturday afternoons each month, taught the cadets to take hard knocks with good temper. It divided the entire cadet body into two groups, drawn up 100 feet apart. On the word 'go', each side would protect its own small flag, mounted on an eight-foot pole, while trying to bend down the pole of its opponents and snatch their flag. It was a veritable Donnybrook, with almost anything permitted. Fortunately, the sport lasted but a few minutes. There was not much in the way of competitive sports. Matches with outsiders were held only on the rare occasions when foreign warships entered Etauchi Bay. 'To sum up,' writes Bullock, 'I would say that the physical part of the Etajima training is, without exaggeration, the most strenuous in the world. It consists of a varied programme of Japanese sports and Western games whose aim is to develop all-round physical fitness, self-discipline and the team spirit, and certain severe tests which demand the utmost courage and endurance. It eliminates the weak and produces a young man who is just about as fit physically as it is possible for anyone to be.'[7]

The rigid discipline which was so marked a national characteristic was all-pervasive at Etajima. It had its origins in the samurai code during the centuries of feudalism, which enjoined unquestioning obedience to heads of families and clans. Discipline was so highly developed that insubordination was practically nonexistent, and punishment for other offences was rare. Bullock writes of the discipline at the Academy:

The new cadet then submits quite naturally and willingly to the strict discipline which prevails at Etajima. Naturally, because a sense of respect

---

[7] Bullock, *Etajima*, p. 36.

and obedience has been drilled into him from birth both at home and school. Willingly, because the Imperial Rescript [see below] says 'Juniors must obey their seniors while those of lower rank must obey those set over them, remembering that in so acting they do but obey Our own direct commands.' . . .

Everything is done with impressive military precision and smartness. The sound of the bugle rules the cadets' day from reveille till lights out. . . . They even march from the changing-rooms on to the playing-fields for their games and back again when the game is over. . . .

. . . the spirit of discipline permeates the College and shows itself in every phase of the cadet's life.

Here you have hundreds of Japanese youths cheerfully accepting a life which for strenuousness has, I believe, no counterpart elsewhere in the world. For over ten months in the year they live on a remote island, confined to the College walls for all but eight hours of the week, with nothing but hard physical and mental labour for six days of the week, and with none of the simple pleasures and luxuries which ordinary schoolboys enjoy. The explanation of this ready submission to such a Spartan life lies in the seriousness of purpose with which the cadet is taught to regard his calling. He is one of those privileged few, chosen from millions to become leaders in the most honourable of all Japanese professions, that of arms. His one duty is to serve his Emperor, and he regards every part of the daily round and common task as part of this service and attaches a corresponding importance to it.[8]

Discipline was also harsh. Captain Hara, who was 'outraged and embittered' by the Etajima discipline, gives us a picture of a sadistic regime—of plebes being treated roughly by the third- and fourth-year cadets (occasionally, a second-year cadet was treated similarly), of hard slaps on the face for a uniform not being properly buttoned, etc. On Sundays during their first six months the plebes were assembled on the parade ground under an open broiling sun and made to stand at attention for four or five hours. This was punctuated by 'almost continuous fist beatings. After a few months of such treatment the newcomers became sheeplike in their obedience.' But, as Hara admits, 'For some of the boys the rigors of this discipline did not seem to be too much of a shock. They had perhaps grown up in a similar environment. In some Japanese homes a stern father chastised his children liberally. In many provincial schools the boys were treated tyrannically by their

[8] Ibid. 52–4.

teachers.'[9] For 'some' of the boys I would substitute 'most'. Most of the cadets felt that the discipline was natural. Hara remembers 'those early days in the Academy with a bad taste in my mouth'. Yet he admits that many of his classmates 'look back on their Academy days with sweet nostalgia'. This was, indeed, the attitude of every one of the Imperial naval officers I interviewed. They look back upon their Etajima experience with what struck me as genuine affection, even if, as Commander Sekiguchi Kōzō says, 'In recollection, it was a life of three years and eight months without a joke or a laugh.'

The values and principles inculcated at Etajima were enshrined in the Emperor Meigi's rescript of 4 January 1882 to the Army and Navy, which might be considered the bible of the Services. Its heart was the five cardinal precepts that should govern the conduct of all members of the fighting forces: *Loyalty, Courtesy, Valour, Fidelity,* and *Simplicity.* The first stressed loyalty to sovereign and to country as the 'essential duty' of the soldier and the sailor. 'A soldier or a sailor in whom this spirit is not strong, however skilled in art or proficient in science, is a mere puppet; and a body of soldiers or sailors wanting in loyalty, however well ordered and disciplined it may be, is in an emergency no better than a rabble. . . . with single heart fulfil your essential duty of loyalty, and bear in mind that duty is weightier than a mountain, while death is lighter than a feather.' The second precept concerned the respect due to superiors and consideration to be shown to inferiors. The third dealt with valour. 'The soldier and the sailor should esteem valor. . . . To be incited by mere impetuosity to violent action cannot be called true valor. . . . Never to despise an inferior enemy or fear a superior, but to do one's duty as soldier or sailor—this is true valor . . .' The fourth precept commanded the soldier and the sailor to 'highly value faithfulness and righteousness. . . . Faithfulness implies the keeping of one's word, and righteousness the fulfilment of one's duty.' The fifth was simplicity. 'If you do not make simplicity your aim, you will become effeminate and frivolous and acquire fondness for luxurious and extravagant ways; you will finally grow selfish and sordid and sink to the last degree of baseness, so that neither loyalty nor valor will avail to save you from the contempt of the world.' 'These five articles should not be disregarded even for a moment by

[9] *Japanese Destroyer Captain,* pp. 15–16.

soldiers and sailors... [They] are the soul of our soldiers and sailors.'[10] First-year cadets received a copy of the Imperial Rescript and carried it wherever they went. Though not told to memorize it, they quickly got the idea when a senior classman would order them to recite from the Rescript. Whereupon they would read and re-read the Rescript until they had learned it by heart. Superintendents of the Academy would read it to the assembled cadets from time to time. In the later years, on Sundays, before being given liberty, first-year cadets were asked to read the Rescript through.

One facet of the third precept, valour, can be summed up in the word *gyokusai*, whose connotation was: when the country is in danger, one must prefer death to dishonour. *Gyokusai* literally means 'broken gem'—the key word in a proverb: 'It is better to be a gem that is smashed to atoms than a tile that is whole.'

The values taught at Etajima were summed up by an officer for me: 'You have to be a patriot, and after that you have to be a seaman, and after that, a gentleman—after which you become an officer.' The three points were parallel. Being a patriot meant in practice having a burning devotion to the Emperor, which was the quintessence of *Loyalty*, the precept in the Rescript that was emphasized for the cadets. In the Meiji Era (1868–1912) there was a transfer of the moral values and standards of behaviour in the code of ethics for the samurai, with its stress on loyalty and devotion to one's master, to the Emperor. Nowhere was this outlook stronger than in the Services. A profound veneration of, and loyalty to, the Emperor constituted the spiritual life of the Academy. The cadet was taught that his sole purpose in life was to enhance the glory of the Imperial House, and that his noblest end was death in battle for his Emperor. The words of the official song of the Imperial Navy express this self-effacing devotion to the Emperor:

> Across the sea, corpses in the water;
> Across the mountain, corpses in the field.
> I shall die only for the emperor,
> I shall never look back.[11]

The centre of the patriotic cult at Etajima was the Great Hall (*Daikōdō*), a dignified light-gray granite building that was used for

---

[10] William T. De Bary (ed.), *Sources of Japanese Tradition* (2 vols., New York, 1954), ii. 198–9.

[11] As translated in William H. Forbis, *Japan Today* (New York, 1975), p. 284.

important lectures by the Superintendents and VIP visitors, and for ceremonies of various sorts, including the paying of homage (bows) to the Imperial portraits on the great national holidays like the Emperor's birthday.[12] On a platform was a throne used by the Emperor on his occasional visits to the Academy for the passing-out ceremony. In a place of honour in the gallery were two large marble tablets bearing the names of all naval officers who had been killed in action. Nearby was a display corner in which were preserved photographs and personal relics of famous naval heroes presented by the Imperial family. 'The cadets were thus constantly reminded of their duty to their Emperor, and are instructed that to have their names included in the list of those who die for him is the greatest honour that a naval officer can achieve.' With the increase in exhibits a special building became necessary. In 1936 the present Naval Museum (Educational Reference Hall), a magnificent Greek classical structure, was built with donations from all ranks in the Navy. There were some 40,000 items housed there before the war.

The three great pre-Pacific War heroes represented in the Museum through photographs and relics, were Admiral of the Fleet Tōgō Heihachirō, Japan's Nelson and the hero of the Russo–Japanese War, Lieutenant-Commander Hirose Takeo, and Lieutenant Sakuma Tsutomu. Hirose was the officer in charge of the death-defying group of 77 volunteers, chosen from 2,000 applicants, who tried to blockade Port Arthur at the outbreak of the war with Russia by placing old merchant ships into position at the entrance. He was killed in this suicide mission. Hirose was posthumously promoted to commander and awarded the Distinguished Service Order (Third Class). He was honoured in the Imperial Navy as a model naval officer for his self-sacrifice, sense of duty and responsibility, and spirit of comradeship. Sakuma was the Commander of Submarine *No. 6*, which sank in the mud of Hiroshima Bay on 15 April 1910 during submarine exercises. Though only at a depth of 52 feet, *No. 6* had no escape hatch or rescue equipment. The entire crew of fourteen died in line of duty, each man performing his duties at the assigned post to the last moment. On exhibit was (and is) the famous letter or report

---

[12] Usually kept locked up, the portraits were hung on the platform on these special occasions. All warships carried a portrait of the Emperor in the commander's cabin. Homage was paid to it on national holidays, and in case of the ship going down, the portrait had to be rescued even at the risk of life.

(actually, a copy) that Sakuma scribbled in pencil, describing the causes of the disaster and the conditions in his ship until the last moment. The catalogue of the new museum says: 'The content never fails to impress the reader and serves as excellent material for the spiritual training of, and a shining example for, naval officers.' The report begins with an apology:

I am sorry that my carelessness sank the Emperor's submarine and killed the Emperor's sailors. ... We are willing to die for our country, but I regret one point, that our deaths might discourage the people of the nation. My sincere hope, gentlemen, is that the accident will give you material to study diligently the problems of submarine design and construction, and thus insure future submarine development. If this be done, we die without regret. ... The crew of a submarine should be carefully selected, for you may have difficulties such as this. Fortunately, my crew have done their duty to the best of their ability, and I am fully satisfied. ... Reverently I write to the Emperor; please do not let the bereaved families of my crew suffer. ... 12.30. very hard to breathe—gasping ...

No. 6 was spotted and raised the next day. The bodies were found calm and peaceful in death—no sign of panic or disorder—each man at his post save Sub-Lieutenant Hasegawa and Chief Petty Officer Kadota, who had died by the break in the petrol pipe they had tried to repair. The rescuers brought the bodies to Kure, and there at the torpedo station the families wept proudly for their dead. The Grand Chamberlain came to Kure to pay the Emperor Meiji's tribute; and at Kure on 20 April 20,000 people mourned at the funeral. The nation gave 35,000 yen for the families of the victims, and 22,000 for a memorial at the Kure naval station. Years later, *No. 6* was placed on land at the submarine school (a half mile north-west of the Kure Navy Yard) in commemoration of one of the proudest episodes of the Imperial Navy. Sakuma in death typified the stiff code of old Japan—the code of the samurai, the code of Bushido.[13]

In 1932 Etajima introduced 'The Five Points of Self-Discipline'. Each student in turn, day after day, would put these points to his classmates after the 18.30–21.30 study period in each of the study rooms. After each point, there was a pause, while the students,

[13] I have relied for the story of Lieutenant Sakuma on an unpublished account by Lieutenant B. A. McMunn, USN, the first complete account of the disaster in English and of the complete text of Sakuma's notes. Today photographs of Tōgō, Hirose, and Sakuma adorn the five study rooms as well as the Museum at Etajima. In the old Navy they were in the Museum only.

heads bowed and eyes closed, silently asked themselves the question. The five points were:

> Ask yourself:
> Whether you have always acted with sincerity.
> Whether you have been careful enough in your speech and behaviour.
> Whether you have been vigorous enough.
> Whether you have ever spared yourself any pain.
> Whether you have ever been indolent.[14]

Officers of the Royal Navy regarded themselves, and were generally regarded, as being what used to be called a 'gentleman'. Indeed, it was rubbed into them as young officers that they were 'officers and gentlemen', an expression that was never used in a snobbish sense, but indicated a standard of conduct. The Superintendents at Etajima emphasized character development, and, as part and parcel of that, the moulding of the cadets into young gentlemen patterned after the Royal Navy. They should, in the words of a former Superintendent, Admiral Inoue Shigeyoshi, 'be looked up to as paragons by the public'. The tradition went back to the 1870s, when Commander A. L. Douglas, who headed a British naval mission to Japan, aimed to make young gentlemen of the cadets at the Imperial Naval College, as well as to teach them naval science. Even after the expiration of the Alliance in 1922, the Japanese continued their practice of hiring two English civilians, university graduates, to teach the English language at Etajima (on a three-year contract, usually). This continued until 1938 (when two American-born Japanese were employed instead), closing a 50-year-old tradition. One of the last of these Englishmen was summoned shortly after his arrival in 1932 to an interview with the Superintendent, who told him: 'Mr. Bullock, I wish you to teach our cadets what an English gentleman is and how he should behave.' Language instruction alone was not sufficient. The following year Bullock received a letter from an Imperial naval officer that read: 'I eagerly hope you enjoy the rest of your stay in Japan, and at the same time please remember to give our cadets the best thoughts of an English gentleman.'

It operated this way. In the pre-war decades the cadets had on an

---

[14] Students at the JMSDF Officer Candidate School at Etajima recite the five points at the end of every day.

average four hours of English instruction a week, three of which were with Japanese instructors, reading and translating English texts and studying grammar. The fourth hour was devoted to English conversation, conducted by an English instructor, with an infusion of instruction on English manners and social customs. They learned about such things as table manners, introductions, invitations, congratulations, apologies, expressions of sympathy, and the making of toasts and speeches. The training cruise of eight months, four in Far Eastern waters and four abroad, that followed graduation was an immediate incentive for the cadets wanting to know all about these matters, so as not to appear crude or foolish in foreign eyes on social occasions. Before the cadets left on the cruise, they attended a Western-style dinner at the Officers' Club, where they were initiated into the mysteries of knives, forks, wine glasses, napkins, and the rest. The English instructors were present to explain these mysteries.

The English gentleman concept included such standards of conduct as that an officer of the Imperial Navy must never be seen in public carrying parcels, and that he must travel first-class in the trains and frequent only the best, or at least the better, restaurants and stay in first-class hotels. This canon applied to all officers throughout their careers; it obviously imposed hardships on the junior officers in particular. The results were impressive. In interviewing dozens of IJN officers in 1976, I was impressed with how much, physical appearance apart, they resembled their opposite numbers in Britain: the similar courtesy, impeccable manners, and neatness of dress, as well as charm (albeit with 'English reserve') and dignity. There was something lacking, however, as I shall point out below.

An extremely important method of inculcating the desired values in the young cadets was *kun'iku* or character-building, which, incidentally, has carried over into the new Navy. *Kun'iku* was carried out by the Superintendent, who would address all the cadets at matriculation and passing-out ceremonies, the beginning and end of the summer holidays, and other special occasions; VIPs visiting Etajima and addressing the cadet corps; and instructors' remarks in the classroom. Beginning in 1935–6, cadet input was added in the form of talks by fourth-year cadets. The subject matter of all these *kun'iku* talks might be the precepts in the Imperial Rescript, ethical principles, heroic incidents in IJN history, especially from the Russian War (e.g. Hirose's exploit), incidents in the careers of Tōgō, Nelson, and John Paul Jones—and cadet misdemeanours when the offending cadet would be mentioned by name and a kind of sermon would be delivered.

A British officer who visited Etajima after the First World War was 'positively frightened by the whole atmosphere of the place and what I was told of what the cadets were put through. There seemed to be no humanity, no sense of humour, no easement at all. But it seemed to me to succeed in producing dedicated, selflessly courageous automata, which, I supposed, looked at one way, is what the Japanese needed.'[15] Or at least wanted.

The fact that only the fittest survived at Etajima strengthened the extraordinary *esprit de corps*, this feeling of brotherliness, which bound officers of the same class together for life and which was often closer than family ties. Whatever professional efficiency they may have attained, the cadets emerged as splendid physical types, primed with patriotism, and with a sense of duty far beyond that of the average male of similar age in Japan—or anywhere else, for that matter. The spirit of *gyokusai* or self-sacrifice, which never deserted them in the war, was deeply imbedded in their outlook, as was a feeling of supreme confidence in their Service.

Class standing was a most important determinant in an officer's career. The brightest Etajima graduates (also a few Maizuru products) would be sent to the Naval War College (*Kaigun Daigakkō*) sooner or later for training as staff officers. In this black four-storied building, a solid, squat structure in the Meguro district of Tokyo, some 25 to 30 lieutenants and lieutenant-commanders were admitted annually for two years' study (reduced to sixteen months during the war until the College was closed in March 1944). The subjects included strategy, tactics, the history of naval warfare (the Falklands action and Jutland were studied with special care), and economics. Other honour students at the naval academies, Maizuru as well as Etajima, were sent to study abroad, especially to the United States and Britain, or to a Japanese university, as a kind of academic prize. These officers and the War College graduates rose to hold the more important jobs in the Navy Ministry, Naval General Staff, and the Fleet.

Before and during the war the more important appointments were determined more by seniority than by merit. This would

[15] Admiral Dick's letter to the author, 9 July 1976.

explain an Oikawa holding such important positions. Vice-Admiral Nakazawa Tasuku went so far as to claim that seniority, regardless of competence, was the operative factor in appointments, together with the academic record at Etajima.[16] The Navy Minister had the last word in appointments (also promotions), although he would discuss the more important appointments with the *Gunreibu* Chief from the mid-1930s onwards. In contrast, the criterion for reaching the higher positions in the Royal Navy was aptitude for command at sea. The selection of officers with this quality was decided by the First Lord of the Admiralty and the First Sea Lord, the latter consulting with the Sea Lords and taking into account the recommendations of Cs-in-C. The extent to which the First Lord involved himself in appointments (or promotions) varied according to the personality of the Minister (*vide* Churchill). We might leave it this way: the highest posts were filled by officers selected almost entirely at the will of the First Sea Lord in agreement with the First Lord. During the war years the Prime Minister—Churchill—brought his influence to bear in the case of the more important commands.

Some comparisons between Etajima and Dartmouth may prove enlightening. In contrast to the Imperial Navy, and with special reference to the inter-war period, the main scheme for entering cadets in the Royal Navy was for 13½-year-old boys (the 'catch 'em young' principle), who competed for places through the Public Schools Common Entrance Examination and entered the Royal Navy through the Royal Naval College, Dartmouth, in January, May, and September.[17] Although a few of the more senior officers, notably A. B. Cunningham and Dudley Pound, had been cadets in the old *Britannia* training ship, the great majority of RN officers in the Second World War were Dartmouth products. To get selected, one had to pass a medical examination, an interview, and written examination. The medical examination was reasonably thorough. The interview was a more daunting experience. The interview board was usually chaired by a frightening admiral (or so they struck the candidates), assisted usually by a senior officer or two and

---

[16] 'Taiheiyō sensō no kaiko to hansei', p. 20.

[17] The early entry was abandoned in 1948, when the age of entry became 16. The Royal Naval College, Osborne, where the cadets had been entered at 13½ since 1903 for two years of study before passing on to Dartmouth, was shut down in 1921 as part of the post-war retrenchment. The cadets then went straight to Dartmouth.

one or two Admiralty civil servants. They looked for character, intelligence, command of the 'King's English', and 'officer-like qualities', in so far as these could be judged at the age of 13 in an interview which might last twenty minutes. Subject to passing the written examinations that followed (mathematics, English, French, and Latin, with the standard expected similar to that of boys taking the common entrance examination for public school), candidates who passed the interview (probably about half of those interviewed) were accepted. On the whole, the system got results in an era when leadership was more important than applied science and when ships were fought from the bridge and not from a computer centre.

Fees of £150 per annum were charged in pre-war days. In addition, parents were required to pay for the initial outfit of uniforms (£40) and to refund any expenses incurred by the cadet for clothing, sports, books, instruments, etc., as well as to provide an allowance of £2 per term pocket money. Reduced fees could be allowed where the circumstances of parents justified it, and there were King's Cadetships for successful candidates whose fathers had been officers in any of the Services and whose deaths had been due to war service or attributable to disease on active service. King's Cadets were entitled to remission of fees in cases where the Admiralty considered that substantial help was needed. (In contrast, Etajima charged the cadets nothing, but on the contrary paid them around 5 yen a month for cleaning, laundry, and shoe repairs. Parents contributed a small sum, perhaps 10–15 yen a month, for pocket money). After eleven terms (3¾ years) in the College—shortly after their seventeenth birthday—the cadets went to sea for eight months of practical training, being promoted to midshipmen at the end of this period. After a further period afloat (total, three years), they returned as sub-lieutenants to the Royal Naval College, Greenwich, for further professional study. Those officers who were to specialize in engineering went to the Royal Naval Engineering College at Keyham (Devonport) for a four-year course. At the outbreak of war in 1939, the sea training of cadets was ended, and the Dartmouth course was reduced by a term for both the 13-year-old and the 18-year-old entry. Thus, all cadets went to the Fleet as midshipmen on completion of their Dartmouth course.

Under a special entry scheme introduced in 1913 a small proportion of boys, about one-sixth of each entry, were entered direct from public school at about 18 (on the basis of a school certificate exam, an interview, and a physical test) and given basic training in a harbour training ship. Thereafter engineer midshipmen proceeded to the Royal Naval College at Keyham, and the others to the Fleet. There was much competition between the two systems. The proponents of Dartmouth believed that their product was more devoted to the Navy and better prepared for naval life. Proponents of public-school entry maintained their product had a clearer and more flexible mind, unclogged by unnecessary lore, and could make better judgements. In truth, proponents of each scheme exaggerated; there was little to choose between the two entries by the time they reached lieutenant's rank. Once at sea, after a time it was difficult in any ship to distinguish between a 'Dart' and 'Pub'.

The great majority of officer cadets of both the 13- and 18-year-old entries came from families who would normally expect to send their sons to a fee-paying public school, and attendance at a fee-paying (private) preparatory school was the normal preliminary to 13-year old entry. Or to put it another way, the Royal Navy drew its officers (both kinds of entry) with few exceptions from the middle and upper middle class, that is, from well-to-do families. Rather more than half of the cadets were the sons of serving or retired officers in the Armed Forces, especially the Navy, or of professional men: in law, medicine, the Church, education, etc. Rather less than half came from families in 'trade', that is, associated with the world of business. It was not until 1941 that the field of selection was greatly widened by the introduction of scholarships.

For the 13-year-old entry at Dartmouth, the aim was to ensure a broad general education on much the same lines as at other public schools, with the qualification that Classics was dropped. History (general European history and British naval history of the sailing-ship era), English, French, geography, and scripture were studied. Because of the technical requirements of a modern navy, every boy did mathematics and science (chemistry and physics) throughout the course. The cadets were also given a limited amount of professional naval training: seamanship, navigation and pilotage, and marine engineering. There was, however, far too much engineering, a hang-over from the days of Jacky Fisher. (The cadets received about 100 hours per year of 'Engineering and Ship Construction' and 'Torpedoes and Electrical' training). But overall the education was unsurpassed. In 1928 a new system (alpha class) was instituted which allowed the more promising cadets to be taught separately with a syllabus based as much on university methods as on school methods. Sports and games were taken very seriously; perhaps too much importance was attached to them, and too much attention paid to those who excelled at them. (In this respect Dartmouth only followed the fashion set by the public schools). Every cadet had to take part in games of one sort or another: rugger, soccer, hockey in the spring and autumn: cricket, rowing, and sailing in the summer. The discipline was strict, and almost everything was done at the double. There was too much unnecessary rushing about. The general tone of Dartmouth is suggested in these two quotations from officers who had been there. 'From the moment of their arrival they were disciplined as if they were delinquents, regimented as if they were both unreliable and untrustworthy and deprived of all means of exercising character or originality ... the cadet was subject to a rigid system of Prussian-like discipline which can hardly have been equalled for severity even in the toughest Borstal of the day.'[18]

We were chased around and kept on the run all day except during studies. We got up with Reveille at about 06.30 and pelted off to the wash place, washed face, neck, ears, and hands, cleaned teeth when told to do so, went through a cold plunge and dressed in about three minutes. That was the pattern for the day. We worked to clear timetable. Time was set aside for games, and everyone had to take some exercise, if not an organized game, then swimming, squash, tennis or a run, etc. There was not much free time—just an hour or so in the evenings and on Sunday afternoon. I think that the great majority enjoyed the life.[19]

[18] 'Manoel', 'Dartmouth, 1931–1935: A Study in Restrictive Education', *Naval Review*, liii, 3 (July 1965), 227, 229. The article *in toto* is on pp. 226–32. It initiated pro and contra replies in the correspondence section. See 'Beagle Ball', 'Dartmouth 31–35', ibid. liv, 4 (Oct. 1966), 360–1, which was in agreement with Manoel's critique, and for letters contra, ibid. liii, 4 (Oct. 1965) and liv, 1 (Jan. 1966). The pot was stirred up again in 1978. Vice-Admiral Sir Louis Le Bailly, in his article, 'All to Be of a Company', ibid. lxvi, 1 (Jan. 1978) painted a picture (pp. 38–40) of Dartmouth in his time, the late 1920s, as a very rigid, harsh establishment. 'Space does not permit a description of these psychological and physical punishments. Today the authorities would be landed in the Law Courts, at least.' Le Bailly quotes an unnamed retired officer (Admiral Sir Frank Twiss, who was at Dartmouth in the mid-1920s), who during the last war had been a prisoner of war of the Japanese, as replying to one of his rescuers, who had asked him how he had been able to stand it: 'Well, four years at Dartmouth helped.' Clearly an exaggeration but indicative of his feelings. My conclusion is that sometime during the First World War Dartmouth became a harsh, rigid place which it had not been before, and did not revert to 'normal' until the Second World War.
[19] Admiral Sir Desmond Dreyer's letter to the author, 12 Aug. 1976.

The effect of these activities, that is, games and always moving at the double (e.g. 'doubling' to the dining hall and from one classroom to another), was to create a fiercely competitive spirit and outlook on life. This competitive policy was quite deliberate: the Navy fostered an intensely competitive spirit, squadron *v.* squadron, ship *v.* ship, the divisions in each ship competing against one another—and it produced results. There was too much corporal punishment, chiefly inflicted by cadet captains. 'Ticks' were awarded by the cadet captain for the most minute offences; three of them might result in a caning. On occasion a cadet captain would inflict a collective 'strafe' for getting 'slack'. Strafes were an abomination—a series of 'evolutions' through which the cadets were put, usually starting at around 05.00 on a Saturday. Everything was done at the double, with laggards receiving a beating.

Reverence for rank—a great stress on seniority—was inculcated and grossly overdone to an extent that would hardly be tolerated in the Vatican. This was partially responsible for the greatest weakness of the Dartmouth system: a certain suppression of individuality and a failure to develop the critical faculty. 'In later life,' Vice-Admiral Sir Peter Gretton tells me, 'some Dartmouth-bred officers were deprived of a critical sense towards all senior officers, and this led to a lack of serious analysis of orders passed down the line.' There was without doubt an excessive unquestioning obedience at Dartmouth. 'Enterprise, initiative, enthusiasm, inventiveness, departure from the official mould, and a host of valuable attributes were all discouraged if not regarded almost as objectionable; even individuality, or a too-inquiring mind were out of place.'[20] Admiral Le Bailly, in the article quoted above, would agree. 'So, wherever we came from, whatever we were, poor or rich, bright or dim, Dartmouth took us and hammered us and beat us, as far as it could, into a pattern. Some could not stand it and left. Others feigned or actually attempted suicide and were removed. Just a few beat the system and retained their individuality unscarred.'

Another serious weakness was that no attempt was made to encourage cadets to have extra-mural interests or to take part in extra-mural activities (debating society, literary society, etc.), in which respect the College fell short of the public schools, with the consequence that the horizons of many officers were not only

[20] 'Beagle Ball', 'Dartmouth 31–35'.

limited when they left Dartmouth, but never expanded afterwards. The situation was, if anything, still worse at Etajima, where the tight schedule of study and physical training left the cadets very little time to consider anything else.

So far we have seen how in many respects the spirit and tone of life at Etajima and Dartmouth were remarkably similar: the emphasis on physical activity, the discipline, the frenetic pace, the discouragement of individuality and the expansion of mental horizons, and how they were different, notably as regards the family background of cadets and the major curriculum differences: much less engineering at Etajima and the infusion of military training. The crucial difference, however, lay in the spirit of Etajima and Dartmouth.

Despite the representation of every social class at Etajima, from Imperial princes to the sons of fishermen, the spirit of Etajima was aristocratic. A former Academy product has written: 'Such emphasis was placed on the sacred duty and prestige of the naval line officer who was educated at Etajima and separated from the secular world, which was called *Shaba*, the external world, that it brought about a consciousness of special privilege and made these officers stand aloof from the nation in general.'[21] The Dartmouth product, on the other hand, though coming from the more privileged classes, was never divorced from the nation. There was a close identification between the two, stemming from the vital and glorious role played by the Senior Service in the history of the British nation. Also besides educating the cadets, Dartmouth aimed at instilling a spirit of loyalty and devotion *to the Navy*. Over the front of the College is inscribed the preamble to Charles II's *Articles of War* (c.1672): 'It is upon the navy under the Providence of God that the safety, honour, and welfare of this realm do chiefly depend.' The cadets had no doubt that this was true; that they had joined an organization with an outstanding record of service for the good of the country; that they should be very proud to wear the King's uniform (and they were proud); that the needs of the Service always came first and their own needs and wishes a poor second.

The qualities required of an officer were stressed at Dartmouth, none more so than leadership. Twenty to 24 per cent of the cadets were lucky to gain an experience of leadership. Ten to twelve cadet

[21] Iguro Takeaki, 'Boeidaigakkō to Kaigun Heigakkō' [The Defence College and the Former Naval Academy], *Gunji Kenkyū* [Military Affairs Review], v, 12 (Dec. 1970), 80.

captains ('prefects') were appointed from each term of 50 cadets in the last three terms to supervise other terms than their own, except, of course, the senior term at the College, which had willy-nilly to have cadet captains from its own term. Most cadets had to wait till they got to sea to learn that initiative and leadership were as important as obedience. Leadership was not stressed to the same degree at Etajima. (See below, pp. 347–8.)

Tradition played a big part in the upbringing of the Dartmouth cadet—a tradition of supreme self-confidence and strong sense of professional pride, summed up in the (ungrammatical) legend emblazoned at one end of the main hall at Osborne: 'There is nothing the Navy cannot do,' a quotation from some admiral. It all went back to a fabulous maritime tradition centuries old—of great commanders and resounding victories. It may have tended to breed in the cadets a resistance to change, and it definitely tended to make them inward-looking. But on the whole the respect for tradition was a good thing.

Speaking of the importance of tradition at Dartmouth (and beyond), there is a precious true story that illustrates a fundamental difference between the two navies. In about the year 1928 the IJN Commander in charge of one of the Japanese commissions which occasionally visited Dartmouth to study the Royal Navy's training methods, went to see the Commanding Officer of the College, Captain Dunbar-Nasmith, with a problem. They had received copies of the time-table which had enabled them to audit classes in seamanship, navigation, etc.; but they could find no listing for a class in tradition, which they wanted to attend. The Captain explained that they had 'no need to teach cadets tradition. It is part of the atmosphere: it is in the air they breathe.' Having discussed the matter with his colleagues, the Commander returned the next day with the request that the members of his commision be permitted to sleep in various dormitories instead of in their hotel.

Knowing the importance attached to tradition by the British Navy they refused to believe that it was not deliberately and formally instilled and had come to the conclusion that this was done by Term officers in the only time for which they could not account—after Commander's rounds and lights out. They could imagine the solemnity of the scene, but they were anxious to witness it for themselves and to hear the impassioned exhortations of the Term officers.

Of course, what the Captain had told the Japanese commander was perfectly true: cadets did learn the value of tradition from their Term officers—not, however, by precept but by catching the infection from them.[22]

2. THE IMPERIAL NAVY OFFICERS: EVALUATION

About 15,000 officers of the Imperial Navy were trained at Etajima in a period of over 50 years (till the end of the Pacific War). How good were the products turned out? To start with a simple point, many of the officers went to seed after their strenuous physical activity in their cadet years. Relatively few took regular exercise. Bullock says that in his first year at Etajima (1932–3) about 24 of the approximately 60 officers on the staff played tennis (only four of them regularly), a figure which shrank in the following two years. The majority took no regular exercise. This is why so many of the flag officers are described as fat. But let us get on with more important considerations.

By Admiral Inoue's standards (above, p. 95), most of the full admirals were in his third or 'C' class. This could apply to most of the world's navies. But what of the Imperial Navy officers? There can be no question of their professional competence, fanatical courage, and extraordinary *élan*. Often quoted in Western literature is this opinion of two officers of the Imperial Navy: 'Perhaps influenced by British naval traditions, the Japanese Navy from its early days had laid great stress on instilling gentlemanly qualities in its officers. Unfortunately, however, a tendency arose to equate a lack of assertiveness and an easygoing affability with gentlemanliness, with the result that there were many bright and likable flag officers, but few real leaders and fighting commanders.'[23] They may have been adequate in peacetime, but too many of them were not up to the challenges of war. In what respects were IJN officers lacking?

The average Imperial naval officer was, in the judgement of many of those whom I interviewed, quite lazy, in the sense that he worked hard at his own job, but made little effort to study and broaden his professional knowledge. Except for those who went to

---

[22] E. A. Hughes, *The Royal Naval College, Dartmouth* (London, 1950), pp. 110–11.
[23] Captain Mitsuo Fuchida and Commander Masatake Okumiya, *Midway: The Battle that Doomed Japan* (London, 1957), p. 90.

the Naval War College, as a group they preferred to drink and play rather than to study war. The explanation may lie in the very fact that at Etajima they were worked so hard and indulged in too much physical exercise. This resulted in a lassitude that was not conducive to mental concentration. The little spare time they had went into leisure pursuits. Bullock writes about the 'dull-eyed and lethargic' average fourth-year cadet. The traits developed at Etajima carried over into the professional careers of the Etajima products. The upshot is that the Imperial Navy had very few students of the science of war, as distinct from competent gunnery and torpedo officers and outstanding navigators.

A weakness was the lack of flexibility—a national trait. This refers to both grand strategy and tactics. Once the Japanese naval officer decided to do something, he was inclined to stick to it to the last moment. Senior officers displayed considerable ability in executing plans, but had difficulty in dealing with the unexpected. A perceptive assessment was made by an RN midshipman after a visit to Japan in 1922: 'Where the Japanese navy would fail in time of war is, I am certain, in the human element. Determined as the men are, yet, cut off from their leaders, they cannot, I am sure, fight on as our own men could. They can doubtless stand any hardship, any wound, but they must be told exactly what to do or they cannot do it. The whole outlook of the officers and men in our own and the Japanese navy is quite different. One has only to watch them at general drill, and especially ashore, to see this.'[24]

The greatest flaw of the IJN officer, and this was a fault of the Japanese people as a whole, was the absence of independent, rational judgement. The learning by rote at Etajima and in all educational establishments contributed to this weakness. Rear-Admiral Yokoyama Ichirō, who was a language officer at Yale University in 1931–2, attended primary school classes in New Haven, Connecticut. He was surprised to find even in the youngest class the teacher asking questions of her pupils.

For example, if you are on your way to a shop on an errand for your mother and you find a small girl crying because of an injury, what would you do? One said: 'It is very important to take care of that girl.' Another said: 'Mother's errand is very important; I'll go to the shop and come back and tell Mother to please help the little girl.' And there were other,

[24] Captain J. S. Litchfield's Midshipman's Journal, HMS *Renown*, May 1922.

different answers. But any answer would be all right. I was surprised that I was taught to make such judgements at the Naval War College for the first time. I had to wait until I got to the Naval War College to get the training that in the United States the children received in primary school, even in the youngest class!²⁵

The problem remains a serious one. As late as 7 June 1976 the *Mainichi Daily News* (Tokyo) could say in a leader on 'Schools at Crucial Stage': 'Children should be taught to cultivate a habit of thinking for themselves and develop individual characters and a sense of self-reliance through classroom education.'

It was a tradition that when an officer got to the top he should delegate most of his responsibilities to his staff officers. If an admiral tried to do everything himself, 'the Navy would say that he was not such a big man!' He would not be respected. (There were exceptions, among them Yonai, Yamamoto, and Ozawa, who tended to concentrate power in their own hands and to make their own decisions). This situation had its good side. There was free discussion between an admiral and his staff. But once a matter was decided, all officers obeyed that decision. Teamwork was stressed and relations were friendly. Indeed, senior–junior officer relations, whether at sea or in the Navy Ministry or *Gunreibu*, were, generally speaking, good, and often cordial, even if reserve officers were sometimes slapped and punched by senior regular officers. Young officers could speak their minds freely. (This was not so in the Army). There was a tendency to look down upon those officers who paid excessive respect to their superiors as servile. The democratic atmosphere stemmed in part from the social background of the officers corps, and from the Imperial Rescript, which enjoined superiors to treat their inferiors with as much kindness and consideration as possible. There is one exception to this on the whole idyllic picture: the bad relations between deck and engineering officers. The Maizuru graduates joined the Etajima graduates for the training cruise, yet the engineering officer was always regarded as a second-class citizen in the Imperial Navy. (The products of the Imperial Naval Paymasters Academy in

---

²⁵ Interview, 4 June 1976. Captain Ōi stresses that the Japanese are 'too emotional and sentimental a people rather than rational. The American approach is: "This is effective or not effective." They analyse. But the Japanese decide at a glance; they don't analyse. Americans and British are analytical. Sometimes, though, they see the trees but not the forest. The Japanese, however, see only the forest.' Interview, 24 May 1976.

Tokyo (*Kaigun Keirigakkō*) rated even lower, professionally and socially). This despite the fact that the entrance requirements at the two academies were identical but for a lower eyesight qualification at Maizuru. For example, until 1943, if a commanding officer was killed or incapacitated, only a deck officer, the next ranking one, could take over the command, even though of lower rank than the senior engineering officer. This created serious problems during the war. From 1943 any higher-ranking officer, regardless of branch, could take over the command of a ship. But the snobbishness of the line officer continued, despite attempts made during the war to eliminate it.

In the Royal Navy, too, senior–junior officer relations were on the whole very good, although the tradition persisted in the inter-war period that the senior officer must be right. Admirals were looked upon as near gods, and it took nerve to criticize them—a relic of the days when an admiral stood supreme on the bridge and did not court advice or criticism. Paradoxically, as mentioned, junior officers were expected to show initiative; those who did not fell by the wayside in the promotion race. Most admirals expected their staff officers to be more than 'yes men'. By the end of the 1930s, however, the products from the Staff Colleges had come to be respected, and senior officers were more prepared to take advice from their staffs. Also, by the 1930s all the old prejudices between the upper deck and the engine-room had completely died away.

The strongest point in the Imperial Navy may well have been the quality of the enlisted men (conscripts and volunteers, mostly the latter, before the war): spirited, diligent, faithful to orders, well trained. Especially splendid were the petty officers, who were the best in the world—skilled specialists who studied and worked hard. Their percentage was high: a third of the total personnel, and in submarines, where initiative and resource were particularly important, it was as high as 80 per cent. The seamen and the petty officers came mostly from the fishermen and farmer classes. The officers had great confidence in the men, above all, the petty officers. In their day-to-day professional relations, officers and men worked together very well. They were not as strictly separated as in the Royal Navy, because, for one thing, both came from the same classes in society. There was, however, no mixing socially. They did not drink or play together.

As for relations between officers and men, off duty, in the Royal

Navy, ship teams for games were chosen on merit from both officers and men, and shipboard concert parties and theatre performances were likewise chosen. Otherwise there was very little mixing, not only for reasons of discipline and long-established custom, but because while most officers came from the middle and upper classes, most men were from the working class. On duty, relations were on the whole admirable. Not only were the officers trained to understand that leadership included concern for the welfare and well-being of their men, but the latter had received a thorough grounding in naval discipline in the training establishments and had a healthy respect for, and confidence in, the professional authority and competence of their officers.

A glaring and grave weakness of the Imperial Navy as an institution, and for which there was no parallel in the Royal Navy, was its totally unsatisfactory relationship with the Army. Conflict was the norm since the early Meiji period. Army and Navy officers were so distinct in outlook that 'they hardly seemed to come from the same nation', as a naval officer remarked to me. One reason lay in the fact that the Services had adopted quite different foreign nations to be their model. This is brought out in a study prepared by the Naval War College in May 1944, which stated that in Meiji Japan the Army and Navy had, respectively, taken the German Army and the British Navy as its model. One result was that the Army went beyond its proper limits and became authoritarian and political, whereas the Navy was liberal and essentially non-political. Another difference was the fundamental discrepancy in strategic perspective, with the Army directing its attention to the north (Russia) and west (China, including Manchuria), and caring little about the US and Britain, and the Navy, looking to the Pacific and the south, was equally disinterested in Russia or China. The nature of the education and training of the officers of the two Services was another factor mentioned. Thus, there was little respect for the individual fighting man in the Army, and the contrary situation in the Navy. Again, the Navy's tradition was one of 'silence', or non self-advertisement, whereas the Army was prone to exaggerate its achievements. Also, the cadets at Etajima (excepting the few enlisted men who would be admitted if they passed the exams) were, with exceptions, middle-school graduates; the Army cadets came from the military preparatory schools as well as from the middle schools, about half from each in the 1920s and 1930s. The former group wore Army khaki and were indoctrinated by the Army at a young age, being taught to think in a certain way.[26]

A major factor in explaining the differences in outlook could not have been stated better than in this memorandum of January 1935 by Captain Vivian, the British Naval Attaché in Tokyo:

The Army has very few foreign contacts and an infinitesimal number of its personnel ever sees a Western country. The Naval officer holds the military officer in some contempt because he is submerged in the details of military fighting and training and thinks of little outside his own profession; the necessary consequence is that his mind becomes intensely nationalistic, not to say narrow, in outlook.

The Naval officer, on the other hand, is comparatively internationally minded. He sees many foreign countries in his career [beginning with his training-ship cruise after Etajima]; the vast majority read English and American books, periodicals and papers; at least 50% of the officers of Captain's rank and above have studied or held appointments in foreign countries, chiefly England and America. It is not unreasonable to suppose that the Army looks on the Naval officer with a certain amount of distrust as having too little of the nationalistic, aggressive spirit.[27]

One important result of this difference between the insular Army officer and the more cosmopolitan Navy officer was that most of the latter had seen for themselves the vast resources of the British Empire and the United States and accordingly knew how formidable a task the defeat of their navies would be. The Army, in contrast, boasted of its ability to fight any Power or Powers that stood in Japan's way.

As a rule the Navy steered clear of politics—that was its tradition since Meiji times, and was in keeping with the Emperor Meiji's admonition to the Services in his rescript of 4 January 1882 that they 'not meddle in politics'. 'There was', Admiral Nagano claimed after the war, 'neither any desire for, nor effort made, to obtain political influence for the Navy in state affairs.' This is not quite true, of course, but the Army was regularly and deeply involved in politics and was far more skilful in the game than the Navy. The Navy, moreover, complained that it had to spend over 80 per cent of its energy in trying to check the Army's aggressive China policies.

[26] Rear-Admiral Takagi Sōkichi, 'Rikukai gunjin kishitsu no sōi' [Differences in Temperament between Army and Navy Personnel], Bōeichō Senshibu Archives.
[27] FO 371/19347.

Finally, and worst of all from the Navy's point of view, the Army was alleged to have little understanding of the role of sea power. The Army and Navy lived in two separate worlds, and each chose to go pretty much its own way, whether in peacetime or wartime. Thus, liaison between the intelligence services of the Army and Navy was minimal. Army–Navy co-operation had been poor in the Russo–Japanese War, and was little better forty years later. The German Naval Attaché in Tokyo testified after the war: 'During my stay in Japan [1933–7, 1940–5] and from my many social and business contacts with various military men, I noticed a decided lack of cooperation between the Japanese Army and Navy. They were constantly suspicious and jealous of each other ... The Army escorted its own convoys and except for those military movements which necessitated the use of the Navy in transporting Army troops the disunity was quite amazing to me.'[28] The lack of co-operation was a not unimportant cause of Japan's defeat in the Pacific War. An Imperial Navy officer, writing soon after the war, commented with bitterness on the inter-Service relationship:

At no time in the history of war was the importance of close cooperation between the army and navy so keenly felt as in the Pacific war ... It was indispensable, imperative, urgent. The United States, which attained perfection in such cooperation, has triumphed. Japan, which has utterly failed in effecting it, has been beaten hollow. There is indeed no name for the mess the disunity between the army and navy did bring about. Now let me ask what kind of studies had been undertaken about such cooperation between the two legs of the defence forces before the war. Just some very limited localized attempts. There were the exchanges of college teachers between the army and navy to study such cooperation. Also some maneuvers were practiced by the joint forces of the college students, but even this only as regards landing operations. Just an academic item to fill up the curriculum! A joint study of the broader aspect of the problem in anticipation of a particular war had never been undertaken.

Instead of cooperation the army had studied how to protect its position against the navy, and vice versa. ... The spirit of rivalry just got the better of both of them. Little else was left in their minds. To expect from such misguided parties a study, however cursory, of cooperation in the event of a war with the United States was out of the question. The case of landing operations excepted, the cooperation between the army and navy

[28] Testimony of Vice-Admiral Paul W. Wenneker, IMTFE, pp. 26,557–8.

on a broad strategical line in the event of war with the United States had never become an object of serious study before the war.

When the war started, instead of cooperation, opposition and antagonism characterized every feature of the relations between the army and navy.[29]

3. 'WAR IS SO EASY COMPARED WITH PEACETIME EXERCISES!'

It was in preparedness for a major war that the Imperial Navy shone. The modern Japan Navy consciously profited from Hideyoshi's mistakes in the Korean operations of the 1590s. It was realized in the Meiji era and afterwards that careful naval preparations must be made in peacetime, regardless of who the enemy might be. Preparations meant, above all, training for battle. The Japanese naval tradition stressed the importance of incessant training for battle. After Tsushima, for example, the ships of the 2nd Division (six armoured cruisers) indulged in target practice, firing at a towed target for over an hour. After the Washington Conference, and especially from 1936, the efficiency of the personnel was tremendously enhanced through war training of a rigour and realism to be found in no other navy. When C-in-C, Combined Fleet, in the 1920s, Vice-Admiral Katō Kanji ordered the Fleet to engage in unrelenting night exercises and manœuvres 'more heroic than under actual battle conditions'. He was determined that, since the Navy had to face a quantitative inferiority, thanks to the humiliating capital-ship ratio accepted at the Washington Conference, this must be fully offset by qualitative superiority, that is, by achieving a level of proficiency second to no navy. 'Tireless effort finally produced a naval establishment whose confidence in its own fighting ability was expressed in the motto, "We rely not upon the enemy's not attacking us, but upon our readiness to meet him when he comes".'[30]

---

[29] Commander Masataka Chihaya, untitled, unpublished typescript in English (on why Japan was defeated in the war), n.d. (early 1947), pp. 29–30; copy in possession of Commander James E. Auer, USN. I have made a few editorial changes. Hereafter cited as Chihaya MS. Towards the end of 1940, General Sugiyama, the Chief of the Army General Staff, proposed to the Navy that there be a combined chief of staff, with the Army and Navy alternating in this post. He recommended Prince Fushimi as the first Combined Chief of Staff. The Navy flatly rejected the proposal. Rear-Admiral Shimamoto Kyūgorō (Chief of the 1st Section, Personnel Bureau, 1939–41) interview, 23 Dec. 1962, Bōeichō Senshibu Archives. It was the general opinion of the IJN that this lack of a unified command was a cause of defeat in the Pacific War.

[30] Fuchida and Okumiya, *Midway*, p. 35.

'WAR IS SO EASY COMPARED WITH PEACETIME EXERCISES!'

The training year started on 1 December, and from then until April, single-ship training and squadron training would be carried on. Combined Fleet training started in May and reached its peak after October, when large and small manœuvres were conducted. The training was exceptionally severe. To preserve secrecy and toughen the men, exercises and manœuvres were often carried out in stormy northern waters from secret bases in the Kuriles. Large manœuvres (about two weeks in duration) took place twice a year—once a year from the China Incident, when many ships were detached from the Combined Fleet for service in China waters—with part of the Fleet opposed to another part of the Fleet. There was very little time for leisure in the pre-war Navy. It was work, work, work. A week, as the refrain went, consisted of 'Monday Monday, Tuesday, Wednesday, Thursday, Friday Friday'. That is, there was no time off on Saturday or Sunday; they were no longer in the naval calendar in the last pre-war years. Shore leave was ordinarily restricted to two or three successive days a month. Combat conditions were duplicated in peacetime exercises and manœuvres, and were sometimes even tougher. Some officers said after the war had started: 'War is so easy for us compared with peacetime exercises!'

Herewith two illustrations of the intensity and realism of the training in the last years. The C-in-C of the British China Station in 1936–8 described how the Japanese were on a war-footing. 'The behaviour of the Japanese Fleet, with the exception of the air arm, is theatrical in that ... they proceed without lights at night and generally behave as if in the presence of an alert and powerful enemy.'[31] Then there was the Mihogaseki incident on 24 August 1927. This was the name of the point in the Sea of Japan off north-western Honshu, the main island of Japan. During a Combined Fleet torpedo exercise on a dark night, with the destroyers dashing forward to occupy a favourable position for a torpedo attack, there were two destroyer–light cruiser collisions. The results were disastrous, since all four ships were steaming at high speed. The destroyer *Warabi*, her hull broken in twain, sank instantly: 104 were killed or injured. The destroyer *Ashi*'s hull was split in two and she suffered 29 casualties. The damage inflicted on the light cruisers *Jintsū* and *Naka* was also serious. There was no radar in those days,

---

[31] Admiral Sir Charles Little to Admiralty, 8 Oct. 1937, ADM 116/3682.

therefore such an exercise was very dangerous. But the Navy was learning to fight in all conceivable battle conditions. The C-in-C, Katō Kanji, addressed his commanding officers, asking that they 'not be demoralized by the disaster, but on the contrary do your utmost to carry on the severe and hard training ... this is the only way our Navy can obtain victory over our hypothetical opponent'.[32]

Under Yamamoto the training of the Combined Fleet became even more rigorous, as, with the outbreak of the war in Europe, the Fleet had to be prepared for any emergency. Although he continued to argue against war with Britain and the United States, he worked hard to prepare the Navy for such a war, so that it might stand a chance. 'With tenacious and timeless spirit,' read a training pamphlet, 'we are striving to reach a superhuman degree of skill and perfect fighting efficiency.'

The Navy made use of the China Incident to train its officers and men to a high state of efficiency. The smaller units were in actual combat with an enemy; the naval aircraft were continuously employed in combat operations; and certain parts of the Fleet carried out joint operations with the Army.

The Imperial Navy was firmly confident in its superior fighting efficiency and fighting spirit. There can be no quarrel with the former: success in war owes a great deal to careful preparation. But the latter can be overstressed, as it was in the Japanese Navy. Ivan Morris reports this wartime conversation, which applies with equal force to the Navy. Captain Sanaka, of the Imperial Army, the leader of an attack group, was trying to persuade his commanding officer that, with the Ki-45 attack planes in short supply, the Army should use the smaller Ki-27s to intercept the American B-29 bombers.

'But how can a Ki-27 possibly take on a plane with the speed and armament of a B-29?'

'I beg your pardon, Sir,' replied Captain Sanaka ..., 'but under the circumstances I think we are obliged to use every available plane in our base to destroy the greatest possible number of American bombers.'

'And what about our pilots? They still aren't properly trained.'

'What counts, Sir, is neither the skill of our pilots nor the quality of our planes but the spirit and morale of the fighters. Everything depends on that.'[33]

[32] *Senshi sōsho*, xxxi. 189.
[33] *The Nobility of Failure: Tragic Heroes in the History of Japan* (London, 1975), p. 311.

'WAR IS SO EASY COMPARED WITH PEACETIME EXERCISES!'

There was an overstress on the value of spiritual qualities in *both* Services. General Genda Minoru, a Captain in the Imperial Navy, had brought out the fallacy in this outlook: 'The psychological factor is an essential element of any operation, but it should never be regarded as the central element in military strategy. It is, on the contrary, a so-called "plus factor" alongside material preparation. The idea of covering material shortages with spiritual power should never be seriously considered by military planners.'[34]

What the Imperial Navy had going for it, apart from a personnel thoroughly imbued with a spirit of self-sacrifice and hardened to battle conditions by realistic exercises and manœuvres, was excellently designed ships and aircraft. Japanese technological progress in *matériel* was one of the surprises in the early stages of the war.

[34] 'Tactical Planning in the Imperial Japanese Navy', (US) *Naval War College Review*, xxii, 2 (Oct. 1969), 49.

XI

The Imperial Japanese Navy: II. Material, Tactics, and Strategy

> Our war plan against Great Britain was nothing but a by-product of our plan to secure the natural resources of the Southern Area in order to fight the United States.
>
> Vice-Admiral Hoshina Zenshirō to the author, 23 June 1976.

> The successful fighter plans his victory and then gives battle: the unsuccessful gives battle and then looks for victory.
>
> Sun-tzŭ (ancient Chinese writer on the art of war).

1. OF SHIPS AND PLANES

THE inter-war Imperial Navy built the largest battleships, the fastest torpedoes, and the most advanced fighter aircraft in the world's navies. Catapult planes aboard large submarines, 18-inch naval guns, and midget submarines were among the other advances. The excellence of the naval technical officers is an important explanation. They were almost all graduates of Tokyo Imperial University, Japan's finest, and the élite among them had studied engineering and related subjects at the top technical universities of Britain, the United States, France, and Germany, including, in the case of Britain, Glasgow and London Universities.

From 1915–16 the Imperial Navy paralleled Royal Navy designs. Before then, as we have seen, the British were building most of the IJN ships. Then, in the late 1920s, the Imperial Navy went its own way, no longer dependent on the Royal Navy, or any other navy, for ideas. The Royal Navy was no longer a model, although all five Chief Naval Constructors in the Imperial Navy, 1916–45, had studied at Greenwich, and British warship designs were not without influence. 'Under the quantitative yoke of the Naval Armament Limitation Treaties, the Chief Naval Constructors laboured to produce naval vessels which would, type for type, be individually superior to those of the hypothetical enemy, even by a single gun or torpedo tube, or by a single knot of speed.[1] High speed and heavy armament were the leading characteristics of warships. The Navy never forgot an important lesson of the wars with China (1894–5) and Russia (1904–5), the immense value of speed,[2] and, from the Battle of Tsushima Straits (1905), of the big gun.

The Imperial navy had imported, from Britain, the idea of the decisive fleet action between fleets, and of the dependence of that kind of encounter on the battleship. Battleships were what mattered. Mahan had demonstrated this from the experience of past wars, and Tsushima and Jutland had confirmed it. Until the Pacific War the principle of the supremacy of the battleship was a vital strategic concept and was enshrined in the Naval Battle Regulations. The Washington Treaty had, however, forced Japan to scrap two 48,000-ton battleships and four 46,000-ton battle cruisers, all with eight 18-inch guns. With the First Vinson Act (1934) the Imperial Navy realized that the ratio of battleships would decline from 6:10 with the United States to less than 5:10. Since it would be difficult to match the American Navy in numbers, the idea of meeting quantity with quantity was abandoned. Quality replaced quantity as the chief desideratum for battleships, and this meant primarily superior striking power and speed. Accordingly, and in direct contravention of the Washington Treaty, in 1934 the Imperial Navy began to stockpile materials and ready blueprints for a new super-battleship that would outgun and outrange existing capital ships or any that might be built in the following decade.

What finally emerged in March 1937 were plans for four 64,000-ton vessels (71,659 at full load, that is, with everything they could carry in the way of extra fuel, stores, ammunition, etc., to give them

---

[1] Captain Shioyama Sakuichi's letter to the author, Aug. 1978. He was an officer in the Ship Construction Division of the Naval Technical Department.

[2] The 12 Japanese battleships in the Second World War had maximum speeds of 25–30·5 knots. (British battleship speeds ranged from the 21 knots of the R-class to the 28·5 of the King George Vs; the three battle cruisers, 28·5 to 31.) On 26 August 1941, NID4 estimated the speed of the battle fleet as 22–3 knots. Japanese Fleet—Effectives', PREM 3/254/4. The fleet carriers had speeds of 28–34·5 knots; the heavy cruisers and light cruisers, 33–6 knots; and the destroyers, 34–8 knots. I have in this section relied mainly on Hansgeorg Jentschura, Dieter Jung, and Peter Mickel, *Warships of the Imperial Japanese Navy, 1869–1945* (London, 1977), for the data on all IJN ships except submarines, where I am greatly indebted to Erminio Bagnasco, *Submarines of World War Two* (London, 1977); for RN ships, Naval Historical Branch records, notably 'Particulars of War Vessels and Aircraft (British Commonwealth of Nations)', Admiralty, Half-Yearly Return, Oct. 1941.

maximum endurance) mounting a main armament of nine 18·1-inch guns. There was nothing like these main batteries in the British or American navies. These guns fired a 3,220 lb shell (50 per cent heavier than a 16-inch shell). They could fire a broadside of 28,800 lb to a maximum range of 44,635 yards, or nearly 26 miles, at an elevation of 45 degrees. The ships were able to steam at 27 knots, with a radius of 7,200 miles at 16 knots. Their protection, too, was extraordinary, making them the most heavily armoured warships in the world. Thus, the belt armour of the *Yamato* was 16·1 inches (*Shinano*, 15·7 inches), bulkheads 11·8 inches, and turrets 9·8 to 25·6 inches. Her deck armour of 7·8 inches to 9 inches, the thickest armour ever laid on a deck, was meant to withstand the heaviest bomb in existence—a 1,100 lb bomb dropped from 11,000 feet—and 18-inch shells fired from 16 miles. There was special protection beneath the magazines against mines and torpedoes. To throw off foreign intelligence agents, the Japanese put out reports about 40,000-ton ships carrying nine 16-inch guns. Twenty-foot fences shielded the construction areas, and strict security measures kept secret what was going on inside. Little wonder that in August 1941 NID4 put down the battleship 'expected to complete this year' (*Yamato*) as a 35,000–40,000-ton ship. Nobody at the Admiralty dreamed that any of the Japanese capital ships had guns exceeding 16 inches.

Two of the Yamato class, the *Yamato* and *Musashi*, were ordered under the Third Replenishment Plan of 1937, and two others, *No. 110* and *No. 111*, under the Fourth Plan (1939). The *Yamato* was laid down in November 1937, launched in August 1940, and completed on 16 December 1941; the *Musashi*, March 1938, November 1940, and August 1942. The keel for battleship *110* was laid in May 1940, but after the disastrous Battle of Midway in June 1942 was converted to the carrier *Shinano* and completed in November 1944. *No. 111* was laid down in November 1940, but work was stopped in March 1942, and she was dismantled in March 1943. The two super-battleships and the super-carrier did not see action until 1944: all were successfully torpedoed within six months, deprived as they were of air cover against carrier aircraft attack. None the less the Yamato class was the ultimate in battleship design.

How did the capital ships of the Royal Navy compare with those of the Imperial Navy in 1941? Putting aside the problem of the number of capital ships that could be sent to the Far East, we find that the most powerful battleships, the *Nelson* and *Rodney* (i.e. before the King George V's were ready), with a main armament of nine 16-inch guns, would have been a match for the two Nagatos (*Nagato, Mutsu*), with eight 15·75-inch guns, and, similarly, the five Queen Elizabeths as regards the two Fusōs (*Fusō, Yamashiro*) and the two Ises (*Ise, Hyūga*) (eight 15-inch *v.* twelve 14·1-inch). The five Royal Sovereigns, though with the same primary armament as the QEs, were too slow and short-ranged for fleet action. Japan's four Kongōs (*Kongō, Haruna, Hiei, Kirishima*), with eight 14·1-inch guns, were too fast for any British capital ship, except the battle cruiser *Hood*, which was sunk in May 1941. Put shortly, the Royal Navy did not have ten capital ships that could meet the ten Japanese on even terms. The construction of the King George Vs in 1940–2 promised to restore the balance, but the two Yamatos drastically upset it in 1941–2. The Japanese had an advantage in damage control, an important variable in judging the sinkability of a warship. The large size of their crews and the excellent compartmentalization, usually at the expense of crew space (which also permitted a heavier armament), gave their capital ships an important advantage over both the British and American. No Japanese capital ship was sunk by gunfire during the war. Indeed, all their surface ships were able to survive large numbers of torpedo and shell hits.

As with battleships, the Imperial Navy, finding it could not compete with the US Navy in numbers of aircraft carriers, tried to compensate in the quality of their new carriers as well as by requisitioning merchant ships. Japan more than doubled her carrier strength between 1936 and the end of 1941: from four to 10. Apart from the obsolete *Hermes*, the Royal Navy had no carriers east of Suez on the eve of the Pacific War; the US Navy had seven, of which only three were in the Pacific. But only six of Japan's carriers were suitable for fleet action in December 1941, that is, able to carry many offensive aircraft, and they constituted the strike force in the Pearl Harbor operation: the *Akagi* (66/25), *Kaga* (72/18), *Soryu* (53/18), *Hiryu* (57/16), and the two Shōkakus (72/12).[3] The

---

[3] The first figure shown in parenthesis is the number of aircraft carried or authorized, the second, that of reserve planes. The exact number carried depended on the mission assigned to the ship. With the sinking of the *Ark Royal* in November 1941 (she carried 54 planes), only the *Indomitable*, among British carriers in commission when the Pacific War broke out, carried as many as 45 aircraft.

last two were ordered under the Third (1937) Replenishment Plan: the *Shōkaku*, laid down in December 1937 and completed in August 1941, and the *Zuikaku*, May 1938 and September 1941. They were of 25,675 tons, had the extremely high speed of 34·5 knots, 84 aircraft (72 operational and 12 spares), and a powerful main AA armament of sixteen 5-inch guns. Their protection exceeded that of any British carrier: belt armour was 8·5 inches, and deck armour, 6·7 inches.[4] The cruising radius of Japan's first-line carriers was about the same as that of the latest British carriers, the Illustrious class: 9,700 miles at 18 knots for the two Shōkakus, and 9,650 for the Illustrious class. A serious deficiency, however, was the vulnerability of their aviation fuel systems, which proved costly. Another British advantage lay in the innovation of the armoured flight deck. Under the IJN's Fourth Plan (1939) a remarkable new carrier, the *Taiho*, the first Japanese carrier with an armoured flight deck, was laid down in 1941, but was not completed until March 1944.

Japan's shipbuilding technology also produced superior ships in other warship classes. Cruisers were distinguished by high speed and heavy armament, including many torpedo tubes. Especially formidable were the heavy (i.e. 8-inch) cruisers. They displaced up to 13,400 tons, carried six to ten 8-inch guns, were equipped with eight to sixteen torpedo tubes (to the British six to twelve), up to double this number of torpedoes (one torpedo per tube in British destroyers), and were capable of 33 to 35 knots. It is instructive to compare the Myōko class of four heavy cruisers (built in 1924–9, modernized in 1939–41) with the contemporary British Kent class. The *Myōko* had ten 8-inch and eight 5-inch dual-purpose guns; the *Kent*, eight 8-inch and four 4·7-inch. The *Myōko* carried sixteen 24-inch torpedo tubes to the *Kent*'s eight 21-inch. The *Myōko* had a 2-knot advantage in speed: 33·8 to 31·7, and her armour protection was superior.

The destroyers were among the largest and most powerful afloat. This stemmed from the requirement that they carry heavy torpedo equipment (the latest classes carried eight 24-inch tubes) to be used for night action. (The full outfit for the latest British destroyer classes was eight or ten 21-inch torpedo tubes in two mounts, but

---

[4] British Intelligence again was off the mark. The two Shōkakus were believed to have aircraft complements of 60 each, the *Kaga* and *Akagi*, 48 and 60, and so forth. NID4, 'Japanese Fleet—Effectives'.

this was reduced to four or five when one mount was sacrificed to ship an extra 4-inch AA gun.) Japanese destroyers carried on deck a full load of torpedoes and gear for reloading their tubes. The speed with which they could reload in action gave them an important advantage. From two sets of four torpedo tubes fore and aft, eight torpedoes could be fired at two-second intervals. Ten minutes later, the reloaded tubes could release another eight. Earlier classes were overloaded and lacked stability and strength: the *Sawarabi* capsized in a storm in 1932, and a powerful typhoon broke off the bows of the *Hatsuyuki* and *Yūgiri* in 1935; but these faults were corrected in the Asashio and Kagerō classes (built in 1937–41) and the Yūgumo class (1941–4).

Unlike the Royal Navy, where the submarine was the Cinderella of the Service (partly because the Navy put too much confidence in the ability of asdic, renamed 'sonar' in 1943, to locate submerged submarines), the submarine played a key role in Japan's naval strategy, and their design was a matter of rightful pride in the Navy. The Japanese developed three types between 1925 and 1940: a cruiser-submarine (*Junsen*), which derived from the British K-class and the German U-Kreuzer type of the First World War (long-range commerce raiders, seven of which had been acquired as post-war booty) and was intended for reconnaissance and in distant operations; only seven units were built. The slightly larger long-range or Fleet type (*Kaidai*), developed from the *Junsen*, was to be employed chiefly in direct co-operation with the battle fleet. A smaller type, the RO classes, was intended for home defence and service near Japanese bases. Despite the example of German near-success in the attack on British trade in the First World War, the Japanese held that the main function of the ocean-going submarine was the support of fleet operations, particularly by the attack on battleships and aircraft carriers. Primary importance was, therefore, attached to the *Kaidai* type (various I classes), which were endowed with high surface speed and range, sea-keeping qualities, and a heavy-gun armament. The most advanced Fleet submarines in 1941 (the 20 units of I-class Type B) had a displacement of 2,589 tons surfaced, 3,654 submerged; a maximum speed of 23·6 knots surfaced, 8 knots submerged; a range of 14,000 miles at 16 knots surfaced, 96 miles at 3 knots submerged; armament of one 5·5-inch and two 25mm guns, and six 21-inch torpedo tubes and 17 torpedoes. (The five units of the contemporary I-class Type C, had eight 21-inch tubes and 20 torpedoes.) They had one catapult and one float-plane. Even the smaller RO-class boats, with a surface displacement of 500–1,000 tons, had a surface range of as much as 8,000 miles at 12 knots and a torpedo armament of four 21-inch tubes. Midget submarines were also built from 1938, with a submerged displacement of 46 tons, a speed of 19 knots (submerged) and 23 knots (surfaced), and armed with two 18-inch torpedoes. They were designed to be carried by surface vessels and by large ocean-going submarines and were intended for use in battle-fleet encounters and to attack big warships in their anchorages.

By contrast, the most advanced ocean-going submarines the Royal Navy had, the T-class, were of about 1,330 tons surfaced displacement (about 1,585 tons submerged), with a speed of 15·25 knots surfaced (9 knots submerged), and a range of 8,000–11,000 miles at 10 knots surfaced and 80 miles at 4 knots submerged. They were armed with one 4-inch gun, a 20mm Oerlikon cannon, three machine-guns, and 10 or 11 21-inch torpedo tubes and 16 or 17 torpedoes.

Yet there were major shortcomings in the Japanese boats related to their high displacements, for these led to slow diving times and poor submerged manœuvrability which made them exposed to air and surface attack. The large hull, in particular, was easy to locate by asdic and vulnerable to depth-charge patterns. 'The conning tower bulk reflected excellent echoes on radar screens, which could locate them at great distances when surfaced.' The redoubtable submarine force was, in the outcome, one of the Imperial Navy's biggest wartime disappointments. The few successes achieved were fortuitous or achieved against a damaged ship. But in December 1941 it was the weapon most feared by the British and American navies.

Japanese warships, unlike the British and American, were designed exclusively for fighting. The Navy tended to put heavier armaments on smaller hulls than the Western navies, at the expense of protection, particularly above the upper deck. These ships, however, could stand up to punishment, a result attained through considerable subdivision of hulls. Generally sacrificed were living accommodations, defensive armament, and radius of action in order to achieve maximum speed and offensive power. These latter were deemed the essential ones in a strategy that called for meeting the expected American naval offensive into the Western Pacific by intercepting and attacking their superior fleet in waters close to Japan proper.

Total Japanese naval strength in ships was:[5]

Classification	Strength possessed at the outbreak of war		Ships under construction at the outbreak of war	
	Number of vessels	Tonnage	Number of vessels	Tonnage
Battleships	10	301,400	2	128,000
Aircraft carriers	10	152,970	4	77,860
Heavy cruisers	18	158,800	—	—
Light cruisers	20	98,855	4	42,700
Destroyers	112	165,868	12	27,120
Submarines	65[6]	97,900	29	42,554
Others	156	490,384	37	57,225
Total	391	1,466,177	88	375,459

The Imperial navy had an overwhelming superiority over the combined British Commonwealth, American, and Dutch, and Free French naval forces stationed in the Far East when war broke out, and a rough equality if we include the US Pacific Fleet in the comparison.[7]

In naval air forces, as we shall see in a moment, the Japanese had a clear superiority over the Allies in the entire Pacific area. The Imperial Navy had a distinct superiority over both the British and American navies in other classes of *matériel*: their parachute flares and starshells were brighter and more dependable, and their binoculars, particularly for night work, were more effective.

[5] Hattori, *The Complete History of the Greater East Asia War*, i. 350, Japanese Monograph No. 160, p. 35. Compare these figures with the NID4 estimate of Japanese Fleet effectives on 26 August 1941: 10 battleships (and one expected to complete that year), 8 aircraft carriers, 13 heavy cruisers (8-inch), 20 light cruisers (6-inch), 126 destroyers, and 80 submarines.

[6] Twenty-one of these boats were obsolete and of small value.

[7] The actual figures on the Allied naval forces in the entire South-east Asia/Pacific area on the eve of war were:

	Battleships	Carriers	Cruisers	Destroyers	Submarines
USA	9	3	24	80	56
Great Britain	2	0	8	13	0
Free France and the Netherlands	0	0	4	7	13
Total	11	3	36	100	69

These figures are from Captain S. W. Roskill, *The War at Sea* (3 vols. in 4, London, 1954–61), i. 560. Considering the dispersion of the Allied ships, from Singapore to Pearl Harbor, the Japanese numerical advantage was greater than these figures reveal.

The Royal Navy did hold important advantages in the development of radar and asdic (the former was of inestimable value for surface gunnery and naval aircraft, the latter, for A/S work); but these were not enough initially to redress the qualitative superiority of Japanese warships, to say nothing of their numerical superiority in Eastern waters. The Imperial Navy did not realize the importance of radar and asdic as war weapons until 1944, and then it was a case of too little too late. Until then the Navy relied upon air reconnaissance, human eyesight (the lookouts of the Combined Fleet developed excellent vision), and their night binoculars, which gave them a pronounced advantage in night sightings.

It was the Fleet Air Arm the progressive thinkers in the Imperial Navy looked to for a decisive blow against the US Pacific Fleet and whatever capital-ship force Britain sent East. In 1941 it was probably the best trained naval air force in the world. The quality of the air officers and their petty officers and enlisted men were even better than their respective line officers and men. But this was not always the case.

After the Tsushima Straits battle anybody who had the ambition to reach flag rank became a gunnery specialist, while officers drawn to naval air in the 1920s were only fifth rate. The air arm had no prestige and did not lead to quick promotion; lip service was paid to it by many senior officers who refused to go up in an aircraft, among them, as late as 1937-9, Yoshida Zengo, when C-in-C, Combined Fleet. Furthermore, the frequency in the 1920s of air accidents, many of them fatal, made a career in the air arm unattractive.

In the 1930s, however, a trend began of able midshipmen wanting to go into naval air; these men, the cream of the young officers, were conscious of the great strides being made in naval aviation. They were given from the start a tremendous, indeed vital, boost by the advocacy of naval air of Admiral Yamamoto from a succession of important posts he held in the inter-war years. He developed a keen interest in air power as early as 1917-19, when he had been sent to the United States to study English. He studied reports on air actions during the war and visited aircraft factories. In 1923-5 he was executive officer of the new air-training base at Kasumigaura, about 40 miles north-east of Tokyo. When Naval Attaché in Washington in 1925-8 he had come under the influence of that fanatical advocate of air power, Brigadier 'Billy' Mitchell. In 1928 Yamamoto predicted that air power would be the nucleus of the Navy. He commanded the carrier *Akagi* in 1928–9 and, in 1933–4, the 1st Aircraft Carrier Division. In 1930–3 he served as Chief of the Technical Division of the Naval Aviation Department, and in 1935–6 as Chief of the Department.

Yamamoto ceaselessly and enthusiastically promoted naval aviation, encouraging men to join the air arm and developing in the process a huge following among navy flyers. He was not lacking in ingenuity. Night flights were very dangerous, and air officers were not keen on making them. When Chief of the Technical Division of the Naval Aviation Department in the early 1930s, Yamamoto decided to do something to encourage night flying. He paid 6 yen to pilots, observers, and flight engineers for each night flight, increasing this sum to 30 for the fifth and subsequent night flights. You had to be airborne at least five minutes each time. These bonuses were attractive to a sub-lieutenant (midshipmen were not permitted to fly), with a regular monthly pay of 85 or 94 yen, plus flight pay of 60 yen. Another incentive plan of Yamamoto's paid 6 yen, up to a 30-yen maximum, for pilots who took off from, and landed on, a carrier, even in daytime, or for those who took off from a land base and landed on a carrier, or vice versa. The extra pay was given regardless of a pilot's rank. Enlisted men received half the sum paid to officers under the incentive plans. Yamamoto's incentive system continued through the war and was responsible, to a degree, for the rapid rise in the efficiency of pilots and observers.

As the possibility of war increased, air training was intensified. By 1941 the pilots were receiving at least 300 flying hours before assignment to a tactical unit. (In the Royal Navy in 1941 pilots had between 110 and 150 hours on first joining front-line squadrons.) Those who participated in the Pearl Harbor attack had averaged about 800 hours, with a minimum of 300 and a maximum of 2,500. (The average flight time of RN pilots at that time is not assessable, though the majority would have had less than 250 hours.) The Fleet Air Arm had achieved a remarkable level of proficiency by 1941. Yamamoto's impact as C-in-C, Combined Fleet, is important here. From the time he took over, in August 1939, priority was given to air training. Just before the war, the pilots of the 1st Aircraft Carrier Division, earmarked for the Pearl Harbor strike, attained these results: 10 per cent of hits in horizontal bombing (at 3,000 metres altitude, against the target of an old battleship steaming evasively at 16–18 knots), but 40 per cent of hits in dive-bombing (against a battleship with high speed and free evasive manœuvre), and 80 per cent of hits in daytime torpedo attack, 70 per cent at night (against a battleship with high speed and free evasive manœuvre).[8]

Yamamoto had much to do with the decision to build the two Shōkaku's, and he was instrumental in the development of the famed carrier-borne and land-based Zero fighter, so named from the 'OO' fuselage marking. This represented the last two digits of the year 2600 in the Japanese calendar (AD 1940), when the plane went into full production.[9] The Zero was a magnificent fighter, highly manœuvrable and with a range more than twice that of contemporary American and British fighters. There were approximately six different types of Zero in service during the war. However, it was the Mark 21 that was the main force of the various air corps deployed in the Southern theatre of operations at the start of the war. It had a maximum speed of 279·5 knots at 14,300 feet, 275 knots at 16,400 feet; cruising speed, 160 knots; service ceiling, 32,800 feet; climb rate, 3 minutes 31 seconds to 9,800 feet, 7 minutes 27 seconds to 19,700 feet; maximum range (flying distance), 1,900 nautical miles at 180 knots at an altitude of 13,100 feet, equipped with detachable extra fuel tanks; armament, two 20mm cannon, two 7·7mm machine-guns, and two 66lb (30kg) or two 132lb (60kg) bombs.[10]

When the Navy designed the Zero (1937), it took the Royal Navy into consideration. 'We calculated the distance from Saigon to Singapore [approximately 600 miles]—and that was one of the reasons why we built a long-range fighter.'[11] Another consideration was the distance between Formosa (Taiwan) and Clark Field, Manila, which was a little over 500 miles. The authors of the

---

[8] Genda, 'Tactical Planning in the Imperial Japanese Navy', p. 49.
[9] An additional word may be helpful. *Shiki* (type) meant the year when the equipment (not only aircraft) was adopted as a regulation weapon. For example, '96' of the Type 96 Nell bomber was the last two digits of 2596, the year according to the year of the Japanese Imperial Reign, or 1936 in the Western calendar. In the same way, the Type 1 Betty bomber was adopted in 2601 = AD 1941.
[10] IJN aircraft performance figures vary with the source. Mine are rounded off from the metric figures in the authoritative *Senshi sōsho*. xcv, *Kaigun kōkū gaishi* [Concise History of Naval Aviation] (1976), Table 1.
[11] Interview with Commander (Lieutenant-General, JMSDF) Okumiya Masatake, 5 July 1976.

standard history of the Zero fighter write of contemporary expectations:

> despite our enemies' awesome industrial might, the Navy had confidence in the ability of our Zeke [Zero] fighters to wrest air control from the enemy over any battle area. Our intelligence and our technical groups stated flatly that the excellent performance and technical superiority of the Zeke fighter meant that, in battle, one Zeke would be the equal of from two to five enemy fighters, depending upon the type. Because of this unshakeable faith in the Zeke, the Navy felt extremely confident of victory in initial campaigns.[12]

The Zero eclipsed the RN fighters of 1941 in every respect except airframe protection and, possibly, sustained speed in a steep dive and the gun-sight design.[13] Moreover, for the first six months of the Pacific War, their air crew were streets ahead of anything that the tired Royal Navy or inexperienced US Navy could put up as Zero-fodder, the Japanese pilots in the carrier- and land-based air groups having had valuable operational practice in China. Not until the edge had been removed through wastage, and the development of superior tactics, was the situation eased, and thereafter the US Navy and Marines got by for a year by superior tactics, not aircraft. By the autumn of 1943, faster aircraft had the measure of the Zero. The Royal Navy's Fleet Air Arm hardly met the Japanese naval aircraft up to mid-1944, combat being limited to 5 and 9 April 1942 and a short encounter with a shadower in August 1942, the last being the only carrier-based encounter.

Details of the armament and tankage of a Zero that had been shot down in China in May 1941 reached Singapore and were passed on at the end of July to the Air Ministry and the Headquarters, Air Command, Far East. Somewhat later these two authorities also received (dispatched on 29 September by Singapore Intelligence, the FECB) performance figures on the Zero that had been sent by the Air Attaché in Chungking and which turned out

---

[12] Masatake Okumiya and Jiro Horikoshi, *Zero! The Story of the Imperial Naval Air Force, 1937–1945* (London, 1957), p. 35. Note that the American and British code-named Japanese aircraft types with Christian names.

[13] The most advanced RN fighters in 1941, the Martlet II and the Sea Hurricane IB, were no match for the Zero; fortunately, neither had ever to fight a Zero. The Grumman Martlet was capable of 292 knots at 6,000 feet; service ceiling, 30,200 feet; climb rate, 8 3/4 minutes to 15,000 feet; maximum range, 780 miles at 10,000–15,000 feet; armament, six 0·5-inch. cannon. My data on RN aircraft is derived from various Naval Historical Branch sources.

to be fairly accurate. The two authorities, in London and Singapore, therefore had a pretty accurate idea of the Zero's capabilities, but the technical data was not passed to the crews of the air squadrons in the Far East command. 'Faulty organization at Headquarters, Air Command, whose establishment did not include an intelligence staff, resulted in this valuable report remaining unsifted from the general mass of intelligence information, and no action being taken upon it.'[14]

The Zero fighter was not the only success story. Other first-class planes included the standard carrier-borne bomber, the Type 97 Kate, which had a much greater range than its British and American counterparts, if slower. The Mark 3 (renamed the Mark 12 when the war broke out) had a maximum speed of 204 knots at 11,800 feet; cruising speed, 140 knots at 9,800 feet; climb rate, 7 minutes 40 seconds to 9,800 feet, 13 minutes 39 seconds to 16,400 feet; service ceiling, 25,000 feet; maximum range, 1,075 nautical miles at 140 knots at 9,800 feet; armament, one 7·7mm machine-gun, and one Type 91 aerial torpedo, or one 1,764lb (800kg) or 1,100lb (500kg) bomb, or two 550lb (250kg) bombs, or six 132lb (60kg) bombs. These were the aircraft that succeeded in firing torpedoes into the shallow waters of Pearl Harbor that hit their marks.

The Type 96 Nell was the Navy's standard land-based medium bomber. It was chiefly the Mark 22 that participated in the naval battle off Malaya: maximum speed, 224·5 knots at 19,300 feet; cruising speed, 160 knots at 13,100 feet; service ceiling, 33,700 feet; climb rate, 9 minutes 43 seconds to 16,400 feet; maximum range, 2,300 nautical miles at 150 knots at 13,100 feet; armament, four 7·7mm machine-guns (the Nells in the naval battle off Malaya had an additional two), one 20mm cannon, and one Type 91 aerial torpedo or one 1,764lb or 1,100lb bomb, or two 550lb bombs, or twelve 132lb bombs. The Japanese Navy was the first in the world to install revolving-type 200mm cannon in an aircraft.

The Nell was gradually replaced from 1941 by the Type 1 land-based medium bomber, the Betty, whose Mark 11 participated in the naval battle off Malaya. Its main characteristics were: maximum speed, 244 knots at 19,300 feet; cruising speed, 170 knots

---

[14] Major-General S. Woodburn Kirby, *et al.*, *The war Against Japan* (5 vols., London, 1957-69), i. 240n. For the result of this gross negligence, see below, p. 428.

at 13,100 feet; climb rate, 10 minutes 36 seconds to 16,400 feet; service ceiling, 30,200 feet; maximum range, 2,000 nautical miles at 170 knots at 9,800 feet, same armament as the Nell Mark 22, including the two extra 7·7s in the naval battle off Malaya.

The standard carrier-borne torpedo-bomber of the Royal Navy in 1941 was the Swordfish. (Swordfish and Albacores operated as torpedo-bombers from land bases, under RAF control, as well as from carriers.) Owen Thetford described it as 'one of the greatest aircraft in the history of air warfare'. Perhaps so; yet it could not stand comparison with the Nell or Betty. The Swordfish had a maximum speed of 121 knots, attained between 2,000 and 4,000 feet (in practice it did almost everything, including cruise, at *90 knots*), a range of 546 miles with normal fuel, and carried one 18-inch torpedo or 1,500lb of bombs.

The Imperial Navy secretly developed the remarkable oxygen torpedo, which was superior to the torpedoes of every other navy. After experimenting in the 1920s with torpedoes powered by oxygen, the Royal Navy had opted for compressed air, which was less dangerous, if also less powerful. In 1927 a Japanese naval officer, visiting the battleship *Rodney* at Portsmouth, had mistakenly identified some apparatus on the deck as an oxygen generator. His report that the Royal Navy had developed an oxygen-powered torpedo spurred the Imperial Navy to continue work on such a torpedo. By 1935, Rear-Admiral Kishimoto Kaneji, Chief of the Torpedo Department of the Kure Naval Arsenal, had produced an oxygen-fuelled 24-inch (61cm) Long Lance torpedo, Type 93 (Model 1), with an extraordinary maximum range of nearly 33,000 yards at 40 knots, and a range of nearly 22,000 yards at 50 knots.[15] It was much faster and longer ranging than anything in the British and American navies, and with a greater explosive charge (1,100lb: 500kg). The warhead was twice the weight of the British 21-inch and four times the weight of their 18-inch. The Type 95 21-inch (53cm) oxygen-fuelled torpedo (Model 1, which went into mass production in 1937), the submarine version of the Long Lance, had a warhead of 880lb (400kg) and a maximum range of 9,800 yards at 49 knots. Compare the Long Lance with the best of the RN surface torpedoes, the 21-inch Mark IX**: 9,000 yards at 40 knots,

---

[15] My information on IJN torpedoes is derived from a highly authoritative work: Rear-Admiral Ōyagi Shizuo, et al., *Kaigun suiraishi* [Torpedoes of the Imperial Japanese Navy] (Tokyo, 1979), especially pp. 21–34.

13,000 yards at 35 knots, and a 725lb explosive charge. The RN submarine torpedo of 1941, the Mark VIII, was a 21-inch weapon capable of 6,000 yards at 45 knots, and had a 725lb charge. The oxygen-fuelled torpedo had the inestimable advantage of being virtually trackless, whereas the conventional hot-air torpedo left an easily detectable track.[16] Although the existence of the Japanese oxygen-fuelled torpedo was known abroad, its capabilities were kept secret. 'When we made mention of this torpedo in the documents of the Navy, we always discounted 10 knots on the speed and one-half on the range, and nobody ever seemed to doubt the veracity of such reports.'[17] The deception was successful, and the revelation of the capabilities of the Japanese torpedoes was one of the nastier surprises to the British and Americans when war broke out.

The Long Lance was for use by surface vessels: all 18 heavy cruisers, selected light cruisers (the *Ōi* and *Kitagami*, which carried 40 torpedoes each, and the flagships of destroyer squadrons), and the latest destroyers, from the Hatsuharu class (built in 1931–5) on (46 in all). (The capital ships did not carry torpedo tubes; the British, other than the King George V-class, did.) The equipment of the Fleet with the Long Lance was completed by the summer of 1941. Only a few destroyers had them before this time. In the final Combined Fleet manœuvres, conducted off Tokyo Bay in the late summer of 1941, oxygen torpedoes without warheads were fired, despite the rough sea, by all the cruisers and destroyers, and at high speed. Although the oxygen torpedoes were the foremost torpedoes in the world at that time, there was trouble early in the war with the Type 93 (surface ships), notably in the Battle of the Java Sea (27 February 1942), such as deviant runs and self-explosions. The mechanical problems were corrected, but it was not until early 1943 that the new model Type 93s were distributed.

[16] The oxygen torpedo was hard to detect because the oxygen fuel, burnt and vapoured up to the surface, did not produce bubbles in the water. Actually, the oxygen torpedo was not entirely trackless, if you could see the point of firing. It did not leave the white wake of the normal hot torpedo, but if you knew where to look for it, and the sea surface was calm and the direction of the sunlight favourable, it was possible to see, though dimly, the disturbance in the water caused by the rotation of its propellers. But the disturbances which appeared on the surface diminished instantly one after another: they did not make a line, and there were no bubbles which produced the white wake of the more normal torpedo breed.

[17] Chihaya MS, p. 11. To ensure against an oxygen torpedo falling into foreign hands and thereby giving away the game, and also because they were so costly, there were strict orders to recover all torpedoes (*sans* warheads) fired in practices.

The torpedo-bombers never used oxygen torpedoes. Type 94 (Model 2) oxygen-fuelled torpedoes were adopted for aerial attack in 1939: 18 inches (45cm) in diameter, with a maximum range of 2,200 yards at 45 knots and a warhead charge of 440lb (200kg). Forty-eight were produced by early 1941, but then its manufacture was discontinued, it having been found unsuitable and impracticable for aerial attack. The reasons were, first, because the attack-plane fired its torpedo at a point close to the enemy ship, there was no necessity to hide its track; second, in comparison with the conventional hot-air torpedo, there was considerable danger in operating and handling the oxygen-fuelled torpedo; and third, arming attack-planes with oxygen torpedoes required a sophisticated and well-protected maintenance system at the air base, which was too costly to be prepared at all shore bases in advanced areas. The aerial torpedo in use when war came was the Type 91, Models 1 and 2 (normal hot-air type): 18-inch (45cm), warhead, 375lb (170kg), Model 1, 450lb (204kg), Model 2; 3,300 yards at 36 knots, 2,200 yards at 42 knots, and 1,600 yards at 44 knots.[18] The main RN aerial torpedo was the 18-inch Mark XII: 2,000 yards at 40 knots, warhead, 465lb.

The tactics of firing torpedoes from carrier aircraft were first attempted in the early 1930s, but were quite crude. The speed of the aircraft at release time was low—90 knots—and the release altitude only 33 feet (10 metres). By the end of 1941, aircraft speed at firing was up to 224 knots, with a release altitude of 33 to 165 feet (10 to 50 metres). In order to give a target as little time as possible to take effective evasive action, the most advantageous dropping distance was believed to be around 2,600 feet (800 metres) from the target. (The main RN aerial torpedo, the Mark XII, was released at up to 150 knots/200 feet from a recommended maximum range of 3,000 feet.)

The only reason that the release altitude was set as low as 10

---

[18] The difference between the two models lay in the stabilizer, a mechanism to prevent the rotation of the torpedo right after it hit the water, and which often led to the torpedo sinking below the required depth or running at the surface. Because the stabilizer of the initial model was not satisfactory, an urgent remodelling order was issued in September 1941, and after desperate efforts at the Kure Naval Arsenal, an effective stabilizer was produced and successfully tested in early November. Model 2 was the Type 91 aerial torpedo which was equipped with this newly developed stabilizer. They were exclusively used in the Pearl Harbor attack. In the naval battle off Malaya only the Kanoya Air Corps (Bettys) used the Model 2; the Genzan and Mihoro Air Corps (all Nells) were equipped with Model 1.

metres was to prepare for the torpedo attack at Pearl Harbor, where the sea depth was no more than 20 metres. Generally speaking, when a torpedo is fired, whether from a plane or the torpedo tube of a surface vessel, after plunging into the sea it sinks quite deeply on account of its own weight, and then comes up through its own buoyancy and starts running, maintaining a constant depth. This depth was set by the functioning of its 'depth adjustment mechanism', normally five metres for a large target like a battleship. In the middle of 1941, the Naval Technical Department succeeded in inventing an apparatus attached to the aerial torpedo which restricted the initial sinking depth to one much shallower than 20 metres. At the same time, releasing the torpedo at a height of 10 metres was found to be absolutely necessary in order to keep the initial sinking depth to the minimum. Although in the Pearl Harbor attack only carrier-borne attack-planes were employed for torpedo attack, land-based medium bombers, Bettys and Nells, adopted the same tactics. To be prepared for shoal-water releasing (the airmen believed that their mission at the outbreak of war would be a torpedo attack against the American ships in Manila Bay, which had a shallow depth), the Genzan, Mihoro, and Kanoya Air Corps from September 1941 practiced releasing their torpedoes at 10 metres.[19]

The battleship *v.* aircraft-carrier controversy was as hot as the contemporary one in British naval circles. The development of naval air was considered mainly in relation to the decisive fleet battle, which was the *idée fixe* of the Service. At first, aircraft were considered for their reconnaissance value, but as their offensive strength improved, the comparison between the offensive power of aircraft and that of the main armament of capital ships became the subject of study. Admiral of the Fleet Tōgō had insisted on battleship supremacy, stating in 1933 that 'the main armament could pour on

[19] It was one of the valuable lessons of the naval battle off Malaya and the Pearl Harbor attack that dropping torpedoes at 10 metres was actually safer than at higher altitudes, because of the depressing limits of the enemy's AA guns. This never occurred to the airmen and war planners during pre-D-day training. Later, however, as a result of these actions the AA guns in US and British ships were remodelled to increase their depressing angles. Although the IJN generally held that releasing torpedoes at around 10 metres was more advantageous than at higher altitudes, this concept was gradually discarded since (1) it was difficult for torpedo attack-planes to descend to 10 metres when the weather was rough and the waves high; (2) it took an extended period of training to level up the skill of pilots who could maintain a 10-metre altitude in the face of heavy AA fire; (3) the increased danger of being shot down by the enemy's remodelled guns.

its fire, whereas aircraft could fire only in small doses', (that is, by dropping bombs).[20]

From around 1934, the year of Tōgō's death, the big-battleship concept was increasingly opposed by air arm officers with the support of men like Yamamoto and Inoue Shigeyoshi (Chief of the Naval Aviation Department, 1940–1). They saw the tremendous importance of air power. It was particularly from his powerful position as Vice-Navy Minister that Yamamoto made his views known and influential. He fought against the construction of the two Yamato-class battleships during the two years (1934–6) their construction was being studied. Even if they built giant battleships, he used to say, there was no such thing as an unsinkable ship. He likened the battleship to 'elaborate religious scrolls which old people hang in their homes—a matter of faith, not reality', and asserted: 'In modern warfare, battleships will be as useful to Japan as a samurai sword.' He challenged the doctrine of the battleship admirals that the primary function of the aircraft carrier was as an umbrella for a striking force of battleships. That torpedoes delivered by carrier-borne planes would be effective against big ships was an article of faith with him: 'The fiercest serpent may be overcome by a swarm of ants.' In short, he believed that victory or defeat in fleet actions would be decided mainly by the result of the air operations. Inoue and two of the Navy's foremost airmen, Captain Ōnishi Takijirō (Rear-Admiral, November 1939) and Commander Genda Minoru, were even more rabid supporters of naval air power. Their position was that money spent on capital ships was a waste, for 'he who commands the air commands the sea'. The air fanatics 'challenged the contention that the battleship remained central to the outcome of the "decisive battle". Since combat aircraft had a range far greater than that of 16-inch shells and since the speed of aircraft carriers was greater than that of battleships, the carrier forces would always have freedom of choice on whether to challenge or evade a battle. The battleship could not be decisive because its big guns would never come within range of the enemy.'[21]

Yet, despite what was revealed by war games and fleet exercises, and despite the advocacy of Yamamoto and Inoue, the young air officers had little impact on the Navy's decision-makers, who, as

---

[20] *Senshi sōsho*, xci, 404. Tōgō's comment is a rather literary allusion: a downpour versus a light rain (*zā-zā* versus *botsu-botsu*).

[21] Genda, 'Tactical Planning in the Imperial Japanese Navy', p. 47.

Commander Seno Sadao puts it, 'felt the opinions of the young officers to be like the barking of young pups'. In the *Gunreibu*, where few of the officers had been closely connected with naval air, the great majority of officers, from the division and section chiefs down, remained to the outbreak of war wedded to the big battleship and the big gun. A leader of the opposition was Vice-Admiral Koga, Chief of the 2nd Division (1935–7) and Vice-Chief of the *Gunreibu* (1937–9). He insisted that they 'need not worry about air attack, since big ships can be protected by stronger defences'.[22] War experience did not impress the Imperial Navy's policy-makers, for there had been no case where a naval air force had achieved a decisive result. They tended to underplay the successful British naval air attack on the Italian Fleet at Taranto on the night of 11–12 November 1940 (torpedo hits from 12 Swordfish torpedo-bombers from the carrier *Illustrious* had sunk three of Italy's six battleships at a loss of two planes), since the Italian ships were 'sitting ducks'. They were no more impressed by the sinking of the mighty German battleship *Bismarck* in the Atlantic on 27 May 1941. The Swordfish from the carrier *Ark Royal* had not been able to sink the absolutely helpless *Bismarck*, though they had crippled her, and she had ultimately to be sunk by the big guns of the battleships *King George V* and *Rodney*, with the coup de grâce administered by torpedoes from the cruiser *Dorsetshire*. In view of such 'lessons', the general trend in the Navy continued to favour the doctrine of the battleship as the principal fighting force.

Around 1939–40 the Navy did turn its attention more towards aircraft carriers, under the stimulus of American carrier expansion. It decided to convert first-class merchant ships into carriers. Work was started on three early in 1941; one, the *Taiyo*, was ready that year. Pearl Harbor and the naval battle off Malaya were products of this shift in emphasis. However, the high-ranking officers who ran the war at sea had little experience in air operations and remained battleship-centred, and it was not until after the catastrophe at Midway (June 1942) that the decision was made to concentrate the navy's efforts on carriers.

Japanese naval air was not without shortcomings on the eve of the Pacific War. Thus, the Zero had serious flaws, as war experience was to reveal. It was a perfectly defenceless plane: its design had not

---

[22] Sorimachi Eiichi, *Ningen Yamamoto Isoroku* (2 vols., Tokyo, 1956–7), ii. 64.

incorporated armour, and the fuel tanks were not of the self-sealing or bullet-proof type, because the added weight would have reduced performance. The fighter pilots insisted on an aircraft with maximum speed, climb, and firepower. Consequently, the Zero was not built to withstand heavy battle damage. Indeed, all IJN aircraft lacked armour and self-sealing tanks when the war broke out. The pilots of the Bettys nicknamed their defenceless Type 1 bomber the 'Ichishiki ['Type 1'] lighter', because it caught fire so easily when hit by bullets from enemy fighters. It was, says Commander Chihaya, 'the nightmare of our pilots'. The Navy did not recognize the vulnerability of its aircraft before the war.

There was an insufficiency of aircraft as well as a lack of aviation fuel for those in service. Admiral Inoue, when Chief of the Naval Aviation Department, informed a conference of bureau chiefs from the Navy Ministry and division chiefs from the Naval General Staff on 3 July 1941 that the Navy's air arm was too weak to permit Japan to begin war with the United States—i.e. the Allied Powers. They had only 52 per cent of the requirement in land-based bombers, 93 per cent in carrier-borne fighters, nought per cent in 'floated Zeros' (a Zero with a float instead of landing gear), and 57 per cent in flying boats. Although the target for the fiscal year 1941–2 (1 April–31 March) was 7,000 aircraft, as of 1 April 1941 the monthly production of all types was a mere 162, with an estimate of 196 on 1 April 1942. There were also, he brought out, marked shortages in machine-guns and their ammunition, most types of bombs, Type 91 aerial torpedoes, and optical instruments. The low production figures were attributed to a shortage of raw materials (especially aluminium and rubber), machine tools, and labour (workers and engineers both).[23]

The expansion in number of pilots also lagged. The Navy was turning out as few as 100 pilots a year in the 1930s.[24] In August

---

[23] Inoue, 'Kōkūhonbuchō Mōshitsugi' (Memorandum by the Chief of the Naval Aviation Department for his successor), Aug. 1941, Shinmyō, pp. 245–54. On hand as of 1 December 1941 were 2,120 aircraft (including 660 Zeros, 240 Bettys and Nells, and 510 advanced trainers, such as the two-seater Zero fighter, which was considered combat worthy). Produced in the four months of December 1941–March 1942 were 981 aircraft of all types, or a monthly average of 245, which was still well below the monthly target for fiscal 1941–2 (583) mentioned by Inoue.

[24] Part of the problem lay in the tough qualifications for flyers. For example, when Sakai Saburō, afterwards the Navy's leading surviving ace, entered pilot training at the Navy Fliers School at Tsuchiura, on the western shore of Lake Kasumigaura, in 1937—enlisted

(*continued*)

1941 the Navy issued a plan for the annual training of 15,000 pilots; but it was too late to supply an adequate war reserve. When war came, there were between 3,000 and 4,000 navy pilots, of whom 1,000–1,500 were trained for carriers. There were not enough pilots to man all available aircraft and maintain a comfortable reserve. But their average flying experience was 800–1,000 hours, with a minimum of 200–300.[25]

In 1941 these imperfections were not discernible to the Imperial Navy or were played down. The air officers were absolutely confident in the ability of the Fleet Air Arm to perform all its duties. Besides, the Royal Navy (and the US Navy) was not aware of the particular weaknesses. And it had its own serious problems in the air, foremost among them the dual control of the Fleet Air Arm by the Admiralty and Air Ministry. Whereas the Imperial Navy had always had complete control of its air force (it had rejected an Army proposal in 1936 to amalgamate the two air forces), in 1918 the Royal Navy had lost control of its Air Arm and henceforth had to rely on the RAF to provide aircraft, all maintenance personnel, and a portion (eventually 30 per cent) of the flying personnel, the remainder being naval but trained by the RAF—hence the name Fleet Air Arm of the RAF. The arrangement was totally unsatisfactory for the FAA, which inevitably came second to the RAF in priority for resources, and one result—there were others—was that its aircraft were poor both in quality and quantity. Contributing to this disaster was the view of the Air Ministry that aircraft operating from carriers were bound to be greatly inferior to shore-based aircraft in performance. This was entirely disproved by both the Americans and the Japanese. Moreover, the Air Ministry estimate of the number of aircraft that could be operated from a carrier was much too pessimistic, as compared to those of

---

men were sent there for basic training before undergoing flight training at Kasumigaura—he was only one of the 70 of the more than 1,500 applicants who had been accepted. When he completed the ten-month course, there were only 25 survivors in his class. No wonder. The training programme included such requirements as swimming under water for at least 50 metres, and remaining below surface for at least 90 seconds. See Saburō Sakai, *Samurai!* (New York, 1957), pp. 32–5, for the rigours of the training course.

[25] These figures are from Captain Genda Minoru's interrogation, 28–9 Nov. 1945, USSBS (Pacific), *Interrogations*, No. 479. *Senshi sōsho*, xcv, Table iii, gives the number of pilots in January 1942 as 3,615. A few RN figures may be instructive. In December 1941 the Navy had (officer and rating pilots) 1,210 trained pilots and 1,324 pilots under training. There were about 560 pilots with squadrons, of whom 279 were with carrier squadrons. Naval Historical Branch figures, 16 Nov. 1977.

other navies. It was an estimate which had its roots in a desire to play down the role of seaborne aircraft altogether, in favour of concentrating everything on building up an effective fighter defence of Great Britain and a strategic bomber force which would be aimed at breaking the enemy's endurance without the necessary intervention of ground forces. There were, of course, strong arguments in favour of these priorities, but they had unfortunate repercussions on the Fleet Air Arm.

In July 1937 full control of the Fleet Air Arm—all ship-borne (but not shore-based) aircraft and their crews—was restored to the Navy, but when the war started in 1939, it was caught halfway through the change-over. As practical consequences, the speed, range, and combat capability of RN naval aircraft were surpassed by those of the IJN. There was a dearth of trained men (the limited pre-war career prospects in naval air was an important factor) as well as of efficient machines when the war began in Europe. The carriers were for the most part obsolete, although replacements had been laid down, and new aircraft designs were only on the drawing board. Moreover, 'the bomb-sight was so poor', remarks a navy flyer writing in 1978, 'that it made high bombing an art rather than a science.' Short of some individually eye-catching episodes, the FAA contributed little to the early part of the European War. In fact, it was not until the arrival of the *Illustrious* in the Mediterranean in September 1940 that the FAA made any noticeable impact on sea warfare. This brand-new ship, with modern equipment such as radar, though still with outdated aircraft, changed the outlook of the Navy to the Fleet Air Arm. The successful attack on the Italian ships in Taranto harbour added to the Navy's understanding of this new weapon. But the Fleet Air Arm had a way to go in December 1941, especially as regards aircraft. Although the IJN was well ahead of the RN in air operations in 1941, being materially superior both in aircraft and in aircraft carriers, there was nothing lacking in the RN in the *quality* of personnel in morale (which was no doubt matched by the more fanatical spirit among the Japanese), and in its training. For instance, the carrier *Eagle*, which was on the Far East Station from May 1937 to August 1939, achieved quite a lot. All air crew by mid-1938 were proficient in night flying and landing on the ship at night under fully dark conditions.[26]

[26] There are other reasons for the backwardness of RN air as compared with American
(*continued*)

2. 'FIGHT THE ENEMY ON SIGHT'

The tactical tradition of the Imperial Navy was an offensive one. This was derived in part from medieval experience and precepts;[27] in part from Tōgō and his success in the Tsushima Straits; and in part from the British naval tradition and experience. The principle of *kenteki hissen*—'fight the enemy on sight'—was inculcated almost from the first day at the Naval Academy and the Naval War College. This was the Royal Navy tradition as understood by the Japanese and exemplified, for example, by Nelson, by Cradock at Coronel, and by Jellicoe and Beatty at Jutland. *Kenteki hissen*, in General Genda's words, 'formed the basis for the tactical bible of the Imperial Navy'.

Closely related to *kenteki hissen* was the concept of the decisive battle between the main fleets. This principle was modified after the Washington Conference and Japan's acceptance of an inferior ratio in capital ships. Pre-war manœuvres generally demonstrated that in fleets of similar composition superior numbers gained the victory. Accordingly, Japan's basic strategy called for the attrition of a superior battle fleet, viz. the US Fleet, before risking a decisive battle. In more specific terms, the Navy would hold a perimeter and make the enemy fleet come to it, and during this expected enemy advance to the western Pacific, would whittle down its fleet to something approaching parity for the decisive battle in waters near the Japanese homeland.[28] The 'quality' of the Imperial Navy was then expected to assert itself.

I will not elaborate on the strategy and tactics of a fight with the US Fleet; they are not part of my study. But I must stress that attritional tactics were regarded as equally applicable to a meeting with the Royal Navy in Eastern waters, if it unexpectedly turned up in force. The 'diminution operations' would consist of surprise attacks by submarines, air attacks by land and carrier-based

---

and Japanese navies than have been suggested here. For the full story see Geoffrey Till, *Air Power and the Royal Navy, 1914–1945* (London, 1979), especially pp. 187–201. One factor was 'The tendency to underrate the performance and the potential of air power at sea, and in consequence to deny it the resources which it needed . . .'

[27] See Arthur Marder, 'From Jimmu Tennō to Perry: Sea Power in Early Japanese History', *American Historical Review*, li, 1 (Oct. 1945), 1–34.

[28] The anticipated theatre for the decisive battle was moved eastward in the 1930s, as the range of warships and aircraft increased, until by 1940 it was placed at the Eastern Carolines/Marshalls.

aircraft, and night torpedo attacks by light craft—cruisers and especially destroyers. The development of the long-range oxygen torpedo in the 1930s opened up exciting possibilities for attritional tactics. Pre-war destroyer training stressed night attacks at high speed, firing torpedoes at battleships, using them only, not the guns, and closing to 3,000–2,000 metres (3,300–2,200 yards).[29]

There was nothing new about attritional tactics. The founder of modern Japanese naval doctrine, Vice-Admiral Akiyama Saneyuki, who was on Tōgō's staff in the Russo–Japanese War, drew up a plan before Tsushima for night destroyer and torpedo-boat attacks which would precede a general fleet action. What was new was the intensity with which the Combined Fleet practiced night-action tactics in the inter-war period. A high level of proficiency in this field was one of the most important of its training targets each year. There was, as has been noted, grave material and human costs involved in the hard and unremitting training in all conditions. The navy persisted because of the deep conviction that proficiency in night action was the only way to win battles against a fleet superior in number of capital ships. Until around 1929, however, it was Combined Fleet policy to evade night actions by the battle fleet with a large force, except for unexpected developments, because complete control and concerted action would be extremely difficult. The battle fleet would leave a night action to the light craft, including cruisers, and resume engagement with the enemy fleet at dawn of the following morning. But by the mid-1930s, with the development of the torpedo, the increasing size of destroyers and their higher speed, excellent seaworthiness, and longer radius of action, and the development of the reconnaissance and offensive capability of naval air power, the doctrine had emerged that the whole Fleet should seek a decisive battle at night when visibility was good. The Navy had great confidence in its night-action capability. This skill brought results in some of the early wartime actions, as at Savo Island against the Americans.

Tactical thought focused on a decisive daylight gunnery duel on parallel lines between the two main fleets—another Tsushima or Jutland—which would follow the 'diminution operations'. The two

---

[29] Standard orders to close within 500 metres (550 yards) before releasing the oxygen torpedoes were not taken seriously. In actual battle the average distance for firing torpedoes was perhaps 4,000–5,000 metres (4,400–5,500 yards), at which distance enemy torpedoes were still outranged.

fleets would bang away at each other, and the war would be finished quickly with this decisive action. An important concept in this duel was the tactics of outranging. From 1910, when 14·1-inch (36cm) artillery, the largest in the world at the time, was adopted for the battle cruiser (later, battleship) *Kongō*, the idea of outranging was stressed not only for the primary armament of surface ships, but for aircraft and torpedoes as well. The 15·75-inch (40cm) guns mounted in the two Nagato-class battleships (completed in 1920–1) were the largest anywhere and gave the Imperial Navy confidence to continue with the development of huge guns. It culminated in the 18·1-inch (46cm) of the Yamatos. In 1938 opening salvoes were fired at 37,800 yards. In 1939 the ranging began at 43,700 yards, and indirect fire at 35,000 yards was conducted against targets, using observation planes, and producing a 12 per cent hitting average. These results generated strong confidence in gunnery combat beyond 35,000 yards. Around June 1939 Combined Fleet Headquarters held the belief that 'the key to victory for our Navy lay in taking advantage of the difference in firing range *vis-à-vis* the enemy main force, and inflicting a heavy blow on the enemy before he opened fire, thus deciding the issue of victory or defeat by upsetting the equilibrium in the battle situation [in our favour]. In order to realize the full power of our gunnery in all sorts of battle situations, it is necessary to use aircraft observation to the utmost'.[30] During this artillery duel, submarines, cruisers, and destroyers would deliver their torpedo attacks against the enemy's capital ships, and aircraft carriers would go into action.[31]

Commander Chihaya makes the point that the concept of the decisive battle was characteristically Japanese—that, as a people, they like gay jobs in which there is much 'show and thrill'. 'The leaders of the Navy had imagined "One Big Battle", further than which they could not think.' They believed that offence was the best defence, and, consequently, little attention was paid to defence

[30] *Senshi sōsho*, xci. 406.

[31] At first the main force of the enemy was considered the primary target of air attacks. With the reinforcement of US carrier strength, however, and the remarkable progress in offensive air tactics (improvement in the bombing and torpedoing capabilities of aircraft), the primary target of Japanese naval aircraft was changed to the enemy carriers from about 1936. The idea, which gathered strength, was to check the offensive threat of the enemy's carriers by launching air attacks (torpedoes and bombs) on them, and then, the control of the skies having been won, the carriers would join the fleet for the decisive action with the enemy's battle fleet.

per se. This neglect found expression in the lack of understanding of an indifference to the protection of vital sea communications. This was considered a secondary problem, and so convoy was slighted until the latter part of the war. The maritime escort mission was allocated to the naval stations: Yokosuka, Kure, Sasebo, and Maizuru were the principal ones.

In these naval stations, from high ranking admirals down to a green seaman, a notion was firmly seated that the major duty of the stations was to offer every possible service and accommodation to the Combined Fleet. The importance these stations attached to the protection of shipping may well be judged by the fact that the duty was attended [to] rather halfheartedly in the station headquarters. For instance, in the headquarters of the Yososuka Naval Station, whose area of responsibility included the sea lanes along almost the entire eastern and southern coast of Honshu (600 miles) and that from Tokyo Bay down to Iwo Jima (700 miles), there was only one officer who attended [to] shipping protection. The same was true with the other naval stations.[32]

At the outbreak of war there was no unit or force solely assigned to escort merchant vessels. This mission was entrusted to the forces engaged in sea patrol: 16 old destroyers, 12 torpedo-boats, 19 minesweepers, 4 coast-defence defence ships, and 201 aircraft, *but these ships and aircraft could be called upon for other duties as required.*

Equally inefficient was the central organization for shipping protection. The responsible section (it was one of its dozen jobs), the 2nd Section of the 1st (Operations) Division of the *Gunreibu*, comprised a chief (captain) and a mere seven members (commanders and lieutenant-commanders), *of whom only one was assigned to shipping protection.* He was Commander Nakamura Takeo, who took over that assignment on 17 November 1941. Later, he was replaced by Lieutenant-Commander Sogawa Kiyoshi, who, with the increasing pressures of the job, was from time to time assisted by a colleague whose primary responsibility was elsewhere. It was not until the end of 1943 that an efficient shipping protection organization came into being.

In view of the lessons of the First World War, in which Britain was at one point in 1917 almost compelled to surrender because of

---

[32] Captain Atsushi Ōi, 'Why Japan's Anti-Submarine Warfare Failed', *United States Naval Institute Proceedings*, lxxviii, 6 (June 1952), 589.

shipping losses inflicted by German submarines, the neglect of shipping protection by Japanese naval strategists, whose country depended as heavily on keeping vital sea communications open as did Britain, sounds almost unbelievable. The most immediate and direct reason for the cursory attention paid to shipping protection (indeed, for the utter lack of interest in the subject outside the Naval War College, and even there the students were bored with the lectures on A/S warfare in the Royal Navy) was the Navy's total emphasis on the decisive fleet action engagement—the Tsushima–Jutland syndrome. But there were other factors. Thus, we have to remember that after the First World War there was a prevalent world-view that unrestricted use of submarines for commerce destruction was criminal. Also, at the London Conference of 1930, Britain and the United States had allowed Japan the same tonnage in submarines as themselves, which attitude may have given Japan's naval authorities the impression that the two Western Powers would not emphasize commerce destruction by means of submarines in time of war. To worsen matters, the Imperial Navy believed that the main purpose of submarine warfare was to attack warships rather than merchant ships. Another reason for the slighting of shipping protection was the influence of the Nazi philosophy of autarky on Japan's expansionists. Under an autarky there is little room for international trade—trade outside one's area of control. This sort of thinking had a tendency, however illusory or self-deceptive it may have been, of assuming that military conquest ensured complete control and exploitation of the resources of that area. In reality, there can be no such thing as a control so complete as to deny intrusion by enemy submarines. Captain Ōi remembers that towards the end of 1940, when he came back to the Navy Ministry from a tour of duty in the South China Sea,

I was told by a naval strategist in the Ministry that the Navy was confident of securing petroleum resources in the Borneo and Sumatra area as soon as war might break out. I presented my counter-argument to the effect that, so far as my own impressions were concerned, acquired through my experience in the South China Sea, it would be next to impossible for us to prevent hostile submarines from entering and haunting the Sea; to occupy the land and produce petroleum there was one thing, but to transport the product from there to Japan in tankers would be quite another. It seemed to me that the Japanese Navy was far from having enough anti-submarine forces to protect the sea lanes.

'FIGHT THE ENEMY ON SIGHT'

His point of view made no impact.[33] Still another factor was twentieth-century war experience. Japanese sea communications not having been seriously threatened by Russia in 1904–5, Germany in 1914–18, or China since 1937, the Imperial Navy was not disposed to regard the problem of shipping protection as an important one. Captain Ōi speculates that racial temperament may have been a factor. 'Compared with the Europeans the Japanese are generally said to be more impetuous and less tenacious. They preferred colourful and offensive fighting to monotonous and defensive warfare. It was only natural that convoy-escorting and A/S warfare were not jobs welcomed by the Japanese naval men'.[34]

Trade warfare was sacrificed to the offensive concept. Whereas the British and Americans loosed their submarines against Japanese shipping, the primary role of the Japanese submarine was, as noted above, in fleet actions. The offensive fetish also resulted in a neglect of air protection for warships: AA armament was grossly inadequate. Another by-product of the Navy's central tactical doctrine that was to cost it dearly in the war was the neglect to think through the problem of wartime shipping requirements. When war broke out, Japan's total tonnage of bottoms over 1,000 tons was nearly 6,000,000 gross tons, including 360,000 gross tons of tankers. Including small vessels over 500 tons and powered sailing craft under 500 tons, the total tonnage figure was 6,630,000. Of this, 2,100,000 tons were reserved for the Army, 1,800,000 for the Navy (to be increased to 2,800,000, at the expense of the Army, after the first four months of the war), and 3,000,000 tons were allocated for civil use. According to the President of the Planning Board, Suzuki, at the Liaison Conference on 5 November 1941, if they could maintain 3,000,000 gross tons of shipping bottoms for civil use, they could secure the supplies called for in the wartime Materials Mobilization Plan of 1941. On the basis of estimated annual shipping losses of between 800,000 and 1,000,000 gross tons, and an annual construction of 600,000 tons, a feasible figure (the normal annual rate was 400,000 tons), the 3,000,000 tons for civil use would be secured. This calculation partly rested on the

---

[33] Letter to the author, 21 June 1976.
[34] 'Why Japan's Anti-Submarine Warfare Failed', pp. 587–8. The same point could be made about the Royal Navy and perhaps all navies. See further, on the reasons for the pre-war neglect of shipping protection, Captain Ōi's *Kaijō goei sanbō no kaisō*, pp. 3–19. He stresses here again (p. 16) the Japanese preference for the colourful and spectacular: for 'fireworks' (*senkōhanabi*).

assumption that the shipping needs of the Services would be reduced once the Southern Operation was finished. This did not turn out to be the case, as the appetites of the Supreme Command grew with the eating. Less tonnage was available for civil use, and the extended lines of communication resulted in greater tonnage losses than had been estimated before the war.

The emphasis on the battleship and on the decisive fleet encounter mesmerized the Royal Navy as well, if not with the same disastrous results. In 1935 Beatty declared that: *'First of all,* the battle fleet needs to be strengthened, for it is the foundation of the whole structure of naval strategy.' Chatfield, Backhouse, and Pound, indeed the Navy generally, anticipated large battle-fleet actions, hence that capital-ship strength was mostly what mattered. Most British admirals, as Liddell Hart observed, 'cherished the battle-fleet with a religious fervour, as an article of belief defying all scientific examination. . . . A battleship had long been to an admiral what a cathedral is to a bishop.' It is fashionable among naval historians (I, too, have been a sinner), and in the Royal Navy itself, to decry the capital-ship fetish. But it is a fact that during most of the inter-war years Japan was Britain's most likely enemy, and such a war would, it was anticipated, probably end with a big fleet action, as indeed it did, for all practical purposes, at Leyte Gulf, though with the US Navy pitted against the Japanese Navy. The Royal Navy's fixation (and the US Navy's, for that matter) on a main-fleet action helps to explain why it (they), too, paid insufficient attention before the Second World War to the teachings of the First as regards the U-boat threat to shipping. It was not until 1937–8 that the protagonists of convoy succeeded in making their point, but it was too late to have the necessary escorts built by the outbreak of the European war; indeed it was 1941 before the system was in full operation.

3. GRAND STRATEGY

It is time that we examined the broad lines of Japanese naval strategy and operational policy, with special reference to Britain. In the first formulation by the Supreme Command of 'National Defence Policy' (*Teikoku Kobubō Hōshin*) in 1907, Russia, the United States, Germany, and France were listed as hypothetical enemies. In 1918, Germany and France were deleted from the list and China was added. That remained the situation until 1936. With the advent of the China Incident and the strained diplomatic relations with Britain as well as with the United States, and the failure of the Second London Conference in 1936, Great Britain was for the first time added to the list of hypothetical enemies in the revision of 1 May 1936. This defence policy statement set forth 'as potential enemies particularly the United States and Russia ... which maintain vast national power and especially strong armed forces and with which Japan is more likely to clash. At the same time we will prepare against China and Great Britain'.[35] When the Emperor questioned the reason for the inclusion of Britain in the revised strategy, Prince Kan'in, the Chief of the Army General Staff, replied: 'We must be prepared for a possible emergency, in view of the acceleration of defence preparations at Hong Kong and Singapore, and the instability of the international situation.'[36]

In the case of the United States, in the 'General principles of Strategy' (*Yōhei Kōryō*)[37] formulated on the same day, 1 May, 'The primary object will be to annihilate the enemy in the Orient, destroy his operational bases, and annihilate the main body of the enemy fleet operating from bases on the American mainland.' As regards Britain, 'The primary object of the operation will be to rout the enemy in the Far East, destroy his operational bases, and annihilate the main enemy fleet that would arrive from its Home waters.'[38] Unlike strategic studies of war with the United States, however, there was no concrete war plan against Britain—only these few general principles. The Navy's thoughts were concentrated on the Pacific, with the US Fleet as its main foe.

The Navy's operational plans for 1937, 1938, 1939, and 1940 (drawn up at the end of the preceding year or the beginning of the year of the plan), so far as Britain was concerned, went only slightly beyond the general principles of 1 May 1936. The main points added up to these: in the first phase the Navy would smash British naval forces in the East by a swift strike, at the same time co-

---

[35] *Senshi sōsho* xci. 316, 318.
[36] Ibid. 325.
[37] The 1st Section of the 1st Division of the *Gunreibu* devised these general principles and also the annual 'operational plan' (*Sakusen Keikaku*). The former preceded and was not identical with the 'operational plan'.
[38] Ibid. 318, 324. By 'operational bases' Singapore and Hong Kong were intended, but were not mentioned by name until the Navy operational plan of 1939, which was prepared early in 1939.

operating with the Army to capture British Borneo and key areas on the east coast of Malaya, also Singapore and Hong Kong. In the second phase, they would annihilate the British main fleet on its arrival in Eastern waters. The 1940 plan stated: 'In case the main force of the enemy fleet tries to hold out, based on India or Australia, we should make efforts to lure the enemy out by diminishing his strength and destroying his line of communications, while securing control of the sea and air north of the Outer South Seas [*Soto Nanyō*], thus strengthening our strategical position.'[39] The 1939 and 1940 plans included submarine attacks on the enemy's shipping in the Indian Ocean, although this was more or less disregarded when war broke out.

As soon as Lieutenant-Commander Ōi Atsushi was put in charge of British Intelligence (8th Section, 3rd Division, of the *Gunreibu*) in December 1937, he was ordered to study Britain's 'traditional strategy—her war philosophy'. He plunged into a study of Corbett, Liddell Hart, *et al.* At the end of 1938 or early in 1939 (the exact date is not known) the first war game ('table-top manoeuvres') that had the Royal Navy as the enemy took place at the Naval War College. Ōi's information on British naval war philosophy was made available to the Commander of the Red Force (British fleet) in this game, Vice-Admiral Takasu Shirō (President of the Naval War College). His staff consisted of *Gunreibu* officers from the 3rd Division. The Commander of the Blue Force (Japanese fleet) was the C-in-C, Combined Fleet, Vice-Admiral Yoshida Zengo, who was assisted by his staff. An umpire directed the war game, in which the two main fleets were supposed to clash. Britain had dispatched her main fleet to the Nicobar Islands in the Bay of Bengal, south of the Andaman Islands. Although the British fleet wanted to wait until the Japanese fleet sailed into the southern part of the South China Sea, so that it could use its Singapore-based aircraft, the umpire forced it to sortie. The game was called before a decision could be reached. Some of the details are interesting. Studies of a war with Britain were so sketchy that some of those participating in the game did not even know the names of the

---

[39] The Navy's operational plan for 1941 against Britain (and China), sanctioned on 17 December 1940, is missing, but from what we know (the Army's operational plan), there were no basic changes. The Navy's operational plans are in *Senshi sōsho*, xci, *passim* , Hattori, *The Complete History of the Greater East Asia War*, i. 315 ff., and Japanese Monograph No. 152, pp. 51 ff.

Andaman and Nicobar Islands, and only Ōi, the operations officer of the British fleet, who had a large-scale map of Nicobar harbour, knew whether it was capable of holding that fleet, so primitive was the Imperial Navy's knowledge at that time. Another facet of the war game was the discussion of what Britain's first line of defence would be, whether Malaysia (i.e. the Malay Archipelago) or Hong Kong.[40]

In the first half of 1941, the urgent need for Indonesian oil, to say nothing of German pressure, caused the Navy to begin to think of Britain, rather than the United States, as the principal enemy. This is brought out in the increasing concern with Singapore: the early capture of the naval base, for which the invasion of Malaya was the prerequisite, and which, it was expected, would lead to the quick disposition of the British Eastern Fleet.[41] When Commander Miyo Kuzunari joined the 1st Section of the Operations Division of the Naval General Staff in November 1939, with, *inter alia*, responsibility for the British war plan, all that his predecessor, Lieutenant-Commander Sasaki Akira, left him was a draft of a plan: two or three pencilled sheets that described the landing of an army on the Malayan coast with naval co-operation. Miyo was too busy with other responsibilities to do much with Sasaki's plan, which remained in skeleton form. When Lieutenant-Commander Prince Kachō, son of the *Gunreibu* Chief, Prince Fushimi, joined Operations at the end of 1940, Miyo handed the plan over to him, with instructions to add detail to it. To assist the Prince, in January 1941 Miyo had seaplanes make a reconnaissance of a part of the north-east Malayan coast, including Kota Bharu, to determine the appropriate places for landing operations. During September three aircraft from Saigon were engaged in photo reconnaissances of the eastern coast of the Malay Peninsula.

The 1941 manœuvres were the first in which the opponent was Great Britain.[42] In the latter part of March and the beginning of

[40] Interview with Captain Ōi, 24 May 1976, *Senshi sōsho*, xci. 389–90.

[41] For what follows in this paragraph I am indebted to Captain Miyo: interview, 17 May 1976, and his letter to me, 31 Jan. 1977.

[42] Naval manœuvres were divided into special grand, grand, and minor manœuvres. Some years had one, other years, another. Each year had one kind of manœuvres. In 1936 the special grand manœuvres featured a big fleet action against the US Navy. In 1937 and 1938 the grand manœuvres were cancelled because of the China Incident. There is no material on the purpose of the minor manœuvres of 1939. The 1940 grand manœuvres consisted of landing operation exercises. In 1941 the joint manœuvres were in lieu of the grand manœuvres that had been scheduled.

April large-scale joint manœuvres were held under the supervision of IGHQ simulating the capture of Singapore, which was to follow the Malay Peninsula landing operation. Japanese Army units departed from the Chusan Archipelago at the mouth of the Yangtze, crossed the East China Sea under air and naval protection, repulsing enemy air and naval attacks *en route*, carried out an opposed landing in northern Kyushu (Karatsu Bay) and then moved some 25 miles south-westward to capture the naval base of Sasebo, which represented Singapore. The Army units were the 5th Division and the 5th Army Air Group; the Navy used the Combined Fleet and the Sasebo Naval District units (small ships). In an exercise that took place in June, an assault force was landed on Hainan Island and moved around its circumference (better than 600 miles, or the approximate distance from the projected landing sites on the Kra Isthmus of southern Thailand to Singapore) to simulate an advance on the British naval base.

The annual operational plans prepared by the Naval General Staff prior to 1940 were drawn up individually for the United States, the Soviet Union, Great Britain, and China, with no provision being made for a war against two or more adversaries. But the problem came to the fore of whether the United States and Britain could be considered separately. When as a result of the sudden change in the European war in the spring of 1940 the idea of expansion to the south came to be considered, it was obviously desirable for Japan to bypass British and American territories and limit the enemy to the Netherlands. It was impossible, however, to isolate the Netherlands from Britain and to take separate measures against her alone: in a war with the Dutch for Indonesia Britain would inevitably be involved, hence war plans had to include Britain. The July 1940 'Outline of the Main Principles for Coping with the Changing World Situation' (above, p. 110) planned so far as possible to limit the enemy to Britain and the Netherlands. There was some hope that this would work—that in the post-Dunkirk period British prospects were so gloomy that the United States would not undertake to support Britain militarily. The subsequent stalemate in the European war caused the idea of the separability of Britain and the US to be given up. When Rear-Admiral Maeda was appointed Chief of the Intelligence Division in October 1940, he 'had a firm conviction that the United States and Britain could not be separated, because they were of one race, the Anglo-Saxon, and my conception never changed'.[43] The Army, however, maintained that they *could* be separated, and that if Japan fought Britain, the United States probably would not intervene. The Army wished to avoid war with the US and take on only the British and Dutch in connection with the drive to the south:

> during the period from late 1940 to the spring of 1941 [writes Hattori], discussions on the settlement of the Southern problems were frequently conducted by the Army and Navy Sections [Departments] of the IGHQ. The Navy Section of the IGHQ concluded that it was absolutely impossible to consider the United States and Great Britain separately and emphasized that a military operation against the Philippines was indispensable to the military advance into the Southern Area.
>
> So long as the Navy ... took the stand that it was strategically impossible to consider the United States and Great Britain separately, the Army had to agree with the Navy. Thus from about the spring of 1941, on the assumption that the United States and Great Britain were inseparable, it was generally accepted that the employment of military action against the Southern Area would mean the commencement of hostilities against the United States, and the persons in charge of operations formulated the plan for occupying the Philippines at the outset of war.... Therefore, in the 'Outline plan ...' decided at the Imperial Conference on 6 September [1941], there was no particular argument regarding the United States, Great Britain and the Netherlands as one bloc.[44]

Already, in June 1941, the Operations Division of the Naval General Staff had begin to draft a plan for simultaneous operations against the ABD Powers.

The discussion of the problem resumed after the formation of the Tōjō Government in October. The conclusion was the same: it was impossible to open hostilities only with the Netherlands or the Netherlands and Britain. There were political and operational reasons for this basic strategical premiss. It was believed that an ABD mutual defence treaty almost certainly existed, to take effect if Japan advanced southward; that in such an eventuality Britain would at once take up arms against Japan if she invaded the Dutch East Indies, and would immediately seek, and receive (not necessarily right away), military aid from the US. That Power considered South-east Asia as within her sphere of influence—she needed its rubber and tin—and, moreover, the Japanese advance

---

[43] Maeda Interview, 19 June 1962, Bōeichō Senshibu Archives.
[44] *The Complete History of the Greater East Asia War*, i. 252–3.

would threaten the Philippines. Also, the US would lose her right to a voice in regard to the China Incident, if she stood apart now. From the operational standpoint, it was considered impossible to conduct the operation against Indonesia without at the same time attacking Britain and the United States, because such an operation would expose the attacking forces to a flanking attack from Singapore, Hong Kong, and the Philippines. Given the existing Anglo-American numerical superiority in ships, and in order not to give these Powers time to strengthen further their war preparations, it was imperative to launch an effective surprise, or forestalling, attack in the initial stage of the war. Finalily, the Japanese could not establish a strong strategic position without occupying Malaya and the Philippines.[45] The upshot is that when the Services and the politicians, above all the Navy, mentioned the United States in any discussion of strategy and operational plans, in the latter part of 1941, that ordinarily did not preclude Britain and the Netherlands.

There was during 1941 an inter-Service clash over the sequence of operations in the south. The Army plan was to attack Malaya first and then reach the Netherlands East Indies and the Philippines from there. If the attack on Malaya were put off, the Army argued, it would give the British time to strengthen their defences. This would render the Japanese attack, when it came, more difficult and would tie down forces for a long time. This operational idea was also in tune with the Army's idea that the US and Britain were separable, i.e. that bypassing the Philippines would delay US participation in the war (as the Germans had always asserted it would). The Navy insisted on attacking the Philippines first and then extending operations to the Netherlands East Indies and Malaya from there. Its reasoning was that if Japan attacked Malaya and the East Indies, the US would inevitably go to war. If the Philippines were initially left alone, the US would hasten a buildup of strength there, which would lead to a difficult campaign when the Japanese attacked the Philippines. Moreover, given the position of the Philippines, astride Japan's sea lanes to the Southern Area, it was obvious that the US Navy and Air Force in the Philippines would try to sever these communications. This would endanger the Southern operations. It was, therefore, imperative to capture the

[45] Ibid. 253–4.

Philippines at the outset of the war. There was no disagreement on the need to capture the Philippines, which would compel US forces to operate from remote bases, remove the threat to maritime communications between the homeland and the South, and provide Japan with an 'intermediate stepping stone' for carrying out operations against the whole Southern Area.

Eventually, in the middle of August, agreement was reached that the pre-emptive operations against the Philippines and Malaya would be commenced simultaneously. In the final agreement between the Army and Navy in November, the capture of Malaya (including Singapore), as well as Thailand to secure a land base for operations against Malaya—Hong Kong and British Borneo would be seized at the same time—and the Philippines would initiate hostilities in the first phase of the basic plan: the seizure of the Southern Area. During the early stages, Dutch Borneo, the Celebes, Sumatra, the Moluccas, and Timor would be occupied. Operations against Burma would be carried out at the appropriate time to cut off the enemy supply route to China. The plan was then to combine all forces for an invasion of Java, the heart of the Netherlands East Indies. The first phase, which included the attack on the US Pacific Fleet at Pearl Harbor, amounted to this: the capture, through sudden and simultaneous attacks, initially against four strategic points, Hawaii, the Philippines, Malaya, and Hong Kong, a wide area extending some 2,000 miles from north to south and from east to west. It was a large-scale operation without historical precedent. The Supreme Command estimated that the Southern Area would be captured within five months. As part of the first phase, they would seize strategic areas required for the establishment of a defensive perimeter to protect the Japanese homeland and the Southern Resources Area. The perimeter to be established was along the line which joined the Kuriles, Wake Island, the Marshalls and Gilberts, the Bismarck Archipelago, New Guinea, Timor, Java, Sumatra, Malaya, and Burma. In the second phase they would consolidate and strengthen this defensive perimeter. In the third phase the Japanese Forces would intercept and destroy any threat to the defensive perimeter or to vital areas within it. Japan would now be secure and self-sufficient and in a position to destroy the Anglo-American will to continue the war. There were, incidentally, no operational plans to invade Australia and New Zealand.

With the Army and Navy in broad agreement by the end of

August on operational plans for the Southern Area, the Navy set to work on the details of its plan. By early September the Navy Department of IGHQ had a draft ready. It was studied in table-top manœuvres on a somewhat larger scale than usual at the Naval War College from 10 to 13 September, under the direction of Admiral Yamamoto and with the participation of the commanders and staff officers of the Combined Fleet, Naval General Staff officers, and a few Navy Ministry staff members. The two operations were studied—one directed at the Southern Area, the other at Hawaii. Hypothetical attacks against the strategically important American, British, and Dutch areas in the Far East were studied in more detail than in previous years. It was judged by Combined Fleet Headquarters that Admiral Kondō's Southern Force (including land-based naval air in French Indo-China) could deal with the British surface forces in the East. Not long after the table-top manœuvres, however, Yamamoto attached the battleships *Kongō* and *Haruna* to the Southern Force to cope with possible strengthening of the British forces. The special problem of the table-top manœuvres was the study in the utmost secrecy of a surprise attack on Hawaii which was made on the last day by a small number of officers.[46] The Army held its own war games in the first five days of October, focusing on Southern Area invasion operations. In agreement with the Army, the naval operational plan was

---

[46] The Hawaiian operation not being part of our story, it may suffice to note its essentials. On 23 January 1941 Yamamoto had written to Admiral Koga: 'If the Government and IGHQ order me as Commander-in-Chief, Combined Fleet, then I will have to commence hostilities, much against my will.' Koga, 'Gohō roku'. It was in that month that Yamamoto conceived the pre-emptive aircraft-carrier strike against the US Pacific Fleet. He saw a good precedent in 1904, when, simultaneously with the declaration of war gainst Russia, the Navy attacked the main Russian Fleet at Port Arthur. Yamamoto's letter to Oikawa, 7 Jan. 1941, Bōeichō Senshibu Archives. See further, Professor Jun Tsunoda and Admiral Kazutomi Uchida, 'The Pearl Harbor Attack: Admiral Yamamoto's Fundamental Concept', *Naval War College Review*, xxxi, 2 (Fall 1978), 83–8. The operation was ostensibly planned and executed as a way of ensuring the success of the Southern operations by inflicting enough damage on the US Pacific Fleet to keep it on the defensive while the Army and Navy carried out the Southern invasions. It is believed, however (at least by the Official Historian), that Yamamoto regarded the basic premiss of the war plans—that Japan could endure a long drawn-out war by capturing the area containing the important resources—as unrealistic, and that he was actually thinking of the Hawaiian operation as the main operation: 'as a means of obtaining conditions for a short war'. *Senshi sōsho*, xci. 552. That is, a crippling of the main US fleet, combined with successful operations in the South and South-west Pacific, might induce the United States to settle for a negotiated peace that would secure some, possibly most, of Japan's gains. The details of the attack had been worked out by September.

(*continued*)

informally adopted on 20 October. The Chiefs of Staff explained their plans in the form of war games in the presence of the Emperor at IGHQ on 15 November.

The feeling in the Combined Fleet as well as in the Navy Ministry and Naval General Staff was that little help could be expected from the German Navy, still less from the Italian. Japan would have to win—or lose—the war by herself. The Tripartite Alliance had scarcely been implemented beyond the technical and political levels. Indeed, as Chapman brings out, 'In spite of, and partly also because of, pre-war and wartime American suspicions of an Axis plan of grand strategy, no joint planning was ever attempted in the vital year, 1941.'[47] There was also a decline in Japanese naval co-operation with the Germans in this period, as, for example, in the matter of naval intelligence. The Imperial Navy had been very co-operative in this field between July 1940 and March 1941, but thereafter it provided the Germans with less and less intelligence about enemy and neutral shipping movements in the Far East. German raiders were finding it more difficult to obtain supplies in Japan, and the Japanese were dragging their feet regarding the provision of such items as tungsten, wolfram ore, and copra. The pressure of the United States and Britain on Japan during 1941 is an important reason for the unco-operative attitude of the Imperial naval authorities, who were 'anxious to avoid creating the impression of active collusion with the European Axis at a time when it was striving with all its might to preserve tolerable relations with the United States'.[48]

There was a serious discussion of the plan with the Naval General Staff on 24 September, when the latter learned of Yamamoto's determination to have his plan accepted. A section of the *Gunreibu*, including Nagano himself as well as Fukudome and Tomioka, did not accept the plan: it was for them too much of a gamble—indeed, reckless. When on 19 October Yamamoto threatened to resign as C-in-C, Combined Fleet, if the plan were dropped, Nagano finally sanctioned it, reluctantly, the next day. The Pearl Harbor strike was regarded as only a temporary departure from the 'decisive battle' strategy. That would come later, after the Combined Fleet had been restored to full strength by the transfer of the bulk of the units in the Southern Area after the successful operations there. The Imperial Navy would lure the US fleet across the Pacific to relieve the Philippines and would catch it *en route* and destroy it in a 'decisive battle of interception'. Nobody, not even Yamamoto, expected the Pearl Harbor operation to achieve anything like the success it did, and the Navy was prepared to suffer heavy losses.

[47] 'German and Japanese Military Co-operation, 1930–1945', p. 485.
[48] Ibid. 450.

XII

Images

A layman reading this [my] paper would, I think, come to the conclusion that the I.J.N. is of the 2nd class, and I think that that is so . . .
    CAPTAIN J. G. P. VIVIAN (Naval Attaché, Tokyo), February 1935.

We were confident that the Royal Navy's Far Eastern Fleet (as of D-Day) could be annihilated without much difficulty . . .
    REAR-ADMIRAL CHŪDŌ KAN'EI (Chief, British Section, Intelligence Division, 1941-3) to the author, 13 July 1979.

1. THE IMPERIAL NAVY LOOKS AT THE ROYAL NAVY

THE Imperial Navy (the Army was no different) tended to underrate the importance of military intelligence. Its Intelligence Division was weak before and during the war. There were only 29 officers in the whole 3rd Division when war came. (NID had 161 officers at this time.) The entire Combined Fleet then had one Intelligence officer. There was no special training for intelligence work, whether at the Naval Academy, the Naval War College, or anywhere else in the Navy. At the War College the students received a general statement on intelligence and some uses to which it might be put. Often the officers assigned to intelligence work were men of rather delicate health, although intelligence officers for the Naval General Staff were chosen for their sharpness of mind and because they had gone through the Naval War College. At lower levels—that is, below the *Gunreibu* and Combined Fleet, in flotillas and smaller fleets—intelligence duties were assigned mainly to communications officers. 'Our intelligence organization was a sparse, scanty affair,' Captain Itō Taisuke, of the Personnel Bureau of the Navy Ministry, reflected after the war.

One important reason for this state of affairs, though perhaps more applicable to the Army, is cited by an official post-war US

Navy study: 'Certain characteristics of the Japanese military mentality tended to nullify the work of intelligence. Corrupted by their own propaganda, military planners, in line with reiterated statements of divinely bestowed Japanese invincibility, overemphasized the importance of the attack at the expense of the preparatory steps necessary for its most effective execution. Being embroiled in internal political administration, suppressing information and bending it to serve political ends became second nature to Japanese militarists, and they became blind to objective intelligence.'[1]

The principal function of the Intelligence Division was the collection and analysis of information, which was then sent to the proper authorities in the Operations Division. Its record here, in peace and war, was spotty. The Chief of the British Section of the Intelligence Division in 1939–41 comments sadly: 'The 3rd Division exercised very little influence on other divisions and bureaux in the Naval General Staff and the Navy Ministry. Although everybody recognized the importance of military intelligence, quite often the valuable intelligence that we offered was treated in a perfunctory way or even ignored.'[2] Tomioka, Chief of the 1st Section of Operations (October 1940–January 1943), then Chief of the 1st Division, never believed what the Intelligence Division sent him on the national power of the United States, whether before or during the war. Indeed, he always paid little attention to intelligence.

The Intelligence Division made use of a vast world-wide network of 'literally thousands of enthusiastic amateur spies', in addition to the reports of naval attachés and other official representatives abroad. In the case of London, the naval attaché reports were not particularly valuable, since the material sent on, especially after

---

[1] United States Strategic Bombing Survey (Pacific), G–2 Division, 'Japanese Military and Naval Intelligence Division' (US National Archives), p. 3.

[2] Rear-Admiral Horiuchi's memorandum for the author, Nov. 1978. One instance he cites is of an Assistant Naval Attaché to Britain who returned to Tokyo, prior to reassignment, and gave a talk to the leading members of the *Gunreibu* and the Navy Ministry. He spoke about what he had actually seen and experienced, and stressed that Britain was not suffering from German air raids to anything like the degree which the Nazis were extravagantly publicizing. This officer was branded thereafter as having been 'brainwashed by the John Bulls'. Admiral Chūdo likewise asserts that 'the information collected and analyzed by the 8th Section on the United Kingdom and the Royal Navy was not treated as significant, or was even disregarded in some cases by the war-planners and policy-makers, while the information furnished by our Attaché in Germany was treated as more valuable and worthwhile'. Letter to the author, 13 July 1979.

war broke out in Europe, was chiefly from BBC broadcasts, cuttings from newspapers and periodicals, and information supplied by Japanese business firms with offices in the United Kingdom. Unlike the situation in the United States, where the Intelligence Division had secret agents, in Britain, apparently, there was none.[3] There were quite a number in Hong Kong and Singapore—retired naval officers serving in the Consulate General but they were not very valuable. The Ship Construction Division of the Naval Technical Department had better luck in procuring technical information.

Once the English alliance was terminated, the details of British warship designs were no longer available to the Imperial Navy.[4] The only useful information then came from representatives (constructor commanders and lieutenant-commanders) of the Ship Construction Division stationed in New York, London, and Berlin. There was also a young Imperial Navy design officer studying at the École de Genie Maritime in Paris who sent reports home. Most of the technical information on British naval vessels was obtained through these officers. They collected cuttings from the newspapers and such technical publications as the *Proceedings* of the Institute of Naval Architects, and they took advantage of festive occasions, or of an invitation, to visit ships and gather first-hand technical information. All this information went to the Ship Construction Division. In addition, new British warships (except capital ships) usually were attached to the China Station. They called on Japanese ports until 1936 (above, p. 24), on which occasions the Imperial

[3] On the naval attachés in London and the secret agents in Britain, I have relied on Rear-Admiral Horiuchi's memorandum of Nov. 1978, Rear-Admiral Chūdō's letter of 13 July 1979, and interviews with Captain Ōi Atsushi, 24 May 1976, and Vice-Admiral Yamamoto Masuhiko (a language officer and student at the Royal Technical College, Glasgow, 1939–40), 1 June 1976. The first three officers were, successively, Head of the British Section of Naval Intelligence, 1937–9, 1939–41, and 1941–3. Admirals Chūdō and Horiuchi flatly state that secret agents were never employed—in the words of the former, 'because our Naval Attaché in London had recognized that the use of this kind of agent would be detrimental to relations between the two countries'. Thus, on his arrival in England, in the summer of 1936, Lieutenant-Commander Yamamoto was told by the Naval Attaché, Captain Yano, not to visit naval ports or British warships, or do anything that might suggest to the British that he was engaged in espionage, and thereby stir up more anti-Japanese feeling. Captain Kondō, who succeeded Yano in 1939, continued this policy. After the signing of the Tripartite Pact, the British regarded Japan as their overt antagonist and, accordingly, severely restricted the activities of the Naval Attaché.

[4] Much of the information in this paragraph and the following three, as well as the material on the *Regulus*, etc. below, is derived from an interview with the naval historian and IJN Technical Branch officer, Lieutenant-Commander Fukui Shizuo, 22 June 1976, and subsequent correspondence with him.

Navy did 'intensive research' (Commander Fukui) on them, taking photographs, etc. One specific *coup* was the acquisition through secret agents of the detailed plans for the aircraft carrier *Hermes*, which were in Japanese hands before she was even laid down. The Imperial Navy also had detailed information on the 10,000-ton County-class cruisers (1924–7 programmes, completed in 1928–31) and the Leander class (1929–31, 1933–6). In 1935 the Ship Construction Division produced the last edition of a reference work which had been revised several times since the First World War, after sufficient new information had been collected. It was entitled 'Tendencies in Foreign Warship Construction.' Volume iii dealt with British capital ships and consisted of blueprints for each: a general arrangement plan and a protection plan. Red indicated a new installation; yellow, the removal of an installation. These blueprints were full of yellow and red markings. Although I have been unable to determine the accuracy of these plans, they do suggest that Japanese naval intelligence had some success in acquiring information on British warships. In the immediate pre-war years, however, the Imperial Navy was ignorant of the details of the latest RN designs, and had therefore no basis for evaluating the latest warships. Nor was there at that time much technical information on the modernized US battleships. The *Yamato* and *Musashi*, accordingly, were designed independently of Western developments. What was known about Britain's latest battleships was a cause of deep concern.

Beginning in late 1940, the Royal Navy fitted AA rocket launchers: the 3-inch UP (unrotated projectile = rocket) 20-barrelled launcher, and these were highly regarded by IJN ordnance officers and line officers when they learned about them. How this came about is a curious tale. When the *King George V* arrived in the United States on 23 January 1941, carrying the new Ambassador, Lord Halifax, and the British delegates to the Washington Staff talks, US civil aircraft flew over her as she steamed up Chesapeake Bay and took many excellent photographs. Some of these were published in *Life* magazine on 3 February 1941. When this issue reached Japan a month later, the Navy learned about the new AA guns and were astonished because they were so unusual. The Imperial Navy had only AA guns and machine-guns. The former were single and twin Vickers AA guns imported from Britain. They did not perform well in tests, and from about 1934 the Navy began to import 25mm and 30mm French Hotchkiss machine-guns, with which the Navy entered the war. The Japanese did not learn that the Royal Navy had replaced the rocket launchers in 1941 with four- and eight-barrelled Vickers pom-poms.[5] (The Japanese developed AA rockets by mid-1944: 12cm 28- to 30-barrelled AA rocket launchers, which worked well in the Philippines actions.) The Imperial Navy was very worried about the Royal Navy's AA guns, not aware of the change and judging the AA rocket-launched guns to be much superior to ordinary AA guns because of their longer range.

Another and still greater cause of concern was British radar. The Imperial Navy had evolved a rudimentary form of radar in 1940, but it was not as good as the British and the Japanese knew it. The photographs in *Life* gave them an inkling of what the Royal Navy had achieved in the field of detection. Clearly visible were the main gunnery radar sets fitted on top of the director, and the main surface and air warning radar sets, which were fitted on top of the control tower. In fact, the surface forces, particularly the light forces, the cruisers and destroyers, though proud of their performance in night operations, were apprehensive that radar might give the British an important advantage, above all, in a night action. Sometime in the last pre-war months Commander Fukui heard an electronics expert, who had been a member of a technical mission sent to Germany early in 1941, 'speak in earnest of the fearful and tremendous effectiveness of British radar'.

Another method of detection where there was much concern was British asdic. The Imperial Navy had knowledge of this development as long ago as 1926, and indeed began to manufacture similar equipment from 1933. However, though the Japanese version improved gradually, it was regarded as inferior to the British system.

Despite these three areas of concern, the Intelligence Division of the *Gunreibu*, which was responsible for assessing the Royal Navy,

---

[5] The UP was not a success. It was removed from all capital ships shortly after the loss of the battle cruiser *Hood* in the *Bismarck* action on 24 May 1941, as it was believed that ready-use UP rounds had been the main fuel for the extensive upper-deck fire (started by a salvo from the *Bismarck* or possibly from the 8-inch cruiser *Prinz Eugen*) before she took the fatal 15-inch hit. In any case, the UP was an interim weapon, to tide the Navy over until deliveries of 20mm Oerlikon and 40mm Bofors could be made in sufficient quantities. The multiple 2-pounder (quadruple or octuple) pom-pom, a Vickers weapon of 40mm calibre, was installed on battleship turret tops in place of the UP launchers.

did not make an extensive or intensive study of the Royal Navy as a possible foe—only of the American Navy. But the Imperial Navy had a high opinion of the capabilities of the British Navy. There was, indeed, a tremendous respect for it: its fighting spirit and tradition of victory, and the sense of duty inculcated in the officers. Vice-Admiral Ozawa Jisaburō, perhaps Japan's leading fighting admiral in the Pacific War, told his staff that the Royal Navy would be a formidable enemy because of its tradition of fighting an enemy on sight.[6]

The Japanese, nevertheless, had confidence in their ability to deal with the Royal Navy. They knew, for example, that the primary armament of their capital ships had a maximum range (38,700–44,600 yards) considerably greater than the British—only the 16-inch guns of the *Nelson* and *Rodney* exceeded 38,000 yards, though merely by 400 yards. Moreover, the Japanese achieved a probability of hits during battle practice (20–25 per cent) that was exceptional. They knew, too, that the older capital ships in the Royal Navy had not been as fully modernized as their own. Again, it was felt that Japanese naval air was superior to the British, especially in comparison to the Royal Navy's performance during the first two years of war, whether in bombing or torpedo work. Japanese naval air officers poohpoohed, for instance, the success of the RN Fleet Air Arm against the Italians at Taranto: 'They were only biplanes and of low speed—Swordfish and the like. Their performance was not outstanding. The British pilots were very brave, but we laughed at their skill.' This opinion was general among IJN airmen and was based on what they knew about air operations in the European war.[7] The Imperial Navy was confident it could destroy the British fleet in a stand-up fight, because of the high level of sea–air integration it had attained.[8] Further, it knew

---

[6] Ozawa made this remark when he got the news that British capital ships were on their way to Singapore. Interview with Captain (General, JMSDF) Sanagi Sadamu, 19 May 1976. Sanagi was then in the Operations Division of the Naval General Staff. Admiral Horiuchi appraised RN officers this way: 'Throughout my naval career, I had deep respect for the quality of the regular-service officers of the Royal Navy, especially for their skill-level and character.' Memorandum for the author, Nov. 1978.

[7] Interview with Commander (Lieutenant-General, JMSDF) Okumiya Masatake, 5 July 1976. His experience was wholly in naval air, as pilot, instructor, and staff officer.

[8] Interview with Captain Sanagi. Captain Ōi informs me that in 1937–9, when he was the *Gunreibu* intelligence officer in charge of the British Commonwealth, the Imperial Navy had a low estimate of British naval aviation. The main reason was that 'the Fleet Air Arm was

(*continued*)

well enough that, with the outbreak of the European war, the Royal Navy would be kept busy fighting the Axis in European and Atlantic waters. As Nagano informed the Liaison Conference of 6 September 1941: 'The naval units that Great Britain could send to the Far East would be rather limited because of the current war in Europe.' Probably only a battleship, ten or more cruisers, and a few aircraft, he told the Imperial Conference of 5 November 1941. This was considered the weakest point of the Royal Navy. As Admiral Chūdo has summed up this essential point,

> We were confident that the Royal Navy's Far Eastern Fleet (as of D-Day) could be annihilated without much difficulty in the early part of the initial phase of the war. If the RN could send a powerful reinforcement to Southeast Asia after that, there would be a problem. However we believed that the RN would never be able to do this, because the United Kingdom had to commit all of her naval power against the German and Italian navies in Europe, especially to protect against possible invasion by Germany and the German Navy's destruction of the British lines of communication in the Atlantic.[9]

There was right up until the commencement of hostilities a residue of strong feelings of friendship, respect, and even affection for the Royal Navy in the Imperial Navy—among senior officers, anyway. The Imperial Navy, after all, had been constructed on the example and teaching of the Royal Navy, and with its material assistance. The cadets at Etajima were taught English and learned about British naval history, traditions, and customs.[10] In a special room at the Naval Museum in pre-war years was a lock of Nelson's hair in a glass container embedded in a miniature of the stern of HMS *Victory*. Elsewhere in the Museum were a bust of Nelson (a gift of E. T. Reed, son of the once Chief Constructor of the Royal

---

organized and trained with a less close relationship with the conventional fleet organization than in the Japanese Navy. In other words, relations between airmen and sailors in the British Navy was deemed by us insufficient. The Japanese Navy learned much more from the American Navy than from the British Navy as far as aviation was concerned.' Letter to the author, 20 Jan. 1979.

[9] Letter to the author, 13 July 1979.

[10] Through the First World War all the textbooks were in English. Then, except for English language study, the textbooks were in Japanese. But for years a large number of naval and technical terms were pronounced in English and printed in *katakana* (one of the two Japanese syllabary alphabets), e.g. 'boat davit', 'shaft', and 'quarter-deck'. Gradually, most of these terms were put into Japanese, though many English naval terms continued in use in a Japanized form, and to the end most of the technical terms used by the Japanese warship designers were English.

Navy, Sir Edward Reed) and reproductions of a Nelson portrait and letter, also a photograph of a painting of Nelson making his last signal before Trafalgar. These latter items were originally presented to Admiral of the Fleet Tōgō by Lord Lee of Fareham, the First Lord of the Admiralty, in about 1921, and were later donated to the Museum.[11] There was indeed an emotional tie between the two navies, at least on the Japanese side. An aspect of this was the fond recollections by officers of the Englishmen who had taught at Etajima.

There was, therefore, a special feeling for the Royal Navy which was not entirely dissipated even after the conclusion of the Tripartite Pact in 1940 and the events of 1941. The American Navy was the primary enemy: war with it had been predicted for so long, and there was a stronger, more positive feeling about fighting it, though there was no sentiment of hatred. Yet, however reluctantly for so many of the officers, whether in the Navy Ministry, Naval General Staff, or with the Fleet at sea, and however much they hated the thought, they realized by 1941 that they would have to fight the British as well as the Americans. It was a sad business when December 1941 found them at war with their old teachers, friends, and allies. It affected all ranks. A midshipman in the cruiser *Exeter* recounts this experience after the Battle of the Java Sea in February 1942: 'When we were prisoners of war, we were visited from time to time by senior ratings from the IJN who asked after their friends in the RN whom they had met at Shanghai and other Eastern ports. There seemed to be a general feeling of regret on their side that the RN and IJN had to be enemies.'[12]

2. THE ROYAL NAVY LOOKS AT THE IMPERIAL NAVY

The IJN evaluation of the Royal Navy was a lot closer to the truth than was the Royal Navy's evaluation of the Imperial Navy. In its

---

[11] The lock of hair was stolen after the war, when Etajima was occupied by Australian, New Zealand, and British-officered Indian troops. Today in the same room, at the head of the landing, are reproductions of portraits of Tōgō, Nelson, and John Paul Jones, the Trinity of the old Navy. Nelson was practically worshipped by the old Navy.

[12] Lieutenant-Commander W. F. B. Faulkner's letter to the author, 26 Nov. 1975. Captain Miyo has told me how one reason for the dilatory way in which the Operations Division worked on a war plan against Britain before 1940 was the absence of any feeling of hatred against their old friends and allies. Interview, 17 May 1976. Another concrete instance of
(continued)

assessment of Japanese naval efficiency the Admiralty's Eastern war plan blithely stated (December 1937): 'In discussing the operations of our fleet subsequent to its arrival at Singapore it has been assumed that the Japanese approximate to our own standard in naval warfare. If, as may well be the case, they prove to be lacking in enterprise, skill, resource or fighting qualities, we should be prepared immediately to exploit our advantages in these respects and increase the boldness of our conceptions accordingly.'[13] Chatfield proclaimed that 'the British Navy had every reason to think that they were more efficient [than the IJN] and could win even with inferior forces, as they had often done in the past'.[14] The efficiency of the IJN was assessed at only 80 per cent of the Royal Navy, because, among other factors, its maintenance standards were believed to be below the RN's, especially owing to the lack of training among specialist ratings, such as ordnance artificers.[15]

The mainstream of naval thinking had a superficial view of Britain's potential adversaries in the East. The Japanese were thought to be rotten shipbuilders, very good at copying Western technology but with no technological background of their own. Their capital ships, photographed in *Jane's Fighting Ships*, looked formidable, but with their towering superstructures, and funnels at funny angles, were objects of derision to British seamen. There was speculation on the effects a 14-inch shell might have on their pagoda-like bridge structures. Cruisers and destroyers seemed to be more heavily armed than the British, and to be carrying a heavy torpedo armament. But the Japanese were said to overdo things by cramming too many guns and torpedo tubes into hulls copied from Western shipbuilding techniques. Submarines, an unknown quantity, were feared. Japanese weaknesses were thought to include their lack of radar and asdic, and a possible oil shortage. On the

---

pro-British attitudes were the sentiments in the heavy cruiser *Chōkai* (4th Cruiser Squadron, Combined Fleet) in the latter part of 1941. The officers were, 'generally speaking, rather pro-Britain'. Vice-Admiral Iwamura Seiichi, Chief of the Naval Technical Department when the war started, was very pro-British and pro-American. Commander Fukui's letter, 5 July 1976.

[13] 'Naval War Memorandum (Eastern)', ADM 116/4393.

[14] COS 209th Mtg., 1 June 1937, CAB 53/7. See also Chatfield at CID 348th Mtg., 24 Feb. 1939, CAB 2/8.

[15] e.g. the COS report, DP(P)61, 'Situation in the Far East', 24 June 1939, CAB 16/183A. The British Army and the RAF (their Air and Military Commanders in the Far East, at any rate) underestimated the efficiency of the Imperial Japanese Army and its air force as badly as the RN *vis-à-vis* the IJN. See Kirby, *Singapore: The Chain of Disaster*, pp. 74–5.

other hand, the Japanese would have the advantage of fighting on more or less home ground. There was, in short, little appreciation of the Japanese capability as weapon developers or their total dedication to achieving great efficiency.

The real failure of the Royal Navy (the US Navy as well) was the underestimation of Japanese naval air power and of the high degree the Japanese had achieved in training, efficiency, and ability to sink warships, although there was a continued awareness of the extraordinary expansion and development of the IJN Air Arm. Curiously, it was the Royal Navy that had done so much to encourage and develop Japanese naval air. In April 1921, with the blessings of its own Government, an unofficial mission of 18 RN officers and 12 warrant officers, nearly all of whom had served in the RNAS, arrived in Japan to supervise the construction of a naval air station at Lake Kasumigaura, and to undertake the organization, equipment, and training of the IJN Air Service. The mission was in Japan for three years, though reduced in numbers during the final year. The members held acting IJN rank; the Chief of the mission, Colonel (retired) W. F. Forbes-Sempill, a Wing-Commander in the RNAS before joining the RAF in 1918, was an acting captain, IJN.

The mission was underwhelmed by the prospects for the development of a first-class fleet air arm. Major H. G. Brackley, a member of the mission, wrote to his fiancée: 'It has been tiring and trying work with the little fellows. They are all very inconsistent and show very bad judgement...'[16] Sempill was frankly critical of both officers and their machines in a mid-term lecture at the Navy Ministry in October 1922. However, by the end of his mission he was able to report:

Nerves seem conspicuous by their absence and pilots are ever ready to undertake the most difficult manoeuvres. The average of ability is perhaps higher than we are accustomed to find in the West, but there is probably a smaller percentage of exceptionally brilliant pilots. The cult of *bushidō*, education, and tradition, aim at producing a racial rather than an individual type. It is not surprising, therefore, that Japanese pilots do not always show that instantaneous and instinctive sense of prompt action under entirely unexpected conditions. Given time, however, they will extricate themselves successfully, and no doubt training and long experience will breed the qualities required. Their courage and

---

[16] 28 Feb. 1922, Frida H. Brackley, *Brackley: Memoirs of a Pioneer of Civil Aviation* (Chatham, 1952), p. 132.

determination to carry out orders under any conditions are most noticeable. They have in general no very great interest for mechanical contrivances, which have, of course, only recently been imported into Japan. They do not therefore appreciate so readily the change of note of an engine that is 'missing' or failing in power from some other cause. In England every pilot is trained in this before he starts flying, and his motor-bicycle has generally provided that valuable schooling, in addition to the natural love of all mechanical things which seems to be born in every British boy. His first plaything is usually a mechanical toy, so that his training has started from his very earliest years, whereas the Japanese pilot never comes into contact with any kind of machinery until he has left school, and sometimes even later than this. That such qualities can be greatly developed by training, however, has been proved in practice. The Japanese petty officers and men are excellent in every way, keen and hard-working.[17]

The Japanese proficiency in torpedo-bombing was noted by an officer lent by the RAF (one of two) who spent about six months at Yokosuka in 1930–1 as an air fighting instructor to the Imperial Navy. 'I heard frequent discussions about torpedo bombing and realised they were pretty well trained even then. I reported this many times in my reports to the Air Ministry. I was, of course, never allowed to see them training in torpedo bombing.' His reports, he understood, were always made available to the Admiralty.[18]

All the same, and despite the supply of much better aircraft to the IJN from about 1930 onwards, there were many RN officers who continued to underrate the effectiveness of the Japanese naval air service—its aircraft and the efficiency of its pilots. The Commander of a destroyer division on the China Station in 1936–8 recalls: 'At this time we had a low opinion of Japanese aircraft, not from any superior attitude, but simply from watching their performance with much interest. They seemed to us sluggish and unadventurous. I have always been puzzled about this in view of the puerile opposition. Whether they deliberately held back or thereafter realised their limitations one will never know, and of course it was a very different story three years later.'[19] As late as 1941 the lighthearted assessment of the Navy was that the Japanese naval air

[17] 'The British Aviation Mission in Japan', 21 Jan. 1925, *Transactions and Proceedings of the Japan Society London*, xxii (1924–5), 42–3.

[18] Air Commodore R. W. Chappell's letters to the author, 3, 23 Nov. 1978. The later famous Captain Genda was his 'star pupil'.

[19] Admiral Dick's letter to the author, 9 July 1976.

force was of no higher quality than the Italian. Thus, on 1 May 1941 the Joint Intelligence Committee estimated the operational efficiency of the Japanese Fleet Air Arm as 'not more, but possibly slightly less than that of the Italians'.[20] On the very eve of war Craigie (presumably on the authority of the Naval and Air Attachés) rated the 'technical and flying efficiency' of the Japanese air force (Army and Navy) as 'similar to that of the Italians', though the 'standard of flying is good, morale is high, and air personnel are capable of great feats of self sacrifice'.[21]

There was a commonly held view—'saloon bar speculation', Vice-Admiral Sir Richard Smeeton calls it, rather than official doctrine—that because of their slit eyes—the epicanthic fold of skin extending from the upper eyelid down over the inner corner of the eye—the Japanese fighter pilots could not shoot straight, and Japanese naval officers could not see in the dark for the same reason!

There were a few highly placed RN officers who saw things differently. Thus, Vice-Admiral Sir Geoffrey Layton had, on the whole, a higher opinion of the fighting qualities of the Japanese Navy, deriving from his pre-war experience as C-in-C on the China Station, than did the Admiralty and most senior officers. Admiral Sir Frederic Dreyer, who was the last C-in-C, China, to visit Japan before the outbreak of the Pacific War (four visits in 1933–5), was impressed with what he saw of Japanese naval aircraft and the quality of the torpedoes. In June 1934 he witnessed aircraft flying on and off a carrier, and ranging on a sleeve target at 12,000 yards, all with great proficiency. In July 1935 he was escorted to sea by 150 naval planes 'flying in excellent formation'.[22] Dreyer was struck by the all-round efficiency of the Imperial Navy. In 1939, in retirement, he sent a memorandum to the First Sea Lord whose main point was to give notice of a possible imminent Japanese *coup de main* against the Netherlands East Indies, but in the process urging that they should not take the Japanese Fleet lightly. It was an efficient instrument. In the same paper Dreyer warned 'how resolute the Japanese are in war in planning operations, which are

[20] JIC(41)175, 'Future Strategy of Japan', Annex to COS(41) 159th Mtg., 3 May 1941, CAB 79/11.
[21] 26 Nov. 1941, FO 371/27971.
[22] Admiral Sir Frederic Dreyer, *The Sea Heritage: A Study of Maritime Warfare* (London, 1955), pp. 312, 314, 326.

carried out with stony courage'. He cited the experience of 1904, when Japanese transports sailed from Sasebo on 6 February, twelve hours before the Japanese Ambassador in St. Petersburg demanded his passport. They landed at Chemulpo (Korea) on 8 February. The Japanese fleet sank two Russian warships there. That night Japanese torpedo-boats attacked the Russian naval base of Port Arthur. 'So we must be ready for action and simultaneous blows...'[23]

IJN officers and men were thought to be brave, tough, and well-disciplined, with a tendency to fanaticism, but with serious weaknesses. These were brought out in the only full analysis of Japanese naval efficiency made in the Royal Navy during the inter-war period. It took the form of a paper in 1935 by the Naval Attaché in Tokyo, Captain J. G. P. Vivian.[24] He singled out four 'national characteristics' that, he claimed, affected the efficiency of the officers and men, and hence of the Navy as a whole. 'Slowness of Mind' was the first: the Japanese were slow in the uptake.

(a) The Japanese have peculiarly slow brains. Teachers in this country have assured me that this is fundamentally due to the strain put on the child's brain in learning some 6,000 Chinese characters before any real education can start.

(b) This inertia shows itself by an inherent disability to switch the mind from one subject to another with rapidity. It requires time to readjust the mental outlook to a new line of thought.

(c) I am convinced that it is for this reason that the Japanese people are a race of specialists. By concentration and intense application a man becomes good, possibly very good, at one particular job but is seldom capable of taking on another, slightly out of his own line, at short notice.

(d) There are, of course, exceptions and it is apparent that these officers who rise to high rank in the Navy are those who are least affected by this disability.

The truth of (a) is questionable.[25] There is, however, something in

[23] Dreyer, 'Some Strategical Notes—Western Pacific', 10 Feb. 1939, ADM 1/11326. Backhouse minuted the paper: 'It will be realised that Admiral Dreyer has made a great study of the Pacific problem and his views are therefore of great value.' But he made no direct reference, nor did the D of P, Danckwerts, to Dreyer's high evaluation of the IJN.

[24] 'Efficiency of the Japanese Navy', 18 Feb. 1935, ADM 116/3862. It was prepared at the request of the DNI. My comments on the points made by Vivian are largely derived from the discussions I had with many IJN officers on this document.

[25] A quarter of a century earlier, in January 1909, the Naval Attaché in Tokyo had made the same claim: 'They are too slow and too methodical, and require time to think where a smart officer should act instantly.' Marder, *From the Dreadnought to Scapa Flow: The Royal Navy in the Fisher Era, 1904–1919* (5 vols., London, 1961–70), i. 236–7.

(b): Japanese society is based on the rule-keeping of Confucianism, which is the main reason for the slowness in switching the mind swiftly from one subject to another. Point (c) is certainly true.

'Concentration' was the second of the four national characteristics Vivian singled out: 'The ability to work hard for long hours ... Nothing, except physical disability, will divert the individual from the object which he has in view.' This, too, is true enough.

Sake drinking, the third characteristic, was a 'national pastime' in which the naval officer excelled. That the Japanese could not (and cannot) hold their liquor is well known.[26] But, he added, excessive drinking apparently did not appreciably undermine the morale or physique of officers. All this was so.

Finally, there was the accurate description of 'super patriotism', which was daily instilled into officers and men and eventually took 'the form of a peculiar exaltation of the spirit capable of producing, at any moment, murder, mutiny, self-destruction or the highest forms of gallantry. In a disciplined Service the dangers are obvious, the benefits not far to seek.'

Vivian thought that the democratic entry had a definite bearing on the efficiency of the Navy. 'It has been admitted to me by more than one highly placed officer, that it is rare for an officer of the executive branch to rise to high rank unless he is sprung from the upper classes. This is not due to lack of "influence" but to the established fact that the peasant class boy lacks the power of command.' The authorities were much concerned at the increasing failure of upper-class boys to pass the stiff medical examination. 'One cannot but conclude from this that the average efficiency of the younger officers is not of a high order.' This is nonsense. An officer from any class, if he had the ability, went to the top; most admirals came from the middle or lower classes.

The training of the young officers at Etajima left much to be desired, Vivian asserted. They were overtrained physically and overcrammed mentally. Worse, 'the inculcation of "Leadership" and the "team spirit" play a very small part in the curriculum'. There is some truth in both statements. Leadership and team spirit

---

[26] William H. Forbis holds that the Japanese intolerance for alcohol (that of all Mongoloids, in fact) is 'apparently due to a genetic factor. A Boston psychiatrist recently proved in experiments that Mongoloids turn red in the face (a spectacle familiar to every visitor to Tokyo) and suffer palpitations, fast heartbeat, dizziness, and sleepiness from amounts of liquor so small as to have no effect on Caucasians.' Forbis, *Japan Today*, p. 74.

were not emphasized at Etajima, certainly not to the same degree as at Dartmouth or Annapolis.²⁷

The staff work was very good when everything went according to plan; 'but should the unexpected intervene there are few, very few, Japanese who would not have to sit down and think out the problem all over again from the start. With the exception of possibly half a dozen officers, I have met none whom I could imagine drafting an operation on a signal pad in a real hurry.' By peacetime standards IJN staff work may have been good, but by the war standards of the Royal Navy and the US Navy, Japanese naval staff work was primitive. This is reflected in the paucity of staff officers at Combined Fleet Headquarters: approximately nine. In contrast, the comparatively miniscule Force Z had about eleven staff officers. As for the latter part of Vivian's statement, the situation was not peculiar to the Imperial Navy.

Another alleged weakness was the remarkably short sea time experienced by the more senior officers; rarely did officers of flag rank have more than one year in command of a ship at sea. The assessment is correct. 'The Imperial Navy generally assigned its brilliant officers to headquarters duty ashore, and so the outstanding men were usually lacking shipboard experience.'²⁸ It was different in the Royal Navy, which was convinced that to produce an efficient sea officer both long training and sea experience were needed. In effect, the Royal Navy trained all its officers to be fit to become admirals.

The engineer officer was 'a highly trained specialist. ... The training is well carried out and no effort is spared to produce a high standard of efficiency.' Very true. As regards the ratings, both

---

²⁷ 'It is true the cadets do read a book on leadership, but the most important practical instrument for developing leadership at Etajima is the *buntai* system, analogous to the house system at our public schools. ... The *buntai*, then, is a small cross-section of the cadet body [32 cadets in each *buntai*, eight from each year], in which the *gocho* [cadet-captain chosen from the fourth-year cadets], the *gocho-ho* [vice-captain] and the 4th year cadets generally are given ample opportunities for developing their powers of leadership. They are, as it were, *ex-officio* instructors of the younger ones.' Bullock, *Etajima*, pp. 49–51. All this did not add up to a widespread and effective training in leadership. 'The lack of real leadership manifested itself on many occasions. For example, when a fleet command or naval district held manoeuvres or battle exercises, the officers usually assembled afterwards for a critique. The fleet or naval district commander presided at such conferences, but it was seldom that he actively guided the discussions or offered any incisive comments. The officers consequently had little idea whether they were on the right track or not.' Fuchida and Okumiya, *Midway*, p. 75.
²⁸ Hara, *Japanese Destroyer Captain*, p. 23.

upper-deck and engine-room, there were, in Vivian's judgement, pluses and minuses. The conscripts, who constituted 20 per cent of the total numbers and 50 per cent of the non-petty officer ratings, were, by RN standards, 'untrained men'. Drawn mostly from industrial and farming districts, they did not have 'the advantage of an inborn sea sense'.

The conscripts' training is superficial in that each man is taught only the specific duties he has to perform in the ship in which he serves. Time does not allow of more....

The low power possessed by the Japanese of assimilating new knowledge quickly must be a grave handicap in a service which is largely manned on a short service basis [five years]....

The Japanese Lower Deck Rating is physically a fine man as the Navy gets the pick of the nation, and from this point of view would be hard to beat. He is intensely patriotic and during his period of service is all out to do his best....

Conclusion

... I cannot believe that the system is capable of producing really efficient ships' companies for war purposes, especially for the smaller classes of ships where initiative and resource are required from others besides the Petty Officers.

The Naval Attaché was off target, for, generally speaking, the Japanese ratings were very good indeed.

Vivian had this to say about the efficiency of the ships. Practically nothing was known about fleet exercises, their number and types. What was certain was that much time was spent in gunnery drills, and there was reason to believe that much effort was expended in achieving rapidity of fire. 'A high rate of controlled and independent fire must be expected from all classes of ships.' However, he had it from the German Naval Attaché that the Japanese were 'years behind the Germans in everything to do with fire control'. The available evidence pointed to fleet backwardness in AA gunnery: the Japanese put little faith in it. As it happened, gunnery efficiency was superb; there was plenty of practice. AA fire was poor, but it had improved greatly by the outbreak of war.

Concerning the Japanese naval air arm (here the Naval Attaché relied on the opinions of the Air Attaché), the aircraft,

though much improved during the last four years, are inferior in performance to those of similar types in use in the Royal Air Force, and it appears extremely unlikely that in the event of war, Japan could keep pace with the rapid changes and progress in design brought on by the necessities of war.

Judging by experience of four years ago, maintenance does not reach a high standard and material in some cases, such as that used for air screws [airplane propellers], was of inferior quality....

With regard to pilots, their personal courage is beyond question, but they are somewhat slow-thinking and lacking in initiative.

There was truth in this estimate, although it was outdated by developments in the following six years.

The Imperial Navy was presumably efficient in combined operations, Vivian continued, since the sailors were 'constantly being exercised in landing operations and tactical training on shore', and combined operations with Army units had been carried out in all naval commands during the past two years. Little was known of sea-going efficiency, but on the two occasions that the Attaché had been able to see ships at sea in company, 'station keeping was bad and would not have been tolerated by a British Admiral'. He assumed that the efficiency of the Fleet was of a high order in bad weather, since normal sea conditions in Home waters were bad—when the sea was not rough, there was a large swell—yet exercises were never cancelled on account of bad weather. Accurate appraisals, as was Vivian's remark that in tactical training great stress was laid on the importance of submarine and aircraft tactics.

In the realm of *matériel*, 'The Fleet is probably provided with first class material in the first place but it is extremely doubtful whether it is kept in first class condition even in peacetime'. The first part of the statement is undoubtedly true, and there was a smidgen of truth in the second part—in 1935. Certainly by 1941 the *matériel* was kept in first-class condition. 'During an oceanic war,' Vivian went on, 'when Fleet units would not have dockyard facilities close at hand, it seems probable that mechanical efficiency would decrease with some rapidity.' This was, he claimed, because of the insufficient training given to mechanics, which must prevent anything more than the simplest refitting work without dockyard assistance, and examinations of machinery and boilers were carried out at irregular intervals.

The Attaché also considered dockyard efficiency, the capacity of dockyards for expansion of the Fleet, and other matters. His general conclusion was: 'I have tried very hard to find some points about the Japanese fleet which one could say with confidence are good. Beyond the devotion to duty of the whole of the personnel and the probability of any naval landing force being a highly efficient fighting force I have failed to do so. If one was allowed to see something of the Fleet at work, or even of the Training Establishments or Schools, one, no doubt, would find many things to praise.'

A private letter from Vivian to the DNI observed: 'A layman reading this paper would, I think, come to the conclusion that the I.J.N. is of the 2nd class, and I think that this is probably so...'[29] And this was the prevalent opinion at the Admiralty, where the Attaché's report generated considerable interest. Chatfield asked that all the Sea Lords read this 'interesting and valuable letter' (29 June 1935). The DNI, Captain G. C. Dickens, agreed 'generally' with Vivian's conclusions (20 May). 'The paragraphs on National Characteristics, Staff Work and Sea Time have been confirmed from many sources.' But he uttered a caveat: 'Against the weakness of the Japanese Navy pointed out in this paper must be set a very high morale and a fighting spirit of the highest order.' The Third Sea Lord and Controller, Admiral R. G. H. Henderson, warned that they 'must be careful not to belittle the general efficiency of a possible enemy' (5 July).

The Director of the Naval Staff College, Captain B. C. Watson, was stimulated by Vivian's report to draw conclusions (*c.* September) regarding Japanese naval efficiency from the conduct of the Russo-Japanese War. 'Provided plans went well, the Japanese showed the utmost determination, but it only required some small upset and their inability to give quick decisions became evident.'

The President of the Royal Naval College, Greenwich, Vice-Admiral Colvin, contributed an astute minute (13 September) that backed up Vivian's opinions regarding Japanese characteristics and Watson's deduction from the war with Russia. The annual study of that war at the Staff College showed that at critical periods the Japanese were apt to fail through 'an inability to change their plans and to act quickly in an emergency and a tendency to panic when things go wrong'. Colvin also questioned 'their coolness and levelheadedness at decisive moments under fire. It would appear that their intense patriotism and their eagerness to die for their country produced a mental state of excitement which may have

[29] Undated ADM 116/3862. The material that follows is from the same file.

lowered their efficiency. As examples of this can be quoted the repeated failure of their torpedo attacks and also their general tactics in most of their naval actions.' The Shanghai operations of 1932 confirmed that

> the initial planning was elaborate and that an unexpected check led to some demoralisation in the command, and revealed the Japanese lack of adaptability in facing a situation not previously studied. . . .
> At the same time, the operations also showed the determination with which, having suffered a reverse the Japanese will re-appreciate a situation and lavish blood and treasure in achieving their aim.
> Nevertheless, it must be remembered that, except at Tsing Tau [1914]—where they were vastly superior in numbers—the Japanese have never met an enemy of enterprise or initiative. They have always been given time to re-appreciate after a check. If this chance is denied them, I have little doubt that they will cut a different and less imposing figure.

The DCNS, Vice-Admiral Sir Charles Little, was 'in general agreement' with the views expressed by Vivian (18 September). 'The fortification of Singapore and the re-building of the British Fleet on an adequate scale for the needs of Imperial defence will, in my view, now have a wholesome deterrent effect on those slow witted but fanatically gallant Japanese.'

There were some cogent observations in these reactions to Vivian's report, but they also displayed a tendency to underrate the Imperial Navy. And no attempt was made after Vivian's assessment down to the outbreak of war to make a fresh, up-to-date one. In the words of Admiral Sir Henry Moore, ACNS (Trade) in 1941, then VCNS when Phillips was appointed C-in-C, Eastern Fleet: 'We grossly underestimated the power and efficiency of the Japanese naval surface and air forces. This may have been due both to lack of intelligence and to a faulty assessment of what we had.'[30] Ship for ship, gun for gun, and man for man, RN officers thought their Navy had the advantage, and that their admirals were probably better. The Royal Navy therefore contemplated with a reasonable equanimity and confidence the possibility of having to take on the Japanese Navy at some future time, assuming that there would be

---

[30] Letter to the author, 30 Aug. 1976. Captain Roskill claims that 'it was Churchill, not the naval staff, which underrated Japanese prowess and efficiency . . .' *Churchill and the Admirals*, p. 196. (In September 1940 Churchill criticized NID for being 'very much inclined to exaggerate Japanese strength and efficiency'.) The evidence is overwhelming that they were equally culpable.

secure bases from which to operate and that numerical comparisons in capital ships on the spot would not be one-sidedly against them.

In general, it must surely be agreed that it is a good thing if fighting forces believe that they are, man for man, and given anything like equal conditions, better men than their foes—superior to them in courage, resolution, enterprise, and devotion to duty, as well as in *matériel*. The trouble in 1941 was that there was an unhealthy *over*confidence, which, wedded to an abysmal ignorance of their opponent's true strength, could only result in initial disasters.

A substantive reason for underrating the efficiency and determination of the Japanese Navy was the fact that from the mid-1930s the growing strength of Germany, the ambitions of Hitler and Mussolini and their activities in the Spanish Civil War, concentrated attention on the Atlantic and Mediterranean, and relegated the Japanese and South-east Asia to the background. Immersed in their own immediate problems west of Suez, the Admiralty and the Royal Navy had, comparatively speaking, little time for or interest in the Japanese Navy.

There was, too, the supreme confidence engendered by the British naval tradition. How could officers brought up on Drake, Blake, Hawke, Howe, St. Vincent, and Nelson believe that little chaps in the Far East who ate rice could ever hope to be a match at sea for honest, beef-eating Englishmen who had had salt water running through their veins for the past 400 years?

Feelings of racial superiority were no doubt an ingredient in the attitude of superiority. There is, for example, the revealing observation by Sir Samuel Hoare, the First Lord of the Admiralty, at a meeting of the Imperial Conference of 1937 (26 May) that a fleet sent to the Far East would, materially, be slightly inferior to Japanese naval strength, but 'relying on the superior fighting qualities of the British race, the Fleet would achieve its object of assuring the Dominions from serious aggression'.[31] The assumed technological superiority of the British was but a facet of this racial superiority complex. The same is, if anything, truer of attitudes in the American Navy. This extract from the reminiscences of the Head of the Far Eastern Section of the Office of Naval Intelligence (1939–42) is even more revealing.

[31] CAB 32/128.

The tendency was to judge technical developments on the basis of our own technology and on the assumption that our technology was superior to any other. So if something was reported that the Japanese did have and we didn't then, obviously, it was wrong.... For instance, we got a report of this Japanese 24-inch [oxygen] torpedo, and we had it about two or three years before the Japanese started using it on us, and we had it in detail [not all of it correct] ... It went to the Bureau of Ordnance.... We said that the source was impeccable ... the Bureau of Ordnance came back and said that, in the first place, a 1,200-lb. warhead would be so long that its center of gravity, which is the origin of the burst, would be so far back that it would have a not materially different effect from our own torpedo which, at that time, carried 800 lbs. of TNT, that the speeds were completely ridiculous, that no torpedo could go that far so fast. ... They only came round to our point of view when the Japanese started blowing the tails off our cruisers down in the Solomon Islands.[32]

The British outlook was no different.

We must remember that all courtesy visits of RN ships and squadrons to Japanese ports were suspended from the autumn of 1936, not that these had ever yielded much valuable intelligence. British ships did observe Japanese naval activity in Chinese waters, but the lack of effective opposition and the fact that few of their more modern units were used in these operations gave the Royal Navy no opportunity to form any worthwhile opinion on the operational efficiency of the Imperial Navy. Inside Japan reliable intelligence on Japanese intentions and preparations was difficult to obtain. Their movements severely curtailed by the Japanese authorities, the attachés were able to produce very little indeed. Useful references to the Navy in the Japanese press were rare—for example, exercises and manœuvres received no publicity—and officers were not accustomed to speak freely to foreigners. As the Naval Attaché observed, 'It must be recognised that no officer under the rank of Admiral dare discuss any naval question with a foreigner. Some Admirals are willing to talk about matters of general interest, but any approach to such topics as tactics or practices is met with a change of subject.'[33] Japanese security

---

[32] *The Reminiscences of Rear Admiral Arthur H. McCollum, U.S. Navy (retired)* (2 vols., Oral History Office, United States Naval Institute, Annapolis, 1973), i. 146-8. The Imperial Navy resented the disparaging opinion in the British and American navies that they were mere copyists incapable of anything original.
[33] Vivian, 'Efficiency of the Japanese Navy'.

measures rendered the job of foreign attachés a most frustrating one. They constructed high fences around shipyards, cleared harbours when ships were launched, played down specifications and capabilities (as with the oxygen torpedo and the Zero fighter), and concealed in every way possible the particulars of their ships and aircraft. It was an iron rule that no foreigner—not even the German Naval Attaché, allies though the Germans were since 1940—be allowed to visit building yards and bases or examine modern naval units. Even their own naval officers were not permitted to inspect the most modern units, so intensive was the policy of secrecy. Naval attachés were able to report the details of the budget, because it was debated in the Diet and the House of Peers; but the debates revealed little more than the general characteristics of the ships and the costs of the building programmes.

NID4 had no more luck than did the Naval Attaché. The Section, which in 1939–41 consisted of two junior naval officers, two or three Royal Marine majors, one or two civilians, and a lady typist, was none too successful in its most important job, that of trying to assess the strength and efficiency of the Japanese Navy. Intelligence from Japan, very difficult to obtain, practically dried up altogether after 1939, and what they did have was suspect. 'It was simply very difficult to infiltrate agents, and the few we did have were usually Chinese merchants, and they were pretty unreliable. To the best of my recollection we had virtually no information from Japan after the war with Japan started.'[34] There was another factor. 'No reliance can be placed on obtaining first hand information of Japanese Fleet movements. Our submarine strength on the China station is only sufficient to allow occasional patrols to be carried out off Japan. Owing to the long distances from Hong Kong, it requires five submarines to keep one on patrol.'[35]

Given these formidable difficulties in obtaining intelligence on the IJN, the achievements of Naval Intelligence deserve respectable marks. NID was one of the Royal Navy's outstanding strengths after Rear-Admiral J. H. Godfrey, a genius at intelligence work, if a ruthless driver, became DNI in February 1939 (–November 1942). Commander Fukui offers proof of some NID *coups* before the war. In March 1942, when one of a group dispatched from the

---

[34] Captain Stephen Barry's letter to the author, 15 Oct. 1975. He was the Head of NID4 in 1940–2.
[35] COS(39), 304th Mtg., 20 June 1939, CAB 53/11.

Naval Technical Department to Singapore, he discovered in the photographic dark room attached to the Operations Room of the former British Fleet Headquarters, despite the destruction, a 1940 track chart of the British submarine *Regulus*, which had, undetected, entered Shibushi Bay, in southern Kyushu. This was a spacious bay often used as a Combined Fleet base prior to the war. There was also a negative showing the flagship *Nagato* and the Combined Fleet in the bay, and attached comments on the speed of elevating and training the *Nagato*'s main battery, and on the speed of the training of her rangefinder. The report was classified 'top secret'.[36]

Fukui also found a large number of good negatives of Japanese warships that showed the Royal Navy knew a great deal about Japanese ships. Photographs of Japanese naval vessels were not made public within Japan because of the extreme secrecy. Every time British merchant ships met Japanese naval vessels off the Yangtze before they entered Shanghai, or when they encountered them off the Japanese main islands, they took photographs. After the China Incident broke out, the Combined Fleet made a show of force off Amoy and Tsingtao, and pictures were taken. When the Combined Fleet changed anchorage in China waters, or was getting under way, invariably a British cruiser would approach for a good look. Among these photographs was one of around 1934–5 (presumably by a British merchant ship) of the inside of the port of Nagasaki when the cruiser *Mikuma* was being fitted. Commander Fukui also came upon a copy of the organization of the Combined Fleet, which had been found on the person of Military Councillor and former Navy Minister Ōsumi Mineo, who had made a forced landing near Canton early in 1941. The Royal Navy must have got this from the Chinese.

Naval intelligence in the Far East was the job of the Far East Combined Bureau (FECB), a combined Services organization,

---

[36] Considering the shallow depth, it would have been very difficult for a submarine to have entered the bay. More likely, Fukui surmises, the *Regulus* had approached the bay and sent in a small boat with an intelligence officer on board to survey the Combined Fleet at its anchorage. It is also his theory that, since the bay was full of Japanese fishing boats, the British boat went unobserved. Another photograph taken by the *Regulus* and discovered by Fukui was one of Osaka Bay. Attached was the remark by the commanding officer that he had entered Kitan Strait, which leads into the bay, and had spent several days in the bay. This was a strictly controlled area. The evidence points to the *Regulus*, operating from Hong Kong, having achieved these successes in a patrol off southern Japan in October 1940. Unfortunately, her patrol report for that period, though noted as received, is missing in the PRO records. See ADM 199/292, 1833. The *Regulus* was lost on 6 December 1940.

under Admiralty administration.[37] The omission of the operative word 'Intelligence' before 'Bureau' was, presumably, a concession to 'security'. When Duff Cooper, representing the War Cabinet, came to Singapore in September 1941 to promote closer inter-Service co-operation, he reported back that the only place where he had found the three Services working in complete harmony was the FECB. The Bureau was formed in Hong Kong in 1935 from existing single-Service intelligence offices in South-east Asia and the Far East, and had moved to the Naval Base, Singapore, in August 1939. Its Head, a naval captain, was the COIS (Chief of Intelligence Staff, 'Far East' being understood). Each of the three Services had its own section—the COIS was also Head of the Naval Section—which communicated directly with the Intelligence division of its own ministry in London. Copies of FECB signals and reports were sent to the local Cs-in-C and, from the autumn of 1940, to the C-in-C, Far East (Brooke-Popham), as well. (I have been unable to learn how the FECB addressed collective messages and reports affecting all three Services, and how they were pooled and disseminated in London.) The Naval Section was much stronger numerically than either of the others, especially on the radio-intercept and cryptanalysis sides, though, as Captain Harkness points out, 'We never saw ourselves as other than three services of equal standing.'

The main pre-war objectives of the FECB were to help in assessing whether there would be war with Japan, and if so, when it would start and what form it would take. This, of course, included building up the Japanese 'Order of Battle' on land and sea and in the air. 'Special Intelligence' or, loosely, 'Ultra' (intelligence

[37] The discussion that follows is based on extensive correspondence in 1978–9 with the late Captain F. J. Wylie and Captain K. L. Harkness, successively, the Heads of the FECB, 1938–40, 1940–2, and a paper prepared for me by Lieutenant-Commander S. W. Francis (see below) in May 1979 ('History of the Special Intelligence Organisation in the Far East for the period of the War, September 1939 to August 1945'). For reasons unknown the FECB records are apparently no longer extant. The remarkably young-looking Harkness, a gunnery specialist with war experience as a destroyer commander, was the COIS in the critical period. It was a complete surprise to him when he was appointed (August 1940) to take charge of the FECB. He had no experience of intelligence work, was perhaps 'too nice' and not sufficiently ruthless when he needed to be, and did not inspire the full confidence of his superiors at that time. He did his best, though well aware of his own limitations. His general attitude was that he had been sent out to take charge of a bunch of experts, the technical aspects of whose jobs he did not pretend to understanding. He had to keep the organization up to the mark, smooth out its difficulties, and see that it was kept in order. At this he was successful.

obtained by the decryption of intercepted radio messages) was their forte, and they made an exceedingly good job of it. (I have been unable to learn precisely how much the FECB knew about Japanese naval ciphers, though they seem to have relied increasingly on the US Navy from about 1939.)

In late 1939 these radio intelligence facilities existed in the Far East: three H/F D/F (high-frequency, direction-finding) stations: Hong Kong, Kranji (Singapore), and Kuching in North Borneo (increased to 17 in 1942); the 'Y' station at Kranji for the interception of enemy wireless signals; and the naval and military Cryptanalysis Section in Seletar Bahru (Singapore).

The 'Y' station personnel in 1939 consisted of 30 WRNS (Wrens: Women's Royal Navy Service) Chief Petty Officer Telegraphists, trained in the meanings attributed by the Japanese to the otherwise universal morse symbols, and approximately 40–50 civilian shore W/T service operators. (These latter personnel also manned the D/F stations as and when they were erected and became operational.) The personnel numbers were increased as necessary. There were three methods of compiling 'Y' information: D/F fixes, study of Japanese naval W/T traffic and air traffic, and identification of call signs. The 'Y' station would intercept a signal from an enemy ship or submarine and immediately pass the frequency to D/F stations, which then got bearings from different positions on the enemy transmitter and plotted them on a chart. The net of the 17 D/F stations, known as the Far East D/F Organization, was very wide, stretching from the Canadian west coast to the east coast of Africa. They were grouped according to their geographical location in such a way that cross bearings of German and Japanese naval transmissions were obtainable. Despite the enormous distances involved the 'cocked hats' obtained by cross bearings were relatively small.[38] The results were sent from the D/F stations to the FECB via the cable 'Flash' system. (Under this system cable authorities would flash a particular cable station or stations, authorizing them to clear all traffic off the line and prepare for an urgent message.) All fixes

---

[38] The 'cocked hat', in the jargon of navigators, is 'the small trianguler space usually found at the intersection of position lines on a chart when a ship's position is determined by plotting three bearings. With perfect observation and plotting, the three position lines should intersect at a common point [marking the approximate position of the signalling ship]; if they do not, a "cocked hat" is formed. ... in general, the larger the cocked hat, the greater the error. Navigators normally take the centre of the cocked hat, when it is not large, as the position of the ship.' Peter Kemp (ed.), *The Oxford Companion to Ships & the Sea* (Oxford, 1976), p. 177.

of German units were sent directly to the DNI. Fixes of Japanese units were used in the FECB daily summaries, which were promulgated to all Far Eastern intelligence authorities affected. In addition to D/F information, details of Japanese naval and air movements as derived from a comprehensive study of intercepted Japanese radio traffic, particularly movements from one area to another, were signalled to the Admiralty, in addition to all Far East intelligence authorities, immediately such intelligence was considered to be reliable. All known methods of confirmation of such indications of movements were employed, i.e. linking up suspected movements in any area with visual and other physical sightings. Working in this manner in conjunction with positive identification of call signs enabled the organization to warn the Admiralty and other directly concerned authorities of squadrons and ships leaving Japan for the Indo-China, South China coast, and Hong Kong areas, particularly during the build up of forces in the Saigon area in late 1941. Similarly, by means of D/F and study of radio traffic, movements and locations of Japanese Air Force squadrons were plotted. Call signs were, in the main, confirmed by the use of RFP equipment (radio finger printing) and sighting reports.[39] The Cryptanalysis Organization was located near the 'Y' intercept station to ensure that interception of any particular traffic requested by the Organization could be quickly and efficiently provided. The 'Crypto' Organization consisted of about 10 naval officer Japanese

---

[39] RFP was an ultra-secret ciné-camera, using a very sensitive film at a very high (lateral) speed, which took photographs of the visual presentation on a cathode ray tube of a wireless set's transmissions. The photographs sometimes allowed the design of the transmitter (e.g. whether it was, say, a Type 48 or a Type 49 set) to be determined; but, if the millesecond or so of the film which followed the pressing of the transmitter's key was examined with a magnifying glass, the film, unless reception conditions were bad, allowed the transmitter to be identified with certainty. An RFP outfit had been installed at the RN W/T Station, Kranji, early in 1941, and by the middle of the year a film library of Japanese transmissions had been built up, which, having been combined with D/F and 'Y' production, was, literally, a dictionary of the transmissions of the main H/F sets of all the major Japanese warships and shore wireless stations. Using this dictionary, ships could be identified without the necessity of identifying the call signs which they used from the traffic which they handled. This great achievement was the work of a man who was sent out from England to instruct the RFP staff in the use of the apparatus: Professor A. C. Hardy, a 'dapper, unassuming University don', who had spent his life studying the growth patterns on minute marine organisms to learn about their life. I am indebted for this information to Captain J. W. McClelland (letter of 26 Feb. 1979), who was until January 1942 in administrative charge of the RFP set as well as the chain of naval D/F stations. Sir Alister (1957) Hardy was Professor of Zoology and Oceanography at Hull, 1928–42, and, after the war, Linacre Professor of Zoology and Anatomy at Oxford.

cryptanalyst-interpreters and two army officer cryptanalysts. It was responsible for obtaining the code words which the Japanese intended to use for declaring hostilities, and for top secret information regarding isolated movements of Japanese warships.

There was full co-operation between the Royal Navy and the US Navy on Japanese Special Intelligence via Lieutenant-Commander Francis, Head of 'Y', D/F, and Special Intercept Organizations (November 1939–September 1942), and the American Naval Liaison Officer, successively Captains Archer Allen and J. M. Creighton.

The Bureau had a Local (security type) Intelligence Section which, among other things, prepared the list of those Japanese residents who should be locked up instantly on the outbreak of war. It worked closely with the local police and with SO(I) Singapore.[40] Reports from British agents were handled by the Local Station, but they were very few. A Shipping Section studied the movements of all known foreign shipping. It was this section that correctly forecast the approximate date of the outbreak of war. Spies were not the province of the FECB, nor was the Bureau told of any information gathered by the Ambassador in Tokyo and the Naval Attaché.

The Naval Section of the FECB never knew what use was made of its signals and reports nor how much credence was attached to them. In fact, its material was sorted out within NID, as between NID4 (political intelligence but no Ultra) and the OIC, which was NID8 (operational and Ultra). The Admiralty's Operational Intelligence Centre (OIC), under the DNI, was, basically, responsible for assessing the state of readiness and disposition of the Japanese Fleet (and other enemy fleets). It co-ordinated, evaluated, and promulgated to the operational staff and commanders afloat all the intelligence relevant to actual operations and the movements of ships, etc. Naturally, Ultra, when available, was the OIC's No. 1 source of intelligence, and here it relied upon the FECB. NID4 was responsible, *inter alia*, for keeping track of the Japanese building programme; there was, therefore, considerable liaison between the

---

[40] The Staff Officer (Intelligence) Singapore, with offices at GHQ, Fort Canning, in Singapore City, was a Royal Marine officer, who with his fellows at Hong Kong, Colombo, and elsewhere acted as the overseas ears and eyes of the DNI. They studied the local press and were in close touch with the local police on security matters. They were not regarded as part of the FECB organization, though SO(I) Singapore worked very closely with the Bureau.

OIC and NID4. The JIC (Joint Intelligence Committee: the three Directors of Intelligence or their Deputies and certain others, with a Foreign Office representative as Chairman) served the COS. The JIC's appraisals, which were based on material from the FECB, OIC, NID4, and other sources, applied this intelligence to the great strategic problems it was asked to examine by the Joint Planners and the Chiefs of Staff—for example, in January 1942, would the Japanese attack Australia and New Zealand?

One scholar claims that 'Where British intelligence slipped up was in the assessment of the Japanese mentality—its ability to do the irrational.'[41] This is true enough, if one is talking about Japan's provocation of the United States and Britain *at the same time*, since there was a general awareness in the Royal Navy of Japan's penchant for the unexpected. However (as the author suggests), this slip-up was common to the British, American, and Dutch leadership, political and military. If at bottom it was the fault of Intelligence estimates, in defence of the FECB, NID4, and other British Intelligence organizations I would say that studies of national psychology and the like are a comparatively recent innovation in the arcane world of Intelligence services. The FECB *did* predict the approximate date of Japan's commencement of war, an estimate, to be sure, based on a practical consideration, Japanese shipping movements in November 1941, rather than on an examination of such factors as the traditions of the Japanese fighting services, which, in any case, was the job of the JIC. The essential point is that, on the whole, considering the very tight Japanese security, the British Naval Intelligence service did not do too badly in getting the information it did.

In reference to the Far East, the Royal Navy was in an impossible situation strategically; but it took comfort, as did its political masters, in the belief that Japan would not go to war, and that if she did, the United States would come in, and that the qualitative superiority of the Royal Navy would do the rest. By 1941 any fellow feeling in the Royal Navy for the Imperial Navy was rapidly diminishing and there was no regret at the prospect of fighting it, except that the Navy, so preoccupied in the Atlantic and the

---

[41] Anthony Wells, 'Naval Intelligence and Decision Making in an Era of Technical Change', in Bryan Ranft (ed.), *Technical Change and British Naval Policy, 1860–1939* (London, 1977), p. 140.

Mediterranean, hoped that the politicians could keep the Japanese neutral.

As so we arrive at the story of the supreme tragedy of the entire war on the RN side—the story of Force Z. The imponderables add a fascination to the brief existence of this Force.

PART THREE
The Saga of Force Z

XIII

Odyssey

> Against the background of haste, muddle, and misconception, Tom Phillips was given an inordinately difficult task.
> ADMIRAL SIR HENRY MOORE to the author, 23 June 1976.

> It was a bold scheme . . . If it had come off as planned it might have changed the face of history: that it didn't come off was one of the saddest tragedies of our time.
> LIEUTENANT-COMMANDER T. J. CAIN, *H.M.S. Electra.*

1. OF MEN AND SHIPS

DIRECTLY following the Defence Committee meeting on 20 October, acting Vice-Admiral Sir Tom Phillips was ordered to hoist his flag in the *Prince of Wales* as C-in-C-designate, Eastern Fleet, with the rank of acting admiral. (The kindly and youthful-looking Vice-Admiral Sir Henry Moore, 'an industrious little brown mouse', Somerville called him, succeeded Phillips as VCNS until June 1943. This made Phillips the youngest full admiral, albeit acting. The double step in rank was unique in the Service. The announcement that Phillips would take command of the force being sent to the Far East was not received with hosannahs in the Fleet. It was the general feeling that it was an unfortunate choice. Not untypical was the reaction of the C-in-C, Mediterranean Fleet: 'What on earth is Phillips going to the Far Eastern squadron for. He hardly knows one end of a ship from the other. His only experience is 8 months as RAD [thirteen months as Commodore, then Rear-Admiral, Destroyers, Home Fleet, 1938–9] and then he had the stupidest collision. However if you have a seat on the Board you can generally manœuvre yourself into a good job—I did!!!'[1]

---

[1] Admiral Sir Andrew Cunningham to Vice-Admiral Sir William Whitworth, 12 Oct. 1941, Whitworth Papers (Imperial War Museum). Admiral Sir Manley Power writes: 'Having been with ABC in the Mediterranean at the time of the *Prince of Wales/Repulse* business, I naturally heard a good deal of comment. His attitude was, before the event, "The
(*continued*)

The incident referred to occurred at 01.00 on 25 September 1938 on passage from Rosyth to Scapa Flow. Weather conditions were overcast with rain, and the ships in the formation were darkened. An alteration of course from 030° to 340° had been made by the main body at 11.50, with which, for some reason, the destroyer *Encounter* failed to conform, and at 01.00 she collided with the aircraft carrier *Furious*. The degree of Phillips's culpability is not clear—there was, it seems, no board of inquiry—but the collision became known throughout the Fleet and did not help Phillips's reputation.

Phillips's staff background was another reason his new appointment failed to generate enthusiasm. In 1941 he was a junior flag officer, a navigation specialist with no war experience at sea. Vice-Admiral Sir James Somerville, commanding Force H in the Mediterranean, 'shuddered to think of the Pocket Napoleon' going out to the East. 'All the tricks to learn & no solid sea experience to fall back on.'[2] Also, we must remember that the Admiralty was seldom popular with officers serving at sea. Admiralty decisions, suggestions, and criticisms were on occasion (to understate it) resented, and some of this rubbed off on the VCNS, whose strong influence at the Admiralty was no secret. He was indeed regarded as the *fons et origio* of all the more tiresome operational diktats originating in the Admiralty.

How can one explain what on its face looked like an extraordinary appointment? There were those at the Admiralty who believed that Phillips received the Far East command in order to get him

---

Eastern Fleet is all poppycock and is doomed to failure. Putting Tom Phillips in command makes it worse." (He did not like Tom Phillips!) After the sinkings, it was "What else could you expect?"' Letter to the author, 21 Dec. 1974. The Admiral makes this further point: 'There was probably a considerable element of jealousy in the dislike [by Cunningham]. I often noticed, with surprise, a strong streak of jealousy where other "up and coming" Flag Officers were concerned. Surprising in a man of such sterling qualities.' Memorandum for the author, 29 Jan. 1976. However this may be, Admiral Dreyer had made the same point about Phillips's incompetence as a sea officer a year earlier. 'Phillips is not an able officer afloat and only survived the blame for a serious collision afloat in 1938 when R.A.(D) Home Fleet because of his aptitude for Admiralty work.' Dreyer to Alexander, 19 Oct. 1940, AVAR 5/4/63(a). On the other hand, the Fleet Signal Officer when Phillips was COS and Flag-Captain to the C-in-C, East Indies, 1932–5, gives him respectable marks for his handling of the flagship, 'at which he was good if not brilliant'. Captain J. W. McClelland's letter to the author, 31 Jan. 1979.

[2] Somerville to Cunningham, 20 Oct. 1941, Cunningham Papers, Add. MS 52563 (British Library).

away from Churchill, with whom he was not on good terms after once having been his blue-eyed boy. Rumours went around the *Prince of Wales* when she left the Clyde that the newly appointed C-in-C and Churchill did not see as closely eye to eye as they had done in the earlier days of the war. Originally, Phillips was one of the few people to whom Churchill would listen, often during weekends at Chequers, and Pound sometimes used him to persuade Churchill when he had failed to do so himself. Churchill had tremendous admiration for Phillips's brains, knowledge, capacity for work, self-assurance, and ability to express himself fluently. Phillips spoke his mind bluntly and argued with the Prime Minister, who nicknamed this clever and volatile little man 'the Cocksparrow', but gradually his aggressive personality began to alienate Churchill. The turning point came in 1941. Phillips remarked sadly to the DNI, Admiral Godfrey, not long before he sailed in the *Prince of Wales*, that the Prime Minister had not even spoken to him for months. He had been relegated to Coventry because he had opposed the expedition to Greece (April 1941), in whose success he had no faith. For him the reinforcement of Malta and the control of the Central Mediterranean was all-important. To achieve this they should concentrate on the North African campaign, pushing their bases and airfields forward into Tripoli, thereby providing a measure of air cover for the convoys between Alexandria and Malta. 'I remember', Godfrey recalled, 'his telling me that the P.M. had got angry and called him a "defeatist", which provoked the rejoinder that it was his job to give his sincere opinion on the naval strategy, which he had done. They parted angrily and Phillips had no more personal consultation with the P.M. and shortly afterwards was "nominated" for the command of the Eastern Fleet.'[3]

It is just possible that Pound decided to make the appointment as a good way to get the VCNS out of the Prime Minister's sight, although Lord Fraser says this was not so. More to the point, surely, are that by October 1941 Phillips had held the VCNS appointment for over two years—it was one which would normally be followed by an important sea-going command—and that Pound had the highest regard for Phillips's abilities. When Pound was COS to Keyes in the Mediterranean (1925–7), Phillips was the right-hand man on his staff. Keyes was a lazy C-in-C—he was essentially a

---

[3] Godfrey to Rear-Admiral H. G. Thursfield, 28 May 1954, in reply to Thursfield's letter of 24 May, Godfrey Papers (Mrs J. H. Godfrey).

fighting man and rather bored with the peacetime Navy—and Pound, then a commodore, virtually ran and trained the Mediterranean Fleet, with Phillips as a very able and energetic assistant. When Pound became First Sea Lord in June 1939, he insisted on having Phillips as his DCNS, although this was a post normally held by the senior vice-admiral, and Phillips had only just been promoted to rear-admiral. The two got on famously at the Admiralty. Phillips was in and out of the First Sea Lord's Room continuously. They also spent a lot of time together in the OIC. The nature of their relationship and the esteem in which Pound held Phillips are brought out in this letter written on the eve of Phillips's departure:

My dear Tom,
This is a very sad moment for me as it means the breaking up of what I hope has been a satisfactory combination. I have been lucky enough, or wise enough to make sure I had your assistance whenever it was possible. ... You have done magnificent work during the last two years and I cannot adequately put into words how grateful I am personally.... it will be a great comfort to know that there will be someone in the Far East who will make the most of the slender resources available and in whom we have complete confidence.

Yours,
Dudley[4]

The First Lord had no reservations about the appointment. It is the impression of Sir Clifford Jarrett, Alexander's Principal Private Secretary (1940–4), that, 'along with his naval advisers, AVA took comfort from the decision to put Tom Phillips in command of the force, since he had—up to then—a well-deserved reputation for an excellently balanced judgment, mixing initiative, resolution and prudence in just about the right proportions.'[5] In view of this

---

[4] Pound to Phillips, 23 Oct. 1941, Phillips Papers (Commander T. V. G. Phillips). After Phillips's death, Pound wrote to his widow (30 Jan. 1942): 'He had such a wonderful combination of brilliance, soundness of judgment and drive and he was head and shoulders above all his contemporaries.' Ibid. At the time of the original appointment in May 1941 Pound had made one reservation. An undated minute to the First Lord reads: 'it would be wise to qualify his appointment by saying that if we had to evacuate the Med^n it is probable that the Med^n Fleet might proceed to Far East in which case it might be desirable that Cunningham should proceed to Far East anyhow for a time and that Phillips should be 2nd in command and take out that part of the Fleet which goes from Home Waters'. AVAR 5/6/16.

[5] Jarrett's letter to the author, 15 Feb. 1975.

assessment, we can take Alexander's letter to Lady Phillips (21 December 1941) at face value: 'I always, throughout the difficult days last year, found in him a constant support and encouragement, not only because of his knowledge and resource, but the impression one always got of complete reliability. When he took leave of me, I tried to thank him, though inadequately, and said how completely my confidence was placed in him.'[6]

The 53-year-old Phillips was unimpressive physically: about 5 feet 2 inches tall, weighing but nine stone, pale-faced, unhealthy looking, and always *seemingly* taking pills. 'When you went in to see him about something, he would keep putting his hand in the drawer and swallowing a tablet!' This, with his pallor, gave visitors the impression that he was not at all fit. Some have even suggested that he used drugs of the amphetamine–benzadrine type, whose after-effects might explain the 'sort of mental paralysis' that allegedly overcame him on the occasion of the fatal sortie of Force Z in December. But there is no evidence that he used drugs, and there was nothing wrong with his health. The pallor is explained by the long hours at his desk, and the 'pills' were nothing but *Peter's* chocolate, which was his weakness! His desk drawer (and safe) was full of chocolate, pieces of which he would be chewing if seen popping anything into his mouth. *Peter's*, the general tonic called Matatone, and vitamins were used as energy boosters. 'Tom Thumb' and 'Wee Tom', he was called in the Service, though in the lower deck more usually 'Tich' Phillips, after 'Little Tich', a famous Edwardian music-hall comedian.[7] Someone coined the description of him as 'all brains and no body'.

Whatever physical qualities Phillips may have lacked were more than made up for by his remarkable drive. A five-oner, he was knowledgeable on all naval matters, extremely hardworking (as much as 20 hours a day),[8] thorough, quick and definite in his opinions, and decisive in action. However overworked, however tired, he never left anything undone. Once he got his teeth into a

---

[6] Phillips Papers.

[7] He was a chap named Harry Relph (1868–1928), but was called 'Little Tich' from the time he was a baby because he was supposed to look like the chap who claimed to be the heir of the Tichborne family, a famous law case in the nineteenth century. Little Tich was all of 4 feet 6 inches in height, and 'Tich' became an idiomatic tag for an unusually short person.

[8] He had two hobbies. He exercised his mechanical flare in tinkering with his car to keep it in perfect order; but sailing, particularly small boats, was his real relaxing hobby. He was keen on boat racing and was a good skipper.

problem, he would never let go until he had got to the root of it. His memory was extraordinary and his knowledge of historical precedents vast.[9] His subordinates always held him in the highest regard. He had three main faults, however, none of them negligible. In his view, he was almost always right. He was too opinionated and not ready enough to listen to what others had to say before reaching a decision—the exact opposite of Pound. But he resembled Pound in being a terrible centralizer. 'He always looks like death and tries to do far too much,' Admiral Somerville remarked. 'Every small detail or minor decision', notes a close observer of the VCNS in action, 'had to be channelled to him, or through him to Dudley Pound, and there was no decentralization of authority on any subject. The result was a dreadful hold-up of decision, and much frustration amongst the Staff divisions.'[10] Finally, there was Phillips's abrasive personality, which made him a difficult man to work with. He was a man of strong will and considerable obstinacy who seldom smiled and was often rude, though he usually had the grace to apologize afterwards. He expected answers from the Directors of Divisions under his superintendence, and

he could be very short-tempered with those who were not able or willing to give them. He could also be very short with anyone who persisted with an argument after he had shewn that he was not disposed to accept it or discuss it further, but differences on particular points had only an immediate effect which disappeared rapidly. I well remember Captain Ralph Edwards (as he then was), the Director of Operations (Home), who stood up for his point of view against both 1st Sea Lord and VCNS, coming into our office one day in the early Autumn of 1941 and expressing his bewilderment because, although on the previous day Tom had told him to get out and hastened his departure by throwing an [weighty glass] ashtray at him [it barely missed], he had just asked him to be his Chief of Staff when Tom went to the Far East. Once he had made up his mind he

---

[9] When Phillips was COS in the East Indies, 'Sometimes a draft would would come back to the staff office with a minute such as, "There is something about the manumission of escaped criminals claiming to be escaped slaves in a Government of India paper on Abu Dhabi about five years ago. Please check."' Captain McClelland's letter to the author, 31 Jan. 1979.
[10] Somerville to Cunningham, 12 Feb. 1940, Cunningham Papers, Add. MS 52563, Admiral Sir Guy Grantham's letter to the author, 29 Aug. 1975. Grantham was Pound's Naval Assistant in 1940–1, and Somerville was at the Admiralty from the outbreak of the war until he went to Force H in June 1940.

could not be easily deflected even though this might mean differences with 1st Sea Lord and the Prime Minister.[11]

Phillips certainly was not an easy person to get to know. He had many friends, but few close ones. Junior officers looked upon him as a cold fish, lacking a sense of humour and in no sense a leader. Yet, to his personal staff he was most considerate and kind, and though he worked them hard, he worked himself far harder. Many of them were utterly devoted to him. He also had a knack of getting on well with people outside the Navy: Army and Air officers, civil servants, diplomats, and particularly foreign naval officers—and wives of his subordinates, one of whom 35 years later was still speaking of Phillips with something amounting to reverence. She maintained he was the finest man she had ever met and had never forgiven Churchill for ordering the move which ended in the Admiral's death.

With all these pluses and minuses the fact remains that Phillips was essentially a staff officer, more theoretical than practical, brilliant, with not very much sea experience in command and no personal experience of war at sea since 1914–18, and with a personality that must have stunted the powers of leadership that a C-in-C was expected to display.

There is a story that Phillips sent a message to Captain L. H. Ashmore, Naval Assistant to the Second Sea Lord: 'I want these chaps' (names on a list) for his staff in the *Prince of Wales*. When Ashmore remonstrated that none had had Second World War sea experience, he was told that that was what the VCNS wanted, and that was that. The story is plausible, as Phillips apparently was more anxious to have a staff he knew and trusted rather than people with war experience not all that relevant to the Far Eastern situation. It was intended to supplement the founder members from officers on Admiral Layton's staff after arrival in Singapore.

The principal Staff officers included the Admiral's Secretary, Temporary Paymaster Captain S. T. Beardsworth, who had been with Phillips in the Home Fleet Destroyer command and at the Admiralty. He was exceptionally able, if rather brusque in manner,

[11] Rear-Admiral K. H. Farnhill's memorandum for the author, 12 June 1975. He was Assistant Secretary to Phillips in 1940–1. Even so formidable a character as the DNI, Godfrey, gave the impression of quaking when summoned to the presence of the VCNS, his immediate superior. Interview with Admiral Farnhill, 9 May 1979. Phillips's explosions were terrible but rare, and, like a summer storm, passed over quickly.

and was highly regarded by Phillips. The tall and thin Acting Captain L. H. Bell, an excellent Staff officer with a pleasant but rather negative personality, was Captain of the Fleet. His duties were administrative. He was responsible to the Admiral for the welfare of all personnel, morale, and all the nuts and bolts of maintenance.

The intention was that there should be two Chiefs of Staff. One, Rear-Admiral A. F. E. Palliser, would be permanently ashore, deputizing for the C-in-C at Singapore in his absence, and the other, Commodore R. A. B. Edwards, would remain afloat in the *Prince of Wales*. Edwards, however, stayed behind when the ship sailed, because of severe dental problems, and was to fly out later. ('That I never joined him before the battle is a tragedy for me, which I shall never get over,' he wrote to Lady Phillips on 19 December 1941.) He reached Ceylon on 16 December, six days after the ship was sunk. There was much lament from those who knew this highly talented officer, and it was even said that all would have been well if he had been on board with the C-in-C as Chief of Staff.

Palliser, who assumed the duties of COS, was a descendent of the famous Sir Hugh Palliser whose contretemps with his senior office, Keppel, after the battle of Ushant in 1778 became a *cause célèbre*. His portly descendent seems to have inherited something of his ancestor's temperament. He was not at all easy to know or to get along with, being extremely reticent and with a rather pompous manner and way of speaking. He took his duties very seriously and was very much the Admiral. Tight-lipped, unsmiling, with not much sense of humour or panache, and possessed of a sharp tongue and fairly rigid standards of personal conduct both for himself and for others, he excited no enthusiasm, let alone affection, in his juniors. The younger officers grumbled that he was too strict—he certainly drove people to work harder—and the Staff found him rather intimidating. But he was also in some ways kind and tolerant, and a much nicer and more charming person than his demeanour and reputation would suggest. He was a first-rate officer, if not in the very highest class—absolutely sound, though somewhat lacking in imagination, 100 per cent reliable, and with the reputation of having a good brain and a keen knowledge of strategy and tactics. He was a distinguished gunnery specialist, who had commanded HMS *Excellent*, the Navy's Gunnery School on Whale Island, in

1938–40. A man of high quality all round, despite deficiencies in personality.

The Staff Officer Plans (SO(P)) was a brilliant officer of great force of character, Commander Michael Goodenough, a heavily built, fleshy, red-faced man with curling iron-grey hair, nephew of 'Barge' Goodenough of First World War fame. He had served in the Plans Division, 1939–41, and had got a DSO for taking a naval party over to destroy the Rotterdam oil tanks before the Germans arrived in 1940. He was not a popular figure, as he was dogmatic and a gunnery specialist who was very 'gunnery', as well as being overbearing and pompous. But he was very bright and quick, and he certainly had Phillips's ear. If anything, he was too 'possessive', resenting 'his' master taking anyone else into his confidence. The tall and handsome Commander J. R. M. Laird, Staff Officer Intelligence (SO(I)), had served in NID for some months before the *Prince of Wales* sailed, and presumably was up-to-date on the latest Admiralty intelligence on Japan. But NID passed little intelligence to the *Prince of Wales* on her way out, probably feeling that the latest and best information would reach him on arrival at Singapore from the FECB. Laird's views were, however, seldom asked for on any intelligence matters. Phillips expected him to provide intelligence facts and not much more, leaving it to him, the C-in-C, to make up his own mind what it all meant and what to do. This was to have unfortunate effects. Commander H. N. S. Brown, Fleet Gunnery Officer, Commander Hilary Norman, Fleet Torpedo Officer, and Lieutenant-Commander William Handcock, the Fleet Wireless Officer, all came with high reputations. Commander Maurice Price, the Fleet Navigating Officer, had been Phillips's squadron navigator in Home Fleet Destroyers. He was on the quiet and reserved side, but an excellent staff officer and navigator much respected by Phillips. Phillips asked the Naval Secretary to nominate candidates for Flag-Lieutenant, and he saw a few of them. There was some amusement that he picked Lieutenant (RNVR) B. Rhodes Armitage, the physically largest of the lot, very much taller than himself, a University Boxing Blue, but with no previous experience of serving a C-in-C. Despite the short notice, Phillips assembled an on the whole first-class staff. It had one, not unimportant, shortcoming. 'In retrospect,' the Fleet Gunnery Officer reminisces, 'there seemed to be a separation in the staff between the Intelligence/Planning/Operational side and the Logistics/Gunnery/Torpedo/etc. side. Whether this was due to the Admiral, his Chief of Staff—or me!—I cannot say, but I never felt we became a properly integrated whole.'[12]

Phillips, singularly lacking in the human touch in his day-to-day operations as VCNS, inspired admiration, devotion, and affection in many members of his Staff. There can be no doubting the sincerity of Goodenough's tribute. 'It is futile for me to tell you of the Admiral's genius or of his kindness and humility. I early surrendered to him my whole devotion.'[13] The widow of Phillips's Flag-Lieutenant, Marjorie Armitage, wrote to Lady Phillips: 'I had two letters from him this week posted in Cape Town, saying that he had never had respect and admiration for anyone as he had for "his Admiral" and that he was a really *great* man.'[14]

Phillips's Flag-Captain was the 47-year-old John Catterall Leach, a tall, broad shouldered, handsome man, with blue eyes and (what there was of it) reddish hair, and a face dominated by a large nose. The latter led to his being affectionately called 'Trunky' by the sailors. His slightly hangdog expression in repose belied a keen sense of humour, or rather a bubbling sense of fun, which was never far from the surface. He had a 'cheerful look in his eyes'. He was a charming person of the most upright character, and he was human—an easy man to talk to, completely devoid of any vestige of pomposity or 'side', and in his dealings with others, gentle, considerate, and fair, natural with all, slow to anger but firm in correcting anything he knew to be wrong. He jollied people along rather than drove them. Of his many attributes the two which surpassed all others were his nearly universal popularity and his natural ability as a sportsman. People in all walks of life regarded him with a degree of affection which can seldom have been equalled in the Service. In an era when the relationship between an officer and a rating in the Royal Navy was rather more austere than it is today, Jack Leach inspired a devotion in the men that was unique. Wherever he served became a 'good ship' with high morale and a wonderful espirit de corps, despite his being a firm disciplinarian. The *Prince of Wales* was no exception. Officers and men were keen

---

[12] Captain H. N. S. Brown's letter to the author, 5 Jan. 1979. Admiral Farnhill refers to the 'considerable rift between the ship's officers and the staff who had of course been imposed upon them'. Letter to the author, 17 Sept. 1979.

[13] Goodenough to Lady Phillips, 22 Dec. 1941, Phillips Papers.

[14] Undated (Dec. 1941), Phillips Papers.

to serve with him, and had complete trust in his ability and leadership. Leach was particularly good at keeping the ship's company informed over the loud speakers as to what was going on. He was renowned for his prowess as a sportsman. Before the last war, sport in the Navy counted for much. Competitive games featured prominently in a ship's routine. Long spells were spent in harbour and the opportunities for such things were good. Leach had an exceptionally good natural eye and sense of timing for all ball games. He won the Navy Racquets, Squash, and Tennis championships over several years in the late 1920s, and with his slow, almost casual, left-handed spinners he often took a devastating toll of wickets on the cricket field. At country pursuits he was also in the top flight: a first-class shot and a gifted salmon and trout fisherman.

Leach had been an outstanding gunnery specialist (his previous appointment was as DNO), and had a well-deserved reputation as a thoroughly competent officer in all branches of his profession, including ship-handling. He had a sharp mind as well. Churchill described him as 'a fine example of what a sailor should be', and that was the general feeling on board. Leach had had battle experience in the *Bismarck* action, and fleet experience, though brief, with the Home Fleet and in the Mediterranean, and was undoubtedly the most battle-tested officer on board the *Prince of Wales* in her final sortie. He had gone to the ship soon after her commissioning, and took her into action against the *Bismarck* before she was properly worked up and her teething troubles rectified. He was the only survivor on the compass platform when she was hit on the bridge, and he had the difficult decision to make to break off the action. He had the courage to show that there are occasions when discretion is the better part of valour. Leach, several of the officers in the wardroom felt, had become quieter and in a way rather withdrawn since the *Bismarck* action, which had been a sad and disappointing one to him personally. And there was the memory of how he had narrowly missed a court-martial. Churchill had persuaded Pound to have Admiral Tovey, C-in-C, Home Fleet, charge Leach and Rear-Admiral W. F. Wake-Walker, who commanded the 1st Cruiser Squadron in the *Bismarck* operations, tried by court-martial for not re-engaging the *Bismarck* after she had sunk the battle cruiser *Hood*. Tovey refused to lend himself to such a travesty of justice, and Pound had dropped the matter.

Instead of a court-martial, Leach was awarded a DSO. The whole incident had a later significance. Leach's son, then a midshipman (today Admiral Sir Henry Leach), met his father when the *Prince of Wales* arrived at Singapore in December 1941. 'I detected that the general rapport between Flag and Flag Captain was somewhat cool.' The Engineer Officer of the *Prince of Wales* (Commander, now Captain, L. J. Goudy) has commented that 'Phillips and Leach were obviously not hand in glove together,' and the Assistant Secretary to the C-in-C (Farnhill) had the same impression: that Leach and the Admiral 'did not entirely hit it off'. Leach may have assumed that the VCNS as well as the First Sea Lord had wanted him to be court-martialled, in effect, for dereliction of duty.

The officer who deserves much credit for getting the *Prince of Wales* operational so quickly was her fine Executive Officer, Commander H. F. Lawson, DSO, nicknamed 'Tarzan'. He was a 'square, hard, tough man with a jaw like a bulldozer blade'. Someone described this small bundle of energy as not having a tired bone in his body. Though a hard taskmaster, he was an efficient administrator who did much for ship morale. The sailors greatly respected this 'terrier' of a man.

The Captain of the *Repulse* was W. G. Tennant, a personal friend of Leach. He was 53 years old and was a true type of British 'officer gentleman'. He was quite tall, grey-haired, a good-looking man with an unlined face. He had a fine sense of humour, great charm of manner, and a ready smile, but he had the highest standards of behaviour and could be tough when the occasion demanded. His calm and dignified bearing inspired confidence in others. 'One felt he would know how to handle any situation and consequently there was no cause for alarm.' He was a country gentleman as well as the best sort of naval officer. His deep love of nature revealed the inner man. He was delighted in peacetime when ordered to the Orkneys, where he could go ashore to observe the birds. He also enjoyed shooting and hunting. Everybody liked and admired Bill Tennant and enjoyed his company, and those in the Navy more than happily served under him. He was a born leader, though a quiet one, who would never exert his authority in any aggressive manner, but would nevertheless get results. The *Repulse*, under Tennant and his tough and amiable Executive Officer, the husky Commander R. J. R. Dendy, was an extremely happy ship.

Tennant may not have had a brilliant brain—his intellectual

powers were a bit limited (he never held an appointment on the Board), and he did not enjoy abstract staff work—but, professionally, he was extremely competent. He was one of the Navy's great ship-handlers. (He had served his apprenticeship as Tyrwhitt's Navigation Officer in the Harwich Force, 1916–19, and as Navigation Officer in the *Repulse* in the 1920s.) When the Second World War broke out, Tennant became Chief Staff Officer to the First Sea Lord, serving as an operational adviser. Everybody knew of his magnificent exploits during the evacuation of Dunkirk in June 1940, when he was the naval controller of movements or 'Beachmaster' (he was one of the last to leave), and for which he received a CB. He assumed command of the *Repulse* in June 1940. At first he was not too popular with the ship's company, because he had such a sense of history. On every spot of ocean he was fond of broadcasting: 'Here 150 years ago, Nelson was doing this-or-that', and so on. But gradually he worked his way into the affections of the ship's company. His Torpedo and Electrical Officer observes: 'Bill Tennant was dedicated to war. He thought and lived war, and on the bridge it was safe to bet that he was the first one to sight smoke, etc. I don't think sailors understood him and I was frightened if he ever spoke to a massed meeting—but they certainly all knew they were on a good thing with him to lead us. He was fearless.'[15] I especially like this heart-warming tribute from one of his Lieutenants, who joined the ship on New Year's Eve, 1940, since, to confess a bias, I glimpsed these very qualities in the man in the course of a few letters exchanged with him after the war:

It was a cold interview with this alarmingly impressive man of immediate presence and austere, though possibly camouflaged, character. For some time I remained in awe of this aloof, utterly professional, puritannical, seemingly stern, obvious leader. As I gained the moral courage to know him, so I found those qualities I had least expected, hidden beneath the austere facade of professionalism. His deep love of Nature, birds and flowers in particular; his humanity and compassion for all his people on board and for whom he never spared himself. A deep Christian faith always practised and never preached. Once you had broken through the veneer of austerity, there was one of the warmest hearts, shy to show itself; but such quality is bound to do so in the end, even to the stokers.

[15] Rear-Admiral Sir Kenneth Buckley's letter to the author, 5 Mar. 1976. He was then a lieutenant-commander.

Quietly, almost surreptitiously, the Captain appeared as the 'pater familias'—for if I had been scared, so had the crew. Men realised that when their case was genuine they had no stauncher advocate. Awe became an undisguised affection and respect for someone in whom they saw a power of discernment and command who would meet in war whatever was asked of *Repulse*. How right we all were when the day came to see that feeling proved. So on going to sea from Freetown on our journey East, it was not as surprising to us as it was to Bill Tennant that a vase of flowers appeared on the desk of his sea-cabin 'From the Stokers'.[16]

The *Prince of Wales*, the second of the King George V class to be completed, was, until the *Yamato*, the last word in modern battleship design: 36,727 tons displacement, 28·5 knots speed, and with heavier protection than any battleship yet built, which gave her the reputation of being 'unsinkable': main belt, 4·5-inch to 15-inch, bulkheads, 4-inch to 12-inch, main deck, 5-inch to 6-inch, and main turrets, 6-inch to 13-inch. She carried 10 14-inch guns (weight of broadside, 15,900lb), with a maximum range of 36,000 yards, and 16 splendid dual purpose 5·25-inch guns that could reach aircraft at altitudes of 30,000 feet and surface ships at about 22,000 yards. For close-range AA armament, she had several eight-barrelled two-pounder pom-poms (nicknamed the 'Chicago piano'), with an accurate range of 2,000 yards, but too unwieldy to deal with really fast-moving and diving aircraft. There were also a 40mm Bofors gun (they were in very short supply), with an accurate range of 3,000 yards, a few 20mm Oerlikons, single-barrelled guns with a maximum effective range of 2,000 yards, of value only at close range, and several Lewis machine-guns. Four extra Oerlikons, shipped at Greenock, were fitted on arrival at Cape Town, and a few Bofors were embarked at Colombo. A definite weakness in the AA armament generally was its inability to range and fire accurately at very low-flying aircraft, of which torpedo-bombers were an obvious example. Two Walrus spotter-reconnaissance aircraft were normally carried, but one had been knocked over the side, while waiting to be catapulted, by the blast from the *Bismarck's* 15-inch shells and had not been replaced.

One of the chief criticisms of the King George V class was that they were designed for the North Sea and the North Atlantic, and

---

[16] Vice-Admiral Sir John Hayes's letter to the author, 25 June 1976.

not for the tropics. Ventilation was very bad and was the subject of much correspondence. Heat exhaustion, to which the poor ventilation contributed immensely, was undoubtedly a factor on 10 December. Lieutenant-Commander A. G. C. Franklin, a Sub-Lieutenant in the *Prince of Wales*, remembers 'very well, after the bomb hit amidships on the catapult deck and when I evacuated my action station, passing through a flat, with literally dozens of sailors—stokers and engine-room—who had evacuated the engine-rooms and boiler-rooms and were out for the count with heat exhaustion. They obviously were there when the ship turned over.'[17] In his post-action report the Medical Officer of the *Prince of Wales*, Surgeon-Commander F. B. Quinn, declared: 'I made certain representations to the Fleet Medical Officer, Home Fleet [September 1941], and also put on paper the inadvisability of employing *Prince of Wales* in hot climates such as Freetown or Singapore owing to defective and inadequate ventilation and of prevailing conditions in working spaces where men were employed in high temperatures. ... Though the morale of the ship's company was good, I am of the opinion that the men were fatigued and listless and their fighting efficiency was below par.'[18] The ventilation arrangements in the much older *Repulse* were far better than the more modern equipment in the *Prince of Wales* because they worked. The *Repulse* was hot in tropical conditions, of course, but not to an extent that impaired efficiency among the officers or men during the battle.[19]

The *Prince of Wales* had been commissioned from the shipbuilders in January 1941, when she was taken to Scapa Flow to work up. Before this could be completed, she was called out to join in the action against the *Bismarck* (a hundred civil contractors staff were still on board, completing the turrets' equipment), scoring the vital hit that sealed the fate of the *Bismarck* by causing a major oil leak. (This was not known at the time, so the *Prince of Wales* received no credit.) But she had suffered damage that required repairs into the summer. She was then transformed into a yacht and took Churchill

---

[17] Letter to the author, 4 Nov. 1975.
[18] Feb. 1942, ADM 199/1149. The Report of the Technical Departments of the Admiralty on the loss of the *Prince of Wales* (May 1942) asserted: 'The extra heat and lack of ventilation below caused rapid fatigue in personnel. This fact requires bearing in mind when considering any omissions which occurred.' ADM 167/116.
[19] Letters from Captain Dendy and Admiral Hayes, 20 July 1978, and Admiral Buckley, 24 July 1978. 'There were no complaints or worrying over the ventilation at all during our action,' says Dendy, who was the Damage Control Officer.

and the Chiefs of Staff across the Atlantic in August for the conference in Placentia Bay. This trip had again interrupted her working up. On her return, she had a three-week work-up of concentrated exercises at Scapa, especially anti-aircraft, and was then off in September to a convoy running job in the Mediterranean: Operation 'Halberd', during which she survived concentrated air and submarine attacks, while helping to account for four of the six Italian torpedo-bombers shot down (27 September), and, regretfully, one of the *Ark Royal's* fighters. On 23 October she was unexpectedly ordered from Scapa round to the Clyde, where she embarked Phillips and his staff.

So, in fact, the ship had never received a proper, progressive, and uninterrupted work-up, and no one was more conscious of that than her Captain. On her journey East there was little one could do to complete it: there were no aircraft available, no targets for gunfire, and no fleet units other than two destroyers (four, when well into the Indian Ocean), and a tight schedule to work to in order to carry out the Prime Minister's unwelcome instructions for maximum publicity on early arrival at Singapore. The one thing Leach really wanted was a quiet spell, when he and his ship could concentrate on suitable targets to achieve efficiency. That opportunity was denied. Before their abortive final operation, the *Prince of Wales's* Gunnery Officer believes, 'We should have had a 2 to 3 week gunnery work-up, but there was no time, and in view of the lack of screen and fighters, it would probably have made little difference. We had, for instance, never exercised with *Repulse*.'[20]

There were boiler problems as well. When at the Clyde prior to sailing, Commander Goudy had difficulty with Leach over getting permission to put a pair of boilers out of action for cleaning purposes. No captain is keen on having 25 per cent of his engine power unavailable at short notice. (The *Prince of Wales* had eight boilers and cleaned them in pairs.) Leach promised Goudy all the time he wanted when they got to the Cape. But the ship did not linger at the Cape. She was ordered to go East at high speed. On arrival at Singapore, all the boilers were much overdue for cleaning, and Goudy gave Leach a 'friendly ultimatum'. On 8 December, when steam was ordered for full speed, Goudy had three pairs open

---

[20] Captain C. W. McMullen's letter to the author, 3 Mar. 1976. McMullen adds that *en route* classes for advancement and seamanship training took a higher priority than gunnery drills for the first time in the ship's commission.

for cleaning (with internal gear out). He told the Captain and the Admiral that he could give them two boilers at once (which would allow of slow movement) and that he could reassemble the other six and raise steam in them and connect up as soon as he could. Leach was not happy about this, but Phillips accepted it without comment. Two of the boilers being cleaned had only just been started and they were quickly reassembled. By the time the ship actually got under way Goudy had four boilers connected, which gave her ample power to go down the Johore Strait. All eight boilers were connected soon after reaching the open sea. The point is that the four pairs of boilers were then in differing stages of cleanliness.[21] The loss of efficiency (there is no record of how much power was lost through the dirty boilers) was regrettable, yet it is doubtful whether the ability of the *Prince of Wales* to make better speed would have been enough to get her 'out of the hole' on the fatal 10 December. For certain, though, it did not help her.

The high morale with which the ship had commissioned under L. H. K. ('Turtle') Hamilton, a 'Band of Brothers' type of captain, who exuded confidence in himself and his officers, received a jolt when he was promoted (over his protestations) and had to be relieved. It was further set back when Leach sent for the Executive Officer (Lawson) and told him he would have to go because he had his own favourite man ready. 'I'm not saying Leach and Lawson were not first-rate officers, but the original fervour evaporated.'[22] It was recaptured by the *Bismarck* action, which had knit the ship's company together, and by the time they sailed for the East they were, if perhaps not the most efficient ship, a reasonably happy one. (Note the qualifications above, pp. 374-5.) The officers were respected and their ship was sincerely believed to be as good or better than any other afloat in the world. She had been used as a showpiece by Churchill for meeting President Roosevelt, and officers and men felt they had a ship to be proud of. The ship's company, however, was a mixed one, mostly 'hostilities only', and the latter could be difficult.

The 33,250-ton *Repulse*, in stark contrast to the *Prince of Wales*, was an old ship, largely unmodernized since her completion in

---

[21] Captain Goudy's letters to the author, 28 May 1975, 11 Mar., 18 Apr. 1978. He was Fleet Engineer Officer to the Eastern Fleet under Phillips (until arrival at Singapore) as well as Engineer Officer of the *Prince of Wales*.

[22] Goudy's letter of 28 May 1975.

1916. Despite one major refit in 1934–6, she was the most out-of-date capital ship in the Navy. She could still make 28.5 knots, but, having been originally designed as a battle cruiser, depending on speed and gunpower for protection, was deficient in the horizontal armour needed for protection against air attack: main belt, 3-inch to 9-inch, main deck, 2.5-inch to 4-inch, main turrets, 7-inch to 11-inch. She mounted six 15-inch guns (weight of broadside, 11,520lb) and a secondary armament of 12 4-inch guns. The latter were anti-surface target weapons, with range of elevation limited to that purpose, though obviously useful against formations of aircraft within those limits. She also had eight 21-inch torpedoes and carried two Walrus aircraft. But her AA armament was juvenile to a degree. She was, in Admiral Hayes's words, 'armed with not much more than an umbrella to push at the enemy like old ladies'; six outdated single-barrelled hand-operated high-angle 4-inch, and, for short range (targets within 1,000 yards: on 10 December, the Japanese released some of their torpedoes outside that range), three eight-barrelled 2-pounder pom-poms, eight single pea-shooting 20mm Oerlikons, and four 0.5-inch four-barrelled Vickers machine-guns (not very effective at any range due to mounting inadequacy). The *Repulse* was indeed the worst-armed from the AA aspect of all the Royal Navy's capital ships. Moreover, she did not do much AA practice after she left the United Kingdom for the East, for the good reason (as with the *Prince of Wales*) that there were very infrequent opportunities for a target-towing aircraft and drogue on the way out. The best they could do was to exercise the full control system at least ten times daily, except when in harbour. Unlike the *Prince of Wales* which had a sophisticated system of bulkheads and watertight compartments to minimize damage through flooding after a torpedo hit, the *Repulse* had old-fashioned underwater bulges to absorb or cushion the effects of torpedo hits. Again, unlike the *Prince of Wales*, which possessed a full complement of radar, the only radar the *Repulse* had was a single set fitted on the way out to the Cape: a surface-warning set (Type 284), which was not married into the gunnery control system. In fact, the ranges were passed by phone to the bridge and then on by voice pipe. Moreover, the movement of the aerial, which was wedged on to the guns of 'B' turret, depended on the training of the turret. When 'B' turret swept the horizon every two or three minutes, so did the aerial, which put a strain on the turret's machinery. The *Repulse* was due for a refit in the United States, like her sister battle cruiser the *Renown* (when her 42 fire-tube boilers would be replaced by eight water-tube ones).[23] She had speed but little more otherwise than a splendid morale and her looks—she was a *distinguished* old lady, being one of the most impressively beautiful ships the Navy has ever produced. 'She had poise and an outward grace and courage, but nothing in her biceps.'

The *Repulse*, much used in peace for carrying royalty in foreign visits, had a reputation unsurpassed for happiness. But during the war she tended to be regarded as a forgotten ship, always on the brink of action, but never quite managing to see it. She had just missed the German battle cruisers *Scharnhorst* and *Gneisenau* on their breakout into the Atlantic in February 1941, and had participated in the early hunt for the *Bismarck*, but had been forced to drop out through a shortage of fuel before the final action. She had been in the Mediterranean, where she never saw action. The closest she had been to action was off Norway, when German planes had bombed her—there were some near misses—but she had not fired a shot. She was, nevertheless, in a high state of efficiency and morale, which was borne out in the action off Malaya. Her ship's company and many of her officers had, before the outbreak of war in Europe, been picked to take King George VI and Queen Elizabeth to Canada. With war threatening, this task was cancelled, but the men remained. She, therefore, had a superb ship's company, 'with morale as high as the Eifel Tower, and this remained to the day so many were decimated' (Admiral Hayes).

Feelings between the two big ships were not the friendliest, due to the fact that the *Repulse* had had a pretty dull war, whereas the *Prince of Wales* was the 'glamour ship', always in the news. On her arrival at Singapore, the *Repulse* was scarcely mentioned in the press (the reason will be indicated below); the *Prince of Wales*—HMS 'Unsinkable'—got all the publicity.

It was during Operation Halberd, in the Malta convoy operation in which the *Prince of Wales* had taken an active role, that the *Nelson* was hit by a torpedo from one of the Italian aircraft. It is of interest

---

[23] When she was half way across the Indian Ocean, the Torpedo and Electrical Officer in the *Repulse* was secretly asked if the ship could stand delaying refit, as otherwise she would have to turn back. 'I said that *Repulse* could soldier on electrically for *years* with the present old-fashioned gear. The Engineer said much the same—and so we went to Singapore.' Admiral Buckley's letter to the author, 5 Mar. 1976.

that the anti-aircraft precautions in defending the Halberd convoy consisted of the *Ark Royal*'s fighters, 3 battleships, 5 cruisers, and 18 destroyers, but still the *Nelson* was nearly sunk. A very different story existed in the *Prince of Wales*'s final operation, when she had a screen of only four old destroyers and no fighter protection. And therein lies a story.

The post-first World War bomb *v.* battleship controversy had reached a crescendo in 1936 with the proceedings of the CID sub-committee on 'The Vulnerability of Capital Ships to Air Attack'.[24] Chatfield's testimony reflected the dominant feeling in the Navy. 'There is no limit', he maintained, 'to the number of guns we can put into a ship. . . . If air attack becomes so severe that all the steps we are taking are not sufficient, and I am almost afraid that we are doing too much for it, to be on the safe side, then all you have to do is to reduce the number of guns and larger weapons and put more weight into the anti-aircraft guns . . .' The idea was more to break up formations of attacking aircraft, or to force them to distances and heights at which accurate bombing would be impossible, than to shoot down individual aircraft. The Air Ministry, of course, did not agree with the naval views as to the efficacy of AA fire from ships, denying, *inter alia*, that gunfire would have any psychological effect on bombing accuracy; but the Conclusions and Recommendations of the Sub-Committee report with qualifications endorsed the position of the Admiralty. When Sir Samuel Hoare, the First Lord, addressed the seventh meeting of the Imperial Conference of 1937, he had 'no hesitation in saying that the report of this committee has justified the continued existence of the capital ship as a type . . .' He spoke of the 'drastic action' taken by the Admiralty to increase the AA armament of warships, and of the 'remarkable advance' in naval AA gunnery since the war.

When our anti-aircraft re-armament has been completed, I feel sure that our Admirals will be able to take their fleets and squadrons into any waters confident that the ships under their command are so strongly

---

[24] The report was issued as a White Paper, Command 5301, but the full confidential publication was CID1258-B, 30 July 1936, CAB 16/147. The First Sea Lord, Chatfield, and the CAS, Air Chief Marshal Sir Edward Ellington, were 'expert advisers' to the Committee, which was chaired by Sir Thomas Inskip, the Minister for Co-ordination of Defence, and whose other members were Lord Halifax (Lord Privy Seal), Malcolm MacDonald (Dominions Secretary), and Walter Runciman (President of the Board of Trade). Witnesses included a variety of civilians and officers from all Services.

defended that air attack by an enemy could only be carried out at such a cost in casualties to aircraft and personnel that he would hesitate before he attempted it.

I make no more claim that ships cannot be sunk by air attack than I claim that ships will not sink under gunfire or as a result of torpedo hits. But in all these respects modern construction has greatly increased the defensive qualities of our ships and decreased their vulnerability.[25]

In 1939 the Parliamentary and Financial Secretary to the Admiralty, Geoffrey Shakespeare, assured the House of Commons that 'Our modern ships can produce a volume of defensive fire, both long range and short range, of such a nature that will drive aircraft to such a height that the efficiency and accuracy of their attacking weapons will be seriously impaired.'[26]

Before the war, therefore, naval officers generally were convinced that the threat of high-level and dive-bombing was greatly exaggerated; torpedo-bombing was taken more seriously, but it was thought that this could also be dealt with and would, in any case, only be likely to be encountered in narrow waters or in range of shore-based aircraft. The barrage of AA fire from British warships would shoot down enemy planes or, at least, put their pilots off their aim. Nothing would make most naval officers understand the air threat to their beloved battlewagons.

Tom Phillips was a foremost and fanatical exponent of this line of thought. When he and Slessor were colleagues in the Joint Planning Committee before the war, the former was so irrational on the subject, at times violently so, that 'we had to have a sort of pact not to discuss aircraft versus ships except when our duty made it inevitable in committee—when there was usually a row'.[27] In 1939, not long before the war, Phillips, now DCNS, sent for the DDNAD, Captain R. M. Ellis, about a paper of his pleading for increased naval air torpedo production. Ellis's figures prophesied hitting rates, attack opportunities, number of hits required to sink a target, and hence a torpedo expenditure rate—the first named

---

[25] 26 May 1937, CAB 32/128.
[26] 16 Mar. 1939, *Parliamentary Debates* (*Hansard*), 5th Ser., Commons, cccvl, cols, 655–6.
[27] Slessor, *The Central Blue*, p. 227. A. T. ('Bomber') Harris, who had preceded Slessor as D of P in the Air Ministry, had the same battles with Phillips. When Phillips was leaving the Plans Division (1938), Harris proposed a jocular toast and said, 'Tom, when the first bomb hits, you'll say, "My God, what a hell of a mine!"' We have this delectable yarn on Slessor's authority.

being reduced by coefficients for AA fire, fog-of-war, etc. The Admiral said that he, Ellis, favoured the aircraft too much, and that the hitting rates would be much lower. 'Then we will need even more torpedoes, Sir.' 'A good point, my boy, a good point,' Phillips said, and approved the paper. But he wrote a minute on it to the effect that the aircraft menace was over-stated, with reasons for saying so. The Japanese obtained an even higher percentage of torpedo hits in the naval battle off Malaya than Ellis had foretold. His percentage of hits to be expected in torpedo attacks on ships under way (at normal cruising speeds, and assuming a normal degree of AA defence) was 15. The actual percentage on 10 December 1941 was 22. 'I later discovered that he was a disciple of the school which held that the British should never start any new "weapon system" that would imperil the ascendancy of the British Capital Ship.'[28]

The Navy retained its blind confidence in sea power when the war broke out in Europe. From Churchill, Pound, and Phillips down, the Navy had faith in the effectiveness of a warship's AA defences. The first months of the war provided no experience to alter these views. The high-level attack on the Home Fleet in the North Sea on 29 September 1939, during which the Germans claimed to have sunk the *Ark Royal*, was completely ineffective. The RAF had attacked the German Fleet at or off Wilhelmshaven seven times between September 1939 and April 1940 with little more success. It needed Norway and Dunkirk in the spring of 1940 to demonstrate the peril to ships operating within range of enemy shore-based aircraft. Norway, in particular, shook up the Navy—Pound included. Whereas he had expressed himself early in 1940 as 'rather optimistic about battleships versus aircraft', basing this on 'the improvements in A/A equipment', towards the end of the Norwegian campaign his tune had changed: 'The one lesson we have learnt here is that it is essential to have fighter protection over

---

[28] Captain Ellis's letter to the author, 17 June 1976, which includes an important appendix (No. 11), 'Pre-War Projections of Hitting Rates ...', to an unpublished book on his part in naval air matters between the wars, in flying and at the Admiralty, and in Combined Operations, 1942–5. The MS ('When the Rain's before the Wind') and a mass of supporting papers are at Churchill College. Table I in Appendix 11, from which I derived the percentage quoted above, 'condenses some of the pre-war forecast figures, expressing them as probabilities of hitting, whereas the original papers expressed them as numbers of torpedoes or bombs needing to be released in order to obtain one hit' (Appendix 11).

the Fleet whenever they are within reach of the enemy bombers.'[29]

There is no evidence that Phillips had undergone a change of heart at that time. During the Norwegian campaign he clung tenaciously to the view that AA fire without fighter cover would provide adequate protection against air attack to surface craft operating close inshore. Thus, he ordered the C-in-C, Home Fleet, Admiral Forbes, to use the cruiser *Suffolk* to bombard Stavanger, though Forbes had warned this could only result in disaster. He continued to underestimate the air threat and remained convinced that warships at sea, if properly equipped with AA armament and efficient gun crews, could repel any attack from the air. Lieutenant-Commander P. K. Kemp remembers Admiral Tovey telling him after the war how he went to see Phillips in the Admiralty on his return from the Mediterranean in October 1940 (he had been Second-in-Command of the Mediterranean Fleet), and being almost accused of cowardice when he said that ships could not operate at sea without air cover. It was indeed a sad irony of fate that decreed that Phillips's first experience of flying his flag at sea should be ended by the aircraft whose value against capital ships he had so long denied.

And yet deeply rooted though his obsession was, there is proof that it weakened from the latter part of 1940 and was all but gone by October 1941. Goodenough, who knew the Admiral's mind as well as anybody, is positive: 'I think the Admiral believed that eventually ships would be able to stand up to aircraft. In this I believe him to have been a very true prophet. One has only to read of the last stages of the Pacific War to see the march of events. But the Admiral most certainly did not believe that ships should be subjected to heavy air attack without the assistance of fighter defence.'[30]

Probably he had learned something from the Navy's rough experience in the Greek and Cretan campaigns and from the crippling of the *Bismarck* by air torpedoes, and had come to realize how ineffective naval anti-aircraft gunfire was at the time. We know that he was by no means convinced that their own air defence measures were adequate, especially the AA control systems (at that stage of the War, without radar warning, ranging, or height-

---

[29] Pound to Cunningham, 7 Jan., 20 May 1940, Cunningham Papers, Add. MS 52560.
[30] Rear-Admiral Michael Goodenough to Lady Phillips, 6 June [1947], Phillips Papers.

finding), and methods of improving them, especially against low flying aircraft, were much in his mind.[31] Vice-Admiral Sir Algernon Willis wrote to Lady Phillips after the disaster of 10 December: 'What seems to me to have been such hard luck is that old Tom should have gone out in circumstances so contrary to all his convictions. As you know he was all for a lot of smaller ships with a large air arm in support—he had *neither*.'[32] The Tom Phillips of the autumn of 1941 was therefore not the Tom Phillips who had made light of the air danger in the Norwegian operations a year and a half earlier. He was certainly alive to the threat imposed by dive-bombers and torpedo-bombers, in particular. The legend, nevertheless, persists, as legends will, that Phillips had undergone no change in his views on the threat from the air.

2. MAIN FLEET TO SINGAPORE

Phillips was not oversanguine about the prospects when he left England. His Assistant Secretary remembers very well Phillips returning to the Admiralty after the Defence Committee meeting on 20 October and his replying, when asked how the meeting had gone, 'glumly and without elaboration, "We are off on Thursday"'. On 22 October, the day before he left for the Clyde, Phillips visited the First Lord at his residence. A. V. Alexander's daughter recalls: 'He was obviously unhappy and must have had serious misgivings about the venture, and I am quite sure my father did, too.'[33] On the other hand, he was glad to be at sea again. When he came to say

---

[31] I rely for this statement on a letter from Admiral Farnhill, 16 Oct. 1975. When the large liner *Empress of Britain* was abandoned, fiercely on fire, after an air attack on 26 October 1940 (she was sunk by a U-boat on the 28th), Phillips told his son that, given enough aircraft to attack a ship, then it would be sunk. 'We went on to talk about defending ships at sea and the inefficiency of the gun armaments of those days to repulse an air attack. That the real defence was your own air cover was obvious, but the facts at the time meant that it was impossible to give air cover to all the places and ships in need of it. There were too few fighters available with too short a range.' Commander Phillips also remembers what his father told him when the heavy cruiser *Southampton* was so badly damaged by air attack (11 January 1941) that she had to be sunk. The admiral said that 'this had started a new era of naval warfare in the Mediterranean, as the introduction of the German Air Force with their dive bombers meant that ships could no longer go about their business in that area with the impunity of the opening phases of the war.' Commander T. V. G. Phillips to Captain S. W. Roskill, 10 Feb. 1962, Phillips Papers.

[32] 17 Dec. 1941, copy of letter in possession of Captain Litchfield.

[33] Lady Beatrix Evison's letter to the author, 25 Feb. 1975.

goodbye to Ismay that day, 'He was blissfully happy at the prospect of flying his flag after so many years in Whitehall.'[34]

The *Prince of Wales* sailed from the Clyde on 25 October, screened by the destroyers *Electra* and *Express*, and a third, the *Hesperus*, for the first part of the voyage. The mood of the ship's company on the way out was relaxed and cheerful (there was, for instance, a very happy 'crossing the line' ceremony), due to the joy of escaping from the monotony and rigours of Scapa Flow to the warmth of the tropics and to the prospect of taking part in great events, although they had little impression of what they might be. Some of the officers would have agreed with this appraisal of the prospect facing a weak and unbalanced force: 'We were sailing into the unknown, with almost complete lack of information on what to expect in the way of opposition. We felt the operation was a gamble and that we were sticking our necks out and that we would be lucky if we got away with it. My belief at the time was that we should never have got ourselves into the situation we did.'[35]

Most officers, however, were optimistic, which, given the remarkable ignorance of Japanese naval capabilities, is not surprising. The lack of air cover was not a matter of too much concern. The Surgeon Lieutenant-Commander recollects how 'at ward room level we had that much publicised misapprehension that the Japanese were all short-sighted and that their planes were reputed to be made of "cardboard" and probably extremely inefficiently piloted'.[36] In similar fashion, another young officer remembers they 'had been told—and I think we believed it even after we had arrived in the Far East—that the Japanese couldn't fly well, particularly at night, because they had the eye-fold, and were really a backward type of flier'.[37] The Engineer Officer overheard some senior staff officers making derogatory remarks about the Japanese airmen, one saying they would bomb Singapore—if they could find it![38] During the ship's dash across the Indian Ocean an incident occurred which revealed current Staff thinking. 'During a Staff meeting in the Plot (Operations Room), someone made a statement to the effect that the Japanese had torpedo planes and

[34] *The Memoirs of General the Lord Ismay* (London, 1960), p. 240.
[35] Captain (then Midshipman) D. G. Roome's letter to the author, 30 May 1975.
[36] Surgeon Vice-Admiral Sir Dick Caldwell's letter to the author, 18 Nov. 1975.
[37] Admiral (then Midshipman) R. H. Leir's memorandum for the author, Oct. 1975.
[38] Captain Goudy's letter to the author, 17 Dec. 1975.

bombers operating from a place with the funny name of Pnom Penh. He said they didn't know the range of the torpedo planes, but based on the performance of the Beaufort he thought it would be about 800 miles, therefore if we stayed outside 400 miles from Pnom Penh we should be all right.'[39] The Japanese Navy's torpedo-bomber was passed off as 'a somewhat inferior edition of the early Swordfish', which was hardly anything to fear.[40] There was great faith in their eight-barrelled pom-poms, which had done good work on the Italian torpedo-bombers in the Mediterranean during Operation Halberd. That experience gave them a lot of confidence, over-confidence really, for an encounter with the Japanese. The only danger the officers in the *Prince of Wales* foresaw was the possibility of the Japanese flying their aircraft into a ship and comitting hara-kiri. The exceedingly high quality of the Japanese naval air arm was to come as a complete and demoralizing bolt from the blue. There was no feeling of regret, from the point of view of sentiment, over meeting the Japanese Fleet if it came to a fight. Gone was any residue of Japanophilism. 'The Japanese were pals with Hitler and that was that' was the attitude.

The *Prince of Wales* escorted a convoy to Freetown, Sierre Leone, her first port of call, and refuelled there for a brief 24 hours. Phillips cracked on at high speed to Cape Town, without his two destroyers, who were left to follow at more economical speeds. Their Lordships were anxious that Phillips reach Cape Town quickly, spend only 28 hours there (to allow a visit to South Africa's Prime Minister, Field-Marshal Smuts), then proceed to Singapore with dispatch for a meeting with British and Dominion naval representatives as a 'necessary preliminary to finally clearing up the Anglo–American plans'. On arrival at Cape Town on 16 November, the Admiral at once flew up to Pretoria for 'a night of very interesting talks' (Smuts) with the Prime Minister. This had been arranged by Churchill, who had great faith in Smuts's judgement. Smuts formed a high opinion of Phillips, but he had grave doubts about Anglo–American naval dispositions in the Pacific. In a telegram to Churchill (18 November) he warned that the Japanese, occupying a central position, might defeat the British and American fleets,

---

[39] Lieutenant-Commander (then Plot Midshipman) W. F. B. Faulkner's letter to the author, 17 June 1975.
[40] Lieutenant-Commander T. J. Cain, *H.M.S. Electra* (London, 1959), pp. 168–9.

each inferior to them, in detail. 'This matter is so vital that I would press for rearrangment of dispositions as soon as war appears imminent. If Japanese are really nippy there is here [an] opening for a first-class disaster.'[41] Smuts told Phillips that his two big ships would have no impact on the far stronger Japanese Fleet, or on its operations, unless their whereabouts was successfully concealed. He urged the Admiral to arrange before leaving Cape Town a series of secret fuelling anchorages and hide-away places in the East Indonesian Islands, and to keep on the move all the time, so that the Japanese would be uncertain and worried. Once the ships showed themselves at Singapore, their presence would be known and their mission would become fruitless.[42] Nothing resulted from this advice, although a very similar strategy came to the fore independently in London at the eleventh hour.

In the meantime, the world was made aware of the arrival of the *Prince of Wales* at Cape Town. She was given the full 'public relations' treatment, the Admiralty having authorized Phillips to give facilities for press photographers and 'controlled interviews' on board the ship. Newspaper headlines flared the news (though, by arrangement, not until the day after she had left Cape Town): 'Eastern Fleet Being Reinforced by *Prince of Wales*', 'Britain's Newest Battleship for Singapore', etc. Actually, nothing was said to the press about the ship's destination. This was hardly necessary. As Pound minuted Churchill, 'The arrival of the *Prince of Wales* at Capetown, taken in conjunction with what you said in your speech at the Guildhall, will, I am sure, leave neither the Japanese, nor our press, in doubt as to the eventual destination of the *Prince of Wales*.'[43]

The ship having refuelled and a battery of four Oerlikon AA guns put aboard at Greenock fitted on the upper deck, and with all ranks surfeited with the 'out-of-this-world' hospitality that had been extended, the *Prince of Wales*, once more alone, left Cape Town on 18 November. There was now a sense of urgency. After further short refuelling stops at Mauritius and Addu Atoll (Gan) in the

---

[41] PREM 3/163/3.
[42] Admiral Grantham's letter to the author, 29 Aug. 1975. He heard this from Smuts when the latter was in Egypt early in 1942 and came on board his ship.
[43] 18 Nov. 1941, ADM 205/10. On 10 November Churchill had given a firm indication to the guests at the Lord Mayor's banquet where the ships were going: 'we now feel ourselves strong enough to provide a powerful naval force of heavy ships, with the necessary ancillary vessels, for service if needed in the Indian and Pacific Oceans'.

Maldives, she reached Colombo in the evening of 28 November and dropped anchor within sight of the destroyers *Jupiter* and *Encounter* (the Admiralty had directed the C-in-C, Mediterranean, to send two destroyers to Ceylon for Phillips's use); the *Repulse* was lying at Trincomalee.

The *Repulse* was not ordered East in any dramatic sense. It was a gradual process that began in August 1941, when she was at Rosyth for a short refit. It then became evident to a few that 'something was up', that the ship was going somewhere abroad. This was a shot-in-the-arm to everybody after the dreary round of Air Defence Stations in Scapa Flow and abortive 'runs' into the Atlantic after the *Hipper* or the *Bismarck*. On 29 August the *Repulse* was suddenly sent round from Scapa to the Clyde as senior officer of the escort for a large troop convoy for the Middle East. She spent October and November in further troop-convoy escort work and in showing the flag, with a bit of raider hunting and gunnery practice. To quote Tennant, they were 'on really what amounted to a yachting trip in the South Indian Ocean, and during that time had two short visits to Durban, when I think the Ship's Company enjoyed themselves more than at any other port they had visited'.[44]

We were all in high spirits [Admiral Hayes recalls]. Sun does much to help after the bleak days of Scapa Flow, the UK ports in winter, skirmishes into the Atlantic amidst the snow flurries and gales looking for the enemy marauder. Young sailors who had never before grilled themselves on a tropic beach began to come to life in a way they could not have guessed possible. People who had not yet tasted war were kindness itself. It all seemed very unreal and good morale soared even higher, ready for anything which everybody sensed was bound to come.[45]

The *Repulse* was at Kilindini, Kenya, awaiting further orders, when she was directed on 11 November to meet the *Prince of Wales* in Colombo and thence proceed to Singapore.

No sooner had Phillips arrived at Colombo than he received an Admiralty signal ordering him to fly to Singapore (which he did on 29 November) in order to get on with his planning, and then to Manila to discuss the co-ordination of naval plans with the

---

[44] 'The Last Action of H.M.S. *Repulse* & H.M.S. *Prince of Wales*', n.d. (Dec. 1941), rough notes for his post-action reports, Tennant Papers (National Maritime Museum). Hereafter cited as Tennant, 'The Last Action'.

[45] Admiral Hayes's letter, 25 June 1976.

Americans. The Admiral turned the combined force, the two big ships and the four destroyers, over to Tennant as the senior captain. The *Repulse* left Trincomalee on the 29th, rendezvoused with the *Prince of Wales* south of Colombo, and proceeded across the Bay of Bengal and through the Malacca Strait at high speed. The fleet steamed up Johore Strait and entered the Naval Base in the late afternoon of 2 December, Phillips rejoining the flagship before the Force entered harbour.

On 3 December Phillips hoisted his flag as C-in-C, Eastern Fleet. Although the Admiralty had informed Vice-Admiral Sir Geoffrey Layton on 21 October that his appointment of C-in-C, China, would be abolished on the arrival of Phillips, it was arranged between the two Admirals that Layton would carry on the local command and administration, flying his flag on shore, until the new C-in-C was able to concert plans for operations with their prospective Allies.

On 28 April 1941 the Admiralty had informed Layton that a separate C-in-C would be appointed who would command the Main Fleet on passage to the Far East, and after its arrival would assume the general command. This had not sat well with Layton, who on the assumption of his command in September 1940 had been given to understand that if war broke out with Japan, his naval force, then negligible, would be strongly reinforced and that he would command it. On 11 May he was told that Phillips had been selected as the new 'Commander-in-Chief, Eastern Fleet', as he was to be designated. Layton never assumed, however, that the Admiralty would be bound by these signals when the balloon went up. To his surprise, an Admiralty signal of 3 October informed him that Phillips had been appointed C-in-C, Eastern Fleet, and would, on arrival in the Far East early in 1942, take over command of the ships and establishments on the China Station, the appointment of C-in-C, China, being abolished. Layton would at that time return to England to take up the appointment of C-in-C, Portsmouth. (This was a prestigious appointment and one that Layton had always wanted as perhaps the final crown of his career.) On 21 October the Admiralty informed him that Phillips would leave for the Far East shortly and that on his arrival the appointment of C-in-C, China, would be abolished, without waiting for the outbreak of hostilities or for the assembly of the projected Eastern Fleet. Layton's disappointment and chagrin were not assuaged by the personal message from Pound that accompanied the official signal on 3 October: 'I realise that the decision conveyed in Admiralty 1151/3 must cause you some disappointment, but it is part of a policy of reducing the age of flag officers in seagoing commands, and you should understand that no-one senior to Tovey will in future be appointed afloat.' (The theory of appointing younger officers to sea-going commands was hardly borne out by the subsequent appointment of Somerville to the Eastern Fleet and the reappointment of A. B. Cunningham to the Mediterranean, both officers considerably senior, in years and in rank, to either Layton or Tovey.) 'Some disappointment!' was Layton's reaction to these signals. 'It's the biggest blow I ever had in my life .... In time of war I've always said that one must do what one is told and not belly-ache. So there it is. But—Tom Phillips!' His *amour propre* was deeply wounded by the fact that, as soon as active naval operations became imminent, he was superseded by an officer who was considerably junior and less experienced, and whom he regarded as an 'unsound' flag officer. This was based, it would appear, on Phillips's views when Rear-Admiral Destroyer Flotillas, and Admiralty comments on operations in the Northern Patrol and in Norway, 1939–40, which Layton believed had emanated from the VCNS. 'He thought Phillips a theorist who clung to his opinions even when all the facts were against him, and who lacked practical experience.'[46]

3. FORCE Z AT SINGAPORE

The *Prince of Wales* and *Repulse* were greeted on their entry into Keppel Harbour, the City's port, 'as though they were the main

---

[46] Doig. 'Geoffrey Layton', a memorandum for the author, 20 Oct. 1978, Doig, 'Misfortune off Malaya', p. 3, and his letters to the author, 1 Oct. 1978, 16 May 1979. Layton no doubt considered himself far better qualified for the new command. He had in turn commanded a battle-cruiser squadron, a battle squadron, and a cruiser squadron, had served continuously at sea for the first nine months of the war, including the Northern Patrol and in the Norwegian campaign, and had had personal experience of being subjected to heavy enemy air attack without adequate resources. I shall introduce Layton properly in my second volume, as he will figure more prominently in our story from 10 December 1941. Enough here to say that he was bullet-headed, aggressive-looking, and aggressive—an unconventional officer with a powerful personality and an imperturbable determination to do his duty no matter what the situation.

attractions of a seaside carnival'. (The destroyers, which received little attention, went on to the Naval Base itself, on the north-east shore of the island, where the big ships joined them later in the day.) The press played up the arrival of the capital ships as though, with the fleet there, the Royal Navy had command of the Eastern seas. The headline in the *Straits Times* (3 December) ran: 'Big Fleet Arrives led by *Prince of Wales*', and the story itself began: '*Prince of Wales*, one of Britain's most modern battleships, arrived in Singapore yesterday with other heavy ships and auxiliary vessels which form the newly-constituted Eastern Fleet, commanded by Admiral Sir Tom Phillips ...' It spoke of these ships making 'a magnificent and imposing sight as they were silhouetted against a background of blue sky and green islands.... Enthusiasm everywhere was very noticeable.' However, only the name of the flagship was mentioned, as efforts were made to conceal the strength of the Force. The name of the *Repulse* was not released by the press or the BBC, to the extreme annoyance of the ship's company, who did not like to be ignored and their whereabouts withheld from their families. The Deputy Director of the Far Eastern Bureau of the Ministry of Information caught the mood of Singapore: 'With what mingled emotions we watched the two ships as they steamed majestically to their anchorage off the Naval Base! Those strange grey shapes on the skyline, they were symbols of our new-found strength, concrete expressions of the confidence with which we faced any emergency that might arise in the Pacific.'[47]

A peacetime atmosphere pervaded the city, which was gay, brightly lit, and, on the surface at any rate, confident that the advent of the Eastern Fleet would counteract and lull the insistent sabre-rattling of the Japanese war lords. Phillips was shaken by the way people in Singapore seemed oblivious of the danger and were still not on a war footing. The old sleepy colonial way of life persisted. Midshipman Henry Leach, who was stationed at Singapore Naval Base (his ship, the cruiser *Mauritius*, was undergoing repairs), had been at Kota Bharu not long before the arrival of Force Z. The general feeling there was: 'They might do it to the Americans, but not to us. They wouldn't dare; it's bluff—they won't come.' The evening of 3 December, Rear-Admiral E. J. Spooner, commanding the Naval Base, gave a party in honour of

---

[47] Ian Morrison, *Malayan Postcript* (London, 1942), p. 16.

the *Prince of Wales*. 'Everybody was cheerful and confident. "There was a sign of revelry by night."'[48] Friends were made, and future plans discussed of meetings, of tennis and golf. Early the following day all leave was stopped.

On that day, 4 December, Phillips, accompanied by Beardsworth and Goodenough, flew to Manila to confer with Admiral Hart, C-in-C, US Asiatic Fleet. Phillips had on his mind the problem of how soon he could start to mould his capital ships and destroyers, which had never worked together and were desperately short of ship, let alone fleet, training, into a coherent task force. But his first priority was with the arrangements for immediate co-operation that he could make with the American and Dutch naval commands. On the 5th the *Repulse* sailed for Port Darwin with a destroyer escort (*Vampire, Tenedos*). It was to be a visit of only a few days, and largely for political considerations. It was Phillips's own idea. He deemed that such a visit 'at the moment may be useful in connection with Australian Government attitude regarding release of any cruiser to serve with Fleet. From what I have heard here I anticipate difficulty in this respect, especially since loss of H.M.A.S. *Sydney*, on whom I was counting.'[49] (A German armed merchant raider had just sunk the Australian cruiser *Sydney* off the coast of Western Australia on 19 November.) The *Prince of Wales* stayed behind. The Bofors guns embarked at Colombo were installed, and small defects were taken in hand, including the retubing of her distillers, a curious defect in so new a ship.

Phillips arrived in Manila at noon, 5 December.[50] He conferred through the following day, with Lieutenant-General Douglas MacArthur, Commander of US Forces in the Far East, present

---

[48] Alfred Duff Cooper (Viscount Norwich), *Old Men Forget: The Autobiography of Duff Cooper* (London, 1953), p. 300.

[49] Phillips to Admiralty, 4 Dec. 1941, Cabinet Office, Great Britain, *Principal War Telegrams and Memoranda, 1940–1943. Far East* (London, 1976), Pt. i. 1. The signals concerning Force Z are in the Naval Historical Branch records. The more important ones are in Pound's memorandum of 25 Jan. 1942, 'Loss of H.M.S. Prince of Wales & Repulse', ADM 199/1149, especially Appendix ii. Operational signals made by the C-in-C and his COS on 9 and 10 December are also to be found in Vice-Admiral Sir Geoffrey Layton, 'Loss of H.M. Ships Prince of Wales and Repulse', 17 Dec. 1941, Supplement to *The London Gazette*, 20 Feb. 1948, pp. 1947–8.

[50] The record of the talks is in Admiral Hart's 'Narrative of Events, Asiatic Fleet Leading up to War and From 8 December 1941 to 15 February 1942', pp. 34–6, World War II Action Reports, US Operational Archives, with some local colour added in Hart's unpublished diary (Mrs Thomas C. Hart).

until the conference became purely naval.[51] Hart was most favourably impressed with Phillips, who 'showed himself to be a remarkably able officer—possessing very broad knowledge, with keen intuition and judgment. Even though our association with him was brief we sensed that he was the best man that we had encountered.' Hart recorded in his diary (5 December): 'I had pictured a big, burly, personable, magnetic sort. He's a bare 5 ft. two and decidedly the intellectual type—good stuff, all right, and has a first rate brain. ... We were quite frank with each other, laid our cards down, and wore no gloves. ... Well I acquired considerable respect for Phillips—looks like as good an Englishman to work with as I have had for some time.' In spite of this evaluation and Phillips's report to London that the discussion was 'very friendly and we can expect full co-operation', there were disappointments on both sides.

Although it was decided that the Malay Barrier must be held against the Japanese, Hart detected 'no decided change in the British Naval attitude in that protection of their sea supply routes as well as of the troop convoys was still primary. There was still the trend toward dispersal of forces. However, the new high command was obviously seeking combat and a coming offensive attitude was clearly seen.' Given the weakness of his A/S screen, Phillips's main concern was to obtain the immediate use of the two divisions of US destroyers (eight ships) from Hart's command to work with the Eastern Fleet which Admiral Stark had offered 'upon the arrival of British battleships in the Far East area ... if the United States is then at war with Japan'.[52] Phillips scaled his request down to one division—four destroyers—to be sent to Singapore at once in view of the situation. Hart agreed to have them join Force Z, but not immediately. The American cruisers needed destroyers to be fully effective; besides, Phillips had four destroyers for his capital ships and could use the two or three on the China Station assigned to the local defence of Hong Kong and which were roughly the equal of

---

[51] MacArthur 'of course talked interminably', Hart noted in his diary. The General was, however, wiser than the sailors where the IJN was concerned. The American journalist T. H. White interviewed him in Manila in December 1940. (MacArthur was then Military Adviser to the Philippine Government): 'he insisted war was coming. He spoke of the Japanese Navy—and he thought it was first class. Beware of the Japanese Navy, he said, and continuing, he said that Japanese carrier-based aviation was superb.' White, *In Search of History: A Personal Adventure* (London, 1979), p. 108.
[52] Ghormley to Pound, 7 Nov. 1941, ADM 205/9.

the US destroyers. Hart assured Phillips that the CNO's promise of the loan of destroyers would be kept, but the time had not arrived. Since the United States was not at war yet, he was on firm ground. However, it was agreed that Manila (1,330 miles east of Singapore) would be a more secure base than Singapore for the British battle fleet, and arrangements would be made to move it there by April;[53] that the British fleet, reinforced by Dutch and American destroyers and a Dutch cruiser, would be used as 'a striking force against Japanese movements in the China Sea, the Dutch East Indies or through the Malay barrier'; that a British–Dutch–American cruiser squadron would operate from eastern Borneo to protect convoys in the triangle North Borneo–Surabaja–Darwin; and that a cruiser force would be earmarked to cover and escort convoys in the Indian Ocean and Australian–New Zealand waters.

The conference was abruptly terminated late in the afternoon of the 6th on the receipt of intelligence from Singapore. In the early afternoon Hudson aircraft of the Royal Australian Air Force No. 1 (Reconnaissance) Squadron based on Kota Bharu sighted three separate convoys of Japanese transports. They totalled 38 ships, had strong naval escorts, and were off the south coast of French Indo-China, steering north-westward and westward towards the Gulf of Siam. Phillips at once signalled to his Chief of Staff to recall the *Repulse*, which was nearing Darwin (Palliser had already taken this step, acting on Layton's advice), and that evening he flew back to Singapore. As Phillips was leaving Manila, Hart said, 'I have just ordered my destroyers at Balikpapan [the four ships of Destroyer Division 57] to proceed to Batavia on the pretext of rest and leave. Actually they will join your force.'[54] They were steaming at full speed to Singapore when Force Z met the Japanese. Their presence with Phillips on 10 December would probably have made no difference, as what he needed most was air cover.

There were no further sightings of Japanese convoys during the

---

[53] The Admiralty had decided in October that, once the Eastern Fleet had been established at Singapore, it 'should look upon Manila as its advance base and probably operate from there'. Rear-Admiral Sir Henry Harwood's (ACNS(F)) minute to Pound, 29 Oct. 1941, ADM 116/4877.

[54] Morison, *History of United States Naval Operations in World War II*, iii. 157. Mrs Hart has her husband telling Phillips just as he was boarding his plane, 'Admiral, you'll get your destroyers and as quickly as they can get to you.' Mrs Hart's letter to Rear-Admiral John D. H. Kane, Jr., USN, 18 Dec. 1978. Balikpapan is in south-eastern Borneo, and Batavia (Djakarta today) is at the western end of Java, about 600 miles south of Singapore.

7th, thick low clouds and intermittent rain hampering air reconnaissance. In the early hours of the 8th, however, reports came in indicating that at last the Japanese had taken the plunge. At 00.30 the War Room, Singapore, received information that gunfire had been seen off Kota Bharu in the extreme north of Malaya, near the border with Thailand.[55] This was followed by the news of a landing at Singora, on the southern coast of Thailand's Kra Isthmus, about 130 miles north of the Malayan border, and at 01.15 of an attempted landing at Kota Bharu. Three hours later, Japanese naval aircraft bombed Singapore. Sixty-six Nell bombers from the Genzan and Mihoro Air Corps, each armed with one 550lb (250kg), two 154lb (70kg), and two 132lb (60kg) bombs, also incendiary bombs, set out from their bases in the Saigon area at 22.24/7th and 23.45/7th, respectively. Their targets were the Island's four airfields. The first attack unit (the 34 Genzan planes) was forced to turn back before reaching Singapore; the heavy rain and winds were too intense. The second attack unit (the 32 Mihoro planes) broke through the storm, although one plane was forced by engine trouble to turn back. The other 31 succeeded in reaching Singapore a little after 04.00. City lights (the street lights were burning throughout the raid), a full moon, and the clear outline of Singapore harbour simplified their task, as did the absence of fighter opposition. They stayed but ten or fifteen minutes, bombing Seletar airfield, the military facilities near British Air Force HQ around the commercial port, and finally Tengah airfield. Military damage was negligible; not so the damage to civilian morale. The city was in an uproar during the raid, with the local population rushing all over the place, hysterical. There were some 200 casualties. Tension was high in the *Prince of Wales*, which, being at anchor, was a sitting duck, although no attack was made on the naval base. One of the gunnery officers announced over the ship's loudspeakers that it was probably only a local exercise. The Leading Seaman in charge of an AA gun was heard to say: 'Exercise, be buggered—open fire!' Whereupon his gun did, and everyone else followed suit. Most of

---

[55] Eastern times given in this chapter and the next are in local (Malayan) time, which the British were using. It was Greenwich Mean Time plus 7½ hours. The 'Z' in the time of a signal refers to GMT. The time used by the Japanese forces, Japan Central Standard (Tokyo) Time, was GMT plus 9 hours. The Japanese always used Japan Central Standard Time during the war regardless of the location of ships and aircraft, and this is the time used in their Official History.

the AA fire was provided by the two capital ships, though severe it was not accurate. Only one plane was hit, and all returned to their base.[56]

Later in the morning, the officers of the *Prince of Wales*, gathered round a crackling oscillating wireless set in the wardroom, learned of the fury and treachery of the Japanese strike at Pearl Harbor (02.00/8th, Malayan Time). At first the news was greeted in Force Z with stupefaction, then with satisfaction. The feeling was: 'Well, the Americans are in: It's round one to the Japs—but now they'll get it!' The crews were not aware at that time of the magnitude of the disaster—that most of the US Pacific Fleet had been eliminated. Late in the afternoon of the same day, 8 December, the ships got the orders they had all been expecting.

Evidence accumulated during November of an early Japanese offensive somewhere in South-east Asia. The COIS reported that the 7th Squadron (four heavy cruisers) had left Japan, 'destination probably Saigon). Two squadrons of long-range Zero fighters were believed to have flown to southern French Indo-China; aircraft in the colony increased during the month from 74 to 245; and the 5th Division, especially trained in landing operations, was said to have moved to southern French Indo-China. All were ominous signs indeed, but none more so than the intelligence arriving during November that the Japanese merchant navy was steadily returning home. These ships, a graph (*c.* 23 November) from the FECB indicated, would all be back in harbour by the first week in December; war would then break out. With this information in hand the FECB suggested to Admiral Layton's staff that reconnaissance units (air or submarine) be sent out to look for an invasion force approaching Malaya. On 29 November, following receipt of a 28 November message from the US Navy Department, warning that an aggressive Japanese move could be expected within days, directed against the Philippines, the Isthmus of Kra, or possibly Borneo, a systematic American, British, and Dutch air reconnaissance was instituted over the South China Sea with the handful of

---

[56] It was learned later in the day that what an officer in the *Prince of Wales* calls 'a very illustrious fifth column' had caused many critical lights, such as the landing lights at one of the airfields, to be switched on as aiming marks for the Japanese. Armed sentries were now placed in the warships alongside the dockyard to shoot at sight any lights appearing in the black-out.

reconnaissance aircraft available, and on 6 December two Dutch submarines left Singapore to patrol in a position about 100 miles south-west of Cape Cambodia.[57]

One school of thought held that the Japanese would first invade Thailand and consolidate there before invading Malaya. Others thought they would cut out the invasion of Thailand and go straight to Kota Bharu. There were important indications at the end of November that Thailand was about to become Japan's target and that this operation would include a seaborne expedition to occupy strategic points in Thailand's Kra Isthmus. This raised the question whether the C-in-C, Far East, Air Chief Marshal Brooke-Popham, should carry out Operation 'Matador', a secret plan adopted in August 1941 for the pre-emptive seizure of the Singora–Patani area in the southern part of the Kra Isthmus to forestall a Japanese attack on the Isthmus. Churchill agreed with the Chiefs of Staff (1 December) that they should not resist or try to forestall a Japanese attack on the Isthmus (or on the Netherlands East Indies) without a satisfactory assurance from Washington that the US would give Britain immediate and full military support. The Chiefs of Staff reiterated their view on this occasion that Japanese aggression in the Kra Isthmus would not by itself constitute an attack on Britain's vital interests. The Isthmus being waterlogged at that season, a Japanese invasion there was not likely to be a prelude to an immediate advance on Singapore. At any rate, Pound affirmed, no Japanese fleet units had been reported south of Hainan, 'which meant that there was no immediate threat of a seaborne expedition to the Isthmus of Kra'.[58] American assurances of armed support having at last been received, on 5 December the Chiefs of Staff finally gave Brooke-Popham the word. He could launch Matador if he learned that a Japanese force 'was advancing with the apparent intention of landing on the Kra Isthmus', or if Japan

---

[57] Between February and June 1940 all 15 submarines on the China Station had been ordered to the Mediterranean. There was only one British submarine in Eastern waters when hostilities commenced with Japan, and she was refitting at Singapore. Layton had invented some bogus British submarines in the hope of giving the impression that British defences were stronger than they were. The date may have been early November 1941, when the FECB's merchant shipping intelligence began to look sinister. The FECB leaked this information in certain quarters and subsequently intercepted the Japanese report on its way to Tokyo. Captain Harkness's memorandum for the author, 31 Mar. 1978, and letter of 6 Sept. 1978.

[58] COS(41) 39th Mg. (O), Confidential Annex, 1 Dec. 1941, CAB 79/86.

'violated any other part of Thailand'. Matador was never carried out, as Brooke-Popham, despite the sightings on 6 December, was not certain of the destination of the Japanese convoys, and by the time Japan's intentions were clear, it was too late to forestall the landings. Force Z was kept on a leash: Phillips did not have permission to attack a seaborne expedition before the Japanese had committed a definite act of hostility against the Associated Powers.

As late as 6 December there was puzzlement in both Washington and London as to what the Japanese were up to. In London there was wishful thinking that the arrival of Force Z might have induced second thoughts in the Japanese. The Head of the British Admiralty Delegation in Washington thought it 'quite possible' that the Japanese would 'hesitate for a moment', as the presence of the *Prince of Wales* would necessitate their dispatch of a capital-ship escort with any expedition southward, 'and they may not feel inclined to do this'.[59]

Whitehall was obsessed with the concept of Singapore as a fixed base, which was deemed to be impregnable from the seaward side. The concept of a more mobile or less rigid set-up was only just beginning to take root. The VCNS, Admiral Moore, clearly remembers:

I tried to persuade Dudley Pound to send Phillips a signal during his passage out [about the time Phillips was at Colombo] to the effect that it would be wise, after refuelling at Singapore, to get himself 'lost' in the Pacific, thereby offering a dangerous and highly mobile threat to any operations the Japanese might contemplate. However, no such signal was sent, for it was Pound's assessment that Phillips, with his very recent Admiralty experience, was sufficiently well in the picture to have a clear idea of the problem. As it was, Phillips' strategy corresponded closely to the more rigid concepts generally (but not universally) held in London.[60]

---

[59] Admiral Sir Charles Little to Pound, 6 Dec. 1941, ADM 205/9. A telegram of 3 December from Craigie (received in the afternoon of the 4th) summarized the indications that Japan was about to attack Thailand and the 'more favourable signs'. Among the latter were the Japanese decision to continue the talks in Washington and the 'absence of any local indication of special strain or excitement such as might be expected to presage Japan's entry into a life and death struggle'. But the latter indication was 'conclusively [?considerably] diminished by the fact that Japan is now on a full war footing with the Government in complete control of information.' FO 371/28127.

[60] Letter to the author, 23 June 1976. Note that Pound had earlier (28 August—see above, p. 221) come out for the Eastern Fleet to withdraw from Singapore to Ceylon if war broke out.

The idea of Force Z vanishing into the ocean wastes had a greater appeal with the growing anxiety at the Admiralty over the difficult position in which Phillips might find himself, now that signs were multiplying that his Force would not succeed in its primary mission of deterring Japan from going to war. 'This force could only be considered as a raiding force and could not in any way be regarded as sufficiently powerful to disrupt enemy sea communications in the South China Seas.'[61] With this consideration in mind, on 1 December a personal message from the First Sea Lord to Phillips suggested the desirability of sending either capital ship, or both, 'away from Singapore in order that the uncertainty of their whereabouts would disconcert the Japanese', while remaining there himself. When intelligence arrived of the sighting of three Japanese submarines off Saigon proceeding southward, probably to watch Singapore, Pound repeated the suggestion on the 3rd—that one or both ships get away 'to the Eastward', or, alternatively, that Phillips reinforce his inadequate A/S screen by asking Admiral Hart to send the promised eight destroyers to Singapore 'on a visit so that they would be immediately available if the balloon went up'. We have it on Goodenough's authority that 'Phillips was already considering on his own the desirability of sending his capital ships away from Singapore before he was committed to that local area by the outbreak of war ... he thought Darwin would probably have to be the base temporarily until our re-inforcements arrived.'[62] However, Phillips's replies (3 December) to the two Admiralty messages did not respond directly to the withdrawal proposal. He reported that the *Prince of Wales* had that day been taken in hand at 72 hours' notice to make good defects in the distiller, which work should be completed in seven days, and that he would discuss the destroyer suggestion with Hart. We have seen how far he got with Hart on this point.

The same reconnaissance reports of the movements of convoys entering the Gulf of Siam that had caused the abrupt termination of the Manila conference and the recall of the *Repulse* to Singapore brought the Chiefs of Staff into an emergency meeting in the late afternoon of 6 December. They discussed the possibilities for two or three hours, without reaching any definite conclusions, there being too much uncertainty about what was happening. Effective action

[61] Pound, 'Loss of H.M.S. Prince of Wales & Repulse'.
[62] Goodenough to Roskill, 8 May 1951, ROSK 4/179.

was not, in any case, possible, as they explained in a minute that was telephoned to the Prime Minister at 6.15 p.m.:

Owing to the time which has elapsed since the convoys were first sighted, the time taken in raising steam, and the distance from Singapore, the *Prince of Wales* could not intercept these convoys unless she was ordered to sea on receipt of the first information. Further, it is not certain that the *Prince of Wales*, owing to trouble with her distillers, would have been ready to go to sea at such short notice. The *Repulse* left Singapore for Port Darwin yesterday. . . .

From the military point of view, it would pay us to attack these convoys at sea, but our present political instructions prevent us from doing so. Unless we are absolutely assured that an attack delivered in these circumstances would have the armed support of the United States, we ought not to make the first move.[63]

On which Churchill tartly minuted: 'If it is not physically possible, the political issue does not arise.' All political difficulties to taking military action against the Japanese were removed with the receipt in the early morning of 7 December of two telegrams from Halifax in Washington that the United States would regard a Japanese invasion of Thailand, Malaya, Burma, or the Dutch East Indies as a hostile act, and that the British should attack Japanese transports sighted steering west or south-west across the Gulf of Siam, 'since they must either be going for Thailand or for Malaya'.[64] An Admiralty telegram to Phillips (1848Z/7, Singapore time 0218/8) apprised him of the new situation: he could act against the Japanese in the event of an attack on British, American, or Dutch territory, or 'an attack on, or entry by invitation into any part of Thailand'.[65] Soon afterwards that evening, news reached London of the Japanese strike at Pearl Harbor and that Japanese troops were now swarming ashore in Thailand and Northern Malaya. At 0415 on the 8th the Admiralty war telegram of 2043Z/7 was received in Singapore: 'Commence hostilities at once.'

It was obvious that Force Z had failed as a deterrent force. What now? At 10 o'clock in the evening of 9 December a staff conference, mostly Admiralty, met in the Cabinet War Room to decide on 'possible naval dispositions and other measures to redress the

[63] COS(41) 44th Mtg. (O), CAB 79/55.
[64] PREM 3/158/6.
[65] *Principal War Telegrams*, Pt. i. 5.

balance of naval power in the Pacific'. Present were Churchill, Alexander, Moore, Harwood, Pound, and the other Service Chiefs, Brooke and Portal. They discussed two alternatives. The *Prince of Wales* and *Repulse* (together with the pre-war target ship, the ancient battleship *Centurion*, which presumably would masquerade as a modern battleship) could go to sea and vanish among the innumerable islands, exercising a vague menace 'as rogue elephants'. 'There was general agreement on that,' Churchill states. But most of the islands were inhabited. The Japanese doubtless would have obtained information of the movements of the Force and attacked with aircraft. It is difficult, in any case, to see how a vanishing trick among the islands could fulfil any strategical object. The alternative plan, which Churchill preferred, was that the Force should cross the Pacific and join the remnants of the US Fleet. 'Thus in a few months there might be a fleet in being on the west coast of America capable of fighting a decisive sea battle if need be. The existence of such a fleet and of such a fact would be the best possible shield to our brothers in Australasia. We were all much attracted by this line of thought. But as the hour was late we decided to sleep on it, and settle the next morning what to do with the *Prince of Wales* and the *Repulse*.'[66] One thing was clear—Force Z must not stay in Singapore. By morning there was no decision to make.

It is an extraordinary fact that 48 hours after the Japanese attack on Pearl Harbor, the authorities in London seemed to be discussing in a leisurely way what the operational role of Force Z should be, and deciding to sleep on it, when that Force was already committed to a hazardous enterprise.

When Phillips returned to Singapore from Manila in the forenoon of Sunday, 7 December (the *Repulse* arrived at noon that day), he plunged into a series of conferences with British and other officers, including Vice-Admiral Sir Guy Royle, the First Naval Member of the Australian Navy Board, and Commodore W. E. Parry, the First Naval Member of the New Zealand Navy Board. These officers had just arrived for an inter-Allied (anticipating the Americans and Dutch as Allies) conference of naval commanders which was

---

[66] Churchill, *The Grand Alliance*, p. 547, COS(41) 45th Mtg. (O), CAB 79/55. The minutes are more specific on the alternative plan, which was intended 'to restore the command of the Pacific by concentrating a superior Anglo–American battle fleet at Hawaii, with a view to offensive action against the Japanese Mainland...'

projected, but which circumstances were to prevent. In the same context Phillips conferred with the Dutch and American Naval Liaison Officers in Singapore, Captains L. G. L. van der Kun and J. M. Creighton.

That evening Phillips received a 'most immediate' Admiralty signal (1229Z/7): 'No decision has yet been taken by H.M. Government but on the assumption that it may be decided that if a Japanese expedition is located in the South China Sea in such a position that its course indicates that it is proceeding towards Thailand, Malaya, Borneo or Netherlands East Indies, report what action it would be possible to take with naval or air forces.' 'The enquiry', Captain Doig suggests, 'must have carried for Admiral Phillips a strong implication that something positive in the way of interference with the enemy was expected, and was the deciding factor which made Phillips decide that he *must* act, however hazardous the enterprise might be.'[67] Phillips replied: 'If relative strength of enemy force permits, endeavour will be made to attack expedition by night or by day. If we are inferior in strength a raid will be attempted and the air forces will attack with bombers and torpedoes in conjunction with our naval forces.' There was no direct reaction from London, but the Admiralty signal 1848Z/7 (above, p. 404) must have strengthened his resolve to disrupt any Japanese landings. His proposed strategy was brought before a conference in the early morning hours of the 8th. It was held in the War Room in the Dockyard Offices at the Singapore Naval Base, began around 0330, and broke up soon after 0430.[68]

Layton, aware of Phillips's intention to call this conference—the evidence suggests that he had decided to call it before he flew to

---

[67] 'Misfortune off Malaya', p. 38. If this were the intention of the Admiralty, they had taken an entirely different position by the time of the staff conference on the 9th, which position was essentially a reversion to their preference on 1 and 3 December for a withdrawal of Force Z.

[68] This important conference is not mentioned in any of the sources or published material. No minutes were kept. I have relied on the account furnished to me by Captain J. W. McClelland (especially in letters of 6, 15 Feb. 1979), who was present quite unofficially. The brilliantly clever McClelland, then a lieutenant-commander, was in charge of the W/T and Signal Station at Singapore. Since he was about to be relieved of his command, Layton would not be attending the meeting; but he was 'particularly anxious that I [McClelland], as an unbiassed witness should the disaster he foresaw occur, should hear what was said and, being aware of my cubbyhole at the far end of the War Room from the conference table, he considered that, in the "Brown out" and with the lights left off at my end, I might easily

(*continued*)

Manila and had asked Layton to arrange the conference in his absence—told McClelland after the war, that he had, in the latter's words,

spent long hours trying to think of some way of avoiding it and its inevitable conclusion, even to the extent of sticking his neck out and sending a signal to the Admiralty saying that he thought that Phillips should be ordered to withdraw westwards, as the two capital ships were at serious risk and their Admiral had been placed in an impossible position. . . . Layton was keen to limit attendance to the actual heads of the Fighting Services, as he saw the problem to be discussed as a joint tactical one, which could be decided quickly and at which long speeches by 'politicians' were unnecessary. And he hoped to exclude the C. in C., Far East, Air Chief Marshal Sir Robert Brooke-Popham, as this would give the AOC in C., Air Vice Marshal C. W. Pulford, who was two grades his junior, a chance to speak his mind, which Layton thought would be more valuable than hearing the ACM, who should have been left on the retired list, he was so little use.

Pulford, who looked rather like a naval officer (he was one at the beginning of his career), was a good solid chap without any particular distinction but did have a reputation for getting on with the other Services.

Present at the conference were Phillips, accompanied by Goodenough and Beardsworth, Greening, the Governor of the Straits Settlements, Sir Shenton Thomas ('accompanied by two elderly men'), Brooke-Popham, accompanied by his Naval Liaison Officer, Captain T. H. Back, Pulford, a Brigadier ('possibly General Staff'), and a Colonel.

The conference was called with the intention of discovering precisely what was desired of Force Z. The Japanese movements looked ominous, and it behoved Phillips not to waste any time. It

escape detection in it. Greening [Commander C. W. Greening, SO(O) China], he thought, might be asked to leave, although in fact this did not happen, because the China Command was due to lapse at midnight.' 'Brown out' was the equivalent of black-out, as, in the climate prevailing, it was impossible to halt the circulation of air. The only lighting in the War Room was the light reflected off the table by pencils of light from the ceiling. Because of the very dim illumination and the distance he was from them, McClelland was doubtful of the identity of some of the participants, and Greening could not enlighten him. 'Greening also had to tell me later much of what was said, as the conspiratorial gloom reduced some of them, particularly Brooke-Popham, to talking in conspiratorial whispers'—conspiratorial because of the presence of the other officers in the War Room. Although Layton had signalled the Admiralty at 01.16/8 that a landing was in progress at Kota Bharu, McClelland is certain that the conference was not aware of the landing.

would not take a genius to decide, in the painfully self-evident circumstances, that early naval intervention was the only possible way of scotching a Japanese invasion, either temporarily or permanently. Nevertheless, Phillips was not the man to risk, in any avoidable way, a couple of valuable ships, only to discover that the C-in-C, Far East, was quite confident that he could repel any invasion without naval help in the early stages. Phillips therefore wanted a statement from Brooke-Popham that early intervention by Force Z was the *only* way of halting an invasion. Note that Brooke-Popham was responsible for the operations of British forces on land and in the air, but had no authority over the Navy.

Phillips opened the meeting and spoke for nearly ten minutes, making these specific points. He felt sure that the Japanese would not deploy any capital ship or aircraft carrier in Malayan waters while the stronger US Fleet remained undefeated. (This was before the news of Pearl Harbor.) To the query of the Brigadier (whoever he was) whether this would be true if Japan declared war only on the British Empire, Phillips replied without hesitation, 'Yes, I do.' The Admiral felt that the threat from Japanese submarines was very serious, as they would be out in force against him, and his five destroyers, two of which were obsolete and a third in dry-dock, could only provide a very inadequate A/S screen. He could only hope that he would not stumble on one and present her with an easy target. Then, putting a better face on the situation, he doubted that they would be sent into confined waters; moreover, the ship in dry-dock would be available in four days and Admiral Hart was sending him extra destroyers, the first of which expected to refuel that day at Balikpapan.

As regards attacks by aircraft, he dismissed high level bombing as only likely to achieve any great result in the face of his anti-aircraft armaments if he was extremely unlucky. Dive bombing was likely to score damaging hits, but should not cripple either of his two capital ships: in any case he understood that the Japanese dive bombers only operated from carriers and he had already said that he did not at all expect to encounter one. As the torpedo was the weapon to which heavy ships were especially vulnerable, the principal danger came from the torpedo bomber, as had been amply illustrated in the case of the *Bismarck*. And to double the number of aircraft taking part in any simultaneous attack quadrupled their chances of scoring hits. [That is, they would swamp the defence, leaving many aircraft unfired at.] But in the thick north-east monsoon weather prevalent the execution of simultaneous attacks was very difficult and the torpedo bomber itself was very vulnerable indeed to attack by fighters during its approach to the dropping position. Against this form of attack his protection by shore-based fighters thus became essential, as his arrival without *Indomitable* meant that he was completely devoid of any fighter protection whatsoever.

He wound up by saying that, if the factor governing the situation was the preservation of his ships so that they could be used with greater advantage later in the campaign, there was no doubt at all that he should retire to the westward and await reinforcements, and sat down. Greening said afterwards that there was a smile on the face of the Tiger. I knew that smile![69]

A dead silence followed which nobody seemed inclined to break. Finally, the Governor gave his views. The heavily built but fit Thomas, a Cambridge man, quiet, scholarly, dignified, even-tempered, and very good at his job, always said that he knew nothing about warfare, except of the tribal kind. But he certainly had a clear mind when the occasion arose to talk about it, as now. It had, he said, come as a complete surprise to him to learn that the arrival of the battleship was only a piece of bluff, and, further, that the Japanese might be about to call it. If they did, would not this change the circumstances completely? Ought they not immediately to ask the Government what they wished the Admiral to do, if war broke out? After all had been said and done, the Japanese must be as aware of the shortcomings of the British Force as the Admiral himself, and would go flat out to exploit them. 'The Brigadier at once rushed to speech, blissfully unaware that the man who was causing the trouble to which he referred, was seated at the table.' Speaking with reference to the Governor's question, to judge by the confusion over, and the delay in, ordering either Matador or 'Krohcol' (a stop-gap in lieu of Matador whose object was to seize 'the Ledge', certain strong positions in the mountains in Thailand

---

[69] 'The Little Man had, for the victim, the unpleasant habit of deciding what was to be done before a conference and getting the victim, even if he had arrived at the conference with quite different views, to state that it was essential to do it. In this instance, the victim was Brooke-Popham. As he [Phillips] very rarely smiled over work, all of which he treated very seriously, he can only have produced the rather puckish grin which told his intimates that he had set his trap for the unwary. Like many others before him, B.-P. fell straight into it.' Captain McClelland's letter to the author, 3 Mar. 1979. Phillips's views on attacks by aircraft are treated more fully below. Note, in particular, his more fully considered views on the torpedo-bomber threat.

about 35 miles above the Thai border, if the Japanese landed before Matador was executed), the War Office had no idea what to do, let alone how to do it. Brooke-Popham, 'obviously shocked by the lèse-majesté and scared stiff that worse might follow', interrupted. He agreed that it was useless to ask for fresh orders, produced his 'usual disparaging remarks about the Japanese', said he did not expect a seaborne attack during the north-east Monsoon, and still hoped that the occupation of Thailand was the Japanese objective. 'His only two useful contributions to the discussion were statements that he had been amazed by the speed at which, according to intelligence reports, the Japanese air forces could both transfer aircraft from base to base and improvise new ones, and that people must remember that, "Once he is in a fight, the only way to get a Jap out of it is to kill him."' Pulford, who had been listening impatiently, spoke very briefly on the limitations of his aircraft and the lack of training of his fighter pilots in a fighter-protection role, stressing the difficulties they would run into out of sight of land. He wound up saying that his operations staff had discussed the Admiral's possible plans with Goodenough and had recommended that he (Pulford) should agree with them within the limitations he had just named. He then nodded a brief 'Goodnight' and left. Thomas spoke again, in the assumed capacity of an 'umpire'. As he saw it, given another week the Admiral would have sufficient destroyers to permit offensive operations as far as Japanese submarines were concerned; but the ships should not be employed on any offensive task unless fighter protection could be guaranteed. The AOC having left, perhaps the C-in-C, Far East, could give the necessary assurances? Brooke-Popham did not reply to this. 'Possibly the realisation that his aircraft were still on the ground when they ought to have been attacking any transports approaching the anchorages, brought something home to him. But, according to Greening, he "suddenly shook himself like a dog" and said, slowly and distinctly, "Do you know, Admiral, that I am beginning to believe that *if* the Japanese intend to attack, your intervention is the only thing that can prevent the invasion succeeding".' He turned to Terence Back and gave him some order which took Back out of the room at the double, then explained to the conference that he had sent him to his office to get on the 'green' line to Pulford's HQ to tell them to carry out armed reconnaissance in force from Singora to Patani and off Kota Bharu and to attack any transport anchored off or approaching the coast. Phillips made no reply to this sudden declaration, but the Governor, after rubbing his chin for a little time, said gently yet very clearly that he sincerely hoped that Brooke-Popham's original ideas (presumably on the inferiority of the Japanese and his conviction that war in the East could not happen) were correct, because, if they were not, it looked as if they would be in a 'regular pot-mess and no mistake'. He then addressed the C-in-C directly, asking how long he thought it would take the Japanese to unload their force. This talk was going on when the 'Air Raid Warning Red' (an attack was imminent) was announced (0400). It being too late to get to the shelters, those in the War Room lay down on the floor under the table. When the sirens sounded the 'All Clear' at 0440, the conference broke up in a hurry.

When only the Admiral remained, the interloper stepped forward to make himself known. 'Why! It's Young James!' exclaimed Phillips and shook him warmly by the hand. The Admiral was in a confiding mood.

It's at present 'most secret', but I'm taking Force Z out this evening to try to scotch the Japs round Singora. I rate the chances of getting there no higher than fifty-fifty, but I am sure that it's the only way in which to halt this invasion and, if it can be halted, they should find it impossible to start it again. Surprise is absolutely essential, but it's just possible in this thick Monsoon weather given even an average amount of luck. But, if we are spotted, which is bound to happen sooner or later, we shall be attacked and *Prince of Wales* will have to shout 'Help'.[70] So see your people stay on their toes and hear the first shout. I've also got a fairly long, urgent signal to send to the Admiralty to tell them what I intend to do. How long is it likely to take to get to them? I said that it would not take more than an hour and a half after I received the cypher version and that that included the time taken to get it to Kranji to transmit it. He replied, 'Splendid! With any luck it'll get 'em up in the middle watch, so see it doesn't go missing.'

What the above amounts to is that Phillips had got the statement from Brooke-Popham that he had sought and expected. In anticipation of this, and well aware that his 'fairly long signal' would take some hours to prepare for transmission, he had (internal evidence would suggest) got that process put in hand before he left the *Prince of Wales* to attend the conference in the War Room. Three

---

[70] The word 'Help', followed by the name of the ship calling, was the standard British method, when attacked by aircraft, of asking for fighter protection.

cipher versions of the Admiral's message reached McClelland within half an hour of the Admiral's departure. He marked it 'Emergency' and sent it direct to Whitehall via Bombay and Simonstown. Whitehall had repeated it back correctly by 0200Z/8, i.e. 0930/8 in Singapore. I have been unable to find the signal; but its gist is as reported by McClelland above. Phillips must have been aware that he was taking a risk, which it was impossible to calculate at all accurately, with two valuable ships. He may have hoped to receive the comments of the Admiralty on his intentions, as expressed in his signal. But he would most certainly have wished to give the First Sea Lord time to instruct him not to take the risk, if, for reasons not known to him, Pound did not wish him to take it. *He received no reaction to this signal, nor to that of 0934* (below). High Authority in London stood transfixed, unable to decide on a course of action in time to influence the unfolding tragedy. Meanwhile, Phillips acted on the brief he had received from the Admiralty on the 7th and the concurrence of the C-in-C, Far East, in his plan.

Phillips had mentioned Singora to McClelland, but this was altered as a result of a conference with Layton and Palliser in the War Room that began at about 0630, and the news that a Japanese landing was taking place at Kota Bharu.

As Captain Doig has reconstructed the scene:

One of the first objects of his visit was to tell Layton that he was taking over full responsibility from 0800. A general discussion then ensued around the chart table and it was then that Phillips made the remark which I have recorded that he could not go to sea until he had some more destroyers. Shortly after this, Phillips, Layton and Palliser went into a private huddle over the chart, and I imagine that it was then that the possibilities of using the big ships to interfere with the Japanese landing operations were worked out, including the time at which they could get there. If so, I am pretty certain that Layton would have said, 'Well, I think you'll have to have some fighter protection if you're going to tangle with the Japs off Singora' or something to that effect ... Layton always afterwards himself insisted that he had given this advice to Phillips, and said in a private letter to Pound that though he understood Phillips' decision, he would not himself have gone ahead without fighter protection. This was undoubtedly based on our experience in Norway in April 1940.[71]

It was at 0934 that Phillips sent off a signal to the Admiralty which

[71] Letter to the author, 20 Oct. 1978.

shows that he had decided to go to Kota Bharu instead of Singora: '[Corrupt group: ? Provided that] as I hope I can make 4 destroyers available intend to proceed with *Prince of Wales* and *Repulse* dusk tonight 8/12 to attack enemy force off Kota Bharu daylight Wednesday 10th. Endeavours will be made to estimate strength of enemy Naval forces by air R/C [reconnaissance] but large proportions of aircraft are naturally required for attack.'

A council of war between Phillips and his senior officers (Palliser, Leach, Tennant) and a few senior staff officers like Bell and Goodenough took place in the Admiral's cabin in the flagship at about 1230 on the 8th. It was held, I believe, only after Phillips had made up his mind to go ahead, and it was really designed to enlist the support of his staff and subordinates, and find out if they saw any snags. The Admiral sounded firm and confident as he outlined the situation and explained his strategy.[72] Landings had been made early that morning between Patani and Singora, and a major landing 90 miles north of Singora, besides a minor landing at Kota Bharu that had been repulsed. British air and military forces were on the move. Japanese naval forces covering the military convoys and landings in the Gulf of Siam were, on the basis of reports from reconnaissance aircraft, believed to include only one capital ship, probably the old battleship *Kongō*, which was no match for the British capital ships, 7 cruisers (of which three were 8-inch and two 5·5-inch), and 20 destroyers. Actually, the Japanese had 8 cruisers (5 8-inch, 3 5·5-inch), 14 destroyers, and 12 submarines in the Gulf of Siam, and, off south-east Indo-China in support, 2 battle cruisers, 2 8-inch cruisers, and 10 destroyers. Neither Phillips nor the Singapore Intelligence authorities had reliable information on the strength, types, disposition, or efficiency of enemy aircraft in the Indo-China area.[73] The operative factor for the C-in-C was that his two-to-one superiority in capital ships gave him a decisive

---

[72] In what follows I have attempted from the sources to give some of the considerations that seem to have been in his mind.

[73] The FECB was, as previously noted, the principal source of naval intelligence at Singapore. Phillips and his staff relied on getting the latest and best intelligence from it, but, unfortunately, the time between the arrival of the *Prince of Wales* at Singapore on the 2nd and departure on the 8th was short. Phillips, moreover, was away from the 4th to the 7th. He never asked the COIS for a personal briefing, nor does Captain Harkness remember talking to Palliser until after the 10 December action. Goodenough apparently told the SO(I), Laird, that he would deal with the FECB, and left him to deal with SO(I) Singapore. Goodenough

(*continued*)

advantage, although he did not minimize the hazardous nature of the operation. Force Z, as the Admiral saw it, had three alternatives. It could stay put and risk being bombed; it could sail to some anchorage or area remote from the enemy and, hopefully, away from the danger of air attack; or it could sally forth and attack Japanese transports and warships off the east coast, between Singora and Kota Bharu. The first alternative being unthinkable—how could they remain sitting in Singapore Harbour with the enemy landing on British soil?—and the second equally so, Phillips opted for the third. But he gave all a free opportunity to speak at the conference in the flagship, and all had agreed with him. At the end of the meeting he asked, 'Does anyone think we shouldn't go?' There were no dissenters. 'All were unanimous that it was impossible for the Navy to attempt nothing while the army and air force were being driven back, and that the plan for a sudden raid, though hazardous, was acceptable. There was also the psychological effect of the fleet putting to sea in this grave emergency.'[74]

And so the Admiral's plan was adopted. One wonders what he would have done, had a majority been against going out. Probably the same. His 0934/8 signal to the Admiralty had mentioned the enemy force 'off Kota Bharu' as his objective if he sailed at dusk that day, but a signal of 1222/8 from Phillips and Brooke-Popham to the Commanding Officers of the RAF and the Army, Pulford and Lieutenant-General A. E. Percival, gave the objective as the 'enemy

---

visited Harkness, but how much detailed information he digested we do not know. This much seems clear: Singapore Intelligence suggested that they could regard Japanese naval air efficiency on a par with the Italian, though possibly slightly inferior. Captain Harkness's letter to the author, 11 July 1978, Captain Bell's letters to the author, 3 Nov. 1975, 16 July 1978. 'We in FECB did not know of the Japanese efficiency in dropping torpedoes from the air [the Naval Attaché, Tokyo, was just as ignorant] . . . but we expected attacks by bombs rather than torpedoes.' Harkness's memorandum for the author, 31 Mar. 1978. But cf. the recollection of Air Commodore R. W. Chappell, below, p. 434 n. Chappell, then Head of the RAF Section of the FECB, was not consulted by any member of Phillips's staff until *after* the sinkings.

[74] Captain L. H. Bell's report, 10 Dec. 1941, ADM 199/1149. The meeting may have lasted a half hour. Not long afterward, at about 1330, Phillips met with a larger group, most of the first group plus Admiral Spooner (Rear-Admiral, Malaya), the commanding officers of the destroyers, and others. About 15 were around the table. It was more for information, the big decision having been taken earlier. The commander of the *Express*, Lieutenant-Commander Cartwright, recollects the Admiral summing up in some such words as: 'We can stay in Singapore. We can sail away to the East—Australia. Or we can go out and fight. Gentlemen, we sail at five o'clock.' Martin Middlebrook and Patrick Mahoney, *Battleship: The Loss of the Prince of Wales and the Repulse* (London, 1977), pp. 105–6.

transports reported between Singora and Patani'. As announced in Phillips's signal to Force Z at 1315 on the 9th it was less precise: 'My object is to surprise and sink transports and enemy warships before air attack can develop. Objective chosen [Kota Bharu or Singora] will depend on air reconnaissance. Intend to arrive objective after sunrise tomorrow 10th. If an opportunity to bring *Kongo* to action occurs this is to take precedence over all other action.' They would then make a quick run back to Singapore, in order to be as short a time as possible in *daylight hours* in range of torpedo attack from hostile air bases at Ca Mau.

What else was running through the Admiral's mind? When the Japanese got into Malaya and started bombing Singapore, Phillips's better judgement told him that the sensible thing was to withdraw both capital ships to the Indian Ocean. Yet, to have done so would have made a mockery of the move to the East as well as doing nothing for the morale of those in Malaya and Singapore. He felt that the publicity which had been given to the arrival of his big ships in the Far East left him no acceptable alternative in the circumstances then obtaining in Malaya. He knew that he was taking serious risks, but he had carefully measured them and decided that the risks were worth taking. Not that he thought he could do more than relieve the pressure on the troops and throw a spanner into the Japanese plans. He reasoned that provided the departure of his Force from Singapore and its passage north went undetected during daylight hours on the 9th, there was a good chance of surprising the Japanese at first light on the 10th and smashing the forces attempting to land. 'The Admiral', Bell stated in his action report on 10 December, 'relied on the speed and surprise of the battleships' attack to avoid damage to these ships sufficient to slow them down, believing that Japanese aircraft would not be carrying anti-ship bombs and torpedoes [i.e. they would be Army planes operating from southern French Indo-China in support of the landing operations] and that the Force on retirement would only have to deal with hastily organised long range bombers from bases in Indo-China'. For these reasons—surprise and the nature of the air opposition to be expected—Phillips expected his two big ships could probably do considerable damage with impunity. He was not too concerned with the possibility of meeting long-range bombers from Indo-China when the Force withdrew to Singapore, being confident that intense AA fire would prevent them from inflicting vital damage to his big ships. Enemy torpedo-bombers could, on his retirement, pose a more serious threat; but they would be beyond their effective range. Phillips stated at that time (the 1230/8th conference?) that no shore-based torpedo attack on ships at the sea had been delivered at a greater range than 200 miles. Singora was nearly 300 miles, and Kota Bharu, over 250 miles, from the nearest Indo-China bases.[75]

The 200-mile limit, according to Captain Bell, 'was based not on British T/B performance, because we well knew the handicap of our absurdly short-ranged T/Bs, but on the statistics of German and Italian attacks on Mediterranean fleets and convoys'. This did *not* mean that Phillips thought the Japanese incapable of delivering an attack at more than 200 miles from base. British Intelligence gave their torpedo-bombers (as well as the Italian) a theoretical range of well over 200 miles—something more in the region of 400 miles. But theoretical capability and practical range are not the same thing, the latter depending on various factors, such as weather, visability, wind strength and direction, the crew's navigational experience and efficiency, and the willingness of crews to outfly their patrol endurance and crash-land anywhere.

It was not reasonable in December 1941 [as Bell summed up the matter] to expect Japanese naval aircraft with no recent war experience to be more efficient at long range torpedo attack than our well-trained Fleet Air Arm after eighteen months of war in May 1941.[76]

I suggest, therefore, that at this time it was a fair assumption that risk of torpedo bomber attack was great inside 200 miles, but that beyond that range the risk progressively decreased until at about 400 miles it became small. It is easy to be wise after the event, but we must put ourselves back into the state of our Intelligence at that time, e.g. past war experience in

---

[75] Calculated from Ca Mau (Quan Long) in the Ca Mau Peninsula of French Indo-China (40-odd miles north-east of Cape Cambodia and about 150 miles south-west of Saigon), which they believed, on FECB intelligence, to be the site of the nearest enemy bomber bases. There was no Japanese air base, Army or Navy, at Ca Mau at that time. The nearest IJN bomber bases were in the Saigon area, over 400 miles from Singora and approximately 370 miles from Kota Bharu. (The nearest IJA bomber base was at Phu Quoc Island, some 260 miles from Singora and Kota Bharu.) 'Aerodromes at Saigon were not considered because they were farther from the vital points than Ca Mau.' Captain Bell to Captain Russell Grenfell, 10 Aug. 1950, Grenfell Papers, GREN 1/3 (Churchill College).

[76] The reference is to the fact that no torpedo-bomber attack was made from the carriers *Victorious* and *Ark Royal* against the *Bismarck* at a greater range than 200 miles, though it was desirable to damage her as early as possible.

the Atlantic and Mediterranean, and the conclusion that the Japanese Air Force was about on a par with the Italian.[77]

Intelligence did not know that the Japanese torpedo-bombers had an operational radius of as much as a thousand miles, and their crews the skill to attack effectively. Phillips likewise grossly underestimated the range of the Japanese torpedo-bombers as well as the efficiency of their crews and torpedoes. He also estimated that, if he were located, the thick monsoon weather would prevent anything like simultaneous attacks, and he hoped to be able to deal with isolated attacking aircraft as they arrived. Finally, there could, in Phillips's view, be no possibility of a really dangerous torpedo-bomber attack until either the Japanese had carriers in the South China Sea or had established land-based torpedo aircraft in Malaya, and there was no evidence of either. In other words, Phillips believed that the air threat was not excessive and justified the risk he had to take. But he still required air support.

Middlebrook and Mahoney (p. 108) make the point that Phillips appears not to have realized that 'the Japanese aircraft that had bombed Singapore the night before had flown nearly twice the distance [of the 400 miles from Saigon to the Singora/Kota Bharu area] and that these same aircraft could operate as torpedo bombers when required'. (Actually, these aircraft had flown about 600 miles to Singapore.) The first part of the statement was doubtful. As regards the latter, it took virtually no time at all to change from torpedo to bombs or vice versa in the Swordfish, Albacore, or Barracuda, as the bombs were carried under the wings and the torpedo slung between the undercarriage wheels. Training for delivery was another matter. Bombs and torpedoes required differing approach and release techniques, and regular practice was essential, particularly as regards torpedoes. The fact is that when the Pacific War began, and for some time thereafter, the crews were inadequately trained for the dual role. Phillips had no reason to believe that the Japanese were any more efficient in this respect. Certainly the FECB had no idea that the Japanese high-level bombers were readily convertible into torpedo-bombers.

At 2210 on the 9th, when Force Z was at sea *en route* to Kuantan (see below), Phillips received a personal message from the First Sea Lord which read: 'As torpedo aircraft attack on ships at anchor in

[77] Bell to Grenfell, 10 Aug. 1950.

Johore Strait cannot be ruled out, I am sure you have in mind M/LD. 02033/41, dated 22 April 1941, paragraph 18–(14), which you took so much interest in.'[78] Admiral Farnhill, who brought the decrypted message to Phillips, says,

When I shewed this to him, Tom asked if I knew what the First Sea Lord was getting at. I said I knew what he was referring to but that I couldn't see any relevance since there was, so far as I knew, no possibility of torpedo bomber attack on the Johore Strait until either the Japanese had carriers in the area or had established shore-based aircraft in Malaya. He said that was what he felt too. I mentioned this because it seems to establish two things. First, that Tom believed that the air opposition was at that time limited to shore-based bombers operating at long range from Cambodia and intended for Army support, and, second, because it implies that the Admiralty was aware that the Japanese had long-range torpedo bombers in the area and believed that Tom knew it too. After I got back to Singapore, Tom's Staff Officer (Intelligence), who also survived the sinking, told me that he had discovered since his return that intelligence about these torpedo bombers had been available in Singapore. When they first got it and why we didn't I have never managed to discover. Even assuming that Singapore believed that we also had this intelligence, it seems odd that the threat from these aircraft was apparently not discussed or raised during Tom's talks at the Shore HQ in Singapore before we sailed.[79]

Phillips was particularly concerned about the Japanese submarines. They were in all probability stationed in numbers between Singapore and their invading forces and were believed to be highly efficient and a serious menace to a force ill equipped with A/S escorts. As Captain Bell explains, 'Admiral Phillips was very conscious of the danger from Japanese S/Ms; our own S/M screen was quite (through complete lack of recent training) inefficient. He certainly rated the danger from S/M attack as greater than that from high-level bombing attack.'[80] Phillips did not place excessive trust in the asdic sets of his destroyers, which were notoriously unreliable. Asdic was the principal submarine detection system, measuring the direction and return time of a sound echo. At its best,

[78] ADM 199/1149.
[79] Letter to the author, 16 Oct. 1975. Naval opinion in Singapore afterwards apparently believed that the torpedo-bombers had been carrier-borne. G. Hermon Gill, *Royal Australian Navy, 1939–1942* (Canberra, 1957), p. 482. The nearest carrier, the *Ryujo*, was 2,000 miles away, east of the Philippines.
[80] Letter to the author, 14 July 1978.

in good water conditions, a detection range of up to 2,500 yards might be expected with all-round sweep other than in the wash of one's own propellers. However, operating conditions in Malayan waters are notoriously tricky, due to shallow conditions causing temperature layers. Another difficulty was that asdic beams went out in a cone. As you approached the target, you lost contact; the deeper the target, the sooner contact was lost. Asdic was unreliable, too, in that the beam produced echoes of fish and disturbances in the water as well as echoes of submarines. And it could not detect a surfaced submarine. In brief, chances of picking up a submarine were not above 50 per cent. If a destroyer did pick one up, her only A/S weapons in 1941 were depth charges (ahead-throwing weapons came later), yet depth had to be estimated. Phillips's judgement was sound. The asdics of his screen did not detect either submarine that sighted his Force: the first, *I–65* was too distant (12 miles), but the second, *I–58*, was quite close in (in the 'near distance', according to the Japanese Official History).

For the Admiral one of the key considerations was surprise. Failing that, the Japanese would have time to disperse their transports, while concentrating air and surface forces and submarines for an overwhelming blow at the British fleet. Air support was nearly as crucial as surprise to the success of Phillips's plan: for reconnaissance, for air cover in the attack, and as insurance—to deal with a possible long-range bomber attack and, more importantly, a torpedo-bomber attack during retirement.[81] At about 09.30 on the 8th he had made his air requirements known to Pulford through Wing-Commander R. A. Chignell, a member of the staff at Air Headquarters. The Admiral's needs were: (*a*) reconnaissance 100 miles to the north of Force Z during daylight on the 9th; (*b*) reconnaissance 100 miles, mid-point Singora, 10 miles from the coast, starting at first light on the 10th; and (*c*) fighter protection off Singora at daylight on the 10th. To get a clearer idea of what was required, and to fix up the details, Pulford visited the Admiral at 10.45. At this stage, apparently, the AOC thought that fighter protection could be arranged. Between 1400 and 1500, however, after determining the general situation (heavy air losses were

---

[81] What follows is based partly on Pulford's record, dated 30 Dec. 1941, of 'The instructions received, orders issued, and action taken regarding air co-operation required for H.M.S. *Prince of Wales* and *Repulse* on the 8th, 9th and 10th December, 1941', AIR 23/4745.

sustained that day in northern Malaya and in attacks on Japanese transports and on airfields in southern Thailand), the AOC gave Phillips a tentative reply through Chignell: that he could provide (*a*), hoped to be able to provide (*b*), and could not provide (*c*). A definite reply was promised through Palliser (whom the Admiral was leaving behind to remain in close touch with GHQ after he had examined the situation more thoroughly. Not being sure that the AOC realized the importance that he attached to air cover, just before sailing, Phillips wrote a final letter to Pulford, stressing the importance he attached to fighter protection over Singora or Kota Bharu on the 10th and gave it to his Captain of the Fleet, Bell, to send by the Chief of Staff's car (waiting at the gangway) for immediate delivery. Pulford's reply to the Admiral's last urgent letter came as the Force was passing through the boom at the entrance to Johore Strait. A visual signal was flashed from the Changi fortress and signal station: 'Regret fighter protection impossible.' Phillips's reaction is said to have been a shrug of the shoulders and: 'Well, we must get on without it.' When Force Z sailed, therefore, Phillips had no assurance that fighter cover would be forthcoming; on the contrary. Yet he remained hopeful. According to his Staff Officer Operations: 'The Admiral decided to continue to operate his ships to the Northward in spite of the postponement partly because he had faith that the fighters would still materialise and partly because his clear brain saw at once what was going to happen to the Army. Under such circumstances he felt that the Navy could not hold back.'[82]

As it seemed undesirable to perpetuate dual control now that hostilities had broken out, and the Admiralty having decided to merge the China command with the Eastern Fleet, Phillips had Layton relinquish command of the China Station to him at 08.00 on the 8th and haul down his flag at sunset. It was shortly before sailing that Phillips code-named his Force 'Force Z'.

4. 'WE ARE OFF TO LOOK FOR TROUBLE'

On 24 November the Admiralty had directed that Phillips consider these units as forming part of the Eastern Fleet: *Prince of Wales*,

---

[82] Goodenough to Lady Phillips, 6 June 1947.

'WE ARE OFF TO LOOK FOR TROUBLE'

Repulse, Revenge, and the destroyers *Electra* (Senior Officer of the destroyers), *Express, Encounter,* and *Jupiter,* 'and such other units of the China Station as desired by C-in-C, Eastern Fleet'. What was actually available when Force Z sailed? He had the *Electra* (Commander C. W. May) and *Express* (Lieutenant-Commander F. J. Cartwright), first-class vessels from the Home Fleet: modern ships of 1,375 tons, built in the mid-1930s and capable of 35 knots. The *Tenedos,* from the China Station (Lieutenant Richard Dyer), and the Australian *Vampire* (Commander W. T. A. Moran) were last-minute substitutions for the Mediterranean Fleet destroyers *Jupiter* and *Encounter,* which were undergoing repairs in Singapore dockyard for various mechanical maladies. (Cunningham, hard pressed in the Mediterranean, had, naturally, not sent his most effective ships to join Force Z.) The substitute pair were small and ancient craft of 1,000 tons (*Tenedos*) and 1,090 tons (*Vampire*), completed in 1919 and 1917 respectively. The endurance of the *Tenedos* at high speed was too short for her to last the whole course. The four destroyers were quite untrained in working together, and their A/S operating capabilities were rusty.[83] Phillips had expected destroyer support from the US Asiatic Fleet and the Dutch, but all he could find to go to sea with him now were these four, the minimum number needed to screen the two capital ships. The *Stronghold*, a China Station destroyer, was at Singapore, but was held back to escort US Destroyer Division 57 in through the minefields on the 10th. Two of the remaining three old British destroyers at Hong Kong were also *en route*, having sailed on the 8th. The *Isis* was in dockyard hands at Singapore for war damage received in the Mediterranean, and the RAN destroyer *Vendetta* was refitting at Singapore. Though early in the morning of the 8th Phillips had said, 'I certainly can't go to sea until I have some more destroyers,' he felt compelled to accept the absence of a sufficient destroyer screen. The cruiser position was no more satisfactory,

---

[83] Phillips's signal of 13.15/9 to the Force reported his intention to send the *Tenedos* back to Singapore before dark, and that the remaining three destroyers might be detached during the night of the 9th/10th, 'should enemy information require a high speed advance'. They would in this case retire towards the Anambas Islands (Netherlands East Indies) until a rendezvous was ordered by W/T. Captain Bell, in his report (10 December), wrote: 'He considered the destroyers would be very vulnerable to air attack; with the exception of *Electra* they were not fully worked up, and their operational endurance was a perpetual anxiety.'

though Phillips was in the process of assembling a cruiser striking force of five modern British ships under cover of his capital ships when the Japanese struck. On the China Station the three 6-inch D-class cruisers, of First World War vintage, were engaged in convoy escort duties. They were hardly fit for serious fighting, and, besides, only the *Durban* was ready to sail. Phillips decided not to take her. Of the projected striking force the practically new 6-inch cruiser *Mauritius* (East Indies Squadron, based on Ceylon) was in dock at Singapore, and the powerful 8-inch cruiser *Exeter* (East Indies Squadron), *en route* from convoy duty in the Bay of Bengal, did not arrive until the 10th. Also on the way were the New Zealand 6-inch cruiser *Achilles* (she had left Auckland on the 8th) and the Australian cruisers *Australia* (8-inch) and *Hobart* (6-inch). The former had left the East Indies Station for Fremantle on the 8th, and the latter had been ordered from the Mediterranean to Colombo, pending decision as to destination. The Dutch light cruiser *Java* was *en route*, but did not arrive at Singapore until the 9th.

Phillips had earlier turned down Pound's suggestion that the battleship *Revenge*, one of the Rs, engaged in convoy duty in the Indian Ocean, join him. He had persuaded the First Sea Lord (8 November dispatch) that only the *Prince of Wales* and *Repulse* should arrive at Singapore. '(A) A force of 2 fast battleships at Singapore should cause Japan concern but should be regarded by her more as a raiding force than as an attempt to form a line of battle against her. (B) The addition of one "R" class might give the impression that we were trying to form a line of battle, but could only spare 3 ships, thus encouraging Japan.' Unless events precipitated matters, he preferred that the *Revenge* stay in the Indian Ocean until, joined by the *Royal Sovereign* and *Ramillies*, the three Rs might come to Singapore early in 1942. Events did precipitate matters, and on 3 December Phillips had asked for all four Rs: the above three and the *Resolution*. This is what he had in mind when he promised Admiral Hart in Manila that he would have six or even seven battleships 'in a few more weeks'.[84] But there was no time on the 8th to bring any of them in. Had Force Z delayed its sailing even two or three days, a much stronger force would have been mustered.

---

[84] Hart's diary, 5 Dec. 1941. The seventh capital ship would have been the *Warspite*. Phillips had proposed (3 December) that advantage be taken of her passage through the station, *en route* to England from repair in the United States, to keep her at Singapore for about a week to give an appearance of strength.

'WE ARE OFF TO LOOK FOR TROUBLE'

The Admiral, however, felt that the situation was too desperate to admit of any delay in his sailing.[85]

So it was a puny force of six ships—puny compared to the forces available to the Japanese in the South China Sea—that sailed off into the bright, red sunset at 1735 on 8 December. (*Electra* and *Express*, which had proceeded to sea at 1400 for minesweeping exercises, rendezvoused with the big ships outside the boom at 1830.) It was a pathetic sight, Admiral Layton said afterwards. He did not expect to see the ships again. Captain Doig was certain they were going to be 'slaughtered'. Nor were they alone in their forebodings. Phillips had asked Palliser and the Fleet Engineer Officer, Captain O. W. Phillips, whom he had inherited from Layton, to stay at Singapore, where they 'could keep the pot a'boiling'. Captain Phillips could see nothing but disaster ahead.

From my office I saw *Prince of Wales* and *Repulse* cast off and leave the naval base, and a deep sense of foreboding came over me. I felt this situation was too much like that existing just before Coronel early in World War I. I said to my Secretary, Commissioned Engineer Albert Wall, who was standing by me, 'Wall, do you know any Latin tags?' 'A few, Sir, which one are you thinking of?' 'Quos Deus vult perdere, prius dementat,' 'Those whom the Gods wish to die, they first make mad.' I think Tom Phillips is going up the east coast of Malaya.' 'Oh! No, Sir,' Wall said, 'he will go down to the Archipelago (Java Sea) or off Darwin.' I had no idea of Sir Tom's intentions, my job was to have the fleet ready to go anywhere from an engineering angle, but I felt strongly that the comparatively small body of troops probably getting it in the neck at Khota Bahru would act as a strong magnet. But, in the circumstances, each ship being roughly the equivalent of an army corps, was this a justifiable risk? Even to sink a few transports? I felt not. I said, 'I wish he was, but I think he is going up the east coast of Malaya and, if he does, I don't think he will come back.' I felt the Japanese were praying for this to happen, they knew the British dislike, even a stronger word, for leaving comrades in desperate straits. I felt I must mention this to Palliser (we had been at Dartmouth together) and went down to his room. He said, 'I advised him to go.' I said, 'That's

---

[85] He apparently intended to have five Dutch submarines follow up his raid by attacking the Japanese transports. Lieutenant-Commander A. Kroese, *The Dutch Navy at War* (London, 1945), p. 36. The Dutch at this time had 3 light cruisers, 6 destroyers, and 11 submarines operational in the East Indies. The irony of the situation is, as Middlebrook and Mahoney point out (p. 296), the decision taken on the 8th to sail that evening 'was already too late', since the landings were completed by the evening of the 9th. Of course, neither Phillips, nor anybody in Singapore (including the FECB), could have foreseen such a swift completion of the landing operations.

just too bad.' He asked me if I wanted to spread 'grief and amazement'? I said, 'Not at all! My Secretary, who is my second self, and you are the only people I have spoken to.'[86]

Captain Leach, too, realized that the prospects were not exactly bright. Doig found his meeting with his old shipmate Leach in the *Prince of Wales* on 3 December 'somewhat saddening. He had always been for me the embodiment of someone who was on top of the world, and willing and eager to tackle any situation. I think he began by saying, "You know, Douglas, they've never really given me a chance with this ship" and of course from the Captain's point of view her history had been maddening.... I was sadly aware that John Leach was conscious of the many deficiencies there might be.'[87] Dining with his midshipman son onboard the *Prince of Wales* the night before she sailed for the last time, Leach asked him what he thought of the situation. In his youthful ignorance Henry Leach replied, 'Let 'em come; let's have a go at them.' To his surprise his father turned a very serious face to him and said, 'I don't think you have any idea of the enormity of the odds we are up against.' The following day, shortly before Force Z sailed, when father and son met at the Base swimming pool, Jack Leach remarked seriously—and prophetically: 'I am going to do a couple of lengths now—you never know when it mightn't come in handy.'[88]

The Fleet Engineer Officer and the Captain of the flagship did not reflect the dominant frame of mind in Force Z. The officers were absolutely confident of beating 'the Jap', should they meet him at sea in anything approaching his strength. In the case of the *Repulse*, the ship's company were looking forward to the first real bit of action most of them had seen in the war so far. A then midshipman in the *Prince of Wales* writes:

We were a pretty confident bunch, particularly as we felt that there was no aircraft that could reach us except the high level bombers that had

---

[86] 'Memoirs of Rear-Admiral O. W. Phillips' (unpublished MS, 1961–2, Imperial War Museum), pp. 337–8.

[87] 'Misfortune off Malaya', p. 11.

[88] Vice-Admiral H. C. (now Admiral Sir Henry) Leach's letter to the author, 21 Apr. 1975. Tennant's mood can be inferred from a message he had pinned up in the *Repulse's* wardroom soon after the Force sailed. It began: 'We are off to look for trouble. I expect we shall find it. We may run up against submarines, destroyers, aircraft or surface ships. We are going to carry out a sweep to northward to see what we can pick up and what we can roar up. We must all be on our toes.'

attacked Singapore, and we had felt that they were not very accurate. Furthermore, we had done some good anti-aircraft work in the Mediterranean. The Japanese aircraft would be literally sitting ducks to the 5.25 and the 8-barreled pom poms of which we had a goodly number. So we felt we were ready for anything when we sailed. We heard, as we were having our dinner that night, of the kind of opposition we could expect. McMullen (on the ship's intercom) told the ship's company about what could be expected. He merely talked of the old battleship *Kongo* and maybe her sister ship. We had our *Jane's Fighting Ships*, and we looked at this old thing and said, 'My, this is going to be a great action. We are going to have ourselves a real good even fight, at which we are superior. Don't forget, we had a healthy respect for modern ships like the *Bismarck*, and this *Kongo* class that we were expecting to meet looked to us like money for old rope.[89]

And from the Surgeon Lieutenant-Commander in the flagship:

There was certainly no regret at the decision to go up and attack them, for I remember very well that the Admiral announced that we were going up North to attack their fleet and convoys and we were delighted, despite the fact that he warned us that we would be very heavily attacked on our way out. We all felt that our much vaunted anti-aircraft defences would be able to cope very adequately with anything that the Japanese Air Arm chose to throw at us—again how wrong we were![90]

This despite the fact that the earliest reports of Pearl Harbor were available to them. Their zest for battle would have been diminished, had they been aware of Pulford's signal flashed from Changi or the W/T signal of 2253/8 from Palliser.

The little fleet had steered east, once clear of Singapore, just south of the Japanese minefield laid off the eastern entrance to Singapore Strait, and then altered course to north-east. (We do not know if Force Z was aware of this minefield.) The big ships disposed in open order in line ahead (i.e. five cables apart, stem to stem), screened by the *Express* and *Electra*, about 2 miles ahead of the flagship and 2 miles apart, and the *Tenedos* and *Vampire* approximately $2\frac{1}{2}$ miles on either beam of the *Repulse* and about $2\frac{1}{2}$ miles from the destroyers in the van. The weather was cloudy and the visibility poor—admirable for the fleet's purpose. Then, because minefields were to be expected between the Anambas and the Malayan coast, and the fact that only the *Electra* of the destroyers

---

[89] Admiral Leir's memorandum for the author, Oct. 1975.
[90] Admiral Caldwell's letter to the author, 18 Nov. 1975.

was fitted with a sweep, which she used for a short period on the passage north (a Japanese minelayer had laid 456 mines halfway between Tioman Island and Djemadja Island, the westernmost of the Anambas, on the night of 6 December), the fleet steered to the east of the Anambas before turning northward at 0400/9th.

At 0125/9th the *Prince of Wales* received a Palliser signal of 2253/8, which confirmed Pulford's decision as regards fighter support. The message stated (cf. Phillips's air needs, above, p. 419) that (*a*) would be arranged and that it was 'hoped' that (*b*) would be carried out. The doubt about (*b*) was whether Kuantan airfield would be usable; the Blenheim IV bombers, which would carry out the reconnaissance, were based there. Both reconnaissances, (*a*) and (*b*), were, in fact, carried out: (*a*) by a Catalina, and (*b*) by two Blenheim IVs in company. As regards (*c*), however, 'fighter protection on Wednesday 10th will not, repeat not, be possible'.[91] It could not be provided, mainly, we know, because fighter protection could only be given in that area by aircraft flying from airfields in northern Malaya. On the 8th, when Phillips had made his needs known to him, Pulford was not aware of the precise situation there, though he knew it was grave. By the evening of that disastrous day out of 110 operational aircraft available in the morning for combat in northern Malaya, only 50 remained in serviceable condition, and the airfields at Singora and Patani were in enemy hands and being used by them. The situation was spelled out in Brooke-Popham's dispatch:

the northern aerodromes were either untenable or else had been badly damaged by bombing; this meant that the fighters would have to operate from aerodromes [in central and southern Malaya] at considerable distance from Singora, and, owing to the short endurance of the Buffalo [with which the fighter squadrons were armed], they would have been

[91] The latter part of Palliser's 2253/8, however, omitted the words 'off Singora at daylight'. 'Although', comments one official source, 'such conditions were inferred in the light of the C-in-C. E. F.'s original request, it is conceivable—even though it cannot be proved—that this abbreviated message may have led Admiral Phillips to believe fighter cover would not be possible anywhere or at any time throughout 10th December. Possibly this may have been why he never advised Singapore of his movements, and in consequence the fighter squadron standing by for Fleet protection remained at Sembawang until it was too late.' Naval Historical Branch records. Although Pulford had been unable to promise continuous air cover, he had earmarked No. 453 Australian Fighter Squadron (11 Buffaloes) at Sembawang, one of Singapore's airfields, as Fleet Defence Squadron. The Squadron Commander had arranged R/T communication between the *Prince of Wales* and the squadron, and was prepared, given the use of Kluang, Kuantan, and Kota Bharu airfields, to keep a small patrol over the Fleet within 80 miles of the coast to a point 80 miles north of Kota Bharu. The range of the squadron was considerably reduced when the Kota Bharu airfield, having become untenable, was abandoned in the late afternoon of 8 December.

able to remain only a very short time over the area before having to return to refuel. The Dutch fighter squadron had not arrived by the 8th; it was uncertain whether it would be available by the 10th and thus there was a shortage of fighter aircraft. These factors meant that a short patrol might possibly have been provided at intervals at Singora, but that it was impossible to guarantee continuous fighter protection.[92]

The aircraft situation was indeed desperate—even before the Japanese struck. The total RAF strength in Malaya on the eve of war was 246 aircraft, including 36 Vildebeeste torpedo-bombers, 'archaic and rickety biplanes with fixed landing gear, masses of rigging wires and braces, and open cockpits'. They had a speed of 100 m.p.h. 'It was noted among the British crewmen after the war began that some Japanese casualties might have been caused when Japanese pilots caught sight of the Vildebeestes and laughed themselves to death.'[93] Ready for action on 8 December were 143 aircraft, only 72 of which were fighters, mainly venerable American-built Brewster Buffaloes, wholly unfit for the defence of a place as important as Singapore—or an important fleet. At a meeting of the Service Chiefs on 25 April 1941 Phillips had pressed 'passionately for Hurricanes to be sent there and not the Brewster Buffaloes [the first had arrived in Malaya in March], but had been overruled by the P.M. and the Air Staff, on what I believe he thought were not valid arguments about ease of supplies and spares of Buffaloes from the U.S.A. As a deterrent to Japan these virtually unknown aircraft had no force. That was one defeat in Committee that he always resented.'[94] The minutes show that the Vice-Chief of the Air Staff, Air Chief Marshal Sir Wilfred Freeman, had asserted that the Buffalo 'compared very favourably with the Hurricane ... [and] would be more than a match' for Japanese aircraft, which were not of modern type.[95] Eventually, approval was given to

---

[92] 'Operations in the Far East, from 17th October 1940 to 27th December 1941', 28 May 1942, Supplement to *The London Gazette*, 22 Jan. 1948, p. 557. Air Vice-Marshal Sir Paul Maltby ('Report on the Air Operations during the Campaigns in Malaya and Netherlands East Indies from 8th December, 1941 to 12th March, 1942', 26 July 1947, Third Supplement to *The London Gazette*, 20 Feb. 1948, p. 1368) duplicates this material, but omits the 'Dutch fighter squadron' sentence and substitutes 'appreciable' for 'continuous' at the end. (Maltby was AOC, RAF, in Java at the beginning of 1942.) The nearest airfield which might possibly be used was at Kuantan, over 300 miles south of Singora.
[93] Martin Caidin, *The Ragged, Rugged Warriors* (New York, 1966), p. 266.
[94] Captain Bell's letter to the author, 24 Mar. 1975.
[95] COS(41) 148th Mtg., CAB 79/11. The VCAS was only repeating the judgement in a

(*continued*)

station four long-range fighter squadrons in the Far East for fleet protection, but it had not been possible to provide them by the outbreak of war.

Noel Barber has alleged that the VCAS's opinion was based on advice of the FECB, the RAF Section being implied.[96] Whatever the truth of the charge against the FECB, it is quite clear that all authorities in Singapore gravely underestimated Japanese air, whether Army or Navy. During the months prior to hostilities, pilots were told that 'the best of the Japanese fighters were old fabric-covered biplanes which wouldn't stand a chance against the Buffaloes'.[97]

Afterwards Pulford and Spooner (the latter was directly responsible for the naval base and the local naval defences) were adamant that the Governor of the Straits Settlement, Thomas, had exercised a malign influence on the conduct of the whole Malayan campaign. They charged that as soon as he knew of the possibility that fighter aircraft might be diverted from the air defence of Singapore to provide air cover for Force Z, he had protested most vehemently against their use for this purpose. This was *before* the loss of the northern airfields adjacent to the operational area.[98]

---

recent COS paper, derived without doubt from the Air Staff, that 'the Buffalo appears to be eminently satisfactory and would probably prove more than a match for any Japanese aircraft'. COS(41)230, 11 May 1941.

[96] *A Sinister Twilight* (London, 1968), p. 45.

[97] Caidin, *The Ragged, Rugged Warriors*, p. 268, on the authority of Gregory-Richmond Board, an Australian pilot attached to 453 Squadron.

[98] Commander R. A. W. Pool's letters to the author, 3 Feb. 1976, 31 Mar. 1978. On 13 February 1942, two days before the surrender of Singapore, Pool, a survivor from the *Repulse*, became responsible for getting a party of 53, including Pulford and Spooner, to Batavia. They left Singapore in a patrol boat and after harrowing experiences were marooned for two months on a small malarial island 20 miles north-east of Banka Island. During this period, when all but twelve eventually died, of exhaustion and malaria, including Pulford and Spooner, the two had bitterly aired their views on the loss of the two ships and Malaya. What Pool heard is borne out by Goodenough's recollection. 'It had been agreed on an inter-Service level before the outbreak of war that, should war break out, fighters should be moved forward to advance air fields to the north of the Malay Peninsular so as to cover the heavy ships should they operate along that coast in the event of a landing. After war broke out, and, I think, largely because of civilian pressure for fighter defence over Singapore, as well as because of the rapid advance of the Japanese overland to some of the fighter air fields envisaged, the A.O.C. went back on his promise and said that he did not think that he could provide fighters.' Goodenough to Roskill, 8 May 1951. In the authorized history of the RAF, Saunders states that the reference in Palliser's 2145/9, 'C-in-C, Far East, hints he is considering concentrating all air efforts on defence of Singapore area', 'would seem to confirm the view that the counsels of Sir Shenton Thomas had prevailed'. Denis

(*continued*)

Palliser, in his 2253/8th signal, was obviously trying to urge caution on Phillips, for in the same signal he reported that the Japanese had large bomber forces in southern Indo-China and possibly also in Thailand, that the Kota Bharu airfield had been abandoned, and that 'we seem to be losing grip' on the other airfields in northern Malaya. Force Z was at this time still south of the Anambas Islands. Here is where many experts, though obviously with hindsight, suggest that Phillips would have been wise to withdraw entirely from those waters, now that one of the two important prerequisites for his plan was no longer operative, and not in fact to return to Singapore.

And so air cover was definitely not on. 'Without air support,' Captain Bell comments, 'it seemed clear that our only hope of success lay in complete surprise, a quick raid at dawn, and high speed withdrawal, helped, it was hoped, by monsoon weather.'[99] Phillips, accordingly, chose to stand on, and at 0400/9th he altered course to northward. The cloudy and rainy weather was probably the decisive factor in his calculations. Palliser's signal, however, ruled out Singora, which depended absolutely on air cover, as the target. Attack on that base at dawn would entail 120 miles further steaming on the return journey, during which they would have been within torpedo-bomber range in daylight hours of the hostile air base believed to be at Ca Mau, than would be the case in a dawn attack on Kota Bharu followed by immediate withdrawal to Singapore; all without fighter cover. So the decision was to make

---

Richards and Hilary St. George Saunders, *Royal Air Force, 1939-1945* (3 vols., London, 1953-4), ii. 25. There is no mention of any such representation by the Governor in either Brooke-Popham's or Maltby's dispatch or in the Brooke-Popham Papers at King's College, London. Thomas himself flatly denied any involvement in the decision. 'I repeat that I had no knowledge of the matter at all, and in my opinion this was right. It did not fall within my province.' Thomas's letter to Sir Folliott Sandford, the Parliamentary Under-Secretary at the Air Ministry, 20 Apr. 1954, Hilary St. George Saunders Papers, 69/64/1 (Imperial War Museum). This all seems persuasive enough. Then how do we explain the Pulford/Spooner accusation?

[99] Letter to the author, 3 Nov. 1975. He has observed (letter of 3 Nov. 1975) that in the final days at Singapore he was far too busy with the fleet's urgent material requirements to have been able to attend all the meetings on the 8th. 'Only after sailing was I fully in the operational picture,' because, when Force Z sailed, he was made Acting Chief of Staff Afloat. He was the Senior Staff Officer, and Ralph Edwards had not arrived. The Admiral, however, appears to have relied more on Leach and Goodenough for advice, Bell being inexperienced in modern war. He had been in the Plans Division until November 1939, then Naval Assistant for the DCNS (subsequently, VCNS) before joining Force Z. Even allowing for the inevitable weakening of one's memory after 35 years and more, Captain Bell's testimony is an invaluable source, he being the only survivor of Admiral Phillips's staff.

for Kota Bharu, In Captain Bell's words, 'The point of attacking at Kota Bharu rather than Singora (*given surprise at dawn*) was that after half an hour in action ships would have 3 to 4 hours less time, in daylight hours, within reasonable T/B range of the hostile air bases. The Japanese were thought unlikely to be able to stage an attack for at least 2 hours.'[100]

The weather on the second day at sea, 9 December, continued favourable for evasion. Except that it was warm, it was quite similar to North Sea weather: low, thick clouds and a fine mist with intermittent rain squalls. Visibility was sometimes down to half a mile. A report of the momentary sighting of an enemy aircraft by the *Vampire* at 0620 was disregarded, since only one lookout reported it. (Its identity remains a mystery.) Unknown to the fleet, it was sighted by a Japanese submarine at 1345. (See the following chapter.) In mid-afternoon the C-in-C had the ships' companies informed as follows:

> The enemy has made several landings on the North Coast of Malaya and has made local progress. Our Army is not large and is hard pressed in places. Our Air Force has had to destroy and abandon one or more aerodromes. Meanwhile fast transports lie off the coast.
>
> This is our opportunity before the enemy can establish himself. We have made a wide circuit to avoid air reconnaissance and hope to surprise the enemy shortly after sunrise tomorrow Wednesday. We may have the luck to try our metal against the old Japanese battlecruiser *Kongo* or against some Japanese cruisers and destroyers which are reported in the Gulf of Siam. We are sure to get some useful practice with the H.A. armament.
>
> Whatever we meet I want to finish quickly and so get well clear to the Eastward before the Japanese can mass too formidable a scale of an attack against us. So shoot to sink.[101]

Unfortunately, at about 1700, an hour before sunset, the sky cleared considerably until 1830. At 1740 the *Prince of Wales* sighted in quick succession what was thought to be three enemy reconnaissance aircraft, 'hovering on the horizon like birds of ill omen before turning away and disappearing towards the East', when darkness set in. (They were from the cruisers *Kinu*, *Suzuya*, and *Kumano*.) The ships' companies cursed the fact that sheer chance had revealed them in that short clear period before darkness fell.

[100] Letter to the author, 14 July 1978.
[101] Layton, 'Loss of H.M. Ships Prince of Wales and Repulse', p. 1244.

The Force was then steering to the north, which it continued to do until dark, when Phillips made a large alteration of course to northwest (1855) and west (1930), ostensibly for Singora, probably to confuse the shadowing aircraft, if they were still in the vicinity. Unknown to him, at 1920 Force Z was only about 22 miles south of Admiral Kurita's four heavy cruisers. The only new information that Phillips received was Palliser's 1855/9 at 1917, reporting the sighting by air reconnaissance of a battleship, a cruiser, 11 destroyers, and a number of transports near the coast between Kota Bharu and Perhentian Island. The Admiral's plans called for the Force to turn back immediately it was discovered by enemy air. At about 2000 Phillips discussed the situation at a brief gathering of senior staff officers—Leach, Goodenough, and Bell—on the Admiral's bridge. The gist of the question the Admiral asked them was this: 'This operation depended for its success on two things—air support and surprise. When air support was lost, I decided to go on as long as we had surprise. That is now lost. Do we go on or call the operation off?' [102] Phillips pointed out that if they sailed on and attempted to disrupt the enemy landings, they would probably find

---

[102] Captain Bell's letter to the author, 31 July 1978. Middlebrook and Mahoney (pp. 137, 298–9) attribute great significance to the *Electra*'s sighting of a flare (actually, five or six flares) dropped by a Japanese reconnaissance plane (actually, three) over the Japanese cruiser *Chōkai* at about 2000/9th (see below, p. 457), and which was estimated by *Electra*'s look-outs to be about 5 miles ahead of the fleet. (The distance was more like 28 miles.) 'The flagship ordered all ships to make an emergency turn to port in order to pass well clear of the flare's position.' 'It was certainly a reckless move on the part of Phillips to steam on after having been so carefully shadowed by the three Japanese seaplanes. Phillips persisted with this for a further two hours, and it is highly significant that he only gave up his course of action after seeing the flare dropped over the Japanese cruiser *Chōkai*. It was this flare, believed by Phillips to be a sign of Japanese surface warship activity, that finally caused him to turn back. It is probable that Phillips would not have persisted in his plan to raid the invasion areas next morning even if that flare had not been seen.... The popular view is that he had decided to give up the operation after realizing that the Japanese seaplanes had reported him before dark ...' In this instance the 'popular view' happens to be the correct one, as Captain Bell makes crystal clear. 'To the best of my belief there was *NO* flare. I certainly saw none, and none was reported to the Admiral. Certainly no action was taken by him or the fleet owing to the dropping of a flare by any aircraft in sight of the fleet. We received no information of any kind of the possible presence of Japanese surface forces in our vicinity. In daylight nothing would have been more welcome to the Admiral than Japanese surface forces which we could engage. We continued our course to N and NW until we had shaken off the reconnaissance aircraft in darkness, and then turned (as previously decided) towards Singapore. The Admiral would not have turned back *before* he knew these reconnaissance aircraft were out of touch with us and could not report our final course. Incidentally, their shadowing was anything but "careful" or close. *No* emergency turn was
(*continued*)

no troop convoys, which would have dispersed, or enemy war vessels. Their own force would be heavily attacked by the whole of the available Japanese air force, which would have had at least 12 hours to concentrate to attack his fleet. It would, therefore, be prudent to abandon the operation and return to Singapore. All agreed with the Admiral's analysis. At 2015, accordingly, Phillips turned to south-east and shaped course for Singapore, about 275 miles away, at high speed, steering to pass east of the Anambas Islands. He was cheered by a Tennant signal that he had made the correct decision. But there was grumbling from the officers and men, who, still inflated with overconfidence, were looking for a scrap. The reaction was especially strong in the *Repulse*. As reported by an American war correspondent aboard the ship:

> In the wardroom there were cries and groans of disappointment and even bitterness. I immediately dashed out of the wardroom into the quarters of the ratings to check their reactions. I went into one sailors' mess and the men were sitting around the long tables. Some of the men had tears in their eyes—two and a half years in the war and never a chance to engage an enemy.
> 'How do you fellows feel about that?'
> The remarks I got were: 'This always happens to the *Repulse*.'
> 'It's a bloody shyme.'
> 'Damned disappointing, we were all keyed up for it.'
> 'We're just an unlucky ship.'
> Back in the wardroom I stood in the doorway surveying the long faces of the officers sitting in chairs and on divans in front of the fireplace and on the railing around the edge of the fireplace in utter dejection.
> Commander Dendy was almost at a loss for words, and the disappointment on his face was pitiful. It was almost like that of a child denied a promised bag of candy.[103]

The Admiral did not share this mood. At about 2100 he invited Commander Goudy, the Engineer Officer who had served with him twice before, into his cabin. 'The Admiral seemed lonely at times in *Prince of Wales* and sometimes asked me into his cabin for a "chat".'

---

ordered to pass clear of *any* flare.' Letter to the author, 2 Aug. 1978. To add to the mystery of the *Electra*'s report (12 Dec. 1941, ADM 199/1149), it gives 1909 as the time of sighting the flare, when in fact the flare(s) was (were) dropped at about 2000. Moreover, for parachute flares to be seen at 28 miles, the weather must be unusually clear, which it was *not* after about 1830. There is no mention of the flare incident in the account by the ship's Torpedo Officer: Cain, *H.M.S. Electra*.

[103] Cecil Brown, *Suez to Singapore* (New York, 1942), pp. 309–10.

'WE ARE OFF TO LOOK FOR TROUBLE'

On this occasion—they were together ten or fifteen minutes at most—'he seemed depressed. One remark he made should have shaken me more than it did. He said, "I would (or will) never again put capital ships in the position we are now in." I was surprised by the remark, but during the two Wars I've heard equally gloomy remarks before and nothing had come of them, so that I just brushed it off as one of those.' 'The impression I got when in his cabin was that we had been in dangerous waters and he was glad to be getting away from them. By this time we were heading for Singapore as far as I can recall. I don't think he would have made such a remark had we still been standing into danger. Phillips had the manner and appearance of being very tired.'[104] A signal of 2145/9 from Palliser, received at 2302, could only have reinforced Phillips in the wisdom of his decision to turn back. The COS warned of the possibility of two carriers in the Saigon area [there was none], and mentioned the presence of enemy bombers in southern Indo-China 'in force and undisturbed', and which could attack his Force five hours after an enemy sighting. It also spoke of the deteriorating position ashore in northern Malaya, where enemy air action had rendered all the airfields untenable.[105]

Just under an hour later, at 2355, a report of 2235 from Palliser was brought to Captain Bell, who was standing in for Phillips on the Admiral's bridge, Phillips having retired to his sleeping cabin for a badly needed rest. The signal reported that a landing was taking place at Kuantan, halfway up the Malayan coast. There was no indication of the reliability of the report, which was a mistake, nor was it followed up within a few hours by a confirmation or cancellation, as should have been done in view of its importance. Kuantan was about 120 miles south of Force Z's position and less than 200 miles from, and not far off the return track to, Singapore.

---

[104] Captain Goudy's letters to the author, 17 Dec. 1975, 15 Jan. 1976. The Executive Officer of the *Prince of Wales*, Commander Lawson, several times after the ship left Singapore made depressing remarks to Goudy, such as, '"If we come out of this alive." He had not spoken like this before over the Bismarck action or Malta Convoy.' Letter of 28 May 1975. Goudy himself 'had no feeling of doom till the night before we were sunk'.

[105] The reference to the bombers seems to have emanated from Brooke-Popham via the FECB. Asked by Palliser to estimate the strength of the air force that the Japanese might bring against Force Z from Indo-China, the C-in-C had given the figure of 50 to 60 bombers, which might be expected to arrive five hours after the ships had been sighted by reconnaissance aircraft. Brooke-Popham's dispatch, pp. 557–8. The Head of the FECB's Air

(*continued*)

It was considered a key military position which every effort must be made to defend, for, ensconced there, the Japanese would command the eastern terminus of the only good east–west road in the peninsula. Controlling this road, the enemy could isolate all British forces to the north. Also, from the Kuantan airfield, one of the best in eastern Malaya, they would have an excellent short-range base for bombing Singapore. All this was well understood by Phillips and his staff. Captain Bell tells us what happened next.

I measured distances on the chart, and it was clear that if we returned to Singapore via Kuantan and *west* of the Anamba Islands, it made little difference to our distance at dawn from hostile air bases at Ca Mau or Saigon. Risk from mines was possibly greater; risk from S/Ms about the same. So, although the report might be false, it seemed to me worth while to return via Kuantan, I roused the Admiral, he discussed it with me over the chart, and agreed; then went up to the Captain's bridge to see John Leach and issue orders to alter course for Kuantan. There was no conference, and so far as I know, only John Leach and I were consulted.[106]

Phillips decided that he could achieve surprise at Kuantan and that the risk was justifiable. At 0052/10th he altered course to southwest for Kuantan and increased speed to 25 knots to investigate the

---

Section remembers being sent for by Brooke-Popham about 4 p.m. on the 8th and told that sailing was at 6 p.m., and that he should prepare an estimate of the amount of bombing that Phillips could expect, if attacked. 'I informed the Admiral that we were sure of the operation of bombing and torpedo aircraft, all from the coast of Indo-China, and that he would be attacked by at least 100 aircraft and possibly more. I presume that this estimate was delivered by Sir Robert's staff to Admiral Phillips. We expected attacks from high level bombing and above all torpedo bombing.' 'I expected the attack to be land based, as a number of aircraft had as far as my memory goes been reported in the vicinity of Saigon and as far as we knew at that time there were no carriers in the vicinity.' Chappell to Harkness, 14 Oct. 1978, and to the author, 6 Dec. 1978. There is no conclusive evidence that Chappell's air appreciation got through Brooke-Popham's Headquarters and reached Phillips before he sailed. It is my guess that it did not, and that Brooke-Popham's estimate for Palliser derived from an earlier estimate supplied by the FECB as soon as they knew where Force Z was going. Note that in his dispatch Brooke-Popham wrote that 'For intelligence I relied almost entirely on . . . FECB.'

[106] Letter to the author, 31 July 1978. It is very probable that Goodenough was also consulted. We know that Laird, though SO(I), was not. Laird sometime after the action declared that, had he been got up to the bridge immediately, as he claimed he should have been, he would have pointed out firmly that (1) there had been a number of *false* reports of landings during the previous days, and (2) the COS's signal had *no* indication of the reliability of the report. When he eventually did see the signal at dawn, when he came up to the bridge, he was livid with rage, holding Goodenough responsible. Vice-Admiral Sir Kaye Edden's letter to the author, 11 Sept. 1978. He had got the story from Laird when they were staff officers under Somerville in the Eastern Fleet.

reported landing. 'It seemed improbable', Bell stated in his report, 'that the enemy would expect Force "Z", last located steering to the northward in the latitude of Singora, to be as far south as Kuantan by daylight.'

The Admiral's failure to notify Singapore of his change of plan and to ask for fighter cover at Kuantan, if only as a precaution, remains a puzzle. One of the considerations was probably his well-known belief in the necessity of preserving radio silence. He thought that, in general, officers at sea made far too many signals and were insufficiently impressed by the virtues of maintaining complete W/T silence in order to deprive the enemy of as much information as possible. If he broke W/T silence now, he risked betraying their exact position, well after they had shaken off the enemy reconnaissance planes. The wireless silence was of no avail, for less than an hour and a half after Force Z had altered course towards Kuantan, it was sighted (and attacked unsuccessfully) by a second Japanese submarine. (See the following chapter.)

Phillips, too, may have assumed that his COS in Singapore would surely have understood what he was likely to do as a result of the signal reporting the Kuantan landing and have arranged to provide air cover there at his estimated time of arrival. Goodenough was

sure that Phillips's attitude was that he believed his Chief of Staff would arrange the provision of a fighter defence. It seemed incredible to him that his Chief of Staff would not appreciate that he had gone to Kuantan in answer to the signal reporting the landing. It was, therefore, quite unnecessary for him to give away his presence by a further signal asking for fighter support or belly aching about his needs. In the event, it is of course proved that he should have broken silence and sent a signal ... But it is understandable that a man with a brain as crystal clear as Phillips should have mistakenly thought that the obvious was obvious.[107]

It was a major error because Palliser could not, or would not, predict how Phillips would respond to his signal—I do not think Palliser ever imagined that Phillips would alter his plans on the basis of this one report—or when he would arrive if he made for Kuantan. No. 453 Australian Fighter Squadron was standing by at

---

[107] Goodenough to Roskill, 8 May 1951. Whatever Phillips may have thought of the performance of his COS during the fatal sortie of 8–10 December, Goodenough put all the blame on Palliser, and when he landed as a survivor in Singapore Base, he refused for several days even to speak to him.

Sembawang, an hour's flight from Kuantan, ready to provide cover if Phillips called for help. It may be that Phillips did not request fighter support when he altered course towards Kuantan because of his very high opinion of the destructive power of the *Prince of Wales's* AA guns, and that, like nearly everyone in the Navy, he sadly and disastrously underestimated the range and quality of the Japanese planes and the efficiency of their pilots. But the key consideration is advanced by Goodenough: 'He still thought, and so did we all, that we were outside really effective fighting range.'[108]

At 1825/9th, when the *Tenedos* was detached to Singapore (due to lack of fuel), she was ordered to request of Palliser by wireless at 0800/10th, when she would be off the Amambas Islands, that all available destroyers meet the Force at one or other of two positions to the east and south of the Anambas at daylight on the 11th. The Singapore authorities inferred in the forenoon of the 10th, when Palliser received this delayed signal with Force Z's anticipated position on the 11th, that the Admiral had changed his plan. The signal indicated that Force Z could not have proceeded as far north as Singora, but nobody in Singapore inferred from it that Phillips might have acted on Palliser's signal and gone to Kuantan.

It was the only signal that Phillips passed to Singapore prior to the latter phase of the action on the 10th. The first knowledge of his actual position came only when the *Repulse* reported she was being attacked by aircraft. Captain Grenfell speculates:

One cannot tell what effect the news that the fleet had turned back might have had on the air dispositions for the next day. Air Vice-Marshal Pulford might or might not have sent fighters to Kuantan airfield to be nearer at hand if the fleet wanted sudden help on its way home. But without that information (except for the very vague signal sent by *Tenedos*), Air headquarters was left in the dark about what was happening at sea. There was no one more acutely distressed at the loss of the big ships than the Air Vice-Marshal, an ex-naval officer and a boyhood friend of some of those who had just lost their lives. 'My God,' he said to Captain

---

[108] Goodenough to Lady Phillips, 6 June 1947. Again, in his letter to Roskill: 'Kuantan was, I seem to recollect, about 450 miles from the nearest air field in Indo-China. This was further by a good deal than our own naval aircraft could have operated in a successful strike. It therefore seemed unlikely that the Japanese would be able to deliver a heavy air strike at this distance.' Kuantan was about 330 nautical miles from Ca Mau, and actually some 450 miles from the nearest IJN air bases. Captain Bell is more precise. 'Certainly he did not expect to meet T/B aricraft as far south as Kuantan.' Letter to the author, 2 Sept. 1979.

'WE ARE OFF TO LOOK FOR TROUBLE'

Tennant that evening, 'I hope you don't blame me for this I had no idea where you were.'[109]

Had Phillips notified Singapore of his change of plan, 'it is conceivable that AHQ might have moved No. 453 (F) Squadron to Kuantan where it could have stood by at call: R/T intercommunication between the two ships and the squadron aircraft had already been arranged. Some effective support might then have been given'.[110] One may wonder how effective a 'passel' of antiquated, lumbering Buffalo fighters could have been against the swarm of bombers and torpedo planes that the Japanese put over the *Prince of Wales* and *Repulse* in the late forenoon and early afternoon of the 10th. More on this anon. Let us return to Force Z, which we left steaming towards Kuantan.

At 0630/10th the *Repulse* reported an 'enemy reconnaissance aircraft', but it is more likely to have been one of the three Hudson reconnaissance planes from Sembawang which were in the area. (If so, *it made no report.*) The Admiral did not allow it to affect his plans and continued to the south–westward. Eight o'clock that morning found the two big ships and their three destroyers off Kuantan. The *Express* and a Walrus seaplane that had been catapulted from the *Prince of Wales* at 0718 conducted an inshore reconnaissance to check the possibility of troop landing-craft hidden under trees on the river bank, etc. (The plane was not recovered aboard but landed ashore.) It proved fruitless, and the *Express* signalled (in one version): 'All is as quiet as a wet Sunday afternoon.' There was nothing to be seen except jungle. The only suspicious objects, a small tug and four barges, had been spotted earlier (0514), but had been passed up in the search for bigger game. When and how this mistaken intelligence of an enemy landing originated is not known for certain, but it was to prove largely responsible for the ensuing disaster.[111]

---

[109] Russell Grenfell, *Main Fleet to Singapore* (London, 1951), p. 128.
[110] Maltby Report, p. 1369.
[111] According to James Leasor, some water buffaloes straying into a minefield near Kuantan had set off the charges. Indian troops manning the beach defences thereupon opened fire, assuming the enemy were attempting a landing, and informed Singapore. Leasor, *War at the Top* (London, 1959), p. 52, and *Singapore* (London, 1968), p. 191. (Leasor has privately stated that he got this information from a secret intelligence report written by Colonel Hollis, of the War Cabinet Secretariat.) The more prosaic explanation is that the
(continued)

One would have expected Phillips to have altered course to south-east for the Anambas Islands and returned to Singapore with all speed, particularly since the weather that day failed to fulfil his hopes and expectations. It was fine and clear, with bright sun and a light breeze—hardly the North-east Monsoon conditions normally met in Malaya in November to March. But when the *Express* rejoined the fleet (0845), the Admiral stood out to seaward, altered course to north and then east (about 0937) to investigate, on Tennant's suggestion, the barges and the tug that had been sighted earlier, on the chance that the barges might be motor landing craft. Without the hour and a half or so wasted in investigating the barges (did Phillips really think that the Japanese would launch an amphibious assault in four barges towed by a tug?), he would very probably have saved his big ships. Japanese charts (*Senshi sōsho*, xxiv, Nos. 33 and 34, pp. 460, 463, and the appended No. 7) indicate that, had Force Z not tarried, but had taken a south-easterly course and maintained 25 knots to the Anambas Islands, there was only a small possibility of being sighted by the Japanese search planes, the attack-squadrons, or the three submarines east of Kuantan, in the southern submarine patrol line, which were thinly disposed on a line extending over 130 miles. The two big ships would almost certainly have been sunk later on, but by then they might have been able to take something worthwhile with them to the bottom.

The Force was still engaged in its investigation when, around 1015, a lookout in the *Prince of Wales* sighted a shadowing aircraft (Hoashi's plane: see next chapter), and the Admiral signalled 'first degree anti-aircraft readiness' (i.e. readiness of the high-angle AA guns). Very soon afterwards the *Repulse's* radar picked up aircraft bearing 220°. Four reports of the sighting of hostile aircraft were received from the *Tenedos*, 140 miles to the south-east (dispatched between 1010 and 1032). The first one (time of origin, 0955) spoke of 'being attacked by enemy A/C', and the last one (1030)

---

troops had fired on a light reconnaissance during the night, and had magnified its size in reporting the incident. Maltby Report, p. 1368. Layton's Assistant Chief of Staff, Captain Collins, has another version: 'As far as we could gather, some ground-staff airmen got the idea that the area was not healthy and decided to get away in motor-boats. These were sighted from the shore defences, the alarm given, and fire opened. Soon the fighting became general, and it was not discovered for some time that there were no Japanese within hundreds of miles.' Vice-Admiral Sir John Collins, *As Luck Would Have It: The Reminiscences of an Australian Sailor* (London, 1965), p. 103.

read: 'Enemy aircraft are dropping bombs.'[112] (Apparently none of these signals was received in Singapore.) And still no signal to base for air protection—not even when the attack commenced, and when, obviously, a signal would have told the enemy absolutely nothing that they did not know already. Why? Even Captain Bell does not know the answer. It may be, as suggested above, that Phillips completely misjudged the efficiency of the Japanese naval air arm. Or 'it may be', as Leasor says, 'that in the excitement he forgot, or assumed that his chief Yeoman of Signals would do so on his own initiative', though this seems farfetched. The most likely explanation is that Phillips was clinging to the hope that all the Force was likely to encounter was a short series of high-level bombing runs, which the capital ships could ride off, if not completely without damage.

Shortly before 1100 Phillips turned south–east to close a vessel that had been sighted. She proved to be a British merchant ship, the SS *Haldis*. Aircraft were sighted just after 1100, approaching from the starboard bow. Phillips now manœuvred the Force by Blue Pendant (Blue 3), the ships turning together 30° to starboard towards the approaching enemy. The capital ships were now in starboard quarter-line formation. At 1113, as a wave of high-level bombers approached on the port bow, altitude, 10,000 feet, fire was opened. Quickly realizing that his Blue 3 signal was a mistake, Phillips countermanded it and ordered 5 Blue: a turn together of 50° to port. Middlebrook and Mahoney (pp. 174–5) describe the resultant confusion graphically:

> both ships were swinging right in answer to the BT3 signal [Blue Pendant 3] and the Control Officers' corrections to the left were thus being counteracted. This turn soon caused all the guns on the starboard side of both ships to cease firing as the superstructure of their ships masked their line of fire....

He [Phillips] soon realized that he had made a mistake in ordering the turn and countermanded it.[113] ... But a big ship cannot reverse course

---

[112] HMS *Tenedos*, 'Report of Proceedings...', 10 Dec. 1941, ADM 199/1149. According to The Japanese Official History, their aircraft did not spot the *Tenedos* until 1013 and did not bomb her until 1044.

[113] The Fleet Gunnery Officer, Commander Brown, 'felt it necessary to proceed from the flag deck to the bridge to advise the Admiral that such rapid and severe alterations of course must have an adverse effect on the gunnery effectiveness. I remember hearing Leach say, "I agree with the FGO, Sir"—but I am not suggesting that this had any great effect on the

(*continued*)

quickly, and *Prince of Wales* and *Repulse* continued to swing right, so much so their port-side guns were able to come into action and fire a few rounds. But then the turn to port started taking effect; the port-side guns had to cease fire; no guns fired for a few moments and finally the starboard-side guns came into action again. By now, of course, the Japanese had completed their approach and were about to bomb.... These cumbersome fleet manœuvres by flag signal had robbed the gunnery officers of the opportunity to settle down to the long 'run' of firing that would have enabled corrections to be steadily applied and more effective fire brought to bear. The unswerving approach of the compact formation of Japanese aircraft at a constant speed and height was really a gunner's dream. Admiral Phillips had made a fiasco out of his first handling of ships in action...

It was not a harbinger of a successful action.

---

final outcome of the saturation attack.' 'I left the bridge, so cannot comment on Phillips's reaction. It is a fact, however, that soon afterwards the two big ships started operating independently.' Letters to the author, 5, 31 Jan. 1979. Phillips immediately afterwards regretted to Leach and Bell 'that he had not negatived the Blue turn already flying and allowed the ships to manœuvre independently to give their guns the best chance. After the first attack the ships were manœuvred independently throughout the action.' Bell to Admiralty, 27 Jan. 1942, ADM 199/1149. The Admiral had not handled his Force as a born seaman.

XIV

Iliad

History shows that they thoroughly understand the importance of getting in the first blow.

Naval War Memorandum (Eastern), June 1938.

The three words, 'folly' in the basic concept of the operation, 'arrogance' in presuming it could be implemented against such impossible odds, and 'waste' in terms of men and ships in its inevitable and predictable result, must sum up the saga which you rightly term a disaster.

VICE-ADMIRAL H. C. LEACH to the author, 16 March 1975.

All accounts agree that in coolness, determination, and cheerfulness in adverse circumstances, the ships' companies of these two ships lived up to the best traditions of His Majesty's Service.

VICE-ADMIRAL SIR GEOFFREY LAYTON, 17 December 1941.

1. CONTACT[1]

THE primary function of the Imperial Navy in the Southern Area was to cover the simultaneous landing operations of the Army in Thailand, Malaya, and the Philippines, and subsequently the Netherlands East Indies and other key areas in the south that would ensure the acquisition of the needed oil and other vital raw materials. Assigned to Southern operations was the Southern Force, one of the task forces of the Combined Fleet, under Vice-Admiral Kondō Nobutake, the former Vice-Chief of the *Gunreibu*. I shall be concerned only with those components involved in the Malayan operation. Under Kondō's direct command was the Main Body: 2 battleships (*Kongō, Haruna*) 3 heavy cruisers (*Atago* (flag), *Takao, Maya*), and 10 destroyers. Its mission was to provide

---

[1] The chapter, on the IJN side, leans heavily, though by no means exclusively, on *Senshi sōsho*, xxiv, especially pp. 425–504, which replaces Japanese Monograph No. 107, *Malaya Invasion Naval Operations* (rev. ed., 1958), as the standard Japanese source. The latter retains some value. *Senshi sōsho*, xcv, the naval air volume, is disappointingly thin on the action.

distant cover for the operations in both Malaya and the Philippines. Under Kondō was the Malaya Force, commanded by Vice-Admiral Ozawa Jisaburō. It had the responsibility for escorting the 25th Army and a regimental-size unit of the 15th Army to Thailand and Malaya, covering the landings, and contacting and destroying the British naval forces. The Malaya Force consisted of (1) the Main Body, under Ozawa: the heavy cruiser *Chōkai* (flag) and the destroyer *Asagiri*; (2) the Main Body of the Escort Force: Rear-Admiral Kurita Takeo's 7th Cruiser Squadron (the heavy cruisers *Kumano* (flag), *Mikuma, Mogami,* and *Suzuya*) and the 11th Destroyer Division (three destroyers); (3) the 1st Escort Force: the 3rd Destroyer Flotilla (the light cruiser *Sendai.* flag of Rear-Admiral Hashimoto Shintarō, 10 latest type destroyers, 6 minesweepers, and 3 submarine-chasers); and (4) the 2nd Escort Force (the training cruiser *Kashii* and the coast-defence ship *Shimushu*). To attack enemy warships coming northward from Singapore and for reconnaissance were 10 submarines of the 4th (Rear-Admiral Yoshitomi Setsuzō) and 5th (Rear-Admiral Marquis Daigo Tadashige) Submarine Flotillas. They were disposed by 7 December in three parallel lines (1–6–3, from north to south) between Singapore and Kota Bharu, with their respective flagships, the light cruisers *Kinu* and *Yura*, patrolling to the north. They, too, were elements of the Malaya Force, as was the Minelaying Group (two minelayers), one of whose units, the *Tatsumiya Maru*, laid 456 mines between Djemadja Island and Tioman Island after nightfall on the 6th. Additionally, 84 mines were laid off the eastern entrance to Singapore Strait by *I-121* and *I-122* in the evening of the 7th. (They comprised the 13th Submarine Division of the 6th Flotilla, employed in another theatre, and were temporarily attached to Admiral Yoshitomi's Command.) There were no more capital ships in the area than the two with Kondō because the more modern battleships, as well as the carriers, were committed to other operations. Yamamoto paid no heed to the strong opinions expressed in the *Gunreibu* and the Combined Fleet that a reinforcement of battleships be dispatched to Kondō's fleet, claiming that aircraft could do the job, if the enemy ships came within range of the air force, and that only planes had the speed to catch and attack the fast enemy ships.

The aircraft upon which Kondō and Ozawa mainly relied were those of the 1st Air Force (Rear-Admiral Matsunaga Sadaichi) of the 11th Air Fleet, whose core was the 22nd Air Flotilla, 99 twin-engined bombers stationed in and near Saigon. It consisted of the Genzan and Mihoro Air Corps, which had moved from Formosa late in October, and to which on the eve of the war was temporarily added half of the Kanoya Air Corps. All were capable of carrying torpedoes or bombs, but none had radar for night operations. Other components of the 1st Air Force were 6 reconnaissance planes (Babs) and 37 fighters. Altogether, including the 6 seaplanes in Kondō's two battleships, 28 seaplanes aboard the cruisers, and the 31 seaplanes of the Navy's 12th Air Flotilla of the 2nd Air Force (Rear-Admiral Imamura Osamu) in three seaplane tenders at Rong Sam Lem Bay (some 45 miles north-west of Phu Quoc Island), there were 207 Navy aircraft in southern French Indo-China and the South China Sea, as well as 612 Army planes in the former, at the outset of the war.[2] It was on 2 December, upon learning of the arrival of the *Prince of Wales* at Singapore, that Yamamoto had had a unit of the Kanoya Air Corps, which was thoroughly trained in torpedo bombing, transferred from the 21st Air Flotilla of the 11th Air Fleet in Formosa to the Saigon area, where it arrived on 5 December.

The Kanoya Air Corps had a long history as a naval air corps. It had been used in bombing missions in China in the summer months. It came under the Combined Fleet in the winter season, when it did bombing and torpedo exercises against the Fleet every year, December to April, dropping dummy torpedoes (no war heads) in deep water, set to pass under the ships. From September 1941, the Kanoya Air Corps began to practise dropping torpedoes in shallow waters against the Combined Fleet. The naval battle off Malaya was fought in such waters. Because the Kanoya Air Corps had been given more opportunities for sea training against surface

[2] As regards the 1st Air Force, at Saigon Air Base was the Genzan Air Corps: 36 Type-96 land-based medium bombers (Nells) with 12 Claudes, older Type-96 fighters, predecessors to the Zero (9 belonged to the Yamada Unit and 3 were attached to Ozawa's command); at Thu Dau Mot, about 20 miles north-west of Saigon, the Mihoro Air Corps: 36 Type-96 bombers (Nells), and the Kanoya Air Corps: 27 Type-1 land-based medium bombers (Bettys); and at Soc Trang, about 80 miles south-west of Saigon, the Yamada Unit (Commander Yamada Yutaka): 25 Zeros with 6 Type-98 land-based reconnaissance planes (Babs). The Yamada Unit had been temporarily dispatched to the 22nd Air Flotilla from the 23rd Air Flotilla of the 11th Air Fleet. The Japanese used the term 'attack-plane' (*kōgekiki*) for the land-based medium bombers—the Nells and Bettys, so far as the naval battle off Malaya is concerned. Strictly speaking, there were two categories of attack-planes: carrier-based (*kanjō kōgekiki*), like the Kates, which participated in the Pearl Harbor attack, and the Nells and Bettys (*rikujō kōgekiki*).

ships than the other air corps, it was no accident that it had the best performance in the action on 10 December. The Genzan and Mihoro Air Corps, in contrast, had been transferred from the China theatre to the Southern theatre shortly before D-day. In China their bombing targets were land objectives, and, accordingly, their training in bombing and torpedo attacks against surface ships steaming at high speed was quite insufficient prior to the outbreak of the Pacific War. Actually, the speed of the two British capital ships during the action was approximately two times faster than the target ships the Japanese air crews had practised on during their training. The Genzan and Mihoro Air Corps had made only one torpedo-dropping exercise immediately prior to D-day, and that was off Hainan Island two weeks before. There were no targets. They simply dropped dummy torpedoes, making sure that they released then properly and that they ran straight. The exercise had been pronounced a success.

The officers of the three air corps, having had experience only of fighting in China, did not know what to expect and what they could do when hostilities commenced against Britain, and consequently were not exactly bubbling over with confidence. They had received no particular information on British naval air, although they had had experience in fighting British aircraft: these were Curtiss fighters which were given to China by Britain and France and which had put up a good show against the Japanese. Because of this experience, some, at least, of the Japanese naval air officers had a high opinion of British naval air. But they had no line on the efficiency of the Royal Navy's AA fire.

It is interesting to note that in the year preceding the outbreak of hostilities the transfer of personnel in the 22nd Air Flotilla had been kept at a minimum, and the organization of units and squadrons had been kept unchanged. There was a sense of solidarity, vertically and horizontally. Everyone knew what his senior commanding officer wanted and expected him to do even without any formal order. The arrival of the Kanoya Air Corps made no difference. 'Although the "Tei Air Attack Force" [the tactical designation of the 27 Bettys] was a unit temporarily attached to the 22nd Air Flotilla, it was not a makeshift one. Each member was fully combat-tested in the China war theatre, and their commanders at each level were on intimate terms with ours and could easily join us as Matsunaga family members. None of us felt any sense of incompatability with each other. There is truth in the saying, "In union, concord is strength."'[3]

Kondō, a gunnery specialist, was not an outstanding sea officer, whether as regards tactics, offensive spirit (he tended to be cautious), or leadership. His officers, while respecting him as a nice person and a gentleman, did not judge him to be a great admiral. Most of his contemporaries would have rated him a 'B' on Admiral Inoue's A–B–C scale. Kondō was typical of Japanese commanding officers in that he did not consult his staff much, other than his COS.

Much abler and smarter, indeed in the 'A' class, was Vice-Admiral Ozawa, a student of war (though only 45/109 in the Etajima class of 1909), a first-class fighting admiral, and the Navy's foremost tactician. He was a torpedo specialist and versed in night operations. No small asset was his ability to work with the Army. Ozawa was taller than the average Japanese, slender, and anything but handsome. Indeed, he, Nagano Osami, and Nagumo Chūichi (the Commander of the Pearl Harbor Striking Force) were by concensus the three ugliest flag officers in the Navy! Ozawa's frightening face earned him the nickname of '*Onigawara*', a kind of tile, with the imprint of a devil, which was used to cover the roof of a shrine, etc. to scare off evil spirits. He was born in the southern main island of Kyushu, which may explain his very dark skin. Normally a man of few words, he could be outspoken when the occasion called for frankness. He never hesitated to speak his mind to the C-in-C, Combined Fleet, or the CNGS. Other fleet commanders might hesitate to do so, but never Ozawa. He was unselfish, never displaying any interest in winning or glory. Thus, towards the end of the war he declined promotion to full admiral, saying that service to his country was more important than rank. He got the best out of each officer on his staff—the younger ones in particular liked him very much—and he made his intentions absolutely clear to them. There was a good deal of feeling in the Navy early in the war that he should have been C-in-C, Combined Fleet (a position he did achieve towards the end of the war, when there was practically no surface fleet left).

Rear-Admiral Kurita (28/149 in the class of 1910) was pleasant

[3] Lieutenant-Commander Takai Sadao's memorandum for the author on facets of the naval battle off Malaya, 12 Mar. 1978 (hereafter cited as Takai MS). Takai was the Squadron Leader of the 2nd (Torpedo) Squadron of the Genzan Air Corps.

and always smiling, yet was reserved. He was a torpedo specialist and a sea dog. He had not attended the Naval War College and had spent his career at sea, scarcely serving ashore. Kurita, with an excellent record in peacetime war games and exercises, was less successful in sea-going commands during the war, despite his strong offensive spirit. Overall, he was a 'B'-class Admiral.

The last of the flag officers intimately involved in the Force Z story was Rear-Admiral Matsunaga Sadaichi, a dark-skinned silent man, who from his headquarters in Saigon commanded the 1st Air Force, which was under the operational command of Ozawa. He was, strangely, not an airman, but a gunnery specialist who had been a sea officer for 25 years. In 1940, when a captain, he had been unexpectedly appointed Commanding Admiral of the 1st Air Force. There was no available air officer of sufficient rank for the job, which went to Matsunaga because he was a War College graduate. Despite Matsunaga's lack of air expertise, his officers and men had much affection for him—the hardships experienced in his youth had made him sympathetic and considerate towards subordinates—and respected his outstanding leadership qualities.

The command channel in the naval battle off Malaya was Nagano–Yamamoto–Kondō–Ozawa–Matsunaga, with Ozawa in command on the spot, though it was Kondō who made the big strategic decisions.

What did the Japanese know about Force Z? On 1 December Nagano had announced at the Imperial Conference that the British were sending to the Indian Ocean 'two battleships for certain, and four battleships less certain'. On the 2nd the British announced that the *Prince of Wales* 'and other heavy units' had been sent as reinforcements to Singapore. The existence of at least the two 'certain' capital ships was thus indirectly acknowledged. IGHQ Navy Department seemed to have judged that one additional battleship might have been moved to Singapore: the *King George V* or the *Revenge*.[4] Combined Fleet HQ believed that the *Prince of Wales* and *King George V* were both at Singapore.[5] Subsequent intelligence on the 6th confirmed the presence of two big ships at Singapore, as

---

[4] See *Senshi sōsho*, xxiv. 361–2.
[5] 'After the *Prince of Wales* has been destroyed, our next target will be the *King George V*.' Diary, 4 Dec. 1941, Ugaki, *Sensō roku*, p. 26.

well as two heavy cruisers. (There were, of course, no heavy cruisers at Singapore.) The two capital ships were photographed in Singapore harbour on the 8th, but until after the action on 10 December there was uncertainty as to the precise identity of the two.

The Malaya Force now 'realized that a decisive battle between the Japanese and British fleets was inevitable, and experienced great strain'.[6] Well might it. In capital ships the number was the same, but not in fighting power. The eight 45-calibre 14.1-inch guns of the *Kongō* and her sister, the *Haruna*, would stand no chance against the new 14-inch guns of the *Prince of Wales*, which were believed to outrange them, in a daylight action.[7] This was Kondō's judgement. He was also aware that the King George V class possessed radar, which would give it a decided advantage in a sea where visability was often bad due to squalls and other adverse weather conditions. He had no information on the capability of British radar, but he dreaded it.[8] Finally, there was the *Prince of Wales*'s reputation of being the 'unsinkable battleship'. Reasonably Kondō was not prepared to approach the British fleet and risk a surface action whose result might jeopardize the amphibious operations in Malaya. He believed his auxiliary forces to be superior, that is, that he had a decided edge in torpedo and air power, though the enemy's speed would make a torpedo attack difficult. His intention, therefore was to attack the ships with aircraft and submarines, then rely on a night torpedo attack by his destoyers, which excelled in night fighting. The *Gunreibu*'s calm in the period leading up to the action on 10 December was based on the same faith in land-based naval aircraft and in their destroyers. Ozawa shared the cautious views of his Chief. He greatly respected and admired Phillips, though he did not know him personally. He

---

[6] *Senshi sōsho*, xxiv. 385.

[7] The two Kongō's had been completed in 1913–15 as battle cruisers, but were classified as 'high-speed battleships' after their second modernization in 1933–4 (*Haruna*) and 1936–7 (*Kongō*). They were of 32,000 tons displacement and could do 30.5 knots after this modernization.

[8] The facts are that the *Prince of Wales* had a surface-warning radar set (Type 271), with an approximate range of 10 to 25 miles, and an air-warning set (Type 281), with an approximate range of 100 miles at 20,000 feet. She also possessed six Type 282 (pom-pom ranging radar), and two Type-284 sets (main armament radar), and four Type-285 sets (AA gunnery radar). The *Repulse* had a single 286 (air warning) set, with an approximate range of 10 to 20 miles. Two of the destroyers, *Electra* and *Express*, had one Type 286 each, which though really AA could pick up a surfaced submarine close to the ship.

was aware that the British Commander had been VCNS and that the Prime Minister trusted him and valued him greatly. Also, Ozawa thought that Phillips understood air operations, since he had requested air cover several times.[9]

The Main Body of the Southern Force (Kondō) rendezvoused in the Inland Sea on 24 November, advanced to the Pescadores by 4 December, and was off the Indo-China coast, south–east of Pulau Condore (Condore Island: Con Son today) early on the morning of the 8th, the scheduled day of the Malayan and Thai landings. The Malaya Force assembled at Samah on Hainan Island by 26 November. On 4 December Kurita steered to a position south of French Indo-China, arriving on 6 December. His 7th Cruiser Squadron and 11th Destroyer Division provided close cover for the three convoys. Ozawa and the Main Body of the Malaya Force and the 1st Escort Force, escorting the main convoy of 18 troop transports, left the port of Samah early in the morning of 4 December; its landing points were to be Singora, Thepha (Tepa), Patani, and Kota Bharu in the southern part of the Isthmus of Kra. The first three were in Thailand, 70–120 miles up the coast from the frontier with Malaya; the last, in the extreme north of Malaya. On the evening of the 5th seven transports, escorted by the *Kashii*, left Cape Saint Jacques (Vung Tau), 40 miles south–east of Saigon, and at dawn on the 7th a convoy of three transports, escorted by the *Shimushu*, left Phu Quoc Island, off the south–west coast of French Indo-China. The destinations of these two convoys were Prachuap, Chumphon, Ban Don, and Nakhon, in the central and northern part of the Isthmus of Kra, all in Thai territory. The main convoy reached the staging area in the Gulf of Siam, about 150 miles north-east of Singora, at about 0900 on 7 December. It was while Ozawa was sailing westward, some 80 miles south of Cape Cambodia, in the forenoon of the 7th that a British plane (a Catalina flying-boat from Singapore) was sighted. To preserve the secrecy of the landing operations timed for the 8th, Ozawa at once ordered the plane shot

---

[9] Interview with Captain Terazaki Takaji, 18 May 1976, who was on Ozawa's staff. The request for air cover is mystifying, since we know that Phillips did *not* request air cover once he sailed. It could be that Japanese Intelligence was aware of the Admiral's position *re* fighter protection before he sailed, and that they had intercepted Palliser's signal (above, p. 426). We know that the Operations Division of the *Gunreibu* was monitoring the (one-sided) flow of messages between Singapore and Phillips. Interview with Captain Sanagi Sadamu of the Operations Division, 19 May 1976.

down, which it promptly was by some 10 French Indo-China-based Army fighters. This was the first act of war committed by the Japanese.

Upon the arrival of the invasion fleet at the staging area, each unit proceeded to its designated landing point, while the Main Body of the Malaya Force moved to waters south of the Gulf of Siam to guard against any British fleet that might come north. All three convoys had moved from the staging area into their designated anchorages at about 2230 on the 7th. By 0230/8th they had succeeded in making surprise landings at Singora, Thepha, and Patani, and about 0830 at the four points to the north. There was no resistance. There were problems only at Kota Bharu, where a landing covered by the *Sendai* and four destroyers of the 3rd Destroyer Flotilla was started in the early morning of the 8th in the face of a rough sea and British land and air opposition. The first two waves were landed, but the landing of the third wave was held up because of strong enemy air attack between 0200 and 0800. One transport was set on fire (it sank the next day) and the other two were badly damaged. At midnight on the 8th/9th, Admiral Hashimoto, having been reinforced by his destroyers which had been in the Singora–Patani area, moved into the anchorage at Kota Bharu once more, escorting the two transports. The landing was resumed at 1600 on the 9th after the landing craft, which had scattered, were assembled. The unloading was completed by evening, this time without interference from the British air force. Air cover and combat patrols over the convoys were provided by both army and naval air forces—in the case of the Navy, the seaplanes of the 2nd Air Force and (at Kota Bharu) the Yamada Unit's Zero fighters.

Ever since the shadowing of the Japanese convoys by the British aircraft on 6 December, Ozawa had judged it highly probable that the British would attempt a pre-emptive air strike against the convoys. When no attack developed, and the Army had succeeded in landing at every point by the 9th, Ozawa had to consider the possibility of an enemy naval attack on the resupplying operations. The only damage such an attack could do would be on some of the supplies and the empty transports. In short, the critically dangerous time for the Japanese forces had passed. Yet Ozawa rated as high the probability of a naval counter-attack. He accordingly intensified the air-and-submarine patrol of the South China Sea, and at the same time planned an air attack on the British fleet at anchor in Singapore to force it to retire to a rear area.

In the early afternoon of the 9th, having received a report from an Army reconnaissance plane that the British capital ships were lying at anchor in Singapore Harbour, Ozawa joined up with Kurita. Both moved towards Camranh Bay with the object of preparing for the next operation, the invasion of Borneo, leaving it to the submarine and air forces to cope with enemy counter-attacks by sea or air. Kondō also left for Camranh Bay at about this time. The sighting of the enemy fleet prevented the completion of these movements.

At 1345 on 9 December, when Force Z was deep in the Gulf of Siam, about 100 miles north of the Anambas Islands, the two big ships were sighted at a great distance (over 12 miles), steering north, from the periscope of *I-65*, the flag submarine of the 30th Submarine Division of the 5th Submarine Flotilla and the most easterly submarine in the second of the three lines deployed in the South China Sea east of Malaya. (She was carrying both her captain, Lieutenant-Commander Harada Hakue, and the CO of the division, Captain Teraoka Masao.) *I-65* reported the sighting of 'two *Repulse*-type battleships' in position 'KOCHISA 11', course 340°, speed 14 knots.[10] It was a quite accurate assessment: 345° at 18 knots were the correct figures. Although the submarine tried to keep contact, mostly while surfaced, and sent further reports, she lost sight of the enemy force in a squall at 1550, rediscovering it later only momentarily before finally losing contact at 1652. Ozawa and 1st Air Force HQ, Saigon, did not receive the first sighting report until 1540. The reasons for the nearly two-hour delay, which greatly affected the subsequent conduct of the operations, are not clear. One reason, however, was that the submarines disposed in this area were all old ones, whose experienced radio men had been taken off before the war to man the new boats, the vacancies in the old boats being filled with radio men straight from the Submarine School. The reported enemy position was 225 miles on the bearing of 165° of Cape Cambodia. This was approximately 350 miles from Saigon, or well within the range of the land-based bombers. At

[10] KOCHISA 11 was part of the Japanese naval grid reference system. One of the two big ships was recognized as of the Repulse class, and the other as a new type battleship that had not appeared in *Jane's Fighting Ships*. It was decided to report them for the time being as battleships of the Repulse class.

1600 Ozawa ordered Matsunaga to 'search for and destroy the enemy'.

I-65's report had been received at 1st Air Force HQ with shouts of joy. Matsunaga had immediately ordered a reconnaissance plane and three attack-planes of the Mihoro Air Corps to search for the enemy. There was a complication, however, in carrying out Ozawa's order. The attack-planes were loading bombs for a dawn attack on the 10th on Singapore harbour, where an Army reconnaissance plane had early that afternoon mistakenly reported (0950) large merchant ships as the two capital ships at anchor.[11] Once this was sorted out in Saigon (on the return of the reconnaissance plane in the late afternoon of the 9th, its photographs of the ships in Singapore harbour, taken at a high altitude, were carefully examined and the error discovered), Matsunaga countermanded the attack on Singapore and ordered an attack 'with all might' on the enemy battleships that had been sighted by *I-65*. The enemy position at 1410 was given as 163 miles on the bearing of 57° of Kuantan. Matsunaga was undeterred by the weather, which was hardly suitable for flying, let alone a night attack, seeing how determined Ozawa was to carry out a resolute night attack. Many of the planes were hastily rearmed with torpedoes, and the air crews were quickly briefed on the difficult technique of night torpedo-bombing. They were full of fighting spirit, despite the weather, and eager to display their skill. The object of the attack was to frustrate the expected descent on the invasion transports off Singora.

At the same time there was uncertainty as to what these British battleships moving north were up to. Did they intend to attack such landing places as Singora? Or were they trying to tempt the Malaya Force to go east, so that another RN unit could attack the landing places? Or were they asking for a showdown with their fleet? Admiral Ugaki's diary for the 9th reflects this uncertainty when the report of the sighting by *I-65* was received at Combined Fleet HQ:

What is the intention of the British fleet in proceeding northward? Is it for the purpose of impeding our landing operations or of bringing confusion

---

[11] Maeda Kōsei, ex-Captain, IJN, 'Ei toyo kantai tsuiyu! Marei oki kaisen' [The Main Force of the British Eastern Fleet was Destroyed! The naval battle off Malaya], *Chisei*, special issue, 'Taiheiyō sensō no zenbō' [The Full Story of the Pacific War], 25 July 1951, p. 66. But *Senshi sōsho*, xcv. 227, says that the examination of the aerial photograph revealed the two 'battleships' to be floating docks berthed inside the harbour.

into the rear of our forces, or of displaying the value of the British Navy's doctrine of fighting any enemy that comes into sight, thereby destroying the enemy even without any specific strategical or tactical purpose? From our viewpoint it is an act of imprudence for the British fleet to advance into an area where our submarines are operating and are awaiting it, our minefields have been laid, and several heavy cruisers, a destroyer flotilla, and two very fast battleships are operating, and further they might have known that a considerably superior air force, consisting of attack-plane squadrons, are stationed in southern French Indo-China. Otherwise, the audacity of the British fleet should be praised.[12]

At 1645 18 attack-planes of the Kanoya Air Corps, nine armed with torpedoes, nine with bombs, took off, heading south, followed at 1734 by 17 attack-planes of the Genzan Air Corps armed with torpedoes, and, lastly, by 18 Mihoro Air Corps attack-planes armed with torpedoes. Those armed with bombs sortied without exchanging them for torpedoes, fearing that the loss of time involved in the exchange might cost them the chance of making an attack. Bad weather forced the Mihoro planes to return to base soon after take-off. When the other aircraft reached Cape Cambodia, weather conditions to the south were so bad that they, too, had to return. The customary practice for attack-planes which had failed to locate the enemy and had to return to base was for them to drop their bombs or torpedoes into the sea, in order to avoid a possible disaster on landing—to themselves and to the planes closely packed on both sides of the runway. On this occasion, however, the air crews, knowing their air-borne arms, especially torpedoes, were in short supply at the base, did not discard them. The planes all landed during darkness without accident: they were kept airborne until the moon rose, at 2245, lighting up the runway, when they were permitted to land. It was an excellent demonstration of the superb training of the pilots. The three Mihoro attack-planes (led by Lieutenant Takeda Hachirō) that had left earlier had braved the foul weather and pressed on. Towards 2000 they discovered what seemed to be an enemy force and dropped parachuted flares—over the *Chōkai*, Ozawa's flagship! At this point we must go back.

Ozawa did not expect that the air force could sink such powerful ships as the *Prince of Wales*, so that when he got news that the two big

[12] Ugaki, *Sensō roku*, p. 39.

ships were at sea, he planned to damage them by night action, using the torpedoes of his five heavy cruisers, and then finish them off in daylight. The problem, of course, was to find the enemy fleet at night. Ozawa realized that if *I-65*'s report was correct, at 1600 his flagship was as close as 110–20 miles to the enemy fleet, with Kondō's force about 300 miles from the enemy. He now ordered *Chōkai*'s seaplane and those of Kurita's four heavy cruisers to search for the enemy fleet. Kondō's battle squadron and the 3rd Destroyer Flotilla (Hashimoto), being some distance away (the latter was still involved in the Kota Bharu operation), could not be expected to join Ozawa for a while. Nevertheless, the surface forces in the vicinity of the enemy's reported position (Ozawa's Main Body, Kurita's Squadron, and the *Kinu* and *Yura*: in all, 5 heavy cruisers, 2 light cruisers, and 4 destroyers) would move swiftly to intercept and destroy the enemy during the night of the 9th/10th. The transports then unloading on the Malayan coast were to withdraw immediately to a safe position. By 1655 Ozawa's force was on the move at 26 knots, course west-south-west. At 1715 speed was raised to 28 knots and the five seaplanes aboard were launched from the heavy cruisers. About 30 minutes earlier, Admiral Yoshitomi had ordered the *Kinu* and *Yura* to launch their two seaplanes to search for the enemy. At 1750 course was altered to 220°, and, because of the wretched weather (heavy squalls that came and went), speed was reduced to 24 knots at 1810. At about this time there was an important change in strategy.

Upon receiving the false report on the 9th that the British capital ships were still in Singapore, Kondō had proceeded towards Camranh Bay for supply. When informed at 1555 of *I-65*'s sighting, his estimate was that the enemy intended to use his capital ships to restrain the movement of the Japanese fleet in the South China Sea and at the same time use his light forces to attack the landing operations. Kondō had immediately proceeded to a position east of Pulau Condore. His intention was stated in his diary at that time: 'I intended to reduce the enemy strength first with aircraft and submarines, and then fight a decisive battle against them (chiefly by the use of torpedoes and, if possible, by a night action), concentrating all the available strength of the Southern Force.'[13]

After further reflection, Kondō judged a night action to be

[13] *Sensho sōsho*, xxiv. 438.

impracticable for these reasons: the 3rd Destroyer Flotilla needed to refuel (it had completed the Kota Bharu operations and was *en route* to Camranh Bay when, at 1805, it, with the *Kinu* and *Yura*, were ordered by Ozawa to join the 7th Cruiser Squadron immediately); the Malaya Force was a makeshift one, a rabble (*ugōnoshū*), without previous training together for a night action; even if the enemy continued to move in the same northward course and at the same speed as when sighted, an engagement would not commence until after midnight; Kondō believed that he could not exercise orderly control of his forces, because they were scattered widely, and therefore there was some danger of being destroyed by the enemy piecemeal. These were the reasons Kondō enumerated after the war for his decision not to seek a night action on the 9th/10th.[14] His Chief of Staff, Rear-Admiral Shiraishi Kazutata added: 'We had information that the British battleships had been equipped with the new weapon called radar, which had the capability of detecting and tracking a target, and thereby measuring the range and bearing of a target even in poor visibility. On that day the visibility was very low, so that it was judged that a night action should not be attempted carelessly.'[15]

Accordingly, Kondō decided to seek a decisive battle after daylight on the 10th, with his entire fleet to rendezvous at 0230/10th in a position about 40 miles to the south-east of Pulau Condore. The order went out to Ozawa at 1630 to draw the enemy force northward, to the south-east of Pulau Condore. He hoped to draw the British to the north by having his ships make free use of their radios. Ozawa, who was heading southward, received the order at about 1800. It differed from his own intention of aggressively seeking a night action with the available forces. He at once issued an order to all his forces: the 1st Air Force and Submarine Force should contact and attack the enemy 'to the utmost' that night; the surface force would fight the decisive battle after daylight the next day, after drawing the enemy towards their main force (Kondō), 'attacking in the meanwhile, as occasion arises, in collaboration

---

[14] The mood in the flagship *Atago* is depicted by one of the junior officers. They were none too confident. 'It would be our first engagement with enemy ships. We were excited, half hoping we didn't meet the British.' Shiraishi speaks of all at headquarters being 'full of grim resolution': they knew the *Prince of Wales* to be 'the most modern crack ship, and it was unknown what secret and powerful fighting power she had'. Interview with Lieutenant-Commander Motora Isamu, 16 June 1976, *Senso sōsho*, xxiv. 498–9.

[15] Ibid. 439.

with attacks by the Air and Submarine Forces'; and, finally, the 3rd Destroyer Flotilla was to join Kurita at the earliest possible moment on the 10th.

At 1800 the *Chōkai* received the first report of the sighting of two enemy battleships from the *Kinu*'s seaplane. It was timed at 1705. A second report of 1745 stated that the enemy had a screen of three destroyers. Ozawa therefore knew the enemy's position about 50 minutes after 1710, when he had received *I-65*'s report that she had lost contact with the enemy. But there was a discrepancy of about 60 miles between the position reported by the *Kinu*'s plane and the enemy's position estimated by dead reckoning on the basis of *I-65*'s report. Ozawa's staff was bewildered at this discrepancy in trying to judge the most probable position of the enemy. The problem was sorted out through a report of 1745 from the cruiser *Suzuya*'s plane (7th Cruiser Squadron) that reached Ozawa at 1810 and which enabled him to estimate that the enemy was about 70 miles in the bearing of 170° of the Main Body of the Malaya Force.

The prospects of drawing the enemy to the north, a difficult operation in itself, were worsened by the poor visibility. And as the *Kinu* and *Yura* had not yet joined the Malaya Force and their positions were not yet clear, there was some danger of the Imperial naval forces fighting among themselves. Besides, Ozawa was finding it difficult to exercise control over the various forces. The Main Body of the Malaya Force (Ozawa) and the Main Body of the Escort Force (Kurita), having lost sight of each other, were continuing their respective advances, maintaining contact by radio telephone. At 1820 Ozawa altered course to 200° in order to approach the British fleet, and Kurita followed suit. At 1846 this report of 1820 was received from the cruiser *Kumano*'s seaplane: 'Two enemy battleships of "Renown" class sighted. Position, 70 miles on the bearing of 185 degrees of point of my departure; course, 50 degrees; speed, 16 knots.' The same aircraft reported directly afterwards that the enemy main body had a screen of five destroyers.

Judged from this position, less than 50 miles separated the two fleets, Japanese and British, at 1830. But the enemy's course was contrary to Ozawa's expectation. He had judged that the enemy intended to attack the Japanese convoy in the Singora area. He accordingly had been heading south-westward so as to occupy a position ahead of the British fleet. Upon receipt of the report from the *Kumano*'s plane, Ozawa's staff were puzzled as to the British intention. Some of the staff officers speculated that the enemy might be trying to confuse them. In any case, since, given the present course of the Main Body of the Malaya Force, it was evident that the distance between it and the British fleet would increase, Ozawa altered course to 165° at 1850. (Kurita conformed and then altered to 130° and decreased speed to 21 knots at 1900.)

It was already an hour after sunset, and the visibility, steadily worsening, was then only three miles. Considering it dangerous to steam at high speed, Ozawa decreased his speed to 16 knots at 1910 and had Kurita conform. Ozawa had now to decide whether to continue the advance towards the enemy fleet. He pondered such considerations as these: *I-65* had not reported the re-establishment of contact after losing it; there were no further reports from the scouting seaplanes, and none from the reconnaissance and attack-planes, which had been expected to make contact with the enemy at dusk; and there was no expectation that visibility would improve, at least until moon-rise (2238); although the *Kinu* had joined the Main Body at 1907, the *Yura* had not (indeed, she did not join Ozawa's Main Body during the night), and although voice communication was kept up with Kurita's force, the Main Body and this force were not in visual contact. Ozawa's conclusions were that there was little possibility of re-discovering the British fleet and of the submarines and aircraft maintaining contact with it, and that it would be difficult to maintain control over his ships during the luring-on strategy. Indeed, there was even danger of his ships fighting each other. He therefore decided it would be disadvantageous to continue his approach towards the enemy until after moon-rise. At 1920 he ordered alteration of course to 90°, and at 1928 to 50°, so as to be on a parallel course with the British capital ships. Kurita's force also, after altering to 170° at 1920, altered again to a parallel course with the Main Body at 1930. When Ozawa altered to 50° at 1928, his staff judged the enemy to be 35 to 40 miles away in the bearing of 110° to 120° of the Main Body. According to the British records, since Force Z altered course to 280° (i.e. north-west) at 1855, it is presumed that the two fleets had approached to some 20 miles (Ozawa, about 18, Kurita, about 22) at 1920, and had Phillips continued his original northward course a quarter of an hour longer, he would have made contact with the Japanese. Who knows, there may have been another Matapan, especially if

Force Z had sighted the Japanese force first, with their capital ships severely mauling the Japanese heavy cruisers. On the other hand, Phillips was no Cunningham, the Japanese were well trained in night combat, and their cruisers and destroyers were equipped with the deadly Long Lance torpedoes. After the two fleets had passed each other, Ozawa steering to the east and Phillips to the west, without sighting each other, the distance between them rapidly lengthened.

Ozawa barely averted a disaster shortly afterwards. This brings us back to the four aircraft that Matsunaga had sent out immediately he had received *I-65*'s sighting report. The reconnaissance plane was frustrated by bad weather. The three attack-planes (Nells), led by Lieutenant Takeda, also met with bad weather but had continued their southward flight. Towards 2000 they sighted two white lines of wakes and two black shapes of ships (*Chōkai, Asagiri*) on the dark sea. The position differed somewhat from the estimated position of the enemy force, but as the ships were steering northward, Takeda was certain they were the enemy. The planes at once began to shadow at low altitude, and at 2000 transmitted this report to Saigon: 'Enemy sighted,' and two minutes later: 'Position, 150 degrees, 90 miles from Obi Island.' When, just before 2000, the *Chōkai* discerned the planes approaching her with flight lights on, the staff judged them to be friendly craft. They were horrified when the planes dropped five or six flares (to illuminate a surface target). The *Chōkai* sent an urgent plain signal to the aircraft by blinker: 'We are the *Chōkai*!' It was not understood.[16] The signal was repeated by searchlight, which, it seems, the planes did not receive. Whereupon the *Chōkai*, fearing that a tragic mishap was about to occur, altered course to 0° (i.e. a turn away to the north) to try to get away, at the same time signalling to 1st Air Force HQ in Saigon: 'Three medium attack-planes are flying over the *Chōkai*,' and: 'The ship illuminated by the flares is the *Chōkai*.' Upon their receipt, Matsunaga at once signalled the planes: 'You are over friendly force. Return to base.' Takeda's unit continued to fly over the *Chōkai* until about 2030, when it finally understood the order.

There is really nothing remarkable about this incident. Identifi-

---

[16] Lieutenant-Commander Sudō Hajime, a Flight Lieutenant in the Kanoya Air Corps, states that Takeda understood the signal but thought it an enemy deception, since he believed that no friendly surface ships were in the area. *Malay oki kaisen* [The naval battle off Malaya] (Tokyo, 1974), p. 59.

cation of warships, difficult enough in daytime, was almost impossible at night, particularly since the IJN air force had not received any training in this area. Another factor was the principle of the Imperial Navy that its surface ships would in self-defence open AA fire against any aircraft, regardless of whether it was friend or foe, that was approaching them as though to attack. Accordingly, the airmen were placed in the difficult position of deciding almost instantly whether the ships below were friendly or hostile. Although indispensable in a night action, there was at this time no urgent light signal for identification of friend or foe between aircraft and surface vessels.

Realizing anew that any systematic and controlled operations to contact and draw the enemy on would be difficult under such confused conditions, Ozawa gave up his plan to approach the enemy after moon-rise and decided to join the Main Body of the Southern Force. At 2030, therefore, he altered course to 20° to effect a junction with Kondō. Kondō and the Main Body of the Southern Force had in the meantime been steering west-south-west. After reaching a position about 30 miles east of Pulau Condore at 2330, Kondō proceeded southward. At 0230/10th the junction of all three surface forces—Kondō, Ozawa, Kurita—was completed, and the entire force increased speed to 24 knots and steered south. Kondō was sill determined to destroy the enemy after dawn in collaboration with air and submarine attacks.

Contact with the British ships had been lost. *I-65*, after losing contact at 1652, had not transmitted any resighting reports. The last report of the *Kinu*'s plane, which had sighted the enemy, was around 1800. Communication with the *Kumano*'s plane was lost after its report around 1846; the plane was deemed to have made a forced landing somewhere. Both planes, lacking radar, had lost contact with the enemy because of low clouds and frequent rainstorms. The *Yura*'s plane had hit a mountain on Pulau Condore and was seriously damaged, and the *Suzuya*'s plane had force-landed on the sea. The reconnaissance plane of the 1st Air Force had returned to base with nothing accomplished, having been hindered in its search by bad weather. And the three planes that had mistaken the Main Body of the Malaya Force for enemy ships had been recalled to base by Matsunaga. In short, after 2030, when Ozawa decided to join Kondō, the only forces that could be expected to rediscover the enemy were the 1st Air Force and the Submarine

Force. There had been no luck here, either. Of the attacking squadrons of the Kanoya and Genzan Air Corps that had taken off in the late afternoon none had got farther than Cape Cambodia before having to return in the face of impossible weather conditions. Nor was the Submarine Force able to learn anything of the enemy's movements. So, from 1820, when the *Kumano*'s plane had last ascertained the position of the British fleet, its movements were utterly unknown.

At about 0210 on the 10th, some 20 nautical miles west of the position where *I-65* had first sighted the enemy force, and 100 miles to the north of the Anambas Islands, the submarine *I-58* (19th Submarine Division of the 4th Submarine Flotilla, Lieutenant-Commander Kitamura Sōshichi), the most westerly boat in the second of the three submarine patrol lines, while moving on the surface suddenly sighted the enemy's two big ships in the near distance. They were steering south, course 180°, in 5° 10′ North, 105° 10′ East, at 22 knots.[17] *I-58* rapidly submerged, but, frustrated by the jamming of one of the torpedo-tube hatches, lost valuable time. By the time the trouble was corrected, the *Prince of Wales* and *Repulse* were disappearing into the distance. She fired a salvo of five torpedoes at the rear ship (*Repulse*) that missed, then surfaced, reported the position of the enemy to Saigon (0211), and followed at 16 knots. She transmitted a further report at 0255: 'Enemy escaping in the direction of 240 degrees [i.e. a course heading towards Kuantan] . . .' There was no mention of the enemy's speed or position. She finally lost contact, and so reported at 0445, but, again, failing to indicate the enemy's last noted course, speed and position.[18]

---

[17] *I-58* gave the British position as 'FUMORO 45', which position is, according to the War Diary of the 7th Cruiser Squadron, as I have given it above. According to another source, it was 140 miles on the bearing of 57° of Kuantan ('Note of Commanding Officer Maeda of the Genzan Flying Corps'). There is a discrepancy of 10 miles between these two positions. The Official History adopted the latter position in its chart after collating the movements of the British and Japanese fleets. This would put the position at 5° North, 104° 30′ East.

[18] The Japanese Official History offers evidence of a probable sighting by *I-58* as early as 2352/9th, that is, while Force Z was on a southerly course but before it had made its sharp alteration of course to Kuantan at 0052/10th. *Senshi sōsho*, xxiv. 452. The reports of 0211 and 0445 were the only ones received by 'higher headquarters' (presumably, the staffs of Kondō, Ozawa, and Matsunaga). Only the 3rd Destroyer Flotilla received those of 2352/9th and 0255. The failure of other Headquarters to receive the two reports greatly affected the subsequent direction of the various forces.

(*continued*)

On receipt of *I-58*'s first report at 0311, it was apparent to Kondō that the enemy fleet was out of his range: it was then 200 miles on the bearing of 240° of the Main Body of the Southern Force and retreating to Singapore. He, nevertheless, increased speed to 24 knots at 0330 (course 170°), intending to give pursuit, and at the same time informed the 1st Air Force and the Submarine Force of the enemy's position at 0211 and ordered them to 'make every possible effort to intercept and destroy the enemy'. The surface forces increased speed to 28 knots at 0614 (course 170°, as before), but the distance was too great to overtake the enemy, and Kondō ordered the chase given up. At 0645 he reversed course for Camranh Bay. The attack was left to the air and submarine forces. At 0900 Kondō cancelled the precautionary measures affecting the transports.

Matsunaga received Kondō's message ordering the attack on the British fleet at about 0430, and at 0500 he received *I-58*'s report of 0211, which put the enemy force almost 350 miles from Saigon base. If the enemy continued their southward movement on the course 180° at 22 knots, as reported by *I-58*, the search planes were expected to catch them about 500 miles from the base at about 0830/10th. At 0455 nine attack-planes of the Genzan Air Corps from Saigon Air Base, each armed with two 60kg bombs, and at 0530 two reconnaissance planes from Soc Trang flew out on a reconnaissance mission covering the South China Sea from the east coast of the Malay Peninsula to the north-west shore of Borneo. The centre part of a fan-shaped search from Saigon as the pivot was to go as far as 500 (subsequently extended to 600) miles south, far beyond the Anambas Islands. At 0600 Matsunaga ordered the Genzan, Mihoro, and Kanoya Air Corps to proceed as soon as preparations were completed to search for and find the enemy force, which was retreating from the position 'FUMORO 45' at 0211. Each corps was to take off when ready. Matsunaga did not receive *I-58*'s 0255 report, but on receiving the 0445 message reporting the loss of contact, he deduced the enemy's position from their 0211 position, assuming that they were holding their course and with speed unchanged from 0211 to 0445. At 0800 a radio

---

After the naval battle off Malaya, when the naval air force was exulting over the great victory, Admiral Ozawa tried to put things in perspective, remarking: 'It is not only yours, because the British battleships were located by the submarines. We should not forget what our submarines have done.' Interview with Captain Terazaki.

message went out to all his aircraft: 'Enemy's estimated position at 0830 is 190 degrees, 420 miles from Saigon, course, 180 degrees, speed, 20 knots,' The British fleet was in no such position.

The attack force was divided into three waves. The Genzan wave (Air Raid Group A, Lieutenant-Commander Nakanishi Niichi) consisted of two squadrons (1st, 2nd) of 9 and 8 Nells[19] armed with one Type-91 Model-1 torpedo each, and one squadron (3rd) of 9 Nells armed with one 500kg bomb each. The Mihoro wave (Air Raid Group B, for which no group commander was appointed) had four squadrons of Nells: one (8th) of 8 torpedo-bombers (one Type-91 Model-1 torpedo each) and three (5th, 6th, 7th) of bombers (8-8-9), the 5th Squadron equipped with two 250kg bombs each, the 6th and 7th, with one 500kg each. The Kanoya wave (Air Raid Group D, Lieutenant-Commander Miyauchi Shichizō) was composed of three torpedo-bomber squadrons (1st, 2nd, 3rd): 9, 8, and 9 Bettys, the Navy's latest, each armed with a Type-91 Model-2 torpedo. Total: 85 twin-engined bombers and torpedo-bombers (34 and 51 respectively). The Bettys had a maximum range of 1,500 nautical miles, and the Nells 1,200.

Before the Pacific War began, the Navy's largest ordinary bombs were 500kg and 800kg. As of D-day, the largest available at the Navy's air bases in French Indo-China were 500kg. The Official History makes this observation about the bombs:

Ordinary 250- and 500-kg bombs were used in this attack, but the strength of the body of the ordinary bomb was insufficient to enable the bomb to penetrate thick steel plate, so that it could not cause fatal damage to a battleship. In our Navy the simultaneous attack by bombs and torpedoes was made the standard attack pattern against the battleship. In this case the main object of the attack with ordinary bombs was to bring about confusion in the target ship through the damage caused by hits, thereby making easier the attack by the torpedo planes. Such armour-piercing bombs as were used in the Hawaii operation were needed, but at the time they were not available in this theatre of war.[20]

The deeper the explosion depth of a torpedo that hits, the greater the effectiveness of the torpedo. In the coming action the Kanoya aircraft, which scored most of the torpedo hits, had their torpedoes

---

[19] The 2nd Genzan Squadron left with eight torpedo planes, but one Nell had to return to Saigon when it developed engine trouble.
[20] *Senshi sōsho*, xxiv. 464.

pre-set at 4 metres, which provided for the appearance of cruisers in the enemy fleet. This decreased the effectiveness of the torpedo hits on the two capital ships. It was recognized after the battle that if the torpedoes of the Kanoya Air Group had been pre-set at 6 metres, the effectiveness of the attack against the battleships would have been greater.

Before the sortie, the Mihoro officers expected pretty high losses: a *third* of the attacking planes.[21] Virtually all the officers were confident of scoring bomb and torpedo hits on the two big enemy ships. At the same time, believing that these were two King George Vs, they were sceptical that their aerial weapons would be destructive enough to send them to the bottom of the sea.

The pilots and crews had worked through most of the night preparing for this mission. Yet, despite an almost sleepless night, spirit was extraordinarily high as the 85 aircraft took off, after Admiral Matsunaga 'painstakingly and kindheartedly gave all the men their orders'. The Genzan Air Corps took off from Saigon Base at 0625; the Kanoya Air Corps from Thu Dau Mot at 0644; and the Mihoro Air Corps from Thu Dau Mot between 0650 and 0800.

The attacking planes flew southward in search of the enemy. At 0947 the Kanoya Air Corps had reached the estimated position of the British fleet, 480 miles from their base. The weather was fine, the mountains of the Malay Peninsula being clearly visible above the broken clouds. At 1028 they were 600 miles from base and could see Singapore about 80 miles to the right. The enemy fleet being nowhere in sight, the squadrons reversed their course and flew northward. The Genzan Air Corps had passed the danger line when, at 1013, at a point south of the Anambas Islands, they spotted a ship below. It was the *Tenedos, en route* to Singapore. It was rather difficult at an altitude of 3,000 metres to ascertain what type she was. The CO mistook her for a light cruiser, a unit of the screening force attached to the enemy battleships. The squadron made two runs over the *Tenedos*, was, seemingly, put off by her evading action, and, finally, on the third run dropped its nine 500kg bombs (1044). All missed, falling 100 yards on the port side

---

[21] Interview with Lieutenant-Commander Takahashi Kassaku, a Mihoro Group Squadron Leader, 16 June 1976. This estimate was contained in a report written by the pilots in the 10 December action. Takahashi himself had expected to lose a third of his squadron in the action, which losses would, he expected, be doubled if the enemy had fighters.

of the ship. 'Suffering from self-reproach,' says Captain Maeda, the Commander of the Genzan Air Corps, who was with the 3rd Squadron as an observer, there was nothing for it but to reverse course and to return to base to reload with bombs.[22] The two torpedo-bomber squadrons had not concerned themselves with the enemy ship and continued their flight south, reaching a point at 1030 approximately 600 miles from base, or well beyond the danger line. The three Mihoro squadrons, the last to leave, had flown south independently of each other. A hundred miles south-south-east of Cape Cambodia the 5th Squadron altered course to south-west and headed towards the offing of Kuantan.

The attacking squadrons had almost despaired of finding the enemy during daylight on the 10th, and were increasingly concerned with the readings of their fuel gauges, when the joyous news was received. The eagerly anticipated report finally came in to Saigon from a Genzan reconnaissance plane in search line No. 3, piloted by Reserve Ensign Hoashi Masane. (The quiet and gentle Hoashi, a graduate of the Buddhist Ryŭkoku College in Kyoto and son of a famous Buddhist priest, always carried his rosary in his hand even aboard a plane. He later received a citation for his outstanding work in the naval battle off Malaya from the C-in-C of

[22] Later the 3rd Squadron Leader, Lieutenant Nikaidō Rokuo, told Lieutenant Takai what had happened. 'The pilots and bombardiers of my squadron's planes had been specially trained as Nell pilots and bombardiers and each of them had had good combat experience in China. When they first sighted a ship below, my bombardier appeared to be dead sure that the target he was aiming at through the bomb-sight was an enemy battleship that we had been seeking. I was suspicious whether she was really an enemy battleship, so I patted his shoulder to warn him to reassure himself about the target. However, he brushed my hand aside, crying "Don't disturb me!" and a few seconds later our bombs were dropped. Directly after the bombs were released, the bombardier became aware that the target was wrong, but it was too late. In retrospect, although it was a case of being "wise after the event", an attack should be commenced by the squadron leader's firm order, and the target should be indicated by him clearly. This is the fundamental procedure taught as Lesson No. 1, and has been practised in bombing exercises again and again. However, this most important item was forgotten by everybody, including myself. I, as the Squadron Leader, am full of remorse and shame. Everything may appear quite abnormal to you, Takai. However, please understand that this is the reality of battlefield psychology. Moreover, I should have thought of the fact that if the ship my squadron was aiming at through its bomb-sights had really been an enemy battleship, the other torpedo squadrons naturally would have manœuvred against her instantly. On this important judgement I admit that I was entirely careless and thoughtless.' On which incident Lieutenant Takai added this comment: 'His story was a quite valuable one, depicting truly the abnormal state of mind everybody experienced in the battlefield more or less. Military men should keep in mind that things do not necessarily go according to what is laid down in the operating manual.' Takai MS. So much for one example of the peculiarities of battlefield psychology. See below for another.

the 11th Air Fleet. He was reported missing in action in March 1942.) He had flown south to a point about 80 miles north of Singapore, and, not sighting any British surface fleet, had reversed course at 0913 and was flying on a north-north-west course along the Malay coast when he discovered Force Z off Kuantan at 1015. He reported immediately: 'Enemy fleet sighted. Position, 4 degrees North, 103·55 East, course, 60 degrees.' This put Force Z 70 nautical miles south-east of Kuantan and roughly 150 miles northwest of the attacking force. At 1020 Hoashi followed up with: 'Enemy Force altered course to 30 degrees'; at 1035: 'Enemy Force has a screen of three destroyers. The cruising order is a "King George"-class ship and *Repulse*'; and at 1045: 'The weather in the vicinity of the enemy, cloudy. Visibility, good. Ceiling, 1,500 metres. Saigon promptly relayed these reports to the three Air Groups, not all of whose aircraft had received Hoashi's signals. The receipt of Lieutenant Nikaidō's report ('Finished bombing of the enemy's main force, 1044') created confusion at Admiral Matsunaga's headquarters, since there was a discrepancy of about 150 miles between the location reported by Hoashi and that by Nikaidō. A staff officer pointed out that 'Ensign Hoashi had participated in the attack on Kuantan yesterday, the 9th, so that he is familiar with that area. Therefore Hoashi could not have made a mistake in fixing the enemy's position.' The Admiral was convinced. At 1140 he had all the aircraft informed: 'Enemy position reported by search plane No. 3 is correct'.[23] The action had already commenced, but the signal may have reassured the squadrons that were late in arriving at the scene—the Kanoya Air Corps and the 6th and 7th (Bombing) Squadrons of the Mihoro Air Corps. Hoashi's first report especially, which reached the Mihoro and Genzan planes directly from about 1030, had more than sufficed for the convergence of the attackers upon the position of discovery. The Kanoya planes failed to receive Hoashi's sighting signal, and it was not until Matsunaga reported the message at 1130 that they were able to turn towards the enemy fleet.

It was 1100 when the first attacking planes sighted the enemy. The initial impression of some of the squadron leaders was that the two big ships might be friendly ships. The *Kongō* was supposed to be in the general area, and she apparently resembled the *Repulse*,

[23] *Senshi sōsho*, xxiv. 465.

superficially anyway. When these big ships began to fire, they were still not sure, but once they were close enough in for a good look, they quickly realized how mistaken they were. We must recall that IJN airmen had not studied RN warships much—primarily USN ships. Equally important, no detailed information on the location of their own fleet and its planned movements had been given to the naval air units based on French Indo-China. On this point Lieutenant Takai comments caustically: 'Presumably, even at that time, our naval leaders were so bigotedly prejudiced that their air force had a secondary position in their strategy; "battle wagons" still maintained their supremacy in naval warfare.' The original plan called for a simultaneous attack on the enemy fleet. This was not feasible, since the 10 December sortie was made on a 'search-and-attack' formula, with each attack squadron of the three air corps flown on a 'search-arc' assigned to it. Moreover, the various squadrons, having received Hoashi's intelligence at different times, and being uneasy over the sufficiency of their remaining fuel, sped on and arrived over the British capital ships at different times. The attacks were, consequently, carried out in succession and independently.

2. THE NAVAL BATTLE OFF MALAYA

The British guns, from capital ships and destroyers, opened fire as soon as the attackers were within range (1113). The noise was indescribable, and was unbelievable to those who experienced it: the roar of the 5·25-inch, the crackling detonation of Oerlikons and Bofors, and the chattering, ear-splitting rhythm of the multiple pom-poms.[24] The attackers left the destroyers alone. (Damaged planes, forced to fly low over the destroyers, dropped bombs on them defensively.) The high-level bombing of the *Prince of Wales* and *Repulse* was carried out at 3,000 or 4,000 metres, the aircraft of each squadron maintaining perfect tight line-abreast formation.

---

[24] Churchill inquired of the Admiralty afterwards why Phillips had not turned away behind a smoke-screen, as the *Tirpitz* had when attacked unsuccessfully by British torpedo-bombers on 9 March 1942. Pound had no way of knowing exactly what was in Phillips's mind, but he presumed that smoke protection was not used because 'whilst smoke would prevent ships using their armament and being able to see what avoiding action to take, it is unlikely to completely hide the ship and would, therefore, be a greater advantage to the attacking aircraft.' Churchill's minute of 13 Mar. 1942 and Pound's minutes of 18, 23 Mar. 1942, PREM 3/163/2, ADM 205/13.

The bombs, released by signal, dropped simultaneously and close together. The torpedo-bomber squadrons approached on a course at right angles to their target, gradually went into a shallow dive while still out of range, at the same time stringing out into a loose, staggered line ahead, then attacked in waves of flights. Each plane in turn released its torpedo at high speed from heights of 10 to 60 metres (greater than in the Royal Navy) and ranges of 100–400 metres, then made a sharp bank that just carried them over the masts of the big ships, while splattering machine-gun bullets over the heads of exposed British seamen.[25]

Cecil Brown, the American war correspondent who was aboard the *Repulse*, told Lieutenant Takai Sadao after the war that he still could not forgive the 'brutal actions of the Japanese' in machine-gunning the British sailors after releasing their torpedoes. 'It was not fair, and was against the spirit of Bushido.' It is difficult to understand what possible grounds for complaint there were, or the need for the Japanese to wish to excuse it. The planes were in action, and after releasing their torpedoes, they were still under fierce fire. Surely, it was the duty of the planes to do all they could to knock out the guns' crews, upset their aim, and sweep the exposed positions on deck and bridges. Be that as it may, Lieutenant Takai informed the author of the facts as they concerned his own squadron, the 2nd (Torpedo) Genzan Squadron, which was one of the culprits. After they had returned to Saigon, he received a report that a considerable amount of machine-gun ammunition had been consumed during the action.

I was sure that I did not issue firing orders during the attack, because we did not encounter enemy interceptors in the air. I assembled all the machine-gunners of my squadron and asked them why they had fired and on what targets. However, most of these gunners could not answer my questions precisely. Nobody remembered why and at what they had opened fire. As a result of the discussion we came to these conclusions: It was only the plane's main pilot who had taken action directly during the battle, and the rest of the crew (seven airmen in a plane, including the main pilot), although each had manned his battle station, had no particular duty to execute during the torpedo attack. They could not endure having time on their hands and waiting until the most critical

---

[25] See the note at the end of the chapter on the basic principles of bombing and torpedoing in the Imperial Navy.

moment of the battle was over. Still, their planes were exposed to severe AA barrages, the enemy's time-fused shells were bursting around them, and some of the bursts of near hits were knocking their planes about heavily. The smell and smoke of the bursts of the enemy barrages were entering their planes. At the meeting we admitted finally that in such a serious survive-or-die situation it was natural and instinctive that the machine-gunners pulled the triggers of their guns automatically and unconsciously when the enemy ship came within the firing range of their guns.[26]

The eight high-level bombers of the 5th Squadron of the Mihoro Air Raid Group (Lieutenant Shirai Yoshimi) carried out the first attack at 1115, directed at the *Repulse*.[27] Flying in close single-line abreast formation, they released their 250kg bombs simultaneously at 3,000 metres on a 340° course. AA fire was intense: five planes received hits, and two of them were forced to return to base. The *Repulse* was straddled: all eight bombs landed within 30 metres of her, making water columns that covered the whole ship. Only one hit was scored, however—on the port hangar. It burst on the armoured deck, below the marines' mess-deck, caused a fire in the catapult deck, damaged the ship's remaining Walrus plane (it was thrown overboard to avoid a petrol fire),[28] and fractured several steam pipes in 'F' boiler room below the armoured deck. Fortunately, the bomb having burst on the armour, no substantive damage was done to the engine or boiler rooms, and the fire was quickly brought under control during the lull that followed the attack.

The *Prince of Wales* and *Repulse* shared the second attack, which was made by the 1st (Lieutenant Ishihara Kaoru) and 2nd (Lieutenant Takai Sadao) (Torpedo) Squadrons of the Genzan Air Corps, attacking in waves of two or three abreast. When it was seen that the enemy aircraft were shaping for an attack with torpedoes, the Torpedo and Electrical Officer in the *Prince of Wales*, Lieutenant-

---

[26] Takai MS.
[27] I have chosen to use the Japanese times for the attacks, as they strike me as being more precise—not that the British times are very different.
[28] The *Repulse*'s other Walrus had flown off to scout ahead of the Force for submarines when it left Kuantan and had not been able to return to the ship when the action commenced. It flew around unmolested during the action, staying in the vicinity until shortage of fuel forced it to return to Singapore. It made a forced landing at Kallang airfield on Singapore Island.

Commander R. F. Harland, observed to Phillips: 'I think they're going to do a torpedo attack,' to which the Admiral replied: 'No they're not. There are no torpedo aircraft about.'[29] The 1st Squadron (one of its nine planes shifted target to the *Repulse*) fired eight torpedoes from both sides of the *Prince of Wales* (1144–1146), losing one plane to fierce AA fire, with three others receiving hits, and the 2nd Squadron and the plane from the 1st Squadron (eight planes) attacked the *Repulse* from her starboard side, dropping eight torpedoes (1145–1147). The firing ranges of the squadrons were 600–1,500 metres (Ishihara) and 700–1,200 metres (Takai); the release altitude at firing, 10–60 metres and 20–50 respectively; and the planes' speed at firing, 145–55 knots and 155–80 knots respectively. The two squadrons were supposed to have attacked simultaneously, so as to divide the AA fire. A slight delay by the Takai Squadron (Takai had hesitated before attacking, not sure whether the ships below him were enemy battleships or Kongō-class ships) had thrown off the timing of this pincer-like movement.

In this attack Squadron Leader Takai approached the *Repulse* as closely as possible in defiance of the intense AA fire and drew the torpedo-release handle. The releasing device did not function (the co-pilot had neglected to unlock the torpedo safety hook) and the torpedo failed to eject. 'I could not believe my eyes for a while.' He reversed course and made a second torpedo run on the *Repulse* (1152), successfully releasing the torpedo when just over the water and skimming right over the ship's superstructure amid a hail of bullets and shells. 'Such coolheaded and imperturbable firings,' notes the Commanding Officer of the Genzan Air Corps, 'the same as those in peacetime training, were seen everywhere, so that it was not by accident that many torpedo hits were scored [in the action].'[30]

It was believed at the time that in this second attack 3 torpedoes had struck the *Prince of Wales* and 4 the *Repulse*. The Japanese Official History figures are 2 and 3 respectively. According to British records, the *Prince of Wales* was hit by two torpedoes and the *Repulse* by none. The *Prince of Wales*'s alteration of course to port to comb her tracks had avoided the other torpedoes. But the two, nearly simultaneous hits (1144), which struck the port side aft and abaft 'Y' turret, were disastrous. The port outer propeller shaft

---

[29] Middlebrook and Mahoney, p. 181, on Commander Harland's authority.
[30] Maeda, 'Ei toyo kantai tsuiyu! Marei oki kaisen', p. 74.

buckled and opened up watertight compartments along the port side. 'B' engine room, 'Y' boiler room, the port diesel dynamo room, and 'Y' action machinery room quickly flooded. Nor was that all. The practical effect was that speed dropped from 25 to 15 knots. Within minutes the ship was listing very heavily ($11\frac{1}{2}°$) to port (counter flooding action reduced the list to 9° before the next attack on her), and by 1220 the port side of the quarter deck was awash. The steering gear was damaged, and the ship was never again under complete control. All this so early in the action. She was left a sitting duck, as in the case of the *Bismarck*, for subsequent attacks. Most of the heavy AA guns (5·25-inch) were put out of action, either because of the list or the failure of electric power. The 'not under control' signal (two black 'NUC' balls) was hoisted at 1210. This brought about the strange situation of Tennant, driving an ancient battlecruiser, closing his modern counterpart, some three miles away, to ascertain her damage and to see if he could be of any assistance. He got no response to his lamp signals.

The six remaining planes of the Shirai Squadron of the Mihoro Air Group carried out a second bombing attack against the *Repulse* (1148) at 4,000 metres, dropping six 250kg bombs that fell around her but did not hit her. This attack and the torpedo attacks of the Ishihara and Takai squadrons were carried out successively at short intervals, so that the attacks of the three squadrons constituted a simultaneous composite bombing–torpedo attack.

The third attack, from 1157 to 1202, was carried out by the 8th (Torpedo) Squadron of the Mihoro Air Group (Lieutenant Takahashi Kassaku) against the *Repulse*, seven planes (one of which could not fire her torpedo because of trouble with the releasing device: see below, pp. 506–7) firing their torpedoes at her port side, and one plane, at the starboard side, from a height of 40 metres and a range of 700–800 metres. There were again no hits (British records), although it was reported that three torpedoes had hit the starboard side (one of which was uncertain), and one the port side. The Japanese Official History accepts three hits.

During the slight lull that followed the third attack, Phillips signalled the *Repulse*: 'Have you been hit by torpedoes?' Tennant replied by visual signal (1214) that he had dodged them all so far, 'thanks to Providence'. One of his officers has observed: 'One felt that it was his sense of Higher Authority to whom he could refer and upon whom he could rely which was the base of his calm and confident approach to problems,' as in this critical situation. Higher Authority in this instance had an invaluable assist in Tennant's supreme skill as a navigator, aided by his skilful Navigating Officer, Lieutenant-Commander H.B.C. Gill. He handled his ship brilliantly throughout the action, while never raising his voice more than necessary to be heard above the gunfire. Concerning the torpedoes, 'We were steaming at 25 knots at the time. I maintained a steady course until the aircraft appeared to be committed to the attack when the wheel was put over and the attacks providentially combed.'[31] He calmly ordered 30° to port, followed by 30° to starboard, then 30° to port, etc. This zigzagging was standard avoiding procedure, and it worked—at first.

The aircraft which carried out the next—the fourth—attack (1220–1232) against both ships were the 26 Bettys of the Kanoya Air Corps, the cream of the Navy's land-based torpedo-bombers, which had just come on the scene. They had reached the west side of the estimated position around 1208 but, unable to find the British force, flew further southward. They did not find the enemy until 1218. They had been flying for six hours, and had the fruitless search continued for five minutes more, they would have been forced to turn back due to the shortage of petrol. The first six planes (four from the 1st Squadron and two from the 2nd Squadron: Lieutenants Nabeta Yoshikichi and Higashi Moritaka) closed in upon the crippled *Prince of Wales* from the starboard side and released their torpedoes. The remaining 11 planes of the 1st and 2nd squadrons (five and six) carried out a pincer attack against the *Repulse*, and were followed by a pincer attack by the nine planes of Lieutenant Iki Haruki's 3rd Squadron, which also released its torpedoes against the *Repulse*. All the Bettys released their torpedoes at an altitude of 30–50 metres and a range of 800–1,000 metres. It was reported that in the fourth attack five torpedoes hit the *Prince of Wales* and seven the *Repulse*, which figures are accepted in the Official History. British records show four hits on the starboard side of the *Prince of Wales* (1223–1224), which resulted in a flooding on that side. She appeared unable to take avoiding action and did not alter course appreciably. The hits had the effect of bringing the ship nearly upright again, but she soon fell into a sinking condition,

---

[31] Tennant's 'Further Report', 14 Dec. 1941, appended to Layton's Dispatch, p. 1241; also Confidential Annex to COS(42) 6th Mtg., 6 Jan. 1942, CAB 79/87.

her speed dropping to 8–9 knots.³² There were, British records show, five hits on the *Repulse* (1222–1225). The cost to the attackers was two planes of the Iki Squadron shot down by the *Repulse*. 'There was no power on any of the anti-aircraft guns and all the guns crews had been obliterated anyway. Out of nowhere six young seaman boys appeared on the firing platform of No. 2 multiple pom-pom, put it into manual control and bagged two Japanese aircraft with a left and a right—they were so close that I can still see the expression of surprise on the face of one of the pilots, as he turned his head and saw that his petrol tank was well and truly alight.'³³

It was in this attack that the *Repulse* received her death blow. Having survived the first two torpedo attacks, combing the tracks of at least 15 torpedoes, even Tennant's skill could not surmount the third attack. 'I found dodging the torpedoes quite interesting and entertaining until in the end they started to come in from all directions and they were too much for me.'³⁴ What happened, to put it simply, was that the attackers were not committing the *Repulse* to comb one attack, and then other planes came at her from several bearings. Dodging the lot was impossible.³⁵ The *Repulse* was hit port side amidships (1222), and soon after by a torpedo that jammed her rudder. The game was up. Although still steaming at approximately 15 knots, she was not under control, as the Japanese were quick to see. In a minute or so she suffered three more hits, two on her port side and one on the starboard side. There was not much they could do about it. They could see the tracks of the torpedo

---

³² At 1220 the flagship finally broke radio silence with an emergency signal. It began: 'Have been struck by a torpedo on port side,' gave the ship's position, and added: '4 torpedoes. *Repulse* hit by 1 torpedo. Send destroyers.' It is my guess that the first part of the signal, through the position indication, was waiting to go off when the next Japanese attack took place. It did not get away till that was over, and then someone added the rest of the message to cover this new development, so I assume that it was meant to convey that the *Prince of Wales* had now been hit by four torpedoes instead of one. Nothing about air support or where the torpedoes came from, with the result that when the message was received in the War Room, Singapore (1240), the first reaction of some of those at the base was that it was probably a submarine attack. In any case, what could be done by way of providing fighter protection had already been done. (See below.)

³³ Lieutenant-Commander O. M. de Las Casas's letter to the author, 24 May 1978.

³⁴ Tennant, 'The Last Action'.

³⁵ In American Service jargon this appeared to be a case of 'real time' tactical learning, i.e. learning a lesson fast enough to apply it to an unfolding problem. But I am assured by Lieutenant-Commander Iki that the attackers were only following the tactics and doctrine in which they had been trained; there were no comments or indication by squadron or flight leaders on how to attack the two ships.

bubbling in the clear water, and only wait for the explosion. Unarmoured, the slender side of the *Repulse* was ripped open, and she listed rapidly and heavily to port, up to 30°.

Knowing that she could not stay afloat much longer, Tennant coolly gave the order over the ship's loudspeakers to cast away the Carley floats and for all hands to come on the main deck (1225). That so many men were saved can be attributed (as Tennant did attribute it) to this timely order about six or seven minutes before the ship went down. A few minutes after his order, when two or three hundred men were assembled on the starboard side, Tennant told them from the bridge how well they had fought the ship. His last words have been variously reported, including: 'Save yourselves and good luck,' and 'Goodbye and God be with you.' All around now men were streaming down the ladders from the various decks to get to the main deck and into the lifeboats. They were wearing lifesaving apparatus, as they had been warned to do 24 hours earlier. But with the *Repulse* now at a steep angle, many were sliding down the side or jumping overboard. There was no confusion, no pell mell, no panic. A number of unfortunates made ghastly jumps, like the officer who dived off the side but who because of the extreme list landed inside a hole caused by a torpedo hit, and so back into the flooded bowels of the ship. Another missed his direction and wound up down the funnel. A group of marines dived from the stern only to find themselves in the blades of the turning propellers.

The ship hung for a minute or two after Tennant's last words to the ship's company with a list of 60° to 70° to port, then, at 1233, rolled over. She was roughly four miles from the starboard quarter of the *Prince of Wales*, from which she had gradually become separated. Vice-Admiral Sir John Hayes, a Lieutenant in the *Repulse*, remembers watching the dying ship plunge on, planing down as she went, with the screws still revolving. 'Then she reared into the vertical as the stern disappeared. Just the bow, half grey, half reddish bottom colour, hung for a moment in a last defiant gesture to the sky; then that too slid back into a cauldron of bubbles while the water blackened from oil in convulsive eddies, and *Repulse* had gone.' It had taken eight minutes from the first torpedo hit. The gallant old ship had fought magnificently against overwhelming odds. Until the last moment her useable AA guns were continuing to fire.

Tennant was saved. As he tells the story:

> There remained on the bridge at least 3 other officers and myself. All knew by this time there was nothing more to be done for the ship and therefore they were free to look out for themselves. I remember wondering whether it would be better to remain on the bridge or to join all the people I could see [on] the starb[oard] side. In the end I climbed down from the bridge towards them. It was strange walking along what was normally a vertical surface. I got as far as, I think it was, B gun deck when without any feeling of the ship going down the sea came up and took me. Almost at once I was sucked down into water that was very black and no light at all.... I suddenly bobbed up to the surface in swirling water and heard a shout from a fellow in a carley float about five yards away saying 'here you are Sir, come on.'[36]

Bill Tennant undoubtedly had idiosyncracies belonging to his generation. His creeds were stern; but he shone for all his men as essentially a good man. When the tragedy eventually overtook the ship and the men he loved, and who loved him, he not only wrote personally to the next of kin of the hundreds of casualties but also to those of the survivors: so typical of his compassion. He enhanced his reputation during those panic days following the disaster off Singapore.

The fifth attack was a dud. The 7th (Bomber) Squadron of the Mihoro Air Group (Lieutenant Ōhira Yoshirō) arrived over the scene of action while the attacks of the Kanoya Air Corps were being carried out. Discerning what he believed to be an enemy battleship through a rift in the clouds. Ōhira had nine 500kg bombs dropped on her. But the targets were destroyers. No hits were obtained, and the squadron had no bombs left.

The sixth and last attack was the work of the 6th (Bomber) Squadron of the Mihoro Air Corps (Lieutenant Takeda Hachirō), which had arrived over the scene of action at 1225, when the *Prince of Wales* and *Repulse* were under attack from the Kanoya Air Corps. Taking the *Prince of Wales* as its target, the squadron dropped seven

---

[36] 'The Last Action'. Cecil Brown's version has Tennant at one point quietly saying to the small group of officers around him on the bridge: 'Well, gentlemen, you had better get out of it now.' When he shook his head negatively and refused to budge after several of the officers asked if he was not coming with them, they pushed their Captain 'forcibly' through the doorway and on to the deck, then grabbed him and pushed him over the side. They then jumped into the sea. Cecil Brown, *Suez to Singapore*, pp. 326–7. This is an excellent example of press nonsense. Tennant was swept clear on 'B' gun deck by a large wave from aft.

500kg bombs over her (1243) at 3,000 metres altitude and a bombing speed of 120 knots. (One of the eight planes was unable to release its bomb.) The Official History claims two hits, British records one, but this was a direct hit (1244) that gave the *Prince of Wales* her *coup de grâce*. The bomb penetrated the upper deck by the catapult, bursting on the main (i.e. armoured) deck below, blowing up a portion of the catapult deck, and causing numerous casualties. This bomb appears to have damaged 'X' boiler room uptakes and downtakes; flash and fumes penetrated to the boiler room, which had to be evacuated. By 1250 the ship was beginning to sink fairly rapidly, probably accentuated by splinter damage to the ship's side in the wake of the bomb hit. By now the whole of this part of the ship's side was under water. The official estimate is that there were finally about 18,000 tons of water aboard. The end was fast approaching.

At 1304 Singapore received a message of 1252 from Force Z giving its position and asking for the dispatch of all available tugs. By 1310 the flagship was a sodden almost static mass of what had been the pride of the Navy. Her speed was reduced to about 6 knots and she was settling rapidly, listing heavily to port, and belching black smoke and steam. At 1315 orders were passed to inflate lifebelts and abandon ship. The fo'c'sle presented an amazing sight, with hundreds of sailors standing placidly smoking and chatting on the sloping deck. They had mostly been driven up from below by the encroaching, rising water. The guns' crews on the upper deck were still at their posts, and there was nothing for the remainder to do but wait for the ship to sink. As she began to heel over more and more, men started climbing over the rails and diving and jumping 30 or 40 feet into the sea below (though 'diving' off the high side of a sinking ship is a euphemism!). There was no panic, just grim determination. The situation, albeit tragic, was not devoid of humorous touches. Many of the officers, with an innate sense of tidiness, after taking off their shoes prior to jumping overboard, placed them neatly together as they had long been accustomed to doing! Again, the British tradition of patient queuing asserted itself. And so the young surgeon officer Caldwell stood for a minute in the orderly crowd waiting their chance to jump, and heard a sailor say to his pal, 'Come on, chum, all them explosions 'll have frightened the blinkin' sharks away!' At one point the ship was listing so much that it was possible for many to walk off the side of the ship. Others were not so fortunate. They slid down the ship's bottom, ripping themselves open on the barnacles, while others tried jumping clear only to land in torpedo holes.

At 1320, her red bottom exposed, the *Prince of Wales* heeled over sharply to port.[37] By a brilliant piece of seamanship Lieutenant-Commander Cartwright had already taken the *Express* alongside the ship's starboard quarter at 1305 to rescue a majority of her company. But her Admiral and Flag-Captain went down with their ship, the tragic epilogue to the whole affair.

Phillips fought the action from the Captain's bridge (also known as the compass platform), not the Admiral's bridge. The Captain's bridge had a better all-round aerial view, but had insufficient space for all the Admiral's staff. Most, if not all, of the officers on this bridge remained with the Captain and the Admiral until the ship capsized, and did not survive. Those on the Admiral's bridge reached the upper deck after 'Abandon ship' was ordered, and before she turned over; most survived. The atmosphere on the Captain's bridge during the action was calm: there was a complete absence of noise or fuss. Phillips had a perfect 'poker face' and displayed no emotion. Even after the first torpedoes struck, he spoke, in ordering tugs from Singapore, in his normal quiet manner.

More than two years after the event Pound still had not been able to learn how Phillips had died, 'but we do know that he had insisted on many of his subordinates leaving the bridge to look after themselves while he still remained there'.[38] We also have these scraps. When the position appeared hopeless and it was obvious that the ship would capsize, Bell and Leach

tried hard to persuade the Admiral to go down to the upper deck where chances of escape would be better, but although he gave orders for all personnel to blow up their life saving belts and set the example himself, he refused to leave the bridge himself until the last possible moment. Before she took her final plunge he did climb out on to the almost horizontal side of the bridge as the ship turned over and that is the last, for certain, that anyone saw of him. I fear that, as happened to the Flag Captain and

---

[37] Middlebrook and Mahoney (p. 254) quote a petty officer as saying that, when the ship was upside down, 'I could see the propellers slowly turning.' Captain Goudy is quite sure that the picturesque phrase has no substance: 'I was watching with interest and the props never came anywhere near to being in sight.' Letter to the author, 4 Aug. 1978. Two, or possibly three, shafts, he adds, were jammed and incapable of turning.

[38] Pound to Lieutenant T. V. G. Phillips, 25 Feb. 1943, Phillips Papers.

several others on or near the bridge, the suction of the ship going down dragged the Admiral so far below the water that he drowned before his belt could bring him to the surface.[39]

One of the rescued crew of the *Prince of Wales*, in an interview with members of the Japanese naval press corps in Singapore on 3 March 1942, added this detail: 'Admiral Sir Thomas Phillips was always standing on the bridge. When our ship was about to sink, a destroyer [*Express*] came close to our ship and signalled to the Admiral, "Please come on board our ship." But the Admiral said: "No. Thank you," and while saluting the crew of the destroyer, he went down with the *Prince of Wales*. Captain Leach of the *Prince of Wales*, who was standing beside Admiral Phillips on the bridge, also raised his hand to the crew and was swallowed into the sea when the ship raised its stern high up in the air.'[40] Goodenough provides this firsthand account of Phillips's last moments in a poignant vignette:

At the last he was on the Compass platform. I was with the rest of the staff on the bridge below. It became obvious that the ship was about to go, her list was increasing rapidly. We were only waiting for him to make a move, and he leaned over to where I could see him and smiled and waved us to go on and abandon ship. He himself got into the water from another deck. I shall carry that last smile of his always with me.[41]

Admiral Farnhill adds: 'The Admiral and Secretary [Beardsworth] were seen literally stepping into the water over the port pom-pom platform. The ship sank to port and all those who went over the port side in the last moments were sucked down.'[42] The Fleet Torpedo Officer, Commander Hilary Norman, described Phillips in the last fatal minutes as slumped on a stool and 'in deep despond'.[43] There is general agreement that Phillips could have

[39] Captain Bell's letter to Lady Phillips, 12 Dec. 1941, Phillips Papers.
[40] From a Japanese report given to Admiral Caldwell by one of the Intelligence people in Malta late in the war. 'Though he was the enemy commander,' writes Captain Maeda, 'these last moments of the Admiral aroused our deep sympathy and made a profound impression on our minds beyond love and hate.' Other survivors have described how they had last seen Phillips and Leach standing alone on the bridge, silent and impervious to entreaties to abandon ship before it was too late. Others recounted seeing the Captain later, floating in the water 'looking very blue and obviously no longer alive'. One report has it that his neck was seen to be broken.
[41] Goodenough to Lady Phillips, 1 Apr. 1942, Phillips Papers.
[42] Letter to the author, 9 Aug. 1978.
[43] After Norman had surfaced and was swimming away, he saw the dead body of the Admiral. He thought momentarily of removing a signet ring or some such object as proof of
(*continued*)

saved himself, had he a mind to. The unfortunate Admiral had been heard to exclaim during the last disastrous minutes, 'I cannot survive this.'[44]

One may speculate whether the grand tradition of an admiral or captain gallantly staying on the bridge until the last moment and going down with his ship is not the most appalling waste. In this instance it seems particularly so, and it is just possible that better communication between the Admiral and his Flag-Captain might have avoided it. This is, of course, pure speculation. What is not is that the loss of the two was a tragedy for the Navy. Phillips had rare talents, and there is no question that Leach would have gone to the top.

On the larger issue of a flag officer's duty when his flagship is disabled, it was generally held in the Royal Navy that the duty of an admiral was to his fleet or squadron and not solely to his flagship, and that if his flagship was disabled, he ought to transfer his flag to any other ship which could fight and steam. It was only the *captain* of the ship who had the duty not to leave her until he had done everything in his power to ensure that all his officers and men had got away. From time immemorial it has been customary for commanders of fleets and squadrons to shift their flags when their flagships were disabled, or in no shape to take a leading part in the remainder of the action. Thus, Beatty had transferred his flag from the *Lion* to a destroyer at the Battle of the Dogger Bank on 24 January 1915, when his flagship was disabled. In the Second World War Stuart Bonham-Carter twice shifted his flag in one Russian convoy. Again, on 11 March 1942 a U-boat torpedoed the *Naiad*, flagship of the 15th Cruiser Squadron. When it was clear to her Captain, Guy Grantham, that she was going to sink, he ordered 'All on deck' and shortly afterwards, 'Abandon Ship.' After a spell, he said to his Admiral, Philip Vian, 'You must go,' and he climbed down from the bridge with his staff and slid into the water. He was saved, lucky for the Navy and the Allied cause. It was the third time that Vian had been sunk, but the first time he had got his feet wet.

Phillips's death, but decided the idea was a trifle macabre, so did nothing. Captain Norman's letter to the author, 10 Sept. 1978.

[44] Doig, 'Misfortune off Malaya', p. 25, letters to the author, 20 Oct., 14 Nov. 1978. The statement was made in his hearing while he and two other officers were in the process of drawing up a narrative of the operation for Admiral Layton. He heard it said by Captain Bell, as he recalls, 'in an almost *sotte voce*, as though he were reluctant to reveal this evidence of the Admiral's despair'.

He was, I believe, the only flag officer who was at sea for practically the whole war—he certainly did not feel he should give up. In Captain Doig's opinion,

> If he [Phillips] had had that experience [of commanding a fleet or a squadron before] he would have appreciated that an Admiral's responsibility does not end if his flagship goes to the bottom; he has a responsibility for the rest of his command, and a duty to transfer his flag to any other vessel which is able to fight and steam. Even with his two big ships gone, Admiral Phillips had the responsibility for commanding three fleet destroyers, with crews of 500 officers and men, and for looking after the survivors of the battleships, who were likely to be numerous. He could best exercise this responsibility if he transferred to a destroyer, and accepted the risk that he would be accused of getting out while the going was good. Moreover, not only was Admiral Phillips in command of Force Z, he was also the Commander-in-Chief, Eastern Fleet, and on his own initiative assumed full responsibility for the naval defence of Singapore and Malaya. This meant that he had a duty to continue to exercise his command at sea as long as he could, and to co-operate fully with the other Service commanders. He would undoubtedly have had to face a severe moral crisis if he had returned to Singapore without his big ships, but strictly speaking it was his duty to do everything that he could to mitigate the disaster, and to do that he had to keep going. He decided to stay.[45]

And yet, naval doctrine notwithstanding, how many flag officers, *placed in Phillips's position on 10 December 1941*, would have acted differently. Indeed, one distinguished flag officer has written to me: 'In similar circumstances, had I been him, I think I would not have made any effort to survive and face the music.' And from another senior officer: 'Tom Phillips would have had great difficulty in facing the situation if he had survived, and for that reason many officers would sympathise with his decision not to leave the ship.'

There were those who felt that Phillips's survival would have made a significant difference. That brilliant officer, Ralph Edwards, writing six months after the disaster—he was then COS to Admiral Somerville, C-in-C, Eastern Fleet—paid his heartfelt tribute to Phillips in writing to his widow: 'As you know I loved Sir Tom but I never realised when I last wrote to you [19 December 1941] what the nation lost when he was killed. He was the man who might have saved the situation in Malaya and heaven knows how many people

---

[45] 'Misfortune off Malaya', Addendum (1978), p. 5.

have told me that in these last painful months. We're still in a pretty pickle in this part of the world and I often feel that his vision and drive are what we're all missing.'[46]

Once the two big ships sank, the attacking aircraft left without bothering the destroyers or molesting the men in the water. Each squadron landed temporarily at Kota Bharu and, except for a few, all the planes returned to their base in the Saigon area. One of the planes was badly damaged in a forced landing in southern French Indo-China. Hoashi's reconnaissance plane, which had first discovered the enemy force, stayed over the scene of action (except for 1220–1250, when it had left to bomb Kuantan airfield), transmitting reports. No sooner had it transmitted its last one (1330) than it sighted oncoming enemy fighters that had suddenly appeared out of the clouds. Hoashi narrowly escaped by taking his plane up into a thick layer of clouds for concealment, and returned safely to Saigon Air Base in the gathering dusk.

What were these British planes doing there? The strange neglect of Phillips to signal Singapore reporting the air attack was corrected by Tennant when he realized that the *Prince of Wales* had failed to do so.[47] Taking matters into his own hands, he made an emergency W/T report at 1158 to 'any British man of war': 'Enemy aircraft bombing,' and giving his position.[48] It was the first indication that

---

[46] 16 May 1942, Phillips Papers.

[47] Perhaps, to be fair, we should say *apparent* neglect. Pound, in his memorandum of 25 January 1942, noted: 'There is no record of any request being received at Singapore from C.-in-C. Eastern Fleet for fighter cover when the attacks commenced. It is possible that the signal may have failed to get through though it is doubtful even if the signal had been passed whether the fighters would have arrived in time.' Grenfell suggests that Phillips may have ordered an attack report, but that such a signal may have been lost in transmission due to the flooding of the W/T cypher office caused by the first torpedo hits. 'In the ensuing hurried evacuation of this office it would have been easy for even an important signal to fall by the wayside.' Grenfell, *Main Fleet to Singapore*, p. 127. The damage certainly caused widespread failures of electric power, and these may well have affected W/T transmission. Yet, the evidence from surviving W/T personnel is that until the flagship went down, she had the ability to send W/T signals; her W/T sets were *not* out of action.

[48] An interesting point is raised by Commander Las Casas, who served as 'Doggie' to Tennant, i.e. a midshipman who virtually shadows his 'Master' and who relays nearly all the important orders that are given in battle. Las Casas is positive that at 1022, just after the *Repulse* got the radar contact (above, p. 438), 'Captain Tennant predicted the outcome and told me to send out an OEAB [Emergency Enemy Aircraft Bombing] in advance, on the assumption that the fighters might arrive at the same time as the bombers. I passed the order down the voicepipe to the Wireless Room, but whether or not it was ever transmitted I shall

(*continued*)

Force Z was under attack, and indeed the first knowledge of its position after the change of plan. The signal was received in the War Room, Singapore, at 1204. At 1219 the AOC rang Fighter Operations to say that he had just received a message that the *Repulse*, 60 miles east of Kuantan, was being bombed by enemy aircraft, and instructed Fighter Operations to take action. At 1225 Fighter Operations telephoned to say that 453 Squadron had taken off. This squadron of 11 Australian-piloted Brewster Buffaloes, which had been detailed for the defence of the fleet, took off from Sembawang and (less one which engine trouble had forced to return) reached the position of the ships, 150 miles away, at approximately 1318, in time to see the *Prince of Wales* go down. All enemy aircraft (but for Hoashi's plane) had made off to the northward. Cover was provided for the destroyers, who had blazed away ineffectually at the attackers throughout the action and were now picking up the survivors from the sunken ships.[49]

Middlebrook and Mahoney have made too much of the importance of an earlier arrival of the fighters. The story of the loss of the ships would not have been any different. To be sure, Flight-Lieutenant T. A. ('Tim') Vigors, temporarily in command of the squadron, was a thoroughly qualified RAF pilot with considerable experience in the Battle of Britain, and the Buffaloes might have picked off a few of the attackers. Yet they would have been no match against the Japanese onslaught, even though the bombers were without fighter escort. There were too many of them, they were better armed than the Buffaloes (one cannon and four or five machine-guns to the four machine-guns of the Buffaloes), and their endurance over the target would have been no less limited than that of their opponents. Moreover, as Captain John Creswell

---

never know.' Las Casas's letter to the author, 19 June 1978. Another mystery! Strictly speaking, OEAB should not have been made until enemy aircraft were actually dropping bombs. The best precautionary signal was OEAS (Enemy Aircraft Shadowing). Why did Tennant fail to wait for the C-in-C to authorize his signal? Las Casas surmises it was because Tennant, who had been responsible for the evacuation of the beaches at Dunkirk, 'fully knew and understood the devastating speed with which modern aircraft could attack'. Letter of 19 July 1978.

[49] The four 4.7-inch of the *Electra* and *Express* had some AA potential, but were 'hitty-missy'. They were also equipped with pom-pom and Oerlikon close-range AA weapons. The *Vampire*'s four 4-inch, one 12-pounder, and a few light and heavy machine-guns were utterly ineffective. The *Tenedos*, had she been present, would have contributed precious little with her three 4-inch guns and a couple of old Lewis machine-guns—.303s of First World War vintage.

brought out, 'If a battleship was to direct shore-based fighters effectively, a degree of experience in cooperation, which here was lacking, was called for.' The crucial point, though, is that the Buffalo was a frightful machine which only the Finns managed to use successfully (probably because they alone had the number of veteran pilots able to make use of such virtues as this aircraft possessed). It was quite manœuvrable, strongly built, and quite well armed: four Browning 0.50-inch machine-guns, two in the fuselage and two in the wings, modified in 453 Squadron for 0.303-inch Brownings in the wings in place of the two 0.50s. But it was slow (its best performance figure was 280 knots at 16,500 feet: in practice, it rarely reached 260 knots) and had a poor ceiling (it was supposed to be 34,000 feet), climb (2,500 feet/minute), and range (650 miles). Its electrical circuits were corroded by tropical conditions, and its radios were obsolescent. The worst problems, however, were the slow climb/poor ceiling and the altitude performance factor: the tendency for speed, acceleration, climb, and manoeuvrability to all deteriorate rapidly above 10,000 feet, or thereabouts. By 20,000 feet, in a tropical sky, the aircraft, which had taken a very long time to reach that height, was wallowing near the stall. It is relevant that, later, in January 1942, the Buffaloes enjoyed little success against the Japanese bombers, Navy Nells and Army Sallys, over Singapore.

The pilots of the four Buffalo squadrons (two Australian, 21 and 453, two mainly New Zealand, 243 and 488) were not much more efficient than their planes. They had been posted direct from pilot-training courses in Australia and New Zealand, where they had only been taught to fly, arriving in batches in Malaya, mostly from the summer of 1941. In the normal course they would have been sent to the United Kingdom for operational training in fighters or bombers, etc., but there was no time for that. When the Pacific War broke out, the vast majority of the pilots had received no formal fighter training, either as regards tactics or air-firing. There were no facilities for such training at Singapore, due to shortage of ammunition (or, at any rate, to the unwillingness of the authorities to allow ammunition to these green squadrons). A thin leavening of experienced fighter pilots, in the main, Battle of Britain veterans, had arrived in the autumn of 1941. Usually, the squadron commander and one of his flight commanders were these experienced pilots. No. 453 was the best of the Buffalo squadrons.

Formed in Australia, it had arrived in Malaya in August 1941 and was the first of the four squadrons to be equipped with Buffaloes (at once). It had, therefore, the greatest experience with these aircraft. It is, however, revealing that the commanding officer of the squadron, Squadron Leader Harper, had gone to Australia in late November to seek 'more suitable' pilots, and Maltby, in his report, admitted that 'some of the personnel were not entirely suitable for a fighter squadron'.[50]

Asked what influence the timely arrival of the 10 Buffalo fighters might have had upon the result of the action, Commander Iki replied that the British fighters would have begun with counter-attacks upon the Nells, since they must have known that they were slower than the Bettys and that the limited field of fire of their 20mm cannons constituted a vulnerability. However, the Nell squadrons, maintaining a bombing altitude of 3,000 to 4,000 metres, and flying in tight formation for mutual protection, would have kept their bombing course unaltered, while firing their 20mm cannons and 7.7mm machine-guns against the enemy fighters. 'Though some of the Nells would have been damaged or set ablaze, the bombings would have been completed against their targets somehow or other.' The Buffaloes would have stood a better chance against the torpedo planes, when releasing their torpedoes, one plane after another, just above the sea-surface, would have been more vulnerable to attack than the bombing planes.

The chances are that some of our torpedo attack-planes would have been severely damaged or shot down before releasing their torpedoes. However, because our torpedo attack planes flew so low, the enemy fighters would have found it difficult to resume their attacks after their initial blow, and the damage to our torpedo attack-planes might have been smaller than expected. The most vulnerable moment for our attack-planes was when they had released their torpedo and had taken a sharp turn just above the battleships' superstructures and ascended for withdrawal. This retiring movement, to be taken by each plane at the discretion of each plane-commander, according to the situation, was the most vulnerable moment for the attacking planes. However, during peace-time exercises with the

---

[50] I have relied for this information on the Buffaloes and their pilots—all but the last sentence (Douglas Gillison, *Royal Australian Air Force, 1939–1942* (Canberra, 1962), p. 197, Maltby Report, p. 1355)— on an interview with Mr C. F. Shores, 9 May 1979, and letters from him of 6 July and 14 Aug. 1979. Shores has corresponded and had interviews with a substantial number of Buffalo pilots who had served in the Malayan theatre in preparation for a large co-operative work on air operations in South-East Asia through May 1942.

'... OR SURVIVED WITH HONOUR'

Combined Fleet, the attack planes were constantly trained to cope with this battle situation, i.e., bombing and torpedoing against surface ships with a heavy fighter cover. The situation on 10 December, when the enemy battleships had no fighter protection, was contrary to our expectation.

Iki's conclusion is that 'assuming our attack squadrons were intercepted by the 10 Buffalo fighters when we attacked Force Z, we would still have sunk the two battleships, although the damage and losses would have been increased to some extent.'[51]

3. '... OR SURVIVED WITH HONOUR'

The one bright spot on the British side in an otherwise depressing day was the exceptionally high spirit and discipline of the ships' companies during the action, the sinkings, and afterwards. There was nothing remotely resembling panic even when it was obvious that the two ships were doomed. In the *Repulse*, as Tennant put it, it was 'evident that the whole ship's company were carrying out their duties as if they were at ordinary peace exercises'. It was no different in the *Prince of Wales*. Tennant said that he could not recommend anyone for a decoration because every officer and man 'carried out his duties to the utmost', and possibly the greatest cases of gallantry were performed by those who did not survive. The Powers that be announced that 'in a disaster of such magnitude no recommendations for awards can be considered', nor were they. (This was not unexpected, since awards for exceptional performance in a disaster are uncommon!) All that the Admiralty would do, and that not until ten months after the action, was to publish a list of 24 officers and men (15 from *Repulse*, 9 from the *Prince of Wales*) who had been 'Mentioned in Dispatches' (13 of them posthumously, including the first three mentioned below)—'the lowest degree of recognition for courage or outstanding service that can be given to a serviceman', as Middlebrook and Mahoney remark.

It is easy to be brave when winning, but hard when losing. Yet many were the acts of bravery, from teenage boys to men on the verge of retirement, of which four instances that must stand for the

---

[51] Memorandum for the author, 14 Dec. 1978.

lot. In Tennant's rough notes for his report ('The Last Action') he felt that

nothing can beat this story. I found an ordinary seaman [J.] Macdonald in hospital at Singapore. He had been wounded by machine gun bullet but was getting on all right. He asked me anxiously was Mr. [J. B.] Page saved. Mr. Page was the Director Gunner. Not wishing to upset the boy I said I was not sure. Macdonald then went on to tell me that before the ship sank Mr. Page found Macdonald wounded on deck and took off his life saving belt and put it on Macdonald. Mr Page was not seen again. It is hard to think of a case of greater gallantry. I am hoping Mr. Page may be given a posthumous V.C.

Another example of extraordinary calm and bravery was provided by a Midshipman in the *Repulse*, A. C. R. Bros, a stripling of 17 who was in charge of the 15-inch transmitting station, the 'brains' of the main armament control system situated in the bowels of the ship and manned by the Royal Marine Band. 'It requires little imagination to picture reactions down there with the holocaust raging around them and the only escape to the deck above, a vertical steel ladder. With not even the main armament engaged, at the order to Abandon Ship there was a natural rush for that ladder. The Midshipman got there first, restored order among his men to evacuate and was last up himself. He did not survive while some under him did.'[52]

The third instance is of another Midshipman, the 18-year-old R. I. Davies (RAN), who only a week before the action had been moved from the role as assistant to the Navigator, a job he loved, to Officer of Quarters for the starboard after Oerlikon, which he did not. '*Repulse* was an old lady with little more than an umbrella and the after oerlikons were just two tiny spokes. When the sinking ship heeled so rapidly to port, only this boy's starboard gun could function—a pop-gun against the Japanese torpedo bombers—and the arc of fire was being fouled by survivors clambering on to the upturned starboard bilge keel. He personally kept the firing operative until he, gun, and ship went down: like Jackie Cornwell at Jutland.'

Then there was Commander Lawson, the Executive Officer in the *Prince of Wales*, buried in Damage Control Headquarters in the

---

[52] Admiral Hayes's letter to the author, 25 June 1976. The instance that follows is from the same letter.

bowels of the ship, attempting to put her steering to rights. Towards the end he ordered the ratings with him to save themselves, while he worked on alone at his impossible task. Lawson's sangfroid never deserted him. When he rang up the Bosun on the fo'c'sle and told him to 'prepare to tow for'rard', thinking that the *Repulse* would be towing the flagship back to Singapore, he was told that the *Repulse* had been sunk and, therefore, unlikely to be in a position to tow anyone anywhere. 'In that case,' said Lawson, 'it is conceivable that you may have to swim!'

There were other instances of humour of the understated sort. When the *Repulse* was sinking and Commander Dendy, the Executive Officer, was washed overboard, he found a Carley float to swim to. 'I was', he relates, 'joined by various ratings. One of these was a minor defaulter that I saw very often. He greeted me with the unoriginal remark, "Ere we are, Sir. Scum always comes to the top." ' We hear of the Irishman serving in the *Prince of Wales* who was saved. Owing to the strict censorship imposed on neutral Eire as a result of pressure by the German Consul in Dublin, no reference to Irishmen serving in the sunken *Prince of Wales* could be made in the press. But a notice did appear: 'His many friends will be glad to hear that Johnny O'Driscoll, who was recently involved in a boating accident, is none the worse for his experience.'

The pilot of the first fighter to reach the spot where the ships sank was the 453 Squadron Commander, Vigors. His report to Admiral Layton on 11 December, though often quoted, is well worth quoting again:

I had the privilege to be the first aircraft to reach the crews of the *Prince of Wales* and the *Repulse* after they had been sunk. I say the privilege, for during the next hour while I flew around low over them, I witnessed a show of that indomitable spirit for which the Royal Navy is so famous. I have seen a show of spirit in this war over Dunkirk, during the 'Battle of Britain', and in the London night raids, but never before have I seen anything comparable with what I saw yesterday. I passed over thousands who had been through an ordeal the greatness of which they alone can understand, for it is impossible to pass on one's feelings in disaster to others.

Even to an eye so inexperienced as mine it was obvious that the three destroyers were going to take hours to pick up those hundreds of men clinging to bits of wreckage, and swimming around in the filthy oily water. Above all this, the threat of another bombing and machine-gun attack was imminent. Every one of those men must have realised that. Yet as I flew around, every man waved and put his thumb up as I flew over him.

After an hour, lack of petrol forced me to leave, but during that hour I had seen many men in dire danger waving, cheering and joking as if they were holiday-makers at Brighton waving at a low flying aircraft. It shook me for here was something above human nature. I take off my hat to them, for in them I saw the spirit which wins wars.

I apologise for taking up your valuable time, but I thought you should know of the incredible conduct of your men.[53]

It would be difficult to improve on Richard Hough's tribute: 'The historical fact that the annihilation of Force Z signalled the end of a maritime era is of little consequence, of purely parochial interest, compared with the way men, who were fated for defeat by misfortune and misjudgment, suffered and died, or survived with honour.'[54]

The three destroyers rescued over 2,000 of the ships' companies that had totalled nearly 3,000. The actual figures are:

	Repulse		
	Rescued	Lost	Total
Officers	42	27	69
Men	754	486	1,240
	796	513	1,309

	Prince of Wales		
	Rescued	Lost	Total
Officers	90	20	110
Men	1,195	307	1,502
	1,285	327	1,612

At higher levels the rescue of the survivors 'was viewed by the Japanese Navy as a grave indication of a deterioration in the morale of the British Navy. The view previously held by the Japanese that

---

[53] Layton's Dispatch, p. 1243. Sceptics have suggested that what the survivors in the water were doing was in fact shaking their fists at the planes and cursing them for not having arrived in time to be of any use. As there were hundreds of men in the water, it is quite possible that some such reaction did exist. See further, below, p. 504.

[54] *The Hunting of Force Z* (London, 1963), p. 242.

even involuntary capture was irreconcilable with honour is again sharply demonstrated.'[55]

Four circumstances explain the large number of survivors. The South China Sea *Pilot*, one of the official guide books for navigation to the oceans of the world, describes this particular sea as being normally other than calm. On this occasion the sea was almost flat calm, so that those in the water were less in danger of getting eyes, nose, and mouth filled with fuel oil with fatal results. Not all were lucky. Some collapsed and died soon after rescue, probably due mainly to the effects of the oil they had swallowed. The minds of many who were in the sea were filled with tales of man-eating sharks in this shark-infested area. But it transpired that not a single man was attacked by them. Nor was the common expectation realized that the Japanese would attack them in the water. That would have made for a massacre. Their aircraft flew over the scene of sinking ships and survivors, many clinging to Carley floats and pieces of wreckage, etc., but they did not attack them with bombs or machine-gun fire, as later they did when boatloads of nurses and others were adrift from torpedoed troopships near Singapore. (But it was *Army* aircraft who were involved on the later occasion.) The unexpected display of decency and clean fighting on the part of their enemies was deeply appreciated by all and was commented on for sometime afterwards. When, after the war, Captain Goudy visited Japan and met IJN officers who had participated in the action, and said a few words of appreciation of the fact that the enemy had made no attempt to interfere with rescue operations, Commander Iki had replied: 'We had no orders other than to seek out and destroy the *Prince of Wales* and *Repulse*.' Finally, one must remark on the rescue work of the destroyers, above all of the *Express*. Commander Cartwright handled his ship in a masterly manner when he came alongside the quarterdeck of the rapidly heeling *Prince of Wales* to pick up survivors, some hundreds of whom were able to walk on to the destroyer without even getting their feet wet. The *Express* stayed alongside the stricken flagship until the last possible moment, and was lifted bodily out of the water by the ship's massive bilge keel as she rolled over. Only the engine-room's

---

[55] German Naval Attaché to OKM, OKW (the Naval and Armed Forces High Commands), 12 Feb. 1942, PG 32146, War Diary, German Naval Attaché, Admiralty Project, Reel 482.

prompt reaction to Cartwright's 'Full astern both' saved the ship from sharing the fate of the *Prince of Wales*.

The destroyers continued collecting their sorry burdens until there was no bobbing head or capital ship to be seen. Then they started for harbour, escorted by 243 Fighter Squadron from Kallang and one flight of 453 Squadron, arriving at Singapore between 2310 and midnight/10th. The survivors were shocked and exhausted, as was to be expected after such an ordeal. Little did they know that many, including the seven surviving midshipmen from the *Prince of Wales*, would shortly join the cruiser *Exeter*, of River Plate fame, and suffer a repetition of this same fate all too soon.

Layton had already embarked in the SS *Dominion Monarch* for passage to England; she was due to sail at 1530. He was lunching with his Secretary, Captain Doig, on the shelter deck forward when he received the sad news from his former Assistant Chief of Staff, Captain Collins, who had rushed aboard. 'That's bad news about Tom Phillips,' the Admiral informed Doig. 'He's run into trouble and lost his ships. We've got to get off and go back.' After some exclamation from Doig, he added, 'I don't know exactly what's happened. But I always said he would make a balls of it, and he has.'[56] And back to the Naval Base went Layton, with Doig, their wives, and their belongings following. He rehoisted his flag in the *Sultan* (a legendary ship name for the naval barracks and naval personnel in the Naval Base) at 1500, and sent a signal to the Admiralty to say that he had resumed command of the Eastern Fleet and the China Station pending further instructions. Late in the afternoon a signal arrived telling him that he was appointed C-in-C temporarily. He was under great duress, and we must therefore make some allowance for his unhappy address to the survivors of the two big ships on 11 December. They had awakened that day still dazed at the loss of the ship they loved. Now they learned they were no longer to be identified as the ship's companies of the *Prince of Wales* or *Repulse*. They were to become HMS *Sultan IV*, a satellite of the main naval base, and many of them, as soon as they were fit, were dispersed throughout the Malay Peninsula to help in the crisis, often in unskilled and dull jobs. 'Physically and mercifully alive, we were inwardly killed by the removal of a proud identity

[56] Doig, 'Misfortune off Malaya', p. 27.

'... OR SURVIVED WITH HONOUR'

in that speech from the C-in-C in a most unsympathetic vein, as if we too had not had a bit to worry about in the previous 24 hours! This of course was not what we had been either hoping or expecting; but with hindsight it was probably inevitable and we did our best to explain this to the disappointed men. Indeed, every one of us shared that sensation.'[57] Morale undoubtedly suffered, too, because most of the survivors had expected a swift passage home and a month's leave at the end of it.

A NOTE ON BASIC PRINCIPLES OF HIGH-LEVEL BOMBING AND TORPEDOING IN THE IMPERIAL JAPANESE NAVY*

The basic formation of a bombing squadron comprising three flights, each composed of three planes, is a indicated in Fig. 1.

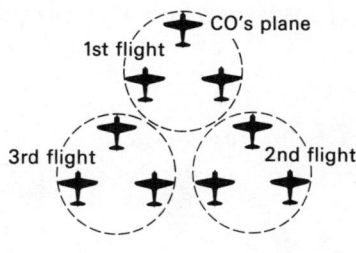

Fig. 1

The commanding officer's plane took the lead, and all the planes dropped bombs simultaneously, following the commander's plane. In this case, the bombing theory was to 'straddle' or 'cover' the target by the 'bomb-triangle', on the principle of CEP (circular error probability). Accordingly, each bomb of each plane was not necessarily aimed carefully so as to hit the target with the first shot; but the commanding officer tried to cover the target with the triangled area of his squadron's bombs. Some called this method 'enveloping the target with a bomb-carpet'.

Unlike the high-level bombing tactics, torpedoing was regarded as a 'duel', i.e. *to beat* or *be beaten*. Whereas the high-level bombing

[57] Admiral Hayes's letter, 25 June 1976.
* From Commander Iki's memorandum for the author of 1 Nov. 1978.

squadron aimed at 'probability coverage' of a simultaneous dropping by a triangular formation, the torpedo attack was made by an individual plane aiming carefully so as to hit the target with the only torpedo it carried. The principle that was taught during training was to attack the enemy ship by squadron (nine planes) in a single-column formation, with the individual attack-plane releasing its torpedo when it reached a point and height most favourable for firing. It was also a principle to make a pincer attack by two squadrons. In Iki's case, in the 10 December action (the Kanoya Air Corps 3rd Squadron: above, p. 470), a pincer attack was effected unintentionally by the 3rd Squadron acting alone. First, observing that the *Repulse* was steaming at 20 knots and was making a sharp turn to starboard to evade the bombs and torpedoes, Iki decided to attack her from her port side with his first flight (three planes) and ordered his second and third flights to attack her from her starboard side, which, naturally, became a pincer-type attack. Each plane of the squadron could release its torpedo at a point in the arc of 65°–120° height 20–50 metres, range 800–1,200 metres. See Fig. 2.

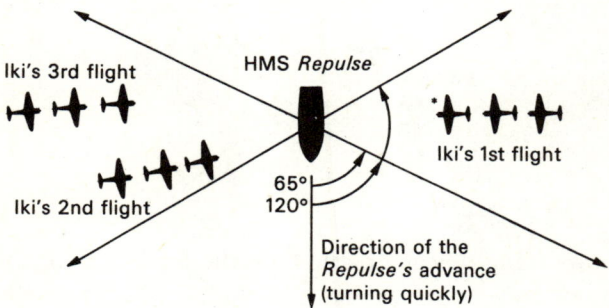

Fig. 2 *This is the plane Iki-san piloted himself. His second and third planes of the flight were hit, and downed in flames.

XV

Post-Mortem

The world is always prone to put the blame for a naval disaster on the Commander of the force concerned.

>> CAPTAIN L. H. BELL to Lady Phillips, 12 December 1941.

The decisions to take his squadron to sea, and later to close the coast, were absolutely right. No shadow of blame can attach to the Admiral.

>> COMMANDER MICHAEL GOODENOUGH to Lady Phillips,
>> 22 December 1941.

I think we all under-rated the efficiency of the Japanese air forces, and certainly did not realise the long ranges at which they could work.

>> ADMIRAL OF THE FLEET SIR DUDLEY POUND to Mrs Mildred Barker,
>> 25 February 1943.

The Jap is not an enemy to be belittled and it is no good thinking that any amateur warfare will do against them.

>> CAPTAIN W. G. TENNANT, *post* 10 December 1941.

The success of our attack should be attributed solely to good luck and divine guidance.

>> LIEUTENANT-COMMANDER TAKAI SADAO to the author,
>> November 1977.

It means that from Africa eastwards to America through the Indian Ocean and Pacific we have lost command of the sea.

>> FIELD MARSHAL SIR ALAN BROOKE, diary, 10 December 1941.

1. 'ATTACKS MAGNIFICENTLY CARRIED OUT'

THE official wartime statistics of the Imperial Navy gave these figures: 14 torpedoes of 34 fired at the *Repulse* scored hits, and 7 of the 15 launched against the *Prince of Wales*, for a total of 21 hits of 49, or 42·9 per cent. The *Repulse* was hit by one of 14 bombs dropped on her (250 kg), and the *Prince of Wales*, by 2 out of 7 (500kg), for a total of 3 out of 21, or 14·3 per cent.[1] More accurate are the figures in the post-war Official History, with the 'British data' added for reference, 'although their accuracy is unknown'.[2] To summarize the tables, 3 of the 21 bombs (two 500kg, one 250kg) dropped on the battleships (7 on the *Prince of Wales*, 14 on the *Repulse*) scored hits, or 14·3 per cent; 18 bombs on the destroyers, no hits; total result, 39 bombs, 3 hits, or 7·7 per cent. The peacetime percentage of hits in high-level bombing by the Navy (Combined Fleet, 1939) was about 12 per cent against battleships under way at about 14 knots. The pre-war estimate of wartime percentage of hits was estimated at a half or a third of the peacetime percentage. In other words, the bombing results on 10 December comfortably exceeded expectations. On the other hand, 'British data' (which is also the figure in the Naval Historical Branch records) show only 2 bomb hits (one on each capital ship, none on the destroyers), which would reduce the percentage from 14·3 to 9·5, still much better than the pre-war estimate. But it was the torpedo aircraft, not the high-level bombers, which Phillips had not feared, that had done the real damage.

The results of the torpedo attacks are given as 20 hits of 49 fired (Lieutenant Takahashi's unreleased torpedo—see below—is not counted): 7 of 14 against the *Prince of Wales*, 13 of 35 against the *Repulse*, or 40·8 per cent of hits. The 'British data', however, show only 10 hits (6 on the *Prince of Wales*, 4 on the *Repulse*), or 20·4 per cent.[3] In peacetime exercises in simultaneous bomb and torpedo attacks against a battleship squadron, with the latter making large

---

[1] These figures were given to the German Naval Attaché in November 1943 and are contained in an eight-page German analysis of the action, mainly from the air tactical aspect, entitled 'Die Seeschlact von der Malayischen Halbinsel', in the German Ministry of Marine records at the Naval Historical Branch, PG 49427.

[2] *Senshi sōsho*, xxiv. 476–7. On 11 December, thanks to the misobservation of an air crew, Matsunaga added a cruiser ('or a flotilla leader') to the list of ships sunk. Of course, there was no cruiser in Force Z, nor had any destroyer been sunk. The battleship, which was presumed to be *King George V*, was found to be the *Prince of Wales* after the official British announcement of her loss.

[3] The *Repulse* figure ('British data') should read 5, which is the figure given in the Naval Historical Branch records. It is also given in the *Senshi sōsho* table as 5, but as 10 when totalled with the *Prince of Wales*'s 6. Using 11, the percentage of torpedo hits becomes 22·2. Actually, British technical experts could not make up their minds whether there were 6 or 7 torpedo hits on the *Prince of Wales*. Their figure for the *Repulse* is 5, which is the officially accepted figure. The report by the Technical Departments of the Admiralty ('Loss of H.M.S. *Prince of Wales*', May 1942) is in ADM 167/116.

evading manœuvres at about 14 knots, the percentage of hits was about 70.

In torpedo attacks [in peacetime training] to approach as closely as possible to the target and fire at the nearest firing point [the position of the plane when the torpedo is released] was the principal factor in raising the percentage of hits, so that much depended upon the spiritual strength of the air crews. But in wartime, since the eye-measurement of the range and speed of the target [i.e. without the use of range-finding instruments] would be difficult owing to the enemy's intense defensive fire and the unfamiliar shapes of the target ships, the percentage of hits would, it was estimated, decrease to less than a half of the peacetime percentage. In this naval battle the British battleships moved at a speed nearly twice that of peacetime target ships, though the evading manœuvres were slow.[4]

The defensive fire of the British ships was so intense that the high-level bombers received serious damage. Even in the case of the 6th Mihoro Squadron (Takeda), which had attacked last, five planes were hit by the AA fire of the *Prince of Wales*, whose speed had already been reduced to about 6 knots and which was on the verge of sinking. On the other hand, the effectiveness of the hail of shells and bullets from small AA guns and machine-guns poured on the torpedo-attacking squadrons by the two capital ships was surprisingly low. A total of three aircraft, all torpedo-bombers (1 Genzan, 2 Kanoya), were shot down during the attacks—and only 21 airmen (petty officers or ratings) were lost—although the British claimed 'about 8'. One Kanoya torpedo plane was hit and was badly damaged when it made a forced landing in southern French Indo-China; 26 other planes required repairs: 4 at the air arsenal; the other 22 were repairable within the Air Groups themselves. An important factor in the small losses and damage torpedo bombers incurred was the relatively low approach and release height that had been selected in view of the shallow sea depth—an average of 40 metres in the whole South China Sea—of the probable battle area.

It was the first experience any British force had had of Japanese efficiency, and the display was indeed awesome. Their pilots had exhibited superb daring, skill, and resolution. Undeterred by the fiercest of AA fire, they had kept coming. Tears were shed when an attack failed to register any hits, so intent were the pilots and crews

[4] *Senshi sōsho*, xxiv. 477.

on scoring hits. The performance elicited Tennant's unstinted praise. 'The enemy attacks were without doubt magnificently carried out and pressed well home. The high level bombers kept tight formation and appeared not to jink. I only observed one torpedo bomber who apparently had cold feet and fired his torpedoes [sic] at a distance of at least two miles from the ship. The torpedoes ran very straight and the tracks were exceptionally easy to see in the calm water and the torpedoes appeared to be running shallow [10–16 feet] ...'[5] The British were impressed with the altitude at which the attackers dropped their torpedoes—much greater than the 20–30 feet that was the practice in British naval aircraft. The *Prince of Wales*'s Gunnery Officer summed up the impossible situation that faced them in these words: 'Due to the lack of an A.A. destroyer and cruiser screen, fighter escort and the determination and skill with which the enemy pressed home their attacks it is doubtful if anything could have prevented torpedo bombers achieving their object.'[6]

2. 'I HAVE BAD NEWS...'

The loss of the two capital ships had an immediate and painful effect on morale in Singapore and Australia, coming as it did on top of the publicity given but a week before to the arrival of the ships.[7] The disaster came as an even greater shock in Britain. Few would have disagreed with J. L. Garvin's mournful leader in the *Observer*, (14 December): 'That day's news was among the worst and saddest in the life-time of any of us.' The public mood was captured in the Ministry of Information's 'Weekly Report':

Last Wednesday, when the public heard of the loss of the *Prince of Wales* and *Repulse*, was described by many people as 'the blackest day since

---

[5] Tennant, 'Further Report', p. 1242. There is the (probably apocryphal) story that, on receiving the news of the sinkings, Lord Sempill declared, 'Well done!'

[6] Lieutenant-Commander McMullen, 14 Dec. 1941, 'Statements by Survivors', ADM 1/12181.

[7] The shocked disbelief with which the British in Singapore (meaning essentially the civilians) received the news of the sinkings lasted but a day or two. Life went on pretty much as before. Lieutenant-Commander Dyer writes: 'Reactions in Singapore after the action? Well, I wasn't mixing much with civilians, but such as I met were mostly quite detached from the war and thinking purely in terms of making money—the atmosphere, almost to within a day of capitulation, was one of unreality. Tennis parties went on, evening drinks, dinner and dancing, and the like. It is hard to believe, but true.' Letter to the author, 10 July 1978. See further, Stanley Falk, *Seventy Days to Singapore* (New York, 1975), p. 123.

Dunkirk', but relief at the high proportion of men rescued has done much to mitigate the public's depression. 'The consternation and distress with which the news was received' gave place, after the first shock, to critical speculation about the amount of air support given to the ships. 'The regard in which the British Navy is held, however, has silenced any criticism of the strategy which resulted in their loss.' Yet many people are said to be making unfavourable comparisons between 'the apparent ease with which the *Prince of Wales* was sunk and the outstanding manner in which the *Bismarck* remained afloat.'[8]

One line of press opinion emphasized the underrating of the air factor in naval warfare and of Japanese air power. Thus, the *Evening Standard* (12 December): 'It is a tremendous and terrible vindication of those who argued that supremacy at sea could only be retained if the fullest possible profit were extracted from the new naval weapon in the air. The lesson is driven home with the impact of a torpedo.' And the *Daily Mail* (11 December): 'There has been a tendency to underrate their machines and airmen. We should hear no more of that.' This, too was the line taken by the Labour *Daily Herald* (11 December). Peter Masefield, the Air Correspondent of the *Sunday Times* (14 December), singled out the necessity of the RAF and the Navy working together, 'a basic fact apparently not yet appreciated, perhaps, even in some naval circles'. *The Times*, the *Daily Telegraph*, the Liberal press, and Lord Chatfield in the *Sunday Times* dwelt on the importance of resolutely facing the consequences of the disaster. The blow summoned them, declared the *Manchester Guardian* (11 December), 'to make a supreme and single-minded effort to bring the country through'.

Here is how Churchill received the news (in the form of a W/T message from Palliser, which reached the Admiralty at 0827 on the 10th):

I was opening my boxes on the 10th when the telephone at my bedside rang. It was the First Sea Lord. His voice sounded odd. He gave a sort of cough and gulp, and at first I could not hear quite clearly. 'Prime Minister, I have to report to you that the *Prince of Wales* and the *Repulse* have both been sunk by the Japanese—we think by aircraft. Tom Phillips is drowned.' 'Are you sure it's true?' 'There is no doubt at all.' So I put the telephone down. I was thankful to be alone. In all the war I never received a more direct shock. The reader of these pages will realise how many

[8] No. 63, 17 Dec. 1941 (covering 8–15 Dec. 1941), INF 1/292 (PRO).

efforts, hopes, and plans foundered with these two ships. As I turned over and twisted in bed the full horror of the news sank in upon me. There were no British or American capital ships in the Indian Ocean or the Pacific except the American survivors of Pearl Harbour, who were hastening back to California. Over all this vast expanse of waters Japan was supreme, and we everywhere were weak and naked.[9]

At 11 that morning he arrived in the House of Commons, together with the First Lord, both looking grave and grim. The House was about to settle down to the question hour when the Speaker announced that the Prime Minister had an important statement to make. He faced a small House of not more than 50 MPs, and in clear, firm tones made a brief statement that began: 'I have bad news...' He was able to provide some details the following day. 'In my whole experience,' he told the House, 'I do not remember any naval blow so heavy or so painful,' and he called for 'a new surge of impulse' to offset the new situation. The shock to the House was manifest. There was a sympathetic cheer when he finished. When it subsided, Churchill was plied with many questions, including one from Admiral of the Fleet Sir Roger Keyes, who asked why the ships had been hazarded without fighter cover.[10] Disaster always brought out all the greatness in the man. The American Ambassador, Winant, who had been with Churchill 'constantly' over the previous days and saw him directly after the announcement, remarked on how 'Discouragements seem only to give him new courage and add to his determination.'[11] Alexander's reaction to the destruction of the two capital ships was one of shock over the loss and bewilderment over why Phillips should have decided to venture his ships up a coast virtually controlled by the enemy devoid of air cover. It seemed out of character, in view of the Admiral's high qualities of judgement. Alexander's daughter remembers how 'completely devastated' he was by the news of the sinkings. 'He always spoke of this afterwards with great emotion, and I really think he was more upset over this than any other single incident during the war.'[12]

---

[9] Churchill, *The Grand Alliance*, p. 551.
[10] *Parliamentary Debates (Hansard)*, 5th ser. (Commons), ccclxxvi, cols. 1501 (10 Dec.), 1686–99 (11 Dec.).
[11] Winant's telegram to Hull, 10 Dec. 1941, *Foreign Relations of the United States. Diplomatic Papers. 1941* (7 vols., Washington, 1956–63), v. 381.
[12] Lady Beatrix Evison's letter to the author, 25 Feb. 1975.

'I HAVE BAD NEWS...'

The First Sea Lord took the news just as hard. It was not so much the loss of the two ships. Here his reaction appears to have been philosophical, rather like it was at the time of the loss of the *Hood* ('Well, we must do without'). It was Phillips's death that affected him profoundly.

I do not think [his Secretary recalls] I have seen Dudley Pound so distressed at the death of anyone as when the *Prince of Wales* and the *Repulse* were lost. He had a small meeting in his room at the time and he asked me to read out the signal from Singapore announcing the loss, and Admiral Phillips's death. The meeting finished shortly afterwards and Dudley Pound picked up his cap and stick and went to walk around the lake in St. James's Park for three-quarters of an hour. Although the loss of the two ships was a disaster, there was no doubt in my mind that it was the loss of Tom Phillips which affected Dudley Pound so keenly.[13]

This comes out in a letter the Admiral wrote to Lady Phillips: 'His death is one of the tragedies of the war—much more so, infinitely more so, than the loss of those two ships. In time we can replace the ships—we can never get another Tom. ... His loss is a blow to the Service of the first magnitude and one which is irreparable. In the P. of Wales incident I regret nothing except Tom's loss. ... I personally know I have lost one of my greatest friends.'[14]

So far as we know, Pound never complained and never spoke a word of condemnation over the disaster. His 25 January memorandum concluded that 'the risks he [Phillips] took were fair and reasonable in the light of the knowledge he had of the enemy when compared with the very urgent and vital issues at stake and on which the whole safety of Malaya may have depended'. He rose to Phillips's defence in correspondence with Cunningham:

I hold most strongly that placed as he was he was absolutely right to do so as he did up to a certain moment, and that was when he was sighted at 6.45 in the morning [evening of the 9th] by an aircraft which presumably was an enemy one. I see no reason why he should not then have asked for fighter cover but he may well have been influenced by the fact that he was 400 miles from the established enemy aerodromes, that the Army was fighting hard in Malaya and wanted all the Air it could get, and that as, not knowing the time of the attack, all he could ask for was a standing

---

[13] Admiral Brockman's letter to the author, 31 Dec. 1975.
[14] 30 Jan. 1942, Phillips Papers.

patrol and what they could have sent him would really have been little good.[15]

His other line of defence of Phillips is contained in the letter of the following day to Lady Phillips already cited:

The whole thing has been considered by the Board of Admiralty who were unanimously of the opinion that he did the right thing in embarking on that operation. It might well have been a brilliant success. But just think what the world would be saying now. The very people who have criticised his action would now be attributing the evacuation of Malaya to the fact that the Navy had done nothing. Of course he should have had an aircraft carrier with him, but there was not a single one available.

The reference in his first sentence was to an Admiralty inquiry into the loss of the ships conducted by Captains William Davis, AD of P, and Angus Nicholl, DOD(F). Their report (20 January 1942) formed the basis of a memorandum by the VCNS (Moore) and ACNS(F) (Harwood) that was put before the Board on 26 January, with the First Sea Lord's 25 January memorandum, and approved with a few changes.[16] I have found only the Davis/Nicholl report, whose conclusions were (*inter alia*): (i) Since the available force was an unbalanced one, the stationing of it at Singapore was strategically unsound. (ii) In the circumstances ruling at Singapore on 8th December C-in-C Eastern Fleet was left with no alternative but to attempt a raid on the enemy's sea communications. For this he had to use his capital ships not as a covering force but as a striking force.'[17]

It should come as no surprise that the debate in the Navy and

[15] 29 Jan. 1942, Cunningham Papers, Add. MS 52561. He added petulantly: 'I do not know why but both the House of Commons and the Public seem to think that the sinking of an important ship is a crime, whilst nobody takes any notice of the loss of 30 or 40 bombers in one night due to inaccurate metereological reports, or to the many failures of the Army.'

[16] It was an inquiry as distinct from a board of inquiry. In the first, evidence is not given on oath; in the second, it is. Pound was of the opinion that no useful purpose would be served by holding a board of inquiry, 'as the salient facts are as clear as we are ever likely to get them without evidence from the late C-in-C himself'. Pound, 'Loss of H.M.S. Prince of Wales & H.M.S. Repulse'. Admiral Layton, who was always opposed to elaborate post-mortems, expected that after the war there would be a formal and official inquiry into the loss of the two ships (and other events connected with the fall of Singapore). 'At one time he certainly understood from Admiral Sir John Cunningham, when First Sea Lord [1946–8], that this was going to happen, but nothing did. On the whole, both the Attlee and Churchill post-war governments viewed the possibility of an enquiry without enthusiasm, and public pressure was never great enough to bring one about.' Doig, 'Misfortune off Malaya', p. 42.

[17] ADM 199/1149.

among naval historians was, and has remained, a lively one, for, as Mahan says somewhere, 'Defeat cries aloud for explanation; whereas success, like charity, covers a multitude of sins.' Critics like Admiral Godfrey and Admiral of the Fleet Sir Algernon Willis have held that, given the lack of a carrier and definite assurance of land-based air cover, better judgement would have halted the two capital ships in Ceylon (Godfrey), or withdrawn them as far west as Ceylon directly Japan went to war (Willis), until proper air support was available, and that this is what Layton would have done had he been in command.[18] Admiral Somerville, Commanding Force H at the time, was furious over the 'thoroughly bad show ... Why the hell don't they send *someone* out there who has been through the mill & knows his stuff'.[19] Sometime after the sinkings, Somerville, then C-in-C of the new Eastern Fleet, declared that his experiences in Force H in the Mediterranean had convinced him that ships could not operate without air cover, and that, had he been in Phillips's place and lost his carrier aground in Jamaica, he would have refused to go to Singapore by some means or other and instead gone to Darwin.[20]

Phillips has not lacked defenders in the Navy, at that time and since, with or without reservations, among them Admirals Sir Frederic Dreyer, Sir William James, Vice-Admiral R. M. Servaes, Commander Stephen King-Hall, the American Admiral Hart, and most of the officers of Force Z who survived. Tennant in his report of 11 December 1941 asserted unequivocally that he had been 'in entire agreement with every action taken by the Commander-in-Chief, Eastern Fleet, with the information that was then, as far as I knew, available to him.'[21] Captain Bell stressed that

in all the decisions that the Admiral took in the last strategic sortie he had the full support of his staff [but see above, p. 434n] and of his Captains. We all felt that he did what was right throughout, and the fault of being in an

---

[18] *Naval Memoirs of Admiral J. H. Godfrey*, vii, Pt. ii. 258–9, Willis's letter to the author, 22 Mar. 1976. Willis says that he suggested this course to Phillips when the latter stopped at Freetown, where Willis was stationed as C-in-C, South Atlantic.

[19] Somerville to Cunningham, 21 Dec. 1941, Cunningham Papers, Add. MS 52563.

[20] Vice-Admiral Sir Kaye Edden's memorandum for the author, 24 Feb. 1977. Edden, his SO(P), had asked Somerville whether he would have done what Phillips did. When Edden asked him if this was not in the light of hindsight, he had replied, 'No, I thought it at the time.'

[21] Layton's Dispatch, p. 1240.

impossible situation did not lie with him. The world is always prone to put the blame for a naval disaster on the Commander of the force concerned, but if they attempt to do so in this case they will be doing the Admiral's memory the greatest injustice. For he, more than any man I know, fought his utmost to prevent ships of the Royal Navy being faced by the position we had to accept on the morning of 10th Dec.—that of being exposed to the full weight of Japanese air attack without the protection of our own air forces.[22]

On the face of it, it would have made good sense if immediately the Japanese began hostilities, he had withdrawn from Singapore. Overwhelming enemy naval and air strength in the South China Sea neutralized his Force, and the weakness of the RAF in Malaya rendered Singapore an unsafe base and made Force Z sitting rabbits for air attack from Indo-China. Naval history is replete with examples of a small force avoiding action with superior forces and disrupting enemy plans by hit-and-run attacks on his lines of communication. In the case of Force Z, the two capital ships could have formed the nucleus of an Allied striking force that might have seriously interfered with Japan's second-phase operations. The flaw in such a strategy is that, before Force Z could have achieved much, it would probably have been hunted down and destroyed by the enemy's vastly superior naval and air forces.

Phillips may not have been prudent in acting as he did, and conceivably he might have been wiser to have sought a safer base and waited for air cover and the formation of a stronger Eastern Fleet. Yet a good case can be made for his strategy. It was unacceptable to him to retain his Force in harbour at Singapore while the enemy were landing troops unmolested on the Kra Isthmus and (with some opposition) at Kota Bharu. One should put oneself in the position of commanding capital ships idling at Singapore while the Japanese advanced practically unopposed, everyone looking at you or seeming to look at you, and asking what are you going to do about it. Had Phillips stayed in Singapore, or sailed to a more secure base, the same critics who lambasted his strategy would have demanded that he be shot for neglect of duty. In Pound's words (repeating what he had told Lady Phillips a year earlier), 'in view of the seriousness of the situation, there was not the slightest doubt that the decision he made was the correct one. Had

[22] Bell to Lady Phillips, 12 Dec. 1941.

he not done what he did I do not think there is a shadow of doubt but that everyone would by now attribute the fall of Malaya and Singapore to his inactivity. The very people who were inclined to criticise him for what they called a rash operation would have been the first to damn him for remaining quietly at Singapore, and making no attempt to interfere with the Japanese landing.'[23]

There is force in the argument that 'If the Air, from whatever cause, had failed Admiral Phillips and by so doing had rendered his force inadequate, was he in turn to let the Army down? The effect would have been far more than local or strategical; it would have jeopardized the confidence of the whole Army in the Navy. It would further have set a new standard of shirking danger with inestimable effect on the Navy's own morale.'[24] I find this line of thought highly persuasive. Had Force Z steamed to Ceylon or Australia for safety sake, not only would the Army in Malaya and the authorities in Singapore have felt betrayed, but the ships' companies in Force Z would have considered themselves disgraced. Any officer of the Royal Navy with any spirit would have gone to Singora/Kota Bharu, or to Kuantan, as matters developed, on being told of the landings in those vital areas.

The comments by Pound and Fauteil raise the question, which would have been better, 'the fall of Malaya and Singapore [due] to his inactivity', or the fall of Malaya and Singapore due to the loss of his fleet? The former is two good ships better. This is the logical answer; but surely 99 per cent of Royal Navy officers would have done what Phillips did.

In fairness we should also bear in mind that monsoon conditions in the South China Sea produced conditions of extemely poor visibility. Had the weather in the morning of the 10th been like that on the 9th, which was the norm, the Japanese attacks on the 10th could not have taken the course they did. This was not easily foreseeable. We must also take into account that Phillips shared the almost universal underestimation of Japanese naval air efficiency and the quality of their aircraft. The Admiral cannot be held responsible for the failures in intelligence. It is easy to be wise after

---

[23] Pound to Mrs Mildred Barker (a close friend of the Phillips family), 25 Feb. 1943, Phillips Papers.
[24] Fauteil, 'Notes on the War at Sea', *Naval Review*, xxxi, 1 (Feb. 1942), 7. The author was Captain Bertram H. Smith, a retired naval officer who wrote his 'Notes' in almost every wartime issue of the *Naval Review*.

the event, but we must put ourselves back into the state of naval intelligence in the Far East at that time. The authorities did their best, which on occasion was very good indeed (as in giving about two weeks' notice of the date when war would begin), but they were unaware of the capabilities of Japanese naval aircraft and of Japanese proficiency in attacking with airborne torpedoes.

Had the Admiral succeeded in his original plan and destroyed a large number of Japanese transports and escorting vessels off southern Thailand and north–east Malaya (his big guns, Admiral Hart thought, would have 'popped off the enemy transports at the rate of one a minute'),[25] he could have seriously, albeit temporarily, have dislocated the Japanese war plan. Larger and more lasting results would have been possible only if the RAF had been strong enough to dispute command of the air over the Gulf of Siam. This would have enabled Force Z to command the sea off the beach-heads, for a time anyway, despite the superiority of the Japanese naval forces in the area.

But should Phillips not have broken wireless silence, if not when his Force was first sighted, at least when he changed his plan and turned towards Kuantan, and requested air cover? (Granted that it made no sense to preserve silence when he was aware that the attack was developing, but, as pointed out, we cannot be absolutely sure whether he had made no attempt to transmit a signal.) He clearly attached a quite exaggerated importance to the maintenance of wireless silence by ships operating at sea, and failed to appreciate how the value of that policy would be affected by evidence of actual contacts with the enemy and the likelihood that the ememy already had adequate information. He had good reasons for the policy of wireless silence, yet, as Captain Doig points out, 'It meant that, having provided ourselves with an elaborate, efficient and rapid means of communication between our forces, we were to deny ourselves any use of it just when it might be of most use to us—because it was feared it might also be useful to the enemy. That was obviously one of the factors to be considered, but only one, and the principle that adequate steps should be taken to ensure that all responsible authorities knew what was going on and what was

[25] Admiral Thomas C. Hart, 'What Our Navy Learned in the Pacific', *Saturday Evening Post*, ccxv, 14 (3 Oct. 1942), p. 10. 'Everyone can see now that the only thing which could have saved Singapore would have been the success of Adm. Tom Phillips' attempt to get his powerful ships into Jap transports at sea.'

intended was the *primary* one.'[26] The delay (or apparent delay) until 1220 to send out the first signal from the *Prince of Wales*, *36 minutes after she was first hit*, is more difficult to explain, since, if her own communications were failing, the flagship could have directed the SO Destroyers to pass any message. Yet we have the evidence of Petty Officer Telegraphist Albert Rose that the ship's W/T sets were working almost to the very end.[27]

Supposing Phillips had broken wireless silence, how much air support would he have received and how effective would it have been? Pound, in his 25 January memorandum, stated: 'In the light of after events it must be concluded that it would have been better if he had asked for this fighter protection firstly when his force was sighted about 0645 [1845, 9 December] and more definitely so when the attack was known to be developing about 1100 [10 December].... Inevitably this patrol would have been so weak that it could not have materially altered the scale of attack on his ships.' Exactly so. As indicated above (pp. 481–3), very probably both ships would have been sunk or very severely damaged even if the sporadic air cover that could have been provided had been sent in time. The weight of the Japanese attack might have been lessened, and a number of attackers shot down. The end result would, however, not have been very different. Of course, all this is hypothetical, as we can never know what actually would have happened.

The attempt failed, and it may be argued that in the absence of air support, the risk was too great. But in war risks must be taken. The operation was a gallant one, commanded by an Admiral who was as brave as a lion in what he did, who took a chance, knowing the risk, and did the best he could with what he had. The fittest epitaph for the whole venture was uttered, ironically, by A. B. Cunningham, a critic of Phillips and the whole operation, when

---

[26] 'Misfortune off Malaya', p. 31. Doig had personal experience in the Home Fleet during the first year of the war of criticisms from the Admiralty that officers engaged in operations were making far too many signals. He feels it 'extemely likely' that these criticisms emanated from the VCNS, Phillips. After one such criticism, Layton, then Vice-Admiral Commanding 18th Cruiser Squadron, asked which signals in a particular operation were thought to be unnecessary; he received no reply. Ibid.

[27] Captain Doig hazards the guess that the 1220 signal was made by Leach, and not by the C-in-C, though probably with the latter's approval. 'Captain Leach possibly came to the conclusion that the safety of his ship was his overriding concern, even though he had an Admiral on board, and he *must* tell someone about her state and condition whether the Admiral liked it or not.' Ibid. 34, Addendum, pp. 3–4.

apropros of his decision to continue the evacuation of the British troops in Crete in May 1941, he told his Chief of Staff: 'It takes the Navy three years to build a ship. It would take three hundred to rebuild a tradition.'[28] In endeavouring to come to the aid of the RAF and the Army, who were in desperate straits, and in 'marching to the sound of the guns', Tom Phillips had followed the great traditions of the senior Service.

There is no truer proverb than 'It is easy to be wise after the event.' The realities as they appeared to a man under pressure are different from those as perceived by historians and others writing long afterwards, seated in comfortable armchairs and *in possession of the facts not available to the man on the spot.*

Of course [as Desmond Morton put it] a historian writing later than the event described may demonstrate how much better it can *now* be seen that some other course would have succeeded in all probability than that chosen at the time. But in no circumstances can he criticise the actors for reaching the conclusions they did *at the time*, unless he can demonstrate that they disregarded facts known to them, acted with duplicity or malice or were demonstrably unfit for the positions they held. ... Democracy judges *solely* by results. Historians must *never* do so.[29]

Therein lies my principal criticism of a particular school of historical thought in the field of military studies.

There was unanimity at the time on the part of naval officers in the two ships that some fighters would have made a difference, and that the RAF had let the Navy down by their failure to provide air cover until too late. 'Where the hell was the air support?' was the attitude of the survivors, who saw in the belated arrival of the Buffaloes the cause of their plight and the loss of their ships. 'If we had had just a few fighters to get their "eye off the ball", we might have got away with it' is a typical opinion. The feeling in the destroyers was equally bitter. A *Prince of Wales* survivor in the *Express* noted that 'if the gun crews on the destroyer had had their way they would have opened fire on the Buffaloes'.[30] A very bitter

---

[28] Admiral Sir William James, *Hotch-Potch*, ii (privately printed, 1971), 71. Cunningham took some of the hardest decisions it has ever fallen to a commander to make when he refused to cut short the Navy's aid in getting the soldiers out from Crete, despite the heavy losses to the German Air Force, the weariness, and the murmurs of his staff. *He* was not going to be the first admiral to let the Army down.

[29] R. W. Thompson, *Churchill and Morton* (London, 1976), p. 100.

[30] Middlebrook and Mahoney, p. 259.

and outspoken critic of the Singapore command on this score, and particularly of the airmen, was Goodenough. He was told to shut up. Tennant, though he was careful throughout the war to avoid any suggestion of blame on anybody's part, talked about how he had deplored the absence of supporting aircraft and felt that it was almost inevitable that they run into trouble. No blame can be put on the RAF. They had asked for reinforcements, but none had come, and, moreover, they were completely ignorant of the whereabouts of Force Z on 10 December until it was too late to help.

There can be no dispute over the complete failure of the inter-Service command at the top. Brooke-Popham and Phillips were informed on 2 December that they were 'jointly responsible ... to H.M. Government for the conduct of our strategy in the Far East'. Yet Phillips went pretty much his own way, barely consulting the C-in-C, Far East (beyond the meeting early on the 8th), in accordance, no doubt, with the Admiralty insistence on operational independence. It did not help matters that the 62-year-old 'Brookham', though an able officer with an outstanding record, was not an inspiring type and lacked up-to-date experience. Indeed, Major-General Sir Henry Pownall was *en-route* to Singapore to take over from him. Admiral Layton summed up Brooke-Popham's deficiencies in succinct fashion:

On the personal side, Sir Robert Brooke-Popham was too old a man to deal with a situation in which it was really essential to have a Commander who was right up to date with the possibilities of land, sea and air warfare in the light of what had happened in Europe and Africa; he had in fact been resuscitated from a Colonial Governorship after some years of separation from the active Service. So far as his impacts on Service and civilian authorities in the Far East went he proved unfortunately to be unimpressive in personality and insufficiently strong-minded to keep a real and effective control over the members of his staff, which contained some very able men.[31]

---

[31] Official source. His unimpressive personality is described this way by Captain McClelland, who had many opportunities to observe him: 'B.-P. was a big, untidy man, going bald, with a [reddish] moustache that might have shrunk from one he had proudly borne as an officer in the cavalry in his youth. He was pleasant and kind to meet, had a good sense of humour of the schoolboy variety, and laughed easily. . . . [He lacked] the profound knowledge of all the aspects of warfare required for high command. I formed the impression, probably influenced to some extent by Layton, that not only had he been told by Whitehall
(*continued*)

It is doubtful, however, that even the most perfect inter-Service cooperation would have made any great difference in the outcome.

At the risk of some repetition, it may be left for us to wonder, with ample hindsight, whether any amount of fighter cover that the RAF could have provided Force Z on 10 December would have made the least difference. On D-day the Japanese had over 800 aircraft deployed in southern French Indo-China and the South China Sea—far more, and far more efficient aircraft, than the British could throw against them. They would have eventually hunted down and destroyed Force Z, even had it succeeded in returning to Singapore. Had Force Z moved into Indonesian waters, as did the naval units that had survived the 10 December action, her fate would only have been postponed. Put shortly, nothing the Royal Navy could maintain in Eastern waters in December 1941 had much chance of stopping the overwhelming force, naval and air, at Japan's disposal.

The fundamental mistake lay in sending out an unbalanced, strategically unsound Force in the first place. It put Phillips in an impossible position. For this neither he nor the Admiralty was responsible. Behind this mistake lay the cardinal error: British strategic policy in the Far East was founded on (as Admiral Sir Herbert Richmond put it in 1946) 'the illusion that a Two-Hemisphere Empire can be defended by a One-Hemisphere Navy.' The British had neither the air nor naval strength to avert the catastrophes that befell her Eastern Empire, the defence of which rested always on bluff unless perfect peace reigned in Europe.

3. 'THE BISMARCK IS AVENGED'

The Japanese exhibited qualities of fanaticism and bravery on 10 December that were harbingers of what the Allies would have to

---

that war in the East was impossible (and therefore considered it was his duty to spread this doctrine), but also that, when the forces planned for the defence of Malaya by the RAF failed to materialize, he did not press too hard for them because Whitehall knew best. As he also considered that all other nations were greatly inferior in fighting to the British, it is not very surprising that he felt that we could at least hold our own against the Japanese with a third of their number of aircraft which were greatly inferior to the enemy in fighting power.' Captain McClelland's letter to the author, 6 Mar. 1979. To complete the picture, Brooke-Popham had what has been described as 'a disturbingly high-pitched voice' and 'a giggling laugh'.

contend with. Lieutenant Iki has been spoken of. There is also the story of Lieutenant Takahashi Kassaku, Leader of the Mihoro Air Corps' 8th Squadron. Seven planes of his eight-plane squadron attacking the *Repulse* dropped their torpedoes at a range of 700–800 metres, altitude 40 metres, except for Takahashi himself, who tried to release his torpedo at a distance of less than 700 metres and a height of 25 metres. Attacking from the port side of the ship, he thought he had released his torpedo. He flew over the bow of the *Repulse* at an altitude of about 50 metres, before beginning a climbing turn, then asked his torpedoman whether the torpedo had been dropped. 'No' was the answer, whereupon Takahashi banked to the right and hurtled himself once more into the deadly enemy barrage, preparing to attack from the ship's starboard side at a range of better than 1,500 metres. This time, he thought, he surely would be shot down. Again he indicated the moment of release to his torpedoman, and again, having flown over the bow of the *Repulse*, he questioned whether the torpedo had been released. Again, '*no!*' Somehow Takashasi's plane had managed to survive the gauntlet of AA fire a second time. Aware that some vital trouble existed in the torpedo release mechanism, and that another attack would mean the death of his crew for nothing, it was his instant judgement that he not try again. *En route* to his base, Takahashi felt disappointed because he had not sunk an enemy ship. Then he received a wireless message that the two capital ships had been sunk. His eyes teared up. He felt deeply for the British sailors and officers as well as for the dead Japanese. It was a sad happening for both navies was his sentiment. This was not a unique experience.

Observing the *Repulse* sinking, an incredible sight, Lieutenant Iki Haruku, Leader of the 3rd Kanoya Squadron, cried '*Banzai!*', and all the way back the crew shouted '*Banzai!*' at the top of their voices.[32] Great was the excitement. Yet, after their return to base, some members of Iki's squadron wondered whether it was 'right' to sink such large and beautiful ships. It seemed a pity to destroy them with a few cheap torpedoes. This puts one in mind of the famous wreath (more properly, bouquet)-dropping incident, the details of

---

[32] *Banzai* is, literally, 'Ten Thousand Years', but should be translated as 'Hurrah'. From the report of Lieutenant-Commander Miyauchi Shichizo, the Kanoya CO: When they observed the hits on the *Repulse*, 'We shouted "*banzai! banzai!*" and shed tears of joy and stamped our feet. Was it a dream or not? I pinched my cheek and realized it was not a dream—it was reality.' Sudō, *Malay oki kaisen*, p. 138.

which have invariably been given incorrectly.[33] After the action, Iki flew to Takao air base (Formosa) to arrange for replacements for the two aircraft he had lost. He was back at Thu Dau Mot Base on 16 December. The next day his squadron was ordered to make a reconnaissance flight over the Anambas Islands on the 18th. This flight would take Iki over the scene of the 10 December action. On the 17th he had one of his petty officers purchase two bouquets of mixed flowers, including hibiscus, in a flower shop near the base. On the 18th the squadron made its reconnaissance flight and, on its way back, the weather being good and the sea calm, Iki could see the two sunken ships. He circled the area at about 200 metres altitude, then dropped the first bouquet over the *Repulse*—for the lost crews of the two aircraft of his flight—and the second over the *Prince of Wales* for the enemy dead. What motivated this chivalrous deed was primarily his feeling of great respect for the two ships which had continued to fight to the last. It was also a tribute to the Royal Navy which had been like a big brother to the Imperial Navy. We must also bear in mind that the honouring of the war dead is very much in the Bushido spirit. Also, in Japanese Buddhist doctrine in death there are no enemies; those who died bravely for their country should be treated with honour. This spirit is captured in what a Mihoro pilot said afterwards: 'We were overjoyed when we learned of our success in destroying two battleships. And yet, when we read about all those English seamen who shared the fate of their ships, we prayed for their souls.'[34] Even today, when the Training Squadron of the new Navy passes the scene of the wrecks, the officers and men stand to attention and bouquets are dropped overboard, honouring the dead of both navies.

Directly after the battle, the Japanese had some ideas of salvaging the ships. Admiral Ugaki's diary of 10 December has this entry: 'The two sunken ships will not be allowed to decay, for the depth of the sea where they sank is 30 metres, so that they can be salvaged and will soon be included in our Navy List.' The Navy sent a salvage ship and an escort ship, with a team of seven divers, in the first week of March 1942, soon after the fall of Singapore, to search for the wrecks. Their priority was the *Prince of Wales*, there being a

---

[33] My account is derived from an interview with Commander Iki, 26 June 1976.
[34] Bessho Naoki, *Senkan Prince of Wales no saigo* [The Sinking of the Battleship *Prince of Wales*] (Tokyo, 1967), p. 256. The pilot was Tahira Ei, a Flight Petty Officer First Class in Takahashi's squadron.

'THE BISMARCK IS AVENGED'

keen interest in the Naval Technical Department in learning what they could about the newest British battleship. They followed a streak of oil to its source, and there was the *Repulse*, at a depth of 147 feet on a soft muddy bottom, with half her bottom upside, listed 130 degrees to port. The divers brought up shells of her AA guns and a number of AA guns, and observed what they could: that her rudders, both smokestacks, and her mainmast were broken, etc. To their great disappointment they could not locate the *Prince of Wales*. They were unable to continue the search when, following a suspension of activity for a week to obtain supplies in Singapore, the salvage ship was ordered to the north coast of Java to tow off a stranded Army amphibious transport.[35]

There was no rejoicing by Kondō. His expression never changed when informed of the victory. The officers in the flagship *Atago*, none of whom had expected that the Air Force would single-handedly annihilate the enemy, at first rejoiced. There were smiles, back slaps, and cries of *banzai*. This was quickly succeeded by a feeling of disappointment because they had had nothing to do with the sinkings. This may explain Kondō's mood, since, after all, the fighting had been done by the aircraft, which were under Ozawa's direct command. The sinkings did, however, mean that Kondō could now act freely: he had secure communications. Ozawa took no pride in the victory. When the Malaya Force was on its way

---

[35] Commander Tōyama Kōichi, 'Chinbotsu ei senkan tansaku ki' [An Account of the Search for the Sunken British Battleships], in Zosen Kai [Ship Construction Society], *Zōsenkan no kiroku* [Records of Ship Construction Officers] (Tokyo, 1966), pp. 116–23. Tōyama, an officer in the Naval Technical Department, was in charge of the project. The ships came to rest with the *Repulse* lying in a depth of 180 feet, and the *Prince of Wales* 8 miles away to eastward in a depth of 216 feet, in, respectively, 03° 37·3′ North, 104° 20·6′ East, and 03° 34·2′ North, 104° 27·8′ East. The former position is about 45 miles north-north-east of Pulau Tioman. Lying in fairly shallow water, the two wrecks are very clear, given suitable weather conditions. When the monsoon is slack and there is little wind to ruffle the reflective surface of the sea, they stand out very clearly when viewed from the air. For interesting material on the status of the wrecks when last surveyed, by RN diving teams in 1965 (*Repulse*) and 1966 (*Prince of Wales*), see 'H.M.S. *Repulse*' and 'H.M.S. *Prince of Wales*' in, respectively, the *Royal Naval Diving Magazine*, xii, 3 (Winter 1965), 39–41, and xiv, 1 (Spring 1967), 10–11. For some years the *Prince of Wales* was marked by a metal ensign staff secured to the wreck, the White Ensign was flown, the immediate vicinity was officially recognized as a War Grave, and about once a year an HM Ship on passage (e.g. from Singapore to Hong Kong) was instructed to close the spot, renew the Ensign, and see that all was well. Local fishermen have since removed the Ensign and staff, but HM Ships still occasionally visit the area on passage, as in 1977, when the Flotilla Chaplain of a group of ships held a single memorial service on board as they passed over the wreck.

back to Camranh Bay and Captain Nomura, the Chief Medical Officer, visited the Admiral in his cabin and offered congratulations on the victory, Ozawa nodded silently and whispered, tears in his eyes: 'It is not an occasion for congratulations. Perhaps I shall suffer the same fate as Admiral Phillips some day.'[36] Admiral Kurita, on the other hand, had been delighted and made no effort to hide his happiness.

The atmosphere in the Operations Room at Combined Fleet HQ (the Fleet was then at sea east of Japan) became tense when it received the report of *I-65*'s sighting. It was expected that the battle, if it developed, would be between aircraft and capital ships in the open sea, the first such battle in world history. If the battle were lost, the Malayan landing operations would come to a standstill, with incalculable effects on Japan's strategy. The atmosphere at Combined Fleet HQ after the Air Raid Groups had taken off in the morning of the 10th is conveyed by the Staff Officer Air Operations:

In the Operations Room of the flagship all the staff officers assembled around the Commander-in-Chief, who was seated in the centre of the room, and were making random guesses and conjectures among themselves as to the anticipated battle between aircraft and battleships. The Admiral said to me casually, 'Do you think that both will be sunk? I think the *Repulse* will be destroyed but not the *King George V*, which at best will be heavily damaged.' I replied, 'Both will be destroyed.' Then the Admiral said, 'Well, let's make a bet on it.' I accepted. It was decided that if I won, the prize would be ten dozen bottles of beer, and if the Admiral won, the prize would be one dozen. The Commander-in-Chief used to resort to such a stratagem, betting contrary to his own thinking so as to test the degree of his opponent's confidence in his conjecture.

The battle began, and the sinking of the *Repulse* became known, but the condition of the *King George V* was uncertain, so that I was worried. More than an hour had elapsed since the commencement of the battle when an extraordinarily loud voice was heard from the radio telegraphy room: 'One more battleship sunk.' They had won! They had won! Won superbly! Aircraft had defeated battleships.

The efforts made by the air personnel for so long a time have been rewarded. Voices of joy were raised spontaneously in the Operations Room. The Admiral was also smiling, with both cheeks flushed. For the

---

[36] Captain Terasaki Ryūji (who was on Ozawa's staff), interview, 18 May 1976, and in Ozawa teitoku denki henshū iinkai, *Teitoku Ozawa Jisaburō den*, p. 56.

first time I saw a bright smile on his face, which usually was almost expressionless. I said to him, 'I will claim from you the prize of the ten dozen bottles of beer.' He replied, 'You may take ten dozen, nay, even 50 dozen, or as much as you like.' And, addressing his ADC, 'Give Miwa any amount of beer that he wants.' His voice was full of joy.[37]

At first, then, Yamamoto and his staff were overjoyed with the news of the achievement of the 22nd Air Flotilla, which had exceeded expectations ('Nothing more brilliant than this remarkable success.' Ugaki wrote in his diary on the 10th[38]), and celebrated the event that evening with toasts in beer to the 22nd Air Flotilla, to the Emperor, and to Victory.

But as the meal progressed, Yamamoto's mood became progressively less buoyant, and after eating, when he played his usual five-game chess match with Lieutenant Commander Yasuji Watanabe, he was not quite up to his game. Though he was a quick player and would almost invariably win three games out of five, he was playing more slowly tonight and Watanabe was beginning to think he might even win this match for a change.

Finally Yamamoto looked up from the chessboard and Watanabe could see he was in a confidential mood. For some reason which Watanabe did not presume to understand, the admiral, who was 19 years his senior, often confided in him.

'In spite of this new victory today,' Yamamoto said to him, 'our success cannot possibly continue for more than a year.' He was silent and thoughtful for a while, then he added, 'I feel great sympathy for the British commander (Vice-Admiral Sir Tom Phillips) who apparently went down with the *Prince of Wales*. The same thing may happen to me someday in the not-too-distant future.'[39]

In the same evening of 10 December Admiral Yonai gave a press interview in his home in Tokyo. The newsmen wanted his reaction to the great victory. 'I really can find no word[s] to thank our Imperial Navy,' he began. It was the result of the 'incessant training

---

[37] Captain Miwa Yoshitake, 'Yamamoto gensui no omide' [Recollections of Admiral of the Fleet Yamamoto] (1943), Bōeichō Senshibu Archives.
[38] *Sensō roku*, p. 42. Ugaki proposed naming the battle 'Sea Battle off Cape Ca Mau [Cape Cambodia].' In the end the navy preferred the 'Naval Battle off Malaya'. The Royal Navy has never seen fit to bestow a name on the action.
[39] Thomas M. Coffey, *Imperial Tragedy: Japan in World War II* (New York, 1970), p. 178. No authority is cited for the passage. It seems odd that Yamamoto did not issue a citation to the 22nd Air Flotilla until 15 April 1942, although the text seems to have been prepared soon after the action. He paid tribute to the 'dauntless and daring attack which destroyed the enemy at one stroke, thereby contributing greatly to the conduct of the subsequent operations. The above brilliant achievement is very remarkable.'

of our Navy, the fierceness of which is beyond description', and of the Navy's 'positive offensive spirit'. 'But,' he warned, 'the war has just begun. We must not be too elated over the victory. With the war prolonged, we cannot expect to go on without some losses.' Also interviewed was Admiral Suetsugu, and, as might have been expected, there were no qualifications in his rejoicing. 'With the successful operations of our Navy, the command of the Pacific and the Indian Ocean has now fallen into our hands, and I feel that world history is making a new turn.'[40]

The general mood in the Services and in the country was one of pride and euphoria. It dawned on few that Japan may have bitten off far more than she could possibly manage by challenging America and the British Commonwealth and Empire, for they did not grasp the fundamental law of maritime war that not only must you have sufficient strength to obtain and exercise control of the seas, but you must have sufficient resources to maintain and strengthen the control once you have it. This the Japanese never had.

The result of the action came as a tremendous surprise to the Navy High Command in Tokyo. 'We did not expect', Admiral Hoshina explains, 'that two such powerful battleships could be sunk by planes like that—*so easily*.' There were *banzais* and a lot of smiling, though not too much excitement, in the Navy Minister's office. Shimada, who expressed himself as 'very glad', joined other Navy leaders in a toast to the victory. There was rejoicing (*sake* drinking and the rest) in the Operations Division of the Naval General Staff, where, too, the result was totally unexpected. Nagano and Shimada lost no time in sending congratulatory messages to Yamamoto and Kondō. Nagano closed the briefing on the action that he gave to Admiral Wenneker on 11 December with the words: 'The *Bismarck* is avenged. We shall tie the knot tighter.'[41]

4. LESSONS AND RESULTS

The naval battle off Malaya was the first case in the history of naval warfare when capital ships under way were sunk by an attack

---

[40] *Japan Times & Advertiser* (Tokyo), 11 Dec. 1941 (evening edition).
[41] War Diary, German Naval Attaché, 11 Dec. 1941, PG 32145a, Admiralty Project, Reel 482. Ugaki had made a similar remark in his diary on 10 December: 'By destroying the

(*continued*)

carried out exclusively by aircraft. Yet the Admiralty apparently made no study of the tactical lessons of the action (torpedo-firing tactics, attack weapons, relation of losses to altitude of attack, etc.), to say nothing of such larger matters as co-operation between air and naval forces, it having been determined from the reports of Tennant and other surviving officers that the action had only confirmed their experience in Home Waters and the Mediterranean. The Staff report of 20 January 1942 (above, p. 498) did make these broad points:

(iii) ... the necessity for providing important units of the fleet with fighter cover either from carriers or shore-based aircraft when a heavy scale of attack is possible.
(iv) If air cover is not available inshore raiding operations should be carried out by light forces rather than by heavy ships. ...
(vi) Once it is clear that the ships' position is known to shadowing aircraft there should be no reluctance in breaking W/T silence to call for fighter protection.

Cunningham found it most interesting that 'the Japs did not synchronise their high level attacks with their torpedo attacks. ... The Italians have learnt that ...'[42] Tennant, who had just passed through, had supplied him with this information. One valuable thing the Admiralty must have learned from Tennant was that the AA shooting was not good: 'we have all got to realise that bursts behind the target at short range AA fire which are missing astern is just a waste of time, and the ammunition might just as well be thrown over the side. I believe that 90% of the short range stuff that is being fired by the fleet at enemy aircraft goes behind them. It is just the same ... [as] the man who goes about with a shot gun who is a bad shot will frequently fire his shot well behind the rabbit or bird, as the case may be.'[43] Captain Bell in his 10 December report was not impressed with the long-range high-angle AA gunfire,

---

Prince of Wales it may be said that we have avenged the *Bismarck* in the Far East, on the opposite side of the earth.' Wenneker added this interesting postscript to his diary entry: 'The entire operation, preparation, and staff work, merit admiration. The brain behind it is Vice-Admiral Ito, Kondo's successor [as Vice-Chief of Staff].'

[42] Cunningham to Pound, 28 Dec. 1941, Cunningham Papers, Add. MS 52561. There is a large measure of truth in this (see above, p. 461, for the exploration), but there was one good example of a co-ordinated attack (above, p. 469).

[43] Tennant, 'The Last Action'. This material is not in his written reports to the Admiralty, but, we may assume, was brought up orally when he made a personal report to the Admiralty on his return to England.

which appeared to leave the high-level bombers 'untouched and unmoved. Fire did not appear accurate, taking some time to get on for deflection, and then being short ... Short range fire was more accurate, but all weapons continued to fire at near targets, which had dropped their torpedoes and were harmless, rather than to select new targets still coming in to attack.'

The problem stemmed in part from the fact that both ships had been without serious AA practice for some months, though the root problem may have lain in the *kind* of AA training the gun crews had been exposed to. As explained by a Japanese writer: 'British torpedo planes of that time launched their weapons at speeds no greater than 100 miles per hour. British gunners, from their training and practice, came to consider that as a near-maximum speed for launching. Japanese [torpedo] planes, however, could launch at speeds of 150 to 190 miles per hour, and British gunners found it difficult to adjust to this unusually high speed. Consequently, ... torpedoes were responsible for most of the ship damage.'[44]

Looking back on the action, Tennant pointed to this as the supreme lesson: 'if 50 or 60 well trained torpedo bombers can be launched to attack capital ships who are without aircraft protection and with very few destroyers, capital ships will be seriously up against it. With luck I think one may well dodge one or two waves of torpedoes but when successive waves come in it becomes very difficult.'[45] The destruction of the two capital ships marked the end of the era of sea power epitomised by Nelson and the teachings of Mahan. The battleship had been toppled from the lordly position it had retained for three centuries. More, it was patently clear that henceforth surface combat could take place only where aircraft were absent, out of range, or at night.

There was concern, not only at the Admiralty, that such an up-to-date ship as the *Prince of Wales* should have failed to survive the attack. 'To allay possible anxiety arising from the loss', the Admiralty appointed a committee to make a study of the technical aspects. The Bucknill Committee (Mr Justice Bucknill), which began its inquiry on 12 March 1942, submitted its report on 25

---

[44] Masanori Ito, with Roger Pineau, *The End of the Imperial Japanese Navy* (London, 1962), p. 48. I would add the ammunition defects: probably due to the hot climate, many of the pom-poms in the two big ships became separated from their cartridges and jammed the barrels.

[45] 'The Last Action'.

April. The Board of Admiralty considered and approved it and directed that its recommendations be implemented.[46]

There is one factor in the loss of the *Prince of Wales* which is known to few. It was after the torpedoes had struck her starboard side that Commander Goudy, the ship's Engineer Officer, came across a Commissioned Warrant Officer who had just opened the flood valve of one of the forward magazines. He asked him 'by whose order?', and was told, 'My own.' Goudy ordered the valve closed, and he saw it closed. He never thought of asking if he had flooded any other magazines. A year or more later, Goudy met an officer survivor who told him that he had seen the same officer flooding other magazines. Goudy can only assume that the misguided officer had lost his head and perhaps had a fear of the ship following the *Hood*'s example—an explosion of her magazines—although there was no question of fire. The Bucknill inquiry being over and done with, Goudy saw no point in 'blowing the gaff'. He has over the years wondered about the effect of the additional weight of water. 'Looking back, it seems unlikely that he would only open one magazine flood valve aft—he certainly intended to open all forward magazine floods.' If all after magazines had been flooded, as Goudy believes was the case, it would have added about 725 tons of water. This would have resulted in the stern settling 15 inches deeper in the sea at a critical time when the stern was low enough, and thereby have accelerated her sinking by exhausting her reserve of buoyancy that much.[47]

The Imperial Navy seriously investigated the lessons of the battle—some of them, that is. A War Lessons Investigation Committee was set up after the outbreak of the war, those lessons related to aviation being carried out chiefly by key staff personnel of the Yokosuka Naval Air Corps. After the action on 10 December, the Committee dispatched the appropriate members to Saigon to collect the necessary data. The Committee's report[48] began by stating that the destruction of the two battleships by air power alone had 'confirmed the enormous offensive power of aircraft against a fleet, although we were favoured by much divine grace and aid'. It urged a re-examination of the traditional doctrine of the

---

[46] The report is in ADM 116/4554. There is a useful discussion of its findings in Middlebrook and Mahoney, pp. 309–13.
[47] Letters to the author, 20 Aug., 4, 16 Sept., 2 Oct. 1978.
[48] *Senshi sōsho*, xxiv. 492–5. There is no indication of the date.

battleship as the main fighting force in a naval battle. While recognizing that there were valid reasons for the attacks on the British fleet being made successively by the different squadrons, with considerable intervals, they urged that 'since such attacks against an enemy fleet on alert are in great danger of being defeated in detail, it is deemed necessary to concentrate as large forces as possible under one commander and to bring the power of concentrated attack into full play'. The Committee approved Kondō's decision to call off the night action by the surface forces and to seek battle the next morning. But as there might be cases where, unless the enemy were caught and destroyed during the night, he would retreat beyond the attacking radius of the Japanese fleet by the next morning, it was necessary 'to expedite immediately the research in and development of the appropriate weapons for night action and conduct training in night-time search and attack'. The collaboration of torpedo- and bomber-planes, as demonstrated in the battle, was approved—that is, 'first of all, the bombing squadrons are to attack and confuse the enemy, and then, taking advantage of this confusion, the torpedo-attack squadrons will charge the enemy, thereby destroying him at one stroke. Such tactics are deemed particularly appropriate when the enemy has strong air cover.' Among the other recommendations were the need for much more incessant and thorough training in measuring target speeds, since this was the most important factor in deciding the firing angle (under present conditions the only method of judging an enemy's speed was that of measuring by eye, which had not proved satisfactory), and the urgent need to revise the 'Umpiring Standard in Naval Exercises' of the aircraft losses that could be expected from enemy defensive gunfire. The results on 10 December were not as serious as shown in the Standard.

		Umpiring standard in naval exercises			
		Torpedo attack squadron		Bombing squadron	
		Before attack	After attack	Before attack	After attack
Shot down	Max.	15	15	10	10
	Min.	6	6	2	2
Result of this naval battle		0	3	0	0

'Such an excessive estimate of damage has a demoralizing influence on the air crews.'

Blinded by the spectacular results, the Imperial Navy failed to absorb all the lessons of the battle. The causes of the many failures and delays in the receipt of important messages, particularly of the submarines, were not investigated thoroughly and remedial measures taken. Again, until the moment the attack groups received Hoashi's 'Enemy in sight' message of 1015, they had to watch their fuel gauges keenly, being concerned about the amount of fuel needed to return to base. After the action, Admiral Matsunaga held a conference, which was attended by his staff and the Commanders and Squadron Leaders of the Air Raid Groups. Lieutenant Takai Sadao reported how he had been kept ill at ease over the fuel problem. On account of the victory, however, 'the acute problem I had raised was not taken up seriously'. Ignored for the same reason was the extremely imprecise initial attack order, which had not indicated the exact location and course of the enemy fleet.

In retrospect [Commander Takai tells us], those two grave problems in the operation, especially the inadequate search plan, did not become valuable war lessons, and were duplicated in every action after the Naval Battle off Malaya throughout the war in the Pacific. ... The famous proverb 'All's well that ends well' should never be applied so far as battles are concerned. On the contrary, there appeared strange tendencies that in cases where we were defeated or unsuccessful in a planned attack, there was no thorough analysis and fact-finding on the causes of failure, mainly because of this tradition: 'Do not speak ill of the leaders who died a heroic death and devoted their precious lives to the country.' This emotional way of thinking was based on the influence of traditional Confucianism, which was deeply rooted in the nation ever since feudal times. Usually, the past deeds and desperate fights of those who had died in battle were glorified and honoured, and their failures were not taken up seriously. We should have thought, however, that the souls of the war dead would have been happy only when the causes of their failures were carefully analyzed and made good use of as war lessons.[49]

In Japan the tremendous initial successes against the United States and Britain raised the morale of air personnel and strengthened the hand of those who maintained that the plane was more powerful than the ship and that even battleships could not

---

[49] Takai MS. On this last point, about the 'tradition of avoiding criticism,' see above, Preface, p. ix.

withstand land-based air power.[50] Thus, Admiral Ugaki was convinced by the battle 'of the real and enormous power of aircraft. The battleship, which had participated in the operations that led to the destruction of the German battleship *Bismarck*, proved unexpectedly vulnerable in her AA defences.... Through the results of this battle the "no more battleships" doctrine and the doctrine of the omnipotence of air power will be the more vigorously advocated. At the same time the paramount power of our naval air force has been displayed to the full in the eastern and western Pacific for the whole world ...'[51] Captain Hashimoto Shōzō, Chief of the 1st Section of the Mobilization Bureau in the Navy Ministry, had, after Pearl Harbor, told the Chief of the 1st Section of the Naval Aviation Department, Captain Yamamoto Chikao, that it was 'still too early to verify the power of naval air. Nagumo succeeded only by a surprise attack.' But after the success off Malaya on 10 December was reported, Hashimoto came to Yamamoto's office and told him, 'Yamamoto, now you have won. I will do my best at the Naval Affairs Bureau to comply with the requests of the Naval Aviation Department.'[52] The Navy Minister, Shimada, would have gone so far as to stop the construction of the battleship *Musashi*, which was completing, but he could not prevail against the general trend of thought in the Navy. There were those naval officers, however, even including many Navy Air Force leaders, who wisely pointed out that on 10 December, as at Pearl Harbor, it had been a case of 'shooting sitting ducks', that the target ships had no fighter cover, so that it was premature to presume the future shape of naval warfare on the basis of this one action.[53]

The upshot was that, despite the brilliant results achieved by naval air power off Malaya and in the other operations in the Southern Area, to say nothing of the surprise attack on Pearl Harbor, many of the Navy's leaders, like Vice-Admiral Fukudome

[50] 'Most of the Naval Air Force personnel concerned, who had laboured for the build-up and improvement of Japanese naval air power, had been advocating, "There is no ship afloat which would not sink." Truthfully, however, this saying was a matter of bragging, and their actual feeling was that destruction of modern battleships by air attack only was hardly feasible—until D-day.' *Senshi sōsho*, xcv. 230.

[51] Diary, 10 Dec. 1941, *Sensō roku*, p. 43.

[52] Rear-Admiral Yamamoto Chikao, 'Malay oki kaisen no kaiko' [Reflections on the Battle off Malaya], in Sudō, *Malay oki kaisen*, p. 174.

[53] The 1943 German analysis of the action (above, p. 492n), too, did not consider that engagement as constituting conclusive evidence of the effectiveness of air attacks on warships, since the capital ships had no air cover and an escort of only three destroyers.

Shigeru, were slow to recognize the change in naval strategical concepts. They still would not discard the doctrine of the battleship as the principal fighting force. For these 'Battlewagon Admirals', air power, whether land-based or in the form of a mobile carrier force, was a powerful *auxiliary* force, no more. The Navy did make some efforts to increase aircraft production, though not of aircraft carriers.[54] The serious effort to increase carrier strength was not started until after the loss of four carriers at one stroke at Midway in June 1942. Even though the Imperial Navy generally operated on the theory that the carrier forces were ancillary to the battle fleet. The Royal Navy was considerably wiser in this respect. At the first Chiefs of Staff meeting after the news of the disaster, Pound reported that the Naval Staff was 'moving in the direction of fighting an aircraft-carrier war' in the Indian Ocean and the Far East.[55] Three fleet carriers (*Indefatigable, Implacable, Unicorn*) were already building. On 14 March 1942, 10 light fleet carriers of the 'Colossus' class were ordered: 13;190 tons, 45 aircraft maximum.

The strategic consequences of the naval battle off Malaya were vast and equally obvious to both sides. Britain's sea power in the Far East was, at least for the near future, shattered. Combined with the American disaster at Pearl Harbor, the battle gave the Japanese an undisputed dominance of the South China Sea as well as the Western Pacific. All that remained to stop their advance in the Southern Area were three American carriers that had escaped destruction at Pearl Harbor, and a few Allied cruisers, destroyers, and submarines in the Far East. As Layton summed up the grim situation in his War Diary for 10 December: 'The tragic loss of *Prince of Wales* and *Repulse* put us back in the "period before relief", with the added factor that their loss meant that that period must be considerably extended. We could only oppose Japanese command of the South China Sea with a few submarines and a few aircraft. We had to do what we could in this direction, and to keep trade and convoys moving on our essential lines of sea communication, while the Army tried to hold as much of Malaya as possible.' It was a lost

---

[54] Admiral Matsunaga told his son some time after 10 December that the prevailing thought had been that land-based air power was only supplemental to the carrier-borne air force, but that the 10 December action had brought about a tactical revolution concerning the role of land-based air power in a decisive fleet engagement. Lieutenant Matsunaga Ichirō's letter to the author, 23 July 1976.

[55] COS(41) 47th Mtg. (O), 11 Dec. 1941, CAB 79/55.

cause. Hong Kong was isolated; Singapore lay exposed—the power of the Royal Navy and the Royal Air Force (the latter down by 10 December to 41 aircraft ready for action) in its defence had been virtually wiped out—and was to fall in February 1942, the largest capitulation in British history (roughly 100,000 troops), and which cost Britain the one base from which she could defend the Pacific Dominions;[56] the Indian Ocean lay open; the Philippines and the Dutch East Indies seemed doomed; Australia, New Zealand, Burma, and India were threatened. Never before had the British Empire fought under such conditions; but never before had a naval Power made war as brilliantly as Japan did between 8 and 10 December, making use of speed, audacity, and a superb *matériel* and personnel. And their Navy was not finished. *The Times* War Correspondent in Malaya wrote in 1942: 'I still remember the chill sense of calamity which was caused by the loss of these two ships. It was worse than calamity. It was calamity that had the premonition of further calamity.'[57]

The loss of the two ships and their Admiral, together with the grievous losses of the US Navy at Pearl Harbor, demoralized not only the Royal Navy and the British people, but all the Allied Powers, governments and peoples. How different in Japan, where the morale and fighting spirit of the Imperial Navy was immensely raised. Almost all the officers forgot their doubts. But there was a harbinger of disaster in what the German Naval Attaché reported as 'excessive conceit and arrogance because of great successes [which] grew to such an extent even among the officers that for some time co-operation was extremely difficult.'[58]

The sinking of the *Prince of Wales* and *Repulse* was a disaster for the Royal Navy, one of the greatest it had ever suffered, and its prestige in consequence tumbled—but not in the Imperial Navy, in the Operations Division at any rate, where the high evaluation of

---

[56] This might be the moment to dispose of the myth that the 15-inch guns in the Singapore defences were pointing the wrong way. In fact, the 15-inch (as well as the 9·2-inch and, to some extent, the 6-inch) had an all-round field of fire. They were, however, provided solely (and in the case of the 9·2-inch and most of the 6-inch, largely) with armour-piercing shell for use against warships, since these guns had been installed to deter the enemy from making a direct naval bombardment from the sea. In this they were successful. It had always been appreciated that if a land invasion force from the north were successful in getting within range of the 15-inch guns, the fate of Singapore would already have been settled, because the enemy would be in possession of the water supply.

[57] Morrison, *Malayan Postscript*, pp. 59–60.

[58] Telegram to OKM, OKW, 12 Feb. 1942.

the Royal Navy was not much affected. It was natural, it was thought, for the two British ships to be sunk, because they had advanced without air cover. But they had displayed 'bravery' in taking the offensive against the Japanese, whereas the US Asiatic Fleet had run away from the Philippines, to Java and Australia.[59] Once the initial shock had worn off in the Royal Navy, there was an implacable determination to pay the enemy back in kind. Ralph Edwards, who had arrived in the Far East after the disaster, expressed the hope that 'I shall be spared to avenge him [Phillips] and his squadron before this war is over.' And a few months later, when he was COS to Admiral Somerville: 'I have several of the Admiral's original staff with me [including Bell and Laird]. They are a fine party and I am lucky to have them. They are all certain that one day they will avenge the First Commander-in-Chief of the Eastern Fleet and his squadron!'[60] What also came into play then was a facet of the British temperament to which Mahan had called attention: 'But the English temper, when once aroused, was marked also by a tenacity of purpose, a constancy of endurance, which strongly supported the conservative tendencies of the race . . .'[61]

[59] Interview with Captain Miyo Kazunari, 17 May 1976.
[60] Edwards to Lady Phillips, 19 Dec. 1941, 16 May 1942, Phillips Papers.
[61] Captain A. T. Mahan, *The Influence of Sea Power upon the French Revolution and Empire, 1793–1812* (4th ed., 2 vols., Boston, 1894), ii. 371.

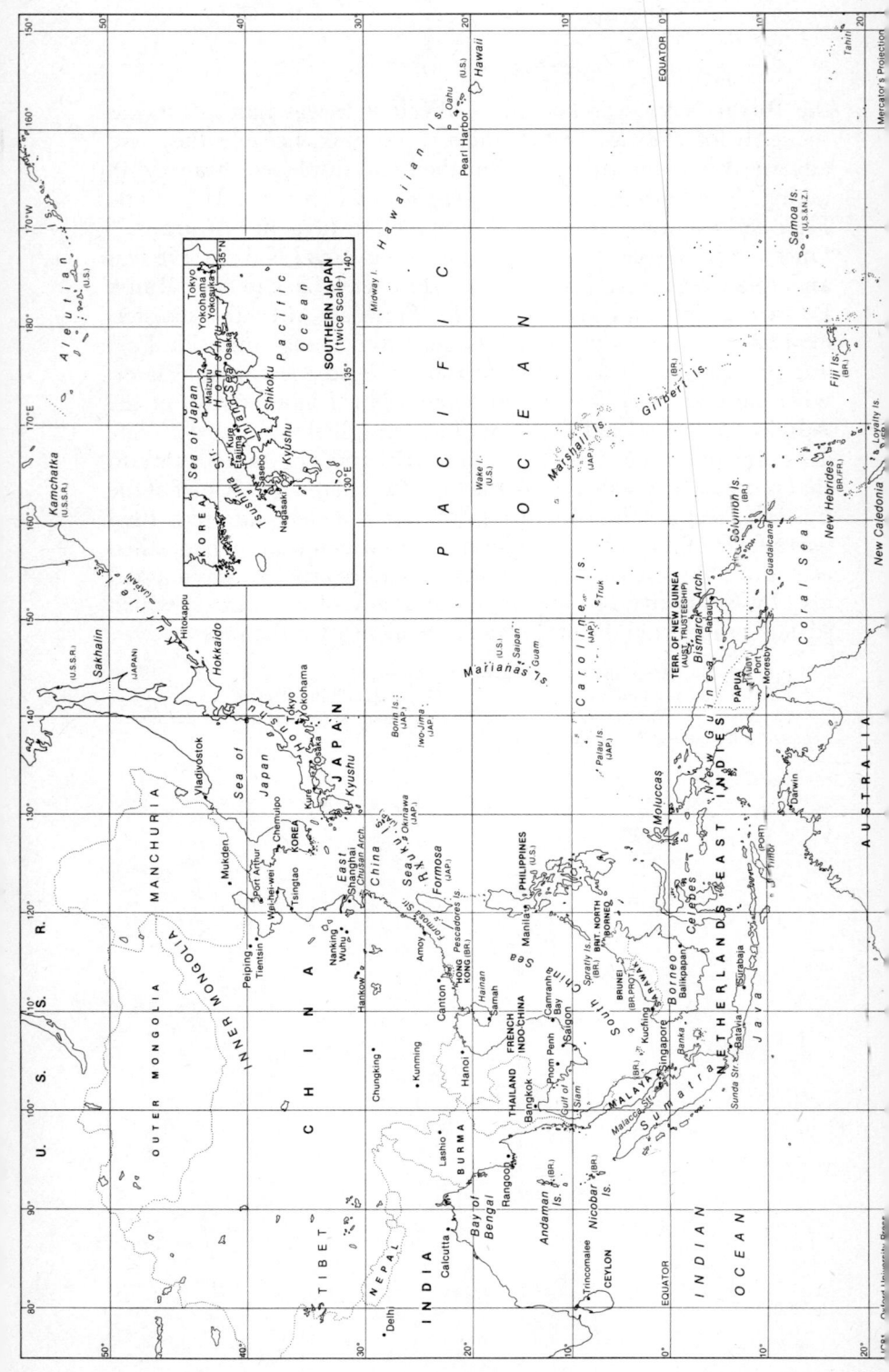

Map 1. South-East Asia, the Far East, and Western Pacific, 1941

INDEX

Abbreviations

Admiral	Adm.	Commander	Cdr
Admiralty	Adm^y	Commodore	Cmdre
aircraft	^{a}/c	cruiser	Cr.
aircraft carrier	A/C	destroyer	Dr.
American	US	Dutch	Du.
anti-aircraft	AA	German	Ger.
Australian	Aust.	Japanese	Jap.
battleship	B	Lieutenant	Lt.
battle cruiser	BC	Lieutenant-Commander	Lt.-Cdr.
British	Br.	merchant vessel	m.v.
Captain	Capt.	Rear-Admiral	R-Adm.
Chief of Imperial General Staff	CIGS	submarine	S/M
Chiefs of Staff	COS	Vice-Admiral	V-Adm.

ABC (US-Br. Staff Conference), opens in Washington 188, differences of opinion 190–7, limited agreement 198, disregarded by US 211

ABCD Powers (US-Br.-Chinese-Du.), Japan's fear of encirclement 122, prevented by Jap. advance 165

ABD Powers (US-Br.-Du.), Jap. fears of war 155, possibilities of war 158, conditions for war 161–2

Abe, Katsuo (R-Adm. IJN), succeeds Inoue 103, favours alliance with Axis 114, approves Tripartite Pact 119, pro-German tendencies 121

Abe, Nobuyuki (Gen. IJA), becomes prime minister 101

Abyssinian Crisis, creates hostile Italy 50

ADA (Br.-Du.-Aust. conference), convenes in Singapore 206, plans for action 206, report approved by COS 207

ADB (US-Du.-Br.) Conference, held in Singapore 207, approved by COS 208, rejected by US Service Chiefs 209

Aircraft carriers (Jap.), strength doubled by 1941 299, over-all strength 303

Akagi (Jap. A/C), plans released to Germany 126, complement of ^{a}/c 299, commanded by Yamamoto 305

Akiyama, Saneyuki (V-Adm. IJN), founder of modern doctrine 319

Alexander, A.V. (First Lord of Admiralty), attributes 30, discussion with Menzies 116, on A/C requirement for Force Z 229, opinion on dispatch of Force Z 241, admires Phillips 368, misgivings about venture 388, devastated by news 496

Anglo-Japanese Alliance (1902), renewed 5, terminated 6, close relationship 7, courses continue 8

Anti-Comintern Pact, signed by Germany and Japan 61, signed by Italy 61

Ark Royal (Br. A/C), unavailable for Force Z 229, sunk 229

Armitage, B. Rhodes (Lt. RNVR), Phillips's flag-lieutenant in Force Z 373

Asagiri (Jap. Cr.), attached to Malaya Force 442, sighted by friendly ^{a}/c 457

Asama Maru (Jap. m.v.), stopped by *Liverpool* 106

Asdic (Sonar), Br. reliance on 301, Jap. S/Ms easy to locate by 302, Br. advantage 304, concern in Japan 338, Jap. weakness in 342

Ashi (Jap. Dr.), sunk in exercises 293

Atago (Jap. Cr.), attached to Southern Force 441

Backhouse, Sir Roger (Adm. of the Fleet, RN), as First Sea Lord 31, attributes 32, on war with Japan 36, impatience with Foreign Office 48–9, doubts Main Fleet strategy 52, anticipates large battle-fleet actions 324

Bailey, Sir Sidney (Adm. RN), chairman of Adm^y Ctee 141, discussions with Ghormley 143, proposes US naval force at Singapore 146

Battleships (Br.), building plans 14, strength 18, speeds 297 n, guns 299, weaker than Jap. equivalents 299

Battleships (Jap.), building plans 14, ships scrapped under Washington Treaty 297, plans for super-Bs 297–8, range of 18·1-inch guns 298, armour 298, stronger than Br. equivalents 299, over-all strength 303, outrange opponents 339

Beardsworth, S. T. (Capt. RN), secretary to Phillips 371, at Singapore conference 407

523

INDEX

Beatty, David, 1st Earl (Adm. of the Fleet RN), suspects Jap. naval ambitions 6, example to Jap. tradition 318, anticipates larger battle-fleet actions 324
Bee (Br. gunboat), fired on by Japanese 20
Bell, L. H. (Capt. RN), Capt. of the fleet in Force Z 372, on Jap. torpedo-bomber, range 416–17, supports Phillips's decision 499–500, unimpressed by AA defence 513–14
Bellairs, Roger M. (R-Adm. RN), in Anglo-Du. talks 140, leads ABC delegation 188, submits paper about Singapore 192–3, criticized by Churchill 195–6
Betty (Jap. land-based medium bomber), capabilities 308–9, lack of defences 315
Bismarck (Ger. B), damaged by naval air 314
Board of Admiralty (GB), duties and constitution 29, critical of decision to dispatch *Prince of Wales* 240
Brooke, Sir Alan (later 1st Viscount Alanbrooke, Field-Marshal), as CIGS 35
Brooke-Popham, Sir Robert (Air Chief Marshal), on defence of Hong Kong 68, proposes deterrent force in Far East 223, considers pre-emptive seizure of Singora 401, at Singapore conference 407, criticized by Layton 505
Brown, H. N. S. (Cdr RN), fleet gunnery officer in Force Z 373
Bruce, Stanley (Australian High Commissioner in London), receives assurance of reinforcement 40
Bucknill, Mr Justice, heads technical committee of investigation 514
Buffalo (Br. fighter in Malaya), inadequate against Jap. a/c 427, performance details 481, inexperience of pilots 481–2
Burma Road, closed by GB 80, reopened 137

Ca Man (Fr. Indo-China), suspected Jap. air base 415
Camranh Bay, Jap. naval base at 138, occupied 166
Caroline Islands, seized by Japan 5
Cartwright F. J. (Lt.-Cdr RN), Capt. of *Express* 421, takes ship alongside *Prince of Wales* 475, masterly seamanship 487–8
Chamberlain, Rt. Hon. Neville (Prime Minister), reassures Australia 40–1
Chatfield, Alfred E. M., 1st Baron (Adm. of the Fleet RN), on Anglo-Jap. Alliance 6, on sharing technical data 8, on Jap. proposal 11, as First Sea Lord 30, on RN role in Eastern war 35, staff talks with France 46–7, advocates larger fleet for Far East 51–2, anticipates larger battle-fleet actions 324, considers IJN inferior to RN 342, on invulnerability of ships to air attack 384, on facing the consequences 495
Chiefs of Staff Committee (COS), difficulties in fighting Japan 26, Australian fears of invasion 38, on limiting number of enemies 43, capital ships available 56–8, defensive strategy in Far East 63, implications of Tripartite Pact 139, invitation to Staff talks 148, approves ABC agreement 200, approves ADA report 207, decision to reinforce Far East 216, considers IJN efficiency at 80 per cent of RN 342 n, authorizes Op.[n] 'Matador' 401
Chihaya, Masataka (Cdr IJN), on lack of Navy–Army co-operation 291–2, critical of Betty bomber 315, on 'one big battle' 320
Chōkai (Jap. Cr.), flagship of Malaya Force 442, flares dropped 452, receives sighting reports 455
Chūdo, Kan'ei R-Adm. IJN), advocates advance in Fr. Indo. China 165, places Tomioka with war party 257 n, confident of defeating Br. fleet 340
Churchill, Rt. Hon. Sir Winston S. (Br. Prime Minister), on danger of Jap. attack 7, as First Lord 30, opinion on Eastern war 49, on defence of Hong Kong 69, as First Lord 75, assurance to Aust. and N.Z. 79, suggests use of Singapore 142, agrees to Staff talks 148, belief that Japan will not attack 188, criticizes Bellairs 195–6, authorizes limited assistance to Du. 204, meets Roosevelt at Placentia Bay 210, proposes squadron for Far East 220, disagrees with Adm^y proposal 224, deterrence of Japan 231, political significances of *Prince of Wales* decision 232, at Adm^y conference 405, reaction at news 495–6, statement to Commons 496
Clarke, A. W. (Capt. RN), member of ABC delegation 188
COIS (Chief of Intelligence Staff), operating in Singapore 357, reports Jap. movements 400
Colvin, Sir Ragnar, (Adm. RN, Pres. RNC Greenwich), on Jap. failures in efficiency 351–2
Committee of Imperial Defence (later, War Cabinet) arguments in 7, constitution 28, approves delay in reaching Singapore 51
Craigie, Sir Robert (Br. Ambassador in Tokyo), warns Japan 13, remarks on Jap. naval strength 17, recommends capital ship reinforcement 42, calls for ships on China station 44, opinion of Yamamoto 97, effects of Tripartite Pact 129, proposes visit of US force to Singapore 137, reassured by Matsuoka 187, on technical efficiency of Jap. air force 345

524

INDEX

Creighton, J. M. (Capt. USN), conference with Phillips 406
Cricket (Br. gunboat), bombed by Japanese 20
Cruisers (Jap.), details of heavy Crs. 300, over-all strength 303, armed with Long Lance torpedoes 310
Cunningham, Sir Andrew (Adm. of the Fleet RN), First Sea Lord 30, appreciation on Far East situation 53–4, opinion of Phillips 365

Daigo, Marquis Tadashige (R-Adm. IJN), commands 5th S/M Flotilla 442
Danckwerts, V. H. (R-Adm. RN), on Allied strategy 150, member of ABC delegation 188, visit to Pearl Harbor 201
Daniel, C. S. (Capt., later Adm. Sir Charles), on US fleet based at Honolulu 70, on Allied strategy 150
Dartmouth (RN College), curriculum and discipline 278–85, encouragement of leadership 283–4
Davis, William (Capt., later Adm. Sir Wm. RN), favours holding Middle East 218, holds Adm^y inquiry into loss 498
Destroyers (Jap.), world's largest 300, torpedo armament 301, over-all strength 303
Deverell, Sir Cyril (Field-Marshal), as CIGS 34–5
Dickens, G. C. (Capt. RN, DNI), agrees with naval attaché's analysis of IJN 351
Dill, Sir John (Field-Marshal), as CIGS 35, recommends assistance to Dutch 202
Douglas, A. L. (Lt-Cdr RN), at Etajima 3, 275
Dreyer, Sir Frederic (Adm. RN), entertained by Jap. Navy 7, proposes US fleet at Honolulu 70, high opinion of IJN 345, opinion of Phillips 366 n, supports Phillips's decision 499
Duff Cooper, Alfred (First Lord of Admiralty), 30, urges caution in reinforcement of Far East 45, chairs Singapore Conference 223 n, reports on working of FECB 357
Dyer, R. (Lt. RN), Capt. of *Tenedos* 421

Eagle (Br. A/C), proficiency of pilots 317
Eden, Anthony (Br. Foreign Secretary), proposes assurance to Du. 202, promises limited assistance 204, warns against Jap. occupation of Thailand 214, proposes deterrent force in Far East 223
Edwards, Ralph (Capt., later Adm. RN), selected as chief of staff to Phillips 370, delayed by dental problems 372, tribute to Phillips 478–9
Electra (Br. Dr.), sails from Clyde 389, sails from Singapore 423

Ellington, Sir Edward (Marshall of the RAF), as CAS 34
Embick, S. D. (US Maj.-Gen.), member of ABC delegation 188
Encounter (Br. Dr.), collision with *Furious* 366, joins *Prince of Wales* 392
Enterprise (Br. Cr.), inspected by Japanese 8
Etajima (Jap. Naval Academy), 4, curriculum and discipline 265–78, 283–4
Exeter (Br. Cr.), absence of Jap. hatred 341, receives midshipmen from *Prince of Wales* 488
Express (Br. Dr.), sails from Clyde 389, sails from Singapore 423, saves men from *Prince of Wales* 475

Farnhill, K. H. (Lt.-Cdr, later R-Adm. RN), assistant secretary to Phillips 371 n, on intelligence of torpedo-bombers 418
FECB (Far East Combined Bureau), operating in Singapore 357, special intelligence 358, operates 'Y' station 358, predicts date of start of war 361, reports Jap. m.v. movements 400, report on Jap. ^{a}/c 428
'First Committee', members of 130, function 132–3, influences Nagano 160, recommends occupation of Fr. Indo-China 161
Fleet Air Arm (Br.), attack on Italian Bs 314, effect of dual control 316, quality of personnel 317, Jap. opinion of Taranto 339
Fleet Air Arm (Jap.), underestimated in RN and USN 343, proficiency in torpedo-bombing 344, efficiency noted by JIC less than Italians 345, bombing formations 489–90, percentages of hits 491–3
Forbes-Sempill, W. F. (Wg-Cdr RAF), heads air mission to IJN 343, criticism of pilots 343–4
Force Z (Br.), formation 224, sails from Singapore 423, alters course for Kuantan 434, manœuvred by Blue Pendant 439, opens fire 440, sighted by *1.65* 450, sighted by reconnaissance ^{a}/c 464, attacked by ^{a}/c 465, as nucleus of striking force 500
French Indo-China, Jap. fear of Ger. influence 124, Jap. ultimatum and occupation 136, negotiations with US for withdrawal of troops 246, failure of talks 247–50
Fukudome, Shigeru (R-Adm. IJN), attributes 160, in favour of negotiations with US 243, votes for war 257, on duration of war 260, slow to recognize power of naval air 519
Fukui, Shizuo (Lt.-Cdr IJN), on Br. radar 338, on Br. intelligence coup 355–6
Furious (Br. A/C), collision with *Encounter* 366
Furstner, (Du. V-Adm.), in talks at Admiralty 140

525

INDEX

Furutaka (Jap. Cr.), technical drawings 8

Fushimi, Prince Hiroyasu (Adm. of the Fleet IJN), as chief of Naval general staff 104, warned by Yamamoto 155, in favour of war 243, suggested as first joint Chief of Staff 292 n

Genda, Minoru (Cdr IJN), supports naval air power 313

Genzan Air Corps (Jap.), practices low-level torpedo releases 312, stationed at Saigon 443, attack ^{a}/c take-off 452, ordered to search for Force Z 460, take-off 462, sights and attacks *Tenedos* 462, attacks Force Z 467

Ghormley, Robert L. (R-Adm., later Adm. USN), negotiations with RN 73, London staff talks 142, receives advice from Pound 150, member of ABC delegation 188

Gill, H. C. B. (Lt.-Cdr RN), navigating officer of *Repulse* 470

Godfrey, John H. (Adm. RN), becomes DNI 355, on Phillips's alienation of Churchill 367, on withdrawal to Ceylon 499

Goodenough, Michael (Cdr., later R-Adm. RN), staff officer (plans) to Phillips 373, at Singapore conference 407

Gort, Viscount (Lt.-Gen. GB), as CIGS 34–5

Goudy, L. J. (Cdr, later Capt. RN), engineer officer of *Prince of Wales* 376, on state of boilers in *Prince of Wales* 380–1

Graf Zeppelin (German carrier), designed on lines of *Akagi* 126

Greening, C. W. (Cdr RN), at Singapore conference 407

Guns, naval (Jap.), largest in the world 320, outrange opponents 320

Hainan Island, occupied by Japanese 25, 45, Jap. concentrations in 78

Hampton, T. C. (Cdr RN), negotiations with USN 73

Handcock, William (Lt.-Cdr RN), fleet wireless officer in Force Z 373

Harada, Hakue (Lt.-Cdr IJN), Capt. of *I.65* 450

Hardy, Prof. A. C., in charge of radio finger printing 359 n

Hart, T. C. (Adm. USN), C-in-C US Asiatic Fleet 209, naval conference in Manila 211, confers with Phillips 397, promises reinforcement 398, supports Phillips's decision 499

Haruna (Jap. B), attached to Southern Force 332, 441

Harwood, Sir Henry (Adm. RN), on Allied strategy 150

Hashimoto, Shintarō (R-Adm. IJN), commands 1st Escort Force 442, covers second assaults at Kota Bharu 449

Hashimoto, Shōzō (Capt. IJN), recognizes power of naval air 518

Henderson, R. G. H. (Adm. RN, Third Sea Lord), warns against belittling IJN 351

Hermes (Br. A/C), at Ceylon 220

Hesperus (Br. Dr.), escorts *Prince of Wales* 389

Hiei (Jap. B) converted from training ship 15, not included in British reckoning 62, faster than Br. Bs 299

Higashi, Mositaka (Lt. IJN, Kanoya Corps), attacks *Prince of Wales* 470

Hinanuma, Baron Küchirō (Gen. IJA), resigns as prime minister 101

Hirohito, Emperor of Japan, exercises supreme command 89, approves Tripartite Pact 119, approves policy towards Fr. Indo-China 157, interview with Nagano 168, decision for war 172–3, supports negotiations with US 242, informed of Liaison Conference decision for war 245, war declared 250–1

Hirose, Takeo (Lt.-Cdr IJN), enshrined at Etajima 273

Hiryu (Jap. A/C), complement of ^{a}/c 299

Hitler, Adolf (German Chancellor), recommends attack on Singapore 155

Hoare, Sir Samuel (First Lord of Admiralty), 30, on British naval superiority 353, on invulnerability of ships to air attack 384–5

Hoashi, Masane (Ensign IJN), pilots reconnaissance ^{a}/c 463, sights Force Z 464, returns to Saigon 479

Hong Kong, problems of defence 67, Jap. decision to capture 326, isolated by loss of Force Z 520

Hori, Teikichi (V-Adm. IJN), victim of purge 95

Hoshina, Zenshirō (V-Adm. IJN), emphasis on military strategy 170, on extremist officers 256, changes his position, 259

Hosokawa, Morisada (Sec. to Konoe), names Ishikawa and Maeda as aggressors 255

Hull, Cordell (US Secretary of State), negotiations with Nomura 158, suspends talks 166, new negotiations 242, delivers final demands 247

I-58 (Jap. S/M), undetected by asdic 419, sights Force Z 459, attacks with torpedoes 459

I-65 (Jap. S/M), beyond asdic range 419, sights Force Z 450

I-121 (Jap. S/M), lays mines off Singapore 442

I.122 (Jap. S/M), lays mines off Singapore 442

Ichimiya Yoshiyuki (Capt. IJN), co-operates with Germans 121

IGHQ (Jap. Imp. Gen. HQ), constitution

INDEX

90, participation in Liaison conferences 91, draft statement 153, on war with ABD Powers 158, decides against war with USSR 163, issues orders for war 251, supervises manœuvres for capture of Singapore 328

Iki, Haruki (Lt. IJN, Kanoya Corps), attacks *Repulse* 470, torpedo-bombing tactics 490, drops wreaths on wrecks 508

Imamura, Osamu (R-Adm. IJN), commands 2nd Air Force 443

Indomitable (Br. A/C), destined to accompany Force Z 229, runs ashore 229, aircraft carried 230

Ingersoll, Royal E. (Capt., later Adm. USN), arrives London for staff talks 71

Inoue, Shigeyoshi, (Adm. IJN), classifies Jap. admirals 95, attributes 98-9, on fears of Army *coup* 255 n, supports air power 313, reports of air weakness 315

Inskip, Sir Thomas (Minister for Co-ordination of Defence GB), uninspiring and unimaginative 30

Ironside, Sir Edmund (Gen. GB), as CIGS 34-5

Ishihara, Kaoru (Lt. IJN, Genzan Corps), attacks with torpedoes 467

Ishii, Viscount (Jap. Foreign Minister), on Anglo-Jap. Alliance 6

Ishikaura, Shingo (Capt. IJN), favours Tripartite Pact 115, strong views against foreign countries 122, member of 'First Committee' 131, advocates war against US 161, leader of the hawks 255

Ishimaru, Tōta (Lt.-Cdr IJN), publishes war book 23

Itō, Seiichi (V-Adm. IJN), replaces Kondō as Vice-Chief of Staff 183, in favour of negotiations with US 243, considers war unavoidable 256

James, Sir William (Adm. RN), supports Phillips's decision to fight 499

JIC (Joint Intelligence Committee, Br.), rates Jap. FAA behind Italians 345, intelligence service to COS 361

Jintsū (Jap. Cr.), damaged in exercises 293

Joint Staff Mission (Br.), set up in Washington 200

Jones, John Paul (Adm. USN), portrait preserved at Etajima 341

JPS (Joint Planning Staff, Br.), constitution 29, served by JIC 361, responsible to COS 361

Jupiter (Br. Dr.), joins *Prince of Wales* 392

Kachō, Prince (Lt.-Cdr IJN), organizes reconnaissance of Malaya 327

Kaga (Jap. A/C), complement of ᵃ/c 299

Kami, Shigenori (Cdr IJN), pro-Axis 100

Kanoya Air Corps (Jap.), practices low-level torpedo attacks 312, units moved to Saigon 443, training 443-4, attack ᵃ/c take-off 452, ordered to search for Force Z 460, take-off 462

Kashii (Jap. Cr.), attached to 2nd Escort Force 442, escorts troop transports 448

Kate (Jap. carrier-borne bomber), capabilities 308

Kato, Kanji (Adm. IJN), backs Navy purge 94, encourages night exercises 292

Katō, Tomasaburō (Adm. IJN), quality 95

Kent (Br. Cr.), comparison with Jap. *Myoko* 300

King George V (Br. B), photographed in Chesapeake Bay 337, radar installations studied by Japs. 338

King-Hall, Stephen (Cdr RN), supports Phillips's decision to fight 499

Kinu (Jap. Cr.), flagship of 4th S/M Flotilla 442, ᵃ/c from sights *Prince of Wales* 430

Kirk, Alan G. (Capt. USN), in London staff talks 142, Pound's message to 145

Kishimoto, Kaneji (R-Adm. IJN), develops Long Lance torpedo 309

Kitagami (Jap. Cr.), armed with 40 Long Lance torpedoes 310

Kitamura, Sōshichi (Lt.-Cdr IJN), commands *1-58* 459, attacks Force Z 459

Kobayashi, Seizaburō (V-Adm. IJN), pro-German tendencies 122

Koga, Mineichi (V-Adm. IJN) as vice-chief of staff 104, attributes 104-5, opponent of naval air power 314

Kojima, Hideo (Capt. IJN), pro-German tendencies 122

Kondō, Nobutake (Adm. IJN), on London Conference 10, attributes 104-5, pro-German tendencies 121, refuses to attack Singapore 154, in command of Southern Force 332, 441, rated B 445, faith in torpedo attack 447, off Indo-China coast 448, moves towards Camranh Bay 450, receives sighting report 453, decides against night action 454, joins Ozawa 458, reverses course for Camranh Bay 460, unmoved by result 509

Kongō: (Jap. B/C), 5; (Jap. B), faster than British Bs 299, attached to Southern Force 332, 441

Konoe, Prince Fumimaro (Jap. Prime Minister), issues policy statements 88, forms new government 111, hopes in Washington talks 164, suggests mission to Hawaii 169, anti-war 177-8, resigns 179

Kota Bharu (Malaya), report of Japanese transports 398, Jap. landing at 412, Phillips decides to attack transports at 413, Br. opposition to landing 449, Jap. planes land 479

527

INDEX

Kuantan (Malaya), reported landing at 433, examined by *Express* 437, no landing apparent 437, airfield bombed 479

Kumano (Jap. Cr.), a/c from sights *Prince of Wales* 430, flagship of escort force 442

Kurita, Takeo (R-Adm. IJN), commands main body of escort force 442, rated B 446, covers invasion convoys 448, moves towards Camranh Bay 450, joins Kondō 458, delighted at result of action 510

Ladybird (Br. gunboat), fired on by Japanese 20

Laird, J. R. M. (Cdr RN), staff officer (intelligence) to Phillips 373, not consulted about Kuantan report 434 n

Lawson, H. F. (Cdr RN), executive officer of *Prince of Wales* 376, forebodings of disaster 433 n

Layton, Sir Geoffrey (Adm. RN), joint Br.-Du. plan 211, proposes deterrent force in Far East 223, high opinion of IJN 345, superseded by Phillips 393, opinion of Phillips 394, sends observer to conference 406, ordered by Phillips to relinquish command 420, rehoists flag as C-in-C 488, opinion of Brooke-Popham 505, sums up situation 519

Leach, John C. (Capt. RN), flag-captain to Phillips 374, attributes 374-5, council of war 413, consulted on Kuantan report 434, lost in sinking of *Prince of Wales* 475-6

Leahy, William D. (Adm. USN), joint plans with RN 70, negotiations with RN 73

Liaison Conferences (Jap.), functions 91, approves foreign policy 112, approves Tripartite Pact 119, procedure in Fr. Indo-China 156, on German invasion of USSR 163, demand for war 171, decision for war 244

Little, Sir Charles (Adm. RN), on Jap. naval training 293, on effects of fortification of Singapore 352

Liverpool (Br. Cr.), stops Jap. m.v. 106

London Naval Treaty (1936), qualitative limitations 12, denounced by Japan 15, GB regarded as enemy 325

Lyons, J. A. (Australian Prime Minister), concerned at Chamberlain's reassurance 40

MacArthur, Douglas (US Lt.-Gen.), confers with Phillips 396

Maeda, Minoru (R-Adm. IJN), advocates advance into Fr. Indo-China 165, leader of the hawks 255, believes US and GB cannot be separated 328

Malaya, air strength in 427

Malaya Force (IJN), escort responsibility 442, covers landing at Singora 449, flares dropped 457

Mariana Islands, occupied by Japan 5

Marshall Islands, occupied by Japan 5

Matsunaga, Sadaichi (R-Adm. IJN), commands 1st Air Force 442, qualities 446, ordered to attack 451, orders a/c to return 457, orders air corps to search for Force Z 460

Matsuoka, Yōsuke (Jap. Foreign Minister), supports Tripartite Pact 111-12, puts pressure on navy 117, visits Hitler and Ribbentrop 154, negotiates pact with USSR 157, reassures Br. ambassador 187

May, C. W. (Cdr RN), Capt. of *Electra* 421

Maya (Jap. Cr.), attached to Southern Force 441

McClelland, J. W. (Lt.-Cdr, later Capt. RN), at Singapore conference 406 n

Medway (Br. depot ship), visits to Formosa 24

Menzies, R. G. (Aust. Prime Minister), Churchill's estimate of Jap. danger 151, asks for capital ships reinforcement 215-16

Mihoro Air Corps (Jap.), practices low-level torpedo attacks 312, stationed at Saigon 443, attack a/c take-off 451-2, ordered to search for force Z 460, take-off 462

Mikasa (Jap. B), Togo's flagship at Tsushima 5

Mikuma (Jap. Cr.), attached to escort force 442

Miyauchi, Shichizō (Lt.-Cdr IJN), commands Kanoya strike-force 461

Miyo, Kuzunari (Capt. IJN), in charge of British war plan 327

Mogami (Jap. Cr.), attached to escort force 442

Molotov–Ribbentrop Pact, upsets Japan 61

Monsell, 1st Baron (First Lord of Adm^y, objects to Jap. proposals 10, on naval aircraft 11, as First Lord 29

Montgomery-Massingberd, Sir Archibald (Field-Marshal), as CIGS 34

Moore, Sir Henry (V-Adm. RN), relieves Phillips as VCNS 223, on underestimation of IJN 352, suggests ships get 'lost' in Pacific 402

Moran, W. T. A. (Cdr RAN), Capt. of *Vampire* 421

Morris, E. L. (Br. Maj.-Gen.), member of ABC delegation 188

Musashi (Jap. B), laid down 298, completed 298, designed independently of Western development 337

Myōko (Jap. Cr.), comparison with Br. *Kent* 300

528

INDEX

Nabeta, Yoshikichi (Lt. IJN, Kanoya Corps), attacks *Prince of Wales* 470

Nagano, Osami (Adm. IJN), heads Jap. delegation at London Conference 9, 10, 11, pro-Axis 124, as Chief of Staff 159-60, endorses policy for war 162, in the driving seat 170, advocates war 177-8, 243, on danger of Army *coup* 254, lacked moral courage 255, on duration of war 260-1

Nagato (Jap. B), photographed by *Regulus* 356

Nagumo, Chuichi (Adm. IJN), typical sea admiral 100

Naka (Jap. Cr.), damaged in exercises 293

Nakahara, Yoshimasa (R-Adm. IJN), consultations for Navy Minister 180, recommends Toyoda, Soemu 181

Nakamura, Takeo (Cdr IJN), responsible for shipping protection 321

Nakanishi, Niichi (Lt.-Cdr IJN), commands Genzan strike force 461

Nakazawa, Tasuku (Capt., later V-Adm. IJN), opposes Tripartite Pact 114, resigns from Naval Staff 127 and n

Natori (Jap. Cr.), French–Thai cease-fire signed on board 185

Naval Intelligence (Br.), difficult to obtain on Japan 355, relies on FECB information 358

Naval Intelligence (Jap.), underrated in IJN 334, receives plans of *Hermes* 337, assesses Br. radar 338

Naval Replenishment Plans (Jap.): Third Plan, new construction 15, holds up drive to south 108, estimated completion 134, super-Bs ordered 298, A/Cs ordered 300; Fourth Plan, worries RN 16, estimated completion 134, two more super-Bs ordered 298, A/C laid down 300; Fifth Plan, adopted in 1941 170; Sixth Plan, envisages more construction 171

Nell (Jap. land-based medium bomber), capabilities 308

Nelson, Horatio (V-Adm. RN), portrait preserved at Etajima 341 n

Nelson (Br. B), suggested force for Far East 199, damaged by torpedo 227

Netherlands East Indies, prospect of Jap. aggression 81-3, included in Jap. 'southern area' 108, Jap. fear of German influence 124, employment of force against 153, breakdown of talks 162

Newall, Sir Cyril (Air Chief Marshal), as CAS 34

Nicholl, Angus (Capt., later R-adm. RN), holds Adm[y] inquiry into loss 498

No. 453 Australian Fighter Squadron, earmarked for fleet defence 426 n, stands by at Sembawang 436, takes off 480

Nomura, Kichisaburō (Adm. IJN, Ambassador to USA), negotiations in Washington 158, final instructions 246

Norman, Hilary (Cdr RN), fleet torpedo officer in Force Z 373

Ōi, Atsushi (Capt. IJN), on tanker protection 322, on offensive and defensive warfare 323, in charge of Br. Intelligence 326

Oi (Jap. Cr.), armed with 40 Long Lance torpedoes 310

Oikawa, Koshirō (Adm. IJN), takes over as Navy Minister 87, not a strong character 95, succeeds Adm. Yoshida 116, approves Tripartite Pact 119, fear of Army *coup d'état* 125, warned against invasion of Fr. Indo-China 157, argues against war with USSR 163, quotes Togo 177, refuses to decide on negotiation 177-8

Oil, Jap. requirements 166-8, war consumption 246 n, possible shortage 342

Oka, Takazumi (R-Adm. IJN), opposes Tripartite Pact 114, as Head of Naval Staff 130, believes Tōjō's appointment means war 184, advised against war 258

Okada, Keisuke, (Adm. IJN), pledges support to government 249, prefers peace 252

Ōnishi, Takijinō (R-Adm. IJN), supports naval air power 313

Ōno, Takeji (Capt., later Adm. IJN), fears German intentions in NEI 109, 124, on the cause of war 130, Member of 'First Committee' 131

Ōsumi, Mineo (Adm. IJN), forces purge of Navy 94, pro-German tendencies 122

Ozawa, Jisaburō (V-Adm. IJN), appointed C-in-C Southern Fleet 255 n, in command of Malaya Force 442, rated A 445, escorts main invasion convoy 448, shoots down Br. reconnaissance [a]/c 449, expects Br. counter-attack 449-50, moves towards Camrahn Bay 450, orders air attack 451, searches for Force Z 453, ordered to draw Force Z northward 454, joins Kondō 458, no pride in victory 509

Palau, occupied by Japan 5

Palliser, A. F. E. (Adm. RN), Chief of staff (ashore) to Phillips 372, attributes 372-3, council of war 413, reports northern airfields abandoned 429, reports landing at Kuantan 433

Panay (US gunboat), bombed and sunk by Japanese 20

Parry, W. E. (Cmdre RN), at conference in Singapore 405

Pearl Harbor, favourable date for attack 170, news of attack reaches Singapore 400

Philippine Islands, threat of US reinforcement 135, Navy's priority of capture 330

Phillips, O. W. (Capt. RN, Fleet engineer

INDEX

officer), sense of foreboding as ships sail 423
Phillips, Sir Tom (Act. Adm. RN), on defence of Hong Kong 68, on US co-operation 69, as D. of P. 71, on Allied strategy 150, discussion with Menzies 216, flies flag in *Prince of Wales* 228, as acting admiral 365, alienates Churchill 367, abrasive personality 370, on invulnerability of ships to air attack 385, on fighter defence 387-8, conference with Smuts 390, hoists flag as C-in-C Eastern Fleet 393, flies to Manila 396, returns to Singapore 398, signals intentions to Adm^y 412, council of war 413, underestimated Jap. torpedo-bomber range 417, makes known air requirements 419, decides to turn back 432, examines tug and barges 438, manœuvres Force Z 439, refuses to abandon ship 475, drowned 476, on adm.'s duty to survive 477-8, on lack of signals 479, 502-3
Plan 'Dog', US strategy for a Pacific war 147, policy reaffirmed 151, not approved by President 194, reaffirmed by ABC delegation 194
Portal, Sir Charles (Air Chief Marshal), as CAS 35, recommends assistance to Dutch 202
Pound, Sir Dudley (Adm. of the Fleet, RN), First Sea Lord 30, attributes 32-3, on stationing fleet in Mediterranean 59, on defence of Hong Kong 68, stresses importance of RN-USN co-operation 143, advice to Ghormley 150-1, suggest US Pacific Fleet based on Singapore 190, against agreement with Du. 202, proposes Eastern Fleet 220, disagrees with Churchill 226, ability to handle Churchill 234-5, health 235-8, anticipates battle-fleet actions 324, admires Phillips 368, changes opinion about need for fighter cover 386-7, advises Phillips to send ships from Singapore 403, distressed by news 497, defends Phillips 497-8, on failure to signal 503, reports on movement towards carrier war 519
Price, Maurice (Cdr RN), fleet navigating officer in Force Z 373
Prince of Wales (Br. B), proposed for Force Z 225, dispatch to Cape Town 227, ordered to join *Repulse* 228, reputation as unsinkable 378, armament 378, poor ventilation 379, action with *Bismarck* 379, Operation 'Halberd' 380, sails from Clyde 389, opinion on board on Jap. naval air 389-90, arrives Cape Town 390, publicity 391, arrives Colombo 392, arrives Singapore 394-5, repairs at Singapore 403, sails from Singapore 423, sighted by Jap. ^{a}/c 430, reconnaissance ^{a}/c sighted 438, hit by torpedoes 468, disabled 469, further torpedo hits 470, sinks 474-5, high spirit and discipline 483, examples of courage 484-6, casualties and survivors 486

Pulford, C. W. (AVM RAF), AOC-in-C Malaya 407, on limitations of his aircraft 410, receives Phillips's air requirements 419, decides fighter cover impossible 420

Radar, Br. advantage 304, Jap. weakness in 342, Kondō's apprehensions 447
Ramillies (Br. B), proposed as part of Eastern Fleet 422
Rawlings, H. B. (Capt. RN, Naval Attaché in Tokyo), remarks on Naval Replenishment Plans 15-16
Reed, E. T., presents bust of Nelson to Etajima 340-1
Regulus (Br. S/M), enters Shibushi Bay 356, photographs Jap. warships 356 n
Renown (Br. BC), to be based in Indian Ocean 150, suggested force for Far East 199
Repulse (Br. BC), suggested force for Far East 199, in Ceylon 228, largely unmodernized 381, A/A equipment 382, high morale of crew 383, ordered to Colombo 392, arrives Singapore 394-5, sails for Port Darwin 396, recalled 398, sails from Singapore 423, picks up ^{a}/c by radar 438, avoids torpedoes 469, hit by torpedoes 471, sinks 472, high spirit and discipline 483, examples of courage 484-6, casualties and survivors 486
Resolution (Br. B), damaged at Dakar 139, proposed for Far East 199, 220, proposed as part of Eastern Fleet 422
Revenge (Br. B), proposed as part of Eastern Fleet 422
Rodney (Br. B), suggested force for Far East 199, 220
Roosevelt, Franklin D. (US President), advised against provocation of Japan 138, in favour of Staff talks 141, freezes Jap. assets 166, warns Jap. Ambassador 187, meets Churchill at Placentia Bay 210
Royal Oak (Br. B), torpedoed in Scapa Flow 76
Royal Sovereign (Br. B), proposed as part of Eastern Fleet 422
Royle, Sir Guy (V. Adm. RN), at conferences in Singapore 405

Saigon, Jap. occupation 165
Sakonji, Seizō (V-Adm. IJN), victim of purge 95
Sakuma, Tsutomu (Lt. IJN), enshrined at Etajima 273-4
Sawamoto, Yorio (V-Adm. IJN), succeeds Toyoda 160, warns Nagano of material

530

INDEX

shortages 253, regrets not resigning before war 258

Scarab (Br. gunboat), bombed by Japanese 20

Sendai (Jap. Cr.), flagship of 1st Escort Force 442, covers assault at Kota Bharu 449

Servaes, R. M. (V-Adm. RN), supports Phillips's decision to fight 499

Shakespeare, Sir Geoffrey (Parl[y] Sec. to Adm[y]), on defensive fire of ships 385

Shanghai, Ch.-Jap. clash leads to war 19, Jap. determination at 352

Shiba, Katsuo (Cdr IJN), pro-Axis 100, fears German intentions in NEI 109, favours alliance with Axis 114, welcomes Tripartite Pact 122

Shigemitsu, Mamoru (Japanese Vice-Foreign Minister), on qualitative limitation, 11, reassures London 187

Shimada, Shigetarō (Adm. IJN), not informed of Midway operation 92, not a strong character 95, warns against invasion of Fr. Indo-China 157, becomes Navy Minister 182, in favour of war 243, self-preservation as cause of war 252, lacked moral courage 255, as man of peace 257

Shimushu (Jap. coast defence ship), attached to 2nd Escort Force 442, escorts troop transports 448

Shinano (Jap. A/C), converted from B 298

Shiraishi, Kazutata (R-Adm. IJN), chief of staff to Kondō 454, doubts about radar 454

Shōkaku (Jap. A/C), complement of a/c 299, speed and armament 300

Singapore, as main base for Eastern war 36, main fleet to 37, defences 66, visit of Dutch CGS 140, Jap. proposal to capture 154, symbol of British prestige 190, Jap. decision to capture 326, Prince of Wales and Repulse arrive 395, bombed by Jap. a/c 399, exposed after loss of Force Z 520

Singora (Kra Isthmus), report of Jap. landing 185, news of landing 399

Slessor, Sir John (Marshal of the RAF), member of ABC delegation 188

Smeeton, Sir Richard (V-Adm. RN), 'saloon bar speculation' on Jap. eyesight 345

Smuts, Jan (Prime Minister of S. Africa), conference with Phillips 390, advice to Churchill 390–1, advice to Phillips 391

Sogawa, Kiyoshi (Lt-Cdr IJN), responsible for shipping protection 321

Somerville, Sir James (Adm. RN), opinion of Phillips 366, on withdrawal to Darwin 499

Soryu (Jap. A/C), complement of a/c 299

Southern Force (IJN), function 441, moves towards Camranh Bay 450, receives sighting report 453, retires to avoid night action 454

Spooner, E. J. (R-Adm. RN, commanding Singapore Naval Base), greets arrival of Force Z 395–6

Spratly Islands, occupied by Japanese 25, 45

Special Intelligence ('Ultra'), Cryptanalysis Organization in Singapore 359, co-ordination between RN and USN 360

Stanhope, 7th Earl (First Lord of Admiralty), 30

Stark, Harold (Adm. USN), instructions to Ghormley 144, rejects Pound's views 146

Submarines (Br.), details of T-class 302

Submarines (Jap.), types 301, midget S/Ms 302, over-all strength 303

Suetsugu, Nobumasa (Adm. IJN), backs Navy purge 94, pro-Axis 124, tipped as Prime Minister 179, press interview 512

Sumiyama, Tokutarō (V-Adm. IJN), succeeds Yamamoto 102, attributes 103

Suzuki, Kantarō (Adm. IJN), prefers peace 252

Suzuya (Jap. Cr.), a/c from sights Prince of Wales 430, attached to escort force 442

Swordfish (Br. carrier-borne T/B), capabilities 309

Sydney (Aust. Cr.), sunk by raider 396

Taiho (Jap. A/C), laid down 300

Taiyo (Jap. A/C), converted from m.v. 314

Takada, Toshitane (Capt. IJN), member of 'First Committee' 131

Takagi, Sōkichi (Capt. IJN), prepares paper on alliances 105

Takahashi, Kassaku (Lt. IJN, Mihoro Corps), attacks with torpedoes 469, returns for second run 507

Takahashi, Sankichi (Adm. IJN), on Jap. expansion 25, as C-in-C Combined Fleet 100

Takai, Sadeo (Lt. IJN, Genzan Corps), attacks with torpedoes 467, makes second run 468

Takasu, Shirō (V-Adm. IJN), in command at war game 326

Takeda, Hachirō (Lt. IJN), drops flares over Chōkai 452, bombs Prince of Wales 474

Takeo (Jap. Cr.), attached to Southern Force 441

Taranto, Battle of, 314, 317

Tatsumiya Maru (Jap. minelayer), lays mines off Anamba Is 442

Tenedos (Br. Dr.), escorts Repulse 396, sails from Singapore 423, escorts Force Z 424, detached for Singapore 436, reports attack by a/c 438–9, sighted by Genzan Air Corps 462

Tennant, W. G. (Capt., later V-Adm. RN), captain of Repulse 376, attributes 376–7,

INDEX

council of war 413, dodges torpedoes 469, abandons ship 473, reports air attack, 479, praises Jap. skill 494, deplores absence of air cover 505

Thomas, Sir Shenton (Governor of Straits Settlement), at Singapore conference 407

Tientsin, crisis in 55–6, negotiations and solution 61, British garrison withdrawn 81

Tōgō, Heihachirō (Adm. of the Fleet IJN), 4, precept quoted by Oikawa 177, represented at Etajima 273, on battleship supremacy 312, offensive doctrine 318, portrait preserved at Etajima 341

Togo, Shigenori (Jap. Foreign Minister), favours negotiations with US 242, attends Liaison Conference 244, agrees to war 250

Tōjō, Hideki (Gen. IJA), as Prime Minister 93, 111, refusal to withdraw from China 176, becomes Prime Minister 179, agrees to continue negotiations 183, 242, opts for war 250

Tomioka, Baron Sadatoshi (Capt. IJN), member of 'First Committee' 131, advocates war against US 161, pressure on NEI 165, on danger of Army *coup* 254, on duration of war 261, disbelieves intelligence 335

Tomita, Kenji (Chief Sec. of Cabinet), on Oka's character 258–9

Torpedoes (Jap.), Long Lance developed 309, ranges and speeds 309, comparison with Br. torpedo 309–10, aerial torpedoes 311, release tactics 311–2

Tovey, Sir John (Adm. RN), criticises despatch of *Prince of Wales* 230–1

Toyoda, Teijinō (V-Adm. IJN), as Vice-Minister, Navy 87, attributes 117, approves Tripartite Pact 119, favours Britain and US 124, becomes Foreign Minister 164

Toyoda Soemu (R-Adm. IJN), favours US and Britain 124, recommended as Navy Minister 180, Tōjō refuses him 181, prefers peace 252, considers war unrealistic 253

Tripartite Pact, signed by Japan 88, opposed by admirals 98–9, favoured by young officers 115, first step towards war 153, fails to destroy pro-RN feelings 341

Tsingtao, seized by Japan 5, Jap. superiority at 352

Tufnell, D. N. C. (Capt. RN, Naval Attaché in Tokyo), estimates building under Fourth Plan 16, warns on Japanese expansion 87, reports Jap. mobilization 215 n

Turner, R. K. (Adm. USN), member of ABC delegation 188, on Br. fleet's dispositions 210

Ugaki, Matrome (R-Adm. IJN), opposes Tripartite Pact 105, on causes of war 252, plans to salvage Force Z 508

USA, imposes trade sanctions on Japan 137

Vampire (Br. Dr.), escorts *Repulse* 396, sails from Singapore 423

Van der Kun, L. G.L. (Du. Capt.), conference with Phillips 406

Vichy government (Fr.), receives ultimatum 165, agrees Jap. occupation of Fr. Indo-China 166

Vinson Acts (US): First (1934), US rearmament 8, Jap. reactions 9, ratio with US 297; Second (1938), spurs Jap. rearmament 16; Third (1940), Jap. countermeasures 170

Vivian, J. G. P. (Capt. RN, Naval Attaché Tokyo), reports on Navy–Army differences 290, on Jap. national characteristics 346–51

Warabi (Jap. Dr.), sunk in exercises 293

War Cabinet (British), assistance to Netherlands East Indies 85, approves ABC agreement 200, discusses assurances to Dutch 205, considers formation of Force Z 226–7

Washington Naval Conference (1921–2), Br. renunciation of Anglo-Jap. Pact 5

Washington Naval Treaty (1922), national limitations 9, denounced by Japan 15, big Jap. ships scrapped 297, contravened by Japan 297

Watson, B. C. (Capt. RN, Director Staff College), comments of Jap. efficiency 351

Wenneker, Paul (V-Adm., German Naval Attaché, Tokyo), sums up Jap. southward policy 108, encourages young officers 121, Minister's coolness towards 127, responsibility of younger officers for war 254, on lack of co-operation between Navy and Army 291

Willis, Sir Algernon (Adm. of the Fleet RN), on Phillips's views on air cover 388, on withdrawal to Ceylon 499

Wireless Intelligence, 'Y' station operating at Singapore 358, radio finger printing 359 and n

Worcester (British T.S.), Togo's training in 4

Yamada, Yutaka, (Cdr IJN), commands fighter and reconnaissance a/c 443 n, fighters at Kota Bharu 449

Yamagata, Seigó (V-Adm. IJN), pro-German tendencies 121

Yamaguchi, Bunjirō (Capt. IJN), reinforces hawks 162

Yamamoto, Gonbei (Adm. IJN), rated class A 95

Yamamoto, Isoroku (Adm. of the Fleet,

INDEX

IJN), at London conference 9, responsibility in planning 92, rated class A 95, attributes 97, favours US and Britain 124, upset by Tripartite Pact 127, on war with US 155, warns against invasion of Fr. Indo-China 157, operation orders for war 245, assembles Pearl Harbor Task Force 245, rates chances of winning as slim 253, practices rigorous fleet training 294, advocacy of naval air 304, 313, opposes building of super-Bs 313, moves torpedo-bombers to Saigon 443, reaction to results 510–11

Yamamoto, Masuhiko (V-Adm. IJN), assistant naval attaché London 336 n

Yamanashi, Katsunoshin (Adm. IJN), victim of purge 94

Yamato (Jap. B), laid down 298, completed 298, designed independently of Western developments 337

Yokoi, Tadao (Capt. IJN), pro-Axis 100

Yonai, Mitsumasa (Adm. IJN), denies Jap. building plans 14 n, claims Japan as greatest naval power 16, as Navy Minister 95, rated class A 95, attributes 96, becomes prime minister 101, cabinet resigns 105, prefers peace 252, press interview 511–12

Yoshida, Toshio (Cdr IJN), Navy could have stopped war 254

Yoshida, Zengo (V-Adm, IJN), succeeded as Navy Minister 87, as Navy Minister 95, 101, attributes 102, suffers breakdown 115, resigns 116, in command at war game 326

Yoshitomi, Setsuzō (R-Adm. IJN), commands 4th S/M Flotilla 442

Yura (Jap. Cr.), flagship of 5th S/M Flotilla 442

Zero (Jap. fighter ^a/c), influence of Yamamoto in design 306, speed, ceiling, climb rate 306, superior to Br. and US fighters 307, defenceless 314–15

Zuikaku (Jap. A/C), complement of ^a/c 299, speed and armament 300